HANDBOOK OF COUNSELING AND PSYCHOTHERAPY IN AN INTERNATIONAL CONTEXT

Many factors in the world today, such as globalization and a rise in immigration, are increasing the need for mental health practitioners to acquire the ability to interact effectively with people of different cultures. This text will be the most comprehensive volume to address this need to date, exploring the history, philosophy, processes, and trends in counseling and psychotherapy in countries from all regions of the globe. Organized by continent and country, each chapter is written by esteemed scholars drawing on intimate knowledge of their homelands. They explore such topics as their countries' demographics, counselor education programs, current counseling theories and trends, as well as significant traditional and indigenous treatment and healing methods. This consistent structure facilitates quick and easy comparisons and contrasts across cultures, offering an enhanced understanding of diversity and multicultural competencies. Overall, this text is an invaluable resource for practitioners, researchers, students, and faculty, showing them how to look beyond their own borders and cultures to enhance their counseling practices.

Roy Moodley, PhD, is Associate Professor of Counseling Psychology at the University of Toronto, Canada.

Uwe P. Gielen, PhD, is Executive Director of the Institute for International and Cross-Cultural Psychology at St. Francis College, New York.

Rosa Wu is a PhD candidate in Counseling Psychology at the University of Toronto, Canada.

HANDBOOK OF COUNSELING AND PSYCHOTHERAPY IN AN INTERNATIONAL CONTEXT

Edited by
Roy Moodley, Uwe P. Gielen, & Rosa Wu

Routledge
Taylor & Francis Group

NEW YORK AND LONDON

First published 2013
by Routledge
711 Third Avenue, New York, NY 10017

Simultaneously published in the UK
by Routledge
2 Park Square, Milton Park, Abingdon, Oxon OX14 4RN

Routledge is an imprint of the Taylor & Francis Group, an informa business

Library of Congress Cataloging in Publication Data
Handbook of counseling and psychotherapy in an international context / Roy Moodley,
Uwe P. Gielen, & Rosa Wu.
    p. cm.
Includes bibliographical references and index.
    1. Counseling. 2. Psychotherapy. I. Gielen, Uwe P. (Uwe Peter), 1940- II. Wu, Rosa. III.
Title.
    BF636.6.M66 2012
    158.309--dc23

                            2012001661

ISBN: 978-0-415-87252-2 (hbk)
ISBN: 978-0-415-87253-9 (pbk)
ISBN: 978-0-203-86490-6 (ebk)

Typeset in Bembo
by Taylor & Francis Book

Visit the Taylor & Francis Web site at
http://www.taylorandfrancis.com

and the Routledge Web site at
http://www.routledgementalhealth.com

Printed and bound in the United States of America
by Edwards Brothers, Inc.

CONTENTS

EDITORS

Roy Moodley, PhD, is Associate Professor of Counseling Psychology at University of Toronto, Canada. He is the Director for the Centre for Diversity in Counselling and Psychotherapy. His research interests include critical multicultural counseling and psychotherapy, race and culture in psychotherapy, traditional healing, culture and resilience, and gender and identity. Roy is the Chair of the Society for Integrating Traditional Healing into Counselling, Psychology, Psychotherapy and Psychiatry (SithCp3.org). He has authored or edited several journal articles, book chapters and books, including *"Outside the Sentence"* (2011).

Uwe P. Gielen, PhD, in Social Psychology, Harvard University; is Executive Director of the Institute for International and Cross-Cultural Psychology at St. Francis College, New York. His work centers on cross-cultural and international psychology, Chinese American immigrant children, Tibetan studies, international family psychology, and moral development. Uwe Gielen is the senior editor, co-editor, and co-author of 19 volumes that have appeared in five languages. Some examples are: *International Perspectives on Human Development; Families in Global Perspective; Toward a Global Psychology: Theory, Research, Intervention, and Pedagogy.* He has served as president of the Society for Cross-Cultural Research, the International Council of Psychologists, and the International Psychology Division of the American Psychology Association.

Rosa Wu, PhD (candidate), in Counseling Psychology at the University of Toronto. She received her MA and EdM at Teachers College, Columbia University. Originally from Taiwan, she has lived in Costa Rica, Panama, Spain, and New York and is proficient in written and spoken English, Spanish, and Mandarin Chinese. Rosa's main research interests include: interethnic couple relationships, multicultural counseling competencies, and traditional and alternative methods of healing. Rosa is currently completing her pre-doctoral internship at Simon Frazier University in British Columbia, Canada, where she works with many students who are first- and second-generation immigrants.

CONTRIBUTORS

Mona M. Amer, PhD, is an Assistant Professor of Psychology at the American University in Cairo, Egypt, where she was awarded the university's Excellence in Teaching Award. She earned a doctorate in clinical psychology from the University of Toledo, Ohio, and a post-doctorate at the Department of Psychiatry, Yale University School of Medicine, New Haven, Connecticut. Mona Amer is the former Editor-in-Chief of the *Journal of Muslim Mental Health* and co-editor of the book *Counseling Muslims: Handbook of Mental Health Issues and Interventions*. Her research interests are in cultural and acculturation factors that impact mental health, and multicultural counseling.

Linah Askari, PhD, is Assistant Professor of Psychology at the Institute of Business Management, Karachi, Pakistan. She received her doctorate from the University of Karachi, Pakistan, where she was a gold medalist in the MSc and Post Master's Diploma programs in clinical psychology. Her research interests include attitudinize psychotherapy and pain management therapy. She is also the founder director of The Ideal Parents, a national trust that aims to help and train parents to raise successful children.

Nicole Baudouin, PhD, is an educator in the field of vocational psychology as well as a lecturer for the master's degree and the training program for the psychologist-guidance counselors. The main themes of her research are group and clinical psychology. She has published the book *Le Sens de L'orientation, une Approche Clinique de L'orientation Scolaire et Professionnelle* (A Clinical Approach to School and Career Counseling) and written articles on counseling interview and supervision.

Robinder P. Bedi, PhD, is an Assistant Professor in the Department of Psychology at Western Washington University and maintains a small private practice in British Columbia, Canada. He previously co-chaired the Canadian Psychological Association Counselling Psychology Section's Executive Committee for a Canadian Understanding of Counselling Psychology – a committee tasked with defining the field within a Canadian context and outlining its scope of practice. His research interests include counseling psychology disciplinary issues and the therapeutic relationship, and he specializes in the practice of substance abuse counseling.

Jalil Bennani, MD, is a Psychiatrist and Psychoanalyst practicing in Rabat, Morocco. He is co-founder and president of the Moroccan Psychoanalytic Circle since 2009. In 2002, he was winner of the Sigmund Freud International Award of the city of Vienna. His publications include: *Dictionnaire de la Psychanalyse* (collective work edited by Alain de Mijolla) and *Psycho-analytic practice and state régulation* (collective work edited by Ian Parker and Simona Revelli), *Le corps suspect, Parcours d'enfants, Le temps des ados* (in collaboration with Alain Braconnier), *Psychanalyse en terre d'islam* and *Traces et paroles* (in collaboration with Mohammed Kacimi).

Behrooz Birashk, PhD, is a Professor of Psychology at Tehran University of Medical Sciences, Tehran Psychiatric Institute and Mental Health Research Center, and ex-dean of the Department of Clinical Psychology and Department of Clinical Psychology—international branch. He is a member of the American Psychological Association (APA), International Cognitive Behavioral Association, Integrative Psychotherapy Association, Iran Academy of Medical Sciences, Iranian Counseling Association and Iranian Clinical Psychology Association. At present he is a member of the Board of Iranian Psychology and Counseling Organization. He is also the ex-president of the Iranian Psychological Association (IPA). He is on the editorial board of nine journals of psychology and psychiatry, a chief editor of a psychology journal, referee for 12 journals, has written and translated 10 books and edited 16 others.

Olaniyi Bojuwoye, PhD, is a Professor of Educational Psychology at the University of the Western Cape, South Africa. He had previously taught in two Nigerian universities before immigrating to South Africa in 1998. He was a Commonwealth Academic Fellow at the University of Reading, U.K., 1990/1991. His research and publication interests include cross-cultural counseling, African traditional healing, counselor training and influences of family dynamics in children's development. He is a member of the International Council of Psychologists (ICP), Southern African Association of Student Counselling and Development in Higher Education (SAACDHE) and the Society for Integrating Traditional Healing into Counselling, Psychology, Psychotherapy and Psychiatry (SithCp3.org).

Jac Brown, PhD, is a Senior Lecturer in Clinical Psychology at Macquarie University, Sydney, Australia. He also practices as a clinical psychologist with individuals and couples. His research interests include intimate partner violence, inter-cultural psychology, body image, relationship dynamics, and homosexual physical and mental health.

Yuping Cao, MD, PhD, is a Psychiatrist and Associate Professor at the Mental Health Institute of Second Xiangya Hospital, Central South University, China. Her interests are in neurosis, stress and psychotherapy. She studied cognitive behavioral theraphy (CBT) and psychoanalysis at Yale University in 2008. Yuping Cao is currently leading a federally-funded study examining standards and best practices for ten types of psychotherapy. She has published 61 articles and co-authored 15 books. She is a member of the Chinese Association of Mental Health's Division of Psychotherapy and Counseling, Division of Suicide and Crisis Intervention, and the Chinese Medical Association's Division of Psychiatry.

Doris F. Chang, PhD, is Associate Professor of Psychology at the New School for Social Research. Her research focuses on ethnic minority mental health and interventions to reduce disparities in mental health care. Since 1994, she has maintained an active program of research in China and is currently collaborating with colleagues to apply Chinese Taoist Cognitive Therapy to Chinese Americans. Doris Chang completed postdoctoral training at the

Department of Social Medicine, Harvard Medical School. In 2006, she received the Early Career Award for Distinguished Contributions from the Asian American Psychological Association. She also maintains a private practice in New York City.

Valérie Cohen-Scali, PhD, is Professor in the Department of Education at the University of Caen-Basse Normandy, France. Her research focuses on: attitudes about work amongst young adults, the transformation of the collective identity of career counselors and individual and collective mentoring. She has published books, notably *Travailler et Etudier* (Working and Studying) and *Les Métiers de la Psychologie Sociale et du Travail* (Occupations and Careers in Social and Work Psychology). She is also regularly involved in several projects with the European Union related to the evolution of different organizations and occupational groups.

Saths Cooper, PhD, is the President of the Psychological Society of South Africa and a Director of the International Association of Applied Psychology (IAAP). He is also the President of the 2012 XXX International Congress of Psychology. Saths Cooper chaired the Professional Board for Psychology, was Vice President of the Health Professions Council of South Africa and IUPsyS, and the last Vice Chancellor of the University of Durban Westville. Associated with the late Steve Biko, he played a key role in the anti-Apartheid struggle, was jailed for nine years (largely in Robben Island in the same cell-block as Nelson Mandela), and was declared a victim of gross human rights violations by South Africa's Truth & Reconciliation Commission.

Andrea L. Dixon, PhD, is an Associate Professor and the School Counseling Program Coordinator in the Department of Counseling and Psychological Services at Georgia State University, Atlanta, Georgia. She received her doctorate at The University of North Carolina at Greensboro in Greensboro, USA in 2002. Her research and teaching interests are in the areas of multicultural counseling with racial/ethnic diverse individuals, adolescents, mattering and meaning making, school counseling and school counselor education. She is the author of a number of articles and book chapters on topics regarding the racial/ethnic minority concerns. She has co-authored several publications regarding counseling in Denmark.

Süleyman Doğan, PhD, is a Professor of Counseling and Guidance, and Department Chair at Ege University, Izmir, Turkey. He spent his sabbatical leave at Ohio University. He is the author of several articles and presentations, especially on the development of counseling and counselor education in Turkey. These presentations were given in Romania, Germany, Greece, Turkey, and the United States. He served on the Turkish Psychological Counseling and Guidance Association Administrative Committee for two years and on the Advisory Council for five years. He has held leadership roles in shaping the counselor education and counseling policy in Turkey.

José F. Domene, PhD, is an Associate Professor in the Faculty of Education at the University of New Brunswick, Fredericton, and Canada Research Chair in School to Work Transition. Additionally, he is serving as Chair of the Counselling Psychology Section of the Canadian Psychological Association. His areas of research interest include: the social contexts of career development, health and wellness in young adults, and counseling psychology research methods and professional issues in Canada.

Juris G. Draguns, PhD, is Professor Emeritus of Psychology, Pennsylvania State University He was born in Riga, Latvia. He completed his primary education in his native country, graduated from high school in Germany, and obtained his undergraduate and graduate degrees in the United States. He holds a doctorate in clinical psychology from the University of Rochester. His areas of interest encompass cross-cultural research on personality, psychopathology, psychotherapy, and counseling as well as interaction among ethnic and cultural groups. He was awarded an honorary doctoral degree by the University of Latvia, served as President of the Society for Cross-Cultural Research, and received the American Psychological Association's Award for Contributions to the International Advancement of Psychology.

Carolyn Zerbe Enns, PhD, is a Professor in the Psychology Department at Cornell College in Mt. Vernon, Iowa. She completed her doctorate at the University of California at Santa Barbara in 1987. She is author of *Feminist Theories and Psychotherapies* and editor (with Ada Sinacore) of *Teaching and Social Justice*. Her primary areas of interest and research are multicultural feminist counseling, psychology and women's issues in international context (especially Japan), and feminist pedagogy. She spent her early years in Japan, served as Resident Director of the Japan Study Program at Waseda University in Tokyo (2006–2007 and 2012–2013), and makes regular research trips to Japan.

Mehmet Eskin, PhD, is a Professor of Clinical Psychology at Adnan Menderes University, Faculty of Medicine, Department of Psychiatry in Aydin, Turkey. Eskin received his doctorate from the department of psychology at Stockholm University, Sweden. His research interests include suicidal behavior, depression, sexual orientation, and adolescent development and family development. He specializes in cognitive-behavioral treatments and prevention strategies. He has published articles in numerous peer reviewed journals. Eskin has written four books in Turkish on suicide, problem-solving therapy and work-family balance and edited a book on youth in Turkey.

Natalia N. Garanian, PhD, is Professor in the Department of Clinical Psychology and Psychotherapy at Moscow State University of Psychology and Education (Faculty of Counseling Psychology) and Founding Fellow of Academy of Cognitive Therapy. She is also a clinical psychologist, psychotherapist, and leading scientist in the Department of Clinical Psychology and Psychotherapy at the Moscow Research Institute of Psychiatry, Russian Federation Ministry of Public Health and Social Development. She graduated from Moscow State University and is trained in cognitive-behavioral therapy (Beck Institute for Cognitive Therapy and Research in Philadelphia), system-oriented family psychotherapy and psychodrama.

María Paz García-Vera, PhD, is a Professor in the Department of Personality, Assessment and Clinical Psychology at the Complutense University of Madrid, and is the Director of the University Psychology Clinic. She is also a registered Clinical Psychologist by the Spanish government authorities, and a registered European Specialist in Psychotherapy by the European Federation of Psychology Associations (EFPA). President Elect of the Division 6 (Clinical Psychology) of the International Association of Applied Psychology (IAAP) (2011–14), her research includes: tobacco addiction, essential arterial hypertension, and psychopathological consequences of catastrophes and terrorist attacks. She has published more than 80 scientific papers, including chapters in books and journal articles, on those topics.

Marco Gemignani, PhD, is Assistant Professor in the Psychology Department at Duquesne University in Pittsburgh, USA. He is the founder and coordinator of the "Mental Health Services for Spanish-Speakers" at Duquesne University. His research concerns psychological aspects of migration and acculturation, including mental health, psychological assessment, prevention, and promotion of wellbeing. His publications in the fields of refugee and migration studies and qualitative research methodologies have appeared in major international journals.

Tony Sam George, PhD, is Associate Professor and Head of the Department of Psychology at Christ University, Bangalore, India. His research interests are in the areas of family violence, psychotherapy research and the issues in professional development of counselors. He holds a doctoral degree from the National Institute of Mental Health and Neurosciences and has pioneered group interventions for persons suffering from Obsessive Compulsive Disorder in India. His clinical practice based in Bangalore revolves around couples, groups and young adults.

Massimo Giliberto, PhD, is Director of the School of Constructivist Psychotherapy of the Institute of Constructivist Psychology (ICP) in Padua, Italy. He is a practicing psychotherapist and acts as consultant for organizations of the ICP. As well as teaching and lecturing at various Institutions in Europe, he is also a co-founder of the European Constructivist Training Network.

William B. Gomes, PhD, is Professor at the Institute of Psychology at The Federal University of Rio Grande do Sul, Brazil. He received his doctorate at Southern Illinois University, Carbondale, USA. He conducts research on history of psychology in Brazil, experimental phenomenology, and psychotherapy effectiveness. He was the founder of *Psychology*, the most prestigious Brazilian scientific journal in the field. He and his colleagues most recent publications are *Remembering and Telling: Narrative Coherence and Phenomenal Aspects of Autobiographical Memories; Clinical Phenomenology; Verbalized Inner Speech and the Expressiveness of Self-Consciousness*.

Nanja H. Hansen, MC, is a licensed Psychologist/Counselor in Copenhagen Denmark. She received her Master's of Counseling at Arizona State University in 2006 and her Bachelor's in Psychology at the University of Illinois Urbana-Champaign in 2003. Her research interests are in the areas of ethics, multicultural counseling and adolescents. She has co-authored several publications regarding counseling in Denmark. Her current work in Denmark included a two year research project working with women with borderline personality disorder and eating disorder using Dialectical Behavioral Therapy.

Shannon Hodges, PhD, is Associate Professor and Director of Clinical Training in the Clinical Mental Health Counseling program at Antioch University New England. He has 20 years of experience teaching, advising and counseling with international students. Shannon's publications include books and numerous journal articles. He has been recognized for excellence in teaching and research. Shannon has recently written a mystery novel (*City of Shadows*) with a counselor as the main character.

Giel J. M. Hutschemaekers, PhD, is the Director of the Academic Centre for Social Studies at the Nijmegen University. He completed his studies in philosophy in Strasbourg (France) and psychology in Tilburg (Netherlands). His doctorate was on cultural trends in psychopathology. In 1990, he became head of the department of mental health care studies at the Trimbos-Institute in Utrecht. His research at that period was oriented toward the professionalization of mental health disciplines. In 2000, he became chair in clinical psychology on the professionalization of mental health care and director of the research department of Pro Persona, a large integrated institution for mental health care near Nijmegen.

Gerard Hutchinson, PhD, is a Professor of Psychiatry and Head of the Department of Clinical Medical Sciences, University of the West Indies, St Augustine. He graduated from the University of the West Indies in Medicine and Psychiatry before obtaining his MPhil and MSc degrees from the University of London in Psychiatry and Psychiatric Epidemiology. Trained in Neuropsychiatry and Psychotherapy he has published over 80 peer reviewed articles and book chapters on a variety of mental health related themes. His research interests include developmental mental health, migration and suicide.

Claudio S. Hutz, PhD, is Professor at the Institute of Psychology at The Federal University of Rio Grande do Sul, Brazil. He received his doctorate at the University of Iowa, Iowa City, USA, in 1982. He was Dean of the Institute of Psychology, President of the Brazilian National Association for Research and Graduate Studies, of the Brazilian Association of Psychological Assessment, and is now president of the Brazilian Positive Psychology Association. He has published more than 100 papers and several books and chapters. His main research interests are in personality and positive psychology.

Shigeru Iwakabe, PhD, is an Associate Professor in the Developmental Clinical Psychology Program at Ochanomizu University in Tokyo, Japan. He received his doctorate at McGill University in Montreal, Canada in 2001. He conducts psychotherapy research on client emotional processes, therapeutic failures and impasses, and therapist empathy. He also conducts and supervises qualitative research focusing on the human change process inside and outside psychotherapy. He and his colleagues started the Japanese Society for Exploration of Psychotherapy Integration. His most recent publication is *Clinical Exploration of Therapeutic Failures: How Therapists Face, Work Through, and Grow from their Mistakes.*

Rebecca Jacoby, PhD, is an Associate Professor of Psychology at the School of Behavioral Sciences, Tel-Aviv Yaffo Academic College, Israel, and she is currently head of the Medical Psychology Graduate Program as well as a clinical and medical psychologist. She was former chairwoman of the Medical Psychology Professional Committee at the Ministry of Health and of the Medical Psychology Division, Israel Psychological Association. Her main research and clinical interests are hope, coping with physical diseases, the body in psychotherapy and doctor-patient communication. She is editor of *Between Stress and Hope* (Praeger, 2003) and editor of the medical psychology section, *Israel Journal of Psychotherapy: Dialogue.*

Naomi James, MA, is a Counseling Psychologist working with Oasis Africa Counseling Centre and Training Institute. She has a master's degree in Counseling Psychology from Daystar University, Nairobi, Kenya. Naomi James is the Counseling Manager at Oasis Africa. Besides other specializations, she has been involved in psychological trauma work especially after the 2008 Kenya's post election violence. She is a member of the Executive Committee of Kenya Psychological Association.

Eunsun Joo, PhD, is a Professor in the Department of Psychology, Duksung Women's University in Seoul. She is also a Certified Focusing Coordinator and Trainer in the U.S. and a Certified Counseling Psychologist and Supervisor in South Korea. She received both her master's and doctorate from the University of Chicago, Department of Psychology, Mental Health Research Program and fulfilled requirements to become a licensed Clinical Psychologist of the State of Illinois. Her main research interests are: cross-cultural counseling, development of psychotherapists, person-centered approach and focusing-oriented experiential psychotherapy.

Nadia Kadri, MD, is Professor of Psychiatry at the Medical School of the University Hassan II of Casablanca. She is responsible for university diploma programs in cognitive behavior therapy, clinical psychology and behavioral medicine and clinical sexology. She is responsible for laboratory research on mental health, cognition and psychopathology. Nadia Kadri is an author of hundreds of communications and papers published at national and international level. She is also author and co-author of books on mental health in general, mental health of women, sexology, stigma and cognitive-behavioral therapy.

Alla B. Kholmogorova, PhD, is the Head of Department of Clinical Psychology and Psychotherapy at the Moscow Research Institute of Psychiatry, Russian Federation Ministry of Public Health and Social Development. She is also Head of the Department of Clinical Psychology and Psychotherapy at Moscow State University of Psychology and Education (Faculty of Counseling Psychology), Founder Fellow of the Academy of Cognitive Therapy and council member of the Russian Society of Psychiatrists and International Federation of Psychotherapy. Kholmogorova graduated from Moscow State University and is trained in cognitive-behavioral therapy (Beck Institute for Cognitive Therapy and Research), system-oriented family psychotherapy and psychodrama.

Brigitte Khoury, PhD, is an Assistant Professor at the American University of Beirut, Department of Psychiatry at the Faculty of Medicine. She is also the director of the Arab Regional Center for Research, Training and Policy Making in Mental Health established in 2010. She received her doctorate degree in Clinical Psychology at the Palo Alto University in California. She did her clinical training at Stanford University and is licensed to practice in California. Her research interests focus on sexuality and reproductive health, diagnosis and classification in international settings, problems of war traumas, and crises interventions. She is the founding president of the Lebanese Psychological Association and a current board member.

Lonzozou Kpanake, PhD, is an Assistant Professor of Cross-cultural Psychology at - Téluq-University of Québec in Montréal, Canada, and a licensed psychologist in Québec. He received his doctorate in psychology from the University of Toulouse II, France and has postdoctoral training in social and transcultural psychiatry from McGill University, Canada. He is originally from Togo, West Africa, where he developed extensive experience in psychological services. His research interests include psychology engaged with African problems and issues.

Valery N. Krasnov, MD, is the Director of Moscow Research Institute of Psychiatry of Russian Federation Ministry of Public Health and Social Development, and past President of the Russian Society of Psychiatrists. He is also a WPA—Zonal representative for Eastern Europe (1999–2005), member of the WPA Committee on Education, and international member of the American Psychological Association (APA). Professional experience of Professor V. Krasnov includes more than 40 years of constant clinical practice and research studies.

Germain Lietaer, PhD, is Emeritus Professor at the Catholic University of Leuven, where he has been teaching client-centered/experiential psychotherapy and process research in psychotherapy. He was also director of a three-year post-master's training program in client-centered/experiential psychotherapy at the same university. Professor Lietaer has published widely (see https://perswww.kuleuven.be/~u0004824/)

Norma Guillard Limonta, PhD, is Adjunct Professor at the University of Havana teaching psychology and gender. Norma is Board member and Executive Secretary of the Cuban Society of Psychology. She is also an advisor to the United Nations Educational, Scientific and Cultural Organization (UNESCO) and to the United Nations Development Program on the issue of gender in the prevention of HIV/AIDS. A psychologist from Santiago de Cuba, she is one of the first Cuban women of her generation to call herself a feminist. She primarily works on the issues of HIV/AIDS, gender, race, sexual orientation, and issues of diversity and identity in a Cuban and Caribbean context.

Del Loewenthal, PhD, is an Analytic Psychotherapist and Counseling Psychologist. At Roehampton University (UK) he directs the Research Centre for Therapeutic Education and Doctoral Programs in Psychotherapy, Counselling and Counselling Psychology; and edits the *European Journal of Psychotherapy and Counselling* (Routledge). His books include: *Post-existentialism and the Psychological Therapies* (2011, Karnac); *Case Studies in Relational Research* (2007, Palgrave); with Robert Snell, *Postmodernism for Psychotherapists* (2003, Routledge); with Richard House, *Critically Engaging CBT* (2010, PCCS Books); *Childhood, Wellbeing and a Therapeutic Ethos* (2009, Karnac Books); and *Phototherapy and Therapeutic Photography in a Digital Age* (2012, Routledge).

Maria Isabel E. Melgar, PhD, is a certified Clinical Psychologist and a faculty with the Ateneo de Manila University Psychology Department. She was formerly the chair of the clinical psychology committee of the Psychological Association of the Philippines (PAP) while sitting as a PAP board member. She also served as the coordinator of the doctoral program for clinical psychology at the Ateneo de Manila University. While maintaining an active practice in psychotherapy, her career and advocacy revolves around public awareness of prevention and holistic care of chronic illnesses and lifestyle diseases. In 2011, the University of the Philippines awarded her a distinguished alumni award in public health promotion.

Andrew A. Mogaji, PhD, is a Professor of Industrial and Organizational Psychology at the Benue State University, Makurdi, Nigeria. He had previously taught at the University of Lagos, Nigeria. His research interests include human resources management, school psychology, organizational behavior and cross-cultural studies. He has represented Africa on the International Association for Cross Cultural Psychology (IACCP) from 2004–2008. He belongs to many professional associations including the International Association of Applied Psychologists (IAAP).

Felipe Muller, PhD, is a Professor in the Department of Research at the University of Belgrano in Buenos Aires, Argentina, and a researcher at the National Scientific and Technical Research Council (CONICET). He holds a chair at both the University of Belgrano and the University of Salvador. He is an affiliate of the International Psychoanalytic Association (IPA). His research interests include the relationship between psychotherapy and theoretical models in Argentina, the relationship between conversation and the conformation of collective memories, and the dimensions of intersubjectivity in psychoanalysis.

Gladys K. Mwiti, PhD, is a Consulting Clinical Psychologist, founder of Oasis Africa, a pan-African professional counseling and training organization. She received her doctorate in Clinical Psychology from the Graduate School of Psychology at Fuller Theological Seminary. Majoring in community trauma and recovery, her past work includes Rwanda post 1994 genocide;

Nairobi post 1998 USA Embassy bombing; and Kenya, post 2008 election violence. Her latest book is *Crisis & Trauma Counseling: A Community-based Approach*. She is the Chair of the Kenya Psychological Association; member of the American Psychological Association; member of the Board of Directors, International Society for Traumatic Stress Studies and the 2010 recipient of the Scholar-Leader of the Year Award by US-based Scholar-Leader International.

Rana G. Nashashibi, PhD (candidate), is the Director of the Palestinian Counseling Center and teaches in the Psychology Department at Birzeit University. She was born in Jerusalem and continues to reside there. She received her BA from Birzeit University in the West Bank in 1982. In 1984 she received a Fulbright Award to continue her master's in the United States. While in the US, she completed a master's in Counseling Psychology from Indiana State University. She received a Humphrey fellowship in 1995 and spent a year at Washington State University in Seattle, Washington. She is currently a doctoral candidate in Expressive Therapies at Leslie University in Boston Massachusetts.

Omar Ndoye, PhD, is a Professor of Psychology at Cheikh Anta Diop University, Dakar, Sénégal. He is a psychologist at Fann University Hospital, Dakar, has collaborated with African traditional healers for over three decades and is an influential contributor to the literature on integrating African traditional healing knowledge into psychotherapy. He obtained his doctorate from Paris X University. He is on the editorial board of *Adolescence-Psychanalyse*, *Évolution Psychiatrique*, *Tradition et Psychanalyse*, and *Psychopathologie Africaine*. He was first President of the Institut Ethno-Psy Afrique Antilles, France. He is a filmmaker and a Deputy in the Senegalese National Parliament.

Wai-Sheng Ng, PsyD, is a Senior Lecturer at HELP University College, Kuala Lumpur, where she spearheaded the Master of Clinical Psychology program and practiced at the Center for Psychological & Counseling Services. She received her doctorate in Clinical Psychology from Argosy University/Illinois School of Professional Psychology, Chicago. She was a Fulbright scholar from 2001 to 2003. An active advocate for the psychology profession, Wai-Sheng serves as a committee member of the Allied Health Professional Bill (Clinical Psychology) Taskforce, as well as a panel assessor of the Malaysian Qualification Agency for program accreditation.

Lionel J. Nicholas, PhD, is the Head of Department of Psychology at Monash, South Africa and was past president of the Psychological Society of South Africa.

María Carolina Palavezzatti, PhD, is Associate Professor in the Psychology faculty at the University of Salvador, Buenos Aires. She is also a supervisor, as well as part of the teaching staff in the specialization of Psychotherapy at the Aiglé Foundation in Buenos Aires, and a psychotherapist working in private practice. Her research interests include psychotherapy and psychotherapy development and she specializes in the practice of personality disorders and serious mental illness. She is the co-author of articles and book chapters on psychotherapy.

Priya Pothan, PhD, is a Clinical Psychologist who specializes in working with married couples and adults with relationship difficulties. She holds a doctoral degree from the National Institute of Mental Health and Neuro Sciences (NIMHANS), Bangalore, and has developed a marital enrichment program for young Indian couples. Her research interests are individual and couple psychotherapies, preventive, and promotive mental health. She works with corporate and wellness centers, conducts group training, and assists in school mental health. Currently, she runs her own psychological clinic and trains postgraduate students in Christ University, Bangalore.

Jacques Pouyaud, PhD, is senior lecturer in the field of vocational and work psychology at the University of Bordeaux Segalen. He is scientific reviewer of the journal *L'Orientation Scolaire et Professionnelle*. His main research themes are: adolescence as a period of transition, the role of activity in career and self-construction, future plans as part of vocational identity, and psychosocial transitions during careers. He is regularly involved in several projects with the European Union and has contributed since 2008 to the constitution of the Erasmus-Nice Network (Network for Innovation in Career guidance studies in Europe).

Şenel Poyrazli, PhD, is an Associate Professor at Pennsylvania State University, and has a part-time private practice. Her clinical background includes working with adolescents, college students, adults, and married/unmarried couples, and dealing with issues primarily related to relationships, psychosocial adjustment, decision making, depression, and trauma. Her research primarily involves cross-cultural competency and processes related to acculturation and psychosocial adjustment. Her research has been published in well-known journals. Şenel Poyrazli is actively involved within the American Psychological Association (APA) and serves as a consulting editor for *International Perspectives in Psychology*. She is also a co-editor of the *Eurasian Journal of Educational Research*.

José M. Prieto, PhD, is Senior Professor of I/O Psychology, past head of Department, and past secretary general of IAAP (1998–2006). He is Communication Officer of International Association of Applied Psychology (IAAP) and Spanish Delegate to IUPsyS and EFPA (committee of Scientific Affairs) and member of the APA, Division 52. His fields of expertise are human resources, psychological assessment and training, development and evaluation programs. He is author of 14 chapters in international handbooks, 23 in international journals and 50 in national journals.

Mingyi Qian, PhD, is Professor and Head of Clinical Psychology in the Department of Psychology at Peking University. Her main work is in the area of clinical psychology, including teaching and research. She is now the Vice Chairman of the Division of Clinical and Counseling Psychology, Chinese Psychological Society and Vice Chairman of the Division of Psychotherapy and Counseling, Chinese Association of Mental Health.

Angélica Riveros, PhD, is currently full professor-researcher in the Postgraduate/Research Division of the School of Business Administration of Mexico's National University, and Director of its Center for Counseling and Psychological Services. She maintains a small private practice in Mexico City and is author of the widely used InCaViSa Quality of Life and Health Inventory. She is a member of Mexico's National Researchers System (SNI) and founding member of Mexico's National Council for Psychotherapy and Counseling. Her research interests include quality of life in chronic patients, cognitive-behavioral psychotherapy and she specializes in cognitive/emotional factors interfering with human performance.

Gargi Roysircar, PhD, is Professor of Clinical Psychology and Director of the Multicultural Center at Antioch University New England. Her research on immigrant mental health, multicultural competencies, and counseling at international disaster sites appears in 85 journal articles and book chapters. She is an APA Fellow and past-editor (2004–2011) of the *Journal of Multicultural Counseling and Development*. Her recent co-authored books are: *Theories and Strategies of Counseling and Psychotherapy: Relevance across Cultures and Settings* (2012); Spanish translation of *Multicultural Counseling Competencies* (2007); and *Handbook of Social Justice in Counseling Psychology* (2006).

Jesús Sanz, PhD, is a Professor in the Department of Personality, Assessment and Clinical Psychology of the Complutense University of Madrid. He received his doctorate in clinical psychology from the Complutense University of Madrid. He was a Fulbright postdoctoral fellow at the University of Yale in 1993–1994. His research interests include cognitive factors in depression, psychometric and cognitive relationships between anxiety and depression, basic structure of personality, and the role of personality and psychological treatments in essential arterial hypertension. He has authored or co-authored more than 110 scientific papers, including chapters in books and journal articles, on those topics.

Shabnum Sarfraz, MD, is a health management professional with over 20 years of experience in research, strategic planning and policy development in the health and social sectors of Pakistan. She has worked with public-private partnerships for the development of healthcare in the Punjab, federal and provincial health departments in Pakistan as well as international bodies such as the World Health Organization (WHO). She is currently engaged in research and consulting for the health and social sectors in Pakistan.

Qijia Shi, PhD, is a Professor of Huazhong University of Science & Technology, and the Vice-President of the Wuhan Hospital for Psychotherapy, where he also works as a neurologist, psychiatrist, and supervisor of trainees in psychotherapy. He has held numerous leadership positions including President of the Counseling and Psychotherapy Association of Hubei Province, President of the Wuhan Mental Health Research Institute, and Board Member of the Chinese Counseling and Psychotherapy Association. He has published over 40 articles in the fields of neurology, psychotherapy, and psychoanalysis, and edited two textbooks on psychotherapy. He is currently conducting a national study of PTSD following the Sichuan earthquake in 2008.

Juan José Sánchez-Sosa, PhD, is a Professor at Mexico's National University (UNAM). He is the author/editor of nine books and over 100 articles/chapters on health, educational, and professional psychology. His main research interests include behavioral factors contributing to the loss of quality of life in persons with chronic conditions, self care, therapeutic adherence and stress management. He also actively trains researchers in the areas intersecting health and human behavior, such as counseling and psychotherapy.

Anan Srour, PhD (candidate), is Head of the Clinical Department in the Palestinian Counseling Center. He has specialized in Educational Psychology while working at the center for psychological services in East Jerusalem. He is team supervisor for several psychosocial organizations in the West Bank and is a doctoral candidate in Ben-Gurion University in the Negev in the Conflict Management and Conflict Resolution program, dealing with collective narratives, perception and openness to the other group among Palestinian Muslims and Christians in Israel.

Roney Srour, PhD, is a Palestinian Clinical and Educational Psychologist. Born and raised in Galilee Israel, he has lived in Jerusalem and pursued his academic education in the Hebrew

University of Jerusalem. He has rich experience in clinical work with the West Bank population. Lately, he is living and working in the city of Haifa. His research interests are in: trauma during war times, cross-cultural psycho-dynamic psychotherapy and parent-child relationship in preschoolers.

Nele Stinckens, PhD, is Professor in the Faculty of Psychology and Educational Sciences of the Catholic University of Louvain at Leuven (KUL), where she is teaching psychological treatments at the master level and coordinating the postgraduate program in client-centered psychotherapy. She is doing research on outcome and process monitoring in psychotherapy at the University Psychiatric Clinic, Campus Kortenberg. She is also working in a group practice for psychotherapy: Naiade. She was past president of the Flemish Association for Client-centered and Experiential Psychotherapy and Counseling (VVCEPC).

Patsy Sutherland, PhD (candidate), in Counselling Psychology at the University of Toronto. Her research and publication interests span areas of cross-cultural counseling and psychotherapy; traditional and cultural healing practices and their integration into psychological treatment; and transgenerational trauma in the context of the colonial encounter and slavery. She has published numerous peer reviewed articles and book chapters and is currently editing *Caribbean Healing Traditions: Implications for Health and Mental Health* (New York: Routledge).

Sarah Tabbarah, PhD (candidate), in the Clinical Psychology program at Palo Alto University specializing in marital and family therapy. She holds undergraduate and graduate degrees in Psychology from the American University of Beirut. She was previously employed as Brigitte Khoury's research assistant at the American University of Beirut Medical Center, during which she collaborated with Brigitte Khoury on multiple publications, including an original research project.

Mercedes Umana, PhD (candidate) and the collaborative graduate program in Women and Gender Studies at the University of Toronto. She is an educator, therapist, researcher and consultant with government agencies, international NGOs, violence against women and children agencies, educational institutions, community health centers and in private practice. Specific areas of interest include anti-oppression praxis, community mental health, health psychology, trauma/post-traumatic growth, HIV, transnational psychology, and intersectional analysis and research methodologies and knowledge translation.

Nady van Broeck, PhD, is a Professor in the Faculty of Psychology and Educational Sciences of the Catholic University of Louvain at Leuven (KUL), as well as the academic director of its postgraduate training programs in psychotherapy. She is vice president of the mental health section of the Belgian Superior Health Council and a member of the Standing Committee on Psychotherapy and the Working Group on Legal Regulations of Psychology in Europe of the European Federation of Psychologists. She is a former president of the Belgian Federation of Psychologists (BFP). She is a trained Behavior Therapist and supervisor of the Flemish Association of Behavior Therapy.

Fiona E. van Dijk, PhD, is the Manager at the Academic Centre for Social Sciences at the Radboud University in Nijmegen. She studied clinical psychology at the Radboud University in Nijmegen (the Netherlands) and followed postmaster training programs of healthcare psychologist (2002–2004), psychotherapist, and clinical psychologist (2005–2009). She worked at

Pro Persona, a large mental health care institute, and at the department of psychiatry at Radboud University Medical Centre in Nijmegen. Her research focuses on the relationship between adult ADHD and borderline personality disorder.

Emmanuelle Vignoli, PhD, is teacher-researcher in the field of vocational psychology at the National Institute for Studies of Work and Vocational Guidance (INETOP). She is lecturer for the master's level courses and training program of the psychologist-guidance counselors. She is also Editor-in-chief of the journal *L'Orientation Scolaire et Professionnelle* (School and Career Counseling Journal). Her main research themes focuses on the relationship between socio-emotional factors and school and career counseling processes during the developmental period of adolescence.

Chun Wang, PhD, is a Psychotherapist in the Department of Psychology, Nanjing Brain Hospital, Nanjing Medical University in China. She is the secretary-general of the Medical Psychology Professional Committee, Jiangsu Psychological Society and a clinical and counseling psychologist registered by the Chinese Psychological Society. Her co-edited books include *Psychiatry* (2005, People's Education Press), *Advanced Abnormal Psychology* (2007, Anhui People Press), *Case Approach to Counseling and Psychotherapy* (2008, People's Medical Publishing House) and *Clinical Psychology* (2009, People's Medical Publishing House). She was also involved in the Chinese translation of *Essentials of Abnormal Psychology*, 3rd ed. (2005, Shaanxi Normal University Press).

Petra Warschburger, PhD, is Professor of Counseling Psychology at the University of Potsdam, Germany. She received her doctorate at the University in Bremen, Germany in 1995 and her habilitation in 1998. Her research interests lie in the area of health psychology in childhood and adolescence, in particular weight-related problems (overweight and obesity, body dissatisfaction, eating disorders) and chronic illness (asthma, atopic dermatitis and chronic abdominal pain). Her research focuses on how these disorders affect the quality of life in children and their parents and how one can promote a healthy lifestyle. In this connection she developed several patient education and prevention programs. One of her most recent publications is *Counseling Psychology,* a German textbook.

Humair Yusuf, EdD (candidate), in Counseling Psychology at the University of Toronto. His research interests include representations of illness, indigenous healing and spirituality in counseling and psychotherapy. He is the publications editor for the Centre for Diversity in Counselling and Psychotherapy. Currently Humair is editing a book on *Islamic Healing Traditions: Implications for Health and Mental Health.*

FOREWORD

This is a book for its time. The second decade of the 21st century has demonstrated, as perhaps never before, that we live in a globally interconnected world. Issues such as worldwide financial instability, climate change (i.e., global warming), unprecedented population aging, ongoing political instability and ideological conflicts, increasingly diverse communities, and rapidly evolving and ever pervasive technologies have all underscored the fact that human beings face a complex set of global challenges. Both individually and collectively, these challenges have the potential to significantly impact human development and wellbeing.

Against the backdrop of these global challenges it is becoming increasingly apparent that those in the mental health professions must develop an international perspective on their helping practices. They must move beyond provincial conceptions of theory, research, and practice to foster notions of mental health and human development that stretch across geopolitical boundaries. As we continue through the century, mental health theory and practice should focus on understanding human nature in a broad global context. In addition, the training of mental health professionals must stress the notion that what happens in any one community in any part of the world must be understood within a larger global context. More than ever it will be crucial for psychologists, counsellors and psychotherapists to be able to "think globally and act locally."

This book represents an important first step in helping us to develop a global view on the nature of helping. The contributors to the book provide insights into the nature of psychology, counseling, and psychotherapy across a broad spectrum of countries and cultural contexts. In reading each chapter one is struck with how the evolution of the professions of psychology, counseling, and psychotherapy in many countries represents a fascinating amalgam of Western psychological constructs with indigenous concepts of helping, which extend thousands of years into the past.

In reflecting on the nature and status of the mental health professions in the countries presented in this book, one is left with a series of questions with respect to the nature of a possible global helping paradigm that would link psychology, counseling and psychotherapy together across national boundaries. These questions include: How do perceptions of health and illness vary across cultures? How do help-seeking attitudes and behaviors vary across cultures? How do models of helping vary across cultures? What is the relationship between indigenous helping practices and counseling? What constitutes ethical helping practice across cultures?

Significantly, this book provides preliminary answers to these questions. It also suggests an important starting point for dialog concerning worldwide collaboration between psychologists, counselors, and psychotherapists. The contributors to this book offer some important direction for how to incorporate what is common in our practices with what is unique to our specific cultural contexts to promote a global mental health agenda for advancing human growth and development.

As you read about the status of psychology, counseling or psychotherapy in the 35 countries explored in this book you will be impressed with both the differences and similarities in the evolution of these disciplines across national boundaries. As you read I urge you to explore the status of helping professions in each country, but then step back and reflect on how the dynamics of these disciplines also transcend cultural boundaries. As I mentioned at the start, this is a book for its time because it allows us to look at the collective global power and possibilities of our professions.

Courtland C. Lee
President, International Association of Counselling and
Professor, Counselor Education Program Department of Counseling,
University of Maryland, USA

ACKNOWLEDGMENTS

We want to express our sincere thanks and appreciation to all the expert contributors in this book for the painstaking research they undertook in writing their respective country chapters. For the patience and understanding that they all have shown to construct and shape their chapters to our specifications and limitations. Their superb chapters are a testament to their commitment and dedication to this project.

During the course of this book's development there were several contributors who for one reason or another were unable to continue, and we thank them for their attempts. Others were invited at short notice to take their place to offer particular country chapters (e.g., Argentina, South Korea, etc.). Our special thanks to you for making the effort to meet our deadlines.

Our deepest gratitude to several colleagues, friends and family who were very supportive of this project; they are Anissa Talahite, Daniel McGrath, James Stuart, Juan Wu, Ingrid Hsing, Irene Wu, Juris Draguns, Maya Florence, Roisin Anna, Tara Isabelle, and Zina Claude.

We are pleased to acknowledge the support of the Centre for Diversity in Counselling and Psychotherapy, Ontario Institute for Studies in Education (OISE) at the University of Toronto; and the Institute for International and Cross-Cultural Psychology, St. Francis College for supporting this project.

Our thanks to Dana Bliss, Senior Editor at Routledge, New York, for his help and guidance. The team at Routledge also require special thanks for their help through the production process.

INTRODUCTION

The motivation to do this book arises from our scholarly engagements in counseling and clinical psychology, psychotherapy and psychoanalysis, and global psychology as well as our personal, socio-political, and geo-cultural experiences in the world. Between the three of us, the following countries of the world are the places where we were born, lived, and worked: Britain, Canada, Costa Rica, United States, Germany, Panama, South Africa, Spain, and Taiwan. And this is not counting those countries where we presented papers, did fieldwork and other forms of research, gave workshops, organized conferences, reviewed dissertations, enjoyed a stroll on the beach, and/or visited family and friends residing in different corners of the world. Indeed, our respective research and scholarly pursuits have also made a deep impression on us regarding the problematics of globalization and the proliferation of psychology, counseling, and psychotherapy. For example, Rosa Wu is analyzing the relationship dynamics of interracial marriages, with a particular focus on Chinese and Euro-Canadian heterosexual couples. Rosa is currently completing her pre-doctoral internship at a post-secondary institution in British Columbia, Canada. In this position she has applied her knowledge of world cultures and her multilingual abilities to a diverse student population. And not too far away from where Rosa resides, perhaps just down the road in global terms, but a long, long way for the three of us, is Uwe Gielen, who together with his American–Chinese–German research team is engaging in his special project that is focusing on how Chinese immigrant youths are acculturating and finding a sense of belonging in New York City. In his role as the Director of the Institute for International and Cross-Cultural Psychology, at St. Francis College, Uwe Gielen has researched, presented papers, given workshops, and lectured in 32 countries on a wide range of topics including international and cross-cultural psychology, traditional healing practices, family studies and family therapy, and migration (see, for example, Gielen & Comunian, 1999; Gielen, Draguns, & Fish, 2008; Gielen, Fish, & Draguns, 2004; Roopnarine & Gielen, 2005). Uwe has also served as the President of, respectively, the Society for Cross-Cultural Research (SCCR), the International Council of Psychologists (ICP), and the American Psychological Association (APA)'s International Psychology Division. Indeed, it was at one of the annual conferences of the latter organization that this book project was born, and it evolved further at the Society for Integrating Traditional Healing into Counseling, Psychology, Psychotherapy and Psychiatry (SithCp3)'s first congress in Toronto. As chair of this organization, Roy Moodley is developing collaborative relationships between indigenous healers and counselors, psychologists, psychiatrists, and psychotherapists.

While we see some of this happening in the middle and low income countries, there is also a growing trend in North America and Europe where integration of indigenous healing practices into counseling and psychotherapy are being explored (see, for example, Moodley & West, 2005). A Canadian Social Sciences Humanities Research Council (SSHRC)-sponsored research undertaken in Toronto has shown that traditional healing practices are thriving and developing at a much faster rate than previously imagined. The role of traditional healers in counseling, health promotion, and education, while currently marginalized and often not valued by mainstream counseling and psychotherapy, is showing great potential for the integration of traditional healing into mainstream health and mental healthcare, indigenous healer-counselor and psychotherapist collaboration, dual interventions by clients, and many more (e.g., Moodley, Sutherland, & Oulanova, 2008; Moodley, 2011a, Moodley & Bertrand, 2011; Moodley & Oulanova, 2011).

However, in relation to psychology, counselling, and psychotherapy, the worldwide situation has long been characterized by the domination of Western views of health and mental healthcare. This is due in part to the well-established status and specialty of Western psychological theories as the standard approach to counseling and psychotherapy. However, questions have been asked about pseudo-scientific racist discourse (Thomas & Sillen, 1972), its cross-cultural relevance (Pedersen, 1991), and its potential for exploitation and appropriation (Fernando, 2010). The consequent growth of cross-cultural psychology (e.g., Draguns, 1997; Gielen, Fish, & Draguns, 2004; Roland, 1988), multicultural counseling (e.g., Carter, 1995; Helms, 1990; Sue & Sue, 2008), intercultural psychotherapy (Kareem & Littlewood, 1993), and transcultural counseling and psychotherapy (Lago, 2011) have made serious attempts to address the issues of racial discrimination, social justice, and social class inequalities in the way we construct theory, practice therapy, and design research methods. There is no argument that multicultural counseling and psychotherapy constitute the "fourth force" in counseling psychology and psychotherapy (Pedersen, 1991). By incorporating the paradigms of Diversity and the Multiple-Identity Models (Moodley, 2011b; Robinson-Woods, 2005), cross-cultural counseling and psychotherapy has solidified its position as the only "psychological force" that engages in a single client the 'group of seven identities' (race, gender, class, sexual orientations, disability, religion, and age) (see Moodley, 2011b for discussion). But this adventure into the interior of Western psychology, counseling, and psychotherapy frequently fails to include the healing traditions of other cultures.

While the integration of foreign values and ideas into native systems of healing and mental health meaning-making has been more apparent in non-Eurocentric countries, places such as Canada and the US have seen a rise in the integrating of indigenous healing traditions, particularly by Aboriginal psychologists, counselors, and psychotherapists (e.g., McCabe, 2007; Stewart, 2008). Resisting what they consider colonial and neo-colonial healthcare experiences, several indigenous healing traditions have now arisen from the underground, such as the medicine wheel, sweat lodge, storytelling circles (McCormick, 1997; Poonwassie & Charter, 2005), to address the health and mental health needs not only of native communities but also of many of the old and new immigrants. This process has opened up the way for the healing traditions of these immigrants to be explored for their health and mental health care potential.

Globalization, internationalization, and a world in transformation

As globalization is intensifying its influence around the world, it is imperative for practitioners, clinicians, educators, and those in training to abandon their sense of self-sufficiency and actively increase their understanding of counseling and psychotherapy practices as they exist across cultures and nations. For many this journey has already begun as the chapters in this book testify. Many, if not all of the chapters, describe the theory and practice of counseling and psychotherapy as they are conceptualized and practiced in North America and Europe. This fact is recognized, and at the same time the author/s of each country have made strong attempts to locate counseling and psychotherapy in their particular sociocultural and geo-political context. In so doing these chapters are offering a narrative of counseling in the respective countries as a process of wellness and healing that not only has universal applications but is also one that is interrogating the very theory of Eurocentric, ethnocentric, and individualistic psychology. As Anthony Marsella (2010) says, "the counseling profession is addressing the many challenges of our global era by examining counseling psychology's assumptions and practices throughout the world, with special attention to the importance of shaping and accommodating its purposes, roles, and functions to cultural and international differences" (p. ix). Marsella's argument is a profound one: when he says that, in a global era, counseling can be beneficial only if it examines and challenges the assumptions and practices of counseling psychology; and, in its proliferation throughout the world it can only function as counseling if it incorporates discourses of cultural and international differences. Indeed, several researchers are concerned about the wholesale "McDonalization" of counseling and psychotherapy. For example, Gerstein, Heppner, Stockton, Leong, and Aegisdottir (2009) state that "there is a 'McDonalization' of counseling and psychology infiltrating countries worldwide ... counseling professionals must seriously think about the consequences of continuing to uncritically export their models...(and) contemplate this issue alongside the importance of respecting and embracing indigenous approaches to counseling found in other countries" (p. 64). Clearly, the message of critically examining current practices for their non-diversity assumptions and Eurocentric approaches was considered long before any contemplation of going beyond its boundaries. The multicultural counseling scholars together with the critical multicultural and diversity movement in counseling and psychotherapy have been engaging in this process for almost 60 years now. Indeed, this process has been unfolding since the discovery of psychoanalysis. As a reflexive process it has always been open to theoretical modifications and cultural processes manifesting themselves over time and across the continents. As a result of North America's social and cultural history, psychologists and counselors have always desired and advocated the need to engage in international collaborations, not as a desire to standardize counseling and psychotherapy but more than ever, at the beginning of the 21st century, to learn from other healing practitioners. As Courtland Lee, when interviewed by Samuel Gladding about his role as the president of the International Association for Counseling (IAC), said, "My international counseling-related activities have shown me the great potential that counseling, as a process and a profession, has in addressing the global challenges that confront humanity ... even though much of the world looks at the US counseling profession for leadership, we do not have all the answers. Indeed, the counseling profession in this country has much to learn from other helping practitioners" (Gladding, 2011, pp. 496–98). Similar sentiments are echoed by Gerstein, Heppner, Aegisdottir, Leung, and Norsworthy in the *International Handbook of Cross-Cultural Counseling* (2009) when they state that counseling, "needs to be responsive to 21st century human, environmental and technological concerns, with particular awareness and sensitivity of, and respect for, the cultural contexts from which they arise ... a dynamic indigenous, cross-cultural, and cross-national counseling movement can greatly enhance our conceptual understanding of common and unique aspects of behavior ... affirm some of the core principles and philosophies of counseling endorsed throughout the world ... the practice of counseling worldwide can only benefit from such an outcome, as can the citizens of this planet" (pp. 4–27).

This book comes together at an interesting and critical time in world history. Not since World War II have we seen a comparable series of world events shaping new ways of thinking about what it means to be human. Throughout the late 20th century and the beginnings of the 21st century, a series of global events occurred that have overwhelmed our collective consciousness which had seemingly arrived at a meaningful equilibrium after the trauma of the 1940s. In North America and many parts of Europe, social scientific fields including psychology with their respective discourses have been preoccupied with so called local issues of race, gender, sexuality, disability, class, religion, language, age and many others. In counseling and psychotherapy, if the focus was not on clinical and DSM-IV-inspired diagnostic issues, the research funding agencies set specific agendas for the investigation of mental health problems such as anxiety and depression, addictions, sexual child abuse, domestic violence, and many others. Scholarly research into these areas of social identities and the intellectual and discursive excursions of scholars and practitioners into the process of meaning-making led to questions of social justice, equity, and the ethics of practice. This, in turn, has led to a considerable preoccupation with concepts such as cultural competency, racial identity, gender and sexual identity, female masculinities and others.

While we as counselors and clinicians were preoccupied with the micro-analysis of clients' psychopathologies together with their coping mechanisms and other forms of resilience, human events across the globe were occurring at a phenomenal pace leaving no room for us to understand and process one event before the next one had already occurred. For example, in the last 25 years, we have seen dramatic global changes: the fall of the Soviet Union, the exponential growth of North American capitalism at a rate not seen since the days of the Industrial Revolution, ethnic cleansing in Africa, the Balkans, and elsewhere, liberation struggles in South America, the rise and fall of dictators in Africa but also of the Apartheid regime, the 9/11 trauma and the ensuing War on Terror, the resurgence of conflict in the Middle East, the Arab Spring and its calls for democracy, the economic crisis in Europe and North America, and the "Occupy Movements" in North America. These events represent just the tip of the iceberg, beneath which one can find the complexity and confusion of a world grappling with the demands and challenges of ever more rapid change, around the globe, and internationalization.

Clearly these fast paced and enormous events are challenging our understanding of the world and the knowledge we have to inform our scholarly and professional pursuits. The adventure and enterprise of creating 'a global village' is underpinned by myriad forms of socio-political discourses that implicitly or explicitly aim to address the question of what it means to be human (Gazzaniga, 2008). Within this context, counseling and psychotherapeutic theories and forms of practice are being challenged philosophically, scientifically, and politically in counseling and psychotherapy. Clients are representing and presenting their psychological distresses and illnesses in a multitudinous number of ways. So it is not just that many proponents of counseling and psychotherapy theories are at a loss but the practitioners endorsing their respective views seem to be in search of new ways of healing as well.

Accompanying the proliferation of discourses of health and mental "illnesses" are capitalistic forces that motivate pharmaceutical companies to attempt to medicalize the agendas of mental health practitioners across the globe. In this effort they are frequently successful—often at the expense of patients who may suffer from disorientation, anxieties, conflicts, discouragement, and so on but not from medical illnesses. Even "health and wellness tourism," e.g., organ transplants, in the middle and low income countries is frequently governed by financial enticements from abroad. Indeed, stating that the world is at a critical juncture constitutes an understatement of the reality of the crisis in which we find ourselves at the beginning of the 21st century.

Beneath the surface of change, unequal relationships between countries continue to inform the world. Globalization, internationalization, and the new technologies, while turning the world into 'a global village' within which the complexity of human encounters is experienced at both the individual and universal levels, has also further enhanced the unequal relations between "the haves and have-nots."

Indeed, confronted by endless possibilities of communicating across the globe through the internet, social-networking websites allow us to continue in our pursuit of connections and attachments with "the other" so that our existential and ontological quests can easily shift from fantasy to reality and vice versa. The growing need for interconnectedness between people around the world in regards to social, political, economic, technological, and cultural forms of exchange cannot be met even by today's advanced technologies. This engagement with global diversity and the illusion that it can create a sense of closeness and intimacy with "the other" has led many to also be fearful and anxious of "the other." We survive by creating physical and psychological boundaries and borderlines, building personal silos and encampments of material objects, and alienating ourselves within one or two identities of the group of seven (Moodley, 2011b). In this attempt to arrive at an imagined safety we hope to feel secure from the psychic terrors that are evoked by the primitive child within us. In allowing for this possibility globalization and capitalism have become key players in our lives.

Cross-cultural psychology, counseling, and psychotherapy: from civil rights to human rights

The global arena is now a playpen within which Western conceptualizations of the self are too often dominating the psychology of the self. It may be critical to remind ourselves that in the practice of therapy, postulated processes such as individuation and self actualization do not constitute the only model within which healing occurs. In many cultures the theory and practice of self/group psychology are interpreted very differently. However, as discussed earlier, globalization has brought Western models of psychopathology to the rest of the world. Indeed, there are positive and negative aspects to this indulgence. Trauma, stress, PTSD, and many other DSM-IV nomenclatures of abnormality are offered to the world's population. The "interpretation of dreams" tends to become the "dream of interpretation of the other" through a variety of post-structuralist, post-modernist, and post-existentialist discourses. Indeed, numerous other post-something-or-other forms of interpretation, meaning-making, and ideas about what it is to be human are being emailed or spread in other ways across continents and cultures. The post-modern client is not one that lies passively on the coach rememorizing narratives of childhood sexuality and adult dreams, nor is (s)he preoccupied with the Oedipus or Electra Complex and theories about childhood seduction. The post-modern client also appears to dissociate or build resistances against the "free association" according to the gospel of Freud. Indeed, patients have become less open to suggestions and Socratic questions from the therapist or to the non-directive approaches of Client-Centered Therapy (Laungani, 1997). These responses against the conventions of counseling and psychotherapy are the very fabric of the healing that allows for the reconstruction of the therapeutic project. The civil rights struggles and subsequent movements seeking liberation from economic and political discrimination, empowered counselors and psychotherapists to address the prevailing inequalities concerning race, culture, and ethnicity in their clinical practices. This was closely followed by the women's movement; with gender discourses providing a safe place to raise questions of discrimination and stereotyping. Questions about sexual orientation, disability, class, religion, and age also found a niche in counseling and psychotherapy. This has been a major transformation in the counseling and psychotherapy profession, and one that has collectively led to the question of human rights in therapy within which the paradoxes and contradictions of multiculturalism and diversity are being questioned. There is no doubt that counseling and psychotherapy theory and practice are constantly being questioned and changed so that the principles of wellness and healing are fundamental to the profession; the very ones in question are the ones that arose when previous theories and practices were under the spotlight. And the process will continue in a similar fashion as clients' mental health needs are generated and transformed in the context of a changing and dynamic world.

The post-modern or global client is one who is adept at surfing, navigating, tweeting, and googling the Internet to verify if their counselor's or their own theory of illness and wellness is consistent with the current scientific literatures as well as with lay persons' tweeted accounts of cure-seeking. Patients come to therapy armed with information not only about the therapist's latest writings but also about recent epidemiological statistics related to their self-diagnosis. Indeed, it seems that the geopolitical and psychosocial worlds tend to grow amorphous and opaque for clients in a globalized world. The omnipotent presence of the counselor, psychologist, and psychotherapist is no more possible in this context. Clients are now empowered to decide their own individual "pursuit of happiness" together with cures to accompanying maladies, by choosing from a menu of therapeutic interventions such as: body massage therapy, Aboriginal sweat lodges, medicine wheel consultation, Voodoo health, traditional spiritual healing, Yoga, mindfulness meditation, Ayurveda, traditional Chinese medicine, and numerous other forms of Western and non-Western healing. Indeed, these therapies themselves are often a combination of each other such as, for example, may be found in combinations of cognitive-behavioral therapy and mindfulness. This then begs the question: Is there a "therapy without borders"?

Since the 1960s, there has been a tremendous growth in counseling and clinical psychology and psychotherapy with culturally diverse clients across most of North America and Europe. One of the founding members of the early movements was Clemmont Vontress (1962, 1976, 1986, 2008, 2010). In his attempt to include culture as part of therapy, Vontress critiqued the foundations of Euro-American theories of counseling and psychotherapy for being ethnocentric, individualistic, and directive in a misleading way. His face-to-face challenge with Carl Rogers on client-centered therapy at which he argued for a culture-centered approach, is one of the many ways in which Vontress can lay claim to putting culture into counseling (Moodley & Walcott, 2010). Indeed, other dedicated scholars, such as Waseem Alladin, Patricia Arredondo, Nancy Arthur, Fred Bemak, Olaniyi Bojuwoye, Juris Draguns, Uwe Gielen, Janet Helms, Farah Ibrahim, Colin Lago, Pittu Laungani, Courtland Lee, Frederick Leong, Anthony Marsella, Tobie Nathan, Stephen Palmer, Paul Pedersen, Karl Peltzer, Wolfgang Pfeiffer, Joseph Ponterotto, Tracy Robinson-Wood, Alan Roland, David Sue, Derald Sue, Stanley Sue, Joseph Trimble and Carmen Braun Williams have been at the forefront of putting culture into the conceptualization and practice of counseling and psychotherapy. Predating all the efforts by the aforementioned scholars are researchers in psychology who shared their work at the first International Congress of Psychology in Paris in 1889 (Evans & Scott, 1978; cited in Gerstein et al., 2009). A century later, numerous international, national, and local organizations and institutions have sprung up to meet the needs of the profession, the professionals, and the clients.

With the advent of electronic technologies, cross-cultural counseling and psychotherapy began to develop and expand in creative and challenging ways. Developments in counseling and cross-cultural psychology programs, new journals, more skill-based training in cultural issues, and an increasing interest in counseling across the globe were being seen. The process is no longer the story of the West completely dominating the rest of the world with its theories and ideas. Thus, globalization has made it possible for mindfulness to be integrated into CBT, for indigenous forms of knowledge to enrich Western models of counseling and therapy, and for traditional healing practices to determine in part how clients can access cultural psychological and physical help.

It therefore should not come as a surprise that the contents of the *Handbook of Counseling and Psychotherapy in an International Context* reflect a weakening of theoretical and conceptual structures in conventional counseling and psychotherapy efforts that were built upon culturally encapsulated and ethnocentric ideologies of the past.

As we write this introduction there are 256 countries in the world. This number varies depending on the context of the focus: for example, we count 196 countries if we consider members of the United Nations; 204 countries if we include those that are not members and those that are applying to become member states of the United Nations, and 256 if we consider those that are still protectorates of the former colonial empires. Interestingly, Montenegro and Serbia joined the United Nations only recently, and South Sudan became a member on 9th July 2011. There are others waiting to join the UN, such as: Kosovo (considered by the US as an independent country), Palestine (currently in the process of seeking recognition), Greenland, and Western Sahara. While counseling and psychotherapy are being practiced in various forms in most of these countries, we have included here only 35 countries due to space considerations; preference has been given to a diverse group of countries on all inhabited continents that show a significant engagement with clinical practice. Finally, we would like to state that although this book is presented in US English, we acknowledge that much is lost in translation. The chapters in this volume were all written in English or were translated into English by the authors. The issue of language in counseling, psychology, and psychotherapy is always an interesting and complex one. Juris Draguns (2001) has forcefully raised the question of linguistic pluralism in psychology and counseling. In *Toward a Truly International Psychology: Beyond English Only,* Draguns states that, "At a minimum, it should be recognized that English is not and should not be the only language of psychological discourse" (p. 1026). He argues that a great many psychological ideas and knowledge of healing methods are lost as a result of the dominance of English in the one way flow of information. As he says, "the flow of information is unidirectional; American psychology radiates to all portions of the world, but is not receptive to the absorption of outside influences" (p. 1020). Through this book we hope that English-speaking scholars and researchers will be motivated to engage with the rich counseling and psychotherapy literatures of other languages and cultures. Juris Draguns reminds counselors, psychologists and psychotherapists that,

> an attitude of active curiosity about the activities and achievements of the psychologists (counselors and psychotherapists) of the world and an openness and receptivity to their contributions is called for ... all over the world, there are thousands of their peers in training, scholarship, and creativity who are eager to contribute on the basis of their own distinctive experiences and outlooks ... as the world moves simultaneously toward indigenization and globalization, let us avoid the pitfalls of encapsulation and homogenization, overcoming them through communication and cooperation.
>
> *(p. 1026)*

The organization of the book

The book is organized into five parts according to geographical location:

Part I: Counseling and psychotherapy in Africa
Part II: Counseling and psychotherapy in the Americas

Part III: Counseling and psychotherapy in Asia
Part IV: Counseling and psychotherapy in Europe
Part V: Counseling and psychotherapy in the Middle East

In each of the above sections, we have placed the countries (in alphabetical order) where counseling and psychotherapy play a significant role in the prevailing mental healthcare practices. In each chapter the following are discussed:

- Brief history of counseling and psychotherapy
- Counselor education programs, accreditation, licensure, and certification
- Current counseling and psychotherapy theories, process and trends
- Indigenous and traditional healing methods
- Research and supervision
- Strengths, weaknesses, opportunities, and challenges
- Future directions

In using such a generalized format we attempted to provide a broad overview of the current state of counseling and psychotherapy and some of the key issues that are preoccupying professionals and the profession.

Part I: Counseling and psychotherapy in Africa

Part I begins with Chapter 1, Counseling and psychotherapy in Egypt: Ambiguous identity of a regional leader, by Mona Amer, who discusses the rich and complex history of European and Middle Eastern intercultural dialogue that has characterized the development of psychiatry, counseling psychology, and psychotherapy in Egypt from the Pharaonic civilization until the current day. Traditional healing practices such as "black magic" and Zar ceremonies are disregarded by the psychotherapy profession, which has adopted a diverse array of Western psychotherapy models. Future directions for Egyptian counseling and psychotherapy include practical skills training at the university level, greater clarity of professional roles, and the establishment of standards for regulating and monitoring the field. In Chapter 2, Counseling and psychotherapy in francophone West Africa: Creating a future vision, Lonzozou Kpanake and Omar Ndoye, focus on Senegal. They argue that counseling and psychotherapy in francophone West African countries are undergoing significant changes, but they are also struggling to establish a relevant identity that is contextually grounded. They discuss past and current developments of counseling and psychotherapy and the factors that are supporting, facilitating, challenging and impeding a future vision that is effective in addressing mental health care. In Chapter 3, Counseling and psychotherapy in Nigeria: Horizons for the future, Olaniyi Bojuwoye and Andrew A. Mogaji trace the history of counseling and psychotherapy. They begin by outlining the development from the practices of traditional healing to the emergence of Western-oriented models. They consider the practice of counseling and psychotherapy in different settings in Nigeria, and then note a number of challenges as well as opportunities and horizons for the future. In Chapter 4, Counseling and psychotherapy in Morocco: The renewal of an ancient tradition, Nadia Kadri and Jalil Bennani review the history and current state of counseling and psychotherapy, including cognitive-behavioral therapy, psychoanalysis and systemic therapy approaches as well as the rich healing traditions of the past. Counseling and psychotherapy are experiencing a period of growth and rapid evolution in response to changing cultural and political trends in Morocco. They discuss the kinds of challenges and opportunities for counseling and psychotherapy in Morocco. In Chapter 5, Counseling and psychotherapy in South Africa: Responding to post-apartheid counseling needs, Saths Cooper and Lionel Nicholas explore the challenges that counseling and psychotherapy face in a post-apartheid era. They describe developments in counseling and psychotherapy in the broader context of South Africa's recent democratic transformation while tracing significant reciprocal international influences over a period of more than a century. The authors argue that serving a multilingual, largely poor black majority, as well as integrating indigenous therapies within mainstream psychology, remain constant challenges. In Chapter 6, Counseling and psychotherapy in sub-Saharan Africa: Brewed in an African pot with Western seasoning, Gladys K. Mwiti and Naomi N. James, review the history of professional counseling and psychotherapy in sub-Saharan Africa with a particular focus on Kenya. They discuss traditional healing practices in African societies together with the inter-weaving of efforts to promote psychological health in indigenous tribal socialization. Counseling and psychotherapy are mushrooming in terms of training and practice, appreciation of indigenous psychologies, contextualization, and the demands for holism in professional practice.

Part II: Counseling and psychotherapy in the Americas

Part II begins with Chapter 7, Counseling and psychotherapy in Argentina: A tango from psychoanalysis to integrative psychotherapies, by Felipe Muller and María Carolina Palavezzatti, who describe the long and extensive history of psychotherapy and counseling in Argentina. Reference is made to the beginnings and evolution of psychotherapy, what the practice is currently like in terms of professional regulations, psychotherapy education and training, and the main theoretical models adopted by practitioners. In contrast to psychoanalytic forms of psychotherapy, counseling is a relatively new field in the country and is beginning to leave its mark as a key mental health discipline. In Chapter 8, Counseling and psychotherapy in Brazil: From private practice to community services, Claudio S. Hutz and William B. Gomes trace the historical aspects of counseling and psychotherapy in Brazil and examine theoretical trends stemming from the intellectual influences respectively of Europe and the USA. While psychotherapy is a well accepted practice by the Brazilian population and a much coveted practice by psychologists, it still requires an increasing reliance on empirical research, particularly with regard to treatment effectiveness and efficacy; advances in skill training programs; and improved regulation of the profession. In Chapter 9, Counseling and psychotherapy in Canada: Diversity and growth, José F. Domene and Robinder P. Bedi discuss the historical roots, varied training and licensure requirements, and diversity of approaches in counseling and psychotherapy in English and French Canada. In response to changing cultural and political trends in Canada, counseling and psychotherapy are expanding rapidly in a context of new challenges and opportunities. In Chapter 10, Counseling and psychotherapy in the (English-speaking) Caribbean: Fidelity, fit or a cause for concern? Gerard Hutchinson and Patsy Sutherland focus on the issues related to the practice and teaching of counseling and psychotherapy in the (English-speaking) Caribbean. They review the training opportunities and resources, and discuss the problems related to practice in the (English-speaking) Caribbean where there has not been a tradition of counseling, psychology or psychotherapy. This region is not a homogeneous whole and the discussion refers to those countries where training has been available. With expanding educational opportunities and links with other health care institutions locally and abroad, counseling theory, research and practice are becoming more prominent. In Chapter 11, Counseling and psychotherapy in Cuba: Interdisciplinarity and community-driven research and education, Norma Guillard and Mercedes Umana explore how the different socio-political and economic changes have influenced counseling and psychotherapy in Cuba. They review the current trends, educational programs, accreditation processes, indigenous and traditional healing methods in Cuban counseling and psychotherapy. In Chapter 12, Counseling and psychotherapy in Mexico: Toward a Latin American perspective, Juan José Sánchez-Sosa and Angélica Riveros examine the main historical conditions that led to the contemporary academic, professional and regulatory aspects of counseling and psychotherapy in Mexico. They discuss the current status and explore how the recent legislative regulations pose an interesting scenario for the development of counseling and psychotherapy. The chapter discusses these and other related issues and considers counseling and psychotherapy towards a Latin American future. In Chapter 13, Counseling and psychotherapy in the United States: Multicultural competence, evidence-based, and measurable outcomes, Gargi Roysircar and Shannon Hodges discuss the two counseling professions in the United States: counseling psychology and mental health counseling. These programs' respective accreditations (by APA; CACREP) and their licenses and training programs are described. These authors trace how the two mental health professions evolved in the past 50 years in their theory, research, training, and supervision from a primarily European American orientation of individualism to embrace cultural and individual differences and diversity, contextualism, multicultural competence, social justice, positive psychology, and the therapist-client relationship as a therapeutic common factor.

Part III: Counseling and psychotherapy in Asia

Part III begins with Chapter 14, Counseling and psychotherapy in Australia: Championing the egalitarian society?, by Jac Brown, who explores how humanistic psychology and cognitive behavioral psychology have developed in Australia. Significant developments in narrative therapy by Michael White and Russell Mears in relation to the conversational model have had major impacts around the world. He also discusses the lack of many significant links with the Aboriginal community and the Torres Strait Islanders in finding common patterns of healing. In Chapter 15, Counseling and psychotherapy in China: Building capacity to serve 1.3 billion, Doris F. Chang, Yuping Cao, Qijia Shi, Chun Wang, and Mingyi Qian review the past and current developments in counseling and psychotherapy in China. They do so in the context of the dramatic social upheavals and transformations of the past century. Counseling and psychotherapy have been flourishing in China in recent years due to greater public acceptance and demand, involvement of foreign experts in psychotherapy training, systematic efforts to elevate professional standards of practice, and innovative approaches to treatment adaptation and development. The authors argue that as the profession enters a period of more thoughtful and critical analysis of Western psychotherapies, it will transform to meet the needs of the rapidly changing Chinese society. In Chapter 16, Counseling and psychotherapy in India: Professionalism amidst changing times, Tony Sam George and Priya Pothan discuss the rapidly changing practice of counseling and psychotherapy. With a rich history of healing practices and Indian philosophical concepts that inform healing, India today stands at the threshold of combining Western counseling approaches with Indian thought and traditional practices. Rapid changes in Indian society and greater psychological mindedness among the public have placed immense demands on practitioners and trainers to provide quality education and service to the public. In Chapter 17, Counseling and psychotherapy in Japan: Integrating Japanese traditions and contemporary Values, Shigeru Iwakabe and Carol Enns introduce the Japanese context in which psychotherapy practice was established, summarize salient themes deriving from its history, and describe contemporary challenges. Problems related to *hikikomori* (social withdrawal), depression, and suicide have received significant attention. A variety of indigenous psychotherapies have informed Japanese practice, including *Morita* therapy, *Naikan* therapy, and *hakoniwa* (sandtray therapy).

Western practices such as humanistic, cognitive-behavioral, and psychoanalytic approaches have been integrated with Japanese traditions. In Chapter 18, Counseling and psychotherapy in Malaysia: Joy and pain of (continuous) pioneering work, Wai Sheng Ng describes and discusses a relatively young profession in the making, due to the sociocultural changes and increased mental health concerns that can be found in Malaysia. Since the 1970s, the practice of Western psychotherapy has evolved from following the psychoanalytic tradition to behavioral and cognitive-behavioral traditions to a more complex one that is now attempting to integrate indigenous cultural beliefs, as well as alternative and complementary practices. In Chapter 19, Counseling and psychotherapy in Pakistan: Colonial legacies and Islamic influences, Humair Yusuf, Shabnum Sarfraz, and Linah Askari discuss how the demographic and political changes and shifts in cultural values have resulted in growing numbers of individuals engaging in counseling and psychotherapy. The treatment of psychological distress has traditionally been dominated by psychiatry and indigenous practices, with psychotherapy limited to an affluent, Anglophone elite based in the main urban centers. The incorporation of Islamic practices into counseling and psychotherapy has made it more acceptable and culturally relevant to Pakistani clients in both the rural and urban areas. They argue that ongoing challenges include the continuing stigmatization of mental illness, negligible government funding, and the absence of a regulatory framework for counseling and psychotherapy. In Chapter 20, Counseling and psychotherapy in the Philippines: A discipline in transition, Maria Isabel E. Melgar charts the young history of counseling and psychotherapy in the Philippines. The American influence on the practice of counseling psychology was reinforced by the return of Filipino scholars who were trained abroad and who helped establish academic programs in psychology in leading universities. The Psychology Law passed by Philippine Congress in 2010 marks a significant transition to an era in which professionals hope to professionalize the practice of counseling and psychotherapy in the country. In Chapter 21, Counseling and psychotherapy in South Korea: Disciplines flourishing in a dynamic and challenging era, Eunsun Joo begins by exploring the historical evolution of counseling and psychotherapy in South Korea. Until the mid 20th century, Shamanistic healing and Chinese medicine were the two main traditional treatment methods for mental illness. With the advent of westernization and modernization, the Western concept of psychotherapy has become prevalent in South Korea. The use of Western therapeutic approaches in a non-Western cultural context is discussed, focusing on the potential conflicts for practitioners between imported methods that embody individualistic values and the traditionally collectivist but changing orientation of Korean society.

Part IV: Counseling and psychotherapy in Europe

Part IV begins with Chapter 22, Counseling and psychotherapy in Belgium: Towards an accessible and evidence-based mental health care, by Nady Van Broeck, Nele Stinckens, and Germain Lietaer. They discuss the role that clinical psychologists, psychotherapists, and counselors play in the assessment and diagnosis of social and psychological problems and in the interventions and treatments as part of the delivery of counseling and psychotherapy in Belgium. In exploring the developments of counseling and psychotherapy, the authors describe the current training standards and programs as well as current trends. In Chapter 23, Counseling and psychotherapy in Denmark: Counseling the "happiest people on Earth", Nanja H. Hansen and Andrea L. Dixon explore the developments of counseling and psychotherapy in Denmark. Even with its long history it continues to evolve, especially during the last thirty years. As this trend continues, so does the research within the field. Moreover, mental health professionals are dedicated to work toward securing mental health services for all Danes. In Chapter 24, Counseling and psychotherapy in France: An evolving heterogeneous field, Valérie Cohen-Scali,

Jacques Pouyaud, Nicole Baudouin, and Emmanuelle Vignoli outline the main developments in counseling and psychotherapy in France, which is currently experiencing a strong public demand for counseling, guidance, and psychotherapy. Counseling and psychotherapy are well differentiated where counseling takes place in schools and in the context of career development, but only rarely in clinical settings. 'Brief Psychotherapies' are now replacing traditional forms of psychoanalysis, which were predominant until the 1980s–1990s. Research is mostly conducted in psychology laboratories, with only a few teams working specifically on counseling. In Chapter 25, Counseling and psychotherapy in Germany: Common past but different present? Petra Warschburger begins with a brief history of counseling and psychotherapy, together with a discussion of the current education and training programs in a unified and modern German context. She discusses a number of key issues confronting counseling and psychotherapy in Germany, such as legal regulations, the regulations for reimbursement, the different target groups for treatment, greater diversity of approaches, and meeting existing mental health needs especially in rural regions and for marginalized groups. In Chapter 26, Counseling and psychotherapy in Italy: Historical, cultural and indigenous perspectives, Marco Gemignani and Massimo Giliberto describe the history and present status of counseling and psychotherapy in Italy. They discuss the complex origins of psychotherapy, current theories, education programs, and regulations. Professional psychology faces significant resistance and pressure from groups that exert great political and cultural influence, like the Roman-Catholic Church and the psychiatric lobby. Despite these difficulties – and general misconceptions about the standing of counseling – an array of lively approaches to psychotherapy and counseling can be found in present day Italy. In Chapter 27, Psychotherapy and clinical psychology in the Netherlands: Settlement of five distinctive psy-professions, Giel J. M. Hutschemaekers and Fiona E. van Dijk describe the history and current state of psychotherapy and clinical psychology in the Netherlands, which the authors refer to as 'the Dutch Case'. Here they point to the very early legislation of a distinctive profession of psychotherapy; however, today, the term also refers to the large number of disciplines who focus on the practice of counseling and psychotherapy. The authors discuss the 'Individual Health Care Professionals Act' (law BIG) that formally recognizes five basic professions and specializations in the field of counseling and psychotherapy by designating specific professional titles. They also explore several issues related to the development of counseling and psychotherapy in the Netherlands, such as education programs, professional training and trends, and the challenge to define profession-specific domains and competencies. In Chapter 28, Psychotherapy in Spain: Rapid growth and vicissitudes of clinical psychology, María Paz García-Vera, Jesús Sanz, and José M. Prieto discuss developments in the field of psychotherapy in Spain which has experienced a rapid growth in the last thirty years. The authors discuss several factors that support this growth, such as, the incorporation of clinical psychology in the Spanish National Health System; the inclusion of psychotherapy services by the private health insurance companies; the development and proliferation of professional training programs and scientific research; the legal requirements to be able to practice as a clinical psychologist; and many more. In Chapter 29, Counseling and psychotherapy in Russia: Reunion with the international science community, Alla B. Kholmogorova, Natalia N. Garanian, and Valery N. Krasnov outline the development of counseling and psychotherapy in Russia by focusing on the long prohibition for scientific psychology beginning in 1936, the domination of a biological orientation in Soviet psychiatry, and the isolation from Western science. In the last decade, there has been increasing growth in psychoanalysis, existential and humanistic psychotherapy, and cognitive-behavioral therapy. Original models in Russia have arisen on the basis of varying syntheses of Russian and Western scientific approaches. The major issues for the future of counseling and psychotherapy are: insufficient financing; low levels of professional training; lack of developed systems of certification, licensing, and supervision; and insufficient understanding by most managers and specialists of the role of counseling and psychotherapy in the prevention and treatment of psychological distress. In Chapter 30, Counseling and psychotherapy in the United Kingdom: Future of talking therapies, Del Loewenthal first provides an overview of counseling and psychotherapy in the UK. He then discusses the Foster report (1971), which proposed that offering talking therapies should be a regulated profession, together with subsequent developments in terms of modalities, professionalization, and the significant impacts of government intervention. The trend within the UK is towards the adoption of what are regarded as 'evidence-based' practices. In this context, the overall standard of what is taken as evidence is determined by the National Institute for Health and Clinical Excellence. Such methods of measurement favor cognitive-behavioral therapies which seem to be favored in training, research, and practice, whereas previously psychoanalytic and humanistic modalities were favored by most practitioners.

Part V: Counseling and psychotherapy in the Middle East

Part V begins with Chapter 31, Counseling and psychotherapy in Iran: A flourishing perspective, by Behrooz Birashk who discusses the impact that Iranian traditional cultural values and religious teachings have had on the development of counseling and psychotherapy. Within this context there are developments to create contemporary approaches, principles, and techniques that incorporate the many theories that can be found in the current counseling and psychotherapy approaches. Iran's mental health profession and the education of practitioners at the university level can be considered to have many strengths, weaknesses, opportunities and challenges. In Chapter 32, Counseling and psychotherapy in Israel: Milestones, disputes and challenges, Rebecca Jacoby discusses the growth of counseling and psychotherapy since the establishment of the state of Israel. It takes into account an increasingly central role in coping with the reality of a young, heterogeneous, stress-ridden society facing continuous threats. She explores several issues by pointing out that the practice of psychotherapy in Israel has not been legislated, public services are unsatisfactory, and tensions exist between different therapeutic approaches and between the realm of practice and the academy. In recent years, there has been a demand, stemming mostly from the academy, to anchor theory and practice in research. In Chapter 33, Counseling and psychotherapy in Lebanon: Towards a Lebanese framework of psychology, Brigitte Khoury and Sarah Tabbarah discuss the state of clinical and counseling psychology in Lebanon. They also explore how traditional and indigenous healing practices, in the form of religious and cultural practices, herbal therapy, and many others are available to the public as mental health services. They suggest that improvements are needed to establish evidence-based and scientist-practitioner model programs necessary for setting up professional standards and maintaining ethical practice. In Chapter 34, Counseling and psychotherapy in Palestine: Between occupation and cultural colonialism, Rana Nashashibi, Anan Srour, and Roney Srour discuss counseling and psychotherapy in relation to the history and culture of living in Occupied Palestinian Territories. We find here a progression beginning with non-violent resistance to occupation, to a transformation into trauma-centered treatment, to becoming part of the mental health system. These transformations were guided by different motives: population needs, the policies of donors, and the capacity of the academic system to qualify and certify professionals. The authors explore several issues confronting counseling and psychotherapy in Palestine, such as the lack of research and model building that takes into account Arab culture and the inability of current Post Traumatic Stress Disorder (PTSD) treatment models to address the continuous traumatizing situation that undermines the importance of the 'post' aspect in PTSD. In Chapter 35, Counseling and psychotherapy in Turkey: Western theories and culturally-inclusive Methods,

Şenel Poyrazlı, Süleyman Doğan, and Mehmet Eskin explore counseling and psychotherapy in modern Turkey with its roots in the Ottoman Empire era. Current developments in counseling and psychotherapy are depending on Western counseling and psychotherapy techniques and approaches. However, in more recent years, there has been a trend to incorporate indigenous and multicultural approaches and methods into counseling and psychotherapy. Efforts are being made by counseling and psychology associations to establish ethical guidelines and develop structures for certification and licensure at the state level.

We conclude the book with Chapter 36: Counseling and psychotherapy around the world: Current state and future prospects, by Juris G. Draguns who attempts to identify some of the current trends in the evolution of counseling and psychotherapy trans-nationally and to sketch some of the discernible directions for its future. In this overview of 'what the book chapters say', Juris Draguns critiques the internationalization of counseling and psychotherapy, while at the same time draws our attention to the influences of Western counseling and psychotherapy across the globe. His analysis focuses on the applied endeavor of counseling and psychotherapy, which has shifted towards an interpretive, hermeneutic study of the various personal narratives which constitute the raw data of the counseling and psychotherapy experience. He argues that the objective of psychotherapy within this framework has become a truly healing enterprise where clients' narratives are honored. He emphasizes that this orientation is more compatible with the exploratory and open-ended humanistic schools of thought than with the directive and focused methods characteristic of CBT. Indeed, he leaves us without any doubt regarding the role of cross-cultural, trans-cultural, and multicultural influences, the use of traditional and indigenous healing methods, and the contemplation of spirituality in any future development of counseling and psychotherapy.

References

Carter, R. T. (1995). *The Influence of Race and Racial Identity in Psychotherapy*. New York: John Wiley & Sons.

Draguns, J. G. (1997). Abnormal behaviour patterns across cultures: Implications for counseling and psychotherapy. In *International Journal of Intercultural Relations*, *21*(2), 213–48.

——(2001). Toward a truly international psychology: Beyond English only. *American Psychologist*, *11*, 1019–30.

Evans, R. B., & Scott, F. D. J. (1978). The 1913 International Congress of Psychology: The American Congress that wasn't. *American Psychologist*, *33*, 711–23.

Fernando, S. (2010). *Mental Health, Race and Culture*, 3rd edn. New York: Palgrave.

Gazzania, M. S. (2008). *Human: The Science Behind what Makes us Unique*. New York: Ecco.

Gerstein, L. H., Heppner, P. P., Stockton,R., Leung, S.-M. A., & Aegisdottir, S. (2009). The counseling profession in- and outside the United States. In L. H. Gerstein, P. P. Heppner, S. Aegisdottir, S.-M., A. Leung, & K. L. Norsworthy (eds), *International Handbook of Cross-Cultural Counseling*. Thousand Oaks, CA: Sage.

Gerstein, L. H., Heppner, P. P., Aegisdottir, S., Leung, S.-M. A., & Norsworthy, K. L (2009). Cross-cultural counseling: History, challenges, and rationale. In L. H. Gerstein, P. P. Heppner, S. Aegisdottir, S.-M., A. Leung, & K. L. Norsworthy (eds), *International Handbook of Cross-Cultural Counseling*. Thousand Oaks, CA: Sage.

Gielen, U. P., & Comunian, A. L. (eds). (1999). *International Approaches to the Family and Family Therapy*. Padua, Italy: UNIPRESS.

Gielen, U. P., Fish, J., & Draguns, J. G. (eds). (2004). *Handbook of Culture, Therapy, and Healing*. Mahwah, NJ: Erlbaum.

Gielen, U. P., Draguns, J. G., & Fish, J. (eds). (2008). *Principles of Multicultural Counseling and Therapy*. New York: Taylor & Francis.

Gladding, S. T. (2011). Courtland Lee: A global advocate for Counseling. *Journal of Counseling & Development*, *89*, 493–99.

Helms, J. E. (1990). *Black and White Racial Identity: Theory, Research and Practice*. Westport, CT: Greenwood.

Kareem, J. & Littlewood, R. (eds). (1992). *Intercultural Therapy: Themes, Interpretations, and Practice*. Oxford: Blackwell.

Lago, C. (ed.) (2011). *The Handbook of Transcultural Counselling & Psychotherapy*. Berkshire: Open University Press/McGraw-Hill.

Laungani, P. (1997). Replacing client-centered counselling with culture-centered counselling. *Counselling Psychology Quarterly, 10*(4), 343–51.

Marsella, A. (2009). Foreword. In L. H. Gerstein, P. P. Heppner, S. Aegisdottir, S.-M., A. Leung, & K. L. Norsworthy (eds), *International Handbook of Cross-Cultural Counseling*. Thousand Oaks, CA: Sage.

McCabe, G. H. (2007). The healing path: A culture and community derived Indigenous therapy model. *Psychotherapy: Theory, Research, Practice, Training, 44*(2), 148–60.

McCormick, R. (1997). Healing through interdependence: The role of connecting in First Nation healing practices. *Canadian Journal of Counselling 31*, 172–84.

Moodley, R. (2011a). The Toronto Traditional Healers Project: An introduction. *International Journal of Health Promotion and Education, 49*(3), 74–78.

——(2011b). *Outside the Sentence: Readings in Critical Multicultural Counselling and Psychotherapy*. Toronto: CDCP Publications.

Moodley, R. & Bertrand, M. (2011). Spirits of a drum beat: African Caribbean traditional healers and their healing practices in Toronto. *International Journal of Health Promotion and Education, 49*(3), 79–89.

Moodley, R. & Oulanova, O. (2011). Rhythm of the pulse: South asian traditional healers and their healing practices in Toronto. *International Journal of Health Promotion and Education, 49*(3), 90–100.

Moodley, R. & Walcott, R. (eds). (2010). *Counseling across and beyond Cultures: Exploring the Work of Clemmont E. Vontress in Clinical Practice*. Toronto: Toronto University Press.

Moodley, R. & West, W. (2005). *Integrating Traditional Healing Practices into Counseling and Psychotherapy*. Thousand Oaks, CA: Sage.

Moodley, R. Sutherland, P. & Oulanova, O. (2008). Traditional healing, the body and mind in psychotherapy. *Counselling Psychology Quarterly, 21*(2), 153–65.

Pedersen, P. (1991). Multiculturalism as a fourth force in counseling. *Journal of Counseling and Development, 70*, 4–250.

Poonwassie, A. & Charter, A. (2005). Aboriginal worldview of healing: Inclusion, blending, and bridging. In R. Moodley & W. West (eds), *Integrating Traditional Healing Practices into Counseling and Psychotherapy*. Thousand Oaks, CA: Sage.

Robinson-Woods, T. L. (2005). *The Convergence of Race, Ethnicity, and Gender: Multiple Identities in Counseling*. New Jersey: Merrill Prentice Hall.

Roland, A. (1988). *In Search of Self in India and Japan: Towards a Cross-cultural Psychology*. Princeton, NJ: Princeton University Press.

Roopnarine, J. L., & Gielen, U. P. (eds). (2005). *Families in Global Perspective*. Boston, MA: Allyn & Bacon.

Stewart, S. L. (2008). Promoting indigenous mental health: Cultural perspectives on healing from Native counsellors in Canada. *International Journal of Health Promotion and Education, 46*(2), 49–56.

Sue, D. W., & Sue, D. (2008). *Counseling the Culturally Diverse: Theory and Practice*, 5th edn. Hoboken, NJ: John Wiley & Sons.

Thomas, A. & Sillen, S. (1972). *Racism and Psychiatry*. USA: Citadel.

Vontress, C. E. (1962). Patterns of segregation and discrimination: Contributing factors to crime among Negroes. *Journal of Negro Education, 31*, 108–16.

——(1976). Racial and ethnic barriers in counseling. In P. Pederson, W. J. Lonner & J. G. Draguns (eds), *Counseling across cultures*. Honolulu, HI: University Press of Hawaii.

——(1986). Social and cultural foundations. In M. D. Lewis, R. Hayes & J. A. Lewis (eds), *Introduction to the Counseling Profession*. Itasca, IL: Peacock.

——(2008). Existential therapy. In J. Frew & M. D. Spiegler (eds), *Contemporary Psychotherapies for a Diverse World*. Boston, MA: Houghton Mifflin/Lahaska Press.

——(2010). Culture and Counseling: A Personal retrospective. In R. Moodley & R. Walcott (eds) *Counseling across and beyond Cultures: Exploring the Work of Clemmont Vontress in Clinical Practice*. Toronto: University of Toronto Press.

PART I

Counseling and psychotherapy in Africa

1

COUNSELING AND PSYCHOTHERAPY IN EGYPT

Ambiguous identity of a regional leader

Mona M. Amer

Introduction

For over 4,000 years Egypt has been a land of intercultural exchanges of which was knowledge, facilitated by its location at the juncture of three continents: Africa, Europe, and Asia. Cultural diversity continues to be evident with a significant population of tourists and non-native residents. Despite this diversity, more than 99% of the population is of Egyptian ethnicity (Central Intelligence Agency [CIA], 2009). Among Egyptians, 90% are Muslim and 10% are Christian (CIA, 2009). The primary language is Arabic, with longstanding geographical, cultural, and socio-political ties with the rest of the Arab world.

In recent decades Egypt has seen the costly impacts of war, rural to urban migration, a flawed educational system, and political upheaval following the January 25, 2011 popular uprising. While the richest continue to gain in wealth, about 9% remain unemployed and about 16 million live in squatter and informal settlements (Rodenbeck, 2010). Egypt leads the world in hepatitis C infection (Rodenbeck, 2010) and its mega-city Cairo lays claim to the highest air pollution levels across the globe (The World Bank, 2007). However, despite such struggles associated with being a developing country, signs of stability and progress are clearly visible. These include the recent growth of extravagant housing and shopping complexes, private schools and universities, and communication technologies. With respect to health, the government has made significant strides in health indicators such as slashing infant mortality rates (Okasha, 2004). On the other hand, the positive health indicators of reduced infant mortality and increased life expectancy have contributed to the chronic challenge of overpopulation; Egypt is the sixteenth most populate country worldwide, totaling nearly 80.5 million people (CIA, 2009).

These complex socio-economic conditions form the backdrop to the mental health practitioner professions, which have similarly been characterized by juxtaposition between growth and stagnation. On the one hand Egypt has been a frontrunner in the Middle East in numbers of psychiatry and psychology educational programs. On the other hand, it is difficult to ascertain a coherent identity or vision for mental health service in Egypt. This chapter discusses this and many other issues that typify the ambiguous identity of present-day Egyptian counseling and psychotherapy. The review begins by tracing the development of the healing professions from ancient Egypt to contemporary times, highlighting the impacts of intercultural exchange and religious healing. Strengths and shortcomings of present-day education, practice, and research are discussed with an eye to future progress and more rigorous regulation of the field.

Brief history of counseling and psychotherapy

Purposive healing of mental and emotional ailments has a long history in Egypt, dating as far back as the Pharaohs. Insight into ancient mental health concepts and treatments can be gleaned from the Ebers, Edwin Smith Surgical, and Kahun papyri (Nasser, 1987; Okasha & Okasha, 2000). These documents, dating from at least 1,600–1,900 BCE, contain physical descriptions of the brain, as well as references to the mind and consciousness. Descriptions of mental illnesses such as hysteria, psychosomatic conditions, melancholia, thought disorder, dementia, and alcohol intoxication were captured in papyri and on temple walls (Nasser, 1987; Okasha, 2005). There is no record of a professional specialized in mental illness; however, the sorcerer, or temple priest, most likely offered mental health care. Treatment methods included temple sleep ("incubation"), dream interpretation, hypnotic methods, and religious methods integrating magic (Nasser, 1987; Okasha & Okasha, 2000).

It is not clear to what extent ancient Egyptian knowledge was transmitted to Europe through Greek visitors (Laver, 1972). However, centuries later, Greco-Roman theories on mental illness and psychotherapy/healing were conveyed to the Arab world, influencing the healing fields (Ahmed, 1992; Ibrahim, 2012). During the Islamic era, especially the ninth to twelfth centuries, great strides in understanding and treating mental illness occurred (Abou-Hatab, 2004). These were spearheaded by eminent scholars such as Najab ud-din Unhammad, Al-Razi (Razhes), Ibn Sina (Avicenna) and others, who catalogued medical and mental illnesses including etiology, differential diagnoses, symptoms, and preferred treatments (Ahmed, 1992; Ibrahim, 2012; Okasha, 2005). The healer was typically the hakim, a medical doctor (Mohit, 2001a).

Modern day mental health practice in Egypt was also influenced by Europe, and can be traced to the time period after the French occupation: during Mohammed Ali's Ottoman rule from 1805 to 1848. One of Ali's policy priorities was education, and as such several colleges were initiated in association with mosques, including a college of medicine in 1827 that sub-sequently offered psychiatry teachings (Abou-Hatab, 2004). The late 1880s saw the earliest noteworthy psychiatry textbook penned by Ismail Najaty (Abou-Hatab, 2004), and the first free-standing psychiatry hospital located in Abbassia (Okasha, 1993). Other trends included state-sponsored postgraduate studies in Europe and translations of textbooks from other countries into Arabic (Abou-Hatab, 2004). A diploma in neuropsychiatry was established over 65 years ago, and for over a quarter of a century medical schools have offered master's and doctoral degrees (Okasha, 2004).

Parallel to the development of psychiatry was the budding profession of psychology. In 1908 the first secular university—The Egyptian University, now Cairo University—opened its gates. Two decades later it established a department of philosophical studies, under which material related to psychology was taught by mostly French professors. Other universities were subsequently founded, and the concepts and methods of psychological assessment were introduced. This stimulated interest in educational psychology, and a significant number of Egyptian students pursued this and other psychology disciplines in England, France, and the USA (Soueif & Ahmed, 2001).

The first Western-trained Egyptian psychologists returned to Egypt in the 1930s and 1940s to lay the foundations for diverse psychology disciplines including clinical psychology. British-trained educational expert Abdel-Aziz El-Koussy established a psychological clinic for school-aged youth in 1934 at the Higher Institute of Education (now the College of Education at Ain

Shams University) (Abou-Hatab, 1992, 2004). Freudian psychoanalytic techniques were introduced to Egypt by French-trained Mostapha Zewar (Farag, 1987), and clinical psychology gained a presence with Somaya A. Fahmy, who studied in France, Switzerland, and the USA (Abou-Hatab, 2004). Other key pioneers were Marcus Gregory, who in 1939 became the first psychologist to practice psychotherapy, and Mohammed Fathy, who was the second (Abou-Hatab, 1992).

The second half of the 20th century saw dramatic developments in the field of modern psychology, including the establishment of independent psychology departments (Abou-Hatab, 1992; Soueif & Ahmed, 2001) and postgraduate diploma, master's, and doctoral degrees (Ahmed, 1992). The psychologist's identity as a clinician (rather than as a researcher or educator) evolved as Egypt imported psychotherapy models; for example, S. H. Mekhaimer promoted psychoanalysis and A. Abdel-Ghaffar endorsed humanistic psychology (Abou-Hatab, 1992). Moustafa Soueif, who was trained in the UK, shared his expertise in behavior therapy (Abou-Hatab, 1992) and took leadership in defining the role of the clinical psychologist (Ahmed, 2004).

Counselor education programs, accreditation, licensure, and certification

Mental health practitioners in Egypt are typically specialized in either psychiatry or psychology, although some social workers also provide supportive family counseling. Psychiatry students complete 6 years of medical school, followed by a 1-year general internship and 3 years of psychiatry residency. Students can pursue further psychiatry specialization at the diploma, master's, and doctoral levels (Okasha, 2004; Okasha & Karam, 1998). Residency and postgraduate training years are typically spent at psychiatric hospitals, where junior psychiatrists develop competencies in medication management, and, depending on the focus and expertise of their supervisors, learn counseling and psychotherapy skills.

At Egyptian universities, practice-oriented psychology degrees are usually housed in the colleges of arts. The bachelor's degree takes 4 years to complete (Abou-Hatab, 2004; Ahmed, 1992). Postgraduate applied practice diplomas can be completed over 1 year at Cairo University or 2 years at Ain Shams University (Farag, 1987). These diplomas emphasize psychological assessment, although theories of psychotherapy are taught. Most universities require 1–2 years of qualifying coursework to gain admission to master's or doctoral programs (Ahmed, 2004). The master's thesis can take 2–4 years to complete and the doctoral thesis another 3–4 years (Farag, 1987). Theoretical coursework in counseling and psychotherapy is taught, but practical skills will depend on onsite training.

Egypt also has over 25 private universities. The oldest private university to offer a bachelor's degree in psychology is the American University in Cairo (AUC). In 2009 AUC launched a master's degree in counseling that aims to be the first practitioner program in Egypt to integrate systematic hands-on training. Other private universities offer psychology courses, and the October 6 University has an undergraduate psychology department with a comprehensive curriculum that includes coursework in clinical and counseling psychologies.

In response to the absence of systematic counseling and psychotherapy skills training at educational institutions, many universities, private clinics, and professional associations arrange for workshops and training courses by visiting psychotherapy "masters" from other countries, particularly from the USA and UK. Workshops also often highlight the expertise of local psychotherapists. Topics are varied depending on the interest of those organizing the events, such as cognitive-behavioral therapy, eye movement desensitization and reprocessing, sex therapy, and substance abuse counseling.

In terms of accreditation and certification processes, at the present time there are no formal mechanisms in Egypt for accrediting mental health practitioner training programs. Efforts particularly in the private sector are currently underway to certify participants who complete some of the lengthier workshops or training courses. Such certification or accreditation would be obtained from international organizations, particularly from the UK. Most of the courses are presently in the evaluation phase required for application for certification, in which data are collected to evaluate the first administration of the course.

As for licensure, the Law No. 198 was passed in 1956 as a response to the tense debate between psychiatrists and psychologists regarding their respective roles (Soueif, 2001) and the abusive practices undertaken by charlatan and unqualified persons. The law stipulated that in order to be eligible for licensure as a psychotherapist, a person must have completed training such as a diploma in psychiatry or neurology from a national or foreign medical school, certification and specialized training from a local or international psychotherapy organization, or a psychology postgraduate degree plus minimum 2 years of clinical practice at an authorized clinic. Therefore, by default psychiatrists with a diploma from Egypt have permission to practice psychotherapy and open private clinics. Persons who completed training abroad, as well as psychologists, must pass an exam offered by the Ministry of Health (Abou-Hatab, 1992; Farag, 1987).

In the past, psychologists have faced challenges obtaining licensure through the Ministry of Health. For example, in the late 1980s Farag (1987) documented only seven clinical psychologists who had a license and operated a clinic, and Ahmed (2004) observed that from psychologists without Egyptian university affiliation, none had been granted the license. To circumvent these challenges, some psychologists have instead opted to work under the license of a psychiatrist or open private practices as "educational training centers" under the regulation of other government ministries.

With the exception of the 1956 law, there is minimal regulation of psychotherapists and counselors in Egypt. As a result of the laxness in regulations, it is possible to find bachelor's-level graduates who call themselves "psychologists" and claim to offer psychotherapy and counseling without having completed any didactic instruction or sustained training in psychotherapy.

Current counseling and psychotherapy theories, processes, and trends

Counseling and psychotherapy are provided in various settings in Egypt, including public and private psychiatric hospitals, private clinics, prisons, juvenile centers, schools, the military, and courts (Ahmed, 2004). A wide array of therapeutic modalities exists, perhaps as a consequence of the diverse and international training backgrounds among practitioners.

Psychodynamic and psychoanalytic methods have a longstanding history in Egypt, beginning in the 1930s and 1940s. For example, French-trained Zewar pioneered psychoanalytic methods at the Ain Shams College of Arts, where this orientation continued to persist for many decades afterwards (Abou-Hatab, 1992; Farag, 1987). According to Safwat Farag, president of the Egyptian Psychologists Association, other psychoanalytically focused psychology departments include the one at Zagazig University (S. Farag, personal communication, August 9, 2010). Psychiatrists were traditionally trained with a psychoanalytic perspective, and therefore conceptualized mental health symptoms with Freudian explanations (Farag, 1987).

In the 1960s behavioral therapy began to gain prominence in Cairo among both psychologists and psychiatrists, including techniques such as systematic desensitization, deep muscle relaxation, and behavior modification. Cognitive interventions were also used (Soueif, 2001). Nowadays these techniques have become increasingly popular and prevalent, with cognitive-behavioral therapy forming the core orientation at Cairo University (S. Farag, personal communication, August 9, 2010). Behavioral modification is widely utilized, particularly by psychologists serving persons with intellectual disabilities (Farag, 1987).

Group therapy is common at psychiatric hospitals and some private clinics. One well-known mode of group psychotherapy is the Egyptian integrative dynamic model, developed by Y. Rakhawy in the 1970s and modified as the "Minia model." It integrates psychodynamic (object relations), existential, and Gestalt concepts and techniques. As a byproduct of the religio-cultural context, these groups in Egypt developed a leadership style that is more directive, prescriptive, active, and emotionally evocative than their counterparts in the UK, where the less directive British group analysis style favors insight through descriptive interpretations. Also unique to Egypt is the tendency to hold very large open groups (with even 30 participants including multiple trainees), mostly as a consequence of the high service demand that outstrips the number of qualified group practitioners available (Taha, Abd-El-Hameed, Hassan, Kamal, and Mahfouz, 2010; Taha, Mahfouz, and Arafa, 2008).

To supplement the traditional psychotherapy models, many hospitals and private centers claim to offer expressive arts therapies (e.g., art, music, dance movement). However, most of the people providing such services do not have degrees in mental health or counseling, but rather have bachelor degrees from other disciplines (e.g., fine arts, music) paired with a personal interest in mental health.

Indigenous and traditional healing methods

Religion is central to Arab culture, and Arabs turn to religion to cope with mental health concerns (Al-Krenawi, 2005). Because of the significant role of religion in Egyptians' lives, traditional healers are often one of the first sources of support for emotional and behavioral problems, including psychosomatic symptoms and mild to moderate affective and psychotic conditions. A significant portion of Egyptian psychiatric patients—particularly those from lower socio-economic classes—have sought religious counseling prior to visiting a mental health professional (Okasha, 1993; Okasha & Karam, 1998).

Egyptians who seek help from a religious healer may do so because they believe that emotional or interpersonal symptoms are due to the evil eye, black magic, or even influence or possession from the *jinn* or spirits (Al-Issa & Al-Subaie, 2004). Religious healers may prescribe religious counseling, incantations, amulets, talismans, or group methods to help rid the person of the symptoms such as the *zar*.[1] Other methods are ingesting herbal remedies, visiting shrines, and holy men (Al-Issa & Al-Subaie, 2004; Okasha, 1993; Okasha & Karam, 1998).

Some native healing practices are sanctioned by religion, and it is the *sheikh* or priest who offers sage guidance. The ill person and his/her family may pray to God, read from the holy book, and attend religious services at the mosque or church. However, other methods are not supported by formal religions. For example, while the Qur'an acknowledges the influence of evil eye, magic, and jinn, Islam does not condone most of the practices mentioned above. Many of the customs described above were transmitted from the Pharaohs (Elworthy, 2003; Nasser, 1987) or imported to the Arab world through intercultural exchanges when the Islamic empire spread to southern Europe and Asia (Al-Issa & Al-Subaie, 2004). It is not permitted in Islam to engage with fortune-tellers, astrologers, or persons involved with magic (Al-Issa & Al-Subaie, 2004); moreover, the zar is prohibited by Egyptian law because of the potential for the public to be scammed by charlatans (Fam, 2001).

Disdain towards traditional healing practices can be seen in the professional mental health community. There is very little collaboration between religious healers and mental health practitioners, with mental health professionals viewing native healers with skepticism (Okasha & Karam, 1998). Some of Egyptian psychologists' disregard for Islamic mental health knowledge can be attributed to beliefs that religio-cultural traditions are antithetical to intellectual progress and modernization (Abou-Hatab, 2004).

Notwithstanding these negative views towards traditional healers, since the 1970s there has been rising interest in Islamic mental health and "Islamic psychology." This was a consequence of growing dissatisfaction with the practice of importing Western theories and methods, and the desire to produce indigenous treatment models. However, proponents of these approaches have mainly focused on either modifying Western theories to align with Islamic terminology or rediscovering and bringing attention to psychological knowledge produced by early Islamic scholars (Abou-Hatab, 1992). As such, a coherent modern approach to Islamic counseling has not been produced, and Egypt thus far has not seen the emergence of indigenous therapies such as those that arose in Asian countries (Ahmed, 2004).

The integration of Christian counseling in mental health service has also gained recent attention in Egypt. For example, one of the most well-known substance abuse rehabilitation centers is located within a church complex, and program residents can elect to receive a religious component to their care plan. Apart from formal mental health services, pastoral counseling is naturally incorporated in many church services throughout Egypt. However, unlike countries in the West where there are pastoral counseling university degrees, professional organizations, and research journals, there is no formalized field of pastoral counseling or even chaplaincy in Egypt.

Research and supervision

Psychological research in Egypt spans a wide variety of specialties, with major trends related to psychometric standardization, cross-cultural replications of Western studies, and timely socio-cultural issues such as prevalence of cannabis use (Ahmed, 2004; Soueif & Ahmed, 2001). Research related to counseling and psychotherapy—such as process and outcome studies or investigations examining empirical support for particular interventions—is virtually nonexistent.

In the 1990s writers (Abou-Hatab, 1992; Farag, 1987) observed that the bulk of research produced in Egypt is self-financed by the researcher, as government and university grants were limited and collaborative research teams were uncommon. These trends persist today. Because most research tends to focus on replicating or modifying Western findings, creative and unique contributions are scarce (Soueif & Ahmed, 2001). Scholars who wish to conduct studies more relevant to their cultural traditions experience a conflict with their desire to publish in Western journals or meet Western research standards (Ahmed, 1992).

The first psychology journal to be published in the Arab World was *The Egyptian Journal of Psychology*, which produced issues focused on mostly theoretical topics from 1945 to 1953 (Abou-Hatab, 1992; Ahmed, 1992). Since then numerous psychology and psychiatry research journals have been established, in addition to books. Research is presented at numerous annual conferences typically sponsored by university departments and professional associations. These conferences not only showcase studies, but often also provide clinical training workshops with well-known university faculty.

With respect to supervision, psychiatry and psychology academic programs generally do not offer in-house systematic hands-on training, but focus on theoretical and didactic instruction. Training and supervision methods that are common in the West (e.g., two-way mirror, video-taping sessions) are rarely utilized. Instead, students and graduates of the programs learn practical skills in the real-world setting through trial-and-error, self-teaching, and shadowing senior colleagues. Many senior professionals have established on-going case discussion groups, and junior clinicians often join these groups to learn therapy skills through case examples. Moreover, psychiatrists and psychologists who can afford to travel abroad may do so in order to obtain specialized training in psychotherapy.

Strengths, weaknesses, opportunities and challenges

Egypt's establishment of the psychology and psychiatry disciplines predated similar developments in other Arab and Middle Eastern countries by decades; this is considered a major strength. As Soueif and Ahmed (2001) observed, "Egypt was the main gateway through which modern psychology was introduced and practiced in the Arab world" (p. 216). When many Arab countries introduced psychology in the 1950s and 1960s (Ahmed, 1992), the Egyptian experience served as the model for those degrees (Melikian, 1984), and a similar trend was seen in psychiatry training. Moreover, a significant portion of Arab psychologists obtained their degrees (including clinical psychology), from Egyptian universities (Ahmed, 1992).

Egypt has also been a leader in the region with respect to publishing Arabic literature on psychology and transmitting psychological knowledge to Arab states. This includes translating key texts (Ahmed, 2004; Melikian, 1984). In 2001 Egypt claimed approximately 70% of psychological research output in the Arab world (Soueif & Ahmed, 2001).

Being at the forefront of psychology and psychiatry has had its drawbacks for Egypt, however, as Egyptian professionals have been in high demand in Arab countries, leading to a "brain drain" (Abou-Hatab, 1992). For example, from the doctoral-level psychologists at departments in the Arab Gulf states, as many as 50–60% are Egyptian, and about 70% of psychologists in the Arab world are Egyptian (Ahmed, 2004). Also contributing to the brain drain is the large volume of professionals who have chosen to immigrate to North America, Europe, and Australia, as well as to richer Arab Gulf countries where salaries are higher (Ahmed, 2004; Farag, 1987). There moreover continues to be a shortage of qualified psychiatrists in Egypt, including those with specializations in child psychiatry and community psychiatry (Okasha, 2004). For example, by the early 2000s Egypt had approximately 1,000 psychiatrists and approximately 9,000 psychiatric beds (Okasha, 2005), rates that fall well below World Health Organization recommendations of 0.25–1 psychiatrist and 5–8 psychiatric beds for every 10,000 citizens (Okasha & Karam, 1998).

Although the mental health practitioners who remain in Egypt have produced a large volume of research, much of it is unheard of in other parts of the world due to language barriers. Moreover, research is constrained by bureaucracy and small budgets (Ahmed, 2004), and tends to be repetitive and unimaginative, without a coherent and sustained national program of inquiry (Soueif & Ahmed, 2001).

Nonetheless, research opportunities do exist. It would be useful for future research to help explore the relevance of Western treatment techniques to the local religio-cultural contexts (Al-Krenawi, 2005), and the effectiveness of interventions designed for specific populations such as refugees, street children, rural residents, and religious minorities. As locally produced theories and methods emerge, these can also be documented and evaluated. Egyptian scholars already have strengths in conducting replications of Western research, so these skills can be applied to psychotherapy studies. Moreover, as Mohit (2001b) suggested, meaningful research can be linked to mental health practice using simple data collection strategies in service settings.

Progress in Egypt's practitioner training and interventions research will necessitate greater availability of resources, including financial, intellectual, and work force. Better access to published literature can come from collaboration on regional journals (Ahmed, 2004) and bilingual translations of Western and Egyptian scholarship to diffuse the language barriers. Joint ventures with scholars from more privileged nations, as well as regional and international professional associations (Mohit, 2001b) could also enhance the fields.

There is great potential for Egypt to continue serving as a regional leader in mental health research and practice. However, a number of practical challenges hamper this potential, many stemming from a serious strain on Egypt's limited resources caused by overpopulation. Societal challenges include urban poverty and slum areas, illiteracy, economic hardships, and unemployment, as well as ongoing health concerns such as malnutrition and maternal mortality (Mohit, 2001b; Okasha, 2004). A full 20% of the population continues to live below the poverty line (CIA, 2009). These socio-economic hardships contribute to the national burden of mental illness, substance abuse, and youth behavior problems (Mohit, 2001b). Egyptians who face these mental health problems, however, often avoid seeking professional services for fear of shame and loss of family honor. This is consistent with other Arab countries, in which under-utilization of services is attributed to stigma and poor knowledge of available services (Al-Krenawi, 2005). Recent public awareness campaigns by the Ministry of Health and World Health Organization have had some success in reducing mental illness stigma.

Economic constraints negatively impact mental health practitioner education programs as well. This is seen with university bureaucracy and inflexible administration, large student-to-faculty ratio, and limited funding support (Soueif & Ahmed, 2001). Specific resources that are lacking in university settings include library collections of books and journals, laboratory equipment, and technology such as educational films (Ahmed, 1992). These multiple resource constraints inhibit opportunities for creative research and practitioner training. Moreover, as a consequence of stigma and public misconceptions, mental health fields tend to carry lower status, and psychology in particular is criticized as being nonscientific (Soueif & Ahmed, 2001). This results in fewer incentives for people to choose to specialize in these fields.

Another challenge concerns the ongoing contentions between mental health professionals of various disciplines about their respective roles and identities. For example, the roles of school versus clinical psychologists are sometimes contested (Soueif & Ahmed, 2001), and psychological practice is often conflated with social work or psychiatry (Abou-Hatab, 2004). A recent letter from an Alexandrian psychiatrist posted in the newsletter of the Egyptian Psychological Association drew ire from psychologists when it argued that their role should be limited to psychological testing and research. Conversely, many psychologists counter that psychotherapy should be under their domain and psychiatrists' work should be limited to medication management (S. Farag, personal communication, August 9, 2010). Despite these tensions, writers have observed that in many settings there is a collegial and complementary relationship between psychiatrists and psychologist practitioners (e.g., Ahmed, 2004; Farag, 1987; Soueif, 2001).

Mental health practitioners in Egypt also face another tension related to identity, and that is the conflict between an allegiance to Western models versus an appreciation of the Egyptian socio-cultural context. A variety of Western theories and models have been introduced and promulgated in Egypt, often without a careful examination of their religio-cultural applications and sometimes even despite a mismatch to the Egyptian culture (Abou-Hatab, 2004; Ahmed, 2004). As Ahmed (2004) stated, "This epistemological dependence inhibits the creativity in Egyptian psychologists and stifles the emergence of indigenous psychology....this has led, among other things, to a psychology lacking in relevance" (p. 400). This friction between imitating the West and cultivating independent, indigenous models is common to many third world nations, and the domination of Western methods has stymied the potential of Egyptians generating and sharing original psychological concepts with the rest of the world (Abou-Hatab, 2004).

Future directions

For psychotherapy and counseling to flourish in Egypt, perhaps the most critical need is for systematic and rigorous theory-informed practical skills training. Many present-day counselors and psychotherapists gained skills in a scattered patchwork fashion: imitating the interventions and therapeutic stances used by their supervisors, self-teaching by reading books by eminent

Western therapists, and attending intervention-specific workshops. Some service providers completed theoretical coursework on psychotherapy methods during their academic years without receiving applied training. Conversely, others acquired practical skills under the tutelage of a senior clinician, but without ever having completed a systematic course of study on the therapy's theoretical underpinnings. These realities can be frustrating for the budding therapist, and raise concerns about the quality of care offered to clients. It will be important for universities to improve applied skills training as part of formal academic curricula. In doing so they should carefully consider which theories to expound; as previous authors have indicated (Ahmed, 2004; Al-Krenawi, 2005; Melikian, 1984), culturally sensitive models of mental health practice are very much needed.

Perhaps an effective catalyst for improving counseling and psychotherapy training in Egypt would be the institution of more rigorous regulations and/or laws to oversee these professions. Changes should include establishing reasonable minimum necessary educational and training standards for those who can obtain licenses as counselors and psychotherapists, as well as monitoring licensed individuals with respect to their educational and ethical standards. Progress should be made to design and operationalize codes of ethical and professional practices that are relevant to the socio-cultural context. Headway has already been made in this domain; for example, the 1995 Egyptian code of ethics for psychologists was ratified in 2005 (S. Farag, personal communication, August 9, 2010). Once standards are established for the helping professions, many university programs may transform their curricula in order to produce graduates who are prepared for licensure. The Ministry of Health's General Secretariat of Mental Health has already initiated dialogue on these issues, but transformative change may take many years to implement.

The respective roles of psychiatrists, clinical psychologists, and other service providers remain to be negotiated (Soueif, 2001; Soueif & Ahmed, 2001), and should be considered when establishing regulations for the fields. Although some psychiatrists are resistant to psychologists working as psychotherapists (Farag, 1987), observers have noted that as of late psychiatrists are less likely to be trained in and to provide psychotherapeutic services. Contributing factors may be the reshaping of the psychiatry field into a primarily biological discipline (Mohit, 2001b), and time constraints in the medical setting that have led psychiatrists to focus on medical management and supportive psychotherapy (Soueif, 2001). Likewise, not all clinical psychologists are interested in psychotherapy, and practitioners may have gained training in psychotherapy from other countries without a formal degree in clinical psychology. As such, the most useful method of identifying and monitoring counselors and psychotherapists in Egypt may be to license practitioners who have qualified training irrespective of their academic disciplines.

As Egypt cultivates a clearer identity for counselors and psychotherapists and establishes rigorous and transparent regulations, it will be important to disseminate these changes to the general public. Effective strategies are needed to avoid the present-day proliferation of often inaccurate and simplistic notions of psychology (Soueif & Ahmed, 2001) and to enhance understanding of the mental health service (Al-Krenawi, 2005). Greater educational awareness through television, print, and Internet media can help to not only reduce the stigma towards mental health services, but also to equip citizens with the tools needed to select practitioners that are best qualified to meet their needs.

Conclusion

Egypt's geographical location has rendered it fertile ground for the growth and exchange of mental health knowledge. From ancient Egypt until the present time, knowledge regarding the explanations and treatments of psychological illness has flowed back and forth across the

Mediterranean Sea with Europe, and across the Red Sea with the rest of the Middle East. As discussed above, even many of the native healing practices in Egypt actually have origins in other cultures.

Over the past century Egypt served as the regional capital of psychology and psychiatry training and research. Yet despite this rich history, the present status of counseling and psychotherapy is mired by limited opportunities for psychotherapy skills training, ambiguous and contentious professional roles, and unimaginative and repetitive research. The importing of and dependence on Western models that are sometimes unsuitable to the religio-cultural context has stymied creativity and prevented the emergence of unique, indigenous models. Harsh economic conditions have contributed to these struggles; resources are insufficient to support an adequate practitioner work force, retain university faculty, or produce creative psychotherapy research. In the next decade it will be important for Egypt to rectify these deficiencies and develop rigorous and contextually relevant regulations for licensing and monitoring counselors and psychotherapists. Reaching these goals will rely on reflective dialogue and organized planning so that Egypt can emerge a pioneer in the mental health field as it once was at the time of the Pharaohs.

Note

1 *Zar* ceremonies consist of rhythmic music and dancing into the late hours of the night, which produces a trance-like state. The jinn affecting the person is identified, and either appeased or exorcised from the possessed person (Sengers, 2003).

References

Abou-Hatab, F. A.-L. H. (1992). Egypt. In V.S. Sexton & J.D. Hogan (eds), *International Psychology: Views from Around the World* (pp. 111–28). Lincoln: University of Nebraska Press.

——(2004). Psychology in Egypt: A case study from the third world. In H. Stubbe & C. dos Santos-Stubbe (eds), *Kölner beiträge zur ethnopsychologie und transkulturellen psychologie* (pp. 9–22). Göttingen, Germany: V&R unipress.

Ahmed, R. A. (1992). Psychology in the Arab countries. In U. P. Gielen, L. L. Adler, & N. N. Milgram (eds), *Psychology in International Perspective: 50 Years of the International Council of Psychologists* (pp. 127–50). Amsterdam: Swets & Zeitlinger B.V.

——(2004). Psychology in Egypt. In M. J. Stevens & D. Wedding (eds), *Handbook of International Psychology* (pp. 387–403). New York: Brunner-Routledge.

Al-Issa, I., & Al-Subaie, A. (2004). Native healing in Arab-Islamic societies. In U. P. Gielen, J. M. Fish, & J. G. Draguns (eds), *Handbook of Culture, Therapy, and Healing* (pp. 343–66). Mahwah, NJ: Lawrence Erlbaum.

Al-Krenawi, A. (2005). Mental health practice in Arab countries. *Current Opinion in Psychiatry, 18*, 560–64.

Central Intelligence Agency [CIA]. (2009). *The world factbook 2009*. Washington, DC: Author. Retrieved from https://www.cia.gov/library/publications/the-world-factbook/index.html

Elworthy, F. T. (2003). *Evil Eye the Origins and Practices of Superstition*. Whitefish, MN: Kessinger Publishing Company.

Fam, M. (2001, June 3). In Egypt, devotees of zar take a spin with spirits. *Los Angeles Time*. Retrieved from http://articles.latimes.com/2001/jun/03/news/mn-5840.

Farag, S. E. (1987). Egypt. In A. R. Gilgen & C. K. Gilgen (eds), *International Handbook of Psychology* (pp. 172–83). New York: Greenwood.

Ibrahim, A.-S. (2012). Saudi Arabia. In D. B. Baker (ed.), *The Oxford Handbook of the History of Psychology: Global Perspectives* (pp. 442–45). New York: Oxford University Press.

Laver, A. B. (1972). Precursors of psychology in ancient Egypt. *Journal of the History of the Behavioral Sciences, 8*, 181–95.

Melikian, L. H. (1984). The transfer of psychological knowledge to the third world countries and its impact on development: The case of five Arab Gulf oil producing states. *International Journal of Psychology, 19*, 65–77.

Mohit, A. (2001a). Mental health and psychiatry in the Middle East: Historical development. *Eastern Mediterranean Health Journal, 7,* 336–47.

——(2001b). Mental health in the Eastern Mediterranean region of the World Health Organization with a view of the future trends. *Eastern Mediterranean Health Journal, 7,* 353–62.

Nasser, M. (1987). Psychiatry in Ancient Egypt. *Bulletin of the Royal College of Psychiatrists, 11,* 420–22.

Okasha, A. (1993). Psychiatry in Egypt. *Psychiatric Bulletin, 17,* 548–51.

——(2004). Focus on psychiatry in Egypt. *British Journal of Psychiatry, 185,* 266–72.

——(2005). Mental health in Egypt. *The Israel Journal of Psychiatry and Related Sciences, 42,* 116–25.

Okasha, A., & Karam, E. (1998). Mental health services and research in the Arab world. *Acta Psychiatrica Scandinavica, 98,* 406–13.

Okasha, A., & Okasha, T. (2000). Notes on mental disorders in Pharaonic Egypt. *History of Psychiatry, xi,* 413–24.

Rodenbeck, M. (2010). Holding its breath: A special report on Egypt. *The Economist, 396*(8691), S1–S16.

Sengers, G. (2003). *Women and Demons: Cult Healing in Islamic Egypt.* Leiden, The Netherlands: Koninklijke Brill NV.

Soueif, M. I. (2001). Practicing clinical psychology in the Egyptian cultural context: Some personal experiences. *International Journal of Group Tensions, 30,* 241–66.

Soueif, M. I., & Ahmed, R. A. (2001). Psychology in the Arab world: Past, present, and future. *International Journal of Group Tensions, 30*(3), 211–40.

Taha, M., Abd-El-Hameed, M. A., Hassan, M. A., Kamal, A. M., & Mahfouz, R. (2010). Power of love and love of power in group psychotherapy. *Group Analysis, 43,* 155–69.

Taha, M., Mahfouz, R., & Arafa, M. (2008). Socio-cultural influence on group therapy leadership style. *Group Analysis, 41,* 391–406.

The World Bank. (2007). *Air pollution.* Retrieved from http://siteresources.worldbank.org/DATASTATISTICS/Resources/table3_13.pdf.

2

COUNSELING AND PSYCHOTHERAPY IN FRANCOPHONE WEST AFRICA (FOCUS ON SENEGAL)

Creating a future vision

Lonzozou Kpanake and Omar Ndoye

Introduction

Known for its beautiful environment, exotic wildlife, and diverse cultures, Francophone West Africa (FWA) has attracted the interest of outsiders for many centuries. With a population of about 115 million (United Nations, 2011), it is a land of some 10 independent nations: Benin, Burkina Faso, Côte-d'Ivoire, Guinée, Mali, Mauritanie, Niger, Senegal, Tchad, and Togo. A large proportion of these populations still embraces animist religion exclusively, or interwoven with either Islam or Christianity. That is, Islam and Christianity do not reduce the psychological commitment to the animistic beliefs and traditions of their ancestors. Furthermore, although these countries display diversity in their ecology, ethnic, and linguistic composition, several authors (e.g., Diop, 1960; Nsamenang, 1993) claimed a cultural unity and common worldview among them, a unity born out of similar cultural practices, beliefs, and patterns of ecological adaptations and political structures. Thus, while this chapter focuses on Senegal, much of what we shall have to say about this country has broad resonances across other countries.

While the aim of achieving and maintaining an optimal state of wellbeing has exercised ancient Africans' minds for thousands of years, the modern fields of counseling and psychotherapy are in their infancy. However, significant changes are taking place, prompted by a greater availability of trained psychologists and counselors from FWA countries and the growing and persistent social stress (including those arising from HIV/AIDS and from post-election violence). Francophone West Africa metropolitan cities such as Dakar, Abidjan, Lomé, Cotonou, and Ouagadougou are at present undergoing rapid social change associated with increasing urbanization, industrialization, social disorganization, and a breakdown of the extended family which in the past has provided personal and social security (Adjamagbo & Antoine, 2002; Antoine, Bocquier, Fall, Guisse & Nanitelamio, 1995). This drastic change has increased significantly social stress and behavior problems (United Nations Office for West Africa, 2007). On

30

the one hand, significant accomplishments have been achieved for mental health promotion. The government's growing recognition of the need and benefits of psychological services has led to increased investments in higher education programs and expansion of mental health services. On the other hand, psychotherapy and counseling remain "underdeveloped fields" in many FWA countries. All these countries suffer from a serious lack of qualified psychologists and counselors, and there is no legislation to protect their practices. There is nowhere for training in psychotherapy and counseling in some of these countries. Where training programs are available, the contents may be inadequate because of various constraints, such as limited qualified faculty and a lot of exposure to "imported" Western theories and perspectives. In addition, the therapeutic potential of local traditional healing practices remains understudied.

The purpose of this chapter is to present in a descriptive and analytical manner the history, current status, strengths, and weaknesses of counseling and psychotherapy in FWA. It proposes some strategies for further advancement of these practices for West African populations. But prior to taking up an examination of these topics, it seems logical to overview briefly how counseling and psychotherapy emerged and became implanted in FWA.

Brief history of counseling and psychotherapy

Counseling and psychotherapy—as a formalized helping profession—arrived in FWA countries during French colonization (1884–1960) in the context of colonial psychiatry and anthropological research (Collignon, 2002). The attitude of colonial psychiatrists reflected that of the colonizers' general attitude to the colonized peoples. For instance, the terms used to think about "madness" in these colonies are nothing more than an accentuation of the discrimination inflicted on those colonized. As underscored by René Collignon working in Senegal, "whereas in Europe, the madman embodies a radical figure of otherness, he is the *other* of reason. In Africa the colonial subject already occupies another place in the colonists' *imaginaire*, that of the Savage" (Collignon, 2002, p. 469). In the book *La Folie au Sénégal*, Mamadou Diouf and Mohamed Mbodj recognize in both decolonization and transcultural psychiatry the common theme of freedom from the colonial denial of Senegalese culture (Diouf & Mbodj, 1997). Under colonialism the wholesale imposition of Western medical knowledge on the Senegalese tended toward the destruction of traditional beliefs and the negation of indigenous culture (Bouvenet, 1955; French Africa High Commissioner, 1941).

Since the early days of the 20th century, psychoanalytic thinking has shown a keen interest in ethnology and anthropology. This interest derived primarily from the wish to explore the "archaic layers of the unconscious," for which psychoanalysts searched for evidence in what they called "primitive cultures" (Freud, Strachey, & Gay, 1990; Jones, 1924). Most French itinerant therapists and scholars found indigenous tributes in the colonies as relevant field for the universal validation of the foundations of psychoanalytic theory.

As independence approached for *Afrique Occidentale Française* (the group of France's colonies in West Africa) in 1960, France built the University of Dakar, Dakar, as a gift and an enduring French legacy for the region. It was at this university in the 1960s that pioneering French mental health practitioners in FWA countries, such as Henri Collomb, René Collignon, and Marie-Cécile Ortigues, initiated a dialogue between Western mental health perspectives and Senegalese cultures, a dialogue that revealed traditional Senegalese methods for understanding and treating mental illness and emotional problems as "modernization" took hold (Bullard, 2005). Dr. Henri Collomb, chief psychiatrist at the University of Dakar until 1978 and the driving force behind the rise of Dakar's medical school program in mental health, deserves much credit for cultivating cultural-sensitized psychotherapy in Senegal (Bullard, 2005; Collignon, 1978, 2002).

Newly independent Senegal and the Fann Hospital under the dynamic direction of Dr. Collomb provided a nourishing therapeutic environment for indigenous people. Their most successful break with the colonial past was engaging Senegalese beliefs and traditions that had been stifled under colonial authority. The Fann Hospital offered an interesting insight into traditional conceptions and therapeutics within the framework of a public healthcare structure (Collomb, 1978, 1973).

The history of counseling in FWA countries cannot be devoid of the pioneering work of Collomb's team in Senegal. They instituted a type of "village council" in the 1960s known by the Wolof name of *penc* for their clients and their families. In order to integrate the healing experience into the patient's social world, each client needed to be accompanied during his or her stay by a family member. Moreover, they created "healing villages" throughout Senegal. The principles of healing villages are (1) the patient and his family are considered as a unit in a sociocultural family situation identical to their own; (2) the healing program respects and incorporates existing administrative structures; the chief of each village remains chief of the healing community; and (3) the existing traditional beliefs and healing concepts are not ignored, but are used. Every attempt is made to recreate the village environment familiar to the patient. The central feature of the system is the participation of relatives in the healing process (Collignon, 1985; Collomb, 1978; Dia, 1976). Today, FWA countries are facing numerous health challenges, most notably the AIDS pandemic and psychological distress related to political violence. Inspired by Collomb's team framework, most programs for health promotion in FWA countries involve local community and spiritual leaders and traditional healers.

Counselor education, accreditation, licensure, and certification

The historical development of counseling psychology clearly reveals its nascent state in FWA. As a matter of fact, most people have neither heard nor seen a psychologist, a counselor, or a psychotherapist. This may be due to the marginal status of these disciplines in academia and the rudimentary but fragmented nature of psychological services (Nsamenang, 1993). Compared to its status in other developing world regions, the training in counseling and clinical psychology in FWA countries is inchoate.

Academic programs in clinical or counseling psychology in FWA countries were not established until the 1980s. Today, each of these countries has a program dedicated to psychological training and education. The Université de Lomé in Togo has an undergraduate and graduate training program in clinical and counseling psychology. Students are provided with a 3-year diploma in applied psychology, then a 2-year master's degree in counseling and clinical psychology. This department's requirements for the master's degree consist of coursework and an internship. Content courses include seminars, methodological courses, and a significant amount of exposure to theories and perspectives in psychological assessments and clinical interventions. The Université de Ouagadougou, Burkina-Faso, has a 4-year undergraduate program with an orientation in clinical psychology during the 2 last years. The content of this program involves an internship and courses such as ethnopsychiatry, projective techniques, and systemic approaches in psychology. In Côte d'Ivoire, the Université d'Abidjan Cocody has a 5-year program within the *Centre d'Enseignement et de Recherche en Psychologie Appliquée* (Center for Studies and Research in Applied Psychology), tailored for graduate students training to become counseling psychologists. Other FWA countries' universities such as Université Cheikh Anta Diop (Senegal), Université de Niamey (Niger), and Université d'Abomey Calavi (Bénin) have only undergraduate training in general psychology. In most of these countries, psychology has not been recognized as a full-fledged academic discipline (Nsamenang, 1993). For example, at the Université de Ouagadougou, the psychology program is included as part of the philosophy department. The typical pattern of faculty is as follows: full professors and Associate professors were trained in Western countries, with most Assistant professors and instructors trained in local universities. Because there are only a limited number of faculty holding a doctoral degree, students with master's degrees often teach in universities in which they receive their degree. Such scarcity of qualified faculty may lead to restricted perspective of the discipline, undermine the quality of teaching, and lower the quality of future counseling and clinical psychologists. Outside of the universities, the ministries of health of each of the FWA countries provide 2–7 day training seminars for health professionals on counseling topics in the context of pandemic diseases such as AIDS.

Communication between therapists is greatly lacking in FWA countries. None of these countries has an association or corporation of therapists, except for Senegal with the Senegalese Association for the Development of Applied Psychology and the Senegalese Association of Family Therapy and Systemic Approach. Further, there is no accreditation or licensing board for those interested in becoming counseling or clinical psychologists or any legislation to protect psychologists. Consequently, untrained people in private practice claim to be able to provide psychological counseling and therapy. However, at least a 5-year degree in psychology is required for a counseling or clinical psychology job in governmental institutions such as healthcare facilities, schools, and incarcerating centers.

In comparison to Europe and North America, the psychologist/population ratio is very low. For example, Senegal's 20 psychologists is too small for an estimated population of 14 million people, so is Togo's nine psychologists for 6 million people. However, these ratios still exceed those of other FWA countries. Most of these psychologists work in public hospitals.

Current counseling and psychotherapy theories, processes, and trends

There exists in FWA countries a broad spectrum of "psychotherapy," all of which were imported from the West by first-generation psychologists trained mainly in France. In terms of basic orientations, methods and goals to be achieved, they may be grouped into three categories: psychoanalytic psychotherapy, cognitive-behavioral therapy, and family therapy.

Knowledge of psychoanalytic theories and therapies was introduced in FWA countries as early as the colonial era (Collignon, 1978). The theorization of insight into traditional healing was one of the most ambitious attempts by Dakar School to link psychoanalysis and ethnology, namely, the universality of the personality structure and the specificity of local culture, explicitly rejecting any culturalistic legacy (see, Ortigues & Ortigues, 1966). Henri Collomb, Andreas Zempleni, and Cécile Ortigues, among others, attempted in their clinical practices to be conversant with the Senegalese culture and worldview. For instance, Ortigues & Ortigues (1966) and Zempleni (1968) use the concept of projection (defense mechanism) to understand their indigenous clients explaining the etiology of their illness in terms of possession. Collomb (1973) believes also that symbols used during traditional healing ceremonies work at an unconscious level because they are related to such fundamental questions as birth and death, fusion and separation. In a seminal book "*L'Oedipe Africain*," Cécile Ortigues and Edmond Ortigues reported an adaptation of Freudian psychoanalytic principles to Senegalese traditional systems of healing (Ortigues & Ortigues, 1966).

Cognitive-behavioral therapy has been generally recognized and accepted in FWA countries. The role and responsibilities of cognitive and behavior therapists are welcomed to alter some of these behavioral problems. More and more psychologists refer to behavioral and cognitive skills to cope with behavioral problems. The emphasis on action, which is basic to behavior therapy, in contrast to verbal interaction, is perceived and accepted more favorably by the clients. That may be explained by cultural and socioeconomic reasons advocating cognitive-behavioral therapy for FWA populations. In fact, the expectations of FWA clients include immediate symptom relief, guidance and advice, and a problem-centered approach. Such a short-term and problem-solving approach is more consistent with the expectations of these populations whose pressing life circumstances demand immediate action.

Because of the extended family structure in Senegal (Diop, 1985; Lambert, Huart & Seck, 2002) and the interdependency of the patient and his family (Collignon, 1985; Ortigues & Ortigues, 1966), many therapists shift their focus on interpersonal issues within a family group in terms of structure and process (Lambert, Huart, & Seck, 2002). The Senegalese Association of Family Therapy and Systemic Approach, formed in 1998, assures training in family and systemic therapy in Senegal and in Mauritania (Lambert, Huart, & Seck, 2002).

Some of the trained therapists have developed an expertise in one of these clinical approaches and use it predominantly with their clients regardless of the clinical case. The others vary their therapeutic approach depending on the client's needs and the diagnostic. For instance, cognitive-behavioral approaches are favored for anxiety disorders, while psychodynamic approaches are favored for somatization cases attributed to external supernatural forces (Nwoye, 2010). Since the great majority of trained therapists are employed in public institutions, they use their therapeutic approaches with clients in hospitals, youth/child centers, refugee camps, and family institutes. This is a trend that shows that the mental health and wellbeing field is no more a preserve of psychiatrists and medical general practitioners. Counseling and clinical psychologists are presently integrated in healthcare settings. They usually work in multidisciplinary teams including psychiatrists, nurses, and social workers.

Indigenous and traditional healing methods

Before colonial times, indigenous populations along the Guinean gulf (West Africa) had an established system of healthcare that included the recognition and management of the mentally ill and was provided by traditional healers. Even nowadays, the great majority of these populations rely on traditional healers when experiencing intellectual, physical, psychological, emotional, or spiritual distress (Ndoye, 2006; Vontress, 1999, 2005). These healers have been found to carry out practices of therapeutic values that are accepted by the people. Indigenous therapy is strongly colored by the African philosophical concepts or value systems, that is, the African worldview. It is based on the concept of the "unity" of life and time, and draws no sharp distinction between animate and inanimate, natural and supernatural, the dead and the living, and material and spiritual (Vontress, 1999, 2005).

Although they are known by different names depending on the country or the ethnic group and the language used to describe them, such as *Marabout* or *Ndöpkat* in Senegal, *Koedu* or *Hoonon* in Togo, and *Komyen* or *Kramo* in Côte d'Ivoire, Vontress's (2005) overview of the variety of traditional healers in FWA notes six categories of traditional healers: indigenous doctors, herbalists, fetish men, mediums, spiritual healers, and sorcerers.

People consult a healer for a wide range of difficulties in their living. A healer in Burkina-Faso interviewed by Vontress (1999) broke down these problems into four categories: (1) the *physical*, including infertility, stomach pains, inability to sleep, and other organic illness; (2) the *psychological*, including clients' complaints that someone has put a hex on them, "going out of" one's mind, and nightmares; (3) *concerns about success in life*, including successfully wooing and winning the heart of another person, finding a good job, succeeding in business, harvesting a good crop, succeeding in hunting, winning an election, and building a good house; and (4) *the spiritual*, which often involves clients' fear of having offended departed ancestors or that spirits are impacting them negatively.

Traditional healers use a variety of procedures to assess and diagnose a client's problems. Commonly, the heads of families bring members needing treatment, explaining their symptoms. Then, the healer tries to understand the cause of the problem by exploring the history of symptoms and the client's behavior at home and in the community, so as to ascertain whether the individual has offended an ancestor or a spirit has been made angry, whether some body has put a hex on the sick person, and whether the sick person or somebody in the family has broken a taboo. The family usually knows if it is so. The healers proceed by asking probing questions to determine any correspondence between one's personal relations and the cause of the sickness. (Collomb, 1973; Ortigues & Ortigues, 1966).

Whatever the method the healers use, diagnosis revolves not around identifying and locating an illness, but rather determining etiology and treatment of the onset circumstances. Thus, diagnosis takes the form of a dialogue between the patient and the healer concerning the recognition of these circumstances, involving interactional changes in the life of the individual. Healers commonly refrain from baldly naming the witch who is responsible for their patient's illness. By oblique reference, they will indicate that the malignant person belongs to this family or environment. For example, "a man in your maternal side family," "a colleague who envy you." This particular healing context not only involves a low degree of diagnostic specificity but also provides an alternative notion of diagnosis in a process (Vontress, 1999; 2005).

Healers use diverse intervention strategies to eradicate, alleviate, or prevent physical, psychological, and spiritual problems of their clients. These interventions include exorcism, incantations, suggestions, music, chanting, dancing, and the use of a wide range of healing ingredients, such as herbs, bones, talisman, animal hides, dried snakes, horns, shells, minerals, and so on. Such interventions are used singly or interactively depending on the patient's needs as shown by the assessment.

Research and supervision

A review regarding research on psychotherapy and counseling in FWA countries seems to indicate the existence of serious problems. Some of the problems emerge from the nature of psychological concepts which are under investigation and deficiency in theoretical background. That is, psychology and counseling lack indigenous concepts and tools to capture local knowledge and points of view adequately. Related to this is the issue of scientific acculturation, which is not simply an imperialist academic domination of local scholars but also a self-imposed emulation of Euro-American models (see Nsamenang, 1995). Another important deterrent to research is political instability. The uncertainty it creates leads to unstable research leadership. This, in turn, makes for short-term planning, which cannot sustain enduring lines of research (Nsamenang, 1995). Political interference in the form of intrusion, such as the several times closure of the Université de Niamey, Niger, by the Government (French Embassy in Niger, 2009) is also inimical to progress. Lack of political stability is also illustrated by a civil war in Côte d'Ivoire in 2002, and a 1992 9-month workers' strike in Togo, paralyzing research activities in these countries. Other factors that militate against research include lack of funding, lack of relevant technological instruments, illiteracy, poor record keeping, and unreliable vital statistics.

However, Senegal has been a central place in research on psychotherapy and counseling. It is mostly the result of the presence of a well-known journal devoted to African mental health issues, which is *Psychopathologie Africaine* (African Psychopathology), a quarterly journal published in Dakar, Senegal, since 1965. It was founded by Moussa Diop and Henri Collomb within the *Société de Psychopathologie et d'Hygiène Mentale de Dakar* (Dakar Society for Psychopathology and Mental Health) to publish the research of Fann School and psychiatric reports and research from across Africa.

In terms of supervision, the few psychology departments providing graduate programs in counseling and clinical psychology in FWA have acknowledged the importance of clinical supervision. These programs have integrated supervision as part of the requirements for graduation. For example at the Université de Lomé, Togo, at least 800 hours of clinical supervision are required to complete the internship. That is similar to the requirements for the 4-year diploma at the Université de Ouagadougou, Burkina-Faso. However, the quality of supervision is undermined by issues related to the nascent state of the field in the FWA. First, because of the serious lack of qualified therapists, trainees cannot be provided individual supervision. For example, it is not uncommon for a qualified therapist to provide supervision to more than 10 trainees during the same period. Also, many trainees complete their internships or practical period in settings where there are no qualified therapists to provide supervision. Furthermore, as a consequence of the dearth of research on effective clinical supervision, many clinical supervisors in FWA lack adequate training and guidelines for supervision competency. In addition, the absence in these countries of any organization that regulates supervision complicate the institution of the supervision criteria and evaluation system.

Strengths, weaknesses, opportunities, and challenges

Counseling and psychotherapy in FWA countries is evolving rapidly in response to the ongoing drastic social changes in this region of the world. Below, we offer an overview of some of the strengths, weaknesses, opportunities, and challenges involved in the burgeoning counseling and psychotherapy in FWA.

Despite the existence of serious problems over decades, there are a variety of strengths in the field. For instance, the population of trained therapists in FWA is increasing. Counseling and psychotherapy services are gaining a wider recognition and acceptance within the populace. There is a consensus among local therapists that the future of counseling and psychotherapy fields in FWA is promising. It is expected that the growing and unrelenting social stresses related to pandemic illness (e.g. HIV/AIDS), and periods of political turmoil and armed conflict in FWA will continue to increase public demand of counseling and psychotherapy services. Indeed, such stressful situations have started to make the needs of counseling and psychotherapy much more visible to FWA governments. Furthermore, the quality of counseling and psychotherapy services has improved significantly as a result of local therapists' efforts to integrate African traditional healing methods into counseling and psychotherapy. Such a trend was inevitable for FWA therapists if we were to find a way to be therapeutic without ignoring our clients' needs.

Weaknesses in the field are also apparent. In contrast to the usefulness of traditional healing, its potential ill effects have not been widely studied and reported. Yet, clinical observation has disclosed that some traditional healers may cause harm to the clients who seek their services through financial deceit or fraud, sexual involvement with a client, prescribing dangerous substances, or physically injuring clients (Pelzer, 1987). Clearly there is a wide range of "professional" quality among traditional healers and different motivations for practice. The major problem, from a public health point of view, is that in most countries there still are no formal guidelines for regulating traditional healing. Traditional healing, whether it is practiced by herbalist, diviner, or medium, should be subject to periodic surveys and re-evaluation by the public health administration, as is modern clinical work, so that its benefits to clients can be protected and any potential malpractice can be prevented. In some countries such as Burkina Faso the government has actually begun implementing an accreditation and regulation process for traditional healers.

In terms of opportunities, psychotherapy cannot successfully develop in FWA without having the local reality as the basis for its growth. Therefore, indigenization as a process of deriving consultation and therapeutic practices from the West African cultural system and feeding them back onto it is becoming an acceptable and legitimate research goal. In Senegal, Dr. Omar Ndoye and his colleagues at the *Société de Psychopathologie et d'Hygiène Mentale* (Dakar Society for Psychopathology and Mental Health) are engaged in studying how the healthy aspects of the traditional culture can be adapted to formulate appropriate psychotherapy.

Numerous serious challenges remain. There is a serious lack of trained therapists to respond to the increasing demands for counseling and psychotherapy in FWA. More psychology departments with graduate programs in counseling and clinical psychology are urgently needed. Second, to elevate the quality of professional training and the delivery of psychological services, each of the FWA countries should institute a professional organization of therapists. Such an organization would establish a licensing process. Thus, therapists who wish to be licensed must meet a set of educational and clinical competencies. In addition, such an organization could take the lead in establishing the supervision criteria and evaluation of therapist training and development. Third, the lack of legal recognition of the profession undermines the development of the discipline. If FWA therapists were to gain legal status, it would be time for serious efforts to lobby for legislation governing their practices. Finally, given the scarcity of opportunities that exist for FWA therapists to interact with each other, more efforts to open up these professionals to themselves should be praiseworthy.

Future directions

The search for relevance and progress in counseling and psychotherapy in FWA should concentrate on their "indigenization." That is, these interventions should be culturally relevant. Some strategies deserving attention are discussed below.

As previously developed, most people in FWA have neither heard nor seen a therapist and have no concept of psychotherapy and what its purposes are. Therefore, the psychotherapeutic rules and the purpose of specific therapeutic techniques need to be explained to the patient and discussed. For instance, dream analysis, free association or interpretation of unconscious dynamics in psychoanalysis; reframing or paradoxical suggestions in family therapy; and positive enforcement or punishment in behavior therapy must be carefully explained and guidance on how to follow them is always needed.

Psychotherapy always involves subtler normative questions of how to live the good life, and its goals are tied to the cultural concept of the person (Kirmayer, 2007). Ignorance of how African people conceptualize their person has led to severe consequences, such as misdiagnosis and inappropriate therapeutic goals (Meyer, Moore & Viljoen, 2002). For decades psychotherapy in FWA has been dominated by the Euro-American egocentric concept of the person, causing a lot of pain to Africans' mental health. Psychological adjustment depends on the degree of match between the patient's cultural ideal of the person and the concept of the person inherent in any given therapeutic practice (Kirmayer, 2007). This implies that we need to consider the way people in FWA conceptualize a person. In fact, the personhood in FWA is grounded on dynamics between a nature-wide self, the spiritual entities, and the social world. Such a personhood is behind the indigenous notions of health, illness, and recovery.

Therapeutic approaches emphasizing introspection and an internal locus of control are not suggested when engaging in healing processes with patients in FWA. Rather, an emphasis should be made on the two fundamental psychic processes inspired by traditional healing: establishing links and containment. Therefore therapists should (1) consider the involvement of the patient's family and community members, (2) respect the patients' spiritual narratives as objective realities, and (3) learn the way local people conceptualize their self boundaries and its implication for successful psychotherapies (e.g., psychotherapy by environmental manipulation). Such a therapeutic approach stresses the whole person's change, rather than to produce a merely internal reorganization of the person. It becomes evident that psychotherapy which does not incorporate the patients' spiritual life, their family members or important ones, their events, their hopes, and their concerns cannot speak to West African clients who are fundamentally spiritual and communal.

Conclusion

This chapter presents an overview of psychotherapy and counseling in FWA with focus on Senegal, and proposes some strategies for its further advancement and relevancy. Psychotherapy is an ethnocentric practice, cultivated mainly in Western societies and then exported to FWA during colonization. It is still nascent and unfamiliar with local populations, who rely on traditional healers for their mental illness and emotional problems. Effective psychotherapy's failure to thrive in FWA is due to its failure to respond appropriately to local clients' needs and expectations, as well as systemic, social, and political factors that militate against personnel training, research, and the mental health service. Contemporary mental health workers have come to realize that cultural dimensions cannot be ignored in the practice of psychotherapy and counseling. In the context of FWA it seems inevitable for counselors and psychologists to find a way to be therapeutic without ignoring their client's needs. Practically, it will be worthwhile to pay particular attention to the cultural adjustment of psychotherapy and counseling. Promising strategies include adapting concepts and theories of psychotherapy to West African realities and integrating traditional healers practice into psychotherapy and counseling.

References

Adjamagbo, A., & Antoine, P. (2002). Le Sénégal face au défi démographique [The demographic challenge in Sénégal]. In M. C. Diop (ed.), *La Société sénégalaise entre le local et le global* (pp. 511–97). Paris: Karthala.

Antoine, P., Bocquier, P., Fall, A. S., Guisse, Y. M., & Nanitelamio, J. (1995). *Les familles dakaroises face à la crise* [Families in Dakar face the crisis]. Dakar: IFAN/ORSTOM/CEPED.

Bouvenet, G. (1955). *Recueil annoté des textes de droit pénal applicables en Afrique Occidentale Française* [Annotated collection of texts of criminal law in French West Africa]. Paris: Editions de l'Union Française.

Bullard, A. (2005). L'Œdipe africain, a retrospective. *Transcultural Psychiatry, 42,* 171–203.

Collignon, R. (1978). Vingt ans de travaux à la clinique psychiatrique de Fann-Dakar [Twenty years of work at the psychiatric department of Dakar-Fann]. *Psychopathologie Africaine, 15,* 133–324.

——(1985). L'idée de 'village psychiatrique': Expériences ouest africaine [The idea of "psychiatric village": West African experience]. *Psichiatria e psicoterapia analitica, 2,* 153–74.

——(2002). Pour une histoire de la psychiatrie coloniale française: A partir de l'exemple du Sénégal [A history of French colonial psychiatry: The example of Senegal]. *L'Autre, 3,* 455–80.

Collomb, H. (1973). Rencontre de deux systèmes de soins. À propos de thérapeutiques des maladies mentales en Afrique [Meeting of two systems of care: Treatment of mental illness in Africa]. *Social Science & Medicine, 7,* 623–33.

——(1978). L'économie des villages psychiatriques [The economics of psychiatric villages]. *Social Science & Medicine, 12,* 113–15.

Dia, A. (1976). Une communauté thérapeutique: le Pinth de Fann [A therapeutic community: Fann's "pinth"]. *African Journal of Psychiatry*, *1*, 147–51.

Diop, A. B. (1985). *La famille Wolof* [The Wolof family]. Paris: Karthala.

Diop, C. A. (1960). *L'Univers culturelle de l'Afrique Noire* [The cultural universe of Black Africa]. Paris: Présence Africaine.

Diouf, M., & Mbodj, M. (1997). L'Administration coloniale et la question de l'aliénation mentale (1840–1956) [The colonial administration and the issue of insanity (1840–1956)]. In L. d'Almeida, M. Ba, P. B. Cou-loubaly, M. C. Diop, M. Diouf, et al. (eds), *La folie au Sénégal* (pp. 13–54). Dakar: Association des Chercheurs Sénégalais.

French Africa High Commissioner. (1941). *La justice indigène en Afrique occidentale française* [Indigenous justice in French West Africa]. Rufisque: Imprimerie du Haut-Commissariat.

French Embassy in Niger (2009). Fiche Niger [Niger sheet]. Retrieved March 05, 2010, from www.diplomatie.gouv.fr/fr/IMG/pdf/Fiche_Curie_Niger.pdf

Freud, S., Strachey, J., & Gay, P. (1990). *Group Psychology and the Analysis of the Ego*. New York: W.W. Norton & Company.

Jones, E. (1924). *Essays in Applied Psycho-Analysis*. London: Hogarth Press.

Kirmayer, L. J. (2007). Psychotherapy and the cultural concept of the person. *Transcultural Psychiatry*, *44*, 232–57.

Lambert, P., Huart, N., & Seck, B. (2002). L'expérience sénégalaise en thérapie familiale systémique [Senegalese experience of systemic and family therapy]. *Thérapie familiale*, *23*, 61–80.

Meyer, W., Moore, C., & Viljoen, H. (2002). *Personology: From Individual to Ecosystem*. Cape Town: Heinemann Publishers.

Ndoye, O. (2006). Vorstellung eines Besessenheitsrituals—"Ndoep" aus dem Senegal [An idea of a ritual of possession—"Ndoep" from Senegal]. In E. Wohlfart & M. Zaumseil, *Transkulturelle Psychiatrie-Interkulturelle Psychotherapie, Interdisziplinäre Theorie und Praxis* (pp. 285–97). Heidelberg: Spinger.

Nsamenang, A. B. (1993). Psychology in sub-Saharan Africa. *Psychology and Developing Societies*, *5*, 171–84.

——(1995). Factors influencing the development of psychology in Sub-Saharan Africa. *International Journal of Psychology*, *30*, 729–30.

Nwoye A. (2010). A psycho-cultural history of psychotherapy in Africa. *Psychotherapy and Politics International*, *8*, 26–43.

Ortigues, M. C., & Ortigues, E. (1966). *L'Oedipe Africain* [African Oedipus]. Paris: Plon.

Pelzer, K. (1987). *Traditional Healing and Psychosocial Health in Malawi*. Heidelberg: Asanger.

United Nations. (2011). *World Population Prospects, the 2010* Revision. Retrieved October 7 from http://esa.un.org/wpp/Excel-Data/population.htm

United Nations Office for West Africa (2007). *Urbanization and Insecurity in West Africa: Population Movements, Mega Cities, and Regional Stabilities*. UNOWA, Issue papers. Retrieved March 05, 2010, from www.un.org/unowa/unowa/studies/urbanization_and_insecurity_in_wa_en.

Vontress, C. E. (1999). Interview with a traditional African healer. *Journal of Mental Health Counseling*, *21*, 326–36.

——(2005). Animism: Foundation of traditional healing in sub-Saharan Africa. In R. Moodley & W. West (eds). *Integrating Traditional Healing Practices into Counseling and Psychotherapy* (pp. 124–37). Thousand Oaks, CA: Sage.

Zempleni, A. (1968). *L'interprétation et la thérapie traditionnelle du désordre mental chez les Wolof et les Lébou du Sénégal* [Interpretation and traditional healing of mental illness among the Wolof and Lebu of Senegal]. Thèse de 3ème cycle en ethnologie, EHESS, Paris.

3

COUNSELING AND PSYCHOTHERAPY IN NIGERIA

Horizons for the future

Olaniyi Bojuwoye and Andrew A. Mogaji

Introduction

Nigeria is the largest of the West African coastal states and, with an estimated population of 158.4 million (United Nations, 2010), it is the most populous country in Africa. With over 250 heterogeneous ethnic groups, Nigeria is one of the most ethnically diverse countries in Africa, and, relative to its size, in the world (World Almanac, 2010). Despite the country's heterogeneous ethnic groupings there are commonalities in traditional or cultural practices including psychotherapeutic and other healthcare practices. Traditional cultural counseling and psychotherapeutic practices have been in existence since time immemorial. However, just before independence in 1960, and as a consequence of foreign cultural incursions, Western-oriented models of counseling and psychotherapy began to take root in various aspects of Nigerian societal life.

While foreign cultural influences have seriously decimated traditional cultural values and practices, Nigerian traditional psychotherapeutic and other healthcare-related practices continue to flourish, servicing more than 60% of the population (Bojuwoye, 2010; Idemudia, 2003). Indigenous knowledge and practices transmitted from generation to generation, mostly verbally, have evolved into unique traditional cultural psychotherapeutic methods and strategies for diagnosis, prevention, treatment, and elimination of physical, mental, and social illnesses, thereby bringing wellbeing to the people (Adekson, 2003). These psychotherapeutic practices are informed by the various paradigms of illness and health which are bound to cultures, social constructions, and/or worldviews (Ipaye, 1995; Olatawura, 2007).

Backed by culturally held beliefs and paradigms of illness, the Nigerian people also recognize certain members of their communities (e.g., traditional healers and or diviners) as experts in psychotherapeutic and other health-related practices due to their unique competencies in the uses of cultural knowledge, tools, and substances as well as methods based on traditional cultural beliefs, social, and religious value systems.

However, this is not suggesting a diminished Western cultural influence. On the contrary, Western-oriented models of counseling and psychotherapy with their ideologies and hegemonic practices, which have been superimposed on Nigerian people by the colonialists, have occupied the center stage and are regarded as "standard" mainstream practice models for Nigeria.

This chapter discusses counseling and psychotherapy in Nigeria starting with an exploration of the history of modern counseling and psychotherapeutic models. This is followed by a discussion on counselor training and certification, the current psychotherapeutic theories that inform practices, indigenous traditional methods, research into traditional practices, and future direction for counseling and psychotherapy in Nigeria.

Brief history of counseling and psychotherapy

Traditional counseling and psychotherapy have been in existence in Nigeria since time immemorial (Adekson, 2003; Ipaye, 1995; Makinde, 1984). However, just before Nigeria attained independence from Great Britain in 1960, and as consequence of foreign cultural incursions, Western-oriented counseling and psychotherapy began to take root in various aspects of Nigerian societal life. The rapid social and economic changes taking place as Nigeria transitioned to independent status as a nation made conditions favorable for Western-oriented psychological practices, which were first directed towards youths who experienced difficulties making decisions about their future. Indeed, Western-oriented psychological practice was first introduced in the form of school psychology in 1959. The school psychology programs were initially geared towards personal and vocational guidance and placement services (Adekson, 2003; Ipaye, 1995; Makinde, 1984). However, later development in school psychological practices which saw the establishment of a USAID (United States Agency for International Development) assisted comprehensive high school in Aiyetoro in 1967, led to the expansion of school psychological services beyond vocational education to program services geared towards all aspects of development. The overarching belief at the time was that society could be improved if youths in the throes of development were assisted through the application of psychological knowledge (Bojuwoye, 1987; 1997).

The formation of the Nigerian Career Council (NCC) in 1963, immediately following the introduction of school psychology in 1959, facilitated the awareness of the need for psychological services. This was carried out through dissemination of information by publication of a newsletter and a journal titled *CAREERS* (Adekson, 2003; Ipaye, 1995; Makinde, 1984). The Nigerian Career Council organized a number of conferences and workshops and through its journal, *CAREERS*, informed the public of the importance of psychological knowledge and the roles of counselors in society.

The development of psychological practice in Nigeria was boosted by the introduction of psychological assessment tools as early as 1947. Aware of the cultural influences on testing instruments, as well as test-taking behavior and performance, there were earlier efforts at modifying and adapting foreign made psychological tests. For instance, the Binet Intelligence Test was modified from the original individual intelligent test to be administered in groups in Nigeria (Ipaye, 1995). In 1958, at the request of the then Western Nigerian regional government, a group of educators from Ohio University were also involved at modifying and adapting foreign-made tests, such as the California Test of Mental Maturity, California Achievement Test, Chicago Non-Verbal Examination, the Iowa Silent Reading test, and the Minnesota Teacher Attitude Inventory, to develop standardized and objective psychological and educational tests for use in the selection and training of teachers (Ipaye, 1995). The results of a 3-year feasibility study into the development of special aptitude tests for use in Africa, which started in 1963 by a Pittsburgh-based non-profit organization, the American Institute for Research, on behalf of USAID led to the establishment of the Test Development and Research Office (TEDRO) of the West African Examination Council. The responsibilities of this psychological testing center included the development and uses of psychological tests for selection of admission into training and education institutions, employment, guidance, and research. Specifically, TEDRO has developed many indigenous aptitude and achievement tests such as aptitude tests for selection into secondary schools (National Common Entrance Examination), technical colleges (National Technical College Examination), schools of nursing and law schools and secondary school achievement tests (West African School Certificate Examination), and tests for manpower selection (Ipaye, 1995).

In the early 1970s, further development in psychology practices in Nigeria was facilitated by university academics and researchers, especially those who had received their training in Western Europe and the USA. Their efforts led to the establishment of academic programs offering research opportunities, training in school psychology and counseling, as well as other specializations such as clinical and industrial psychology. Some of these Nigerian university researchers are also responsible for further development of psychological assessment tools, for example, the Students' Problems Inventory, Study Habits Inventory, Motivation for Occupational Preferences and the Adolescent Personal Data Inventory (Akinboye, 1980, Ipaye, 1995).

Moreover, with the expansion in healthcare services as Nigeria transitioned into independence in 1960s, also came the development of counseling and psychotherapy within the health sector of the nation. This latter trend led to more hospitals and health centers being built, and many young Nigerians who had been sent abroad to receive Western education in various disciplines were returning home to take over from the colonial masters. For instance, one of the first hospitals, the Neuropsychiatric Hospital in Aro, Abeokuta, Western Nigeria, was built in 1954 and managed by Adeoye Lambo, a Western-trained psychiatrist who had returned to the country after receiving his qualifications and practicing for many years in Britain. Lambo, reputed as being the father of African psychiatry, introduced the innovative approach to mental healthcare by combining the practice of psychotherapy with community services (Association of Psychiatrists in Nigeria, 2011; Oyebode, 2004). He was among the first to describe psychiatric disorders as they presented in Africa and as conceived by native African traditional psychiatrists. He was also among the very first clinicians to observe comparatively quick recovery, lack of chronicity, and better therapeutic response among schizophrenic patients who benefited from favorable social and environmental factors inherent in the community to which they were exposed (Oyebode, 2004). In 1961 Lambo organized the first Pan African Conference of Psychiatrists at Aro, Nigeria. His contributions to the integration of traditional and Western psychotherapies may have influenced the choice of Nigeria as part of the World Health Organization (WHO) Multicentre International Pilot Study on Schizophrenia (Association of Psychiatrists in Nigeria, 2011). In 1973 he became the Deputy Director General of the WHO, a position he occupied until 1988 when he retired (Oyebode, 2004). He inspired the training of many psychiatrists who have contributed greatly to the practice of psychotherapy and psychiatry as well as research into mental health and the integration of traditional and Western-oriented practices.

Psychotherapy in Nigeria has also been contributed to by Peter Ebigbo, also a Western-educated clinical psychologist, who in 1978 was a founding member of the Department of Psychological Medicine at the University of Nigeria, Nsukka. His contributions include that of motivating the establishment of many NGOs and therapeutic projects utilizing psychotherapeutic methods, which take into consideration a patient's cultural factors (Uwakwe, 2007). He is the founding president of the Nigerian Society for Psychotherapy and has held the position since 1995. Further, he built a psychotherapeutic laboratory in Enugu, Eastern Nigeria, where he developed many psycho-diagnostic tools as well as the adaptations of projective tools, such as Draw-A-Person (DAP) and Rorschach Inkblot techniques, for uses in Nigeria. He is also reputed for having founded the African Network for the Prevention of and the Protection against Child Abuse and Neglect (ANPPCAN), the Association of Institutions and Initiatives for the Care of Mentally Retarded Children in West and Central Africa (Nigeria Chapter) and was for many years the president of the African Regional Chapter of the International Federation for Psychotherapy (IFP) (Ezenwa, 2010; Uwakwe, 2007). His works with mentally retarded children won him the UNICEF Merit award in 1995. Through his works on child abuse, child neglect, and mental retardation he has been able to spearhead the moves for a major review of Nigerian laws relating to Child Abuse and Neglect (Ezenwa, 2010).

The works of Lambo and Ebigbo, as suggested earlier, have made significant contributions to a better understanding of mental disorders in Nigeria and have also inspired many others not only to seek training in psychology, psychotherapy, and psychiatry but to also make careers of these by practicing in hospitals, health clinics, businesses, and/or private practice. Needless to say that in doing so psychological health and wellbeing are brought to millions of Nigerian citizens.

Counselor education programs, accreditation, licensure, and certification

Psychology as an academic discipline started in Nigeria in 1964 with the establishment of a department at the University of Nigeria, Nsukka (Wedding & Stevens, 2009). Soon after, other institutions followed suit and also began offering psychology as an academic discipline. While specialization in different areas of psychology was being offered, the initial emphasis was on the production of school psychologists or counselors for the rapidly expanding secondary education of the nation.

Psychology in Nigeria is a social and health science and training in psychology is provided at the bachelor's, master's, and doctoral levels in universities (Egwu, 2005), mainly in the Education and Social Sciences departments. Some courses, however, are provided at Polytechnic Institutes. Egwu (2005) further notes that sub-degree (diploma) programs in psychology are also offered in some Nigerian universities. These cater mostly for non-psychology professionals who require familiarity and appropriate knowledge of various aspects of psychology in their professional training programs.

In terms of accreditation, the Nigerian Universities Commission (NUC) is the recognized body for accrediting academic programs in Nigerian universities. Programs offered in Nigerian universities also receive policy backup from the highest national education decision-making body—the Federal Ministry of Education. Further, standardized training for psychologists exists in Nigeria, with training requirements geared towards satisfying the mandatory minimum academic requirements stipulated by the NUC (Egwu, 2005). Different psychology-related professional associations have also developed a code of ethics to guide professional training and practice in psychology (Egwu, 2005). For instance, the blueprint on counselor education programs in Nigerian universities was developed by the Counseling Association of Nigeria and approved by the Federal Ministry of Education (Idowu, 2004). The Nigerian Psychological Association has also developed a formal code of ethics to guide professional training and practice (Egwu, 2005). The Association of Psychiatrists in Nigeria, like other psychology-related professional associations, plays a very significant role in stipulating curricular program and training standards, admission requirements, and certification in psychiatry. Continuous professional development is assessed through presentations at conferences and publications as well as through post-qualification training and examinations.

Current counseling and psychotherapy theories, processes, and trends

The Nigerian colonial university heritage was responsible for the introduction of Western-oriented training programs for psychologists and this in turn led to the emphasis on Western-oriented clinical consultative models of psychological practices (Adekson, 2003; Bojuwoye, 1987; 2006). Academic training programs feature several Western-oriented counseling and psychotherapeutic theories and models. In terms of actual practice the theories informing treatment methods are primarily eclectic with varying aspects of cognitive-behavioral therapy, family therapy, humanistic methods, relaxation techniques, hypnosis, and analytic-oriented sessions, especially in settings outside of education (Peltzer & Ebigbo, 1991). However, in educational settings, emphasis has generally tended to be more on relationship-centered therapies (Bojuwoye, 2010). The major factor responsible for the employment of relationship-centered therapy approaches, such as psychodynamic approaches, is their close relationship with the collective group and traditional family-oriented psychotherapeutic approaches (Bojuwoye, 2010).

Adekson (2003) also reports on the widespread use of approaches to therapy similar to Carl Rogers' client-centered psychotherapeutic approach. Again, this is connected with the use of interpersonal interaction strategies for healing as commonly practiced in traditional cultural healing. Socio-cultural inclusions in psychotherapy are important characteristic features of practices in hospital settings (Ebigbo, 1989; Makanjuola, 1987; Olatawura, 2007). Peltzer (1995) asserts that Africans (including Nigerians) generally have a group awareness tendency and so any individual approaches are bound to fail. For instance, the failure of individual approaches to psychotherapy is often associated with the infrequent use of psychoanalysis as the treatment method. Practitioners have had to resort to modifications of this approach so that it is more active, didactical, inclusive of supportive group methods, and sensitive to the cultural reality of the patients (Peltzer, 1995).

Modification of counseling in educational settings has also been witnessed, with counseling gradually moving away from the clinical consultative model as it became more apparent that there is a need to fit practice appropriately within the cultural context. Counseling transitioned from being seen solely as therapy or one-on-one individual or personal counseling to being also of educational process involving a series of activities and services. In other words, the theory and practice of school counseling moved from a therapeutic medical model to a health promoting and illness prevention educational model—re-education rather than catharsis as the preferred mode of helping (Conger, 1983; Gothard & Bojuwoye, 1992; Ipaye, 1995). In some cases the approach to school counseling assumed the status of a specialized instructional approach or as subjects in the school curriculum (e.g., Health Education, Sexuality Education, Career Education). An instructional mode of counseling is considered to be associated with the traditional directive mode of helping, as it conveys necessary knowledge or information and develops attitudes, skills, and values systematically through formal and informal learning experiences to influence personality development and strengthen behavior competencies (Bojuwoye, 1992; 1997). Furthermore, the instructional nature of school counseling makes possible the integration of traditional collective group and family-oriented approaches to helping, due to the necessary collaboration with students' primary or secondary caregivers, including parents and family members (Bojuwoye, 2010; Ipaye, 1986; Olayinka, 1973).

Indigenous and traditional healing methods

As is the case in many African countries, most psychotherapeutic care in Nigeria is provided by traditional, religious, or faith healers (Peltzer, 1995). The growing popularity of African Indigenous churches, in particular the Pentecostal and Charismatic churches, is attributable to the very essential community mental health services they provide (Peltzer, 1995). "Psychotherapy," as practiced by religious faith healers, is geared towards health promotion and behavior or lifestyle changes. It is backed by the establishment of outreach networks through church services, follow-up visits, group visitations, and cell meetings, all of which anchor members in the supportive feeling of fellowship and solidarity with their Christian groups (Nwoko, 2009; Peltzer, 1995). The practice is further reinforced by Sunday church services when believers convene and in their perceived presence of God, have their spirits reinvigorated so as to experience relief from their problems.

The general attitude of faith healers is that health is religion (Bojuwoye, 2010). In many Nigerian cultures, religion (or the spiritual) and medicine (or health) are almost indistinguishable—religion is medicine and medicine is spiritual (Owusu-Bempah, & Howitt, 1995). According to Mbiti (1989), for Africans, generally, the pursuit of health for the fulfillment of the whole of existence is a religious affair. Therefore, to the faith healers and their followers, illnesses, regardless of their forms, are spiritual in nature. For example, AIDS and alcohol addiction are considered to be results of sinful behaviors and the purpose of medical treatment is to work for God (Peltzer, 1995). Treatment methods include prayer, scripture study, and inspirational counseling as well as uses of social system methods such as group support, mutual participation, communal spiritual experience, and group identification. Within the African Indigenous churches, one of the methods used by religious faith healers is to convert patients to the healer's religion; doing so causes fundamental changes in the patients' lifestyles (e.g., changing attitudes towards detrimental behaviors like drinking alcohol, multiple sexual partnerships, overspending, or other poor self-management habits). Thus conversion is therapeutic in that it involves an enormous amount of habit breaking from the old lifestyle to a number of desirable habits of a new lifestyle (e.g., a drinker exchanging his bar and bar friends for the church and non-drinking members) (Peltzer, 1995). However, it is important to note that indigenous and traditional healing practitioners do not require their patients to share their religious beliefs. On the contrary, Nigerian traditional healers respect their patients' religious values and work within the patients' cultural systems.

In terms of counseling and psychotherapeutic practice, the Yoruba traditional healers are arguably the most widely documented Nigerian traditional healers. According to Adekson (2003), these Yoruba traditional healers, otherwise called *babalawo*, combine their leadership role in their traditional religion with their roles as "psychologists" or "counselors." They deal with social and medical problems ranging from issues around self-understanding; decision making; educational, career, and lifestyle choices; marital and family problems; personal, psychological, and emotional distress to more severe forms of psychological disorders, such as depression, schizophrenia, and major personality disorders. The *babalawos,* who are also described as *Ifa* priests, welcome clients with open arms, visit or invite clients suspected to be in trouble and employ counselor-initiated interviews and human relationships for procuring health, similar to Carl Rogers' client-centered approach to therapy (Adekson, 2003). Abimbola (1977) and Ipaye (1995) also note further that counseling strategies employed by *babalawo* include information-giving, consultation with significant people in clients' social and familial networks, and assistance to clients in building community cohesion and social harmony as well as activation of traditional care and support. Ipaye (1995) asserts that the *odu ifa* literary corpus used by *babalawo* for diagnosis of problems comprises bodies of knowledge in dealing with virtually any problem that humans may confront, such as illness and death, poverty and debt, getting married and having children, marital conflicts, owning new land and building a new house, choosing a chief or community leader and appointments into leadership positions, undertaking a business venture, making a trip, and recovering a lost property.

Research and supervision

Research studies in counseling and psychotherapy in Nigeria take place mainly in the universities and are geared towards application of psychological knowledge, problem solving, and social policies (Egwu, 2005). Some research studies in counseling within education settings include school psychological and counseling services (Bojuwoye, 1997), adolescent problems or behavior tendencies, HIV and school-based sexuality education (Adegoke, 2004; UNESCO, 2011), guidance counseling and career education (Ipaye, 1995), psycho-educational assessment (Umoh, 2004), and personality styles of Nigerian school children (Oakland, Mogaji, & Dempsey, 2006). As for research studies in counseling and psychotherapy carried out outside of educational settings, topics have touched upon issues in such areas as productivity; motivation; job satisfaction; alcohol and drug abuse prevention and treatment (Egwu, 2005); child abuse and neglect (Ebigbo & Aboh, 1990); socio-demographic and clinical features of patients (Ebigbo & Aboh, 1990); self-efficacy, job security, and organizational commitment and burnout (Adebayo, 2006; Idemudia, Jegede, Madu, & Arowolo, 2000); traditional psychiatric and psychotherapeutic practices (Ezenwa, 2010); and orthodox, traditional, and faith healing (Makanjuola, 1987; Olatawura, 2007). There is also a strong research focus on better understanding of the various Nigerian indigenous medical or healthcare systems, individual and community wellbeing, and African traditional healing practices (Adekson, 2003).

Research in counseling and psychotherapy in Nigeria is supported by several journals, both locally and internationally. These include the *African Journal of Psychiatry; Culture, Medicine and Psychiatry; Psychopathologie Africaine; Nigerian Journal of Clinical Psychology; Nigerian Journal of Guidance and Counselling; The Counsellor; The Nigerian Medicine Practitioner; International Journal of Family Psychiatry; Nigerian Journal of Psychiatry; Nigerian Journal of Psychology and Journal of Psychology in Africa.*

Funding supports for research are poor and are provided by relevant Federal government departments such as the Federal Ministry of Health and the Federal Ministry of Culture and Social Welfare. Generally speaking, universities are the main sources of funding for research in counseling and psychotherapy in Nigeria. A few international organizations such as the British Council, WHO, and UNICEF have also provided funding support for research.

Supervised practice in Nigeria is part of the counselor education program, and it is conducted by placement in both educational and non-educational settings including schools, guidance clinics, career centers, community-oriented agencies, and health clinics (Gothard & Bojuwoye, 1992; Idowu, 2004). In these settings trainees are assisted to acquire knowledge, skills, values, and behaviors appropriate for their practice. In other psychology-related training programs, as in psychiatry and clinical psychology, supervision is conducted through internship training and before trainees become members of professional bodies. Internship training is conducted in hospitals and other health centers and lasts for a whole year. In the medical and psychiatrist professions there exists a system of continuous professional development (CPD), which consists of passing post-qualification professional examinations, attending conferences, and contributing to research and publications.

Strengths, weaknesses, challenges, and opportunities

Counseling and psychotherapy as practiced in Nigeria is experiencing some measure of growth from original confinement to education to now featuring in social and health-related settings. Psychology can also be said to be gaining popularity as almost all accredited Nigerian universities have departments of psychology and offer academic programs in various areas of psychology at both undergraduate and postgraduate levels. Psychology is also taught in foundation courses for many training programs. Moreover, the practice of psychology is also supported by professional organizations. The strength of counseling and psychotherapy in Nigeria is also attested to in terms of attempts to make the counseling and psychotherapy practice context sensitive. For instance, Peltzer (1995) reports on research efforts at adapting psychoanalysis to local cultural milieu.

Adekson (2003) also indicated that much of the research in Nigeria is currently striving towards a better understanding of traditional and culturally sensitive practices related to healthcare delivery with a view to integrating them into mainstream Western-oriented practices.

One major area of weakness in counseling and psychotherapy practice in Nigeria revolves around counselor education and training, which although Gothard and Bojuwoye (1992) suggested it many years ago, remains to be adequately addressed. An externally moderated student assessment system is still largely employed in counselor education. This colonial student assessment heritage has the tendency of placing more emphasis on the theoretical aspects of training and less emphasis on the practical aspects. The implication of this unequal emphasis on the two parts of training is that more time is spent at the beginning of employment trying to acquire practical skills and adjusting to practice and trying to link theoretical to practical knowledge.

Another area of weakness in the practice of counseling and psychotherapy in Nigeria is with regard to the fact that counseling practice is not being regulated by law, despite the existence of standardized training programs and the outlining of codes of ethics by professional associations (Egwu, 2005). The implication is that there is no legal protection for the identities and practices of professional counselors and psychologists in Nigeria (Bojuwoye, 2006).

Finally, another weakness in the practice of counseling and psychotherapy in Nigeria is the lack of funding support for research. With universities being the major and perhaps the only visible source of funding, this, no doubt, limits the amount of research being generated.

Despite the aforementioned weaknesses, many opportunities to strengthen the field of counseling and psychotherapy are currently evident in Nigeria. The help seeking behavior of many Nigerians is still in favor of traditional practitioners, as it is reported that more than 60% of the population still consult traditional and religious faith healers for almost all social and health-related problems (Idemudia, 2003; Uwakwe, 2007). Since cultural sensitivity is the hallmark of effective practice, the opportunity here is in the intensification of efforts at integrating traditional and culturally sensitive practices into Western-oriented psychotherapeutic approaches. For instance, Peltzer (1995) suggested the adaptation and modification of Western-oriented methods, such as psychoanalysis.

Further, with many Nigerians becoming educated, the country is becoming increasingly industrialized, and people are living in better conditions, it is expected that the likelihood of the need for counseling and psychotherapy will increase. With more education, people are more likely to understand psychotherapy and become more psychologically minded, thus providing opportunities for the expansion of counseling and psychotherapeutic practice in Nigeria. Moreover, as the country continues to open up to the rest of the world and exist in a globalized community, this too will lead to increased acceptance of counseling and psychotherapy.

Counseling and psychotherapy in a Western sense is still relatively new in Nigeria, which is perhaps responsible for the challenges being encountered in the field, especially in terms of acceptance of "expressive" psychotherapies (Peltzer, 1995). This lack of acceptance is explained by the lack of psychological mindedness, lack of interest in introspection, and reluctance to speak of family problems beyond the confines of the family (Ebigbo, Oluka, Ezenwa, Obidigbo, & Okwaraji, 1995). Peltzer and Reichmayr (1999) also assert that African patients (including Nigerian) have the tendency to want to depend on psychotropic drugs (especially antidepressant drugs) for neurotic illness since psychotherapy takes much longer in giving satisfactory results. Moreover, intensive psychotherapy is often rejected since a patient's aim is immediate symptom relief and not self-understanding or personality change. There is, therefore, the need to discover more effective psychotherapy methods of helping patients. This challenge is linked to the attempts to modify and adjust psychotherapeutic practice more appropriately to the context of practice.

Future directions

Looking at counseling and psychotherapy practice in Nigeria, as described in this chapter, there is, without a doubt, much promise for future expansion. However, this will depend on continued efforts in research into finding ways to making counseling and psychotherapy practice more context sensitive and more acceptable to the Nigerian people. In this connection, efforts at adapting psychotherapy approaches and the development of psychological assessment tools, as reported in this chapter, should continue with greater vigor. Research direction should also be at evolving programs and methods for collaboration between traditional and religious faith healers and Western-oriented practitioners. Any meaningful future direction in the applications of psychological knowledge in Nigeria should, therefore, be towards evolving a hybrid system of practice which incorporates both models (traditional and Western) in mutually beneficial and collaborative partnerships, thus making the advantages of the two systems available for the benefits of the Nigerian people. Moreover, along with this future direction of integration of Nigerian indigenous psychology with Western-oriented psychological practice should be the modification of training programs with a view to ensuring that these are adapted to the realities of the context. This, of course, would mean that training programs feature more practical-oriented skills as well as aspects of psychology-related indigenous knowledge and applications in the curricular training programs.

Finally, the strengthening of the professional identities of psychologists, psychotherapists and counselors should also be an important future direction. Professional associations need to intensify efforts at ensuring that the practices of both their counselor and psychotherapist members are accorded legal protection over their titles.

Conclusion

The chapter has described the history of counseling and psychotherapy in Nigeria including the emergence of Western-oriented models. Standardized education programs in various aspects of psychology at various levels of training exist in Nigeria, thus leading to a production of various professionals including school psychologists; counselors; clinical, industrial and research psychologists; and psychiatrists. Psychological practice is also backed by professional organizations and by several journals for the dissemination of research findings in various aspects of psychology, including traditional and culturally sensitive psychotherapeutic practices. Although the very strong influence of culturally bound and traditional healing methods tends to create the impression that Nigerians generally lack psychological mindedness in terms of Western-oriented consultative model of psychology, this is likely to change with more education and exposure to mental healthcare through globalization. With current attempts at modifying and adapting psychotherapeutic practices to suit Nigerian cultural contexts, these would go a long way at making available the advantages of both traditional and Western-oriented psychotherapeutic systems of counseling and psychotherapy.

References

Abimbola, W. (1977). *Ifa Divination Poetry*. New York: NOK.

Adebayo, D. O. (2006). The moderating effect of self-efficacy on job insecurity and organizational commitment among Nigerian public servants. *Journal of Psychology in Africa, 16*(1), 35–43.

Adegoke, A. (2004). Adolescent and adolescent problems in schools. In A.O. Idowu (ed.), *Guidance and Counselling in Education* (pp. 21–35). Ilorin, Nigeria: Indemac Publishers.

Adekson, M. O. (2003). *The Yoruba Traditional Healers of Nigeria*. New York: Routledge.

Akinboye, J. (1980). A study of self-concept, behavior and health attributes of male and female Nigerian adolescents. *Journal of African Child Studies*, *1*(1), 21–32.

Association of Psychiatrists in Nigeria. (2011). *Daycare centre in London remembers Professor Adeoye Lambo*. Retrieved September 14, 2011 from: http://schoolvilla.com/nigerianpsychiatrists.org/index.php?option=com_content&task=view&id=15&Itemid=28

Bojuwoye, O. (1987). A Nigerian undergraduate counsellor training programme. *School Psychology International*, *8*, 167–171.

——(1992). The role of counselling in developing countries: A reply to Soliman. *International Journal for the Advancement of Counselling*, *15*, 3–16.

——(1997). Student counselling in a Nigerian University. *International Journal for the Advancement of Counselling*, *19*, 1–13.

——(2006). Training of professional psychologists for Africa: Community Psychology or community works. *Journal of Psychology in Africa*, *2*, 161–66.

——(2010). Clemmont E. Vontress, African cultural imperatives and traditional healing. In R. Moodley & R. Walcott (eds), *Counseling Across and Beyond Cultures* (pp. 187–99). Toronto: University of Toronto Press.

Conger, D. S. (1983). The training of counselors. *The School Guidance Worker*, *38*(5), 23–25.

Ebigbo, P. O. (1989). Vigrant psychotic healers. In K. Pelzer & P. O. Ebigbo (eds), *Clinical Psychology in Africa* (pp. 482–84). Enugu: WGAP.

Ebigbo, P. O., & Aboh, U. (1990). Sociodemographic and clinical features of psychology clinic attenders at the University of Nigeria Teaching Hospital, Enugu. *Journal of African Psychology*, *1*(3), 33–43.

Ebigbo, P. O, Oluka, J. I., Ezenwa, M. O., Obidigbo, G.C, & Okwaraji. F. E. (eds) (1995). *The Practice of Psychotherapy in Africa*. Enugu: Chumez Enterprises (Nigeria).

Egwu, U. (2005). *National Tour of Psychology Throughout the World—Nigeria*. Retrieved September 29, 2011 from: http://ebook.lib.sjtu.edu.cn/iupsys/Pages/National/ngnc.htm1

Ezenwa, M. O. (2010). *Opening up to Gestalt Therapy in Africa*. Enugu, Nigeria: Immaculate Publication Limited.

Gothard, W. P., & Bojuwoye, O. (1992). Counsellor training in two cultures. *International Journal for the Advancement of Counselling*, *15*, 209–219.

Idemudia, S. E. (2003). Trado-therapy and psychotherapy in Africa: A synthesis. In N. S. Madu (ed.), *Contributions to Psychotherapy in Africa*. (pp. 32–44). Polokwane, South Africa: World Council for Psychotherapy African Chapter.

Idemudia, S. E., Jegede, A. S., Madu, N. S., & Arowolo, F. (2000). Type A behaviour and burnout among bank managers. *Journal of African Psychology*, *10*(2), 189–200.

Idowu, A. (2004). *Guidance and Counseling in Education*. Ilorin, Nigeria: Indemac Publishers (Nig.) Ltd.

Ipaye, B. (1986). Roles and functions of counselors in Nigerian schools. *Nigerian Journal of Guidance and Counselling*, *2*(1), 87–106.

——(1995). *Guidance and Counselling in Nigerian Schools*. Ilorin, Nigeria: Chayoobi Ltd.

Makanjuola, R. O. A. (1987). Yoruba traditional healers in psychiatry: Traditional healers' concepts of the nature and aetiology of mental disorders. *African Journal of Medicine and Medical Sciences*, *16*, 53–59.

Makinde, O. (1984). *Fundamentals of Guidance and Counselling*. London: Macmillan.

Mbiti, J. S. (1989). *African Religions and Philosophy* (2nd edn). Oxford: Heinemann Educational Books Inc.

Nwoko, K.C. (2009). Traditional psychiatric healing in Igbo Land. *African Journal of History and Culture*, *1*(2), 36–43.

Oakland, T., Mogaji, A., & Dempsey, J. (2006). Temperament styles of Nigerian and U.S. children. *Journal of Psychology in Africa*, *16*(1), 27–34.

Olayinka, M. S. (1973). *Counsellor Preparation and his Functions in the Nigerian Educational System*. Seminar paper presented on Lagos counselling and guidance at the Child Guidance Clinic, Yaba, Lagos.

Olatawura, M. O. (2007). Orthodox, traditional treatment and faith healing in perspective *Nigerian Journal of Psychiatry*, *5*(1), 50–52.

Owusu-Bempah, J., & Howitt, D. (1995). How Euroccentric psychology damages Africa. *The Psychologist*, 462–65.

Oyebode, F. (2004). Obituary: Thomas Adeoye Lambo O.B.E. *Psychiatric Bulletin*, *28*, 469.

Peltzer, K. ((1995). *Psychology and Health in African Cultures: Examples of Ethnopsychotherapeutic Practice*. Frankfurt/M: IKO Verlag.

——(1996). Psychotherapy and culture in Africa. *World Health*, *49*, 18–19.

Peltzer, K., & Ebigbo, P. O. (1991). Clinical psychology in Africa. *Journal of African Psychology*, *1*(4), 96–97.

Peltzer, K., & Reichmayr, J. (1999). Psychoanalysis in Africa: Background paper for discussion. *Journal of African Psychology, 9*(2), 139–47.

Umoh, S. H. (2004). Continuous assessment procedures in schools. In A. O. Idowu (ed.). *Guidance and Counselling in Education* (pp 108–24). Ilorin, Nigeria: Indemac Publishers.

United Nations. (2010). *World Population Prospects: The 2010 Revision Population Database.* Retrieved October 20, 2011 from http://esa.un.org/wpp/unpp/panel_population.htm

United Nations Educational, Scientific and Cultural Organization, UNESCO. (2011). *UNESCO HIV and AIDS Education Clearinghouse.* Retrieved October 20, 2011 from http://hivaidsclearinghouse.unesco.org/fileadmin/user_upload/pdf/2010/2011/Newsletter_September_October_2011.pdf

Uwakwe, R. (2007). The views of some selected Nigerians about mental disorders. *Nigeria Postgraduate Medical Journal, 14*(4), 319–24.

Wedding, D., & Stevens, M. (eds). (2009). National tour of psychology throughout the world – Nigeria, 2005. *Psychology: IUPsyS Global Resource (Edition 2009) [CD-ROM]. International Journal of Psychology, 44 (Suppl. 1).*

World Almanac. (2010). *The World Almanac and Books of Facts – Nigeria.* New York: Best Seller.

4

COUNSELING AND PSYCHOTHERAPY IN MOROCCO

Renewal of an ancient tradition

Nadia Kadri and Jalil Bennani

Introduction

Morocco (officially the Kingdom of Morocco) is a country located in North Africa. It has a population of nearly 33 million and an area of 710,850 km^2 (National Institute of Statistics and Applied Economics, 2007). Morocco, being situated between many civilizations because of its unique position between Africa, the Middle East, and the Iberian Peninsula, also possesses a rich culture and civilization itself. The population is a mix of Arabs and Berbers and this can be seen in their dialect, which is within the Maghrebi Arabic continuum. As in other countries in the world such as France or Spain, other regional languages are spoken in Morocco besides Arabic (Khatibi, 1985).

Moroccan society is in a transitional phase from the social and economic points of view. During the last two decades, for the first time in its history, the urban population has become more prevalent than the rural one. The Ministry of Health has responded to this process of urbanization by making great efforts in training mental health professionals and establishing mental health hospitals and outpatient facilities across the major cities.

The training in psychotherapy and counseling in Morocco officially started at the end of the last century, coinciding with the establishment of the Moroccan Psychotherapy Association in 1992. While the Moroccan background in psychotherapy is in psychiatry and psychology, counseling has no official position here (Bennani, 2002). Its meaning is closely related to "le soutien" in French, which means "support." It is a mixture of good therapeutic alliance and other psychotherapies, without applying a specific technique. Nonetheless, many mental health professionals in Morocco practice counseling despite the absence of formal training opportunities in this approach. This may be attributed to the fact that there is a deep-rooted tradition of this form of healing in Morocco.

This chapter explores the history, present status, and future prospects of psychotherapy and counseling in Morocco within the context of its socio-cultural development. Emphasis is placed on the different types of available psychotherapies in Morocco, namely psychoanalytic, cognitive-behavioral, and systemic therapies, how they were installed, and their place within the community and scientific society. Furthermore, therapy education programs, traditional healing practices, and their comparison to scientific models of treatment, as well as issues around research and supervision, are discussed. Lastly, the authors offer a critical examination of the strengths, weaknesses, opportunities, and challenges of counseling and psychotherapy within a Moroccan context, along with possible directions to take to strengthen the field.

Brief history of counseling and psychotherapy

Morocco has witnessed numerous periods and events throughout its history, swinging between glory and misery. During the pre-colonial period in the 20th century, Morocco was a wretched country in the grip of a serious political crisis marked by a major weakening of central power, the disintegration of state structures, and social and economic involution. As a result, infrastructure, technological equipment, and basic healthcare institutions specific to modern states were virtually nonexistent. The country turned inwards and existed in isolation. Its economy was based mainly on trade and agriculture with no industrial activity. Exchange of knowledge took place at the University of Al Quaraouiyine,[1] the remains of a glorious past and the only academic institution at the beginning of the century, though the courses offered mainly focused on theology and law. Granting of degrees in mathematical sciences, pharmacology, or medicine did not occur until 1957.

Owing to the aforementioned social, political, and economic conditions at the beginning of the 20th century, there was no modern facility for the mentally ill or for other types of patients. Relying on the splendor and contributions of Arabic scientific medicine, traditional healers and *Berbers* (the country's indigenous population) took on the role of treating the mentally ill with the use of traditional healing techniques and certain surgical procedures. Their patients were generally considered as being "possessed" by evil or demonic forces and were recluses in the family home (especially if it was felt they were dangerous to themselves or others), *maristans* (a term of Persian origin etymologically denoting a place for patients), centers of neighboring *marabouts* (tomb of a saint or place of worship known to heal and even bring about miracles) or *zaouias* (mosque attached to a religious brotherhood) (Paes, Toufiq, Ouannas, & El Omari, 2005).

The practice of "counseling" may have begun in the so-called *maristans* at the turn of the century. Originating from an Arabo-Muslim tradition, they were the only available health institutions during this period.[2] The more notable ones were the *maristans* of Fès Marrakesh and Salé. In the beginning, these establishments received patients without making a distinction between physical and mental disorders and both medical and surgical training were provided. Later on, they served as refuges for the mentally ill and contained various facilities. Music therapy was known to have been practiced there.

In Morocco, the practice of modern psychotherapy goes back several decades and has been associated with psychiatry and psychology. It was first practiced in the 1950s by French psychiatrists during the colonial period (Igert, 1955). The training of Moroccan psychiatrists (mainly in France and some in Morocco), however, started in the mid-seventies (Bennani, 2008). In 1992, a founding congress was held in Casablanca with the theme "Psychotherapies of Maghreb Patients," organized by Jalil Bennani, author of this chapter, and Driss Moussaoui (Bennani & Moussaoui, 1992). The Moroccan Psychotherapy Association was subsequently born out of this. The need for training in three disciplines was therefore realized: cognitive-behavioral therapies, systemic therapies, and psychoanalysis. Several associations consequently came into being: The Moroccan Association of Cognitive and Behavioral Therapy in 1997, The Moroccan Association for the Research and Systemic Therapy of the Family and other Human Systems in 2000, The Moroccan Psychoanalytical Society in 2001, and The Moroccan Psychoanalytic Circle in 2009.

Morocco's socio-cultural, political, and historical characteristics have made this country one of the pioneers in psychoanalysis in the Muslim world (Azouri & Roudinesco, 2005). Until only a few years ago, the Arabo-Islamic world seemed impermeable to studies in psychoanalysis, which was viewed as bourgeois, elitist, or Judeo-Christian. However, as we know, there are different Arabo-Islamic societies and they are highly different in their degree of openness to the West.

The history of psychoanalysis in Morocco has been a long journey which started during colonial times in the 1950s (de Mijolla, 2002). Morocco was the only Maghreb country where psychoanalysts were active during that period (Igert, 1955). A major transition occurred with the emergence of Moroccan psychiatrists and psychoanalysts in the 1970s, some of whom settled in Casablanca and Rabat. Psychoanalysis was thus reintroduced, this time by local experts. It can be said that the post-colonial period (post 1956) was marked by the foundation and sometimes the dissolution of a number of psychiatric and psychoanalytical foundations which were in the process of reinventing themselves.

Concerning cognitive-behavioral psychotherapy, it was initially the interest of a few but gradually gained momentum. The first interest group was formed in Fez with the creation of the Moroccan Association of Cognitive and Behavioral Therapy in 1997 by Dr. J. Chiboub and his colleagues. The association has organized several national meetings and training sessions for its members over the years.

The introduction of systemic thought in Morocco started at the end of the 1980s by Dr. Amina Bargach, a child psychologist who studied systemic family therapy in Milan and Rome in the 1970s and 1980s and became trainer and supervisor of the first group of family therapies. The group was first active in Rabat at the University of Sciences of Education, then in a private capacity in Tetouan, the town where The Moroccan Association for Research into Systemic Therapy is based.

Counselor education programs, accreditation, licensure, and certification

In Morocco there are no university degrees offered in "counseling" or "psychotherapy." Instead, universities of human sciences train students and offer degrees such as a master's of psychology. Practical training in psychotherapy is held in psychiatric institutions. For instance, an education program leading to certification in psychotherapy is held in the medical school of the University of Hassan II, in the shape of a university diploma (equivalent to a master's degree). To be able to have the authorization to practice as a psychotherapist, it is mandatory to prove that the trainee has spent a fixed number of hours and training in a center recognized by the authorities, such as a university psychiatric center.

In Morocco, there is no specific training for counseling. However, in psychotherapy training, various types of psychotherapy, such as psychoanalysis, cognitive-behavioral, and systemic therapies, are taught in the university and in private training organizations. Bridges are built between these modalities and therapists use these techniques in a mixed manner to help their patients. These therapies are, in general, short-termed and nourished from other therapies in both education and training.

Training in psychoanalysis is mainly carried out by private training organizations such as the Moroccan Psychoanalytic Society and the Moroccan Psychoanalytic Circle. The Moroccan Psychoanalytic Society, founded in 2001, has committed itself to an unorthodox path that had already been practiced in Latin America, Lebanon, and even in Freud's time. It consists of inviting one or two analysts to come from other countries, once a month for up to a week at a time for training. This option meant that the sessions were spaced out (Chemla & Bennani, 2008). Six years after its foundation, serious disagreements appeared between the founding members. The history of psychoanalysis is punctuated with conflict, and Morocco is no exception.

The Moroccan Psychoanalytic Circle, established in 2009, aims to train, research, and teach psychoanalysis in Morocco. The analysands have the freedom to select the analysts of their choice, wherever they are, thus taking charge of their analysis. As in several European countries, there is no diploma of psychoanalysis. Training may last several years until the trainee becomes an analyst him/herself.

Training in cognitive-behavioral therapy is primarily carried out in academic institutions. The first cycle started in the medical school of Casablanca, the University of Hassan II, by Professor Nadia Kadri, one of the authors of this chapter, in 2002. Means of training include teaching of theoretical aspects of cognitive-behavioral therapy (CBT), clinical cases, and supervision with role play. The mandatory training to obtain the diploma is 2 years, with at least eight modules a year. Each module includes 24 hours of training. Also, due to the high demand of Moroccan health professionals with expertise in the care of psychological disorders associated with medical illnesses—chronic illnesses, cancer, and pain—a second university diploma was created in this particular field by the same department in 2006. The target public is medical doctors, other specialists who are not psychiatrists, clinical psychologists, and occupational psychologists. The content of the academic training centers on psychological aspects of diabetes and other chronic illnesses such as cancer, stress, chronic pain, insomnia, and some common child disorders.

Training professionals at the University of Hassan II are mainly psychiatrists, psychologists, and specialists in CBT working in the national and international domain. These teachers, coming from all over the world (e.g., France, England, United States, Canada, and Switzerland), allow students to benefit from their unique experience and expertise. Training focuses on the most prevalent mental disorders in Morocco: mood and anxiety disorders, addiction, and alcohol problems. Also, it includes the study of conditions such as psychosis, personality and sexual disorders, and eating disorders, as well as the most prevalent mental disorders in child psychiatry. More recently, the third wave of CBT, which focuses on emotion, has introduced the application of mindfulness techniques. The fifth cycle of this training is currently underway.

With respect to systemic therapy training, the second international symposium held in Casablanca in 2001 with the theme "Towards a New Conceptualization of Therapeutic Change," marked a turning point for the founding members of the *Association Marocaine pour la Recherche et la Thérapie Systémique de la Famille et autres Systèmes Humains* (Moroccan Association for Research and Systemic Therapy in Family and other Human Systems, AMRTS), which, with the moral support and encouragement and confidence of national and international therapists, Mony El Kaim, Odette Masson, and Giuliana Prat, has allowed for the creation of a private training space in Casablanca and Rabat for all participants concerned with the human sciences (psychiatrists, pediatricians, educators, and so on).

In sum, training in psychoanalysis and systemic therapies is carried out in psychological associations, although theory is taught at the Faculty of Letters in universities. Training in CBT is taught at the University Hassan II and by the Moroccan Association of Cognitive Behavior Therapy. The two work in a collaborative way to perform this training. As mentioned earlier, CBT is also taught in hospitals (clinical training) and touched on most mental disorders in which efficacy was clearly approved. Training in cognitive and behavioral therapies is taught in the same conditions and touches on psychiatric and psychological disorders related to physical illnesses.

Until now, accreditation, licensing, or certification processes have not existed in Morocco. There are no professional associations or regulatory bodies governing the practices of psychotherapy. With the multiplication of associations dealing with specific therapeutic modalities (psychoanalysis, CBT, systemic therapies), regulatory practices are becoming increasingly complex and challenging. However, those involved in the field of psychotherapy and counseling (educators, students, and practitioners) all recognize the need for some degree of state regulation.

Current counseling and psychotherapy theories, processes, and trends

As previously suggested, the three most favored theories in Morocco are psychoanalysis, CBT, and systemic therapies. The following section will discuss the settings in which they are applied and any issues and processes associated with their use.

The Moroccan Psychoanalytic Circle is watchful in setting up a mechanism to carry out control analyses, an indispensable supervision for the training of analysts. The accent here is on the different methods of transmission of psychoanalysis and the impetus for research on new means relative to this transmission.

The members of the Moroccan Psychoanalytic Circle are psychoanalysts practicing in Morocco, mainly in private practice, and are people who are committed to a sufficiently advanced analytical training process (personal analysis, control, and teaching). There are also psychoanalysts practicing abroad and whose practices are recognized either within an institution or by their work. Taking into consideration the social and cultural context, the Moroccan Psychoanalytic Circle aims to reinforce the specificity of the analytical discourse by placing it firmly in the cultural domain. The Moroccan Psychoanalytic Circle takes into account the role and the place of psychoanalysis as a study of the unconscious processes, which are behind all thought and creativity. It includes in its research all the disciplines likely to contribute to the knowledge of the psyche (Bennani, 2010).

CBT practice is currently practiced at hospitals and in private practice. The Group Therapy for Bipolar Disorders at the University Psychiatric Center in Casablanca has been active for 6 years and is a member of the French-speaking network of cognitive and behavioral therapy in bipolar disorders among French colleagues (Clinic of Mental Illness and the Brain [CMME] at the Sainte-Anne Hospital in Paris and Centre for Psychiatry and Neurosciences, INSERM U894, in Sainte-Anne, Paris). Practice is disseminated progressively in all regions of Morocco since trained psychiatrists and psychologists in the university are working in hospitals and private practices around Morocco.

The first international symposium held in Tetouan in 1992 with the theme "Underperforming Pupils" allowed for the creation of a systemic group faced with a very complex social structure with significant repercussions on the construction and maintenance of the nation's personal family and national identity. This group consisted mainly of women based in Casablanca, Rabat, and Tetouan: Dr. Amina Bargach, a child psychiatrist and systemic family therapist, and Marya Jaïdi, Salima Mrini, and Aïcha Rabeh Sijelmassi, clinical psychologists and systemic family therapists.

It is important to stress that while the mother tongue in Morocco is Moroccan Arabic (spoken by 89.84% of the population) (High Commissioner Office of Planning of Morocco, 2009), training for all psychotherapeutic methods as well as communication between teachers and trainees in universities and associations are carried out in French, as it is regarded as the scientific language. Doctors and psychologists are accustomed to think and write in French; however, in the presence of a non-French-speaking client, they must translate their thoughts into Arabic. One could question whether the discrepancy between the medium of education and the language spoken by the majority of the population would complicate or enrich the therapeutic process. We are in need of studies exploring this phenomenon.

Indigenous and traditional healing methods

Traditional medicine in Morocco has its own logic. Illness is due to occult power, entering from outside the body and acting on people via an external agent called a "djinn" (Stein, 2000). Thus, by placing the person in the cosmos, traditional medicine answers questions that modern medicine cannot answer. A traditional healer in Morocco seeks to chase away bad spirits by various magico-religious processes. For many Maghrebi patients, modern medicine is not necessarily opposite to traditional healing methods; the former merely stresses the materiality of the phenomenon while the latter explains the spiritual causes of the illness. Traditional healers (who are also called "marabouts" in Morocco) and religious people provide consultations on various cases such as delirium, neurosis, sterility, impotence, and couple conflicts (Stein, 2000). Unfortunately, however, many charlatans wrongfully use these traditional healing methods with the aim to profit at the expense of human suffering.

One can speak with ethnologists of *Maghreb Islam* (North West African) about the intermingling of religion with marabout and magic practices (El Ayadi, Rachik, & Tozy, 2007). For instance, Moroccan ethnologists claim that magic is associated with desire. Because it is concerned with desire, magic is of interest to psychoanalysis. It may be suitable to give magic-religious tradition a place in psychoanalysis if addressing it is merely a matter of semantics. In line with this notion, differences between the terms "magic" or "desire" are mainly due to language effects and not necessarily cultural effects. The psychoanalyst, integrating magic and religious expressions within language, is watching out for signifiers present in the culture. It is not a question here of creating new specificities but of reappropriating the tradition within universal values (Bennani, 2009). This example illustrates that in order for traditional methods to be understood within the context of psychotherapy, practitioners must take language and culture into account. It is through words driven from culture that psychotherapeutic process progresses.

Despite the belief that traditional societies are more supportive of the weak and the sick, stigma is a major burden in addition to the illness itself. Similar to findings in non-Western countries and many other parts of the world, various studies conducted in Morocco found that patients and their families suffer from stigma associated with mental illness and therefore resort to traditional healers first (Kadri, 2005; Kadri, Manoudi, Berrada, & Moussaoui, 2004). Frequently, however, patients come to consult a psychotherapist after having failed with traditional methods. For example, when healers are not able to cure a man's impotence, a psychoanalyst may be able to help him by exploring his conflict and life trauma, thereby helping remove his inhibition.

Research and supervision

Funds allocated to research by the government and NGOs are generally small. Research laboratories are generally responsible for finding their own funding sources.

With the aim of making a link between clinical practice and research, the Research Laboratory in Mental Health, Psychopathology and Cognition at the University of Hassan II organizes a doctorate training (PhD equivalent) course with research subjects on CBT, cognition, and emotion. Areas of ongoing research are neurocognitive models of mental disorder, the neurobiology of stress, the relationship between bipolar disorder and fasting during Ramadan, behavioral addiction and neuropsychology, addiction and stress, attachment disorders between mother and infant, rape, neurocognitive and emotional disturbances, sleep and cognitive disorders, pain and cognitive disorder.

Various studies in the field that are already published at national and international level touch on topics such as religious obsessions and religiosity (Khoubila & Kadri, 2010); the contribution of behavioral and cognitive therapies to treating bipolar disorders (Mirabel-Sarron, 2006), a self-help guide to dealing with generalized anxiety disorder (Kadri & Chiboub, 2011), religious obsessions and Ramadan (Kadri & Khoubila, 2010), humanization of death in the intensive care unit (Barouti, Khoubila, & Kadri, 2010), and post-traumatic stress disorder in victims of the Mohammedia flooding (Rhoulam, Khoubila, and Kadri, 2010). These papers are published in national journals such as *Revue* (University of Hassan II), international ones like *Canadian Journal of Psychiatry* or as books by Editions Lefennec.

With regard to supervision in Morocco, it is still linked to the individual's initiative. There is no regulation that psychotherapists have to submit to; ethics are the only constraint. Morocco has its own ethical codes that are drafted by the ethical committee of the University of Hassan II, Commission of Ethics of the Ministry of Health, and Moroccan Association of Bioethics. Though they serve to protect mentally ill patients, there are no specific codes regulating supervision in psychotherapy. Supervision may be provided to student trainees in hospital settings. Patients seen by both senior clinicians and trainees are discussed during case conferences, as well as the modalities involved in treating them. Supervision meetings at the Moroccan Association of Cognitive Behavior Therapy, for instance, involve watching videos of therapy sessions and role playing, followed by an in-depth discussion of the therapeutic process.

Strengths, weaknesses, opportunities, and challenges

Counseling and psychotherapy in Morocco are evolving in parallel to the shifting social, cultural, and economic landscape. Below, we offer our appraisal of some of the strengths, weaknesses, opportunities, and challenges involved in providing counseling and psychotherapy in Morocco.

Despite numerous cultural and social difficulties, psychotherapy services are progressively spreading around Morocco as a result of increased public demand and the teaching effort made in the country. Leaders in the field are working to increase the professionalism, normalization, localization, and globalization of psychotherapy, with promising results. The most noticeable strength in Morocco, however, is the increasing rate of literacy and the number of people engaging themselves in psychotherapy either as professionals or as clients seeking quality psychotherapeutic and counseling services.

Various weaknesses in the field may be stressed. First, a system of continuing professional development is currently not mandatory in Morocco. Today, once psychologists have met the requirements and obtained licensure and/or the specialist and supervisory degrees there are no requirements for maintaining these credentials. Second, the dominant psychotherapy schools in Morocco are located in big cities and continue to rely on Western theoretical frameworks such as CBT, psychoanalysis, and family therapy. Third, psychotherapists are primarily trained in French, despite the fact that the mother tongue of the Moroccan population is Arabic. Consequently, therapists have had to think and elaborate in French while verbally translating their material into Arabic for patients who do not speak French. One would question the validity of this process: What is given to the patient? We can suppose that the quality of care offered to patients is therefore uneven. Fourth, there continues to be a lack of access to health services in general for many residents of rural areas of Morocco. Mental health services and psychotherapy are perceived as luxuries not a need. Further, the very low salary offered to psychologists working in the public sector is a crucial weakness and has led to the concentration of psychotherapists in private sectors. Finally, psychotherapy consultations are not covered by the health insurance system, unless they are prescribed by a physician or a psychiatrist. To make matters worse, health insurance covers less than 30% of Morocco's population, thus resulting in a large portion of the population being left uncared for.

Improvements in the standard of living and education, efforts made by the government to lower the rate of illiteracy, accompanied by a greater willingness to seek professional help have, however, facilitated the growth of counseling and psychotherapy over the past 30 years. Collaboration between professionals from the two sides of the Mediterranean has led to developments in psychotherapy to reach Moroccan practitioners. There is also a growing potential for interprofessional collaboration and interdisciplinary training between not only the mental health professionals themselves but also the various types of health professionals. Other opportunities in training, practice, and research are evident with the ongoing establishment of new facilities and universities around the country. For example, during the 1960s, one medical school was available in Morocco. Nowadays there are four around the nation providing adequate training and high quality services.

A number of challenging tasks remain which render the aforementioned opportunities difficult to capitalize on. For instance, a standardized licensure and certification process for clinical psychologists has yet to be realized. At present, different institutions including the Ministry of Labor, the Ministry of Health, and the various universities have not been able to collaborate and develop a standard and centralized system of training, licensure, and certification. This results in practitioners with varying levels of competencies and clients receiving quality care in some instances and inadequate care in others. Moreover, the lack of success on the part of the Moroccan government to generate a funding system to allow people to benefit from psychotherapy in public facilities further exacerbates the conditions of those in need of psychological aid. Challenges in developing practices that are "Moroccan" and not solely dependent on Western philosophies also delay the process of meeting the unique needs of the Moroccan population.

Future directions

Looking ahead to the future, we expect that professional standards and guidelines for clinical training, education, and practice will be implemented in Morocco. We also encourage continued efforts in research and scholarship aimed at clarifying the universality versus cultural specificity of clinical theory and practice in Morocco. Because culture shapes individuals' thoughts, values, and behaviors, culturally grounded forms of counseling and psychotherapy may be more readily accepted and are likely to be more effective. Studying these culture-specific elements in counseling and psychotherapy may contribute to greater understanding of the universal and culture-specific elements of effective clinical practice.

Furthermore, practitioners have to push and lobby on the establishment of counseling and psychotherapy as primary and adjunct treatments for many mental and physical illnesses. The field should continue to work towards legislation to regulate and protect the practices of counseling and psychotherapy across Morocco. Finally, it has to advocate for the inclusion of counseling and psychotherapy services in Moroccan public healthcare coverage and the expansion of services in rural regions.

Conclusion

Psychotherapy in Morocco is a growing field in terms of practitioners' training, professional affiliations, and work settings. The nation is in need of a regulatory system that ensures quality of psychological services and supervision on a par with international standards. Morocco's rich history with traditional healing and the ancient wisdom embedded within it provide a fertile ground from which to advance the field. It is our hope that as Morocco enters a new stage of modernization and urbanization, helping professionals will seek ways to renew these traditions and incorporate them into their training and learning of Western methods so that psychotherapy and counseling are adapted to meet the unique needs of the Moroccan population.

Notes

1 Located in Fez, Al Quaraouiyine's origins date back to 859 and it was known as 'Al Quaraouiyine madrasa' until it was elevated to university status in 1947. The institution is considered by the Guinness Book of Records to be the oldest academic institution in the world.
2 In Morocco, they were first built by the Almohad dynasty during the twelfth century.

References

Azouri, C., & Roudinesco, E. (2005). *La psychanalyse dans le monde arabe et islamique* [Psychoanalysis in the Arabic and Islamic world]. Beirut: Presses de l'Université Saint-Joseph (in French).

Barouti, O., Khoubila, A., & Kadri, N. (2010). Humanization of death in intensive care unit. *Revue l'Université Hassan II, 8*(2), 45–64.

Bennani, J., & Reverzy, J.-F. (1981). Corps-langue-tradition [Body-language-tradition], *Transitions, 6,* 7–14.

Bennani, J., & Moussaoui, D. (1992). Psychothérapie des patients Maghrébins [Psychotherapy with Maghreb patients]. *Revue Maghrébine de Psychiatrie, 2*(2), 66–113.

Bennani, J. (2002). Morocco. In A. Pritz (ed.), *Globalized psychotherapy* (pp. 569–74). Vienna: Facultas Universitätsverlag.

——(2008). Psychoanalysis, women and Islam. *Journal of the Center of Freudian Analysis and Research, 8,* 69–99.

——(2008). *Psychanalyse en terre d'islam* [Psychoanalysis in the land of Islam], Strasbourg: Arcanes Erès.

——(2008). Regulation, ethics, and freedom. In I. Parker & S. Revelli (eds), *Psychoanalytic practice and state regulation* (pp. 123–32). London: Karnac Books.

——(2009). La psychanalyse au Maroc [Psychoanalysis in Morocco]. In N. Benjelloun (ed.), *Le Sacré, cet obscur objet du désir* (pp. 33–40). France: Éditions Albin Michel (in French).

——(2008). La psychanalyse au Maroc: Ruptures et transmission [Psychoanalysis in Morocco: Ruptures and transmission]. In P. Chemla (ed.), *Entre deux rives, exil et transmission* (pp. 121–30). France: Editions Erès.

——(2010). *Psychanalyser au Maroc* [Psychoanalysis in Morocco]. In S. de Mijolla-Mellor (ed.), *Topique n° 110: La psychanalyse au Maghreb et au Machrek* (pp. 7–21). France: L'esprit du temps.

de Mijolla, A. (ed.). (2002). *Dictionnaire international de la psychanalyse* [International dictionary of psychoanalysis]. Paris: Éditions Calmann-Lévy.

El Ayadi, M., Rachik, H., & Tozy, M. (2007). *L'islam au quotidien* [Islam in everyday life], Casablanca: Éditions Prologues.

High Commissioner Office of Planning of Morocco. (2009). *Demographics*. Retrieved November 11, 2011 from www.hcp.ma/downloads/Demographie_t11876.html

Igert, M. (1955). Introduction à la psychopathologie marocaine [Introduction to Moroccan psychopathology]. *Maroc Médical, 365,* 22–24.

Kadri, N. (2005). Schizophrenia and stigma in a transcultural perspective. In A. Okasha & C. N. Stefanis (eds), *Perspectives on the Stigma of Mental Illness* (pp. 57–69). Geneva: World Psychiatric Association.

Kadri, N., & Chiboub, J. (2011). *Guide de l'anxieux* [Guide to anxiety]. Casablanca: Éditions Le Fennec.

Kadri, N., & Khoubila, A. (2010). Religious obsessions and Ramadan. *Revue de l'Université Hassan II, 8*(2), 73–78.

Kadri, N., Manoudi, F., Berrada, F. & Moussaoui, D. (2004), Stigma impact on Moroccan families of patients with schizophrenia. *Canadian Journal of Psychiatry, 49*(9), 189–93.

Khatibi, A. (ed.) (1985). *Du bilinguisme* [Bilingualism]. Paris: Éditions Denoël.

Khoubila A., & Kadri, N. (2010). Obsessions religieuses et religiosité [Religious obsessions and religiosity]. *Canadian Journal of Psychiatry, 55*(7), 458–63.

Mirabel-Sarron, C., Siobud-Dorocant, E., Cheour-Ellouz, M., Kadri, N., & Guelfi, J.-D. (2006). Apport des thérapies comportementales et cognitives dans le trouble bipolaire [Contribution of behavioral and cognitive therapies in bipolar disorder]. *Annales Médico-Psychologiques, 164,* 341–48.

National Institute of Statistics and Applied Economics. (2007). *Some numbers on Moroccan demographic statistics*. Retrieved November 9, 2011 from www.inseadima.com/t665-quelques-statistiques-sur-la-demographie-du-maroc

Paes, M., Toufiq, J., Ouannas, A., & El Omari, F. (2005). Psychiatrie au Maghreb. La psychiatrie au Maroc [Psychiatry in the Maghreb. Psychiatry in Morocco]. *L'Information Psychiatrique, 8,* 471–80.

Rhoulam, H., Khoubila, A., Houri, J., & Kadri, N. (2010). *Post traumatic stress disorder in victims of Mohammedia flooding.* Paper presented at the 20th World Congress of Social Psychiatry in Marrakech, Morocco.

Stein, D. (2000). Views of mental illness in Morocco: Western medicine meets the traditional symbolic. *Canadian Medical Association, 163*(11), 1468–70.

5

COUNSELING AND PSYCHOTHERAPY IN SOUTH AFRICA

Responding to post-apartheid counseling needs

Saths Cooper and Lionel Nicholas

Introduction

We describe developments in counseling and psychotherapy in the context of historical forces that determined the shape of psychology and the transformation of South Africa into a democratic society. Almost 80% of South Africa's 50.6 million inhabitants are Black African. The next biggest group is the 4.6 million Whites, followed by the 4.5 million Coloreds and 1.3 million Indians (mid-year 2011 census estimates). Coloreds is the term used for persons of supposed mixed ancestry and was entrenched during Apartheid, which classified some seven different groups of coloreds. The overwhelming majority of South Africans are Christian (80%), followed by Muslims (1.5%), Hindus (1.2%), African traditional beliefs (0.3%), Judaism (0.2%), and 15% indicated no religion (Statistics South Africa, 2005). South Africa has 11 official languages, with Zulu being the majority (23.8%), followed by Xhosa (17.65%), Afrikaans (13.4%), Sesotho (9.4%), English (8.2%), SePedi (7.9%), Xitsonga (4.4%), SiSwati (2.7%), Tshivenda (2.3%), and Ndebele (1.6%). Most South Africans are multilingual and are able to speak English (Statistics South Africa, 2005).

Apartheid racism beddeviled the development of psychology in South Africa and shaped the direction of counseling and psychotherapy, making it largely the preserve of the White minority (Holdstock, 2000; Nicholas & Cooper, 1990). An ahistoric and narrowly defined ambit for psychology, counseling, and psychotherapy was propagated (Cooper, 1990; Stevens, 2001). It is hardly surprising that a ruling minority group that identified itself as European on the southern tip of the African continent should seek to underscore its actual behavior and explanations thereof in terms of borrowed Western mores and culture (Holdstock, 2000) and actively seek to repudiate anything indigenous and African.

On October 31 2009, there were 9,704 professionals licensed in the various Registers of the Professional Board for Psychology (Health Professions Council of South Africa [HPSCA], 2009). The ratio of officially qualified and licensed counselors and psychotherapists does not exceed 1:8,000 people. With nearly one-third of the population being younger than 15 years of age (some 7.5% being 60 years of age or older), an average life expectancy at birth of 53.5 for males and 57.2 for females, huge wealth differentials, and high unemployment (Statistics South Africa, 2009), appropriate counseling in South Africa is lacking.

Given South Africa's history of White minority racial domination, perhaps it is under-standable that all professional disciplines have been impacted by the erstwhile oppressive apart-heid system that sought to protect and promote White interests at the expense of the Black, largely ethnic-African, majority (Cooper, 1990; Magwaza, 2001; Nicholas, 1990, 2001; Seedat, 1990, 2001; Suffla, Stevens, & Seedat, 2001). Consequently, psychology, counseling and psy-chotherapy in South Africa have reflected such racially biased origins.

In this chapter, "counseling" and "psychotherapy" refer to professional interventions con-cerned with all aspects of psychological adjustment, distress, and dysfunction. These terms are largely unregulated in South Africa but among the five categories of registration as a psycholo-gist, "clinical" and "counseling" psychologists are designated to perform these practice areas. Counseling and psychotherapy are used interchangeably in South Africa and we will distinguish between them only when it is important to do so.

A brief history of counseling and psychotherapy

The first South African to be rated as an important psychologist internationally was Jan Christiaan Smuts, Prime Minister of South Africa (Annin, Borig & Watson, 1968). He produced the first psy-chological manuscript in 1895 that analyzed Walt Whitman's personality (Smuts, 1895 [1973]) and proposed a holistic perspective of personality, which had a significant impact on Individual psychology and Gestalt therapy (Blanckenberg, 1951; Perls, 1947). Smuts (1895 [1973]) was interested in how the mind develops and acts as a whole, which he further explored in his book *Holism and Evolution* (Smuts, 1926). After studying current psychology textbooks he concluded that:

> Psychologists first divide the mental or psychic phenomenon of human life into the unconscious and the conscious. The unconscious phenomena they set aside as not properly within the scope of their subject. The conscious mental phenomenon is then divided into intellect, feeling or emotion, and volition, and these are then separately anatomized in their historical development in the growing individual. This seems all very ingenious; and the results arrived at are no doubt of importance and interest. But where is the synthesis?
>
> *(p. 32)*

His holistic approach was intended to move beyond the purely psychological. Smuts believed that every individual form of life is a unity that operates according to its own inherent laws and forms. This fundamental property shapes the products of life into a harmonious whole. This distinct unity Smuts called the personality. He cautioned against confusing this term with the transcendental ego or with the "self-consciousness" of "our friend the psychologist." He intended to consider personality from a biological point of view and he chose to study Walt Whitman because "biological phenomena are best studied in the most perfect and fully developed speci-mens" (Blanckenberg, 1951, p. 38). His subsequent accession to political power may have underscored the racialization of counseling and psychotherapy in South Africa.

Smuts wrote to a friend in 1938 after the death of Adler about the extended conversation they had in Berlin, commenting that Adler's theory points to very important facts which had been left unconsidered by his predecessors. Smuts believed that Adler uncovered the most important aspects of human personality and what lies behind human endeavor. He agreed with Adler's questioning of the role of sex in human personality and Adler's inferiority and power complexes, which he believed were generally accepted by psychologists and the public (Blanckenberg, 1951).

In addition to Smuts, several other historical figures are worth mentioning. Fritz and Laura Perls established the South African Institute of Psychoanalysis and a thriving analytic practice in Johannesburg from 1934 and 1946. While fleeing Germany via Holland, they learnt from Ernst Jones (Freud's biographer) in London of a request for a training analyst in South Africa. Fritz Perls also worked as an army psychiatrist in Pretoria from 1942 to 1945. Clarkson and Mackewn (1993) contend that, although Perls met Jan Smuts only once, he was deeply influenced by Smut's book and that a large number of Perls's later ideas can be traced to it.

In a survey of trends in counseling and psychotherapy conducted in the 1980s, Smith (1982) found that two South Africans, Joseph Wolpe and Arnold Lazarus, were selected as the fourth and fifth most influential psychotherapists, with Perls selected sixth most influential. Respondents also rated Lazarus's Multimodal Behavior therapy as the second most representative of the *zeitgeist* in counseling and psychotherapy at the time and Wolpe (1958) was rated eleventh.

Wolpe received the Distinguished Scientific Award for Applications of Psychology in 1979 for his innovative work that led to the establishment of behavior therapy (American Psychologist, 1980), though it was Lazarus (1958) who coined the term. He discovered systematic desensitization and published *Psychotherapy by Reciprocal Inhibition* (Wolpe, 1958). In his pioneering work in sex therapy, Wolpe suggested systematic desensitization for erectile dysfunction and other sexual difficulties, which started a shift from psychoanalytic approaches. Finally, two of Wolpe's students, Stanley Rachman and Arnold Lazarus, later became distinguished contributors to behavior therapy. Rachman did extensive work with Eysenck, jointly establishing the first behavior therapy journal, *Behavior Research and Therapy*.

South African psychology was taught in philosophy departments until 1917, when R. W. Wilcocks was appointed Professor of Logic and Psychology at the University of Stellenbosch (Louw & Foster, 1991). Wilcocks established the first experimental psychology laboratory in South Africa at the University of Stellenbosch. He modeled it along the lines of Wundt's laboratory, having received his doctorate on the analysis of productive thought at the University of Berlin in 1917. Hugh Reyburn was appointed Chair of Psychology at the University of Cape Town (UCT) in 1920, and other universities followed suit.

In October 1946 the 34th Congress of the South African Medical Association accepted proposals for the registration of medical psychologists. The professionalization of psychology was facilitated by a proposal to register psychologists in a supplementary category to medical doctors (Nicholas, 1990). This led to the committee for supplementary services of the South African Medical and Dental Council (SAMDC) approaching a number of psychologists and psychiatrists to consider the registration of medical psychologists. The committee recommended using the term *clinical psychologist* rather than *medical psychologist*. It was not accepted because the tasks of the clinical psychologist would be equal to that of a medical doctor and would therefore not fit into the category of a supplementary service. The committee decided not to register clinical psychologists until an association was established which would represent the interests and sentiment of South African psychologists. The psychologists at the meeting arranged another meeting for the following day to discuss the formation of a psychology association.

The South African Psychological Association (SAPA) was officially founded in July 1948 in Bloemfontein, with a membership of 34 (Nicholas, 1990), soon after the apartheid government came into power. After the controversy of the admission of the first Black psychologist, which took some 5 years to resolve, there was a right-wing breakaway after H. F. Verwoerd (referred to later in this chapter, and who later became South African prime minister) resigned his membership. Eventually, the Psychological Association of South Africa (PASA) was formed in 1983, although the leadership remained White and overwhelmingly Afrikaner male until the dawn of democracy in South Africa in 1994. This racial political trajectory has indelibly impacted on the form and content of counseling and psychotherapy in South Africa.

Organized university and technical higher education institution (called technikons during the apartheid era) counselors were mainly represented by the Society for Student Counseling in South Africa (SSCSA), which had been established in 1978 (Cloete & Pillay, 1998). The role of the SSCSA was to provide a platform for student counselors to debate and present research at annual conferences. The Organization of Appropriate Social Services in South Africa (OASSSA) was established in 1983 by a Johannesburg-based group of graduate psychology students. Its main goal was to unite social workers, psychologists, and other social service workers who were interested in working towards appropriate social services in South Africa. OASSSA's membership consisted mainly of White psychologists based in largely White university psychology departments. The organization had several annual conferences and published the proceedings of its conferences (Flisher, Skinner, Lazarus, & Louw, 1993).

In 1989 a group of largely Black psychologists, under the leadership of the second author, convened at a *Psychology and Apartheid* conference to address neglected psychological issues related to oppression, followed by a second conference on a similar theme *Apartheid and the Crisis in Psychology* in 1990. Given the small number of Black psychologists in South Africa and the neglect of themes related to oppression in South Africa, the focus of the Psychology and Apartheid Committee was supporting the development of Black psychologists through workshops, seminars and training. The current professional psychology association, the Psychological Society of South Africa (PsySSA), was formed on January 21 1994, uniting all the separate organizations, setting the tone for a less racialized conceptualization of and praxis for counseling and psychotherapy in the country.

In the past 20 years Blacks have dominated the leadership of psychology and Black psychology professors have been appointed at all psychology departments. Participation in national conferences, workshops, and continuing education has grown over the years as has research and publication.

Counselor education programs, accreditation, licensure, and certification

The following universities offer degrees in counseling and psychotherapy: Cape Town, Free State, Fort Hare, Johannesburg, Kwazulu-Natal, Limpopo, Nelson Mandela Metropolitan, North-West, Pretoria, Rhodes, South Africa, Stellenbosch, Western Cape, Witwatersrand, and Zululand.

Licensure occurs at the master's level and started in the 1970s. A year of academic course work in the categories of clinical, counseling, educational, and industrial, including a thesis requirement, is followed by a year of full-time paid internship in the relevant category. All master's students would have completed 4 years of psychology. Some honors graduates practice as "registered counselors" after completing an honors degree and a 6-month practicum. Registered counselors are expected to refer clients with more serious and embedded issues to appropriate professionals for resolution. Master's students also complete practicum requirements of usually 8 hours per week during their first year of coursework.

Counseling interns do internships after completing their first year of coursework and a thesis. In a minority of master's degree offerings the degree is awarded after completing the coursework and thesis. Most universities award the degree after coursework, thesis, and internship have been completed at university counseling centers.

Clinical psychologists are placed in mental hospitals and are required to complete a year of community service after qualifying as psychologists, if they wish to practice privately, which most do.[1] Educational psychologists are placed at universities, colleges, and schools, where appropriate supervision is available and industrial psychologists are placed in an industrial or corporate setting. Over the last decade, because of the paucity of internship sites, training sites have diversified to include private practices, general hospitals, university clinics and non-governmental organizations. All psychologists are required to pass a Board exam set by the Professional Board for Psychology (the Board) before they are allowed to practice.

In terms of accreditation, the Board accredits programs after evaluating the patient/client profile, senior supervision staff, and the availability of a multiprofessional team, psychological assessment tools, one-way mirror rooms, and training program content (HPCSA, 2009). The Board also evaluates training sites periodically, requires all registered psychologists to engage in continuing education activities and does individual evaluations of such activities. The Board accredits trainers and organizations for this purpose and one's registration as a psychologist and ability to practice depends on obtaining continuing education credits (Pillay & Johnston, 2011). The foregoing provides a complete description of accreditation and certification processes in South Africa.

Current counseling and psychotherapy theories, processes, and trends

There is no discernible dominant trend in counseling and psychotherapy in South Africa. University training programs expose their students and interns to the core mainstream psychological theories and also offer electives that are often linked to the particular expertise of the trainers and teachers. The subsequent practice is therefore linked to the training received and could be, among others, eclectic, psychodynamic, cognitive-behavioral, community, or person centered. A range of family therapy models, hypnotherapy and developmental oriented therapy has a large following as is evidenced by the content of psychology conferences and workshops.

South African psychology, from its earliest inception, has been informed by international trends in psychology. A number of South African psychologists traveled abroad to acquaint themselves with the latest psychological trends and some remained abroad. Malherbe studied under Thorndike and returned to South Africa to establish widescale psychometric testing in the 1930s and eventually headed the University of Natal (Malherbe, 1981). Wilcocks returned from Berlin to join Malherbe in his testing endeavors, and recommended the formalization of a range of apartheid measures. He further mentored H. F. Verwoerd, professor of psychology at Stellenbosch University and later the prime minister, who would become known as the architect of apartheid.

Gordon Allport and Thomas Pettigrew made an extended visit to the University of Natal in 1954. Pettigrew presented a paper entitled "Conformity and personality in race attitudes" and Allport summarized the proceedings of the conference. Their visit stimulated South African research on authoritarianism and race attitudes (Louw & Foster, 1991). Carl Rogers visited South Africa in 1986 to facilitate groups to modify intergroup attitudes. The idea was that group members (the first author was in an initial group in Johannesburg) would in turn facilitate other groups and ultimately lessen intergroup conflict (Swartz, 1986). Jack Mann, head of psychology at the University of the Witwatersrand, completed his doctorate on the marginal personality under the supervision of Gordon Allport (Louw & Foster, 1991).

As for other trends, Nicholas (1997) surveyed over 9,000 first-year university students about their counseling needs and found that a high number of respondents expressed the need for counseling. Nicholas (2002) surveyed 1,292 first year university students about their counseling needs and preferred counseling sources and found that more than half the respondents indicated a high or moderate need for counseling assistance, with the top nine ranked personal concerns:

public speaking anxiety, increasing self-confidence, increasing motivation, controlling anxiety, fear of failure, relationships with academic staff, adjustment to campus, finding greater purpose in life, becoming assertive, and career and learning skills concerns. Respondents also indicated a preference for counseling from indigenous healers for eight of the listed concerns. Nicholas, Damianova and Ntantiso's (2011) survey of 567 first-year university students found that more than a third of respondents indicated a high or moderate need for counseling for the nine top-ranked personal concerns and all career and learning skills concerns. Only 10 students indicated a preference for assistance from an indigenous healer.

Indigenous and traditional healing methods

The traditional Health Practitioners Bill was adopted in 2007 enabling the establishment of the Traditional Health Practitioners Council of South Africa and facilitating the regulation of approximately 20,000 traditional healers (Ramgoon, Dalasile, Paruk & Patel, 2011). In response to the new democratic government's call for collaboration between the medical establishment and traditional healers and the lack of information about traditional healers' contribution to mental health, Robertson (2006) conducted three studies to explore the basis for such collaboration. He found substantial agreement among diviners about treating the following conditions (expressed in isiZulu): (1) *Ukuthwasa* (calling to a healer),[2] (2) *amafufunyane* (possession by evil spirits, a concept which has resonance with traditional cultures the world over), (3) *ukuphambana* (madness), (4) *isinyama esikolweni* (bewitchment at school),[3] and (5) *ukuphaphazela* (episode of fearfulness).

Over 90% of the 349 adults surveyed by Robertson reported that they were satisfied with their treatment and would consult the healers again.[4] Traditional healers operate intuitively, interpreting their client's behaviors and experiences in the context of their relationships with ancestors and bewitchment. For instance, *amafufunyane* is believed to be contracted when soil and ants from graves are mixed into a *muti* (traditional medicine) and ingested. The ants are believed to carry the spirits of the dead, who create internal disturbance in the form of symptoms such as listlessness, appetite loss, and social withdrawal. The acute presentation is ritualized episodes of faintness, grunting, and collapse to the ground. Following this, the afflicted person is usually amnesic for the event (Baumann, 1998). Sorsdahl et al. (2010) found that traditional healers used multiple explanatory models for psychotic and non-psychotic disorders. They presented four vignettes of schizophrenia, panic depression and somatization to 32 traditional healers and found that the multiple causes of illness were presented as witchcraft, spirit possession, substance abuse, and life stressors. Many respondents also did not believe that schizophrenia was a mental illness but rather a calling from the ancestors to become a traditional healer. Sorsdahl et al. (2010) provide an account of its treatment:

> I have a mentally ill patient, who had gone to the Western doctor and did not get cured. His family took him to me and he stayed with me for 5 months. He took 1 teaspoon of muti (traditional medicine) 3 times a day with food. Although he does not live with me anymore, he still takes his muti. He is much better now and will soon be cured.
>
> *(p. 286)*

Research and supervision

Much of the research on counseling and psychotherapy is problem focused and largely quantitative. South Africa's main research journal, the *South African Journal of Psychology* (SAJP), has been in continuous publication since 1962. The most recent issue of the journal (i.e., 2011 issue) includes research on family resilience, family therapy for schizophrenia, intervening with violent men, career success, HIV risk and prevention, post-divorce children, and cognitive-behavioral counseling.

Funding for psychological research in South Africa comes mainly from the National Research Foundation (NRF), which receives the bulk of its funding from the fiscus. The NRF rates psychologists and other scientists in terms of their research productivity and quality and then funds their research projects with no limitation as to topic. The South African government funds universities specifically for research productivity (e.g., on notification of a publication in an accredited journal, the university would receive approximately $18,000, which they would use to facilitate further research). The Human Sciences Research Council (HSRC) also receives such funding and in turn commissions research (HSRC, n.d.). No specific priorities have been set but the expectation is that psychological research should respond to the high profile problems of South Africa. Cabinet has given principled approval for the formation of a Social Cluster of critical national government departments that will oversee human quality of life and wellbeing issues, to enable greater cohesiveness for the consistency of delivery of services to the South African population (GCIS, personal communication, September 21, 2011).

For instance, several needs assessment studies have been conducted via surveys. Flisher, de Beer, and Bokhorst (2002), in their survey of students who had received counseling, found that female students were more likely to receive counseling than males. First-year students were also more likely to receive counseling services than more senior students. Cilliers, Pretorius & Van der Westhuizen (2010) found in their survey of student counseling in centers in South Africa that the demand for counseling had increased with an accompanying increase in the severity of students' problems. They recommended that future research should obtain student perspectives of counseling services and that such services should be matched to the expectations and needs of students. Anderson (1994) found that all of the traditional counseling services were provided at university counseling centers in South Africa and that the goals of counseling were conceptualized within traditional counseling endeavors.

While studies have shown that student needs surveys have a range of benefits, Morrison, Brand & Cilliers (2006) cautioned that counseling centers will have to provide more explicit and tangible proof of their impact in relation to specific concerns and goals of the university to ensure continued funding (Nicholas, 1997). Apart from support programs, which appeared not to function at their optimum, there is also the issue of non-use of counseling services by students (Nicholas, 2002).

Some concern has been expressed that counseling and psychotherapy in South Africa rely on invalidated therapeutic procedures, clinical experience and intuition (Kagee, 2006). However, as pointed out by Cooper, Nicholas and Bawa (2011), Kagee (2006) provides no evidence for his assertion, though it must be noted that there is indeed a paucity of outcome-based research in South Africa on the effectiveness of different psychotherapies.

With respect to supervision in South Africa, the Board requires that all students and interns receive supervision of their contact with clients. In the first year, students have limited practice exposure and are supervised by academic staff and psychologists at the training site. Psychology interns are required to attend weekly supervision sessions and are exposed to case presentations, usually attended by a multiprofessional team. Internship sites are required to have senior psychologists (at least 3 years' experience) available to supervise and expose interns to assessment measures and therapy experiences during a 40 hour week for an unbroken period of a year (HPCSA, 2009).

Strengths, weaknesses, opportunities, and challenges

Counseling and psychotherapy in South Africa have been engaged with international psychology since the systematic development of psychology in the 19th century, thus responding to international trends as well as influencing the direction of behavior therapy and individual psychology worldwide (Blanckenberg, 1951). Wolpe (1958), for instance, is still cited as one of the 40 studies that changed psychology (Hock, 2009). However, there is very little that is African in the theory and praxis of psychology. We offer our view of some of the strengths, weaknesses, opportunities, and challenges of providing counseling and psychotherapy to potential clients speaking a multitude of languages and whose levels of poverty preclude access to most formal contexts of counseling and psychotherapy.

A major strength in the field of counseling and psychotherapy in South Africa is the significant increase in participation and formal leaderships of Black psychologists, despite psychology being reserved for Whites in the early years of its development and most psychologists still being White. The national professional society and the regulatory professional board have had a largely Black leadership for over a decade. The psychological issues of the Black majority have increasingly become the focus of research and training in counseling and psychotherapy. An additional strength is that journal publishing and professional institutions have endured for over half a century and a productive network of researchers publishes collaborative research locally and internationally. The training offered at accredited universities is comparable with the best available elsewhere, as is evidenced by the ease with which South African psychologists and academics are welcomed in the English-speaking world. Finally, rigorous monitoring of standards of training and continuing professional development ensures a strong foundation for counseling and psychotherapy.

Counseling and psychotherapy in South Africa, however, are dominated by Western models and South African's unique healing and therapeutic traditions have not been integrated into our training programs. This is a prominent weakness that has yet to be adequately addressed. Further, access to master's programs is very limited where up to 80% of applicants for training programs that lead to registration as psychologists are excluded. Research in counseling and psychotherapy involves only a minority of psychologists and those in practice rarely publish their work.

With the advent of democracy in 1994, more clients and students of psychology have access to training and therapy. Technological developments have also opened up opportunities for education and training worldwide. Greater participation by previously excluded groups enables their involvement in research, publishing, supervision and training and allows excluded indigenous groups into mainstream South African counseling and psychotherapy. Previously excluded groups now form a larger percentage of those selected for training in psychology, auguring well for the greater receptivity of counseling and psychotherapy by the population at large.

Several challenges still remain unresolved. The number of psychologists qualifying annually is unable to adequately serve the client population; limitations on the number of entrants to the profession at universities lack systematic engagement; and research on the extent and nature of indigenous therapies is limited and their integration into counseling and psychotherapy presents a significant challenge.

Future directions

The gains of South African psychology need to be disseminated beyond our immediate borders while considering cultural contextuality. International collaborative research and academic exchanges will enable greater understanding of the applicability of dominant Western models. Currently the Psychological Society of South Africa has memoranda of understanding with a number of African psychological societies which could be utilized to embark on a number of mutually beneficial projects: mutual recognition of degrees and training programs, joint conferences and workshops and reciprocal staff and student visits. Universities should be encouraged to be more responsive to the objective needs of the country's population by increasing the number of places available to master's students wishing to pursue counseling and psychotherapy. The shortcomings in the field, which we have already alluded to in this chapter, require a compact of the Psychological Society of South Africa, the Professional Board for Psychology, the various postgraduate training institutions, and the respective leadership of these constituencies, to ensure that these shortcomings are meaningfully addressed. A new trajectory, based on objective measures, can then be fashioned for the future of counseling and psychotherapy in a post-democratic society.

Conclusion

South Africa's engagement with psychology is over a hundred years old and its rich history and contributions to international psychology have been delineated. Despite distance and isolation from the powerhouse of psychology in the West, a vibrant counseling and psychotherapy enterprise persists in South Africa. Its formal engagement in the African continent and internationally has strengthened its organizational capacity and it has the ability to enable more development of psychology in Africa. The hosting of the Africa Regional conference in 1999 on behalf of the International Union of Psychological Science, and the forthcoming 30th International Conference of Psychology in July 2012 attest to its stature in international psychology. Without a doubt, South African psychologists will continue to make contributions to the advancements of the field in the African continent and beyond.

Note

1 Pillay and Johnston (2011) found in their survey of 150 intern clinical psychologists, that around three-quarters of respondents felt adequately supported in their training, received adequate clinical supervision and were satisfied with the internship overall.
2 Sorsdahl, Flisher, Wilson and Stein (2010) reported that when ancestors call an individual to become a traditional healer, they inflict a mental disorder on that person before the period of spirit possession begins.
3 Predominant symptoms are the inability to see a book or paper, and the afflicted person's eyes are red and sore. Associated symptoms are hearing difficulties, dizziness, weak fingers, and cardiac palpitations (Nicholas, 2008).
4 In its ongoing quarterly tracking of perceptions of government, the Government Communication Information Services (GCIS) reports that 75% of the population use public health services, with 14% visiting traditional healers (GCIS, 2011).

References

American Psychologist. (1980). Distinguished Scientific Award for the Applications of Psychology: 1979. *American Psychologist, 35*(1), 44–51.
Anderson, B. (1994). *Student counseling in a new South Africa.* Paper presented at the 14th annual conference of the Society for Student Counseling in South Africa, Cape Technikon, Cape Town, South Africa.
Annin, E. L., Borig, E. G., & Watson, R. I. (1968). Important Psychologists, 1600–1967. *Journal of the History of the Behavioral Sciences, 4*(4), 303–15.
Baumann, S. E. (1998). *Psychiatry and Primary Health Care.* Cape Town: Juta.
Blanckenberg, P. B. (1951). *The Thoughts of General Smuts.* Cape Town: Juta.
Cilliers, C. D., Pretorius, K., & Van der Westhuizen, L. R. (2010). A national benchmarking of student counseling units in South Africa. *South African Journal of Higher Education, 24*(1), 48–65.
Clarkson, P., & Mackewn, J. (1993). *Fritz Perls.* London: Sage.
Cloete, N., & Pillay, S. (1988). *The Shifting Allegiance of Neutral Counselors.* Paper presented at the First International Conference on Counseling Psychology, Portugal.

Cooper, S., Nicholas, L. J., & Bawa, U. L. (2011). The imminent demise of South African (SA) psychology: A response to Kagee (2006a,b) and Kagee (2009). *South African Journal of Psychology, 41*(2), 250–52.

Cooper, S. (1990). Social control or social empowerment? The psychologist as social activist. In L. J. Nicholas & S. Cooper (eds), *Psychology and Apartheid* (pp. 60–65). Johannesburg: Vision Publications.

Flisher, A. J., De Beer, J. P., & Bokhorst, F. (2002). Characteristics of students receiving counseling services at the University of Cape Town, South Africa. *British Journal of Guidance and Counseling, 30*(3), 299–310.

Flisher, A. J., Skinner, D., Lazarus, S. & Louw, J. (1993). Organising mental health workers on the basis of politics and service: The case of the organisation of appropriate social services in South Africa. In L. Nicholas (ed.), *Psychology and Oppression: Critiques and Proposals* (pp. 236–45). Johannesburg: Skotaville.

Government Communication Information Services. (2011). *Public Perceptions on Social Human Development Issues in South Africa*. Pretoria: GCIS.

Health Professions Council of South Africa (HPCSA). (2009). *Annual Report: Health Professions Council of South Africa*. Pretoria: HPCSA.

Hock, R. R. (2009). *Forty Studies that Changed Psychology: Explorations into the History of Psychological Research*. New Jersey: Pearson Educational International.

Holdstock, L. T. (2000). *Re-examining Psychology: Critical Perspectives and African Insights*. London: Routledge.

Human Sciences Research Council (HSRC). (n.d.). *About the HSRC*. Retrieved from www.hsrc.ac.za/Corporate_Information-1.phtml

Kagee, A. (2006). Where is the evidence in South African clinical psychology? *South African Journal of Psychology, 36*, 255–58.

Lazarus, A. A. (1958). New methods in psychotherapy: A case study. *South African Medical Journal, 32*, 660–64.

Louw, J. & Foster, D. (1991). Historical perspective: Psychology and group relations in South Africa. In D. Foster & J. Louw-Potgieter (eds), *Social Psychology in South Africa* (pp. 57–92). Isando: Lexicon.

Magwaza, A. (2001). Submissions to the South African Truth and Reconciliation Commission: The reflections of a commissioner on the culpability of psychology. In N. Duncan, A. van Niekerk, C. de la Rey & M. Seedat (eds), *"Race," Racism, Knowledge Production and Psychology in South Africa* (pp. 37–44). New York: Nova Science Publishers.

Malherbe, E. G. (1981). *Never a Dull Moment*. UK: Howard Timmins.

Morrison, M. J., Brand, H. J. & Cilliers, C. D. (2006). Assessing the impact of student counseling service centers at tertiary education institutions: How should it be approached? *South African Journal of Higher Education, 20* (5), 655–78.

Nicholas, L. J. (1990). The response of South African professional psychology associations to apartheid. *Journal of the History of the Behavioral Sciences 26*, 58–59.

Nicholas, L. J. (1997). Counseling students in tertiary educational settings. In D. Foster, M. Freeman, & Y. Pillay. (eds). *Mental Health Policy Issues for South Africa* (pp. 284–85). Pinelands: Medical Association of South Africa Multimedia Publications.

Nicholas, L. J. (2001). The history of racism in professional South African psychology. In N. Duncan, A. van Niekerk, C. de la Rey & M. Seedat (eds), *"Race," Racism, Knowledge Production and Psychology in South Africa* (pp. 17–25). New York: Nova Science Publishers.

Nicholas, L. J. (2002). South African first year-students" counseling needs and preferred counseling sources. *International Journal for the Advancement of Counseling, 24*, 289–95.

Nicholas, L. J. (2008). *Introduction to Psychology*. Cape Town: UCT Press.

Nicholas, L. J., & Cooper S. (eds) (1990). *Psychology and Apartheid: Essays on the Struggle for Psychology and the Mind in South Africa*. Johannesburg: Vision/Madiba.

Nicholas, L. J., Damianova, M., & Ntantiso. (2011). *A Comparison of South African and International First-year Students Counseling Needs and Preferred Counseling Sources*. Unpublished manuscript.

Perls, F. S. (1947). *Ego, Hunger and Aggression*. London: Allen & Unwin.

Pillay, A.L., & Johnston, E. R. (2011). Intern clinical psychologists" experiences of their training and internship placements. *South African Journal of Psychology, 41*(1), 74–82.

Ramgoon, S., Dalasile, N. Q., Paruk, Z., & Patel, J. (2011). An exploratory study of trainee and registered psychologists" perceptions about indigenous healing systems. *South African Journal of Psychology, 41*(1), 90–100.

Robertson, B. A. (2006). Does evidence support collaboration between psychiatry and traditional healers? Findings from three South African studies. *South African Psychiatry Review, 9*, 87–89.

Seedat, M. (1990). Programmes, trends and silences in South African psychology: 1983–88. In L. J. Nicholas & S. Cooper (eds), *Psychology and Apartheid* (pp. 22–49). Johannesburg: Vision Publications.

Seedat, M. (2001). Invisibility in South African psychology (1948–88). A trend analysis. In N. Duncan, A. van Niekerk, C. de la Rey & M. Seedat (eds), *"Race," Racism, Knowledge Production and Psychology in South Africa* (pp. 83–102). New York: Nova Science Publishers.

Smith, D. (1982). Trends in counseling and psychotherapy. *American Psychologist, 37*(7), 802–9.

Smuts, J. C. (1926). *Holism and Evolution*. New York: McMillan

Smuts, J. C. (1895 [1973]). *Walt Whitman: A study in the Evolution of Personality*. Detroit, MI: Wayne State University Press.

Sorsdahl, K. R., Flisher, A. J., Wilson, Z., & Stein, D. J. (2010). Explanatory models of mental disorders and treatment practices among traditional healers in Mpumulanga, South Africa. *African Journal of Psychiatry, 31*, 284–90.

Statistics South Africa (2005). *Census 2001*. Retrieved August 9, 2011 from www.statssa.gov.za/census01/html/c2001products.asp

Stevens, G. (2001). Racism and cultural imperialism in the training of blacks in South Africa: Identity, ambiguity and dilemmas of praxis. In N. Duncan, A. van Niekerk, C. de la Rey & M. Seedat (eds), *"Race," Racism, Knowledge Production and Psychology in South Africa* (pp. 45–60). New York: Nova Science Publishers.

Statistics South Africa. (2009). *Mid-year Population Estimates*. Pretoria: Statistics South Africa.

Stone, C. R. (2001). *Socio-political and Psychological Perspectives on South Africa*. New York: Nova Science Publishers.

Suffla, S., Stevens, G., & Seedat, M. (2001). Mirror reflections: The evolution of organised professional psychology in South Africa. In N. Duncan, A. van Niekerk, C. de la Rey & M. Seedat (eds), *"Race," Racism, Knowledge Production and Psychology in South Africa* (pp. 27–36). New York: Nova Science Publishers.

Swartz, L. (1986). Carl Rogers in South Africa: The issue of silence. *Psychology in Society, 31*, 133–43.

Wolpe, J. (1958). *Psychotherapy by Reciprocal Inhibition*. Palo Alto, CA: Stanford University Press.

6

COUNSELING AND PSYCHOTHERAPY IN SUB-SAHARAN AFRICA

Brewed in an African pot with Western seasoning

Gladys K. Mwiti and Naomi N. James

Introduction

Formal counseling and psychotherapy in sub-Saharan Africa (hereon referred to as SSA) can be placed within a continuum, with vibrancy and growth in some nations like South Africa and Kenya while others like Somalia have many systems in need of recovery and reconstruction. This region of Africa hosts an estimated population of 800 million people, 54% of whom are under 19 years of age (World Bank, 2009). In this regard, the most threatened population are children, adolescents, and young adults affected by poverty, rapid urbanization, changing lifestyles, HIV and AIDS, drug and substance abuse, and various insecurities that have contributed to the fast unraveling of the family and community fabric (Jamison, Feachmen, & Makgoba, 2006).

Mental disorders are increasingly prevalent in SSA, the result of endemic poverty, hunger, malnutrition, and persistent conflict in regions such as the Horn of Africa (Jamison et al., 2006). Studies indicate that poor and less-educated people are more likely to suffer from depression (Das, Do, Friedman, McKenzie, & Scott, 2006; Friedman, 2004). Owing to the persistent prevalence of a combination of various psychopathologies in places of abject want, leading mental disorders such as anxiety and depression have been grouped together as common mental disorders (CMDs) (Baingana, Alem, & Jenkins, 2006). The challenge for counselors and psychotherapists in SSA will continue to be diagnosis and management of these disorders within a biomedical model setting that emphasizes physical ailment above psychological struggles (Solarsh & Hofman, 2006).

Besides poverty, counseling and psychotherapy in SSA are also shaped by the AIDS pandemic that has negatively impacted mental health. Etiologies of HIV/AIDS include clinical psychological and psychosocial factors such as depression, anxiety disorders, manic symptoms, and even psychosis. Studies in Zaire revealed that 41% of patients who tested positive for HIV also presented with high levels of emotional symptomatology (Perriens et al., 1992). In another WHO study, depression was higher in patients who tested positive for HIV compared with those who tested negative (Maj et al., 1994). In Lusaka, Zambia, 85% of women who found out that they were HIV positive while pregnant were diagnosed with major depressive episodes and suicidal thoughts (Kwalombota, 2002).

In SSA, 43 million children under the age of 18 have lost one or both parents to AIDS, conflict, or other causes (UNAIDS, UNICEF, USAID, 2004), implying that psychosocial support for these children is an overwhelming necessity. Various organizations and governments are beginning to understand that beyond food and shelter, psychosocial support is critical. This implies the need for ongoing quality training of counselors and psychotherapists for clinical practice, research, and innovative community-based interventions.

Over the past two decades and in response to these vulnerabilities, formal counseling and psychotherapy in SSA has been rapidly intensifying and developing. Western psychological theory and models of counseling and psychotherapy continue to dominate practitioner training. However, there is a growing awakening to examine and adopt indigenous psychologies for the purpose of developing practices that are contextualized, relevant, and sustainable. Mental health practitioners recognize the fallibility of older Euro-American methodologies and systems of reliability and validity that emphasize universal characteristics for various disorders. These, as well as the generation of universal interventions for psychopathology, are coming into question. To this end, professional training and practice in SSA is embracing the reality that psychological disorders are a product of one's culture, that resources for healing abide in the same ethos, and so the need for integration of ethnographic and epidemiological techniques for sustainable solutions in mental health is imminent (Patel & Patel, 1998).

Brief history of counseling and psychotherapy

African psychology was mainly oral and undocumented. Traditionally, Africans approach psychology from a mental wellness perspective as opposed to one that focuses on mental illness and psychopathology. At the onset of colonialism, African psychology was confused with witchcraft and superstition, labeled pagan and retrogressive, and left out of formal education and training curricula. In a study of Kenya, Mali, Mozambique, and Nigeria, Woolman (2001) observes that several Africans who experienced colonial education report that it introduced an individualistic Eurocentric value system that undermined African communal mores and consistently isolated students from their local communities.

Many colonizers perceived SSA as amoral and bereft of value systems. Some individuals believed that they had come to rescue Africa from herself, arguing that "many of the Bantu tribes (of SSA) were actually on the way to extinction through their beastly immorality," (Smith, 1923, p. 70). With this mindset, colonizers assumed that African minds were like empty vessels to be filled with Western knowledge, and that this emptiness was reflected through inferior culture, mentality, and personality (Berinyuu, 1989). In spite of these negative beginnings, SSA has slowly evolved to embrace formal practice of counseling and psychology.

Historically, formal counseling and psychotherapy in SSA began as educational psychology with teacher training and student career counseling in a bid for human resource development (Stockton, Nitza, & Bhusumane, 2010). Then came pastoral counseling through churches, counseling and clinical psychology in the general public, and finally community counseling that offered Voluntary Testing and Counseling (VCT) in response to the AIDS pandemic (Denis & Becker, 2006). Traditionally, religious communities in Kenya, for example, have provided spiritual counsel and guidance to their members for as long as the churches have been in existence. Pastors were trained in theological matters as well as pastoral care and counseling beginning with the diploma level. Examples are the Friends Theological Seminary in Kaimosi,

Kenya, founded in 1942; St. Pauls University in Kenya, founded in 1903; and the AMECEA Pastoral Institute, which was first established in Uganda in 1967 and later moved to Kenya in 1976. These schools prepare clergy to offer pastoral counseling as ministry to congregants within the church.

Beyond pastoral counseling, formal counseling has slowly developed over the years. Some of the earliest counseling programs in Kenya are the Amani Counseling Centre and Training Institute founded in 1979 and the Oasis Africa Counseling Center and Training Institute founded by Dr. Gladys Mwiti in 1990 (American Association of Christian Counselors, 1997). These two have continued to shape the practice of counseling and counseling training in the region over the years. Counseling psychology, clinical psychology and marriage and family therapy have evolved slowly in the region as well as a multiplication of helpers working in various forums in counseling and psychotherapy.

Counselor education programs, accreditation, licensure, certification

SSA counselors and psychotherapists have continuously played an active role in the reconstruction of the continent as its people grapple with the aftermath of neo-colonization and the various "social changes in this century in terms of race, ethnicity, politics, violence, labor relations and industrialization" (Makgoba, 1997, p. 180). Makgoba adds that to respond to these needs, universities are instrumental in training and nurturing highly skilled practitioners and scholars and that would contribute significantly to a new Africa.

Growth of universities offering counseling and psychology training has been incremental. The earliest experimental and educational psychology programs were opened at the University of Zambia in 1965 and Kenyatta University in 1970. Other countries soon followed suit, opening departments of educational psychology located mainly in national universities: Zimbabwe and Ethiopia in 1974, Uganda in 1975, Malawi in 1980, and Tanzania in 1990 (Myambo, 2000). In particular, educational psychology was made a component in universities and teacher training colleges to ingrain upon teachers an understanding of the learner, the learning process, and the learning situation.

Outside the realm of education, mental health training in SSA historically followed a biomedical model emphasizing psychiatry at the exclusion of counseling and psychotherapy (Mpofu, Zindi, Oakland, & Peresuh, 2011). Currently, however, there is a need for clinical and service-oriented training to prepare counselors and psychotherapists who can respond to increasing psychological problems, the result of urbanization, people mobility, war, and the AIDS pandemic in SSA. To this end, more and more universities in Kenya and Uganda are offering counseling psychology programs at graduate levels, producing increasing numbers of practitioners with master's degrees. The oldest of these programs is Kenya's United States International University, which started in 1979, followed by Daystar University (Kenya), and more recently Moi University in Eldoret (Kenya) and Uganda Christian University. The University of Nairobi recently established a MSc and a PhD Clinical Psychology program, though they struggle to find enough clinical psychologists to teach the program and have ended up with more psychiatrist lecturers and a doctoral program that tends to focus on research more than clinical practice. In the near future, it is expected that more Kenyan universities will commence quality clinical psychology graduate and doctoral programs.

Furthermore, with the increasing industrialization in Africa, organizational psychology became relevant for example in Malawi in the 1980s and Uganda in the 1990s. Psychometrics for personnel assessment especially for the mining industry started in earnest in South Africa then moved to Zimbabwe and Zambia in the 1960s. Currently, using Western-trained human resource personnel, employers in Kenya and Uganda are utilizing psychometrics for employee selection and evaluation, pointing to the need for industrial psychology training in the region.

Commissions for Higher Education are stringent regarding program accreditation. This commitment has kept training standards high. In Kenya, the Commission issues rules and regulations for institutions of higher learning that include a qualified faculty, a well-equipped library including online facilities, research, and clearly stipulated plans for student practical training (Kinyanjui, 2007). Professional associations monitor the same curricula, create student practicum and internship placements, and stipulate requirements for personal therapy and practitioner continuing education. Just like other vital areas in the practice of counseling and psychotherapy, accreditation in SSA can be placed within a continuum, where some nations are well ahead and others are yet to begin professional counselor and therapist training. In South Africa, the Board of Psychology is the accrediting body for psychology training (Health Professions Council of South Africa [HPCSA, 2010]) while in Kenya the Bull of Psychology is in progress to enable the formation of a Board of Psychology.

Currently, licensing and certification processes exist only in a few nations in SSA. South Africa utilizes a certification process through the Education Committee of the Professional Board for Psychology (HPCSA, 2010) while Kenya is expected to have the same in the near future as the Bill of Psychology is in progress. Principal licensing members currently existing in some of the SSA nations are the Kenya Psychological Association (KPA), the Kenya Counselors Association (KCA), the Psychological Society of South Africa (PsySSA), and Uganda National Psychological Association (UNPA). They are some of the membership bodies that promote ethical practice, encourage research, and monitor quality continuing education. As counseling and psychotherapy grow in the region, more and more membership bodies are in formation to meet the demand for diversification and specialization in service provision.

Current counseling and psychotherapy theories, processes, and trends

The majority of psychologists and counselors in SSA have been trained to follow major models of psychotherapy developed in Western countries, such as Carl Rogers's Person-Centered Therapy, Albert Ellis's Rational Emotive Therapy, and the Existential Model that includes Victor Frankl's Logotherapy. Play therapy is also gaining popularity due to large numbers of children experiencing bereavement and loss related to war and AIDS.

Owing to the multiplicity of needs and few helpers, many psychologists and counselors serve a cross-section of the population utilizing some form of eclectic approach (Ruxin, 2005). Group counseling and psychotherapy are used in community-based prevention and intervention programs, e.g., in HIV and AIDS and mass trauma with documented efficacy (Bolton et al., 2003; Parekh & Inge, 1996). For instance, a study in Western Kenya examined the effectiveness of group therapy to reduce alcohol use among HIV-infected men and showed significant increase in abstinence at the end of the treatment (Papas et al., 2010). This therapeutic approach enhances social support and empathy, reduces stigma, and synergistically grows community resiliency through creating a forum for shared resources (Stockton, Morran, & Nitza, 2000).

The person-centered approach has gained popularity because of the client–therapist relationship as the basis for change and qualities of the therapeutic relationship such as unconditional positive regard, warmth, empathy, respect, and genuineness that resonate with African value systems (Okun, 1982). Cognitive-behavioral therapies have been effective for substance abuse. Family system therapy works well for African families although factors like underdevelopment and poverty have extremely compromised the family fabric (Nwoye, 2004). Psychodynamic therapies find relevance in exploration of issues of early childhood especially from families of origin (Shacham et al., 2008). Individual counseling is gaining popularity especially in urban areas where there is a higher concentration of trained helpers, although this service may be out of reach for individuals in poor communities (Bott, Morrison, Ellsberg, 2005)

All these individual, family and group therapeutic approaches are heavily inlaid by the African desire for transcendence that is eschatological, emphasizing hope versus despair. Resiliency is empowered by narrative therapy and shared experiences commonly used when individuals or people groups are threatened with annihilation, as in the case of the Rwanda genocide that produced 6 million likely candidates for post-traumatic stress disorder.

Owing to the complexity and immensity of mental health problems in SSA, there is a growing trend to create multidisciplinary teams of caregivers to meet needs related to disasters like HIV and AIDS, mass trauma and Africa's orphaned generation. Various programs report success; for example, the Regional Psychosocial Support Initiative (REPSSI)[1] works in 13 countries in eastern and southern Africa to promote vulnerable children's healthy development, enhance survival skills, increase self-confidence, and help them deal with grief, loss, and stigma. Such programs create a safety net for the children through mobilizing multidisciplinary partnerships with governments, school teachers, caregivers, faith-based organizations, and radio programs so as to stabilize the children socially and psychologically. A major focus is the creation of a caring community where separation of the vulnerable child from cultures and families of origin is discouraged in recognition of the value of indigenous connections for holistic child development. However, there is much more to be done and resources needed for the care of millions of these children (Stover, Bollinger, Walker, & Monasch, 2010).

Many psychotherapists and counselors in SSA realize that since human needs are as unique as the individual seeking help, flexibility in the selection of an appropriate theoretical model and the wisdom to exercise integration should be the practical therapeutic approach (Okun, 1982). In this regard, the client's spirituality, culture, and the community of origin play a major role in shaping psychotherapy.

Indigenous and traditional healing methods

In SSA, working from a health versus psychopathology mindset, indigenous healing begins with the prevention of psychopathology. When illness presents, healers work with their clients to help them comprehend the basis of their psychopathology and how they can identify and access resources to restore health and build resiliency. Examples of such indigenous interventions include relaxation techniques such as the use of drum beats; medicinal herbs; psycho-cultural education; dream interpretation; storytelling; use of proverbs; cleansing; libation; music; and ceremonies such as ritual cleansing, circumcision, and marriage (Mpofu, Peltzer & Bojuwoye, 2011).

Both prevention and healing found in African indigenous healing methodology are woven around a traditional worldview where beliefs regarding the human psyche and behavior inform counseling and psychotherapy, beginning with prevention of psychopathology. Deterrence is woven through valuing and celebrating life with rituals and rites of passage that breathe life into the community. They create resiliency during times of hardship and empower individuals to live with hope. In traditional Africa, Marah (2006) explains that young men were socialized in a cohort, and through various programs adults communicated rules, regulations, and values. Socialized together, young people belong to a cohort marked by shared experiences and values that enhance discipline, accountability, and mutual concern. These ingrained mores of behavior create caution, discourage negative unacceptable behavior, and underscore self-identity and focus.

In Kenya, reinforcement of appropriate behavior occurs through social sanctions, approvals, rewards, and punishments. Fathers stayed close to their sons and modeled appropriate behavior while girls' education differentiated their roles from those of boys (Kenyatta, 1965). To this end, psychopathology, healing, and wholeness are understood within a developmental perspective. The cycle of life—birth, child naming, growing up, marriage, and death—is marked all through life with communal observances that reinforce stage-to-stage maturation. From a psychological perspective, positive elements of community-based puberty rites of passage form identity and belonging (Mugambi & Kirima, 1976). For individuals who deviate from the norm in terms of graduating through the age group rites of passage (M'Imanyara, 1992), the family would seek Shaman wisdom to deal with the pathology. He might prescribe appeasing ancestral spirits, herbal treatment for developmental delays, or family reconciliation, and so on.

Africans believe that an individual does not exist in the universe alone but belongs to a community that consists of the living, the dead, and the unborn. This network of connections does not camouflage the person's identity but enriches it with a synergistic network of support and resiliency (ya Azibo, 1996). The interconnectedness finds expression in such instances where the extended family or community takes part in an individual's healing through shared diagnosis of the problem and treatment. For example, a man, angry that his brothers swindled him of land after their father's death, may act out his anger on some helpless family member. Here, the Shaman leads the family in diagnosis followed by mutual confession, repentance, forgiveness, restitution, and restoration (Kingah, 2004). Other forms of group therapy utilizing African interconnectedness are sustenance groups (Mwiti, 2009), used extensively in community trauma healing after disaster. To illustrate, Lowey, Williams and Keleta (2002) used an indigenous ceremony called the Kaffa (a traditional East African coffee drinking event) to demonstrate the efficacy of group trauma psychotherapy among East African refugee women living in the USA.

In SSA, spirituality also plays a major role in shaping communal living and psychotherapy (Awolalu, 1972; Idowu, 1975; Igenoza, 1994; Mbiti, 1969; Willoughby,1970). Many believe that life without religious observance is akin to self-excommunication from the entire life of the society. The worldview is that faith in God ensures individual and group identity and that communal worship creates spiritual connections that enhance social support and resiliency (Ma Mpolo, 1994). When these connections are deliberately broken, for example, through blatant disobedience of morals or ethical behavior, psychopathology may result. It is common practice for a spiritual leader to apprehend a thief through ritual, and to cleanse the wayward fellow through the same. After cleansing, elders help restore the person back to the community through payment of a fine or some other prescribed means of cleansing (Asagba, 2009; Kiriswa, 2002).

Another worldview is communal ownership of pathology. Just as healing is shared, psychopathology is also collective, and the bearer of the illness is taken care of by the group. To this end, no psychopathology is strong enough to cause excommunication of an individual. Instead, the community would share the care of the patient and together seek help for the same. Excommunication happens only in cases where there was blatant disregard for life and communal ties, for example: murder, incest, or witchcraft (Penal Reform International, 2000).

Research and supervision

Research and publishing are encouraged, especially in institutions of higher learning and among members of professional bodies, such as associations of psychologists, psychotherapists, and pastoral counselors. Findings are published locally and internationally in journals of psychology or medical practice. Most psychological research is carried out at universities, since institutions attract a large portion of donor funding. In Kenya, there are no journals devoted to psychology so most Kenyan publications have appeared in international journals. Myambo (2000) has provided a bold attempt at summarizing the growth of psychology in some sub-Saharan countries. She states that in Kenya, most research topics have been in educational psychology, although there is ongoing research in traumatic stress and coping.

In Malawi, psychology is not offered as a separate discipline at degree level but is a part of the social science discipline. Research topics are mainly in AIDS, orphan care, personnel selection, and marketing with publications carried in the *Journal of Social Science*. For Ethiopia, psychological research topics include social problems such as gender studies and domestic violence, with publications in the *Ethiopian Journal of Education*. As for Tanzania, psychology has been operating primarily within the field education, with research mainly focusing on the AIDS epidemic.

Established in 1965, the University of Zambia has a department of psychology with a strong orientation towards mental testing, and graduates are mainly recruited to work in applied educational and industrial psychology. Most research is in community health and alcohol use, with publications in the *African Social Research Journal* and the *Journal of Adult Education*. In Zimbabwe, most psychologists serve in education or private practice. Research is mainly carried out in the universities and focuses on HIV/AIDS, unemployment, forensics, and organizational psychology. Publications are carried out in the *Zimbabwe Journal of Educational Research* and the *Central African Journal of Medicine*.

Funding for HIV/AIDS research has come from partnerships, for example, with the Institute for Health Policy Studies, Center for AIDS Prevention Studies, and AIDS Research Institute at the University of California, San Francisco; National Institutes of Health, USA; Wellcome Trust, UK; and Department for International Development, UK. Such research outcomes have been published in international journals such as the *Lancet*, *PubMed*, *Journal of the American Medical Association*, and *International Journal of Mental Health Systems*.

Since psychotherapy is on the increase in SSA, counselors, and psychotherapists are recognizing the need for evidence-based practice, although most findings remain unpublished due to lack of trained expertise to carry the load of treatment, assessment, research, and publishing (Jamison, et al., 2006). Currently, research partnerships between local and international universities are on the increase, thus enhancing the capacity of African-based practitioners (Sexual Violence Research Initiative, 2010).

Supervision in SSA is part of counselor and therapist training curricula and a minimum number of supervised clinical hours is mandatory for licensure by professional associations. In Kenya, the Kenya Psychological Association requires 25 hours for personal therapy, a minimum of 500 supervised client contact hours for MA Counseling Psychology, MA Clinical Psychology and MA Marriage and Family Practitioners. Holders of PhD in Counseling Psychology require a minimum of 1,000 supervised clinical hours while Doctor of Psychology (PsyD) and PhD Clinical Psychology will require a minimum of 1,500 supervised clinical hours. At Oasis Africa, an active clinical training location, practicum and internship students receive personal therapy as well as individual, peer, and group supervision for rotations where they practice individual and group therapy (children, adolescents, and adults).

As more and more countries in SSA form Boards of Psychology, there will be an increase in coordinated licensure and standard setting as well as mandated supervision and therapist Continuing Education (Gureje & Jenkins, 2007). As much as many see the need for seasoned counselors and psychotherapists, gaps in terms of qualified faculty and supervisors still exist. Currently, to close this gap, peer supervision is encouraged.

Strengths, weakness, opportunities, and challenges

A major strength in the field of counseling and psychotherapy in SSA stems from its people's resiliency and undying hope for a better tomorrow, which stimulate existential attitudes, narrative therapy, and the eschatological plot for life and living (Garcia, Pence, & Evans, 2008). Where contemporary psychology focuses on current life crises, African psychology equips the person through rites of passage before the onset of crises. Finally, the interweaving, interconnection, and sanctity of life systems create a net of care and belonging. There is community life, love for children, protection of the most vulnerable, care for the environment including wild life protection, deep spirituality, awareness of God's presence, and interest in the affairs of humanity. Africans also love formal education, and so these strengths create endless opportunities to document African psychologies and healing interventions.

Currently, in many nations in SSA and cognizant of the growing need for professional help, there is scarcity of quality counseling and psychology training programs, poor integrative approaches, lack of or inadequate mental health policies, and absent or low national budgeting for service provision. These inadequacies are closely linked with poverty of research, professional practice, and supervision, all in the face of major challenges that are fast compromising mental health (Jenkins, et al., 2010). A major threat is the encroachment of a global value system through social networks, media, music, and people mobility, aspects that tend to dictate values that are more illusion than reality. Implications exist for counselor and therapist training to keep pace with a volatile populace.

SSA is home to many identified and unrecorded authentic healing modalities that need identification and affirmation. The region holds the capacity to set foundations for scholarship, research, practice, and innovative psychotherapies. Set in a capsule of people diversity, a youthful population, multiplicity of language and culture, racial and tribal intermarriage, as well as growing opportunities for trade and communication, SSA mental health practitioners have endless opportunities to grow and enrich their professions (Nsamenang, 1993). Currently, SSA Africa is known for HIV/AIDS, millions of orphaned children, malaria, armed conflict, and poverty. Most of the aid resources coming to Africa tend to address one of these pandemics, and interventions do not seem to be producing a lasting solution. Counselors and psychotherapists in SSA therefore have the opportunity to expose factors that contribute to resiliency in the continent. Utilizing African cultural values of resiliency creation, they have immense opportunities to create intervention programs that can promote dialogue and so enhance cultures of mutual understanding (University of Lubumbashi, 2002). To this end, the practice of counseling and psychotherapy in SSA will continue to face the challenge of cultural relevance that brings healing, change, and transformation to the masses.

As much as SSA is endowed endless opportunities towards the development of authentic indigenous psychology and counseling models, funding for research, and affordability of treatment exist. Part of the reason is that to many African governments, mental health provision and research are not budgetary priorities (Kiima and Jenkins, 2010). In addition, following hard on the heels of colonialism, the perception of mental health is still influenced by the colonial biomedical model that emphasizes psychiatry over counseling and psychotherapy. With the absence of mental health policies in many countries in this region, the need for quality research-driven practice will continue to suffer.

Future directions

For a society continuing to experience many psychosocial challenges, SSA is coping relatively well due to resiliency created by strong indigenous values, the African family, and community fabric as well as reliance on faith and spirituality. This is the hope that emerging therapists need to explore (Garcia, Pence, & Evans, 2008). This reality also means that health psychology other than models of psychopathology offer more promise for sustainable healing for Africa (Evans, Marks, Murray, & Estacio, 2005).

Informed by African indigenous worldviews of wholeness and integration, counselors and psychotherapists in SSA will need to assume a vocational perspective of an integrated mentor, teacher, and trainer with a bio-psycho-social-spiritual-relational perspective cognizant of individual and group survival. Such an all-enveloping model demands insightful curricula, intense holistic training, sound professional practice, research, publishing, supervision, and mentoring, as well as partnerships that will realize these milestones (Berinyuu, 1989). To maintain focus and ensure quality, national and pan African professional bodies will pursue networks as a platform for mutual exchange, training, and encouragement. Although concerted efforts and a bigger share of resources for research and interventions in mental health has gone to psychiatric training and mental illness programs (Jenkins, et al., 2010), it is hoped that similar enthusiasm will be shown in the field of counseling and psychotherapy since the two are codependent.

Conclusion

SSA is home to millions, with a diverse population from different heritages, practices, and cultures. However, sub-Sahara Africans are united by a common overarching sense of what it means to be human and how this existence is linked with the other, with God the Creator, with his creation, with the unborn, and the departed (Mbiti, 1978). Rich traditions exist and will continue to influence and inspire new approaches to mental health that can enrich contemporary psychology. Therapist training, research, and practice in this region face great opportunities but also great challenges in terms of exploring and cultivating practical interventions that are created from integration of sound psychological theory, African indigenous cultural riches, and eschatological faith that hopes for a better future (Hetsen & Wanjohi, 1982). SSA can begin to share its methodologies and take its place in informing global holistic approaches to psychological, mental, relational, emotional, spiritual, and behavioral healing and wellness.

Note

1 The Regional Psychosocial Support Initiative (REPSSI) is supported by Foundation for Sustainable Development with Swiss and Swedish development agencies (Norvatis Foundation, 2011).

References

American Association of Christian Counselors. (1997). Retrieved from www.richardnethercut.org/16-pioneers-in-christian-counseling.html

Asagba, R. B. (2009). *Logotherapy: Issues from an African Perspective*. Ibadan: University Press, PLC.

Awolalu, J.O. (1972). The African traditional view of man. ORITA: *Ibadan Journal of Religious Studies*, 4,101–18.

Baingana, F. K., Alem, A., & Jenkins, R. (2006). Mental health and the abuse of alcohol and controlled substances. In D. T. Jamison, R. G. Feachem, M. W. Makgoba, E. R. Bos, F. K. Hofman, K. J. Hofman, & K. O. Rogo (eds), *Disease and Mortality in Sub-Sahara Africa* (pp. 329–50). Washington, DC: The World Bank.

Berinyuu, A. A. (1989). *Towards Theory and Practice of Pastoral Counseling in Africa*. Frankfurt: Peter Lang.

Bolton, P., Bass, J., Neugebauer, R., Verdeli, H., Clougherty, K., Wickramaratne, P., & Weissman, M. (2003). Group interpersonal psychotherapy for depression in rural Uganda. A randomized controlled trial. *Journal of the American Medical Association, 289*, 3117–24.

Bott, S., Morrison, A., & Ellsberg, M. (2005). Preventing and responding to gender-based violence in middle and low-income countries: A global review and analysis. *World Bank Policy Research Working Paper, 3618*, 61.

Das, J., Do, Q., Friedman, J., McKenzie, D., & Scott, K. (2006) *Mental Health and Poverty in Developing Countries: Revisiting the Relationship*. Retrieved from http://siteresources.worldbank.org/DEC/Resources/84797–1114437274304/Mental_Health_and_Poverty_Aug2006.pdf.

Denis, P., & Becker, C. (eds) (2006). *The HIV/AIDS Epidemic in Sub-Saharan Africa in a Historical Perspective.* Retrieved from http://rds.refer.sn/IMG/pdf/AIDSHISTORYALL.pdf.

Evans, D., Marks, D. F., Murray, M., & Estacio, E. (2005). *Health Psychology: Theory, Research and Practice.* London: Sage Publications.

Friedman, E. (2004). *Mental Health Effects of the Indonesian Economic Crisis.* Development Economics Group Discussion Paper. Washington, DC: World Bank.

Garcia, M., Pence, A. & Evans, J. (eds) (2008). *Africa's Future, Africa's Challenge: Early Childhood Care and Development in Sub-Saharan Africa.* Retrieved from www.ecdgroup.com/docs/lib_005310613.pdf.

Gureje, O., & Jenkins, R. (2007). Mental health in development: Re-emphasizing the link. *The Lancet, 369*(9560), 447–49.

Health Professs Council of South Africa (HPCSA). (2010). *Handbook for Intern Psychologists and Accredited Institutions.* Retrieved from www.hpcsa.co.za/downloads/psychology/intern_psychology_hand_book.pdf

Hetsen, J., & Wanjohi, R. (1982). *Anointing and Healing in Africa.* Eldoret, Kenya: Gaba Publications

Idowu, E. B. (1975). *Olódùmarè: God in Yoruba Belief.* Ikeje: Longman Nigerian Plc.

Igenoza, A. O. (1994). Wholeness in an African experience, Christian perspective. In E. Lartey, D. Nwachuku, W. K. Kasonga (eds), *The Church and Healing: Echoes from Africa* (pp. 124–37). Frankfurt: Peter Lang.

Jamison, D. T., Feachem, R.G., & Makgoba, M. W., Bos, E. R., Baingana, F. K., Hofman, K. J., & Rogo, K. O. (eds). (2006). *Disease and Mortality in Sub-Saharan Africa* (2nd edn). Washington, DC: The World Bank.

Jenkins, R., Baingana, G., Belkin, G., Borowitz, M., Daly, A., Francis, P., & Sadiq, S. (2010). Mental health and the development agenda in Sub-Saharan Africa. *Psychiatric Services, 61*, 229–34.

Kenyatta, J. (1965). *Facing Mount Kenya.* New York: Vintage Books.

Kiima, D., & Jenkins, R. (2010). Mental health policy in Kenya – an integrated approach to scaling up equitable care for poor populations. *International Journal of Mental Health Systems, 4*, 4–19.

Kingah, S. (2004). Using the palaver settlement paradigm as a means of fortifying the search for the democratic ideal in Sub-Saharan Africa. *Recherches et Documentation juridiques africaines, 8*(30), 109–45.

Kinyanjui, K. (2007). *The transformation of higher education in Kenya: Challenges and opportunities.* Retrieved from http://chet.org.za/manual/media/files/chet_hernana_docs/Kenya/Other/Transformation%20of%20Higher%20Education%20in%20Kenya.pdf.

Kiriswa, B. (2002). *Pastoral Counseling in Africa: An Integrated Model.* Eldoret, Kenya: AMECEA Gaba Publications.

Kwalombota, M., (2002). The effect of pregnancy in HIV infected women. *AIDS Care, 14*, 431–33.

Lowey, M. I., Williams, D. T., & Keleta, A. (2002). Group counseling with traumatized East African refugee women in the United States: Using the Kaffa ceremony intervention. *Journal for Specialists in Group Work, 27*, 173–91.

Maj, M., Janssen, R., Starace, F., Zaudig, M., Salz, P., Sughondhabirom, B., Luabeya, M. A. (1994). WHO neuropsychiatric AIDS study. Cross sectional Phase 1. Study design and psychiatric findings. *Archives of General Psychiatry, 51*, 39–39.

Makgoba, M. W. (1997). *MOKOKO, the Makgoba Affair: A Reflection on Transformation.* Florida Hills, FL: Vivlia Publishers and Booksellers.

Ma Mpolo, J. M. (1994). Spirituality and counseling for healing and liberation: The context and praxis of African pastoral activity and psychotherapy. In E. Lartey, D. Nwachuku, W. K. Kasonga (eds), *The Church and Healing: Echoes from Africa* (pp. 11–34). Frankfurt am Main: Peter Lang.

Marah, J. (2006). The virtues and challenges in traditional African education. *The Journal of Pan African Studies, 4*, 15–24.

Mbiti, J. S. (1969). *African Religions and Philosophy.* London: Heinemann Publications.

Mbiti, J. (1978). Christianity and culture in Africa. In M. Cassidy & L. Verlinden (eds), *Facing the New Challenges: The Message of PACLA* (pp. 272–284). Kisumu, Kenya: Evangel Publishing House.

M'Imanyara, A. M. (1992). *The Restatement of Bantu Origin and Meru history.* Nairobi, Kenya: Longman Kenya.

Mpofu, E., Peltzer, K. & Bojuwoye, O. (2011). Indigenous healing practices in sub-Saharan Africa. In E. Mpofu (ed.). *Counseling People of African Ancestry* (pp. 3–21). Cambridge: Cambridge University Press.

Mpofu, E., Zindi, F., Oakland, T., & Peresuh, M. (2011). *School Psychology Practices in East and Southern Africa: Special Educators' Perspectives.* Retrieved from http://sed.sagepub.com/content/31/3/387.abstract

Mugambi, J. & Kirima, N. (1976). *The African Religious Heritage.* Nairobi: Oxford University Press.

Mwiti, G. K. (2009). *Crisis and Trauma Counseling. A Community-based Approach for Resiliency, Reconciliation and Renewal.* Nairobi, Kenya: Evangel Publishing House.

Myambo, K. (2000). Sub-Saharan Africa. In A. E. Kazdin (ed.), *Encyclopedia of Psychology, Vol.* 7 (pp. 499–505). American Psychological Association: Oxford University Press.

Norvatis Foundation. (2011). Regional psychosocial support initiative: Bringing hope to AIDS orphans in Africa. Retrieved from www.corporatecitizenship.novartis.com/downloads/cc-in-action/Bringing_Hope.pdf.

Nsamenang, A. B. (1993). Psychology in Sub-Saharan Africa. Special Issue: Psychological research in developing countries: Progress, problems and prospects. *Psychology and Developing Societies,* 5(2), 171–184.

Nwoye, A. (2004). The shattered microcosm: Imperatives for improved family therapy in Africa in the 21st century. *Contemporary Family Therapy, 26,* 143–164.

Okun, B. F. (1982). *Effective helping: Interviewing and counseling techniques.* Monterey: Brooks/le.

Papas, R. K., Sidle, J. E., Gakinya, B., Martino, O., Mwaniki, M., Baliddawa, J. B., & Maisto, S. A. (2010). Systematic cultural adaptation of cognitive-behavioral therapy to reduce alcohol use among HIV-infected outpatients in western Kenya. *AIDS Behavior, 14,* 669–678.

Parekh, A. & Inge, P. (1996). The role of mental health Ngos in South Africa: Before and during political transition. *Journal of African Psychology, 2,* 2–13.

Patel, V., & Patel, D. (1998). *Culture and Common Mental Disorders in Sub-Saharan Africa.* Hove: Psychology Press.

Penal Reform International (2000). *Access to Justice in Sub-Saharan Africa: The Role of Traditional and Informal Justice Systems.* Astron Printers, London: Penal Reform International.

Perriens, J. H., Luabeya Mussa, M. K., Kayembe, K., Kapita, B., Brown, C., Piot, P., Jansen, R. (1992). Neurological complications of HIV-1 seropositive internal medicine inpatients in Kinshasa, Zaire. *Journal of Acquired Immune Deficiency Syndrome, 5,* 333–40.

Ruxin, J. (2005). *Shared Imperatives in Battling HIV/AIDS in the South.* Retrieved from http://ssc.undp.org/uploads/media/3Josh-Ruxin.pd

Sexual Violence Research Initiative. (2010). *Parenting, Gender Socialization and the Prevention of Child Abuse and Neglect in Low- and Middle-income Countries.* London: Sexual Violence Research Institute.

Shacham, E., Reece, M., Owino, W., Omollo, O., Monahan, P., & Ojwang, O. (2008). Characteristics of psychosocial support seeking during HIV-related treatment in western Kenya. *AIDS Patient Care STDS, 22,* 595–601.

Smith, E. W. (1923). *The Religion of the Lower Races.* New York: The MacMillan Co.

Solarsh, G., & Hofman, K.J. (2006). Developmental disabilities. In D. T. Jamison, R. G. Feachem, M. W. Makgoba, E. R., Bos, F. K. Hofman, K. J. Hofman, & K. O. Rogo (eds), *Disease and Mortality in Sub-Sahara Africa* (2nd edn) (pp. 125–147). Washington, DC: The World Bank.

Stockton, R., Morran, D. K., & Nitza, A. G. (2000). Processing group events: A conceptual map for leaders. *Journal for Specialists in Group Work, 25,* 343–355.

Stockton, R., Nitza, A., & Bhusumane, D. (2010). The development of professional counseling in Botswana. *Journal of Counseling & Development, 88,* 9–12.

Stover, J., Bollinger, L., Walker, N., & Monasch, R. (2010). Resource needs to support orphans and vulnerable children in Sub-Saharan Africa. *Oxford Journals Health Policy & Planning, 22,* 21–27.

UNAIDS, UNICEF, & USAID (2004). *Children on the Brink: A Joint Report of New Orphan Estimates and a Framework for Action.* Retrieved from http://data.unaids.org/publications/External-Documents/unicef_childrenonthebrink2004_en.pdf

University of Lubumbashi. (2002). *Conditions de prévention des crises et d'une paix durable en République Démocratique du Congo* [Conditions of crisis prevention and sustainable peace in Democratic Republic of Congo]. Lubumbashi: Presses Universitaires de Lubumbashi.

Willoughby, W.C. (1970). *The Soul of the Bantu.* Westport, CT: Negro Universities Press.

Woolman, D. C. (2001). Educational reconstruction and post-colonial curriculum development: A comparative study of four African countries. *International Education Journal, 2,* 27–46.

World Bank (2009). *SSA World Development Indicators Database.* Washington, DC: World Bank.

ya Azibo, D.A. (ed.) (1996). *African Psychology in Historical Perspective and Related Commentary.* Trenton: World Press Inc.

PART II

Counseling and psychotherapy in the Americas

7

COUNSELING AND PSYCHOTHERAPY IN ARGENTINA

A tango from psychoanalysis to integrative psychotherapies

Felipe Muller and María Carolina Palavezzatti

Introduction

Argentina has a population of 40,117,096 people, with women outnumbering men by 1 million (National Institute of Statistics and Census, 2010). The urban population represents 89.4% of the country's total population (Pan American Health Organization & Ministry of Health Office of the President, 2010). It is a country that is deeply rooted in the Catholic tradition, where 76% of the citizens identify themselves as Catholics (Mallimaci, Esquivel & Irrazabal, 2008). Life expectancy at birth is 75 years.

Regarding mental health, 21% of the population in Argentina over the age of 15 suffers from some sort of mental disorder. Alcoholism is the principal diagnosis, followed by depression, with the two representing 54% of the consultations (Ministry of Health, n.d.). Psychotherapy services offered extend from the public sphere to the private in a nation where 57,631 psychologists are currently active, and where there is one psychologist for every 696 inhabitants. The vast majority of them work as clinical psychologists (Alonso & Gago, 2008) and 85% of these psychologists are female. In Argentina, 80% of the mental health field is mainly in the hands of psychologists.

Argentina is characterized by having a long tradition in psychotherapy. However, psychotherapy is not recognized as a formal profession and its practice is closely linked to the profession of a psychologist. The link is so strong that among the responsibilities of the psychologist and those with degrees in psychology is that of providing psychotherapy based on any specific psychological model (Ministry of Education and Justice, 1985).

Previously, in 1956, it was decreed that only medical doctors were able to perform psychotherapy, and it was not until the start of the 1980s, with the resolution of the responsibilities of psychologists and following broad and complex debates regarding the professional practice of psychotherapists, that psychologists were finally able to legally practice psychotherapy.

The latest milestone in the field of mental healthcare is the enactment of the Mental Health Act of 2010, which describes psychologists as professionals with a bachelor's degree who are qualified for positions of leadership and management of services in institutions involved in mental health; their suitability for these positions and their ability to integrate different knowledge surrounding the field have been adequately assessed (Mental Health Act, 2010). Until recently the institutional management positions for mental health services could only be occupied by psychiatrists.

Within the various psychological traditions in Argentina, psychoanalysis was the first to occupy the clinical field, and for much of the 20th century it became the hegemonic discipline in mental health (Fernández-Álvarez & Pérez, 1993). Thus, the country became an important center for psychoanalysis in Latin America in particular and the world in general, and an area where psychotherapy found fertile ground for development.

At the start of the 21st century, psychotherapy in Argentina underwent internal transformations as part of its continuous development and faced several challenges imposed by the realities at the time. In recent years, the map of psychotherapy has been characterized by a growing trend toward integration of theories on the one hand and a predominant majority of the psychoanalytic tradition on the other. Only recently has an incipient growth of cognitive psychotherapy been observed (Muller & Palavezzatti, in press).

Counseling as a profession was formalized only about 15 years ago, and its general focus is on the areas of prevention, health promotion, and human development. This specialty is not analogous to psychotherapy, but instead operates in support for issues such as decision making, understanding of life situations, or resolution of specific dilemmas.

By virtue of the differences in development between psychotherapy and counseling, the former with its long history and tradition and the latter with its new beginnings, this chapter is oriented to focus on the history and status of the field of psychotherapy, as counseling is merely taking its first steps as a discipline in this country.

A brief history of counseling and psychotherapy

The origins of psychological aid in Argentina can be traced back to the late 19th century and are strongly linked to psychiatry (Vilanova, 1994). In those times, Argentine psychiatry was predominantly under the influence of positivism, leaning towards the French and Italian schools of thought.

In this context, figures such as José Ingenieros are noteworthy, because although he was a positivist, he was interested in sociology, psychology, and philosophy and was the primary promoter of hypnosis and psychotherapy in the early 20th century (Plotkin, 2001). Ingenieros further promoted the idea that patients should be listened to. Despite being an opponent of psychoanalysis, he was also responsible for opening up new areas for its reception (Vezetti, 1996).

The most significant shift towards the formalization of psychotherapy was the decline of positivism starting in 1910. This shift opened doors to alternative therapeutic theories to mainstream psychiatry, as it was moving from a somatic approach to treating mental illness to one that included its psychological dimension (Plotkin, 2001). Thus, a path from a hereditary-degenerative paradigm to a mental hygiene movement, from viewing "cerebral" illnesses as a "mental" illnesses, had begun and it was finally consolidated in the 1930s (Dagfal, 2009).

The first offerings of systematic training in psychotherapy arose in the early 20th century, prior to the creation of a career in psychology: the Visiting Course of Social Hygiene at the School of Medical Sciences of the University of Buenos Aires in 1924; a social work program which started in 1930 at the University of Argentine Social Museum; the Polytechnic School of

Biotypology, Eugenics and Social Medicine, which was created in 1934 and depended on the General Technical Direction and the Welfare Section of the Argentina Association of Biotypology, Eugenics and Social Medicine; and the School of Social Visitors of Mental Hygiene, which was founded in 1934 as an initiative of the Argentine Mental Hygiene League. The beginnings of clinical psychology and its development during this crucial period were marked by an absence of psychologists working in the field (Rossi, 2009). Terms and concepts related to psychotherapy in Argentina at the time were products of doctors, lawyers, and teachers.

In January 1936 a new journal called *Psicoterapia: Revista de Psicoterapia, Psicología Médica, Psicopatología, Psiquiatría, Caracterología, Higiene Mental* (*Psychotherapy: Journal of Psychotherapy, Medical Psychology, Psychopathology, Psychiatry, Characterology and Mental Hygiene*) was published for the first time. It was the first direct reference to the discipline and a turning point in traditional psychiatry to date. Its editors expressed their admiration for Freud, Jung, Adler, Jaspers, Janet, and Pavlov, among others, and expressed that psychotherapy was a modern response to the social conditions of the time. For them, psychotherapy would have an increasingly important role in the construction of a new society (Plotkin, 2001). It was in the same journal where Ángel Garma, a Spaniard who would become one of the founders of the Argentine Psychoanalytic Association (APA), published his first psychoanalytic articles in the country.

In the same decade psychoanalysis was introduced in Argentina. While during the last years of the 1920s psychoanalysis was incorporated as a therapeutic arsenal by psychiatrists, during the 1930s it took hold as an autonomous specialty, occupying a central place in urban cultural life. In the 1940s, with the formation of the APA, recognized by the International Psychoanalitic Association (IPA), psychoanalysis developed and acquired an undeniable strength, and its place would be central to the development of the field of clinical psychology in Argentina (Dagfal, 2009).

Another important milestone in the development of psychotherapy was the establishment of psychology as a formal profession. During the 1940s and 1950s psychology prevailed in non-clinical settings such as schools and workplaces, which marked the creation of the first careers in psychology in the 1950s. It was during the 1960s, however, that careers in psychology became clinically driven. This was the beginning of conflicts among related professions (medicine, for example) regarding roles and responsibilities. These conflicts, mainly experienced between clinical psychologists and psychiatrists, were issues that were being resolved between 1980 and 1985 (Klappenbach, 1995) and ultimately reaching their way to the mental health law as previously mentioned this chapter.

Although the clinical field was dominated by psychoanalysis, pathways leading to different specializations started in the 1970s. Developing specialties was a necessary response to the growing social acceptance and demand for psychotherapy (Fernández-Álvarez & Pérez, 1993). The field was therefore expanded through the importation of new theoretical models from abroad, and in subsequent years there emerged a trend among psychotherapists to integrate local and foreign theoretical models.

At the end of the 1990s, treatment options increased exponentially when health insurance companies and prepaid healthcare systems were legally mandated to offer psychotherapy to their clients. This has favored the growth of short-term psychotherapies.

Despite all the changes, the map of psychotherapy in the new millennium shows that psychoanalysis is still a driving force within the field of psychotherapy. Furthemore, the increasing presence of different schools of thought has replaced the pure cognitive systems, or behavioral psychotherapists with more integrative psychotherapists, in a technical hybrid that conforms a new trend in itself. Furthermore, during this new millennium, amidst well-established disciplines, counseling has begun to develop as a formal career but faces numerous obstacles as a newcomer in the field.

Counselor education programs, accreditation, licensure, and certification

In the early 1990s, the Ministry of Culture and Education granted preliminary approval of the career title "Psychological Counselor," which later was finally adopted as a tertiary higher education degree. As it is an undergraduate degree, a counselor cannot officially practice psychotherapy in Argentina.

For the professional practice of clinical psychology and psychotherapy it is mandatory to obtain a license through completion of requirements of an official study program. In most cases, the degree awarded that enables the recipient to practice psychotherapy is a bachelor's degree in psychology (*Licenciado en Psicología*). As discussed later, the problem is that these programs do not include any supervised clinical practice.

In 1995, the Higher Education Act (Law 24.521) was passed in Argentina. This Act regulates and accredits the degree in psychology, as it is a degree corresponding to a profession regulated by the state, and the exercise of this profession involves the public interest and its practice has the ability to directly threaten the health of the inhabitants. On the other hand, it is the National Commission for the Assessment and Accreditation of Universities (CONEAU), a decentralized organization that operates under the Ministry of Culture and Education of the Nation, which has among its functions accrediting this undergraduate major, as well any post-graduate[1] clinical programs (Klappenbach, 2000).

In the last few years, postgraduate clinical psychology programs have been incorporated into formal education. They offer an official degree issued by public and private universities and are accredited by the CONEAU. In many cases, these programs are taught jointly by universities and specific institutions representing different theoretical models.

The professional councils or schools of law (e.g. College of Psychologists in the Province of Buenos Aires) (Klappenbach, 1998) are the institutions in which the state delegates the function of regulating professional practice through registration processes and ascertaining that practitioners comply with ethical standards. It is mandatory to be a member of these key institutions. The city of Buenos Aires has no such school and therefore the body responsible for registering psychotherapists is the National Ministry of Health.

In Argentina, unlike in other countries, there is no certification system for professional practice. For psychotherapists, once they receive their undergraduate degree, there are no subsequent evaluations of their competencies. Once the degree is achieved and the license is attained, psychologists who practice psychotherapy are not obligated to further their education or undergo any supervision.

The psychological associations representing the different theoretical models (e.g., for psychoanalysis, the Argentina Psychoanalytic Association) certify and accredit their members based on fulfilling the requirements imposed by the respective educational and training programs; but this certification is merely voluntary and they carry no official value for the state.

Current counseling and psychotherapy theories, processes, and trends

There are two main theories that Argentine psychotherapists rely on to orient and organize their psychotherapeutic practice: psychoanalysis and integrative psychotherapy (Muller, 2008). In a survey of 525 psychotherapists in the city of Buenos Aires and the provinces of Buenos Aires, Santa Fe, La Pampa, Neuquén, Chubut, and Rio Negro, 53% of the psychotherapists stated that they apply psychoanalytic theory as the main theory in their clinical practice (Muller, 2008). The second largest group in the survey, totaling 39.8% of the sample, reported that they integrate theories in their clinical practice.

Among Argentine psychoanalysts, a Freudian–Lacanian combination was reported by 41.9% (Muller, 2008). In total, 32.6% of the psychoanalysts reported to be Freudians, while 15.4% defined themselves as Lacanians. Surprisingly, "other schools" represented only 5% of this sample population, with 1.1% identifying themselves as Winnicotians, and 0.4% as Kleinians. Some (3.6%) did not specify a particular kind of psychoanalytic theory that they use in their practice.

A more detailed analysis of the integrative group was done, considering two elements: (a) a base theory into which other theories are integrated; and (b) other theories that are integrated into that base theory. The most widely reported base theory was psychoanalysis, reported by 63.2%, followed by cognitive theory at 12.9%, and systemic theory at 12.4%. On the other hand, systemic is the most frequently reported theory (34.9%) that is being integrated into a base theory. Next is cognitive at 19.6%, followed by psychoanalysis at 14.4%.

Taken together, Argentine integrative psychotherapists reported three combinations that are most frequently adopted. In first place was psychoanalysis–systemic, reported by 34.4% of the integrative group. The second most frequently applied combination was psychoanalysis–cognitive (20% of the sample), followed by systemic–cognitive, reported by 8.6% of the integrative psychotherapists.

There are two good predictors of whether an Argentine psychotherapist would integrate theories or adhere to psychoanalysis. One is the importance they attribute to specific and non-specific factors. Argentine psychoanalytic psychotherapists tend to attribute more weight to theories in any psychotherapeutic achievement, while integrative therapists perceive factors such as the experience and personality of the psychotherapist and the therapeutic alliance as having more weight than theory in those achievements. The other predictor is the type of university where psychotherapists have studied. Argentine psychotherapists who have studied in public universities tend to choose psychoanalysis as their main theoretical framework; those who studied in private universities, on the other hand, tend to integrate various theories.

The majority of Argentine psychotherapists are unaware of which theory of knowledge informs their clinical practice. In a sample of 415 psychotherapists (Muller, 2008), those who did not know the main epistemology supporting their theory and practice represented the largest group (29.4% of the sample). It was followed by the constructivists with 24.6%, and by structuralism/psychoanalysis with 14.7%. When the sample was divided between psychoanalysts and integrative psychotherapists, the first group was less aware of the kind of theory of knowledge behind their theories. Of these participants 39.1% indicated that they "do not know" the epistemological basis for their theories, while 21.3% define themselves as structuralists. On the other hand, integrative psychotherapists were more aware of the epistemological basis they apply: only 16.6% answered they "did not know," while 36% defined themselves as constructivists.

While all these data correspond to a 2003–2005 sample, a more recent but smaller sample could help indicate future trends and movements. A sample gathered 6 years after (2010–2011) the previous one (Muller & Palavezzatti, 2005) at the same public hospitals and corresponding mental health departments in the City of Buenos Aires shows that the amount of psychotherapists defining themselves as integrative has increased to almost 48% of the sample (Muller & Palavezzatti, in press). A bigger presence of cognitive therapists was also found among the participants.

There are no data about the main theories of counselors. The training programs in the country are based, as expected, on two main theories: Carl Rogers' person-centered therapy, with its existential and humanistic approach to the self, and the systemic approach, with its interactional approach to the self and its relationships.

Indigenous and traditional healing methods

Between 2004 and 2005, a national survey revealed that 600,000 people defined themselves as indigenous or as having an aboriginal descent. Argentina is a country largely populated by immigrants and their descendants.

The history of Argentina owes a great deal to its indigenous people. Traditionally, the elite always looked to Europe (Plotkin, 2001). This is evident in various health fields, especially in psychotherapy. Throughout the history of psychotherapy in Argentina, the experiences, customs, and healing methods of indigenous people have existed in isolation from the psychotherapeutic developments based on European and North American traditions. In some areas, few psychotherapists worked closely with traditional healers, respecting the traditions and beliefs of the indigenous population. The early eighties marked a milestone when Dr. Arturo Philip incorporated a Mapuche shaman into the Neuropsychiatric Hospital in Carmen de Patagones as a therapeutic assistance. She worked together with the staff, participating in meetings and decision making. She achieved positive results with the Mapuche population and in one instance treated a white, non-indigenous patient. Other exchanges with Mapuche tribes have also followed suit (Arrué & Kalinsky, 1991; Bekes, 2000).

Traditional folk healing and shamanism are recognized as belonging to the indigenous societies of Argentina (Idoyaga Molina, 2002). The former is a result of combining old forms of biomedical knowledge, practices of traditional immigrants, and rituals from Catholicism. In some regions of the northeast some indigenous elements are also incorporated (Korman & Idoyaga Molina, 2010). To date, neither traditional folk healing nor shamanism have been incorporated or integrated into any healthcare plan or any form of psychotherapy in Argentina. The experiences mentioned in the preceding paragraph are extraordinary.

Research and supervision

Very little research has been done on psychotherapy in Argentina. While the history of psychotherapy in the country is extensive, the history of psychotherapy research is short, which may explain why there is limited development in the field. Until the early 1990s, no psychotherapy research was carried out in the country. In 1992, with the aid of Horst Kachele, a world-renowned psychoanalyst from Germany, a group of psychoanalysts from the APA and the Buenos Aires Psychoanalytic Association (APdeBA) began to promote psychotherapy research in Argentina (Primero, 2002). Formal meetings were led by the Society for Psychotherapy Research (SPR), and clinical researchers from other theoretical backgrounds began to attend these meetings.

There are three main reasons that would account for this late start. One is the dominance of psychoanalysis as the primary psychotherapeutic modality and psychoanalysts' general refusal to have their clinical work be evaluated by means of empirical research. Another cause is the lack of need to evaluate psychotherapy before third parties. Only recently has there been an interest in investigating what specific types of psychotherapy are the most effective. In Argentina there are neither public nor private entities that look into the effectiveness of different psychotherapies. Finally, the third cause is the lack of resources devoted to research in general (Fernández-Álvarez & García, 2001).

With regard to funding resources, there are three sources of funding for research: two internal and one external. Funds for research are available internally through the National Agency for Promotion of Science and Technology (ANCyT), and to a lesser extent, from the universities themselves. In terms of external funding, the International Psychoanalytic Association (IPA) has allocated research funds since the creation of its committee to promote empirical research. According to the IPA, between 2007 and 2009, 10% of all applications received came from Argentine researchers, showing an increasing trend to investigate psychonalaytic-oriented psychotherapy from an empirical point of view.

The main issues in psychotherapy research in Argentina center on therapy processes and outcomes. For example, empirical process-oriented research studies have looked into the therapeutic alliance in psychoanalytic psychotherapy (Zukerfeld, 2001), the therapist's personal style (Castañeira et al., 2006), different types of interventions (Roussos et al., 2010), and the construction of clinical inferences (Leibovich de Duarte, 2010). Other research topics investigate the prevalence of different theoretical frameworks in clinical practice in Argentina (Muller, 2008; Muller & Palavezzatti, 2005), and the relationship between clinical supervision and psychoanalytic psychotherapy (Moreno et al., 2005).

Supervision in psychotherapy is, as in other countries, a requirement in the majority of clinical training programs for postgraduate students. The requirement for these programs is internal and is not part of any national or provincial regulations. In other words, psychotherapists are not required to have their cases monitored through supervision once they have obtained their medical or psychological degrees. They are obligated to do so only insofar as they are enrolled in training program and want to meet the requirements. For example, to obtain the title of Psychoanalyst through the Argentine Psychoanalytic Association (APA), students need to undergo at least 200 hours of supervision with a faculty member of that institution. To register as a member of the Argentine Association for Cognitive Therapy (AATC), 100 hours of certified supervision are required.

On the other hand, hospitals and other healthcare provides, both public and private, generally make room for supervision. While it is an established practice among psychotherapists, there are no data on the frequency of supervision of their cases when they are not working within an institutional framework.

Strengths, weaknesses, opportunities, and challenges

One aspect that strengthens the discipline in Argentina is its plurality; in its development, psychotherapy welcomed and encouraged the emergence and development of a variety of models and approaches. Its remarkable expansion allows for a large repertoire of theories and techniques to be available for a wide range of applications (Fernández-Alvarez, 2011).

The historical development of psychotherapy in the country is another of its strengths, and it has contributed to the creation of psychotherapists with an Argentine identity and its prestige in the world. Argentina is recognized as a center for psychotherapy and psychoanalysis within the region and the world at large.

This plurality, nevertheless, has one more step to take, that of building a constructive dialogue. Among the opportunities for the field is that of extending the theoretical debate on the basis of proposals of *common grounds* in psychoanalysis (Wallerstein, 1992), *principles for unification* (Fernández-Alvarez, 2003), and *common factors* in psychotherapy (Imel & Wampold, 2008; Lambert & Barley, 2001). Therapists increasingly recognize the significance of specific and common factors as two central aspects of their work. The debate on these issues can contribute to further development of the discipline in our country.

The scarcity of research groups in Argentina is a significant weakness. In a world increasingly oriented towards the search for evidence, the lack of research projects results in the nation receiving little international recognition, despite its great potential.

The lack of certification is also a major weakness. The lax approach to regulation homologizes trained and responsible professionals with those who are indifferent about training, supervision, and actualization in the field. Argentina needs to have a system that regulates, at least, some aspects of the practices and training of psychotherapists.

The trend toward integration is a phenomenon observed in Argentina (Muller, 2008). In spite of this, training programs adhering to an integrative perspective are nearly non-existent. Those who define themselves as integrative thus form a group of practitioners who have no specific training in specific models of integration. For the aforementioned reasons and the type of postgraduate training offered in the country (rich in diversity of models), it is possible to assume that those who integrate do so on the basis of incorporating various models in a more eclectic fashion as opposed to one that clearly articulates the different views among those models.

Argentina has a traditionally close relationship with psychotherapy. The main challenge is whether its future potentials can be discerned. As integrative forms of therapy continue to develop at such a fast pace, the challenge would be to identify the potential new trends that would further the discipline in a way that could make important contributions in the field. Further, it would be interesting to see how psychotherapists address the theoretical contradictions and technical incompatibilities. So far, there is no one addressing these inconsistencies, particularly the theoretical ones, perhaps due to the pragmatic nature associated with integrative practices.

Another challenge is to consolidate more interdisciplinary approaches. Pathologies like alcoholism and drugs addiction have a high social component (Di Nanno, 2008) and require interdisciplinary approaches. One big challenge for psychotherapy would be establish common areas of intervention with other disciplines for these types of interventions.

A final challenge is to integrate the concept of training in cultural clues (Korman & Idoyaga Molina, 2010) that allow greater sensitivity when working with the ethnic multiplicity and cultural diversity. In Argentina, psychotherapy training programs do not contemplate topics such as the need to recognize and respect social diversity. As Argentinean society becomes more pluralistic and socially inclusive, this would be a challenge to attend to.

Future directions

Psychotherapy in Argentina should be organized and regulated using measures that seek to locate the professional practice in a place of greater prestige. The recertification of the degrees in Psychology (Licenciatura en Psicología) and the increase in offerings of graduate programs with official degrees are demonstrations of a future path that envisions the possibility of having, at some point, accreditation procedures that the country does not have today.

Psychoanalysis and psychotherapy as disciplines have been homologized. The trend to set themselves apart as separate disciplines, with the emergence of psychotherapy as a discipline in its own right, may appear near in our horizon.

One last point refers to the need for empirical support in the validation of treatments. Most psychotherapists, with very well-sustained arguments, do not see the need for empirical support of their practice. In the future, researchers would have to show, through their work and results, how the practice itself can be benefited with the increase of research programs in psychotherapy.

Conclusion

Psychotherapy, with its long history in Argentina, has continued to expand and reinvent itself for over a century. Present challenges and weaknesses need to be addressed so as to ensure a future as promising and fruitful as the past has been. To accomplish this, there needs to be ongoing intellectual and theoretical exchanges between professionals committed to psychotherapy, for the field can only thrive when there is a bridge of dialogues among scientists.

Counseling, on the other hand, started its course a little more than a decade ago. Its challenges make way for opportunities and space for it to grow. It would be interesting to observe if they could establish these same bridges with psychotherapists. So, far, it is the new discipline that should find its place in a country overpopulated with psychotherapists.

Both psychotherapy and counseling share a similar goal, which is to contribute, in the best way, and each in its own way, to people's quality of life. Psychotherapy has not only become a well established discipline in Argentina but also continues to be a lively field undergoing constant transformations. Its long history tells us that it has indeed contributed to the well being of our nation, but there remains a place for counseling to come and make its own contribution to Argentine society.

Note

1 In Argentina, MAs and PhDs are *postgraduate* degrees, whereas "Licenciatura en psicología" is a *graduate* degree similar to a bachelor's degree in North America.

References

Alonso, M., & Gago, P. (2008). Psicologas/os en Argentina. Actualización cuantitativa 2008 [Psychologists in Argentina. Quantitative update]. *Anuario de Investigaciones, 17*(1), 375–382.

Arrué, W., & B. Kalinsky. (1991). *De "la médica" y el terapeuta. La gestión intercultural de la salud en el sur de la provincia del Neuquén* [On "the medical" and the therapist. Intercultural management of health in the southern province of Neuquen]. Buenos Aires: Centro Editor de América Latina.

Bekes, M. (2000). Intercambio medicinal entre Alemania y los mapuches [Medical exchange between Germany and the Mapuche]. *Alcmeón, 9,* 31–33.

Castañeiras, C., García, F., Lo Bianco, J., & Fernández-Álvarez, H. (2006). Modulating effect of experience and theoretical-technical orientation on the personal style of the therapist. *Psychotherapy Research, 16,* 587–593.

Dagfal, A. (2009). *Entre París y Buenos Aires. La invención del psicólogo (1942–1966)* [Between Paris and Buenos Aires. The invention of the psychologist (1942–1966)]. Buenos Aires: Paídos.

Di Nanno, A. (2008). Hacia la construcción de una política en Salud Mental. Rescatar la historia, destacar los logros del federalismo, fortalecer la institucionalidad. [Toward the construction of a Mental Health Policy. Rescue history, highlight the achievements of federalism and strengthen institutionality]. *Revista Argentina de Clínica Psicológica, 17,* 155–166.

Fernández-Álvarez, H., & Pérez, A. (1993). La psicología en distintos países: La psicoterapia en la Argentina. Evolución de la clínica psicológica en los años 1940/70 [Psychology in different countries: Psychotherapy in Argentina. Evolution of the psychological clinic in the years 1940/70]. *Revista Argentina de Clínica Psicológica, 2,* 91–97.

Fernández-Álvarez, H., & García, F. (2001). *Investigación en psicoterapia: Un puente entre teoría y clínica* [Investigation in psychotherapy: A bridge between theory and clinical]. Vertex, *12,* 204–210.

Fernández-Álvarez, H. (2003). Claves para la unificación en psicoterapia (más allá de la integración) [Keys in the unification in psychotherapy (beyond integration)]. *Revista Argentina de Clínica Psicológica, 12,* 229–246.

Fernández-Alvarez, H. (2011). Perspectiva de la psicoterapia [Perspective on psychotherapy]. In H. Fernandez-Alvarez (Comp.), *Paisajes de la psicoterapia. Modelos, aplicaciones y procedimientos* (pp. 269–295). Buenos Aires: Polemos.

Imel, Z., & Wampold, B. (2008). The importance of treatment and the science of common factors in psychotherapy. In S. Brown & R. Lent (eds), *Handbook of Counseling Psychology* (4th edn) (pp. 249–262). Hoboken, NJ: John Wiley & Sons Inc.

Idoyaga Molina, A. (2002). *Culturas, enfermedades y medicinas. Reflexiones sobre la atención de la salud en contextos interculturales de Argentina* [Culture, illness and medicine. Reflections on health care in intercultural contexts of Argentina]. Buenos Aires: CAEA-CONICET.

Klappenbach, H. (1995). El proceso de profesionalización de la psicología en la Argentina [The process of professionalization of psychology in Argentina]. *Idea, 22,* 17–35.

Klappenbach, H. (1998). Formas organizativas de la psicología en la Argentina. Notas históricas y situación actual [Organizational forms of psychology in Argentina. Notes on its history and current situation]. *Idea, 25,* 137–158.

Klappenbach, H. (2000). El título profesional de psicólogo en Argentina antecedentes históricos y situación actual [The professional title of psychologist in Argentina: Historical background and current situation]. *Revista Latinoamericana de Psicología: Colombia, 32*, 419–446.

Korman, G., & Idoyaga Molina, A. (2010). *Cultura y depresión. Aportes antropológicos para la conceptualización de los trastornos mentales* [Culture and depression. Anthropological contributions to the conceptualization of mental disorders]. Buenos Aires: Akadia.

Lambert, M., & Barley, D. (2001). Research summary on the therapeutic relationship and psychotherapy outcome. *Psychotherapy: Theory, Research, Practice, Training, 38*(4), 357–361.

Leibovich de Duarte, A. (2010). Psychotherapists at work. Exploring the construction of clinical inferences. In R. Schwarzer & P.A. Frensch (eds), *Personality, Human Development, and Culture: International Perspectives on Psychological Science* (Vol. 2) (pp. 29–43). New York: Psychology Press.

Mallimaci, F., Esquivel, J., & Irrazabal, G. (2008). *Primera encuesta sobre creencias y actitudes religiosas en Argentina* [First survey on religious beliefs and attitudes in Argentina]. Retrieved from www.culto.gov.ar/encuestareligion

Ministry of Health (n.d.). *Analisis de la Salud Mental en Argentina* [Analysis of mental health in Argentina]. Retrieved October 20, 2011, from www.msal.gov.ar/saludmental/

Ministry of Education and Justice (1985). Resolución N° *2447/85* [Resolution N° 2447/85]. Buenos Aires: Mimeo.

National Institute of Statistics and Census (2010). *Censo 2010 Argentina* [Argentina 2010 census]. Retrieved October 25, 2011, from www.censo2010.indec.gov.ar.

Moreno, C.L., Schalayeff, C., Acosta, S., Vernengo, P., Roussos, A., & Lerner, B. (2005). Evaluation of psychic change through the application of empirical and clinical techniques for a 2-year treatment: a single case study. *Psychotherapy Research, 15*(3), 199–209.

Muller, F. (2008). Psychotherapy in Argentina: Theoretical orientation and clinical practice. *Journal for Psychotherapy Integration, 18*, 410–420.

Muller, F., & Palavezzatti, C. (in press). La psicoterapia y los modelos teóricos en los hospitales públicos de la ciudad de Buenos Aires [Psychotherapy and theoretical models in public hospitals of the city of Buenos Aires].

Muller, F., & Palavezzatti, C. (2005). Modelos teóricos y practica clínica en Argentina: Psicoterapia en Capital Federal [Theoretical models and clinical practice in Argentina: Psychotherapy in Capital Federal]. *Revista Argentina de Clínica Psicológica, 13*, 73–82.

Pan American Health Organization & Ministry of Health Office of the President, 2010. (2010). *Indicadores básicos Argentina 2010* [Basic indicators for Argentina 2010]. Retrieved from www.ops.org.ar

Plotkin, M. (2001). *Freud in the Pampas: The Emergence and Development of a Psychoanalytic Culture in Argentina.* Stanford, CA: Stanford University Press.

Poder Legislativo Nacional (2010). *Boletin Oficial: Ley de Salud Mental 26.657.* Retrieved from www.forumadd.com.ar/documentos/ley-26657-SM.pdf

Primero, G. (2002). *Investigación en psicoterapia. Entrevista a Fernando S. García* [Research in psychotherapy. Interview with Fernando S García]. Retrieved November 2, 2011, from www.psiquiatria.com/articulos/tratamientos/psicoterapias/8017/

Rossi, L. (2009). Antecedentes en la profesionalización de la psicología en Argentina. Proyectos de formación sistemática, supuestos implícitos y proyecto político [Historical background of the professionalization of psychology in Argentina. Systematic training projects, implicit assumptions, and political project]. *Revista de Historia de la Psicología en Argentina, 2*, 27–47.

Roussos, A., Waizmann, V., & Etchebarne, I. (2010). Common interventions in 2 single cases of cognitive and psychoanalytic psychotherapies. *Journal of Psychotherapy Integration, 20*, 327–346.

Vezetti (1996). Los estúdios históricos de la psicología en Argentina [The historical studies of psychology in Argentina]. *Cuadernos Argentinos de Historia de la Psicología, 2*(1/2), 79–93.

Vilanova, A. (1994). La psicoterapia en diferentes países. La psicoterapia en la Argentina (II). Evolución de la clínica psicológica hasta 1940 [Psychotherapy in different countries. Psychotherapy in Argentina (II). Evolution of clinical psychology until 1940]. *Revista Argentina de Clínica Psicológica, 3*, 79–86.

Wallerstein, R. (1992). *The Common Grounds in Psychoanalysis.* New Jersey: Jason Aronson.

Zukerfeld, R. (2001). Alianza terapéutica y encuadre analítico. Investigación empírica del proceso y sus resultados [Therapeutic alliance and the analytic framework. An empirical research of process and outcomes] *Vertex. Revista Argentina de Psiquiatría, 12*(45), 211–220.

8

COUNSELING AND PSYCHOTHERAPY IN BRAZIL

From private practice to community services

Claudio S. Hutz and William B. Gomes

Introduction

Brazil was a Portuguese colony since its discovery in 1500 until 1808, when Napoleon troops invaded Portugal and the Portuguese court moved to Rio de Janeiro and created the United Kingdom of Portugal, Brazil, and the Algarves. Today, Brazil has a population of more than 190 million people (Brazilian Institute of Geography and Statistics [IBGE], 2010). The three main groups were the indigenous peoples who were the original inhabitants, the Africans, originally brought there as slaves, and the Portuguese, who were the first settlers. However, the Dutch, Spanish, Germans, Italians, Jews, Japanese, and, more recently, Syrians and Lebanese immigrants, among many others, have also left their mark and influenced the culture. Despite this diversity, Portuguese is the official language and is spoken by almost everybody. The last census (IBGE, 2010) showed that most of the population is Catholic but the Evangelicals and Spiritualists have been consistently growing. There is considerable influence of African religions (Ubanda, Quibanda) in all regions of the country.

Over the past 15 years the country's economy has modernized to become the seventh largest in the world. Today, Brazil is part of the emergent BRIC countries and has a stable situation with sustained growth. There has been a large reduction in poverty and a considerable increase in the middle class; however, Brazil still faces problems with corruption in government and crime in large cities, and efforts are being made to increase security and transparency of government actions.

Against the backdrop of the aforementioned demographic and socio-economic conditions, the development and dissemination of psychotherapy in Brazil are associated with the growth of the profession of psychologist. Brazil was one of the first countries to recognize and regulate the profession by federal law in 1962. Since then, there has been an enormous growth of programs for training of psychologists.

Counseling and psychotherapy are widespread psychological practices which are very much appreciated in Brazil, although today there are not clear distinctions between them. The term "counseling" was used to describe psychological assistance in psycho–pedagogic and career guidance services. The distinction is maintained as a technical and didactic reference in training programs for psychologists. At present, psychotherapy is defined by the Federal Council of

Psychology (CFP, 2000) as a scientific process of understanding, analysis, and intervention, using psychological methods and techniques to provide conditions for people to cope with conflicts or psychological disorders. Although psychotherapy is a practice associated with the work of the psychologist, it is not restricted to that profession or even regulated.

Because of the proven positive effects, psychotherapy has been extended to various segments of the population, leading to pressure from professional bodies and health insurance companies to regulate the activity and cost reduction. In this sense, Brazil is following what already occurs in the USA (Reed & Eisman, 2006), Germany (Müller, 2011), and France (Roudinesco, 2005). In Brazil, the CFP has been speaking out strongly on the regulation of psychotherapy since 2000, having chosen the year of 2009 as the "Year of Psychotherapy." In this sense, it follows the example of the above nations, where psychotherapy must meet strict regulations for inclusion in universities, pension systems, and health insurance. The idea is to establish parameters for the practice of psychotherapy performed by psychologists to become accessible and comprehensive (Regional Council of Psychology of São Paulo, 2008).

The difference between counseling and psychotherapy has been kept in the curriculum of training programs in psychology. However the term "psychotherapy" prevailed because of its greater scope and application. Thus, in this chapter there will not be a distinction between counseling and psychotherapy. Psychotherapy is most prevalent and the most commonly used term in Brazil. A more detailed and specific history and description of counseling in Brazil can be found in Hutz-Midgett and Hutz (2012).

Brief history of counseling and psychotherapy

In Brazil, the practice of psychological counseling originated in the American psychological movements of the first half of the 20th century, such as the centers of juvenile guidance for parents and children, the vocational guidance services, services of mental hygiene, social welfare services, and psychological services for companies. These counseling centers and first psychological services in major Brazilian cities flourished between the years 1930 and 1950 (Lourenço-Filho, 1955). In 1964, Ruth Scheeffer published the first book on counseling psychology in Brazil, describing her experience as an adviser to guidance counselor candidates at the Institute of Career Guidance and Professional Selection of the Getulio Vargas Foundation in Rio de Janeiro. Scheeffer's study helped disseminate the nondirective counseling of Carl Rogers in Brazil. Another example of dissemination of counseling techniques is represented by the work of one of the first Brazilian psychologists, José Arvedo Flach, who already in the 1950s became a major promoter of the work of Carl Rogers in Brazil (Cavalcante Junior & Montenegro, 2009).

In contrast, psychotherapy has its origins in the strong influence that psychoanalysis has exercised. Since the first decades of the 20th century, psychiatrists began to study and to include psychoanalysis in medicine programs (Sagawa, 2004).

Freud's early works were read and studied in German. Between the 1910s and 1920s, psychoanalysis was studied and disseminated in a move unrelated to training and professionalization. In the 1920s, Brazilian psychiatrists not only exchanged letters with Freud but they also visited him in Europe. The first Brazilian to correspond with Freud was Durval Marcondes, trained in São Paulo. He was also the first Brazilian to recognize the need to seek didactic analysis training for the practice of psychoanalysis.

In 1938, after insistent requests from Durval Marcondes, psychoanalyst Adelheid Lucy Koch (a member of the Berlin Psychoanalytic Institute) was sent to Brazil by Ernest Jones, then president of the International Psychoanalytical Association (IPA) (Uchôa, 1981) for training purposes. Soon after her, other training psychoanalysts arrived in Brazil and psychoanalysis began to develop in the cities of São Paulo, Rio de Janeiro, and Porto Alegre. The Psychoanalytic Society of São Paulo was recognized by the IPA in 1951, and in Rio de Janeiro two societies were formed because of dissension among local psychoanalysts. The Psychoanalytic Society of Porto Alegre was recognized by the IPA in 1963. It was founded by psychoanalysts trained in Argentina and in Brazil with the support of the Psychoanalytic Society of Rio de Janeiro. Finally, in 1967, the Brazilian Association of Psychoanalysis was founded, bringing together the societies of Sao Paulo, Porto Alegre, and Rio de Janeiro.

In the 1940s and 1950s, psychotherapy was practiced by psychiatrists following a psychodynamic orientation. However, Marcondes (1955) defended that the practice of psychotherapy should also be undertaken by clinical psychologists and psychoanalysts who are not physicians, provided they receive training in an institution supervised by the IPA, and that they would work under the supervision of a physician. The two positions concerning the making of a psychoanalyst—one maintained that it should be restricted to medical doctors and the other accepted non-medical doctors provided they received adequate training—would affect the practice of psychotherapy and interaction between physicians and psychologists, including important theoretical implications, for several years.

The practice of psychotherapy grew enormously in the 1950s and 1960s, driven by the organization of societies of psychoanalysis and the creation of training programs in psychology. Simultaneously, the conflicts between psychiatrists and psychologists contributed to interest in other theoretical approaches which had expanded in different directions in the second half of the 20th century.

More recently, in 2004, the Brazilian Association of Psychotherapy (ABRAP) was founded with the aim of bringing together and promoting exchanges between psychotherapists of the different theoretical backgrounds that exist today. It is an association that covers a broad spectrum of psychotherapeutic lines, such as psychoanalytic, psychodrama, cognitive-behavioral, systemic, body behavior, analytical psychology, and others. The creation of ABRAP underscores the maturity of this field in Brazil and points to future trends to foster dialogue across theories and to promote the critical integration of methods with empirical support.

Counselor education programs, accreditation, licensure, and certification

The largest number of psychotherapists in Brazil comes from psychology programs. These programs are offered by universities or colleges, lasting 5 to 6 years, and are characterized by a general curriculum, including basic areas (experimental, development, personality, social, psychopathology, statistics, and research methods) and applied (school, organizational, clinical, forensic, etc.). Upon completing the program in psychology, the new psychologist may register in the CFM, through one of its regional agencies. Registration is very simple as it requires only the psychology degree diploma and payment of a fee. With this application, the psychologist receives a license and can engage in any activity in any area in the field of psychology. This license is permanent and need not be renewed.

For physicians, training in psychotherapy occurs in a psychiatric internship that follows the general training program of medicine. The medical internships are much disputed in Brazil and meet only 50% of the demand. However, just like the psychologist, the physician can register at the CFM, obtain a license and start to work in any field of the profession. However, psychiatry is a specialty that requires specific training and registration.

Training in psychotherapy outside academic institutions also exists. It is also offered by training centers in psychotherapy, formed by professionals with no ties to universities, and characterized by several theoretical representations (psychoanalytic, behavioral, cognitive, psychodrama, gestalt, person-centered approach, systemic, etc.). These training centers accept both psychologists and psychiatrists, and some of them may also accept other professionals, such as social workers, educators, speech therapists.

The professional training programs, in both public and private universities, are recognized by the Ministry of Education. The Ministry maintains a system of continuous evaluation of the degree programs through national sample surveys for graduating students and regular assessment of the conditions of each program, which includes an assessment of the its curricula and general infrastructure. However, this assessment is poor and there is a great variation in quality of training offered at several universities. It is deemed that a higher quality of training is obtained at public universities and Catholic universities in the main cities.

Psychotherapy is now recognized as a specialty for both physicians and psychologists. Thus, it is common for these professionals to seek further training shortly after they graduate. Programs that offer this training within accredited universities do not require any certifying agency. However, when they are offered by private training centers in psychotherapy or clinical psychology they are certified by the CFP. The specialties in medicine are certified by the Federal Council of Medicine. Note that such programs do not provide a degree of specialization. They merely provide a certificate of completion of a training program.

Master's and PhD programs in Brazil are recognized as postgraduate training, the main purpose of which is research and technological innovation. These programs are rigorously monitored and evaluated by CAPES (Coordination for the Improvement of Higher Education), an agency of the Ministry of Education. Thus, Brazil has advanced postgraduate studies strongly dedicated to research, occupying thirteenth position in scientific production, according to the ISI (Institute for Scientific Information, National Science Indicators) in the USA (ISI, 2007).

Current counseling and psychotherapy theories, processes, and trends

One of the characteristics of psychology practiced in Brazil is the confluence of the European and US schools of thought. The general curriculum of psychotherapy training programs provides a comprehensive overview of psychological theories and their histories, though the overview can sometimes be superficial. Nevertheless, many different psychotherapeutic approaches have found fertile ground to grow in Brazil.

A recent study of theoretical preferences among Brazilian psychologists (Gondim, Bastos & Peixoto, 2010) brings a reliable picture of current trends. Using questionnaires, the authors gathered data on theoretical preferences of 1,190 Brazilian psychologists working in the clinical area (605 worked exclusively in the clinical area and 585 combined work in clinical and some other area). Psychoanalysis was still the predominant theoretical framework, both for those who are dedicated solely to the clinical area (n = 162, 27%) and for those who work in clinics and other areas (n = 150, 26%). The two preferences that follow are cognitive-behavioral (15% and 17% for both groups) and humanistic-existential (with 9% and 6%, also for both groups). What impressed the authors was the high proportion of psychologists who combined two or more approaches: For example, 20% of the psychologists who worked only in the clinical area reported that they combine two theoretical approaches, and 18% combine three or more approaches. The authors interpreted that the combination may have resulted from a lack of experience, as is evident in more recent college graduates. In contrast, psychologists who were more specialized and involved in research tended to focus on a single approach. An alternative interpretation is that new professionals seem more open to theoretical integration, either because they do not have much experience or because of the complex demands of clinical practice. Highly specialized professionals with more training time can be more committed to their own beliefs, which may restrict being open to new possibilities and theories.

Cognitive-behavioral psychotherapies are expanding in Brazil, even more in private clinics than in hospitals. A study conducted by Range, Falcone and Sardinha (2007) with 248 professionals (228 psychologists and 20 psychiatrists) indicated that most professionals based their practice on the combination of models of cognitive restructuring and cognitive-behavioral therapy. For the authors, the results point to the integration of approaches, which they deemed to be the future trend in psychotherapy.

In terms of other trends in the field, Bastos & Achcar (1994) reported that Brazilian psychologists are beginning to turn their attention to their social role in meeting collective demands, gradually moving away from an individualistic model of treatment. Bastos (1988) had criticized the hegemonic dominance of the medical model, based on individual and private care, considered by the author as inappropriate in meeting the unique demands of Brazilian society. Adherence to this view of social psychology reverberated strongly in psychology programs, reducing somewhat the interest in psychotherapy, and leading the exploration for forms of psychological interventions that are more community oriented. These psychologists use research and policy advocacy to influence public policy and thus bring psychological services to segments of the population that need them most (Medeiros, Bernardes, & Guareschi, 2005).

Indigenous and traditional healing methods

Brazilian culture was formed by Portuguese, indigenous, and African influences. These populations have bequeathed to the new country their beliefs and mysticism. However, these mystical practices continue to exist as such in the field of faith and religion. In the 1990s there was heated debate in the CFP on emerging practices that could be characterized as alternative therapies because of the great attraction they exerted on many psychologists (Tavares, 2003). The list of these practices was great, including treatments such as crystal healing, energy therapy, shamanic psychotherapy, esoteric psychotherapy, transmutation of energy therapy, past life regression therapy, spiritual psychotherapy, and meditation therapy.

In this debate, Marques (1996) argued that the alternative psychotherapies could be signs of new psychological paradigms. However, Tourinho and Carvalho (1995) pointed out the logical incompatibility between the conjunction of events and results with their statement of explanatory rules; that is, these models were simply not scientific. The first initiative of the CFP— resolution 016 of 1995—was to curb such practices. However, in a meeting in 1996, the CFP reviewed its position and recommended further study and research, collaborating with other professions in the health area (Tavares, 2003).

In a qualitative study of patients who sought alternative psychotherapies (Gauer, Souza, Molin, & Gomes, 1997),[1] improvements were reported in the patients' ability to handle their own problems, changes in worldview and relationship with other people, and remission of physical symptoms. Such changes were noticed not only by the patients themselves but also by family members and friends. In interviews with therapists, responses did not contain magical or mystical elements. In fact, they seemed to be aware of aspects of conventional therapy structures (e.g., differentiation of symptom expression versus process perception). It was interpreted that therapists made efforts to provide answers that they believed would be comprehensible to researchers (Gauer et al, 1997).

In recent decades little has been published on the subject. In fact, interest turned to the growth of neo-Pentecostalism and its promised cures for a variety of health problems, including mental health (Costa-Rosa, 2008; Próchino, Paradivini, & Gonçalves, 2008). In any case, it is expected that these studies may broaden the understanding of these phenomena and subsidize preventive and remediation psychological interventions, having as a context a universe of cultural beliefs.

Research and supervision

Within academia, psychotherapeutic practices are the subject of research in postgraduate programs with a major area of research in clinical psychology. Yamamoto (2010) pointed out that of the 64 existing programs at that time, most programs were in the area of social psychology (28%), followed by research in clinical psychology (17%), and developmental psychology (11%). However, summing up the lines of research in clinical psychology and health psychology, which also conducts research on psychotherapy, the amount of programs jumps to 27%. As mentioned previously, there is a major attraction among Brazilian psychologists for social psychology, an approach rooted in socio-history. Although these researchers are not concerned with psychotherapy in the classical and traditional way, they propose alternative treatments that are not elitist and restricted to private clinics, and that may include groups, communities, schools, clubs, clinics, hospitals, or even take place on the streets, as is common when caring for at-risk populations (Mendes & Machado, 2004).

The number of published papers on psychotherapy in Brazil is relatively large. There are many journals devoted to psychotherapy. Practically every psychotherapeutic approach has its own journal and some, like psychoanalysis, have several journals (see Brazilian indexes such as SciELO and IndexPsi). A recent study using Brazilian databases (Pieta, DeCastro & Gomes, 2011) located 235 papers that were classified as (1) theoretical or literature review (n = 131), (2) technique proposal, instruments or evaluation (n = 53), (3) profile description of clinical populations (n = 26), (4) experience reports (n = 14), and (5) research results (n = 19). As the study suggests, the number of research results is low, which leads us to interpret that evidence-based psychotherapy has much to develop in Brazil. In these articles, there was an even distribution between efficacy studies (n = 6) and effectiveness studies (n = 7) in psychiatric journals. It was observed also that research with experimental control pre-intervention and post intervention are being used both in cognitive-behavioral psychotherapy (Habigzang et al., 2009) and in psychoanalytic psychotherapies (Hauck et al., 2007; Santeiro, 2008).

Clinical supervision is a requirement of training in both psychiatry and psychology in Brazil. The curriculum guidelines for psychology courses, approved in 2003 by the National Board of Education, require supervised internships in professional emphases chosen by students. The tradition of non-academic training centers provides clinical supervision and initial basic conditions for professional training in psychotherapy to psychologists and psychiatrists. There are also residency programs, which are more related to psychiatry than to psychology. Activities in these programs are all supervised. Taken together, clinical supervision is a practice recognized and coveted by professionals interested in the practice of psychotherapy in Brazil.

In discussing the supervision of psychotherapy trainees in psychoanalysis, Saraiva and Nunes (2007) note that there is little empirical research, and the literature does not discuss the steps that the supervisor and supervisee must follow to achieve the necessary skills. The papers address the contemporary dilemmas concerning supervision, but have no suggestions for changes in technique and strategy oversight. As for supervision of cognitive-behavioral psychotherapies, Wainer and Piccoloto (2007) concluded that it is well structured, favoring both the evaluation of therapeutic results and the actual performance of the therapist. However, it has yet to be defined what are the most significant variables in the proper formation of new cognitive therapists. In phenomenological-existential psychotherapy, Boris (2008) suggested the use of a reflective instrument called "versions of the senses" to transform the mechanics of supervision into an existential moment fruitful for the training of the therapist. In short, the three studies mentioned have pointed out some of the concerns voiced by supervisors in the field, but they clearly indicate the need for further empirical research and a delineation of the skills required for psychological treatment.

Strengths, weaknesses, opportunities, challenges

In view of the strengths of the field of psychotherapy in Brazil, it can be said that it is an established practice in the field of mental health and is recognized by the population. The number of psychotherapists, especially with a background in psychology, is growing, and scientific and professional organizations such as the CFP and the Brazilian Psychiatric Association are working to regulate the practice (Abreu, 2002). It is also recognized that there is a great diversity of psychotherapeutic approaches currently being represented in Brazil, thus calling for the need for greater openness to debate across theories. In Brazil, there are many journals representing the different psychotherapeutic approaches that publish regularly and plenty of training opportunities in well-recognized training centers.

Among the major weaknesses are the need for greater regulation of psychotherapists in training and a lack of empirical research on treatment effectiveness and efficacy. In addition, clinical practice and supervision activities all require closer and more rigorous monitoring from regulatory agencies (Osório, 2006). Although there is a real demand for treatment, payment for psychologists and psychotherapists is relatively low, which discourages more qualified students (Heloani, 2010). Finally, a major weakness lies in the ongoing territorial disputes among mental health practitioners in Brazil. For instance, psychiatrists who fought so hard for exclusivity in psychotherapeutic care have now switched from talking therapy to psychoactive drugs. The same trend is observed with psychologists, who are opposed to social workers becoming family therapists (Osório, 2006).

In Brazil, there is a good range of training programs in psychotherapy, most of them are independent of the universities. They are centers in which the major activity is to provide training, but many of them also require that the candidate undergoes psychological treatment at the same institution, especially in treatments based on psychoanalysis. However, although opportunities for training are plenty and offered at different levels, professional employment may be difficult, especially without contacts offered by these training centers.

In Brazil, the number of qualified psychotherapists has not met the high demand for their services. On the other hand, socio-historical social psychologists working in the area of psychological health have had the opportunity to extend their services to provide psychological assistance to the low-income population through public policies. Further, secretaries of state and municipal health services have hired psychologists to provide assistance to families and communities on the outskirts of large cities and even to rural populations.

The biggest challenge lies in the provision of remuneration compatible with the characteristics and demands of the field and its training requirements. As for the training of psychotherapists, the biggest challenge still lies in the dialogue between these professionals. Incompatibilities between theoretical approaches hinder teamwork and communication between psychotherapists and other professionals. Another major challenge lies in encouraging graduate programs to become more involved in empirical research and the training of psychotherapists. One possibility is the creation of *professional* masters in psychotherapy who could train qualified professionals and also develop research for innovation in treatments. Certainly, these programs could encourage theoretical integration, enhancing diagnosis and outcomes research. These programs could have a clinical school that would serve both training and research. For instance, the graduate program in clinical psychology at the Pontifical Catholic University of Campinas has a school clinic that could serve as a model.

Future directions

The great expectation is that in the near future the practice of psychotherapy will be regulated in Brazil and that it will be considered a multidisciplinary activity. Thus, professionals from various health areas could engage in the practice of psychotherapy. This will require strict criteria for certification of training programs in psychotherapy that are expected at the postgraduate level. In the psychoanalytic tradition certification of training centers has been recognized since the time of Freud. However, theoretical disagreements led to forming alternative traditions, many of which disregard or are against certification. In the cognitive-behavioral tradition there are still no certification requirements, but the openness to empirical research will contribute to the improvement of techniques and applications. The same occurs with the phenomenological-existential psychotherapy which, curiously, still refers to psychological counseling (Forghieri, 2007).

The most hopeful trend in the development of psychotherapy in the country is the strengthening of scientific research. Even sectors that are more resistant to research, such as psychodynamic psychotherapies, are gradually admitting and considering the conduct of research, in the strictest sense, using interviews, questionnaires with quantitative and qualitative methodological criteria. Certainly, there will be a movement in favor of integrative psychotherapy, but the identification of principles, with clear relevance to the ontology of therapeutic purposes, must be carefully examined in empirical research.

There will probably be a reduction in the number of candidates for psychotherapists, but there will be an increase in the quality of services. Providing psychotherapy services to large groups and communities will be strengthened. However, there should be a greater understanding of the coexistence of care in clinics and health centers and in private clinics. Practices should not be opposed to one another, and professionals should understand the reasons for their choices and vocation. Similarly, the combination of pharmacological and psychotherapeutic treatment will become common practice. The improvement in professional qualifications will also lead to improvements in ethical standards.

Conclusion

The practice of counseling and psychotherapy in Brazil developed gradually over the 20th century, with a significant increase in the last two decades. The former is commonly associated with educators and psychologists, whereas the latter with medical doctors. The regulation of the profession of psychologist in the 1960s increased the interest in the study and provision of health care. Disputes between medical doctors and psychologists as to the practice of psychotherapy have been overcome, but present-day educators, philosophers, social workers, and nurses are struggling to exercise their right to offer treatment and to be accepted at training centers. If psychotherapy were to function as a true multidisciplinary discipline, the need for specific regulation and supervision of its practices is perhaps imminent.

Among the positive aspects of psychotherapy in Brazil are its recognition among health professionals and the general population, the wide range of training programs in psychotherapy, and the existence of diverse approaches. Among the challenges is the need to enhance the qualification and regulation of professional practice. It is expected that in the near future there will be greater theoretical integration, increased dialogue among professionals, an increased number of studies that address the efficacy and effectiveness of psychotherapeutic practices considering the peculiarities of Brazilian culture, and public policies by the National Health Service that ensure access to these services among disadvantaged populations.

Note

1 A similar study was conducted a few years prior with patients who underwent recognized traditional treatments (Gomes, Reck, Bianchi & Ganzo, 1993).

References

Abreu, J. R. P. (2002). Psicanálise e psicoterapia no Brasil: Crise e desenvolvimento [Psychoanalysis and psychotherapy in Brazil: Crisis and development]. *Psicanálise, 4*(2), 339–360.

Abreu, J. R., Piccinini, W., Cacilhas, A., Trahtman C. E., & Thormann, N. J. (2000). Psicoterapias no Brasil: Duas décadas através das publicações psiquiátricas. [Psychotherapies in Brazil: Two decades of psychiatric publications]. *Revista Brasileira de Psicoterapia, 2*(1), 89–104.

Bastos, A. V. B. (1988). Áreas de atuação: Em questão o nosso modelo profissional. [Areas of work: Our professional model in question]. In Conselho Federal de Psicologia (ed.), *Quem é o psicólogo Brasileiro* (pp. 163–193). São Paulo: Edicon.

Bastos A. V. B. & Achcar, R. (1994). Dinâmica profissional e formação do psicólogo: Uma perspectiva de integração [Professional dynamics and training of psychologists: A perspective of integration]. In Conselho Federal de Psicologia (ed.), *Psicólogo brasileiro: Práticas emergentes* (pp. 299–329). São Paulo: Casa do Psicólogo.

Beck, A. T., Rush, A. J., Shaw, B. F., & Emery, G. (1982). *Terapia cognitiva da depressão* [Cognitive therapy of depression] (V. Ribeiro, Trans). Rio de Janeiro: Zahar. (1979)

Boris, G. (2008). Versões de sentido: Um instrumento fenomenológico-existencial para a supervisão de psicoterapeutas iniciantes [Versions of meaning: An existential-phenomenological tool for the supervision of psychotherapists beginners]. *Psicologia Clínica* (PUCRJ), *20*(1), 165–180

Cavalcante Junior, F.S. & Montenegro, A. (2009). Irmão Henrique Justo: um pioneiro da psicologia humanista no Brasil. [Brother Henrique Justo: a pioneer of the humanistic psychology in Brazil]. *Memorandum, 16*, 85–91.

Costa, R. P. (2001) A chegada do psicodrama no Brasil: Sua história de 1960 a 1970 [The arrival of psychodrama in Brazil: its history from 1960 to 1970]. *Revista. Brasileira de Psicodrama, 9*(2), 11–36.

Costa-Rosa, A. (2008). Práticas de cura místico-religiosas, psicoterapia e subjetividade contemporânea [Mystical-religious healing practices, psychotherapy and contemporary subjectivity]. *Psicologia USP, 19* (4), 561–590.

Cunha, R. (2004). História da perspectiva do behaviorismo radical [History from the perspective of radical behaviorism]. In M. Massimi (ed.), *História da psicologia no Brasil do século XX* (pp. 199–216). São Paulo: E.P.U.

Federal Council of Psychology (CFP) (2000). *Resolução CFP N° 010/2000: Especifica e qualifica a psicoterapia como prática do psicólogo* [CFP Resolution N° 010/2000: Specifies e qualifies psychoterapy as a psychologist practice]. Retrieved from http://pol.org.br/legislacao/pdf/resolucao2000_10.pdf

Féres-Carneiro, T. & Magalhães, A. S. (2008). Novas configurações familiares e as repercussões em psicoterapia de família [New family configurations and the impact on family psychotherapy]. *Revista Brasileira de Psicoterapia, 10*(2), 7–16.

Ferro-Bucher, J. S. N. (1989). Dos estudos da família a terapia familiar no Brasil [From family studies to family therapy in Brazil]. *Psicologia: Reflexão e Crítica, 4*, 43–58.

Forghieri, Y. C. (2007). Aconselhamento terapêutico: Origens, fundamentos e prática [Therapeutic counseling: Origins, foundations and practice]. São Paulo: Thompson.

Gauer, G., Souza, M. L., Molin, F., & Gomes, W. B. (1997). Terapias alternativas: Uma questão contemporânea em psicologia [Alternative therapies: A contemporary issue in psychology]. *Psicologia Ciência e Profissão, 17*(2), 21–32.

Gomes, W. B. (2003). Pesquisa e prática em psicologia no Brasil [Research and practice in psychology in Brazil]. In O. H. Yamamoto & V. V. Gouveia (ed.), *Construindo a psicologia brasileira: Desafios da ciência e da prática psicológica* (pp. 23–59). São Paulo: Casa do Psicólogo.

Gomes, W. B., Reck, A., Bianchi, A., & Ganzo, C. (1993). O uso de descritores qualitativos e indicadores quantitativos na pesquisa em psicoterapia [The use of qualitative and quantitative descriptors in psychotherapy research]. *Psicologia: Teoria e Pesquisa, 9*(2), 415–433.

Gomes, W. B., Holanda, A. F., & Gauer, G. (2004). História das abordagens humanistas em psicologia no Brasil [The history of humanistic approaches in psychology in Brazil]. In M. Massimi (ed.), *História da psicologia no Brasil do século XX* (pp. 105–130). São Paulo: E.P.U.

Gomes, W. B., & Gauer, G. (2006). Psicólogos versus médicos psicanalistas. [Psychologists versus medical psychoanalysts]. In W. Gomes (ed.) *Psicologia no Rio Grande do Sul*. Porto Alegre: MuseuPsi.

Gondim, S. M. G., Bastos, A. V. B., & Peixoto, L. S. A. (2010). Áreas de atuação, atividade e abordagens teóricas do psicólogo brasileiro [Work areas, activities, and theoretical approaches of Brazilian psychologists]. In A. V. B. Bastos & S. M. G. Gondim (eds), *O trabalho do psicólogo brasileiro* (pp. 174–199). Porto Alegre: ArtMed.

Habigzang, L. F., Hatzenberguer, R., Stroeher, F., Cunha, R. C., Ramos, M., & Koller, S. H. (2009). Grupoterapia cognitivo-comportamental para crianças e adolescentes vítimas de abuso sexual [Cognitive behavioral group therapy for children and adolescents victims of sexual abuse)]. *Revista de Saúde Pública, 43*, 70–78.

Hartmann, H. (1958). *Ego psychology and the problem of adaption*. Madison, CT: International University Press.

Hauck, S., Crestana, T., Mombach, C. K. Almeida, E. A., & Eizerik, C. L. (2008). Pesquisa em psicanálise e psicoterapia psicanalítica: um novo instrumento para avaliação de aderência à técnica em estudos de efetividade [Research in psychoanalysis and psychoanalytic psychotherapy: A new tool for the evaluation of adherence to the technique in studies of effectiveness]. *Revista Brasileira de Psiquiatria, 30*(3), 293–294.

Heloani, R. (2010). O exercício da profissão: Características gerais da inserção profissional do psicólogo [Practice of the profession: General characteristics of the professional insertion of psychologists]. In A. V. B. Bastos & S. M. G. Gondim (eds), *O trabalho do psicólogo brasileiro* (pp. 107–130). Porto Alegre: ArtMed.

Hutz-Midgett, A. & Hutz, C. S. (2012). Counseling in Brazil: Past, present, and future. *Journal of Counseling & Development, 90*, 238–242.

IBGE (Brazilian Institute of Geography and Statistics) (2010). População residente, por sexo e situação do domicílio, segundo a religião [Resident population, by sex and place of residence, according to the religion]. Retrieved from www.ibge.gov.br/home/estatistica/populacao/censo2000/populacao/religiao_Censo2000.pdf

IBGE (2010). Brazil in numbers. Retrieved in Nov. 24, 2011 from www.brasil.gov.br/sobre/brazil/brazil-in-numbers/demographics/br_model1?set_language=en

Institute for Scientific Information (2007). *Essential science indicators*. Retrieved from http://thomsonreuters.com/products_services/science/science_products/a-z/essential_science_indicators/

Ito, L. (ed.). (1998). *Terapia cognitivo-comportamental para transtornos psiquiátricos*. [Cognitive behavioral therapy for psychiatric disorders]. Porto Alegre: Artes Médicas.

Jacó-Vilela, A. M., & Rodrigues, H. B. C. (2004). Aquém e além da separação: A psicologia interpelada pelo social [Before and beyond separation: Psychology challenged by the social]. In M. Massimi (ed.), *História da psicologia no Brasil do século XX* (pp. 217–230). São Paulo: E.P.U.

Lourenço-Filho, M. B. (1955). Psicologia no Brasil [Psychology in Brazil]. In F. Azevedo (ed.), *As ciências no Brasil* (Vol. II) (pp. 143–151). São Paulo: Melhoramentos.

Mahoney, M. J. (1974). *Cognition and Behavior Modification*. Cambridge: Ballinger Publishing Company.

Marcondes, D. (1955). *Parecer sobre o exercício da psicoterapia por psicólogos clínicos e psicanalistas não formados em medicina* [Opinion on the practice of psychotherapy by clinical psychologists and psychoanalysts not trained in medicine]. São Paulo: Tipografia Edance SA.

Marques, L. F. (1996). Práticas alternativas em psicoterapia num cenário de mudança de paradigma [Alternative practices in psychotherapy in a setting of a paradigm shift]. *Psico, 27*(1), 161–184.

Medeiros, P. F., Bernardes, A. G., & Guareschi, N. M. F. (2005). O conceito de saúde e suas implicações nas práticas psicológicas [The concept of health and its implication on the psychological practices]. *Psicoterapia Teoria e Pesquisa. 21*(3), 263–269.

Mendes, A. A., & Machado, M. F. (2004). Uma clínica para o atendimento a moradores de rua: direitos humanos e composição do sujeito [A social clinic to attend homeless: Human rights and the identity]. *Psicologia, Ciência e Profissão, 24*(3), 100–105.

Müller, J. M. (2011). Evaluation of a therapeutic concept diagram. *European Journal of Psychological Assessment, 27*(1), 17–28.

Osório, C. (2006). *Novos paradigmas em psicoterapia* [New paradigms in psychotherapy]. São Paulo: Casa do Psicólogo.

Pieta, M. A., DeCastro T., & Gomes, W. (2011). *Psychotherapy and Research: Challenges for the Next 10 Years in Brazil*. Manuscript submitted for publication.

Ponciano, E. L. T., & Féres-Carneiro, T. (2006) Terapia de família no Brasil: Uma visão panorâmica [Family therapy in Brazil: An overview]. *Psicologia Reflexão e Crítica, 19*(2), 252–260.

Próchino, C., Paradivini, J., & Gonçalves, M. (2008). Subjetivação e cura no Neopentecostalismo [Subjectivity and cure in the Neopentecostalism]. *Psicologia Ciência e Profissão, 28*(3), 586–601.

Rangé, B., & Guilhardi, H. (1995). História da psicoterapia comportamental e cognitiva no Brasil [History of cognitive and behavioral psychotherapy in Brazil]. In B. Rangé (ed.), *Psicoterapia comportamental e cognitiva. Pesquisa, prática, aplicações e problemas* (Vol 2) (pp. 55–69). Campinas: Editorial Psy.

Rangé, B. P., Falcone, E. M., & Sardinha, A. (2007). *História e panorama atual das terapias cognitivas no Brasil* [History and current situation of cognitive therapies in Brazil]. Retrieved from http://pepsic.bvsalud.org/scielo.php?pid=S1808–56872007000200006&script=sci_arttext

Rapaport, D. (1951). *Organization and Pathology of Thought*. New York: Columbia University Press.

Reed, G. M., & Eisman, E. (2006). Uses and misuses of evidence: Managed care, treatment guidelines, and outcomes measurement in professional practice. In D. Goodheart, A. E. Kazdin, & R. J. Sternberg (eds), *Evidence-based Psychotherapy: Where Practice and Research Meet* (pp. 13–25). Washington, DC: American Psychological Association.

Regional Council of Psychology of São Paulo (2008). *Sistematização do seminário nacional "2009: Ano da psicoterapia"* [Systematization of the national seminar "2009: Year of psychotherapy"]. Retrieved July 1st, 2011 from www.crpsp.org.br/psicoterapia/sistematizacao_1.aspx

Roudinesco, E. (2005). *O paciente, o terapeuta e o Estado* [The patient, the therapist and the State] (A. Telles, Trans.). Rio de Janeiro: Jorge Zahar ed.

Sagawa, R. Y. (2004). História da psicanálise no Brasil: Importação ou descoberta? [History of psychoanalysis in Brazil: Import or discovery?]. In M. Massimi (ed.), *História da psicologia no Brasil do século XX* (pp. 35–74). São Paulo: E.P.U.

Santeiro, T. V. (2008). Psicoterapia breve psicodinâmica preventiva: pesquisa exploratória de resultados e acompanhamento [Brief preventive psychodynamic psychotherapy: Exploratory research on results and follow-up]. *Psicologia em Estudo, 13*(4), 761–770.

Saraiva, L. A., & Nunes, M. L. T. (2007). A supervisão na formação do analista e do psicoterapeuta psicanalítico [The supervision in the training of psychoanalytical psychotherapist]. *Estudos de Psicologia (Natal), 12*, 259–268.

Scarparo, H. B. K., Moraes, M. L. A., Almeida, C. C. R., & Ballardim, G. (2010) Psicodrama Moreniano no Rio Grande do Sul: Memórias não encenadas [Moreno's psychodrama in Rio Grande do Sul state: Unenacted memories]. *Psicologia Argumento, 28*(62), 199–208.

Scheeffer, R. (1964). *Aconselhamento psicológico* [Psychological counseling]. Rio de Janeiro: Editora Fundo de Cultura.

Suassuna, D., & Holanda, A. (2009). *"Histórias" da Gestalt-terapia no Brasil: Um estudo historiográfico* ["Stories" of Gestalt therapy in Brazil: A historiographic study]. Curitiba: Juruá.

Tavares, R. S. G. (2003). Legitimidade terapêutica no Brasil contemporâneo: As terapias alternativas no âmbito do saber psicológico [Therapeutic legitimacy in contemporary Brazil: Alternative therapies in the context of psychological knowledge]. *Physis, 13*(2), 83–104.

Todorov, J. C. (1996). Good by teacher, good old friend. *Journal of the Experimental Analysis of Behavior, 66* (1), 7–9.

Tourinho, E. Z., & Carvalho, M. B. N. (1995). As fronteiras entre a Psicologia e as práticas alternativas: Algumas considerações [The boundaries between psychology and alternative practices: Some considerations]. In Conselho Federal de Psicologia (ed.), *Psicologia no Brasil: Direções epistemológicas* (pp. 81–110). Brasília: Conselho Federal de Psicologia.

Uchôa, D. M. (1981). *Organização da psiquiatria no Brasil* [Organization of psychiatry in Brazil]. São Paulo: Sarvier.

Wainer, R., & Piccoloto, N. M. (2007). Formação e supervisão em psicoterapia cognitivo-comportamental [Education and supervision in cognitive behavioral therapy]. *Revista Brasileira de Psicoterapia, 10*(2) 219–228.

Yamamoto, O. H. (2010). Pesquisa na psicologia: Reflexões sobre a formação. [Research in psychology: Reflections on the training]. In XIII Simpósio de Pesquisa e Intercâmbio Científico em Psicologia, Fortaleza, *Anais / Pesquisa em Psicologia: formação, produção e intervenção* (Vol. 1) (pp. 183–195). Fortaleza: Anpepp/Expressão Gráfica.

9

COUNSELING AND PSYCHOTHERAPY IN CANADA

Diversity and growth

José F. Domene and Robinder P. Bedi

Introduction

In Canada, there are countless advertisements for counseling services. However, besides offers for psychological counseling services are advertisements from nutrition counselors, spiritual counselors, holistic healing counselors, credit counselors, and travel counselors, among others. This conflation reflects the current Canadian situation where the word "counseling" is recognized by the general public, but is used in such different contexts that it has virtually lost its meaning. This confusing situation requires any substantive discussion of counseling and psychotherapy in Canada to clearly define its scope.

In this chapter, the terms "counseling" and "psychotherapy" refer to professional practices primarily concerned with mental health and applied human development. We also focus our discussion on professions that define counseling or psychotherapy as a core part of their regular scope of practice (e.g., guidance counselors, counseling therapists, marriage/family therapists, professional psychologists), rather than professions where counseling or psychotherapy is only part of the range of services that are typically provided by its practitioners (e.g., nurses, psychiatrists, social workers). These somewhat arbitrary boundaries are required because, in Canada, the term "counseling" is largely unregulated and the meaning of the term "psychotherapy" is contested, being defined differently by different stakeholders (Gazzola, Drapeau, Synard, Horvath, Page, & Toukmanian, 2009). We distinguish between counseling and psychotherapy only when it is important to do so; the terms will be used interchangeably in the contexts where it is not meaningful to distinguish between them.

Counseling and psychotherapy in Canada have also been shaped by linguistic and sociopolitical history. Census data reveal that 57% of the population is unilingual Anglophone and 22% are unilingual Francophone, with the remaining being multilingual or reporting a mother tongue other than English or French (Statistics Canada, 2006). The Canadian population is also characterized by substantial cultural diversity, housing one of the largest per capita immigration rates in the world, and with a large proportion of its immigrants currently from developing areas of the world (Becklumb, 2008). Another contributor to Canada's diversity is its indigenous population, that is, individuals who are of Inuit, Métis, or First Nations/North American Indian background[1] and represent approximately 4% of the population. Politically, Canada has a federal governance structure where provinces and territories retain substantial legislative control over areas such as health and social services, labor and employment, and education (Forsey, 2005). Canada also has a publicly funded healthcare system, although counseling and psychotherapy are generally not covered by provincial healthcare plans.

Brief history of counseling and psychotherapy

In the first half of the 20th century, the development of counseling and psychotherapy paralleled that of the United States, being rooted in Frank Parsons' efforts in vocational guidance, the mental hygiene movement and, later, the counseling process work of Carl Rogers. The discipline in Canada began to gain momentum in the 1950s and 1960s, with the introduction of formal training programs in school counseling at Canadian universities (Young, 2009) and the incorporation of national associations for counselors (Canadian Counselling and Psychotherapy Association [CCPA], 2011) and psychologists (Canadian Psychological Association [CPA], 2011). Since that time, the field has grown and diversified with a proliferation of associations focused on particular practice areas and/or geographic regions (e.g., Canadian Association for Child and Play Therapy; l'association francophone des conseillères et des conseillers en orientation du Nouveau-Brunswick), a growing number of specialized journals with national and international mandates (e.g., *Transcultural Psychiatry*; *Canadian Journal of Career Development*), and numerous counseling and psychotherapy-related training programs at both master's and doctoral levels.

Despite differences in regulation and a lack of awareness of disciplinary advances in the other language on the part of both Anglophone and Francophone practitioners (Young & Nicol, 2007), the development of counseling and psychotherapy has followed the same broad pathway in English and French Canada. Fifty years ago, the practice of counselors was primarily associated with education and guidance while the practice of psychotherapists was more closely associated with the treatment of clients with psychological and psychiatric conditions. However, this division no longer reflects the reality of practice in Canada: numerous professions that span both counseling and psychotherapy have emerged, and the scope of practice of many professions has expanded to the point that the distinction is no longer valid.

Counselor education programs, accreditation, licensure, and certification

Most psychotherapy-related doctoral level programs are in clinical psychology, although doctoral programs in counseling psychology, educational counseling, and sciences de l'orientation (guidance sciences) also exist. The situation is more varied at master's level, with the CCPA (2011) listing over 50 counseling-related master's degree programs on their website. These programs have various names, including clinical psychology, counseling psychology, educational counseling, guidance, and marriage/family therapy. Various short-term (6 months to 1 year) training programs that provide diplomas or certificates in counseling can also be found in Canada. These programs have few prerequisites in terms of prior knowledge or a bachelor's degree. Regulatory bodies and many professional associations (e.g., CPA, CCPA) do not recognize graduates of these non-degree programs. However, the general public is typically unaware of the discrepancies in training between graduates of these certificate programs and practitioners with advanced degrees.

Government and regulatory bodies do not require counseling or psychotherapy education programs to follow a specific curriculum. However, the major national professional associations for psychology (the CPA) and counseling (the CCPA) have developed accreditation standards and processes for education programs. Accreditation is voluntary, and many programs, especially master's level programs, remain unaccredited.

In Canada, professional regulation is defined as a provincial responsibility. Thus, licensure for counseling and psychotherapy differs not only according to practitioners' specific professions, but also their provinces of residence. The provincial government of Quebec has created legislation and separate professional organizations to regulate the practice of (a) guidance counseling and psychoeducation; (b) psychotherapy and psychology; and (c) social work and marriage/family therapy. These regulatory bodies issue licenses contingent on applicants meeting specific education standards and demonstrating French language competency. In English Canada, the situation is more varied. In most jurisdictions, psychotherapy is recognized as being within the scope of practice of psychologists, although not limited to that profession. Professional psychology is regulated in virtually all provinces and territories (Bedi, Haverkamp, Beatch, Cave, Domene, Harris & Mikhail, 2011), but licensure requirements vary across jurisdictions. Additionally, some provinces set the minimum educational standard at the master's level, while others require a doctoral degree to register as a psychologist. Licensure and regulation of other counseling practitioners in English Canada has only begun to occur, with two provinces creating regulatory bodies for the profession of counseling and psychotherapy within the past decade: the Ontario College of Psychotherapists and Registered Mental Health Therapists (Legislative Assembly of Ontario, 2007), and the Nova Scotia College of Counseling Therapists (Legislative Assembly of Nova Scotia, 2008). Efforts to pursue regulation are also actively underway in British Columbia, Prince Edward Island, and New Brunswick.

In terms of certification processes, many national and regional professional associations for counseling or psychotherapy in Canada exist independently from legal regulatory bodies. At the national level, the principal professional associations are the CPA and the CCPA. There are also a multitude of provincial associations for practitioners of a particular specialty within counseling and psychotherapy. These associations promote practice and research within their specialization and advocate for their members. Some associations, such as the CCPA, also maintain quality control over the practice of their members through certification processes involving minimal educational and supervised practice standards, and the requirement to engage in continuing education activities. However, certification is voluntary, and these associations have no legal authority to define or restrict practice.

Current counseling and psychotherapy theories, processes, and trends

The counseling and psychotherapy theories that are commonly employed in Canada have been substantially influenced by literature from the United States and Europe. In fact, Hiebert and Uhlemann (1993) claimed "it would seem that [counselors and psychotherapists] have been willing to accept American perspectives and positions as being appropriate for Canadians (p. 286)." At the same time, the work of Canadian scholars such as Lynne Angus in narrative psychotherapy (e.g., Angus & Hardtke, 1994), Les Greenberg in emotion-focused therapy (e.g., Greenberg, 2004), Karl Tomm in marriage/family therapy and supervision (e.g., Collins & Tomm, 2009) and Richard Young in action theory applied to counseling (e.g., Young, Marshall, Valach, Domene, Graham, & Zaidman-Zait, 2011) have contributed substantially to the advancement of theory and practice all over the world. Similarly, numerous practice-oriented organizations with an international mandate are located in Canada and led by Canadians, such as Roy Moodley and colleagues' Centre for Diversity in Counseling and Psychotherapy (2011), and Paul Wong and colleagues' International Network on Personal Meaning (2011).

Established European–North American theoretical orientations (e.g., cognitive-behavioral, humanistic/existential, psychodynamic) are frequently practiced in English and French Canada, along with newer European–North American models (e.g., narrative, solution-focused, feminist). There are estimates that up to 75% of Canadian practitioners use an integrative or eclectic model (Gazzola & Smith, 2007; Hadjipavlou & Ogrodniczuk, 2007; Hunsley & Lefebvre, 1990). Practitioners tend to rely on a small handful of theories to primarily guide their work, and then incorporate aspects of various others at either the level of theory or the level of techniques and interventions to meet client needs or practical constraints. These estimates also suggest that CCPA-affiliated practitioners primarily draw from client-centered/humanistic, cognitive-behavioral, or postmodern theoretical approaches, and least from psychodynamic approaches, while those trained in clinical psychology or psychiatry seem to draw most from cognitive-behavioral, systemic and psychodynamic approaches, and least from existential, gestalt, and humanistic ones.

One of the largest trends for counseling and psychotherapy in Canada is the movement into private practice, although this is often combined with work in other settings (Hiebert & Uhlemann, 1993; Gazzola & Smith, 2007). These other settings include college/university student services, community agencies, mental health settings, schools, medical/rehabilitation settings, the private sector, and government (Bedi et al., 2011; Gazzola & Smith, 2007; Smith & Drodge, 2001). The movement towards private practice places these practitioners at the mercy of economic market conditions and larger sociopolitical trends, some of which run antithetical to their training.

Despite efforts to define the discipline as encompassing a full range of practice (Bedi et al., 2011), most contemporary counseling and psychotherapy in Canada is provided for remedial therapeutic purposes (e.g., treating psychological disorders), rather than for preventative (e.g., working with high risk youth) or educative/development efforts (e.g., improving conflict resolutions skills of the general population) (Hiebert & Uhlemann, 1993; Young & Nicol, 2007). There is also structural pressure for practitioners to focus on remediation generated by circumstances such as higher proportion of third party funding and referrals for treating psychological and psychiatric disorders, cuts in government funding for preventative and developmental services, popular acceptance of the medical model of mental health, and the high costs of self-payment for services outside of severely limited government-funded services. Consequently, practitioners in Canada, even those working in educational settings, require a working knowledge of psychiatric diagnoses. Hiebert and Uhlemann note that this movement away from prevention, education, and development is especially apparent amongst younger practitioners. Despite this situation, there is a notable minority of practitioners who strongly oppose the trend towards the psychopathologizing, diagnose-and-treat model of service provision (Bedi et al., 2011).

Two additional trends are currently occurring in English Canada. First, the practice of psychotherapy and associated professional titles (e.g., mental health therapist, counseling therapist, psychotherapist) are increasingly being regulated, while the activity of counseling continues to remain unrestricted. Thus, a legislative distinction is being drawn between the regulated activity of psychotherapy and the largely unregulated activity of professional counseling. Second, the same legislation that regulates psychotherapy acknowledges that it can be practiced by a diverse range of professionals (e.g., psychiatric nurses, counseling psychologists). This second trend reflects the increasing overlap in scopes of practice and employment settings of mental health professions. For example, individuals with master's degrees in educational counseling can obtain employment in a medical setting and be deemed to be providing psychotherapy, while clinical psychologists with specialized training in psychotherapy provide counseling services in university counseling centers. Furthermore, an examination of the field concluded that the workplace activities of counseling and clinical psychologists are largely indistinguishable in Canada (Linden, Moseley, & Erskine, 2005). Therefore, rather than labeling oneself as a counselor or psychotherapist on the basis of training, such a proclamation depends more on one's work setting and clientele. Overall, although the terms "counseling" and "psychotherapy" are becoming differentiated in law, the actual practices are increasingly overlapping. Reflecting this situation, in 2009, the Canadian Counseling Association changed its name to the Canadian Counseling *and Psychotherapy* Association.

Despite this blurring of practice boundaries, there remains a hierarchy of status and prestige among different practitioners who provide counseling or psychotherapy in Canada, in terms of public perception and professional deference (Gazzola & Smith, 2007; Smith & Drodge, 2001). Psychiatrists and other medical doctors are granted the highest status, followed by clinical psychologists and then practitioners commonly employed in medical or forensic settings (e.g., psychiatric nurses, clinical social workers, counseling psychologists). The third tier appears to consist of master's level practitioners employed in other settings (e.g., schools, private practice). Finally, practitioners with less than a master's degree (e.g., graduates of certificate or diploma programs in counseling) have the least status and usually receive substantially less remuneration and professional recognition.

Indigenous and traditional healing methods

Canada's high rate of immigration and government policies that promote cultural diversity facilitate the retention of many traditional practices by cultural and ethnic minority groups, including traditional approaches to health and wellness. Therefore, many traditional healing practices from other countries (see other chapters for details) may be found in communities comprising people in Canada who are from the same cultural background. Research on these practices in the Canadian context is beginning to emerge (Centre for Diversity in Counseling and Psychotherapy, 2011). However, these traditional healing methods are predominantly confined to members of specific cultural groups, rather than being widely adopted by counseling and psychotherapy practitioners. The exception is that some Asian healing practices are beginning to be incorporated into mainstream practice. For example, some Canadian hospitals have begun to include yoga as a treatment strategy (R. Wu, personal communication, July 18, 2011). Also, paralleling the movement internationally, mindfulness meditation techniques are increasingly being incorporated into psychotherapy practice in Canada. For example, mindfulness was specifically mentioned in the 2010 Canadian Psychological Association's presidential address on advances in the treatment of anxiety disorders and, as early as 1988, the *Canadian Journal of Counseling and Psychotherapy* has been publishing research about the effectiveness of this traditional healing practice (Greene & Hiebert, 1988).

In the past 20 years, there has also been increasing interest in adapting indigenous healing methods for counseling and psychotherapy practice, particularly with Aboriginal Canadian clients. This interest has generated far more articles in the *Canadian Journal of Counseling and Psychotherapy* about Aboriginal Canadians than any other ethnic minority group, including a special issue, published in 2000, devoted entirely to Aboriginal counseling. These publications discuss how to effectively work with these clients and describe indigenous healing methods that can be incorporated into conventional counseling and psychotherapy practice. Specific examples of these methods include healing circles, sweat lodge ceremonies, the medicine wheel, therapeutic use of Aboriginal culture (e.g., traditional dancing, storytelling, use of the eagle's feather or talking stick, drumming, potlatches), and seeking a stronger connection with nature and one's tribal community (Heilbron & Guttman, 2000; Malone, 2000; McCormick, 1997; Neumann, McCormick, Amundson, & McLean, 2000; Poonwasshie & Charter, 2001). Although limited, the existing empirical research on the integration of traditional aboriginal healing methods into counseling practice by both Aboriginal and non-Aboriginal practitioners has yielded positive results (e.g., Neumann et al., 2000; Oulanova & Moodley, 2010; Thomas & Bellefeuille, 2006). It must be noted, however, that virtually all the literature on the use of these traditional healing methods has been written in the context of working with Aboriginal clients. It is not yet clear whether these methods can also be successfully incorporated into counseling with clients from other cultural backgrounds.

Many Aboriginal communities also promote the notion of culture as treatment; that is, connecting with Aboriginal communities and traditional beliefs as part of the healing process (McCormick, 1997). Some of these beliefs include the necessity of a collectivistic life orientation; the inseparable interconnection between the family, community, nature, and spiritual world; prioritizing the wellbeing of the community as much as the wellbeing of the individual; and the importance of holistic wellness and balance between the physical, mental, emotional, and spiritual dimensions of the person (Heilbron & Guttman, 2000; McCormick, 1997). Other important concepts include encouraging the inclusion of family members and other important community members (e.g., elders) as influential collaborators in healing activities, and for practitioners to become actively involved with a client's Aboriginal community despite the multiple relationships that may develop (McCormick, 1998).

Research and supervision

Canadian scholars have a long history of researching every aspect of counseling and psychotherapy, including career and guidance (e.g., Baudouin et al., 2007), marriage/family therapy (e.g., Beaton, Dienhart, Schmidt, & Turner, 2009), theories and processes of psychotherapy (e.g., Angus & Hardtke, 1994), counselor supervision (e.g., Gazzola & Theriault, 2007), and a wide range of research methodologies (e.g., Bedi & Alexander, 2009). Canadian research is particularly characterized by openness to diversity, not only in terms of areas of inquiry and methodology, but also populations studied (e.g., Juraskovic & Arthur, 2009; Sandhu, 2005; Wong & Piran, 1995). Moreover, Canadians have made substantial contributions to the literature on counseling and psychotherapy research methods, particularly approaches to program evaluation and qualitative inquiry (Bedi et al., 2011; Hiebert, Domene, & Buchanan, in press).

Counseling and psychotherapy research in Canada is supported by the existence of several publication venues, most of which publish in both French and English. These include the *Canadian Journal of Behavioural Science*, *Canadian Journal of Career Development*, *Canadian Journal of Community Mental Health*, *Canadian Journal of Counselling and Psychotherapy*, *Canadian Journal of Psychiatry*, *Canadian Journal of Psychoanalysis*, and *Canadian Psychology*. Canadian researchers also publish extensively in journals from other nations. Research is also supported by funding from federal and provincial governments, non-government organizations, and the private sector. The federal government is the major source of research grants, providing funding through agencies such as the *Social Sciences and Humanities Research Council* and the *Canadian Institutes of Health Research*. These agencies fund research on a competitive basis, with applications being peer reviewed. Unfortunately, as Hiebert and colleagues (in press) explain, the official policies and unwritten practices of these agencies sometimes work against counseling-related scholars in Canada, particularly those whose focus is at the intersection of normative human development and health, and those who use qualitative methods in psychotherapy research.

Practicing under supervision is a core component of virtually every graduate-level professional psychology and counselor education program in Canada. Programs typically require completion of hundreds of hours of client contact in actual practice settings as part of their degree requirements. What varies more widely is the type of setting in which a student will complete their internship/practicum. For example, Smith and Drodge's (2001) survey of master's students from their counseling program reported internships in community agencies, schools, college/university counseling centers, the civil service, medical and rehabilitation settings, and private practice. Education programs accredited by the CCPA and CPA must ensure that the number of client contact hours, the types of practice experiences, and the quantity and quality of supervision that is provided conforms to the standards laid out by their accrediting association (CCPA, 2011; CPA, 2011). The CPA also accredits internship sites, which must provide adequate quality and quantity of supervision.

Despite the demand for supervisors in the field, few formal training opportunities in the supervision of counseling and psychotherapy are offered in counseling and psychotherapy education programs. Instead, supervisors usually receive "on-the-job" training, operate under the assumption that a competent practitioner will inherently know how to supervise other practitioners, or seek post-graduation continuing education opportunities. Fortunately, opportunities for supervision-related continuing education are readily available. For example, for the past five years, the *Canadian Journal of Counselling and Psychotherapy* has published at least two articles per year on counselor education and supervision, including supervision in diverse contexts.

Strengths, weaknesses, opportunities, challenges

Counseling and psychotherapy are strong and growing areas of professional practice in Canada, with reputable and well-established programs of training and research. Practitioners belong to robust professional groups, numbering well over 40,000 (CCPA, 2011). There is steadily growing membership in their primary national professional associations, the CCPA and CPA. Additionally, some surveys of counselors reveal high levels of job satisfaction and the sense that they would make the same career decision again, despite recurring complaints about low salaries (Gazzola & Smith, 2007; Smith & Drodge, 2001).

Further, practitioners, educators, and researchers have sought to ensure that counseling and psychotherapy remain relevant in the increasingly diverse cultural context of Canada. This has included tailoring practice to meet the needs of specific ethnic and religious minority groups, including clients with Aboriginal (Malone, 2000), Chinese (Wong & Piran, 1995), South Asian (Shariff, 2009), Buddhist (Cohen & Bai 2008) Christian (Olthuis, 1994), and Sikh (Sandhu, 2005) backgrounds. There is also strong Canadian scholarship on topics such as acculturation, immigration, racism, and cross-cultural counseling (e.g., Arthur & Januszkowski, 2001; Beharry & Crozier, 2008).

Despite these strengths, several circumstances hinder the progress of counseling and psychotherapy in Canada. One weakness is that there is no regulatory protection of the term "counseling." Although some counselors are well trained and belong to established professional associations, others are paraprofessionals with little formal training, and no professional affiliation. This creates confusion about the nature of counseling and lowers the professional status of counselors (Bedi et al., 2011; Smith & Drodge, 2001; Young & Nicol, 2007). In contrast, laws protecting the act of psychotherapy and the title of psychotherapist (or associated titles such as "mental health therapist" and "counselor therapist") have begun to emerge in several Canadian provinces (Gazzola et al., 2009). It is probable to the practice of counseling, it is probable that psychotherapy will become regulated and restricted in many Canadian jurisdictions within the next decade. The current inconsistent regulatory environment and the growing legislative divide between counseling and psychotherapy also impede the mobility of some mental and applied human development professionals who wish to relocate to a new province.

Another weakness arises from the fact that Canada has two official languages, but a majority of the population is unilingual. This linguistic divide impedes research collaboration and awareness of practice advances across the two languages. For example, there is relatively little citation of French language research in English language publications. Bilingual journals mitigate this problem to some degree. However, most journals only publish abstracts in both languages; the text of articles still tends to be available in only one language.

Finally, the geography of Canada imposes another difficulty for counseling and psychotherapy: there is a lack of access to services for many residents of rural and northern areas of Canada. Individuals residing in rural communities must often rely on practitioners who travel to remote areas for brief periods of time to provide very time-limited services or simply do without professional assistance. Additionally, many practitioners remain unaware of key practice and ethical issues in providing services in rural areas (Schank, 1998).

Currently, one of the major opportunities for Canadian counseling and psychotherapy practitioners is the growing potential for interprofessional collaboration and interdisciplinary training. Because many professions perceive counseling or psychotherapy to be within their scope of practice, practitioners of one profession are able to use scholarly literature from many other professions to inform their work. A psychotherapist may draw upon literature from counseling psychology, clinical psychology, counselor education, educational psychology, industrial-organization psychology, psychiatric nursing, clinical social work, child and youth care, marriage and family therapy, and psychiatry. Although the potential for interdisciplinary engagement exists, it is currently more prevalent amongst researchers and educators, than practitioners. One exception is a recent move towards interprofessional collaboration in Ontario, motivated by the desire to influence the process of regulating psychotherapy (Gazzola et al. 2009). Nevertheless, there remains substantial untapped potential to improve service provision through increased interdisciplinary training and sharing of advancements from allied professions.

Through immigration patterns and government policies that are designed to maintain Canada as a "cultural mosaic," the cultural diversity of Canadian society will continue to expand at a rapid pace. This provides counselors and psychotherapists with ample opportunities to work with clients of ethnically diverse backgrounds. Similarly, Canadian scholars and practitioners have an extraordinary opportunity to advance evidence-based, cross-cultural and multicultural competencies that promote the acculturation, mental health, life adjustment, and career development of immigrants and refugees

The Canadian population is aging, with a greater proportion of individuals approaching retirement age. This provides increased opportunity to demonstrate the effectiveness of counseling and psychotherapy for successfully navigating key life transitions such as retirement and end of life. In addition, practitioners will have more opportunities to assist in treating and managing a variety of health conditions, especially those associated with age-related and degenerative diseases and disabilities, as well as promoting the wellbeing for those with terminal illnesses. Research clearly demonstrates the important role of counseling and psychotherapy in promoting positive physical health outcomes, including recovery from surgery and limiting disease progression (Lalande, 2004; Rejeski, Brawley, Ambrosius, Brubaker, Focht, Foy, & Fox 2003). Therefore, there are opportunities for practitioners to engage in health promotion, physical wellness, and disease recovery, particularly for older Canadians (Arnett, 2001; Young & Nicol, 2007).

There are two fundamental challenges and threats to the professional activities of counseling and psychotherapy that may systemically restrict the access to these services for Canadians. First, despite a shared expertise, individuals who practice counseling or psychotherapy tend to be a highly diverse group in terms of educational background and professional preparation. This contributes to considerable tension among the different stakeholder groups, including the question of who is qualified to provide various services. Overlapping scopes of practice contribute to competition and territorial disputes that threaten to limit who can provide or bill for such services (Hiebert & Uhlemann, 1993; Young & Nicol, 2007). For example, in Ontario, psychotherapy can only be billed to the provincial healthcare plan when it is practiced by physicians and psychiatrists; other psychotherapists must rely on clients' private insurance plans or direct payment. Similarly, in 2009, the province of Quebec passed legislation requiring practitioners other than physicians and psychologists to meet specific training criteria and obtain a permit from the Quebec Order of Psychologists to practice psychotherapy. This territoriality restricts widespread access to counseling or psychotherapy services.

Although Canada has a publicly funded medical system, counseling and psychotherapy are, for the most part, not covered by provincial healthcare plans. Therefore, another challenge is that outside of limited services provided through hospitals, correction facilities, and educational institutions, Canadians must directly fund counseling and psychotherapy, often through supplemental insurance and employee assistance programs. Consequently, many individuals are unable to afford to pay for needed counseling and psychotherapy. This situation has been exacerbated by government policies in most provinces that, over the past 10 years, have increasingly restricted publicly funded counseling and psychotherapy services. Many practitioners address this issue by billing on a sliding scale, but this merely shifts the burden of lack of public funding to counselors and psychotherapists themselves, rather than truly addressing the challenge of access.

Future directions

Building upon their strengths, counselors and psychotherapists should continue to respond to the increasingly diverse nature of Canadian society and ensure that the rights and perspectives of members of disadvantaged groups are respected in the provision of mental health services. Practitioners also have an opportunity to establish counseling and psychotherapy as bona fide primary and adjunct treatments for many physical diseases and illnesses. Also, the field should continue to work towards legislation to regulate and protect the practices of counseling and psychotherapy across Canada, and to permit increased professional mobility across provinces and territories. Another key future direction is to resolve ongoing interprofessional conflicts in order to improve mutually respectful cooperation and collaboration to best serve the mental health needs of Canadians. Finally, addressing the issue of access, it will be important to advocate for the inclusion of counseling and psychotherapy services in Canada's public healthcare coverage and the expansion of services in rural and northern regions.

Conclusion

In conclusion, there is currently such diversity in terms of practitioners' training, licensure/certification, professional affiliations, and work settings that it makes little sense to refer to a single discipline of counseling and psychotherapy in Canada. Instead, many different mental health and human development practitioners engage in counseling and/or psychotherapy as part of their practice. Nevertheless, counseling and psychotherapy have a long history in Canada, and Canadian practitioners and scholars will continue to make substantial contributions to the advancement of the field around the world. Although practice has been shaped by the geographic, cultural, linguistic, and political context of the country, there is great potential for individuals in the counseling and psychotherapy professions to take an active role in shaping the future.

Note

1 In this chapter, these distinct groups will collectively be referred to as Aboriginal peoples.

References

Angus, L., & Hardtke, K. (1994). Narrative processes in psychotherapy. *Canadian Psychology, 35,* 190–203.

Arnett, J. L. (2001). Clinical and health psychology: Future directions. *Canadian Psychology, 42,* 38–48.

Arthur, N. & Januszkowski, T. (2001). The multicultural counselling competencies of Canadian counsellors. *Canadian Journal of Counselling, 35,* 36–48.

Baudouin, R., Bezanson, L., Borgen, B., Goyer, L., Hiebert, B., Lalande, V. & … Turcotte, M. (2007). Demonstrating value: A draft framework for evaluating the effectiveness of career development interventions. *Canadian Journal of Counselling, 41,* 146–157.

Beaton, J., Dienhart, A., Schmidt, J., & Turner, J. (2009). Clinical practice patterns of Canadian couple/marital/family therapists. *Journal of Marital & Family Therapy, 35,* 193–203.

Becklumb, P. (2008). *Canada's immigration program.* Ottawa, Ontario, Canada: Parliamentary Information and Research Service.

Bedi, R. P. & Alexander, D. (2009). Using multivariate concept-mapping for examining client understandings of counselling. *Canadian Journal of Counselling, 43,* 76–91

Bedi, R. P., Haverkamp, B. E., Beatch, R., Cave, D., Domene, J. F., Harris, G. E., & Mikhail, A. (2011). Counselling psychology in a Canadian context: Definition and description. *Canadian Psychology, 52,* 128–138.

Beharry, P. & Crozier, S. (2008). Using phenomenology to understand experiences of racism for second-generation South Asian women. *Canadian Journal of Counselling, 42,* 262–277.

Canadian Counselling and Psychotherapy Association (CCPA) (2011). *CCPA Website.* Retrieved from www.cpa.ca/en/

Canadian Psychological Association (CPA) (2011). *CPA website.* Retrieved from www.cpa.ca/aboutcpa/

Centre for Diversity in Counseling and Psychotherapy (2011). *The role of traditional healers in health promotion, counselling, and education.* Retrieved from: http://cdcp.oise.utoronto.ca/traditionalhealers.html

Collins, D., & Tomm, K. (2009). Karl Tomm: His changing views on family therapy over 35 years. *The Family Journal, 17*(2), 106–117.

Cohen, A. & Bai, H. (2008). Suffering loves and needs company: Buddhist and Daoist perspectives on the counsellor as companion. *Canadian Journal of Counselling, 42,* 45–56.

Forsey, E. A. (2005). *How Canadians govern themselves* (6th edn). Ottawa, Ontario, Canada: Library of Parliament.

Gazzola, N., Drapeau, M., Synard, J., Horvath, A., Page, L., & Toukmanian, S. (2009). *The Psychotherapeutic Professions in Canada.* Paper presented at the annual meeting of the Society for Psychotherapy Research, Barcelona, Spain.

Gazzola, N. & Smith, J. D. (2007). Who do we think we are: A survey of counsellors in Canada. *International Journal for the Advancement of Counselling, 29,* 97–110.

Gazzola, N. & Theriault, A. (2007). Relational themes in counselling supervision: Broadening and narrowing processes. *Canadian Journal of Counselling, 41,* 228–243.

Greenberg, L. S. (2004). Emotion-focused therapy. *Clinical Psychology & Psychotherapy, 11*(1), 3–16.

Greene, Y. N., & Hiebert, B. (1988). A comparison of mindfulness meditation and cognitive self-observation. *Canadian Journal of Counselling, 22,* 25–34.

Hadjipavlou, G. & Ogrodniczuk, J. S. (2007). A national survey of Canadian psychiatry residents' perceptions of psychotherapy training. *Canadian Journal of Psychiatry, 52,* 710–711.

Heilbron, C. L., & Guttman, M. A. (2000). Traditional healing methods with First Nations women in group counselling, *Canadian Journal of Counselling, 34,* 3–13.

Hiebert, B., Domene, J. F., & Buchanan, M. J. (2012). The power of multiple methods and evidence sources: Raising the profile of Canadian counselling psychology research. *Canadian Psychology, 52,* 265–275.

Hiebert, B., & Uhlemann, M. R. (1993). Counselling psychology: Development, identity, and issues. In K. S. Dobson & D. J. G. Dobson (eds), *Professional Psychology in Canada* (pp. 285–312). Cambridge, MA: Hogrefe & Huber.

Hunsley, J., & Lefebvre, M. (1990). A survey of the practices and activities of Canadian clinical psychologists. *Canadian Psychology, 31,* 350–358.

International Network on Personal Meaning (2011). *INPM Website.* Retrieved from www.meaning.ca/

Juraskovic, I., & Arthur, N. (2009). The acculturation of former Yugoslavian refugees. *Canadian Journal of Counselling, 43,* 18–34.

Lalande, V. (2004). Counselling psychology: A Canadian perspective. *Counselling Psychology Quarterly, 17,* 273–286.

Legislative Assembly of Nova Scotia (2008). *Bill 201: Counselling Therapists Act.* Halifax, Nova Scotia, Canada: Author.

Legislative Assembly of Ontario (2007). *Bill 171: Health System Improvements Act.* Toronto, Ontario, Canada: Author.

Linden, W., Moseley, J., & Erskine, Y. (2005). Psychology as a health-care profession: Implications for training. *Canadian Psychology, 46,* 179–188.

Malone, J. L. (2000). Working with Aboriginal women: Applying feminist therapy in a multicultural counselling context. *Canadian Journal of Counselling, 34,* 33–42.

McCormick, R. M. (1997). Healing through interdependence: The role of connecting in First Nations healing practices. *Canadian Journal of Counselling, 31,* 172–184.

McCormick, R. M. (1998). Ethical considerations in First Nations counselling and research. *Canadian Journal of Counselling, 32,* 284–297.

Neumann, H., McCormick, R. M., Amundson, N. E., & McLean, H. B. (2000). Career counselling First Nations youth: Applying the First Nations career-life planning model. *Canadian Journal of Counselling, 34,* 172–185.

Olthuis, J. H. (1994). God-with-us: Toward a relational psychotherapeutic model. *Journal of Psychology and Christianity, 13,* 37–49.

Oulanova, O., & Moodley, R. (2010). Navigating two worlds: Experiences of counsellors who integrate Aboriginal traditional healing practices. *Canadian Journal of Counselling and Psychotherapy, 44,* 346–362.

Poonwasshie, A., & Charter, A. (2001). An Aboriginal worldview of helping: Empowering approaches. *Canadian Journal of Counselling, 35,* 63–73.

Rejeski, W. J., Brawley, L. R., Ambrosius, W. T., Brubaker, P. H., Focht, B. C. Foy, C. G., & Fox, L. D. (2003). Older adults with chronic disease: Benefits of group-mediated counselling in the promotion of physically active lifestyles. *Health Psychology, 22,* 414–423.

Sandhu, J. S. (2005). A Sikh perspective on life-stress: Implications for counselling. *Canadian Journal of Counselling, 39,* 40–51.

Schank, J. A. (1998). Ethical issues in rural counselling practice. *Canadian Journal of Counselling, 32,* 270–283.

Shariff, A. (2009). Ethnic identity and parenting stress in South Asian families: Implications for culturally sensitive counselling. *Canadian Journal of Counselling, 43,* 35–46.

Smith, J. D., & Drodge, E. N. (2001). A portrait of counselling: Counsellors' work roles and career satisfaction. *Canadian Journal of Counselling, 35,* 237–249.

Statistics Canada (2006). 2006 Census. Retrieved December 15, 2009 from www12.statcan.gc.ca/census-recensement/index-eng.cfm.

Thomas, W., & Bellefeuille, G. (2006). An evidence-based formative evaluation of a cross cultural Aboriginal mental health program in Canada. *Australian-Journal for the Advancement of Mental Health, 5*(3), 1–14.

Wong, O. C., & Piran, N. (1995). Western biases and assumptions as impediments in counselling traditional Chinese clients. *Canadian Journal of Counselling, 29,* 107–119.

Young, R. (2009). Counseling in the Canadian mosaic: A cultural perspective. In L. H. Gerstein, P. P. Heppner, K. L. Norsworthy, S. Aegisdottir, & S. A. Leung (eds), *International Handbook of Cross-cultural Counseling: Cultural Assumptions and Practices Worldwide* (pp. 359–367). Thousand Oaks, CA: Sage.

Young, R. A., Marshall, S. K., Valach, L., Domene, J. F., Graham, M. D., & Zaidman-Zait, A. (2011). *Transition to Adulthood: Action, Projects, and Counseling.* New York: Springer Science + Business Media.

Young, R. A., & Nicol, J. J. (2007). Counseling psychology in Canada: Advancing psychology for all. *Applied Psychology: An International Journal, 56,* 20–32.

10

COUNSELING AND PSYCHOTHERAPY IN THE (ENGLISH-SPEAKING) CARIBBEAN

Fidelity, fit or a cause for concern?

Gerard Hutchinson and Patsy Sutherland

Introduction

The English-speaking Caribbean (from hereon referred to as ESC) is best understood through its history. The indigenous people were mostly exterminated by the marauding European settlers and populated by transplanted people. Its current inhabitants are descendants of these transplanted Africans, Indians, Chinese, and Europeans, with the Africans in the majority on the islands. The history is a colonial and postcolonial one with the prefix English-speaking reflecting the period of British colonial rule as compared to the Spanish (e.g., Cuba, which was mostly colonized by Spain), French (e.g., Guadeloupe), and Dutch (e.g., Curacao) speaking islands. The population of the ESC, which politically also includes the South American country Guyana, is approximately 5 million (Hillman, 2009), and this number is significantly less than the number of Caribbean-descended people in the diaspora residing in the metropolitan countries, particularly the United States of America, Britain, and the rest of Europe (Conway, 2009).

A defining characteristic of this postcolonial history is a sense of, "What's wrong with me?" A psychologist working in Jamaica has described it as a chronic sense of inadequacy and low self-esteem (Doorbar, 2008). V. S. Naipaul (2001) laments the lack of self-created history and this may be the central problem of the inhabitants of the Caribbean—how to assert oneself in the context of a globalized world that no longer acknowledges these island colonies as places of value? Given that every Caribbean institution is an inheritance of its colonial past, it is becoming necessary to rebuild and/or reshape these institutions with models that are more culturally sensitive to our history and geography. This is so because there is a persistent distrust about these institutions and who they best serve. It is felt that they are almost inevitably elitist in their orientation and designed to serve the interests of the privileged, rich, and powerful, which therefore are seen as not representing the interests of the masses (Henry & Buhle, 1992). The sense of privilege is also still perceived to be equivalent to skin color and hair texture. In 2008, dancehall singer Queen Ifrica (2008) was admonishing Jamaicans to 'nah bleach' as they sought to seek the advantages of lighter pigmentation through chemical means, another illustration of the longstanding, damning, and traumatic effects of the colonial process.

These issues inform any consideration of counseling and other psychological treatment in the Caribbean. For example, a central question that needs to be established is what issues need treatment? While issues related to trauma, violence, underachievement, and substance abuse seem to predominate in the social sphere, individual complaints of anxiety and depressive feelings may just be a response to these wider social pressures. Some theorists have questioned whether these issues relate specifically to defects in personality and mental state or are simply consequences of our history (Hickling, Martin, & Harrisingh-Dewar, 2008). Furthermore, there is a sense that the societies in the Caribbean are unraveling because of high crime rates, falling academic and professional standards, and an inability to construct paradigms that resonate with wide sections of the population that would encourage them to develop their mental and cognitive structures in a positive way. Therefore, the emergence of a Caribbean-oriented psychology as a means to address these issues is long overdue.

This chapter explores the history, practice, and challenges to psychological treatment in the ESC. We first review the history of counseling and psychotherapy, provide a brief overview of current practices, and explore the educational system relative to the profession of psychology. This is followed by a discussion of how psychological distress is conceptualized and treated in the ESC, and lastly we explore the challenges for the future development of counseling and psychotherapy services for this population.

Brief history of counseling and psychotherapy

There is little perceived difference between counseling and psychotherapy in the ESC. For much of the 20th century, formal psychotherapy in the Caribbean was non-existent, so the discussion to distinguish between the two has not occurred (Ward & Hickling, 2004). Psychology as a profession only came into prominence in the last 25 years; in fact, an account by a Jamaican psychologist returning home to work in 1974 explained that the medical doctor in charge of the hospital did not know what her skill set included and loosely associated it with a kind of counseling (Doorbar, 2008). In Trinidad and Tobago, psychological services were initially provided in the early 1970s by one returning psychologist who had been trained in Britain. For close to 10 years, she was the only psychologist employed in the public health system providing service to over 1000 patients. This remained the case until three others returned from national scholarships in the early 1980s (J. Hinkson, personal communication, March 30, 2009).

Mental health treatment in the ESC has been mostly influenced by psychiatric training which began in Jamaica, the only site for the University of the West Indies (UWI) in the 1960s (Beaubrun, 1992). As late as 2007, psychologist Kai Morgan was still lamenting the lack of presence of psychology in the mental health landscape in Jamaica (Collinder, 2007). This has since spread to the other island campus sites, for example, Trinidad, Barbados, and Bahamas. However, such training is grounded in the Western paradigm and heavily influenced by the medical model with its focus on psychopathology and the belief in psychopharmacology as the only therapeutic option available to clinicians (Hickling, Matthies et al., 2008). Consequently, the role of psychology in health and mental health matters in the ESC has been nebulous when compared to other parts of the Caribbean. For example, psychological services are well established in Cuba and the remaining French territories of Guadeloupe and Martinique. A similar situation exists in Haiti in spite of its many economic challenges. In sharp contrast, in the ESC, counseling and psychotherapy have been effectively nonexistent until recently (Ward & Hickling, 2004).

UWI's first undergraduate program in psychology began in 1995 in the St. Augustine campus, which was spearheaded by social psychologist Professor Ramesh Deosaran. The same program was later established in the Mona campus in Jamaica by a group of psychologists including Peter Weller, Rose Johnson, and Orlean Brown. Their work had been preceded by Delroy Louden, who had pioneered a master's program in 1983 at the Mona campus but which trained a single cohort. After the first cohort, he left the university and the program was discontinued. Dr. Leachim Semaj later provided leadership in the development of Psychology in Jamaica in the 1980s and 1990s, taking over from Louden as lecturer in the medical faculty (Ward & Hickling, 2004). Driven by the burgeoning number of graduates from the undergraduate program, the master's program was thus restarted in Mona in 2002. Other UWI campuses followed suit, with the UWI in Trinidad offering its first master's program in clinical psychology in 2006 (Hutchinson & Rose, 2010). The Cave Hill campus in Barbados began offering undergraduate training in psychology in 2000. By 2003, the UWI campus in Jamaica introduced its first PhD program in clinical psychology (Office of Vice Chancellery, 2009).

A master's degree in counseling psychology was introduced in Jamaica in 1987 by the School of Theology, now known as the Caribbean Graduate School of Theology (Caribbean Graduate School of Theology, n.d.), followed by the opening of undergraduate programs in the same field in the UWI campuses in Jamaica and Trinidad in 1995 and then in Barbados in 2000. In 1998, the UWI in Jamaica also began offering a master's in counseling psychology. There are now such courses in UWI, Barbados (2008), and at various other institutions in Jamaica (Northern Caribbean University) and Trinidad (University of the Southern Caribbean, Caribbean Nazarene College) (Hutchinson & Rose, 2010).

In 2000 the Trinidad and Tobago Association for Psychologists was established, followed by the Bahamas Psychological Association in Jamaica (Ward & Hickling, 2004). Their main functions were to promote psychological wellbeing of all persons, interests and honor of the profession of psychology and welfare of psychologists; maintain standards of conduct; disseminate knowledge through research and educational activities; and represent interests of psychologists both locally and internationally (Trinidad and Tobago Gazette, 2000).

Counselor education programs, accreditation, licensure, and certification

Currently, there are six undergraduate programs in psychology across the region. In addition, there are at least five postgraduate training programs in counseling psychology in the ESC and two in the discipline of clinical psychology. All of the programs are 2 years in duration and generally comprise taught courses, practicum placements and a research project/thesis. Because independent practice is not currently licensed or legislated in any of the islands, it is generally accepted that a master's degree is sufficient to practice as a psychologist.

There are no known psychotherapy training programs outside of academia but psychologists have sought training and offer services in areas such as eye movement desensitization (EMDR) and neurolinguistic programming (NLP). (K. Lequay, personal communication, January 2009).

The burgeoning presence of cable television and the internet have resulted in greater awareness, and counseling and psychotherapy are becoming more in demand. The undergraduate programs in psychology at UWI are now the most subscribed to in the UWI curriculum (Hickling et al., 2008). The purpose and therefore the focus of this training are now demanding attention as the enrolment numbers increase and more embark upon clinical practice. Given that a cogent and coherent Caribbean philosophy of psychology is now developing, the presence of these programs suggests that there will eventually be a shift from the Western epistemological stranglehold currently dominant in the thinking in this area. This critical

transformative process that would accelerate the process of self-understanding and self-acceptance among the ESC is still very much needed.

The number of trained practitioners in clinical psychology remains relatively small and while
they are increasing in UWI and other academic institutions, their practice has yet to be regulated.
The recency of the field and perhaps the slow working of the bureaucratic machinery in these
postcolonial islands have resulted in the lack of formal licensing and certification for practitioners in psychology (Ward & Hickling, 2004). They are subsumed under the rubric of professions allied to medicine and therefore lumped together with social work, physiotherapy,
pharmacy, and chiropody. The tardiness of the bureaucratic machinery is yet another reflection
of the lack of confidence which these postcolonial societies express when attempting to define
new professional structures. Further, the need for legislation to specifically govern the practice
of these professions has not been given attention.

Academic programs provide certification and are accredited within the general accreditation
that is afforded by the institutions that offer them. This general accreditation is a function of
accrediting bodies within each island; however, no attempts have been made to make them
internationally accredited by professional psychology associations such as the American Psychological Association or the British Psychological Society. Licensure remains difficult without
legislative support and while Jamaica, Trinidad and Tobago, and Bahamas all have established
psychological associations, a legal framework for governing professional practice remains elusive.

Current counseling and psychotherapy theories, processes, and trends

Approaches to treatment in the ESC also reflect Western theoretical orientations with practitioners drawing upon client centered/humanistic, cognitive-behavioral, and family/systemic
theories to inform their work. At the same time, counseling and psychotherapy in the ESC are
still in their early stages of development; hence, these theoretical orientations are mostly used
among practitioners engaged in private practice and little has been written about their prevalence,
appropriateness and effectiveness with this population. One approach that has been documented
to have good success is family/systemic therapy. A review of treatment conducted in the Virgin
Islands revealed that adolescents with conduct disorders and their families were greatly assisted by
using a culturally sensitive set of family therapy interventions (Dudley-Grant, 1996). These
interventions were based on the multisystems approach developed by Boyd-Franklin (1989),
which seeks to intervene on multiple levels in a family system ranging from the nuclear and
extended family to the community and environment in general. Moreover, it incorporates the
cultural and psychosocial realities within which these families exist (Dudley-Grant, 2001).

Another emerging trend in the ESC is the use of cognitive-behavioral therapy (CBT); in fact,
there is a growing movement to culturally adapt the traditional CBT model to a more flexible
treatment protocol that addresses clients' values, contexts, as well as a host of other variables (see
Bernal, Jimenez-Chafey & Domenech Rodriguez, 2009; Duarté-Vélez, Bernal & Bonilla,
2010). In their work on the types of psychotherapy relevant to the needs of Caribbean clients,
Lefley and Bestman (1977) identified a number of indicators. They argue that effective psychotherapy with this population must be problem oriented and focused on attainable goals, the
therapist should position him or herself as the authority figure and adopt a more directive stance
to fit in with clients' expectations of being counseled and given advice, and it must be short-
term. More importantly, it must be oriented on the present, as they aptly note that "with
people whose futures have always been problematic, looking ahead for relief seems an additional burden" (p. 19). Based on their assessment, a short-term, evidenced-based, goal-directed
psychological therapy like CBT shows promise for the ESC given financial and other

considerations; however, the question of whether simply adapting standard practices and manuals is enough to produce culturally sensitive CBT remains to be seen.

One approach that shows great potential for use in the ESC is relational cultural therapy (RCT). The socio-cultural milieu of Caribbean life is grounded in relationships and a rich interweaving of culture and history that informs belief systems and, consequently, behavior. Problems in living can often be traced to neglected or corrupted relationships; consequently, healing is considered a relational process which takes place in the relational or in-between space between entities (Brown, 2003). For example, understanding relational family dynamics in the Caribbean context may involve identifying the critical developmental influences which may originate from the extended family or the community in which the individual has had his or her developmental experience. RCT challenges some of conventional psychology's notions of self, autonomy, independence, individuation and competition and proposes that a central human necessity is the establishment of authentic and mutual connections in relationships; consequently, disconnection in relationships is the source of psychological problems (Walker, 2004). These notions are central to Caribbean culture and worldview.

An additional emerging trend in the Caribbean is the presence of Employee Assistance Programs (EAPs), programs that are engaged in promoting personal and psychological well-being in their regional institutions. In Trinidad and Tobago, for instance, these have flourished perhaps because of its industrialized focus, but they have served to enhance employment opportunities for psychologists and increase the acceptance of prevention and early detection as goals of intervention. These EAPs, a product of North America, are now beginning to surface in the other islands as well. Multisector collaboration is critical but the inputs must be sought and respected.

Indigenous and traditional healing methods

The most popular and well documented therapeutic process and trend in the Caribbean is traditional healing. Despite the hegemonic influence of Euro-American values, it has not negated the strength of this socio-cultural and historical orientation; a belief in magic and the supernatural, for example, continues to transcend social class and education.

Caribbean cultures are deeply rooted in spiritual dimensions; a commonly held perception is that mental health problems are caused by spells, curses, spirits, and demons, and that such problems represent a punishment for wrongful deeds (Laguerre, 1987; Nicolas, DeSilva, Grey & Gonzalez-Eastep, 2006; Waldron, 2003). Consequently, there is a plethora of bush medicines, practices, rituals, and spiritual cures available on demand. Furthermore, there is a strong religious element that supports the idea of miracle interventions from the gods that are served. This tacit investment in religion, spirituality, and traditional healing practices inevitably reinforce beliefs about the presence of evil, and that psychic harm can be inflicted on the unsuspecting by those maliciously or jealously motivated. Because illness is linked to spirituality, psychological and other holistic treatment is often sought from religious leaders (Griffith & Mahy, 1984).

This worldview is not surprising given that the vast array of healing forms in the Caribbean are based on retentions from the predominantly African and, to a lesser degree, Indian past and represent an extraordinary complexity of interacting cultural influences (Edmonds & Gonzalez, 2010; Fernández-Olmos, 2003; Laguerre, 1987; Wane & Sutherland, 2010). For example, Shango, Revival Zion, and Spiritual Baptist have their origins in the multifaceted religious practices found in West Africa. While these practices are separate ritual traditions, they are interconnected in significant ways. They are all characterized by ancestor veneration, spirit possession, the use of herbs and oils, divination, and a general belief in the Orishas or deities (Glazier 1993; Henry 2001; Wedenoja, 1988). Public possessions during which the deity or spirit takes over the bodies of their devotees are by far the most prominent characteristic of these religions (Glazier, 2008). Similarly, Rastafari practiced predominantly in Jamaica also combines African traditions with elements of Christianity.

Hinduism and Islam practiced predominantly in Trinidad, Suriname, and Guyana have their origins in India. However, perhaps due to the process of having to adapt to the new and harsh climate of the colonial Caribbean, the myths, rituals, festivals, and healing practices have taken on forms of expressions that appear to be distinct from their place of origin (Desmangles, Glazier & Murphy, 2009).

Healing in the Caribbean context also takes place within Christian-based religions in the form of faith healing. The foundation of faith healing is based on the healing and restorative rituals of priest-healers within their specified religious tradition (Lartey, 2002). Within this system, miraculous, and immediate recovery that is beyond the understanding of conventional approaches to health and well-being is commonplace. Furthermore, there is an emphasis on the spiritual as an important dimension of the person and according to Allen (2001), it is this emphasis that opens up the possibility of prayer as a healing modality.

These traditional healing forms were brought to the Caribbean by enslaved Africans and indentured laborers from India and evolved under the inhumane and life-threatening conditions of slavery and colonialism. They are practiced in almost every country in the ESC, at various social levels that reflect the ethnic, socioeconomic, and historical background of the people (Aarons, 1999; Fernández-Olmos, 2003). As Edmonds & Gonzalez (2010) note, "all of these traditions sought to connect people to spiritual and divine power in order to heal their personal and communal afflictions and to dismantle systems of oppression" (p. 184). Not only are these healing systems used habitually as a psychotherapeutic method and alternative to the medical system, they have also taken on the role of support systems (Pasquali, 1994; Nuñez-Molina, 2001; Reyes, 2004) and are often accessed in place of conventional health and mental healthcare.

The choice of traditional healing in place of conventional psychological treatment is due to a number of factors, which include different values, beliefs and conceptualizations of distress which make the continued use of intervention models based on Eurocentric assumptions and values ineffectual (see Sutherland & Moodley, 2010; Moodley & Sutherland, 2009; 2010). In many instances, the role of the traditional healer/priest/pundit in Caribbean society is probably the closest model to psychotherapy that people experience, either first hand or through observation and vicarious experience (Griffith & Mahy, 1984). These healers would be considered legitimate by polite society but there is also an active use of obeah-men/women, healers, seers, prophets, and prophetesses even among the leaders in business and politics. Therefore, psychological practice has to seek a balance between this cultural imperative and the professional demands which are a natural consequence of the therapeutic process.

Research and supervision

There has been a lack of active research in counseling and clinical psychology in the ESC, though this may be gradually changing due to the recent establishment of the *Caribbean Journal of Psychology* in 2008. Some research funding comes from the UWI Graduate Studies fund and from postgraduate students doing their theses and research projects. Various research projects have begun the task of developing and validating interventions, measures and instruments for use in the Caribbean. For instance, the ANSA McAL Psychological Research Centre, with a presence at all three campuses of the UWI, seems to be pioneering the growth of psychology in the region. The research projects undertaken by the center over the years incorporate various themes and subjects including psychonomics, crime, psychology of juvenile behavior, social norms, HIV/AIDS stigmatization, environmental attitudes, attitudes towards work, psychology of risk and perception of victimization, civic and community and family life (Ramdhanie, 2001).

The other issue related to the practice of psychology is the need to do research, standardize tests and validate measures for the Caribbean region (see Sutherland & Moodley, 2011, for a discussion). This scientific aspect of the practice has been underserved as practitioner demands have overwhelmed those whose training and skills would have prepared them to tackle these important areas. The value of Caribbean professionals working abroad to establish collaborative linkages is critical here as the research capacity is compromised by the demands of practice and the relative lack of resources. However, it must be stressed that the need to maintain a Caribbean identity and to not lose sight of the priorities in the Caribbean when inviting these linkages are also essential.

Clinical supervision in the ESC is provided by practitioners in either public or private practice. The issues for supervision arise out of the lack of boundaries between clinical and counseling psychology and the detachment of many practitioners from the academic environment. In a more practical sense, there is also a lack of trained psychologists in the field, resulting in clinical supervision being provided by psychiatrists and social workers at some sites. In light of these deficits, a clear definition of the role and function of a psychologist in the public, private and academic domains of the Caribbean context is needed, and it is hoped that this goal will be achieved through the work of the various psychological associations and their collaboration with the political directorate (Doorbar, 2008). For instance, the formation of a number of psychological associations in Trinidad, Jamaica, Barbados and the Bahamas represent some of the first steps towards advancing psychology as a discipline and establishing a professional framework for the region.

Strengths, weaknesses, opportunities, challenges

Counseling and psychotherapy are growing fields in the ESC. This is evident in the tremendous growth in education and training programs as well as the number of professional associations throughout the region. In addition, the launch of the *Caribbean Journal of Psychology* (CJP) and the upcoming Caribbean Regional Conference of Psychology 2011 are critical steps in providing a forum for discussing issues relevant to the Caribbean and for disseminating research. These endeavors may go a long way in transforming the way mental health issues are perceived and treated in the Caribbean, which has typically followed the British model where the mentally ill were locked away in "mad houses" for extended periods of time (Hickling & Gibson, 2005). With the development and expansion of counseling and psychotherapy, the region can seek alternative ways to treat people outside of these institutions, for example, through community-based mental health services (World Health Organization, 2011) and in so doing, address the negative stigma associated with mental illness and its treatments.

That being said, a major weakness is that the implications for education, training and indeed living systems are firmly rooted in European values. This applies to most areas of life in the Caribbean with the partial exception of religion. This also means that the predominant model of psychological intervention is also strongly grounded in Western ideals and values and as previously mentioned, firmly entrenched in the medical model. Some practitioners and theorists have argued that even in the Euro-American system, traditional models of psychotherapy have limited relevance for minority groups and cultures (see Bhugra & Bhui, 1998; Kareem & Littlewood, 1992; Moodley, 1999). Therefore, a monumental shift is required to make counseling and psychotherapy appropriate and useful in the Caribbean context.

In spite of the difficulties and complexities of the region, the recency of the discipline must be seen as a great opportunity for influencing development, improving mental health practice and improving the lives of Caribbean people. It is also an opportunity to learn from the pitfalls of the West more generally and failure of the multicultural movement in particular, to adequately address the needs of diverse populations (see Sutherland & Moodley, 2011). The region is fertile ground for the proliferation of research; however, the tools and methodologies used to penetrate this virtually untouched domain must be culturally appropriate and relevant to the needs of this population. Hence, behavior change research that addresses growing regional problems such as obesity, homophobia, and interpersonal relationship breakdown is necessary. Changing gender roles, the need for improved child care facilities, and the tackling of problems such as child abuse, domestic violence and old age care are also rich areas for psychological intervention.

A major challenge in the region is the parallel system of beliefs and actions derived from the retentions of African and Indian traditions that makes it difficult for Western models of counseling and psychotherapy to satisfactorily explain some of the experiences of the Caribbean people. This is partly due to a conceptual schism of the prevailing psychotherapeutic model that focuses on individual action and responsibility as the preferred mechanism to deal with life's problems. With this approach, the therapist retains a neutral and objective perspective as the client is encouraged to take charge of his or her responses to the environment. The greatest difficulty is to merge these sometimes competing belief systems into a cogent and relevant whole through education and practice. Research and formal training is still validated through its synchronicity with Western ideals and philosophy as the existence of a true and consistent Caribbean philosophy remains debated and unresolved. Furthermore, the heterogeneity of Caribbean people becomes an issue here as diversity in ethnic identities, religions, and social classes, all impact the experience, understanding, and acknowledgement of psychological distress, and perhaps more importantly, they dictate how help will be sought.

Additionally, migration from the Caribbean continues to be a major issue, particularly for those who have been educated there but choose to seek their fortune in the metropolitan world ("brain drain" phenomenon). While the value of financial and material reparations is significant to most Caribbean economies, there is also the contending loss of human resources and brain power to tackle the many social problems. Attracting some of these professionals back to work and teach in the Caribbean must be a priority.

Future directions

Clearly, counseling and psychotherapy in the ESC has the potential to be a wellspring for theory development as well as hypothesis testing (Dudley-Grant, 2001). Nevertheless, the emergence of this field highlights critical questions regarding the universal applicability of psychological theories and interventions in view of the Caribbean's enduring colonial legacy of imposition and historical wounding. For instance, should counselors maintain 'fidelity' to evidence-based treatments that have not been validated for Caribbean clients or should they adapt a treatment protocol that 'fits' the client's culture but is not supported by research (Morales, 2010)?

In view of this conflict, it is imperative that future research in the ESC target (1) the integration of traditional healing practices in counseling/psychotherapy and/or (2) an indigenous psychology based solely on the Caribbean experience. To do otherwise would ignore salient aspects of Caribbean history, devalue the coping strategies used by this population for centuries and perpetuate the kind of psychological violence and hegemonic practices that are reminiscent of colonialism.

These are important considerations that counselors and psychotherapists need to respond to as they attempt to define new structures for the Caribbean in the years ahead. Practitioners have an opportunity to engage in dual interventions in counseling and psychotherapy; that is, traditional healing alongside conventional counseling and psychotherapy to address the mind–body–spirit holism that many clients in the ESC currently seek (Moodley & Sutherland, 2009).

Finally, poverty and limited access to psychological services is another area of grave concern that must be addressed to accelerate the process. It is also critical that the traditional rivalries between the islands that have been engendered in the colonial past do not obstruct us from forging a collective and mutually supportive future. These critical transformative developments are necessary in order for counseling and psychotherapy to be deemed relevant to the ESC.

Conclusion

In order to ensure that a positive developmental trajectory of Caribbean life is shared and facilitated for the majority of its population, it is imperative that the mental health services function effectively. This functioning must be holistic and embrace assessment, prevention and treatment strategies that are grounded in the experiences of Caribbean people. This represents a major challenge but one that must be met if the generations to come and indeed those presently coping with so many socio-cultural and economic challenges are to survive as healthy and independent people.

References

Aarons, D. E. (1999). Medicine and its alternatives: Health care priorities in the Caribbean. *The Hastings Center Report, 29*(4), 23–27.

Allen E. A. (2001). Whole person healing, spiritual realism and social disintegration. A Caribbean case study in faith, health and healing. *International Review of Mission, 90*(356/357), 118–133.

Beaubrun, M. H. (1992) Caribbean psychiatry, yesterday, today and tomorrow. *History of Psychiatry, 3*(11), 371–382.

Bernal, G., Jimenez-Chafey, M. I., & Domenech Rodriguez, M. M. (2009). Cultural adaptation of treatments: A resource for considering culture in evidence-based practice. *Professional Psychology: Research and Practice, 40*, 361–368.

Bhugra, D. & Bhui, K. (1998). Psychotherapy for ethnic minorities: Issues, context and practice. *British Journal of Psychotherapy, 14*(3), 310–326.

Boyd-Franklin, N. (1989). Black families in therapy: A multisystems approach. New York: Guilford Press.

Brown, K. M. (2003). Healing relationships in the African Caribbean. In H. Selin & H. Shapiro (eds), *Medicine across Cultures: History and Practice of Medicine in Non-Western Cultures*. Dordrecht: Kluwer Academic Publishers.

Caribbean Graduate School of Theology. (n.d.). *Masters of Arts in Counselling Psychology*. Retrieved from http://cgstonline.org/index.php?option=com_content&task=view&id=8&Itemid=37

Collinder, A. (2007). *On the Mind of Kai Morgan*. Retrieved from http://jamaica-gleaner.com/gleaner/20071202/out/out1.html

Conway, D. (2009). The Caribbean diaspora. In R. S. Hillman & T. J. D'Agostino (eds), *Understanding the Contemporary Caribbean* (2nd edn) (pp. 367–390). Boulder, CO: Lynne Reinner.

Desmangles, L. G., Glazier, S. D., & Murphy, J. M. (2009). Religion in the Caribbean. In R. S. Hillman & T. J. D'Agostino (eds), *Understanding the Contemporary Caribbean* (2nd edn) (pp. 263–304). Boulder, CO: Lynne Reinner.

Doorbar, R. (2008). Reflections of a psychologist in Jamaica. In F. W. Hickling, B. K. Matties, K. Morgan, & R. C., Gibson (eds), *Perspectives in Caribbean psychology* (pp. 516–526). Carimensa: University of the West Indies, Mona, Jamaica.

Duarté-Vélez, Y., Bernal, G., & Bonilla, K. (2010). Culturally adapted cognitive-behavioral therapy: Integrating sexual, spiritual, and family identities in an evidence-based treatment of a depressed Latino adolescent. *Journal of Clinical Psychology, 66*(8), 895–906.

Dudley-Grant, G. R. (1996). Conduct disorder (delinquent behavior) as coping mechanism: Family therapy in the U.S. Virgin Islands. In F.W. Kaslow (Chair), *Family Therapy in Various Countries*. Symposium conducted at the 104th Annual Convention of the American Psychological Association, Toronto, Ontario, Canada.

Dudley-Grant, G. R. (2001). Eastern Caribbean family psychology with conduct disordered adolescents from the Virgin Islands. *American Psychologist, 56*(1), 47–57.

Edmonds, E. B., & Gonzalez, M. A. (2010). *Caribbean Religious History*. New York: New York University Press.

Fernández Olmos, M. (2003). *Creole Religions of the Caribbean: An Introduction from Vodou and Santería to Obeah and Espiritismo*. New York: New York University Press.

Glazier, S.D. (1993). Funerals and mourning in the Spiritual Baptist and Shango traditions. *Caribbean Quarterly, 39*(3/4) 1–11.

Glazier, S. D. (2008). Demanding deities and reluctant devotees belief and unbelief in the Trinidadian Orisa movement. *Social Analysis, 52*(1), 19–38.

Griffith E. E. H., & Mahy G. E. (1984). Psychological benefits of spiritual Baptist "mourning". *American Journal of Psychiatry, 141*, 769–773.

Henry, F. (2001). The Orisha (Shango) movement in Trinidad. In S. D. Glazier (ed.). *The Encyclopedia of African and African-American Religion* (pp. 221–223). New York: Routledge.

Henry, P., & Buhle, P. (1992). Caliban as deconstructionist. CLR James and post colonial discourse. In P. Henry & P. Buhle (eds), *CLR James' Caribbean* (pp. 111–142). Durham, NC: Duke University Press.

Hickling F. W., & Gibson R. C. (2005). The history of Caribbean psychiatry. In F. W. Hickling & E. Sorel (eds), *Images of Psychiatry: The Caribbean* (pp. 15–41). Kingston, Jamaica: University of the West Indies.

Hickling F. W., Martin, J., & Harrisingh-Dewar, A. (2008). Redefining personality disorder in Jamaica. In F. W. Hickling, B. K. Matthies, K. Morgan, & R. C. Gibson (eds), *Perspectives in Caribbean Psychology* (pp. 263–288). Carimensa: University of the West Indies, Mona, Jamaica.

Hickling, F. W. Matthies, B. K., Morgan, K., & Gibson, R. C. (2008). Introduction. In F. W. Hickling, B. K. Matthies, K. Morgan, & R. C. Gibson (eds), *Perspectives in Caribbean Psychology* (pp. x–xiv). Carimensa: University of the West Indies, Mona, Jamaica.

Hillman, R. S. (2009). Introduction. In R. S. Hillman & T. J. D'Agostino (eds). *Understanding the Contemporary Caribbean* (2nd edn) (pp. 1–18). Boulder, CO: Lynne Reiner.

Hutchinson, G., & Rose, J. (2010). The development of clinical psychology in Trinidad and Tobago. *Psychology Forum, 215*, 40–42.

Kareem, J., & Littlewood, R. (eds). (1992). *Intercultural Therapy: Themes, Interpretations and Practice*. Oxford: Blackwell.

Laguerre, M. S. (1987). *Afro-Caribbean Folk Medicine*. South Hadley, MA: Bergin & Garvey.

Lartey, E.Y. (2002). Pastoral counselling in multi-cultural contexts. In J. R.Farris (ed.), *International Perspectives on Pastoral Counseling* (pp. 317–329). New York: The Haworth Pastoral Press.

Lefley, H. P., & Bestman, E. W. (1977). *Psychotherapy in Caribbean Cultures*. Paper presented at the Annual Convention of the American Psychological Association, San Francisco, California.

Moodley, R. (1999). Challenges and transformation: Counselling in a multi-cultural context. *International Journal for the Advancement of Counselling, 21*, 139–152.

Moodley, R., & Sutherland, P. (2009). Traditional and cultural healers: Dual interventions in counselling and psychotherapy. *Spirituality and Counselling Journal, 28*(1) 11–31.

Moodley, R., & Sutherland, P. (2010). Psychic retreats in other places: Clients who seek healing with traditional healers and psychotherapists. *Counselling Psychology Quarterly, 23*(3), 267–282.

Morales, E. (2010). Evidence-based practices with ethnic minorities: Strange bedfellows no more. *Journal of Clinical Psychology: In Session, 66*(8), 821–829.

Naipaul, V. S. (2001). *The Middle Passage*. New York: Picador (paperback edition).

Nicolas, G., DeSilva, A. M., Grey, K. S., & Gonzalez-Eastep, D. (2006). Using a multicultural lens to understand illnesses among Haitians living in America. *American Journal of Orthopsychiatry, 77*(4), 702–707.

Nuñez-Molina, M. A. (2001). Community healing among Puerto Ricans: Espiritismo as a therapy for the soul. In M. O. Fernández (ed.), *Healing Cultures: Art and Religion as Curative Practices in the Caribbean and its Diaspora* (pp. 115–132). London: Palgrave.

Office of Vice Chancellery. (2009). *The University of West Indies: 2007–2008* Annual Report. Retrieved from http://sta.uwi.edu/resources/documents/vc_report_0708.pdf

Pasquali, E. A. (1994). Santeria. *Journal of Holistic Nursing, 12*(4), 380–390.

Queen Ifrica. (2008). The ultimate reggae dancehall x-Perience: Mi nah rub [CD]. Plantation, FL: Island Entertainment.

Ramdhanie, I. K. (2001). *The Ansa McAL Psychological Research Centre: The Miracle of St. Augustine, 1989–1999*. St. Augustine: Ansa McAL Psychological Research Centre.

Reyes, A. R. (2004). Illness and the rule of Ocha in Cuban santeria. *Transforming Anthropology, 12*(1/2), 75–59.

Sutherland, P., & Moodley, R. (2011). Research in transcultural counselling and psychotherapy. In C. Lago (ed.). *Handbook of Transcultural Counselling and Psychotherapy.* Berkshire: Open University Press.

Sutherland, P., & Moodley, R. (2010). Reclaiming the spirit: Clemmont Vontress and the quest for spirituality and traditional healing in counselling. In R. Moodley & R. Walcott's (eds), *Counselling Across and Beyond Cultures: Exploring the Work of Clemmont Vontress in Clinical Practice* (pp. 263–277). Toronto: University of Toronto Press.

Trinidad and Tobago Gazette. (2000). *Legal Supplement part A to Act No. 84 of 2000-Trinidad and Tobago Association of Psychologists (incorporation) Act.* Retrieved from www.ttparliament.org/legislations/a2000–84.pdf

Waldron, I. R. G. (2003). Examining beliefs about mental illness among African Canadian women. *Women's Health and Urban Life: An International and Interdisciplinary Journal, 2*(1), 42–58.

Walker, M. (2004). How relationships heal. In. M. Walker & W. B. Rosen (eds), *How Connections Heal: Stories from Relational-cultural Therapy* (pp. 3–21). New York: Guilford Press.

Wane, N., & Sutherland, P. (2010). African and Caribbean healing practices in therapy. In R. Moodley (ed.), *Building Bridges for Wellness and Psychotherapy* (pp. 335–347). Toronto: CDCP Press.

Ward, T. & Hickling, F. (2004). Psychology in the English-speaking Caribbean. *The Psychologist, 17*(8), 442–444.

Wedenoja, W. (1988). The origins of revival, a Creole religion in Jamaica. In G. Saunders (ed.), *Culture and Christianity: The Dialectics of Transformation* (pp. 91–116). New York: Greenwood.

World Health Organization (2011). *WHO-AIMS Report on Mental Health Systems in the Caribbean.* Retrieved October 10, 2011 from www.who.int/mental_health/evidence/mh_systems_caribbeans_en.pdf

11

COUNSELING AND PSYCHOTHERAPY IN CUBA

Interdisciplinarity, community-driven research and education

Norma Guillard Limonta and Mercedes Umana

Introduction

The Republic of Cuba is an archipelago comprising over 1,600 islands and islets with a total population of approximately 11 million people, with 63% between 20 and 64 years of age (Government of the Republic of Cuba, 2010). The official language of Cuba is Spanish.

Cuba is a middle-income country with high human development, ranking 51 out of 187 countries in the 2011 Human Development Report (United Nations Development Programme [UNDP], 2011). In spite of the negative impact of the US commercial and financial blockade to the country and the fall of the socialist bloc in the 1990s, Cuba has achieved the Millennium Goals related to universal primary education, gender equality, and reduction of infant mortality (UNDP, 2008). According to the UNDP Cuba office (2008), for 2015, the Cuban government seeks to achieve the Millennium Goals related to elimination of extreme poverty and hunger, improvement of maternal health, fighting against HIV/AIDS and other infections, as well as environmental sustainability and worldwide alliances for development. The same office reports that for over 40 years, Cuba has not accessed any international funding from the World Bank or the International Monetary Fund, and since 2003 Cuban economy has not received funds from the European Union.

Over the past 5 years, Cuba has implemented measures aimed at strengthening international exports of nickel, and pharmaceuticals and biotechnology. Additionally, Cuba has adopted measures to increase international investment in the country and to develop new forms of agricultural production, as well as opening up to other economies, including China and Venezuela (UNDP, 2008).

Cuba has achieved world-renowned successes with respect to education, health, public safety, social security, territorial development, protection of vulnerable groups, gender equity, citizens' active participation in decision making at the local and national level; these are some of the outcomes that provide evidence of a paradigm in public policy and programming that conceives development is only achievable when interrelating the social and economic development of the population. These outcomes are particularly relevant as Cuba has surpassed other countries with similar incomes with respect to social development (UNDP, 2010).[1]

Cuban conceptualizations and praxis of counseling and psychotherapy are very similar. Hernandez (1996) conceptualizes "psychological counseling" as short-term interventions that focus on situations with a relatively low level of complexity, usually derived from the client's lack of proper information in regard to how to deal with a specific situation or problem, or from difficulties in decision making with regard to areas such as career, the workplace, school, and family to name a few. He considers that the main distinction between the two terms is that psychotherapy focuses on long-term interventions and/or more complex mental health issues involving psychopathologies. He characterizes counseling as a cognitive emotional learning process, strongly focused on prevention, where the individual is dedicated to finding the most convenient decision for a specific circumstance, while learning skills that will enhance optimal functioning in all spheres of his/her life. Both counseling and psychotherapy constitute domains of specialization within psychology in Cuba. Throughout the year, training opportunities in these areas can be found in undergraduate and graduate courses as well as within professional conferences or as stand-alone workshops.

Brief history of counseling and psychotherapy

Cuban counseling and psychotherapy have been deeply influenced by the socio-political and economical processes the Republic has undergone throughout the years. Simultaneous with the struggle for independence from Spain in the 1800s, Cuban intellectuals departed from dogmatic traditionalist epistemologies in favor of materialistic empiricism. Enrique José Varona (1849–1933) is considered one of the main academic contributors to the development of psychology as a distinct discipline from philosophy in Cuba (Bernal, 1985). In his second series of philosophical conferences, Varona (1888) presented an in-depth overview of the domains of psychology as a science with topics including introspective and experimental methods, sensation, perception, memory, illusions, hallucinations, relationship between physiology and emotional states, to name a few. In 1900, Varona taught courses on psychology, logic, ethics and sociology at the University of Havana (Becerra, 2008).

Following the struggle for independence from Spain, the United States of America occupied Cuba in 1899 as a result of the Spanish–American War (Institute of History of Cuba, 2011). This political development marked a period of strong North American influence on Cuban counseling and psychotherapy that was characterized by the tension between those who rigidly applied North American psychological perspectives (i.e. using psychological testing instruments without standardization or appropriate norming procedures) and those who advocated the development of psychological instruments and approaches based on Cuban realities (Bernal, 1985). During this period most clinical, educational, and industrial psychologists were predominantly US trained with strong behavioral, humanistic, and developmental North American and European influences from theorists/psychologists such as Rogers and Piaget. Additionally, during this period psychology courses in Cuba were offered only within high school or in academic programs for other professions (Corral, 2008).

Cuban psychology was profoundly impacted by the Revolution of 1959. The first Cuban Faculties of Psychology were founded in 1961 (University of Las Villas) and in 1962 (University of Havana) (Bernal, 1985; Corral, 2008). The main objective of these new faculties pointed towards supporting the revolutionary socio-political process, which was translated into research projects that identified the diverse needs of Cuban society, and proposing changes, particularly in relation to health, education, and industry (Bernal, 1985). Notable historical contributions of the School of Psychology included the foundation of a psychology group in the new Ministry of Public Health, as well as conducting research projects requested by the new Revolutionary government such as the one commissioned by then Minister of Industries, Ernesto (Che) Guevara, looking into the situation of rural communities (Corral, 2008).

During the 1970s and early 1980s special efforts were made by the Revolutionary government to overcome the shortage of professionally trained psychologists by providing scholarships for students to be trained in the discipline in Eastern Europe and in the Soviet Union. At the same time, a new psychology curriculum was established with strong Soviet influence, incorporating social-historical perspectives in psychology in a somewhat rigid or dogmatic fashion (Corral, 2008). Some of the theories that influenced academia and professional praxis at this time included those of Rubenstein, Leontiev, and Vygotsky.[2] During the late 1980s and into the 1990s, Cuban counseling and psychotherapy appeared to become more flexible, attaining equilibrium between rigorous research and social praxis based on different theories and models. The strength in counseling and psychotherapy was supported by guaranteed employment upon graduation from university-level programs, and the academic programs' openness to explore new lines of inquiry linked to emerging approaches (cognitive therapy, family therapy, other innovative therapeutic modalities), and issues in counseling/psychotherapy such as gender and sexuality (Corral, 2008).

From the late 1990s and into the new millennium, Cuban society has been impacted by global socio-economic and political changes that have presented new challenges for psychologists. Some of these changes have undeniably increased the levels of stress in Cuban society, as in the case of the US Cuban embargo. In response to these changes, Cuban universities have trained new generations of psychologists who now work on finding solutions to old and new challenges, such as epidemics, natural disasters, addictions, and sexual exploitation, among others, while continuing to promote the best of Cuban society's qualities, such as community participation in mental health promotion.

Pérez-Stable (1985) traces Cuba's shift towards strengthening community participation in mental health promotion to major decisions within the Ministry of Health taken between 1965 and 1975, which resulted in the establishment of the *polyclinic* as the main unit for health service delivery and planning. This decision was also accompanied by specific measures to deal with nationwide criticisms which indicated that the healthcare system at that time had a passive attitude towards health promotion, lacked continuity of care and teamwork, was impersonal, and used consultations inappropriately (Pérez-Stable, 1985). As a result, Cuba developed and implemented a notion of "Medicine in the Community," establishing seven principles to guide the work of the new polyclinics. These principles included integrated healthcare, sectorization of full-time polyclinic work, regionalization of healthcare, continuity of care, active medicine, team work, and citizen participation in the definition of community-based healthcare priorities through local municipal assemblies, local health commissions, and mass organizations such as the Committees for the Defense of the Revolution, the Federation of Cuban Women, trade unions, and the Association of Small Farmers (Pérez-Stable, 1985).

The changes in the healthcare system that developed early on after the Cuban revolution also resulted in a reconceptualization of the role of psychologists in Cuba, as psychology professionals moved from narrowly focusing on individual testing and diagnosis to participating in different levels of the healthcare system, such as direct community healthcare service delivery, policy development, planning, and research (García-Averasturi, 1985).

Today, interdisciplinarity and community involvement are prominent characteristics of counseling within Cuba's healthcare system. Healthcare service provision on the island comprises a network of family physicians who deliver primary care in *consultorios* (clinics) and secondary care in polyclinics (specialty clinics). *Consultorios* address approximately 80% of the health problems in Cuba and stress health promotion (Dresang, Brebrick, Murray, Shallue, & Sullivan-Vedder, 2005). Each *consultorio* serves around 600–700 patients (or 150 families) within the area surrounding it (Dresang et al., 2005). Between 15 and 20 *consultorios* integrate a working group (Dominguez-Alonso & Zacca, 2011), which comprises a team of healthcare providers including specialists in internal medicine, gynecology–obstetrics, and stomatology; additionally, the working group also comprises psychologists, nursing supervisors, social workers, a statistician, and an epidemiology technician. Patients requiring care beyond the scope of the *consultorio* are referred to a polyclinic. More specialists from other disciplines provide services at these specialty clinics depending on the specific needs of the population served (Luna-Morales, Sierra-Perez, & Gandul Salabarria, 2009). There can be up to four psychologists providing services within a polyclinic, whose tasks often include knowledge exchange and training of professionals from other disciplines within the polyclinic; collaborative interdisciplinary assessment of a patient's needs; and direct counseling/psychotherapy to self-referred or family doctor-referred patients. Additionally, psychologists provide counseling and psychotherapy services (tertiary care) within hospital settings (Pérez Lovelle, 2003).

Counselor education programs, accreditation, licensure, and certification

Cuban post-secondary education is regulated by the Ministry of Postsecondary Education (Ministry of Justice, 2007). Under this ministry's authority, the National Board of Accreditations is responsible for the evaluation and accreditation of all university-level programs, including psychology (Organization of Ibero-American States, 2006). Both the Ministry and the Board are responsible for ensuring consistency and quality of training for all university programs in psychology, across all locations (faculties in different provinces) and modalities (full time vs. part-time) of the program. Therefore, psychology programs in Cuba all follow a similar curriculum. Examples of undergraduate courses offered at the University of Havana include counseling psychology, personality theories, clinical psychology, counseling/psychotherapy in relation to sexuality, developmental psychology of children, adults and seniors, psychological assessment, and diagnostics (University of Havana, 2011).

There are three Faculties of Psychology based in the Universities of Havana, Las Villas, and Oriente. Psychology programs are state funded, and include undergraduate and graduate programs at the diploma, bachelor, master's, and doctoral levels. Completion of a bachelor's degree in psychology constitutes accreditation to work as a psychologist in clinical, organizational, and educational settings. Master's, doctorate, and diplomas focus on specialized areas of interest for psychologists who have already graduated from an undergraduate degree; these programs focus specifically on the development of research and other skills directly related to areas of interest of the student (Organization of Ibero-American States, 2006).

Cuban undergraduate psychology programs last 4–5 years, after which the graduate obtains the degree of *licenciatura universitaria* (university licensee), a title that accredits the graduate to work as a psychologist wherever he/she is given employment. Bill 1254 (Council of Ministers of the Republic of Cuba, 1973) and Decree 3771 (Presidency of the Republic of Cuba, 1974) establish that all graduates in different fields (including psychology) are required to work in an assigned position in their field of expertise for a total of 2 years following their graduation as part of a social service or paid practicum. Professional certification (acquired through graduation from an undergraduate program in Psychology by a recognized university) qualifies all graduates to take on all responsibilities and duties of the profession of psychology, while also providing eligibility to pursue studies at the master's and doctorate level.

All psychology graduates are entitled to practice as psychotherapists, without requiring any additional special license, certification, title or degree. A certification process is currently being discussed in response to the increasing diversity of psychology programs and psychotherapeutic modalities.

Over the past 50 years the faculties of psychology have produced around 3,020 graduates from the bachelor's program. Cuba has approximately 3,020 psychologists trained in three Faculties of Psychology (Las Villas, Havana, and Oriente), with an estimated 2,000 specializing in health psychology, and the remainder specializing in psychology of education, social psychology, organizational psychology, sports psychology and public relations (Ares Mucio, 2010). Currently, there are 26,881 undergraduate psychology students throughout the country, out of which it is estimated that 785 will specialize in health psychology (Ares Mucio, 2010). This number of enrolled students represents a significant increase, given that in previous years the average number of graduates from the undergraduate program in psychology was around 20–30. This increase is due to the recent implementation of policies and programs that decentralized post-secondary education, opening university satellites in previously underserved municipalities and neighborhoods (de Armas & Espi, 2004). In recent years, social workers and teachers have also registered in psychology programs offered in training sites throughout the 14 Cuban provinces. In Havana alone it is estimated that there are 333 students registered in the undergraduate program in psychology.

The Cuban Society of Psychology (Sociedad Cubana de Psicología) is the main organization of psychologists in Cuba. Its mission focuses on building a scientific community of professionals in psychology and related sciences, to contribute to the development of psychology as a science and profession in Cuba and internationally. It also seeks to promote the socio-cultural development and wellbeing of Cuban society as a whole, and that of its professional members in particular (Cuban Society of Psychology, 2002). The organization comprises 18 working groups or sections focusing on specific areas of interest of its members. Some of these groups are psychology and society, psychoballet, psychoanalysis, Lacanian psychoanalysis, group modalities and psychodrama, historical cultural group, identity and diversity, youth, and sport psychology to name a few.

The Cuban Society of Psychology's main activities include continuous education of its members and members of other disciplines, through conferences, workshops, and other educational forums. Additionally, the organization promotes educational activities for the general public.

In relation to regulatory instruments for the profession of psychology, the Cuban Society of Psychology has developed an ethics code which outlines the general principles of the profession, including a description and guidelines of the main areas of competence of the profession, as well as ethical guidelines and disciplinary procedures in cases of failure to adhere to the code (Cuban Society of Psychology, 2002).

Current counseling and psychotherapy theories, processes, and trends

Cuban counseling and psychotherapy can be said to be based on critical analysis and integration of different epistemologies and approaches, which have manifested in the development, adaptation and application of approaches such as cognitive-behavioral, psychodynamic, cultural-historical, humanistic, hypnosis, systemic, and feminist perspectives at the individual, group, family, and community levels in a variety of settings. As an illustration of this, a quick review of the recent Intercontinental Conventions on Psychology, Humanities and Social Sciences Hominis 2002 and 2005 programs demonstrate the centrality of symposiums focusing on discussions on the use of Vygotsky's social historical perspectives in combination with different psychotherapeutic approaches. Keeping with the world-renowned Cuban tradition in research informed psychotherapeutic praxis, the conventions have showcased a wide range of workshops, panel discussions, and group meetings focusing on specialized areas such as psychodrama, psychoanalysis, the use of yoga in psychotherapy, psychological assessment, hypnosis, approaches to family therapy, and addressing diversity in counseling, among others (Hominis Organizing Committee, 2002, 2005).

Other examples of psychotherapeutic approaches practiced in Cuba include body–mind therapies from a social historical perspective (Febles, n.d.), an approach that highlights the role of the body in self-regulation and personality development. Other approaches used in individual, group, family, and community counseling include psychoanalytic psychodrama, as well as different expressive arts such as puppetry, drawing, and painting. Similar to recent emerging trends in counseling and psychotherapy, Cuban psychologists have also integrated social historical perspectives with what resembles positive psychology or even solution-focused perspectives in counseling, as in the work of Roca (2007, 2010), which emphasizes clients' strengths and resources rather than focusing on weaknesses and limitations.

Indigenous and traditional healing methods

One of Cuba's most notable indigenous/traditional healing methods is the *Regla Lucumi* spiritual practice (also known as Santería), which is popularly known also as *Regla de Ocha*, *Regla de Santo*, *babaorichas*, *iyaorichas*, and *omorichas* (Cros Sandoval, 2006). The origins of this spiritual practice are rooted in the resistance of enslaved Africans who arrived in Cuba after being violently removed from their land via the transatlantic slave trade (Orozco & Bolivar, 1998).

Historical documents reveal that a significant number of well-trained priests and priestesses were among the men and women who had been forced into slavery and taken to Cuba from Yorubaland, including the new and old Oyo Empires and the sacred city of Ile Ife (Cros Sandoval, 2006). The *Regla Lucumi* provided African men, women, and children a life line of physical and emotional survival and resistance in the face of the genocide of slavery. In this sense, it has been documented that multiple revolts originated within the *cabildos*, a form of organization utilized by colonial Spanish authorities for the purpose of dividing enslaved Africans, where they instead implemented diverse ways to continue practicing and transferring their identity and spiritual practice to new generations (Argyriadis, 2005; Wedel, 2004). The worldview, rituals, emancipatory and clandestine nature of the *Regla Lucumi* are not an isolated phenomenon exclusive to Cuba, but rather an expression of collective and transnational resistance. As Adefarakan (2011) explains, "Yoruba culture and spirituality was forced to go underground, to move, shift and syncretize, yet continue and take root in the form of Shango and Spiritual Baptism in Trinidad and Tobago, Vodun in Haiti, Santería/Lucumi in Cuba and Candomble in Brazil" (p. 12).

Currently, it is estimated that the *Regla Lucumi* is practiced by 60–85% of the Cuban population versus 2–3% who actively practice Catholicism (Wedel, 2004). In spite of the popularity and richness of Santería, mainstream Cuban psychotherapy has not yet extended its critical analysis, adaptation, and integration processes to this area. Just as in the case of different religions and spiritual practices throughout the world, Babalaos and Regla Lucumi priestesses (Santería practice leaders) are the preferred community healers, providing guidance and advice in times of distress and celebrating personal and collective milestones. Without any doubt, Cuban psychotherapy has yet to tap into the vast potential of African indigenous spirituality that remains in Cuban society and has resisted the centuries of colonial violence. Some of the barriers in this regard constitute transnational racist representations that continue to reduce African spiritualities to stereotypes that speak of "witchcraft" or "black magic." From a health psychology perspective, emerging efforts are promising, as in the case of Afroache (Anderson, 2009), an HIV education, prevention, and counseling program that was developed as a collaborative initiative between personnel from the Centre for Prevention of HIV/AIDS and STIs and Regla Lucumi leaders and practitioners.

Other traditional healing methods utilized in Cuba include the use of herbs, homeopathic remedies, floral essences, universal energy courses, yoga, and tai-chi. Workshops and trainings in this area are advertised as part of the programs of professional conferences (Hominis Organizing Committee, 2002, 2005). The use of these traditional healing methods is also common in other disciplines, as in the case of medicine, where family physicians learn complementary and alternative medicine, commonly known in Cuba as natural and traditional medicine. This knowledge is integrated into courses on physiology, anatomy, and other clinical courses physicians take as part of their training. Some of the methods utilized by physicians include the use of herbs, floral essences, acupuncture, meditation exercise training, and music and art therapy (Dresang et al., 2005).

Research and supervision

Cuban research in counseling and psychotherapy has continued with the tradition of critical analysis, adaptation, and development of new interventions looking at the specific needs determined by Cuba's unique context. Current research areas include emotional intelligence, the role of psychotherapy in disease prevention, and national and community identity development among others (N. Guillard, personal communication, June 29, 2010). Particular emphasis has been placed historically on researching the role of psychology in relation to acute and chronic diseases. This research has resulted in the inclusion of psychologists in a new model of family health services (previously discussed), making it easier to provide psychotherapy in a more direct and personalized way targeting groups such as the elderly, adolescents, pregnant teens, young smokers, high-risk youth, and people living under extreme stress.

In addition to research conducted within Cuban universities, the Center for Psychological and Sociological Research (Centro de Investigaciones Psicológicas y Sociológicas, CIPS) plays an important role. This center was created in October of 1983 and is part of the Social Sciences Council within the Ministry of Science, Technology, and the Environment (CIPS, 2008). The creation of the center resulted from the restructuring of the then Social Sciences Institute and the Cuban Academy of Sciences. Whereas originally the Center divided its research areas into psychology and sociology, currently it has shifted into organizing its structure around research issues or programs from an interdisciplinary approach. Some of the main areas of research include social structures and inequity, family, youth, religion, psycho-social studies in health, learning for change, creativity for transformation, and human change, among others. Results from research conducted are published in books, *cuadernos* (notebooks), and in local and international journals. One of the main journals in counseling is the *Journal of Cuban Psychology*, which originated in 1984 with the objective of contributing to the education of professionals in psychology and other disciplines, and disseminating knowledge generated from Cuban research in psychology (University of Havana, 2007).

Clinical supervision in Cuba is provided by Faculty of Psychology members. The Cuban Society of Psychology is currently considering elaborating guidelines for supervision within its ethical code. There are no additional provisions related to clinical supervision for practitioners beyond those included during their training at the undergraduate and graduate levels. A network of provincial groups from the Society of Health Psychologists assists those psychologists of different specializations requiring advice or support with particular cases locally. Clinical supervision, however, is a standard practice by psychologists who adhere to psychoanalytic approaches. The Cuban Society of Psychology is currently considering including requirements related to clinical supervision in its by-laws (N. Guillard, personal communication, June 29, 2010).

Strengths, weaknesses, opportunities, and challenges

Cuba's creative responses to the socio-political and economical challenges have resulted in a strong body of psychotherapists who have integrated different epistemologies and approaches to respond to the particular needs of their clients. The emphasis on social historical perspectives along with the development of participatory community-based interventions have become a significant contribution Cuban psychologists have made to Latin American psychotherapeutic perspectives. Additionally, the state's commitment to fund training and research in counseling and psychotherapy, as well as its provision of employment to all graduates has resulted in some degree in the stability professionals require to dedicate fully to practicing and innovating in their fields. Another strength in Cuban psychology is its interdisciplinarity and community focus, which has resulted in a rich practice that has expanded from individual diagnosis into richer interactions with diverse communities, with other professions, and in diverse areas including service delivery, planning, and policy development.

Some of the weaknesses found in Cuban psychotherapy relate to the previously mentioned difficulties of integrating traditional healing methods that can increase the impact of mainstream approaches. Another weakness mentioned by García-Averasturri (1985) that persists today relates to the need for more scientific publications in psychology to facilitate knowledge translation across different community and professional generations. From the 1990s and into the new millennium, Cuban psychotherapists have also been forced to fight against the limitations imposed by the American embargo, which sought to isolate Cuba economically and intellectually. In spite of this, significant efforts are made continuously to foster transnational dialogues with counselors and psychotherapists from around the world via exchanges, conferences, and research.

The need for effective responses to regional and continental phenomena such as violence, economic recession, poverty, natural disasters, and their resulting impact on mental health have provided an opportunity for Cuban psychotherapists to share their expertise beyond their national territory, continuing with a long tradition of Cuban professionals as ambassadors for the development of excellence in healthcare and assisting other countries in responding to national emergencies, as in the case of Haiti following the earthquake of 2010. Measures adopted by the government of Cuba related to decentralization of services particularly looking into advancing the Millennium Goals in all provinces, along with the increased number of students registered in psychology undergraduate programs, and Cuban society's interdisciplinary healthcare system, can provide opportunities for innovative research.

The main challenge for Cuban psychology relates to the need to maintain the richness of community, interdisciplinary mental healthcare in a global context where individual fees for service paradigms are predominant. Cuban psychologists need to continue to engage in knowledge production and research to facilitate transitions among different generations of practitioners. For this purpose, promotion of local, national, and international research partnerships can greatly benefit not only Cuba, but also practitioners from other countries who would be enriched by Cuba's experiences in community participation and interdisciplinarity in mental health promotion and counseling.

Future directions

As previously indicated, imminent high numbers of new graduates in psychology and the emergence of new specializations call for the need to establish an institutional body dedicated to the accreditation, coordination, specialization, and expansion of counseling and psychotherapy in Cuba. In this regard, the Cuban Psychological Society is expected to play a pivotal role.

Continuing with its tradition, Cuban counseling and psychotherapy is expected to review, innovate, adapt, implement, and exchange psychotherapeutic perspectives tailored to the specific needs of Cuban society. Additionally, the increase in the number of psychotherapists will provide an excellent opportunity to expand coverage to particular communities and to continue to contribute to mental health initiatives transnationally.

Conclusion

This chapter has provided a brief characterization of counseling and psychotherapy in Cuba. Day-to-day psychotherapeutic practice in a dynamic socio-political-economical environment has strengthened Cuban practitioners by looking at developing dialectical approaches that emphasize the interrelation of the individual, community, and society at large, while critically examining diverse perspectives and theories that respond to the particularities of Cuban contexts. This praxis in resistance against hegemonic forces that have sought to isolate Cuban knowledge production has also resulted in conscious efforts towards epistemological flexibility, where different perspectives are examined, adapted, innovated, and applied to Cuban society's day-to-day old and new mental health challenges and opportunities.

Notes

1 Other analyses pertaining to Cuba's economic performance with respect to the Human Development Index (i.e., Gross National Income per capita or Gross Domestic Product) are inadequate to measure the country's economic performance in comparison to other countries given that it does not participate in the International Comparisons Program (UNDP, 2010).
2 For a discussion on these theorists see Daniels (2005).

References

Adefarakan, E. (2011). *Yoruba indigenous knowledges in the African diaspora: Knowledge, power and the politics of indigenous spirituality* (doctoral dissertation). Retrieved from https://tspace.library.utoronto.ca/handle/1807/29656

Anderson, T. (2009). HIV/AIDS in Cuba, a rights based analysis. *Health and Human Rights, An International Journal, 11*(1), 93–104.

Ares Mucio, P. (2010). *Speech on Occasion of the National Day of Psychology.* Havana, Cuba: Cuban Society of Psychology.

Argyriadis, K. (2005). Religión de indígenas, religion de científicos, construcción de la cubanidad y Santería [Religion of scientists and indigenous peoples, the construction of Cuban identity and Santería]. *Desacatos, 17*, 85–106.

Becerra, J. (2008). *Varela, Martí y Varona: Padres fundadores de la psicologia cubana* [Varela, Martí, and Varona: Founding fathers of Cuban psychology]. Retrieved from http://cubapsi.blogia.com/2008/121501-varela-marti-y-varona-padres-fundadores-de-la-psicologia-cubana.php

Bernal, G. (1985). A history of psychology in Cuba. *Journal of Community Psychology, 13*, 222–235.

Centre for Psychological and Sociological Research (CIPS) (2008). Experiencias de investigacion social en Cuba [Social research experiences in Cuba]. Havana, Cuba: CIPS.

Corral, R. (2008). Historia (mínima) de la facultad de psicología de La Habana [(Brief) history of Havana's faculty of Psychology]. Unpublished manuscript.

Council of Ministers of the Republic of Cuba. (1973). *Ley 1254* [Law 1254]. Havana: Gaceta Oficial de la República de Cuba.

Cros Sandoval, M. (2006). *Worldview, the Orichas, and Santeria.* Gainesville, FL: University Press of Florida.

Cuban Society of Psychology (2002). *Código de etica* [Ethics code]. Retrieved from http://cubapsi.blogia.com/2007/030202-codigo-de-etica.php

Daniels, H. (ed.) (2005). *An Introduction to Vygotsky.* New York: Routledge.

de Armas, R., & Espi, N. (2004). *El sistema de educación superior de la república de Cuba, junta de acreditación nacional ministerio de educación de Cuba* [Postsecondary education system of the Republic of Cuba, National Accreditation Board Ministry of Education of Cuba]. Retrieved from http://tuning.unideusto.org/tuningal/images/stories/presentaciones/cuba_doc.pdf

Dominguez-Alonso, E. & Zacca, E. (2011). Sistema de salud de Cuba [The health system of Cuba]. *Salud Pública de México*, *53*(2), 168–176.

Dresang, L. T., Brebrick, L., Murray, D., Shallue, A., & Sullivan-Vedder, J. (2005). Family medicine in Cuba: Community-oriented primary care and complementary and alternative medicine. *Journal of the American Board of Family Medicine*, *18*(4), 297–303.

Febles, M. (n.d.) *El cuerpo como mediador de las funciones psíquicas superiores en busca de fundamentos de la terapia corporal* [The body as a mediator of superior psychological functions, in search of the foundations of body therapy]. Unpublished manuscript.

García-Averasturi, L. (1985). Community health psychology in Cuba. *Journal of Community Psychology 13*, 117–123.

Government of the Republic of Cuba. (2011). *Sitio del Gobierno de la Republica de Cuba* [Website of the republic of Cuba]. Retrieved from www.cubagob.cu/

Hernandez, F. (1996). Aproximacion al concepto de orientacion psicologica [Introduction to the concept of psychological counselling]. *Revista Cubana de Psicologia 13*(1), 17–26.

Hominis Organizing Committee. (2002). *Programa Hominis 2002: Hominis* [2002 Hominis Conference Program]. La Habana, Cuba: Sociedad Cubana de Psicologia.

Hominis Organizing Committee. (2005). Programa convencion intercontinental de psicologia y ciencias sociales y humanas: Hominis [Program of the intercontinental convention on psychology, social sciences and humanities. La Habana, Cuba: Sociedad Cubana de Psicologia.

Institute of History of Cuba. (2011). *The US military occupation of Cuba.* Retrieved on January 10th, 2011 from www.cubagob.cu/otras_info/historia/home.html

Luna-Morales, E., Sierra-Perez, D., & Gandul Salabarria, L. (2009). La transformacion del policlinico en Cuba de cara al siglo XXI [The transformation of the Cuban polyclinical towards the 21st century]. *Revista Cubana de Medicina Integra, 25*(2). Retrieved from http://bvs.sld.cu/revistas/mgi/vol25_2_09/mgi16209.htm

Ministry of Justice. (2007). *Reglamento para el trabajo docente y metodologico en la educacion superior* [Postsecundary education teaching and methodology bylaws]. Havana: Gaceta Oficial de la Republica de Cuba.

Organization of Ibero-American States. (2006). *Estructura y titulaciones de educacion superior en Cuba* [Structure and titles in postsecondary education in Cuba]. Retrieved from www.oei.es/homo logaciones/cuba.pdf

Orozco, R., & Bolivar, N. (1998). *Cubasanta, comunistas, santeros y cristianos en la isla de Fidel Castro* [HollyCuba, communists, Santeria practitioners and Christians in the island of Fidel Castro]. Madrid: Ediciones El Pais.

Pérez-Stable, E. (1985). Community medicine in Cuba. *Journal of Community Psychology, 13*, 124–137.

Pérez-Lovelle, R. (2003). La psicología de la salud en Cuba [Health psychology in Cuba]. *Revista psicología científica.com, 5*(16). Retrieved from www.psicologiacientifica.com/bv/psicologia-112-1-lapsicologia-de-la-salud-en-cuba.html

Presidency of the Republic of Cuba. (1974). *Decreto 3771* [Decree 3771]. Havana: Gaceta Oficial de la República de Cuba.

Roca, M. (2007). *Es legítima la integración en psicoterapia? ... polemicemos un poco* [Is it legitimate integration in psychotherapy? ... let's debate]. Keynote presentation at the University of Nuevo León Congress, Monterrey, Mexico.

Roca, M. (2010). Profundizando en las terapias constructivas [In depth analysis into constructivist therapies]. Presentation at CIMEQ Conference, Havana, Cuba.

United Nations Development Programme (UNDP) (2008). Plan de acción para el programa de país entre el gobierno de Cuba y el programa de las Naciones Unidas para el Desarrollo [Country action between the government of Cuba and the United Nations Development Program]. Havana, Cuba: UNDP Cuba.

United Nations Development Programme (UNDP) (2010). *Human Development Report 2010, 20th Anniversary Edition.* New York: United Nations Development Programme.

United Nations Development Programme (UNDP) (2011). *Human Development Report 2011.* New York: United Nations Development Programme.

University of Havana. (2007). *Revista Cubana de Psicologia: Acerca de esta revista* [Cuban psychology journal About this journal]. Retrieved from http://pepsic.bvsalud.org/revistas/rcp/eaboutj.htm

University of Havana. (2011). *Plan de estudio facultad de psicologia* [Curriculum of the faculty of psychology]. Retrieved from www.uh.cu/

Varona, E. (1888). *Conferencias filosoficas, segunda serie, psicologia* [Philosophical conferences, second series, psychology]. Havana: Imprenta El Retiro.

Wedel, J. (2004). *Santeria Healing, a Journey into the Afro-Cuban World of Divinities, Spirits, and Sorcery.* Gainesville, FL: University Press of Florida.

12

COUNSELING AND PSYCHOTHERAPY IN MEXICO

Moving towards a Latin American perspective

Juan José Sánchez-Sosa and Angélica Riveros

Introduction

Mexico is a widely diverse country in many respects. It currently has slightly over 120 million inhabitants (INEGI, 2011). Mexicans' main language is Spanish, although a number of regional pre-Columbian languages are still spoken on the streets by approximately 6% of the population including, in descending order, Nahuatl (the language of the ancient Aztecs), Maya, Zapotec, and Mixtec; but mostly in addition to Spanish. In terms of religion, approximately 88% of Mexicans are Roman Catholic; other religions in descending order include Protestant, Other Christian, Jewish, "other," and "none" (INEGI, 2011).

Ethnic groups in Mexico are normally defined in terms of region-predominant languages but it is difficult to ascertain ancestor predominance since most medium to large communities tend to reflect various degrees of ethnic mixtures. It is widely accepted, however, that a majority of the population in Mexico involve some degree of "mestizaje"; that is, some degree of combination of European (or other) and indigenous ancestry (Cosío-Villegas, 2009; Miller, 2004; White, 2002).

The predominant use of the terms *psychotherapy* and *counseling* by both professionals and the general public in Mexico is related to the main antecedents of the development of these concepts as professional specialties. Psychotherapy is perceived as a much more defined mental health-aimed set of procedures or interventions than that of counseling. Psychotherapy is widely perceived as done mainly by psychologists and psychiatrists, while counseling is perceived as done by anyone with specialized training to provide problem-solving advice in such settings as schools, health facilities, churches, community centers, sports organizations, industry, or the armed forces.

Although both counseling and psychotherapy are expected to be carried out by professionals whose training involves research-based decisions and interventions, in Mexico psychotherapy is widely perceived as requiring more advanced, in-depth formal training than counseling. Also, in comparison to counselors, psychotherapists are generally expected to deal with more severe human problems usually involving intense emotional suffering and serious maladaptation, often accompanied by deleterious interpersonal, family or immediate community conflict. Counseling, on the other hand, usually implies more focused, brief interventions aimed at helping individuals or small groups make relatively specific decisions which, in turn, are expected to help solve particular problems in the near future. In fact, in contrast with the term *psychotherapist,* the term or title *counselor* is neither formally defined nor legally protected under Mexican law. Thus, in this chapter the terms psychotherapy and counseling will be used as reflecting these general characteristics.

In the scope of the background mentioned above, the purpose of the present chapter is to describe and reflect on some key historical antecedents of psychotherapy and counseling in Mexico as well as their current status, perspectives and some challenges, regarding such issues as education, training, ethics, and regulatory aspects of their professional practice.

Brief history of counseling and psychotherapy

Early accounts of healing practices in pre-Columbian Mexico include descriptions of interventions by priests to help alleviate emotional and psychosomatic suffering. People during the times of the Aztec empire referred to *susto* (fright) and other types of distress as complaints involving both emotional and physical components (Estrada, Ponce-de-León, & López, 2004; López-Austin, 1997; Martínez, 2006). Although oral tradition accounts of caring for such conditions collected by Catholic Spanish monks by the late 16th century rarely included other ethnic groups and regions, it is highly likely that earlier civilizations such as the Maya and Teotihuacan engaged in similar practices. Those are probably the earliest documented accounts of some type of psychosomatic suffering assumed to require a relatively specific expert intervention in the American continent (Sánchez-Sosa, 1998).

Psychology in general and psychotherapy in particular in Mexico developed within, or in very close ties with academic settings. For example, teachings of early scholars such as Friar Alonso de la Veracruz (1507–1584) at the University of Mexico, founded in 1551, included his own treatises, one of which was titled *Physica Speculatio* (better translated as physical research) and included psychology. Although his writings had religious overtones, Veracruz was known for his naturalistic approach to knowledge and a keen interest in man as a changing being (Ricard, 1986; Robles, 1942). This approach probably helped stabilize the acceptance of conceptions combining religious with natural views, even in conservative colonial times (Sánchez-Sosa & Valderrama-Iturbe, 2001).

Up to the second decade of the 19th century, numerous scholars in Latin American universities gradually adopted other philosophical notions. The works of Rene Descartes, and others, introduced more mechanistic conceptions of the world. In this context, some Mexican scholars published texts dealing with the application of these new traditions to psychological issues. For example, Benito Díaz de Gamarra (1745–1783), who published extensive reviews of proposals by Descartes, Nicholas Malebranche and Christian Wolff, proposed: " … it should certainly be affirmed that the spirit has its own seat only in the brain, even though we cannot be certain about its exact location inside it" (Navarro, 1983, p. 105). Although it would be difficult to ascertain how much these early academic teachings specifically influenced the development of psychology in general and psychotherapy or counseling in particular, they certainly helped set the historic stage for easier acceptance of modern scientific views (Navarro, 1983).

By the late eighteenth and early nineteenth centuries, the context propitiated by both the industrial revolution and the growing independence *zeitgeist* in most American colonies facilitated new scientific and technological developments which ended up affecting psychology in key but gradual ways. This was especially true in Latin American countries where several decades of political unrest still persisted after their declarations of independence occurring during the first three decades of the 19th century. Psychological applications more specifically aimed at solving mental health problems actually started developing during the early 20th century. Thus, a relatively large leap in Mexican history would end up placing us in times when more specific factors are known to have influenced contemporary psychotherapy and counseling.

By the mid-1930s, psychology and its applications in Mexico were acquiring a clear-cut academic and professional image and were regarded as contributions able to help solve human problems. Many key advances continued their development linked with Mexico's flagship university, now called the National Autonomous University of Mexico (*Universidad Nacional Autónoma de México* or UNAM). The basic program curriculum in the section of Psychology within the Faculty of Philosophy and Letters added courses in genetics and psychology, mental hygiene (prevention), projective techniques, psychophysiology, psychopathology, and psycho-dynamics (Korbman-Shein, 1997). Psychology students in training started to fulfill new training requirements such as supervised clinical training in hospitals and clinics. The total number of students in professional training in psychology had increased to approximately 100, most of whom were at UNAM. In 1945 Mexico's public health system founded a psychiatry–psychology department in its largest public pediatric hospital, with three specific service areas: diagnostics, psychomotor development, and psychotherapy (Korbman-Shein, 1997).

By the 1950s some key developments and transitions had occurred in Mexican psychology. Professional training received a renewed impact from two psychodynamic approaches through the initiative of two main groups of clinicians working at UNAM: one aligned with the culturalistic Frommian tradition after Erich Fromm himself permanently settled near Mexico City. Some key sponsors of this movement included three well-known professors: Guillermo Dávila, Abraham Fortes, and Ramón de la Fuente. The second modality remained within the orthodox Freudian tradition through the initiative of Ramón Parres, Santiago Ramírez, José Remus, Fernando Césarman, and José Cueli, also professors in either or both UNAM School of Psychology and its School of Medicine.

By the early 1960s, training options in psychotherapy and counseling widened after the foundation of the first large private school of psychology at the Ibero-American University (*Universidad Iberoamericana* or UIA) headed by professor Ramón Arias. The UIA departments of psychology and human development involved the second largest facilities for the education of psychotherapists in Mexico. This university set the stage for the development of a strong third clinical group, often referred to as *the third school* linked to the humanistic tradition of Carl Rogers, a new movement led by Juan Lafarga, SJ (Galindo, 2004). In the domain of public education, the expansion of programs has been even stronger since all Mexican states have at least one significant public university.

The last three to four decades have witnessed highly significant advancements, especially in the field of psychotherapy. First, professional, academic, and social recognition of psychologists as therapists is now widely and firmly established in Mexico and other Latin American countries. This is in stark contrast with the predominant panorama in the 1960s, when only physicians trained as psychoanalysts or psychiatrists were perceived as professionals able to address serious psychological problems. Second, Mexican psychotherapists are incorporating research-based interventions in their professional practice and an ever-increasing number of training programs are also adopting them for their curricula. Third, probably as a consequence of this advancement, psychologists with postgraduate training in either cognitive-behavioral therapy or behavioral medicine are occupying job openings in the public and private sectors in never before seen proportions. Fourth, serious, peer-reviewed outlets for research in health-related applications of psychology have increased from nearly nil, to having a 4:1 proportion to outlets in psychiatry. Finally, training and ethical standards as well as Mexican laws regulating the practice of psychotherapy are now almost comparable to those of developed nations both in terms of requirements and social acceptance.

Counselor education programs, accreditation, licensure, and certification

Currently, public and private universities offer an entry-to-practice degree called *Psychology Licentiate* or licensed psychologist, which is a strictly professional degree but *not* a specialized one. Overall, after 12 years of elementary, high school, and BA education (with a duration of 6, 3, and 3 years respectively), in order to become a psychologist one attends a specifically designated professional program exclusively in psychology for 5–6 years at a university. All specialized and advanced training needed to formally become a psychotherapist or a counselor occurs in post-graduate (post-licentiate) programs.

With the exception of those aimed at educational and career guidance, formal university-based programs to train counselors in Mexico are very recent. Most likely one of the reasons for this is the conceptual and professional dispersion of a counselor's function and expected services. The predominant public perception is one of an *orientation* expert, who mainly functions in career (vocation) guidance and school counseling. Within this specific area of career or occupation guidance, the training of counselors in Mexico occurs as part of teacher training, mainly for the high school and bachelor levels or in training programs for entry level practice (licentiate) in pedagogy and education. Although most such programs still include some basic courses with psychological content, their curricula tend to revolve more around educational theoretical approaches such as constructivism (Gavilán, 2007; López-Carrasco, 1991) than around research-based or empirically supported counseling interventions.

In areas more closely related to severe problems of human adaptation or mental health, the distinction of programs dedicated to training counselors or psychotherapists is somewhat difficult because their formal titles tend to revolve around such terms as *health psychology* or *clinical psychology*. This is likely to change because a new law regulating the practice or the mental health professions and specialties such as psychotherapy is more specific regarding education and credentials of psychotherapists and about the term *psychotherapy* itself. Since the law does not include counseling in any section, this is likely to widen the conceptual gap between the two disciplines instead of making them appear more similar. When accredited through the process implemented by the Council for Accreditation of Higher Education (COPAES) (described below), many of these basic entry to practice-level programs resemble those designated as *Combined and Integrated* in the USA (CCIDPIP, 2009). Nearly all such programs involve course, laboratory and practicum work, and a formal examination, which grants the corresponding licentiate diploma (for a detailed description of the system see Sánchez-Sosa, 2004). There are currently some 700 such basic entry-level to practice programs in Mexico, but no more than 75 are actually accredited. Perhaps the two most important differences between these general, basic licensing degrees (common to most Latin American Countries) and those of CCIDPIP is that they involve only a small number of hours of clinical practicum work under supervision and only about half of them involve research-based contents. For an updated list of accredited programs at this basic entry to practice level in psychology visit www.copaes.org.mx/home/motor/resultado_programas.php.

The quality of postgraduate (post-licensing) degrees from either public or private universities is evaluated in Mexico by the National Council for Science and Technology (CoNaCyT), which registers and lists postgraduate (master's and doctorate) programs in all disciplines and specialties along a four-level program classification system in terms of characteristics, quality, and performance. There are currently only five doctoral programs and eight master's programs related to health–clinical psychology registered and supported by the CoNaCyT system nationwide and nearly all are, so far, in public universities. For details see www.conacyt.gob. mx/Becas/Calidad/Paginas/Becas_ProgramasPosgradosNacionalesCalidad.aspx.

Although this CoNaCyT evaluation and register does not formally constitute an *accreditation* process, it works as such in the sense that its registered programs are in higher demand from students; they have more stringent admissions criteria, they are more likely to get funding for postgraduate training and research, and their graduates frequently obtain better professional or academic positions. The Council also administers federal funds from the Ministry of Education to support research and postgraduate training. So, for instance, all postgraduate students of programs registered by the CoNaCyT system get a scholarship and additional funding for national and international academic collaboration activities. Also, faculty from those programs normally have a better chance to obtain funding for research projects and many belong to a nationwide researchers system (also administered by CoNaCyT) which gives university professors who are productive (in terms of publications) researchers a supplementary monthly stipend along a peer-reviewed four-level ranking system. At the higher level cases the corresponding monetary amount may be nearly as large as the professor's monthly salary. It should be pointed out that private universities can also apply for evaluation and registry of their postgraduate programs with the CoNaCyT.

Programs of private universities, for both entry level (licentiate) and postgraduate, are to be registered, and are expected to obtain the *Official Recognition of Studies Validity* (RVOE) certificate from the Ministry of Education. The authorities grant the certificate through either of two paths: first, a joint committee designated by the Health and Education ministries recommends the latter to issue the program certificate. Second, the program becomes affiliated with the equivalent program of a recognized public university. This means that the new (private) program actually adopts the structure, curriculum, academic criteria, operating systems, etc., from one of Mexico's recognized public universities.

It is important to point out that the RVOE recognition certificate, more than actually involving the detailed evaluation of the academic quality of a program, as expected of an accreditation process, includes the registration of the *basic* legal and academic features required to provide education in any area or discipline.

In terms of accreditation processes, the only entity and process formally recognized by the higher education federal and state authorities in Mexico is based on a series of boards or councils independent from universities or the educational federal or state authorities and administered by an overarching body called the Council for the Accreditation of Higher Education (COPAES). COPAES promotes and facilitates the inception of accrediting boards by disciplines or professions, and supports and oversees their operation. It should be pointed out that, up to the present, this system accredits only basic entry-level to practice (licentiate) psychology programs but not yet specialty-level (master's or higher) programs, so counseling or psychotherapy are yet to be included.

Private programs and universities can also choose to advertise their accreditation by foreign boards such as the Council for the Accreditation of Counseling and Related Educational Programs in the USA (CACREP), though very few counseling master's programs from private universities are listed as accredited by this body. It should be pointed out that this type of accreditation, however, has relatively little bearing on the legality of professional practice by their graduates in Mexico, since regulatory laws specify that graduates from programs of private universities lacking the RVOE designation will not be issued the corresponding license (*cedula*) and their university diploma will not be endorsed or validated by the Vice Ministry of Higher Education (SEP-SES, 2011).

Regarding certification of counselors and psychotherapists, there is not yet an officially recognized board or council in Mexico; this process is at its initial stages and some self-designated certifying entities are beginning to appear. Some such boards contend that counseling and psychotherapy are the same or equivalent, and therefore encompass both. Charters of some such organizations include almost any activity which will purportedly lead to the advancement of counseling and psychotherapy and their purposes involve all the way from training to continuing education, to certification of counselors and psychotherapists.

Finally, licensure for professional practice in Mexico is tied both to the designation of the corresponding training program and its registered level (licentiate, master's, or doctorate) with the Ministry of Education. The formal process for postgraduate licensure for either counselors or psychotherapists is conducted through the same official channels as those for basic entry-level practice. Once a master's or doctorate university diploma is issued upon graduation from a registered program it becomes, in turn, registered by the Ministry of Education's Office for the Regulation of the Professions. After formally authenticating the corresponding paperwork, this office issues an actual master's or doctoral-level license called *cedula* which legally authorizes the recipient to practice the corresponding specialized professional services. It should be pointed out, however, that penalizing individuals who practice without complying with this process has not been easy to enforce as it usually depends on some formal complaint being filed by a user or consumer. New legislative initiatives currently in progress are aiming at addressing and regulating these possibilities.

Current counseling and psychotherapy theories, processes and trends

Including intra-theoretical variations in emphasis or conceptions linked to specific authors, the predominant five psychotherapy theories in Mexico in order of historical appearance are the Freudian psychodynamic approach, the Frommian psychodynamic approach, the Humanistic approach of Carl Rogers, various systemic approaches, and the contemporary cognitive-behavioral traditions. Other approaches also have some representativeness but they constitute a minority.

Psychotherapists frequently join associations, which vary widely in type, level of activity, academic or public visibility, and influence. Most such societies purport to be nonprofit organizations and some function only as long as their original founders remain at the helm. Some exceptions include societies founded by scholars of particular clinical psychology departments or schools (mostly private) but end up functioning as guilds aimed at promoting or guarding relatively specific interests. Many such establishments end up as multipurpose businesses; they provide training, offer psychotherapeutic services, promote client demand through talks and short courses and even offer certification, thus engaging in conflict of interests along various lines. The training provided by many such groups is almost never recognized by any of the systems described earlier and their admission criteria are frankly negligent. Again, in the absence of a formal complaint it is difficult to "fish out" and penalize them. On the other hand, psychotherapeutic organizations that do not entail some level of business activities show wide variations in permanence, activity and cohesiveness and, in time, some either disappear or end up as paper organizations.

Most Mexican psychotherapists work in private practice. Many of those who hold a faculty position at a university or a baccalaureate level college, or work at a public healthcare facility will still tend to conduct a private office in the evening. Public institutions such as those in the National Institutes of Health network have specialized research hospitals that are currently showing a booming interest in hiring graduates from registered cognitive-behavioral master's programs. Some significant examples include the hospitals of the National Institutes of

Psychiatry, Cancer, Nutrition, Pediatrics, Respiratory Diseases, and Rehabilitation, and three large general hospitals. One public research hospital that runs most of its psychotherapeutic services within the Frommian psychodynamic tradition is the National Institute of Perinatology.

Indigenous and traditional healing methods

Ancient Mexicans developed healing methods for the treatment of problems such as impotence, "nervousness," "fright" hysteria, insomnia, and anger (Berenzon & Saavedra, 2002), many of which are still used today by traditional healers. The explanations for the development of such distress normally include an intense emotional reaction to an event, the impact of negative emotions such as jealousy or envy, or interpersonal conflict, as causes of discomfort and suffering. The recovery of health implies some form of balance restoration (emotional, spiritual, energy, etc.) through practices that allow for such recovery (Vallejo, 2006; Villatoro & PIES, 2001). Most healing procedures start by symbolizing the disease as a battle in which the suffering takes on a sense of earthly or divine significance for the person. This process will also involve spiritual guidance to give meaning to what happened in terms of a spiritual learning and/or "cosmic" balance. In some cases, the individual is expected to pay or compensate any harm he/she did to the natural or cultural environment, by performing activities prescribed by the healer (Vallejo, 2006).

One of the most developed areas is herbalism, since there is evidence of the effectiveness of chemical substances in plants which were applied to address problems of emotional regulation through taking certain herbal teas and cleansing rituals. The effectiveness of these practices often lies in a cultural environment that assigns healing value to these practices. Thus, they tend to be more common in relatively isolated rural areas for individuals with little schooling.

Healers acquire their knowledge through oral tradition, usually from other family members, and are expected to have the right vocation or the "gift," which refers to a divine predisposition to healing. The training begins in adolescence, at first observing and listening to explanations of the guide, then as assistant and then healing others under supervision. Healing is considered a craft and an art (Villatoro & PIES, 2001). Learning specifics include the type of symptom, learning rituals, spiritual communication, and/or the effects of specific plants, the proper way to use it and even the time of collection (Berenzon & Saavedra, 2002).

Cultural competence is crucial for therapeutic activities for Mexicans in general and indigenous communities in particular, and this applies also to many Hispanic communities in the USA and Canada. Lacking such competence will affect the credibility of the therapist and patients' adaptation or interaction with their community. The notions of meaning resignification, balance, and searching for it are especially valuable for interpreting the events and to foster the feeling of doing something to solve problems that lie outside the control of the person. Few mainstream psychotherapists actually incorporate these notions or tools in their practice and probably do so more in terms of recognizing their cultural origin; still, only some are likely to use them as part of conventional interventions.

Research and supervision

Perhaps as much as 70–80% of all peer-reviewed research publications in the applied sciences, including psychotherapy, in Mexico stem from projects conducted in public facilities and they tend to be financially supported by public funds (OECD-CERI, 2004). Most funds are jointly provided by grants from the National Council of Science and Technology (CoNaCyT) or its state equivalents, and the research offices of public universities in all 31 states and the Federal District. There are some peer-reviewed journals in Latin America; most are published in Mexico,

Colombia, Chile, Brazil, and Argentina. Some researchers make a point of publishing in Spanish almost as a statement of principle, even if they risk reducing the number of international citations to their articles. There are currently approximately 20 journals with some specific reference to research in psychotherapy or clinical and counseling work edited and published in Latin America, but only about 10 are actually peer reviewed.

Mexican psychologists currently conduct research studies on psychotherapy and counseling with a larger proportion of publications on psychotherapy. Recent examples of some of the most researched areas include anxiety (e.g., Robles, Flores, Jurado & Páez, 2002), depression (e.g., Alvarez, Cortés, Ortiz, Estrella & Sánchez-Sosa, 2007), chronic pain (e.g., Domínguez, Martínez, Olvera & Victorio, 1997), quality of life of chronic patients (e.g., Riveros, Cortazar, Alcázar & Sánchez, 2005), dysfunctional eating behaviors (e.g., Vázquez-Arévalo et al., 2005) social phobia (e.g., Gil & Hernández, 2009; Morales, López & Antona, 2010), abused children (e.g., Rojas, 2007), and addictive behaviors (e.g., Oropeza, Medina & Sánchez, 2007). Some recent examples of studies in counseling include such areas as: communication skills with sexual partners (e.g., Robles, Moreno, Frías, Rodríguez, Barroso, et al., 2006), alcohol abuse by adolescents (e.g., Martínez, Pedroza, Vacío, Jiménez & Salazar, 2008), marital guidance (e.g., Barragán, González & Ayala, 2004), sexual guidance (e.g., Moral, 2011), career counseling (e.g., Fuentes, 2010), and drug abuse prevention (e.g., Rodríguez, Díaz, Gutiérrez, Guerrero & Lucio, 2011).

Supervision requirements vary widely depending on the service institution or the training program. Basic entry level to practice licentiate training in Mexico and other Latin American countries normally requires a minimum of 500 hours of supervised work, which usually occur during the fifth year and frequently tend to coincide with the thesis work of students. Since the new mental health law specifies required postgraduate training (master's or higher) for psychotherapists, most specialized training programs provide between 500 and 1000 hours of supervised clinical work. Perhaps the most noticeable exceptions are UNAM's behavioral medicine master's program, which requires 2000 hours, and its sleep disorders and school counseling master's programs, which involve 1600 hours. All three programs are rated as *consolidated* by the CoNaCyT system. In residence-like activities, the supervision process within these programs is usually carried out in vivo or in weekly or bi-weekly sessions where an expert faculty discusses cases with small groups of students and reach treatment decisions to follow. Many supervisors have a doctoral degree and none has less than a postgraduate (post-licensure) master's. Program coordinators or chairpersons normally appoint supervisors among those professors with the longest clinical and academic experience. Again, this will depend on such conditions as amount of resources and consolidation level of the program, among other factors.

Strengths, weaknesses, opportunities, and challenges

Only a few decades back psychotherapists in Mexico were perceived as practicing some obscure craft aimed at people with obscure problems. The notion of a reliable professional educated and trained through systematic research-based knowledge, just as physicians or any other well-respected health practitioner, is only now losing its novelty.

Another strength resides in the fact that, for the first time in Mexico's history, psychologists actually helped draft a law that regulates much of the professional practice of mental health caregivers. This experience proved invaluable in terms of the establishment of close connections with legislators, politicians, and representatives from other health professions, the media, and professional and scientific organizations. These connections helped further a goal set almost a decade ago by Mexican psychologists, in the sense of educating politicians, the media, and the public regarding psychology as science and profession.

A third strength stems from the fact that the health sector (public or private), normally a closed and conservative establishment which used to look down on psychologists as helpers only, is now realizing that human behavior is a key component of all health problems, physical or psychological, and that such problems demand in-depth expert knowledge of psychological mechanisms and their application. This has led to openings in health services previously out of the reach of psychologists, not only in Mexico but also in other Latin American countries.

Most weaknesses still relate to slow development of legal frameworks, scarcity of resources typical of countries in the majority of the world, and lack of professional accountability of therapists graduating from "diploma mills."

The new mental health law allows for providing feedback to high education institutions, politicians, lawmakers, policymaking entities, and the media. Another opportunity relates to taking advantage of increased mutual knowledge among psychologists and psychotherapists from Canada, Mexico, and the USA on such issues as those addressed in the present volume and in other publications on psychotherapy education, practice, ethics, etc., in order to reach viable regional agreements.

Addressing some contemporary challenges seems especially vital for further advancement of psychotherapy and counseling in Mexico. First, regulatory laws for the practice of psychotherapy and counseling are very recent and are not yet applicable in all jurisdictions. This is a consequence of decades of a legislative and regulatory vacuum which currently draw a somewhat bleak panorama. Hundreds of self-called psychotherapists and counselors have very deficient training or nearly no training at all, some of which have made clever use of advertising so consumers find it extremely difficult to distinguish serious psychotherapists or counselors from charlatans. Thus the challenge consists of speeding up strategies to educate the media and the public and caution them about the risks of using services of such dubious quality.

Second, closely linked to the previous point, the aforementioned longstanding regulatory vacuum also led to a proliferation of diploma mills which call themselves "schools" or "institutes" offering training in psychotherapy and/or counseling. Again, these instances not only admit nearly anyone but lack serious program components and find ways to benefit from legal loopholes in order to, for example, disguise the fact that graduates from their programs cannot obtain an actual license to practice. Since the regulatory system is clearly insufficient in terms of means to penalize such "schools" and their graduates, the challenge consists of devising and putting into effect strategies to enforce the law.

Third, the systematic requirement to develop training programs based on scientific research is not evolving as fast as would seem desirable. There has always been (and will be) a widespread respect in academic and service institutions for all kinds of psychotherapeutic approaches, but still in this context, the new law specifies that training and practice are to stem from sound scientific findings (Article 48). Thus the challenge consists of complying with the law through such means as continuing education and providing feedback to new proposed programs or to those about to undergo revision, among other strategies. Also, the law currently regulates psychotherapy in a jurisdiction of 22 million people but another 31 jurisdictions with some 100 million inhabitants are still in need of coverage; thus the careful lobbying task ahead seems enormous.

A fourth challenge stems from a meager culture in Mexico about demanding accountability from healthcare providers in general and psychotherapists and counselors in particular. Perhaps this is precisely one factor contributing to the scarcity of instances of complaint filing by users or consumers of psychotherapeutic services, which in turn (and in time) contributes to maintaining lenient standards for selecting a training program or to seek certification from a serious entity. A few capable and interest- and conflict-free certifying organizations have recently started operating but their impact on the field will probably be seen only in years to come.

147

Finally, the sheer scarcity of resources typical of developing nations has become a heavy burden for a faster and more consolidated development of psychotherapy and counseling in Mexico and other Latin American countries. Indeed, scarcity affects all the way from education and training, accreditation and certification, effective regulation, and scientific development. To complicate matters further, some instances of incompetent administration of resources or even corruption make it even harder to achieve satisfactory results in these areas.

Future directions

Counseling and psychotherapy in Mexico and Latin America are to benefit from a series of agendas undertaken by serious organizations, higher education institutions, regulatory bodies, and influential professionals and scientists in psychology. An important goal is to internationalize psychotherapy and counseling through joint research or applied projects. A key aspect of this endeavor must involve cultural and theoretical sensitivity to conceptions other than their own. Mastering or at least becoming closely familiar with a foreign language seems a future direction bound to improve research and professional communications as well as mutual respect. It should be noted that this is needed for all psychotherapists in the world. The authors hope that the widespread knowledge of the impressive effort by Mexican psychotherapists and counselors (all the way from faculty, researchers, practitioners, and disseminators) to further the development of these disciplines will help open some international doors. It is becoming critical to achieve well-deserved recognition by colleagues and organizations of the developed world.

Another future direction consists of strengthening research methodology skills in psychotherapists and counselors. It should be mentioned that the narrowness of the prevalent conceptions of counseling in Latin America seem particularly related to this need. Finally, both psychotherapists and counselors would greatly benefit from increasing their professional accountability in terms of the effectiveness of their interventions.

Conclusion

Both counseling and psychotherapy are alive, well, and growing in Mexico and Latin America. Strong academic, research, professional, and public image scenarios are benefitting from increasingly solid communities, especially in psychotherapy. While counseling is a little behind in some of these respects, recent circumstances point toward viable and encouraging perspectives, although further Latin American integration of efforts is still a task to be addressed more forcefully. In a context of increasing diversity, the recent development of these disciplines in Mexico denotes consolidation, growth, and increased social impact. As recent developments give evidence, the richness of history and traditions in Mexico, even from ancient times, has blended with contemporary science and society in such a graceful way that it has engendered a landscape that can only be portrayed in optimistic terms. Strengths are well preserved, weaknesses are well identified, and challenges will continue to receive enthusiastic and appropriate attention. It is precisely systematic efforts like those which led to the publication of the present volume, the kind of sign that points toward showing the way for the future.

References

Alvarez, L. M., Cortés, J. F., Ortiz, S. L., Estrella, J. & Sánchez-Sosa, J. J. (2007). Computer program in the treatment of major depression and cognitive impairment in university students. *Computers in Human Behavior, 24*(4), 816–826.

Barragán, T. L., González, V. J. & Ayala, V. H. (2004). A marriage guidance model based on conflict solution and reciprocal reinforcement. *Salud Mental, 27*(3), 65–73.

Berenzon, S., & Saavedra, N. (2002). Presencia de la Herbolaria en el Tratamiento de los problemas emocionales: Entrevista a los curanderos urbanos [Presence of herbalism in treating emotional problems: Interview with urban healers]. *Salud Mental, 25*(1), 55–66.

Consortium of Combined-Integrated Doctoral Programs in Psychology (CCIDPIP) (2009). *Consensus Conference on Combined-Integrated Doctoral Training in Psychology.* Retrieved from www.jmu.edu/ccidpip/

Cosío-Villegas, D. (2009). *Historia general de Mexico* [General history of Mexico]. Mexico City: El Colegio de Mexico.

Domínguez, T. B., Martínez, G. S., Olvera, Y. & Victorio, A. (1997). Stress management with hypnosis and sensorial-emotional reversal in chronic-pain cases. *Experimentelle und Klinische Hypnose, 13*(2), 125–132.

Estrada, D. M., Ponce-de-León, P. I. & López, V. R. (October, 2004). *La importancia de las enfermedades inexplicables mágico-religiosas de los diferentes grupos étnicos de México y su relación con la práctica médica* [The importance of intricate, magical-religious diseases in diverse Mexican ethnic groups and their relation to medical practice]. Proceedings of the Fourth Virtual Congress of Anthropology and Archeology. Retrieved from: www.antropologia.com.ar/congreso2004/ponencias/rosa_maria_estrada_dominguez. htm.

Fuentes, N. T. (2010). Professional orientation for fundamentally choosing an occupation: An alternative proposal. *Revista Mexicana de Psicología, 27*(2), 237–246.

Galindo, E. (2004). Análisis del desarrollo de la psicología en México hasta 1990 [Analysis of the development of psychology in Mexico up until 1990]. *Psicología para América Latina. Revista Electrónica Internacional de la Unión Latinoamericana de Entidades de Psicología* Retrieved from: http://psicolatina.org/Dos/analisis_psicol.html#1.

Gavilán, M. (2007). La formación de orientadores en contextos complejos con especial referencia a Latinoamérica [The training of counselors in complex context with special reference to Latin America]. *Orientación y Sociedad, 7*(1), 1–15.

Gil, B. F., & Hernández, G. L. (2009). Cognitive behavioral treatment of Mexican children with social phobia. *Anuario de Psicología, 40*(1), 89–104.

INEGI, Institute for Statistics, Geography and Informatics (December, 2011). *Population, housing and dwelling census, 2010.* Retrieved from: http://cuentame.inegi.org.mx/poblacion/habitantes.aspx?tema=P.

Korbman-Shein, R. (1997). The beginning of professionalization and the establishment of the licensing degree in Psychology [El principio de la profesionalización y el establecimiento del grado de licenciado en psicología]. In J. J. Sanchez-Sosa (ed.), *One Hundred Years of Psychology in Mexico* (pp. 59–68). Mexico City: National University Press.

López-Austin, A. (1997). *Cuerpo Humano e ideología, Tomo I* [Human body and ideology, Vol. I]. Mexico City: Institute for Anthropological Research, National University Press.

López-Carrasco, M. A. (1991). El psicologismo dentro de la práctica cotidiana del orientador educativo [A psychologistic view of the everyday practice of the educational counselor]. *Diorama Educativo, 3*(1), 36–40.

Martínez, G. R. (September, 2006). El ihiyotl, las sombras y las almas aliento en Mesoamérica [The "Ihiyotl", the shadow and the breath-souls in Meso-America]. *Cuicuilco, 13*(38), 177–199.

Martínez, K. I., Pedroza, F. J., Vacío, M. A., Jiménez, A. L., & Salazar, M. L. (2008). School-based brief counseling for teenage drinkers. *Revista Mexicana de Análisis de la Conducta, 34*(2), 247–264.

Miller, M. G. (2004). *Rise and Fall of the Cosmic Race: The Cult of Mestizaje in Latin America.* Austin: University of Texas Press.

Moral, R. J. (2011). Sexual orientation among 12 to 19 year old Mexican adolescents and youths. *Psicología Desde el Caribe, 27*(2), 112–135.

Morales, M. G., López, R. E., & Antona, C. C. (2010). Methods of affective facilitation for identifying the impact of the clinical treatment of social phobia. *Revista Intercontinental de Psicología y Educación, 12*(2), 181–201.

Navarro, B. (1983). *Cultura Mexicana Moderna en el Siglo XVIII* [Modern Mexican culture in the eighteenth century]. Mexico City: National University Press.

OECD-CERI, Organization for Economic Cooperation and Development: Centre for Educational Research and Innovation (2004). *Revisión nacional de investigación y desarrollo educativo* [National review of education research and development]. Retrieved from: www.oecd.org/dataoecd/42/23/32496490.pdf

Oropeza, T. R., Medina, M. E., & Sánchez S. J. J. (2007) Evaluation of a brief treatment for cocaine users. *Revista Mexicana de Psicología, 24*(2), 219–231.

Ricard, R. (1986). *La conquista espiritual de México* [The spiritual conquest of Mexico]. Mexico City: Fondo de Cultura Económica.

Riveros, R. A., Cortazar, P. J., Alcázar, L. F., & Sánchez, S. J. J. (2005). Effects of a cognitive-behavioral intervention on quality of life, anxiety, depression and medical condition of diabetic and essential hypertensive patients. *International Journal of Clinical and Health Psychology, 5*(3), 445–462.

Robles, O. (1942). *Investigación filosófica natural: Los libros del alma de Fray Alonso de la Veracruz* [Philosophical & natural research: The books of Animae by Fray Alonso de la Veracruz]. Mexico City: National University Press.

Robles, G. R., Flores, E., Jurado, S., & Páez, F. (2002). Assertiveness training for improving depressive and anxiety symptoms. *Psiquiatría, 18*(3), 176–179.

Robles, M. S., Moreno, A. D., Frías, C. V., Rodríguez, V. M., Barroso, G. R., Díaz, A. E., ... & Hernández, P. R. (2006). Behavioural training in partner communication and correct condom use skills. *Anales de Psicología, 22*(1), 60–71.

Rodríguez, K. S., Díaz, N. D., Gutiérrez, V. S. Guerrero, H. J., & Lucio, G. M. E. (2011). Evaluation of a drug abuse prevention program for adolescents. *Salud Mental, 34*(1), 27–35.

Rojas, R. M. (2007). Group therapy with victims of child abuse in a shelter of Mexico City. *Revista Colombiana de Psiquiatría, 36*(3), 411–428.

Sánchez-Sosa, J. J. (September, 1998). Clinical Psychology in Mexico: Background, current developments and future trends. *International Clinical Psychologist, Newsletter of the International Society of Clinical Psychology, 1*(1), 3–5.

Sánchez-Sosa, J. J. (2004). Psychology in Mexico: Recent developments and perspective. In M. J. Stevens & D. Wedding (eds), *Handbook of International Psychology* (pp. 93–128). New York: Brunner-Routledge.

Sánchez Sosa, J. J. and Valderrama-Iturbe, P. (2001). Psychology in Latin America: Historical reflections and perspectives. *International Journal of Psychology, 36*(6), 384–394.

SEP-SES Ministry of Education, Viceministry for Higher Education (2011). *¿Qué es un RVOE?* [What is the RVOE?]. Retrieved from www.sirvoes.sep.gob.mx/sirvoes/jspQueEsRvoe.jsp

Vallejo, A. R. (2006). Medicina indígena y salud mental [Indigenous medicine and mental health]. *Acta Colombiana de Psicología, 9*(002), 39–46.

Vázquez, A. R., Mancilla, J. M., Mateo, G. C., López, A. X., Alvarez, R. G., Ruiz, M. A. & Franco, P. K. (2005). Eating disorders and risk factors in an incidental sample of young Mexicans. *Revista Mexicana de Psicología, 22*(1), 55–63.

Villatoro, E. & PIES (Organization for Research, Education and Promotion of Health) (2001). (2001). *Promoción de la medicina y terapias indígenas en la atención primaria de salud: El caso de los Maya de Guatemala* [Promotion of indigenous medicines and therapies in primary health care: The case of the Maya of Guatemala]. Washington, DC: Division of Development of Health Systems and Services, PAHO-WHO.

White, P. (ed.). (2002). *Larousse gran diccionario* [Larousse grand dictionary]. Mexico: Larousse.

13

COUNSELING AND PSYCHOTHERAPY IN THE UNITED STATES

Multicultural competence, evidence-based, and measurable outcomes

Gargi Roysircar and Shannon Hodges

Introduction

The population of the United States is roughly 300 million people with an increasingly aging population and a low birth rate (US Census Bureau, 2010). English remains the dominant language, though an increasing percentage of US citizens speak Spanish as their first or second language. Through immigration, the US has become a montage of cultural diversity particularly in urban areas with Latinos and Asians as the fastest growing ethnic minority groups (US Census Bureau, 2010). At the onset of this millennium, people of color comprised roughly one-third of the population (US Census Bureau, 2010). The racial and ethnic minority population is expected to rise to at least 50% by the year 2050.

Additionally, school-aged children are the most diverse age group in the United States, with 37% of this group being non-White as opposed to 28% non-White people in the general population (American Psychological Association [APA], 2003); this is because minority families have more children than White families. The APA (2003) noted further that under these demographic trends, by the year 2025, the typical public school classroom will be 50% non-White. Some cities and towns in Texas, New Mexico, and California are already 50% minority people. Significant immigration has altered the social landscape of the United States, particularly in certain regions.

This societal complexity of the United States interacts with individuals, families, and social groups, affecting all people's life, work, and relationships, which could benefit from psychological helping services. Counseling, in fact, has become an accepted practice in mainstream US culture. A perusal of the internet will show numerous advertisements for individual, couples, family, and group counseling. There are daily television shows with Dr. Phil, a psychologist, and Dr. Drew, a psychiatrist. Psychotherapy experts are called on regularly on the cable network to give interpretations about addictions, family violence, sexual and physical abuse, suicide, homicide, and other individual and societal problems. Talk show hostess, Oprah's huge popularity with women was influenced by her counselor-like empathic listening and verbal responses and emotional self-disclosures. Counseling services are now in full view in public advertising, the media, and community clinics.

In this chapter, counseling refers to practitioners in the distinct fields of counseling psychology and professional counseling. The two counseling fields are presented here in separate sections because they represent different professions. They have a different history, belong to different professional organizations, and have separate accreditation bodies that oversee their training. They have different orientations to training and deliver education at different graduate levels, for a different number of years. The two professions have their respective licenses. Because counseling psychologists and counselors have distinct identities and may even be competitive or adversarial with each other over resource allocations, the authors thought it best to describe their professions separately. First, counseling psychology is described (Part I) by the first author, Gargi Roysircar, followed by a description of professional counseling (Part II) by Shannon Hodges. Gargi Roysircar is a licensed psychologist and Shannon Hodges is a licensed mental health counselor.

Part I: Counseling psychology in the United States

Counseling psychologists are doctorate level psychologists (PhD, PsyD, or EdD; the last two degrees being less frequent) who have received general education in the core areas of psychology, specialized education in interventions and treatments, extensive supervised practice, and have completed a dissertation in the field of psychology. Counseling psychologists, in contrast to clinical psychologists, focus on the adaptive functioning of individuals in their personal and interpersonal lives across the lifespan. In particular, counseling psychologists focus on adaptation problems that occur emotionally, socially, vocationally, developmentally, organizationally, and those related to health. The settings in which their education, research, intervention, or treatment occur are numerous, such as colleges and universities, local hospitals, veterans hospitals, community clinics, and private practices.

While both clinical and counseling psychologists provide psychotherapy, they differ in the means they deliver treatment. When the two subfields were developed, clinical focused on care of the ill or bedridden. The term clinical even derives from the Greek, "kline," which means bed. Counseling psychology focused on consultation with those who were generally well. Counsel is from the Latin, "consulere," which means to consult, advise, or deliberate. Clinical psychologists typically use more assessment and treatment methods of psychopathology than counseling psychologists, who use more psychotherapy and prevention methods.

A brief history

Counseling psychology as a formal discipline in the United States is about 100 years old, being launched by the mental hygiene (1920s), vocational guidance (1940s), and psychometrics (1940s) movements. Its professional affiliation with APA started in 1946, with the founding of the Personnel and Guidance Psychology Division, Division 17 (Div 17) of APA. Div 17 subsequently had two name changes: Counseling Psychology, and since 2002, Society of Counseling Psychology. Div 17 has the largest membership in APA. It has evolved beyond one organization and includes collaborative relations with the Council of Counseling Psychology Training Programs (CCPTP) and the Association of Counseling Center Training Agencies (ACCTA). Both these organizations are strong forces within professional psychology and university-based national and regional accredited bodies.

Counseling psychology evolved over 50 years but faced substantial problems in the 1980s and 1990s with competing demands for changes in training (more applied work), national and state licensure requirements (formal knowledge-based exams), and reduced professional opportunities.[1] Overall, owing to institutional budget cuts, there was a significant decrease in the number of psychologists working in hospital settings and community mental health centers. The younger generation of counseling psychologists was less involved in settings that focused on preventative and developmental services (e.g., business and industry, university administration, schools, non-profits) and more interested in remedial and therapeutic activities of private practice. The number of counseling psychologists working in college and university settings, however, had remained constant since the inception of counseling psychology, with a significant focus of college counseling centers on vocational psychology and assessment, career counseling, a combination of brief and long-term therapy, and campus prevention outreach, such as alcohol abuse and suicide prevention (Lichtenberg, Goodyear, & Genther, 2008).

The 1980s were wrought with societal changes. National training conferences and groups and task forces (e.g., Task Force on the Scope and Criteria for Accreditation of the APA) proposed a shift in pedagogy expanding curricula to include diversity issues, consultation, policy formation, supervision, and program development (Lichtenberg et al., 2008). Psychology was written into Medicare statutes, which ultimately intensified battles between medicine/psychiatry and psychology. Ethical complaints about dual relationships (i.e., sexual relationships with clients), diversity, and HIV/AIDS status came to the fore. For the first time, attention was given to the "distressed psychologist" because it was naïve and dangerous to ignore the stressors counseling psychologists faced in their work and personal lives.

In the new millennium, the evolution of counseling psychology has changed with the increase in managed care, prescriptive authority, and expansion of practical roles for counseling psychologists. Counseling psychologists' roles were equally divided between academician (40.2%) and clinical practitioner (39.7%), with less self-report for administrator (14.1%), and other (6.0%) (see Lichtenberg et al., 2008). Counseling psychologists began to move from the relative security of salaried, academic, or administrative positions to work as independent, fee-for-service professionals. Counseling psychologists who are now in private practice must deal with managed care, for which they were not prepared by their prevention-, developmental-, and research-focused academic training programs.

Managed care has always been around but it did not begin to have a broad impact on healthcare delivery until recently as a response to skyrocketing healthcare costs. The managed care organizations' increasing emphasis on improving the quality of care is one of the major trends shaping the delivery of mental health services. Practitioners are rewarded for quality performance. The Centers for Medicare and Medicaid Services for the retired/elderly (i.e., Medicare) and indigent populations (i.e., Medicaid) are working with at least several states to implement pay-for-performance (or quality-based purchasing) Medicaid programs.

Performance might be measured, for instance, by client satisfaction, symptom reduction, and indexing the client's subsequent healthcare usage. As a result, there has been increasing emphasis on "medically necessary" treatments, reducing services overall, including psychological care, and restricting reimbursement rates. The cost of healthcare and the fact that millions of Americans have no health insurance create a unique problem to ensure access to care, which contradicts counseling psychology's multicultural and social justice advocacy. Added worry about ethical issues working with managed care has been a growing concern among practitioners and further complicates clinical practice. Practicum students may be afforded fewer training opportunities as managed care directs who can provide treatment to clientele. Moreover, with budgetary cuts being made across the mental health sector (e.g., hospitals and community mental health centers), training opportunities for students will continue to dwindle while there is an increased enrollment of students in professional psychology training.

At the turn of this century, APA responded to two pressures: (1) the increasing pressure from managed care companies and government funding agencies to verify the necessity and utility of psychotherapeutic interventions; and (2) pressures as well from the practitioners of psychology who did not want their craft to be controlled by bodies outside of psychology (e.g., Fox, 1995; Roysircar, 2009). APA (2005) officially endorsed a policy statement advocating the use of evidence-based practice (EBP) as a means for delivering quality and cost-effective treatment for mental disorders. While treatment is research-based, standardized, and time-limited, good clinical judgment and cultural competence in client characteristics are valued in making accurate diagnoses and facilitating successful outcomes. APA (2002, 2003) also recognized that responding to a client's culture and worldview arouses clinician reactions, which require the therapist to become aware of his or her own worldview, assumptions, values, and biases and to control these from impeding good practice.

Education programs, accreditation, licensure, and certification

Initial accreditation by APA of counseling psychology programs occurred more than 50 years ago. There are currently about 70 APA-accredited counseling psychology programs. In the 1980s, a standardized licensing system for all professional psychology disciplines of counseling, clinical, school, and industrial organizational was begun in every state in the United States.

The APA Commission on Accreditation's (APA-CoA) (APA-CoA, 2007) goal is to provide consumers of educational services with sufficient information to make an informed decision about which program in professional psychology they want to attend. The APA-CoA review is not to be considered an adversarial process, but rather a process of APA-CoA and a program under review working together to ensure that an acceptable level of quality is maintained in professional psychology. The APA-CoA does not accredit schools or universities, or programs at the bachelor's or master's levels. In addition, accreditation applies only to programs—it is not a credential that individuals can obtain.

APA-CoA is recognized by both the US Department of Education and the Council of Higher Education Accreditation as the national accrediting authority for professional education and training in psychology. Accordingly, the APA-CoA's accreditation policies, procedures, and guidelines are intended to be consistent with national recognized purposes and values of accreditation, as articulated by governmental and non-governmental groups with an interest in accreditation.

The APA-CoA accredits doctoral graduate programs in clinical, counseling, and school psychology, and programs offering combinations of two or more of these areas. Accredited programs provide broad and general training in scientific psychology and in the foundations of practice, and have as a goal to prepare students for the practice of professional psychology. Practicum and predoctoral internship programs are a required component of doctoral training.

APA accreditation (APA-CoA, 2012) has an outcome-oriented evaluation focus. Accreditation standards evaluate eight areas: Program Eligibility (Domain A); Program Philosophy, Objectives, and Curriculum Plan (Domain B); Program Resources (Domain C); Cultural and Individual Differences and Diversity (Domain D); Student-Faculty Relations (Domain E); Program Self-Assessment and Quality Enhancement (Domain F); Public Disclosure (Domain G); and the application to and completion of the Predoctoral Internship by students in the fifth year of training.

Postdoctoral residency programs provide preparation for professional practice at an advanced level of competency in traditional and specialty practice areas of psychology. Upon defending a dissertation which is predominantly psychological in nature and graduating with a doctorate, a graduate does one year of fulltime postdoctoral supervised clinical work. The postdoctoral work is followed by taking the national psychology licensure exam, which is a test of 200 multiple choice items. Upon passing the national exam, whose passing grade is 70% to 75%, depending on the state, and an exam on the ethics and laws of the state where the person will practice, a doctoral professional becomes a licensed psychologist. Any licensed psychologist who independently provides or offers to provide to the public health services must be certified as a health service provider by the psychologist's state mental health board.

APA-CoA emphasizes the inclusion of diversity education in all coursework, and evidence exists to support this emphasis of accreditation. Smith, Constantine, Dunn, Dinehart and Montoya (2006) used a meta-analysis to show that practitioners who received diversity education in professional psychology programs performed better on multicultural competency measures than these who had not. In addition, Griner and Smith (2006) showed that culturally adapted interventions were more effective in treating racial and ethnic minority populations than interventions that were not adapted. According to S. Sue (1998), clinicians who are diversity competent are scientifically minded and have skills in dynamic sizing. In other words, they are in the practice of making cultural hypotheses on the status of a client, including knowing when to generalize and when to exclude the experience of others in individual client case conceptualization and treatment.

Training facilities and programs that hope to train diversity competent psychologists must incorporate the multicultural competencies of knowledge, skills and awareness into every aspect of the program (Roysircar, Dobbins, & Malloy, 2009). Faculty and administrators must use an ongoing developmental approach that focuses on the developmental levels of pre-practicum, readiness for pre-doctoral internship, and doctoral graduation (Roysircar et al., 2009). This integrated system allows for a congruent and natural approach for teaching new clinicians about diversity competence.

Current counseling psychology theories, processes, and trends

Two theories currently popular in counseling psychology are the bioecological perspective and positive psychology. A focus on therapist process includes multicultural and diversity competence and therapists' recognition of indigenous healing methods. A description of these theories, processes, and trends follows.

The ecological perspective (EP) explicates interactions of the individual client with contexts at multiple levels in five concentric systems in order to organize the relative influences of contextual influences on the client (Bronfenbrenner, 1995). First, the individual system includes the interactions of the client with one's own multiple identities, gender role beliefs, personality, biology, developmental status, interests and occupation, social make-up, and everyday life. Second, the microsystem includes the client's family, school, work, peer groups, religious institutions, as well as the counseling center where the client is seeking help. Third, the mesosystem includes the interactions among the client's above-mentioned local groups. Fourth, the exosystem includes the context of social policies that promote/advocate for parity across healthcare, law, education, and employment. Fifth, the macrosystem encompasses all subordinate systems (one to four) and represents the broader societal mores, values, and sociopolitical responses that effectively structure life implicitly or explicitly for members of society, including the client. Sixth, the chronosystem represents changes over time in all the five systems. Thus, the systems are interpenetrating, interactive, and change with time and history. As a therapeutic tool, EP provides a template for therapists to conceptualize the multiple layers of a client's problems and, thus, create appropriate interventions at each level of the client's interactions. EP is consistent with multicultural assessment and counseling (Roysircar, 2012a). Although individuals have genetically based propensities for behavior, whether and how these propensities are enacted within a client's life are likely to be moderated by the client's interactions with the five contexts and changes of time. From the EP stance, the most significant contextual interactions can be connected with meaning-making by the client.

Positive psychology is described by Seligman (1998) as the scientific pursuit of optimal functioning. This theory is the opposite of the well-established study of and practice in psychopathology, which relies on the Diagnostic and Statistical Manual of Mental Disorders (American Psychiatric Association, 2000) and dominates the clinical psychology profession. Positive psychology has become a movement, philosophy, science, practice, and a professional specialty that attends to *positive individual traits, positive emotions,* and *positive institutions* (Lopez & Edwards, 2008). *Positive personal traits,* such as hope, optimism, self-efficacy, emotional intelligence, wisdom, courage, and more generally human strengths have received the most attention. *Positive emotions,* such as, attachment, flow, spirituality, and mindfulness have also garnered current attention (Roysircar, 2011). While the concern for *positive institutions* has not attracted as much attention, the multicultural and social justice movements to increase access, equity, a more diverse workforce and student body, and an affirming social climate have resulted in institutional changes and pluralistic organizations.

There is one counseling approach in strength-based practice that has not yet undergone empirical scrutiny. Strengths-centered therapy is grounded in social constructionism, designed to leverage character strengths and virtues as facilitators of the change process. It is hypothesized that clients begin to attach their life experiences to that which is positive and adaptive. This is done by naming strengths (*explicitizing*), identifying desired strengths (*envisioning*), facilitating a burst of agency (*empowering*), and encouraging this cycle to continue in a neverending process that transcends psychotherapeutic process (*evolving*).

Finally, APA (2003) has mandated diversity competence. According to Roysircar et al., (2009), diversity competence is characterized by

> (a) *knowledge* of the unique dimensions of clients' worldviews, the historical backgrounds of diverse groups, and the current sociopolitical influence on these groups; (b) *skills* to devise and implement interventions that are relevant to clients' cultural values, beliefs and expectations; and (c) *awareness* of their own attitudes of privilege, beliefs, and biases that might influence therapeutic perceptions and subsequent therapeutic dynamics.
>
> *(p. 187)*

Knowledge, skills, and attitudes (KSAs) influence quality of care in five domains. These five domains that cut across the 3 KSA competencies and are located in the same order within each competency one: 1) multiple identities, 2) power, oppression and privilege, 3) cultural and individual differences and diversity (CID) and (CID)-specific knowledge, 4) culturally competent service provision, and 5) ethics (Roysircar et al., 2009). Student KSAs are developed through training, research on CID factors, personal introspection, and diversity supervision.

Indigenous and traditional healing methods

The indigenous healing practices of traditional Native Americans, Mexican immigrants, or Vietnamese/Cambodian refugees tend to be organic, natural, and "mind–body–spirit" holistic in nature. The worldview of a technological society and of a traditional agrarian society has different answers to the questions: "How" to heal? and "What" is healing itself? Multicultural counseling is most concerned with issues of cultural relevance and adaptability of counseling in order to provide culturally sensitive treatment (Roysircar, 2009). Cultural relevance of theories can be enhanced by adaptation based on the knowledge of local researchers and practitioners about local culture and contextual characteristics. Adapted counseling theories can be tested by using local samples and diverse research methodologies in the natural context of local participants and generating alternative models and frameworks, where both the indigenous and universal elements are addressed and integrated. This type of an accommodation model of counseling theory is different from "indigenization from within," such as the use of prayers, rituals, and espiritsmo (Roysircar, 2012b), which is the more authentic approach to indigenizing psychology. This "emic" approach, however, will require time as well as efforts and resources from those within the target indigenous cultures (e.g., Native American psychologists' articles in a special issue of the *Journal of Multicultural Counseling and Development*, 2012, *40*, 4).

While awaiting new learning in spiritual healing, counseling psychologists keep in mind that supernatural explanations of mental illness are deeply embedded in traditional religious societies. Supernatural occurrences to which mental illnesses are attributed include possession by a spirit, sorcery, the evil eye, or effects of God or the devil (Roysircar, 2012c). Supernatural causes are often blamed for bizarre behaviors or psychotic symptoms, and, as a result, traditional spiritual rituals tend to be the most common initial solution for these types of diagnoses. Reliance on mystical cures for mental illness is present in many non-Western cultures, even among their highly educated and scientific people.

Research and supervision

Counseling psychology is based on APA's scientist-practitioner model. Counseling psychologists in research universities and their teams of doctoral students maintain an active program of empirical research with increasing methodological sophistication and rigor, and they provide important new knowledge that furthers the development of theories and practice relevant to counseling process and outcome, vocational psychology, measurement instrumentation, and multicultural counseling. Research courses, supervised research, a dissertation, supervised clinical work, a supervision course, and supervision of master's practicum students are integral to the 5-year, doctoral APA-approved curriculum that qualifies a graduate for the licensure examination for psychologists.

In counseling psychology research, a common factors approach has been popular (Imel & Wampold, 2008). It allows generalizations to be made regardless of paradigm by not placing emphasis on specific interventions. Instead, common factors that are applicable to all successful therapeutic intervention are highlighted and encouraged by counseling psychology researchers. Common factors, in contrast to the medical model that emphasizes specificity, suggests one of two things: (1) therapies are different but are equally effective or (2) therapies look different, but actually have a common factor that causes them to be effective.

Since psychotherapy and the common factors do not fit the medical model, some psychologists question the true effectiveness of therapist relational interventions. Therefore, psychologists, who are most consistent with the medical model, state that specific interventions would be best suited to specific psychopathology or problems. For instance, they may argue that the common factor of therapeutic alliance may be enough to aid mild depression, but exposure therapy is a better treatment for phobias. Common factors place the source for change on the clinician. Common factors are typically standard about therapist interpersonal characteristics, but are grouped and labeled differently based on the researcher's theory. The process of making psychology more medical-model-oriented limits the treatments available for clients.

Finally, because counseling psychology in the United States is committed to serving multicultural populations, it demonstrates its advocacy through consistent publication of multicultural articles in its top-tier journals, *Journal of Counseling Psychology* and *The Counseling Psychologist*, and by its required textbooks for students, such as, Lent and Brown's *Handbook of Counseling Psychology*; Ponterotto, Casas, Suzuki, and Alexander's *Handbook of Multicultural Counseling*; Toporek, Gerstein, Fouad, Roysircar, and Israel's, *Handbook of Social Justice in Counseling Psychology*; and Gerstein, Heppner, Aegisdottir, Leung, and Norsworthy's *International Handbook of Counseling*. The reason for multicultural training, also required by APA accreditation and for licensing, is the increasingly diverse population of the United States.

Supervision in the United States is either a psychotherapy-based supervision, where supervision is like psychotherapy, or supervision based, where thoughts and information are exchanged between the supervisor and supervisee, and is acknowledged as a unique training experience unlike any other (Ladany & Inman, 2008). In supervision, the *integrated developmental model* focuses on the supervisee's level of development, motivation, autonomy, and self- and other-awareness. The *systems approach* to supervision focuses on the supervisee-supervisor relationship, the client, the trainee, the institution, the supervisor, the functions of supervision, and supervision tasks. *Critical events in supervision* focuses on learning based on remediation of difficulties and deficits, heightening multicultural awareness, negotiating role conflicts, working through countertransference, managing sexual attraction, repairing gender-related misunderstandings, and addressing problematic supervisee emotions and behaviors. The working alliance between supervisor and supervisee guides the critical events in supervision process regardless of approach.

Bordin's *working alliance* (Hovarth & Greenberg, 1994) can be adapted to a model of supervision with eight goals: mastery of specific skills; expanding one's understanding of clients; expanding one's awareness of process issues; increasing awareness of self and its impact on process; overcoming personal and intellectual obstacles towards learning and mastery; deepening one's understanding of concepts and mastery; providing a stimulus to research; and maintaining standards of good clinical practice. Taping supervisees and following supervisor ethics are recommended for all supervisors. Similarly, supervisee evaluation is based on goal-setting and feedback, which should be both formative (ongoing) and summative (formal documentation and evaluation on overarching themes).

Strengths, weaknesses, opportunities, and challenges

Within APA, counseling psychology's major strength is its goal of serving marginalized populations through knowledge, skills, and awareness that are sensitive to cultural and individual differences and diversity. Thus, counseling psychology has uniquely positioned itself within APA as a major resource for meeting the many pressing challenges of our global era. No other professional psychology specialty has been as unrelenting and constant as counseling psychology in reminding practitioners of its obligations, responsibilities, and duties to promote diversity, to respond to injustice, and to advance the human condition. This is evidenced by counseling psychology's teaching curriculum, research, community services, and advocacy regarding ethnic, racial, and cultural minorities.

Counseling psychology's weakness may be its ever-expanding interests, roles, and openness to new social movements that may result in a shifting professional identity and a diffuse curriculum, requiring one to periodically define "what a counseling psychologist is." Another weakness is that counseling psychologists in universities are focused on statistical methodology and publications in premier APA journals. Unfortunately, academic theoreticians, researchers, and measurement experts are removed from the real problems of real people and encapsulated in the ivory tower of APA's Division 17. There is a gap between these researchers who are trainers and their graduate students who want to be in private practice.

The flexibility of counseling psychology, viewed as a weakness from one perspective, is also its capacity to integrate into its core values the zeitgeist of the times. New social movements, theories, knowledge, and training paradigms give its discipline and profession many opportunities for growth and change. One such pressing opportunity is the inclusion of geropsychology. The Association of Psychology Postdoctoral and Internship Centers' (APPIC) 2003 conference on training in competencies included knowledge, skills, and awareness of geropsychology in the competency domain of Cultural and Individual Differences and Diversity (CID) (Daniel, Roysircar, Abeles, & Boyd, 2004). Interweaving aging issues into existing course work in training programs will be in keeping with the approach widely applied in the ongoing movement to increase students' multicultural competencies, as noted by APPIC's 2003 recommendations for CID (Daniel et al., 2004). This interweaving of aging issues is most salient given that 14 to 19.6 million elderly individuals may be seeking mental health services just a decade from now. It will be important to increase the number of geropsychologists as well as the awareness among generalists of geropsychology issues to meet the burgeoning demand predicted by APA.

Counseling psychology's approach of prevention, positive psychology, and common factors of therapy can be viewed as a weakness by clinical psychology's disease model of psychopathology, diagnosis, assessment, and specific treatments that has popular appeal, media appeal, and the approval of third-party payers. Private practice, forensics, placements in hospitals and the military, and collaboration with psychiatrists and other medical professionals become possible for clinical psychologists. Thus many counseling psychologists may not retain their original professional identity to do what clinical psychologists do because both counseling psychologists and clinical psychologists carry the same license. Thus, counseling psychologists come in many different stripes, which is not necessarily a bad thing.

Future directions

Counseling has become a global profession, with diverse helping services, not necessarily based in university higher education, and offered on every continent. International counseling is critical to the US profession of counseling psychology because the US is the world leader in the psychotherapy field and, as such, will be responsible for setting standards, offering training, developing credentialing procedures, and forming partnerships with counseling training programs overseas. However, the exportation of US counseling must not be one of educational and professional colonization, but rather the indigenization of US psychology.

Part II: Professional counseling in the United States

A brief history

The American Counseling Association (ACA) is the largest organization devoted to providing counseling services (Gladding, 2009). ACA began existence as the American Personnel and Guidance Association (APGA). Conceived in 1952 by a loose confederation of organizations, APGA was primarily "concerned with vocational guidance and other personnel activities" (Harold, 1985, p. 4). ACA has evolved from its "guidance" infancy into a multifaceted profession of some 46,000 members and 19 divisional affiliates (Cashwell, 2010, March). The State of Virginia passed the first counselor licensure law in 1976, followed by 49 other states, Washington, DC, and Puerto Rico. Counselors now bill private health insurance, and the Veteran's Administration

(VA) has recently approved counselors to work in VA hospitals. Currently, some 635,000 counselors work in a variety of settings and this number is "expected to grow much faster than the average for all occupations through 2016" (Bureau of Labor Statistics, 2010–2011, p. 209).

Education programs, accreditation, licensure, and certification

Counselors must complete a 2- to 3-year master's degree program that typically includes a 700–1,000 hour field placement. Though counselors may attain a doctorate in counseling, the master's is the practitioner's degree, whereas counselors holding doctorates usually are seeking to become professors.

Accreditation was a latecomer to the counseling profession, but in 1981 the Council for the Accreditation of Counseling and Related Programs (CACREP) was created (Hollis & Dodson, 2001). CACREP is now an independent agency recognized by the Council for Higher Education Accreditation to accredit the master's degree in eight counseling specialties (e.g., school counseling, clinical mental health counseling, addictions counseling) and doctoral programs in counselor education. Though counselor accreditation is voluntary for counseling programs, CACREP requirements form the basis for most state licensure laws (Remley & Herlihy, 2007).

CACREP's popularity has grown with nearly 600 counseling programs currently accredited (Cashwell, 2010). Because ACA—unlike APA which also is an accrediting organization—has delegated accreditation responsibility to CACREP, this has created an identity issue for counselors. There has been an informal opinion within the counseling field that CACREP accreditation should be dropped in favor of "ACA" accreditation. Though some counseling professionals would like to see the change for clarity purposes, CACREP will likely remain the accrediting organization (Cashwell, 2010).

In the US, counselors must become "licensed" to practice and receive insurance reimbursement. Unlike psychologists who must hold doctorates (with rare exceptions like in Vermont), counselors are licensed at the master's degree. To attain licensure, counselors must graduate from a master's level counseling program, work under supervision of a licensed mental health professional (e.g., counselor, psychologist) for a 2- to 3-year period, and then pass the state counseling examination. Licensure requirements are set by the individual state or territory and may vary considerably, making it difficult for a counselor who relocates from say, the State of Arkansas to the State of New Hampshire, to retain licensure. The counselor may have to take a second examination, accrue more hours of supervision, and possibly complete additional course work, as required by the state licensing body (Remley & Herlihy, 2007). The American Association of State Boards of Counseling (AACSB) currently represents an effort to centralize disparate state licensure requirements (Cashwell, 2010, March).

Another complication regarding vagaries in counselor licensure lies in the various licensure names and acronyms. Many states' name for licensed counselors is "Licensed Professional Counselor" (LPC); others title it "Licensed Mental Health Counselor" (LMHC), "Licensed Clinical Mental Health Counselor" (LCMHC), or Licensed Clinical Professional Counselor (LCPC). Furthermore, some states have a "two-tiered" licensure system, meaning initial licensure is given at the completion of a master's degree, passing the state examination, and accumulation of the required supervised hours of counseling practice. Because the first tier is limited, counselors must continue to be supervised by a counselor holding the higher tier license. Some states require the higher tiered license to bill health insurance. Most states have not instituted a tier system, though as the field matures they may become more common.

National certification is a voluntary credential, second in importance and function to state licensure. National certification is the purview of the National Board for Certified Counselors

(NBCC), a separate credentialing organization overseeing national certification in a variety of specialty areas including mental health counseling, marriage and family counseling, clinical supervision, and others (NBCC, 2011). National certification once was the only credentialing option counselors had prior to state licensure. This coexistence of state licensure and national certification may be confusing to professionals outside the counseling field.

NBCC offers several credentials most notably the "Nationally Certified Counselor" (NCC) credential, and the "National Certified Clinical Counselor" (NCCC). For certification, a counselor must complete a master's degree and then pass the National Counselor Examination (NCE) to become NCC or the National Clinical Mental Health Counselor Examination (NCMHCE) for certification as NCCC. These examinations have also been adopted by numerous states as their licensure examination.

Some counseling professionals have questioned the validity of certification as state licensure because national certification does not provide counselors the vehicle to practice, bill health insurance, supervise beginning counselors, etc. (Weinrach & Thomas, 1993). Remley (1995) has argued that a license should be for general practice while national certification should identify specialty areas. The field has moved towards Remley's model, though debate regarding certifications' necessity persists.

Current counseling and psychotherapy theories, processes, and trends

The counseling profession has enjoyed enormous popularity in the US and abroad for several decades. Numerous theoretical approaches have become popular, including cognitive-behavioral therapy (CBT), rational emotive behavior therapy (REBT), eye movement desensitization reprocessing (EMDR), reality therapy, and Adlerian therapy to name some common approaches.

"Eclectic" approaches, popular since the 1970s, refers to a counselor's practice of picking the best techniques from a variety of theoretical approaches to fit the needs of the individual client. Eclecticism has always been controversial, as some view the practice as lacking a coherent, driving theory (Corey, 2009). Corsini, however, opined that "all good therapists adopt an eclectic stance" (2008, p. 10), implying that "technique and method are secondary to the clinician's sense of what is the right thing to do with a given client at a given moment in time, irrespective of theory" (p. 10).

Interestingly, in a national survey conducted by the *Psychotherapy Networker* (2007), only 4% of respondents identified being aligned with one exclusive model, while 96% claimed an *integrative approach*. Integrative has come to be preferred over eclectic, as integrative implies more organization and cohesion in the manner approaches and techniques are combined and utilized (Norcross, Karpiak, & Lister, 2005), with the common factors approach likely the most popular (Corey, 2009).

The common factors approach integrates factors common to all theoretical approaches, e.g., therapeutic alliance, catharsis, and nurturing positive change. (Norcross et al., 2005). These common factors may be more important than the particular theoretical approach. Hubble, Duncan, and Miller (1999) reviewed 40 years of research on psychotherapy and found the following four factors account for positive change in psychotherapy: Client factors 40%; Alliance factors (the therapeutic relationship) 30%; Expectancy factors (hope and allegiance) 15%; and theoretical models and techniques 15% (reported in Corey, 2009, p. 477).

The most significant impact within the counseling profession is that of multiculturalism. Multiculturalism may be defined in broad ways utilizing sociological variables such as race, ethnicity, nationality, sexuality orientation, socioeconomic standing, religion, etc. Just as the term culture is multidimensional, multiculturalism has been defined in numerous ways with no one particular definition of the term. The most common definitions of multiculturalism are distinct group uniqueness (e.g., ethnicity, gender, culture, religion, national origin, etc.) and concepts that facilitate attention to individual differences (Locke, 1990).

Multiculturalism has become ubiquitous as every counseling text will integrate multiculturalism into its book, and virtually all journal articles address issues of multiculturalism as related to the article's topic. The Association for Multicultural Counseling and Development (AMCD) is an organization solely dedicated to multicultural practice. AMCD also offers a website, newsletter, and the *Journal of Multicultural Counseling and Development*. Originally founded as the Association for Nonwhite Concerns in Personnel and Guidance (ANWC), the division affiliated with ACA in 1972. AMCD has been instrumental in promoting the multicultural counseling competency movement in 1992 (Sue, Arredondo, & McDavis, 1992), sponsoring training and educational material to assist counselors and counselor educators in understanding and applying the multicultural competencies, with updates on the competencies in 1996 and 2003. See p. 156 of this chapter for the most accepted definition of multicultural competencies.

Complications with multiculturalism abound. The reality is that the vast majority of counselors and counselor educators are White. Resistance to the multicultural movement has been noted by researchers (Sue & Sue, 2003) and a prime reason for such resistance may be due in large part to the profession's European American ethnic makeup. Similarly, there are the ongoing disagreements regarding what should be included. Sexual orientation, though accepted by all major counseling and accreditation organizations, remains controversial. Some counselors object to inclusion of sexual orientation on the basis of religion. Other counselors object to gay and lesbian inclusion for fear it weakens the impact of race, which they see as the dominant theme in multiculturalism (Sue & Sue, 2003). Sexual orientation is probably the most debated multicultural issue and is likely to remain controversial for some time.

Indigenous and traditional healing methods

Prior to the arrival of Europeans in what is now the Unites States, the country was populated by numerous indigenous tribes, with different languages, cultures, customs, spiritual beliefs, and their own particular healthcare approaches. However, there is very little research on indigenous people relative to other cultural groups. A key search of journal articles reveals that far more research has been conducted on other cultures, such as African American, Latino, and Asian American. The researchers of these groups are themselves members of the minority groups, and they intend to increase psychological knowledge about their own people. American Indians represent the smallest percentage of college students by ethnicity (around 1%), but have the highest attrition rate of all ethnic groups (*The Chronicle of Higher Education*, 2010), which may explain the limited number of Native American scholars in counseling, and, consequently, limited Native American counseling literature. This situation is different from that of Canada, where research on indigenous people generally exceeds that of any other ethnic group (McCormick & Ishiyama, 2000).

Some publications on indigenous people can be found scattered throughout journals such as the *Journal of Counseling and Development, Journal of Mental Health Counseling*, and *Journal of Multicultural Counseling and Development*. Many of these publications discuss the importance of how to counsel indigenous clients and describe traditional indigenous healing methods that can be integrated into counseling practice. Specific indigenous healing approaches include the sweat lodge, medicine wheel, story telling, drumming, dancing, vision quest, traditional spiritual rituals, and mentoring from an older member of the community.

In indigenous communities (e.g., Navaho, Cherokee, Apache, etc.), mental health approaches will generally incorporate healing approaches that vary greatly from mainstream mental health practice (Garrett, 2006). While counseling services typically utilize a Western, individualistic framework for diagnosis, treatment planning, and counseling, indigenous approaches will stress the importance of family ties, collective decision-making, and an exploration of returning to harmony with the environment.

Research and supervision

Research in the counseling field has evolved since Sprinthall's statement that "counseling has had a 'long and ambivalent relationship with research'" (1981, p. 465). US counselor education scholars have been instrumental in promoting scholarship with research study in the areas of counselor education (Gladding, 2009), multiculturalism (Harper & McFadden, 2003; Lee, 2006), career (Zunker, 2006), couples and family counseling, psychiatric diagnosis (L. Seligman, 1999), wellness (Myers & Sweeney, 2005), and a wide array of topics beyond these areas. Counseling research in the US is primarily supported by counseling faculty in universities and by the existence of the ACA and 19 divisional affiliates which publish professional journals such as the *Journal of Counseling & Development*, the *Journal of Mental Health Counseling*, *Counselor Education and Supervision*, and many others.

The federal government is the major source of research grants, providing funding through federal agencies such as the National Institute for Drug Abuse (NIDA) and the National Institute for Mental Health (NIMH). These and other federal agencies fund research on a competitive basis, with proposals being peer reviewed. Perhaps the most concerning aspect is that much research on mental health is funded by the pharmaceutical industry. This is problematic as drug companies have a vested interest in promoting psychopharmacology over counseling. The *New England Journal of Medicine* (Turner, Matthews, Linardatos, Tell, & Rosenthal, 2008) reported selective bias in the publishing of research articles on the effectiveness of antidepressant medications (2008). Favorable results were reported at a of 94% as opposed to 14% for unfavorable results. A report in the *Journal of the American Medical Association* (Hochman, Hochman, Bor, & McCormick, 2008) documented the frequent practice of drug manufacturers paying academic scientists to take credit for research articles.

The effectiveness of psychoactive medications is also much debated (Glasser, 2003). Drug manufactures are required to state the increased risks for suicide in some populations (e.g., adolescents) when taking certain antidepressants. Psychoactive medications remain controversial, though popular as evidenced by the ubiquity of drug advertisements on television, the internet, in magazines, etc.

Supervision of counseling practice is a core component of all graduate-level counseling programs (Gladding, 2009; Remley & Herlihy, 2007). CACREP standards stipulate that accredited programs must require students to complete a practicum and internship consisting of a minimum of 600 supervised hours in a clinical setting (CACREP, 2009). While there is agreement on the number of internship hours, there is considerable variation in internship settings. Counseling students may complete their clinical hours in psychiatric hospitals, out-patient centers, P-12 schools, university counseling centers, addictions treatment, etc. (Gladding, 2009). Some states, however, require mental health counselors to have completed their placement in a setting where diagnosis and treatment planning is conducted, though not all states have this requirement.

Training opportunities for counselors are provided in two ways. Doctoral counseling programs offer courses in counselor supervision. Supervision training is also offered through professional continuing education (CE) training at state and national conferences and other venues. For master's level counseling supervisors, the supervision training they receive likely is

on-the-job. The Association for Counselor Education and Supervision (ACES), an ACA affiliate organization, promotes formal supervision training and research on counselor supervision.
ACES publishes a quarterly journal, *Counselor Education and Supervision*, a national newsletter
(*VISIONS*), operates a web-site (www.aces.org) and listserv, sponsors conferences, and publishes books and DVDs on supervision training. As ACES membership is low compared to the
number of professional counselors, supervision training remains a concern.

Strengths, weaknesses, opportunities and challenges

The counseling profession has begun a major effort at unification. *20/20: A Vision for the Future of
Counseling* represents a significant step towards reducing splintering and strengthening the profession (Rollins, 2010). The 20/20 initiative represents an opportunity to provide more unity to
the counseling profession and its numerous affiliates. Among other endeavors, 20/20 delegates
reached consensus on the definition of counseling: "Counseling is a professional relationship that
empowers diverse individuals, families and groups, to accomplish mental health, wellness,
education, and career goals" (Rollins, 2010, p. 36).

Multiculturalism is well integrated into the profession. It is no stretch to state that multiculturalism has become the major force in the US counseling profession over the past 25 years.
Having made this statement, however, there are still many disagreements regarding the
parameters of multiculturalism and the challenges in moving the profession towards a more
culturally inclusive version of counseling (Hodges, 2009; Weinrach & Thomas, 1993).

There are several issues that serve to weaken the counseling profession in the United States.
A major weakness is the professional "turf battles" that occur between the various mental health
professions that offer counseling services. Currently, counseling is performed by counselors,
psychologists, social workers, marriage and family therapists, and psychiatrists, to name the
major helping professionals. Turf battles have been waged over licensure and the right to conduct counseling, insurance billing, assessment, etc. This infighting has often made for contentious relationships between the various mental health professions and the organizations
representing them (Remley & Herlihy, 2007).

Another weakness for the counseling profession has been the long journey towards achieving
parity with colleagues in psychology. Though the counseling profession has grown significantly
and achieved numerous professionals goals (e.g., licensure, billing privileges, accreditation, etc.),
the profession remains in a subservient relationship to that of psychology. Though both professions provide counseling services, psychologists will be paid more. Psychology, by virtue of
being a doctorate-level profession, holds a loftier position in the mental health profession.
Counselors also have an issue regarding their recognition, as the general public will refer to
them as psychologists. While it could be argued this confusion hurts psychologists more, it also
means the counseling profession receives less recognition.

As previously stated, the counseling profession has achieved numerous milestones and currently is focused on achieving Medicare reimbursement privileges. Though this goal has yet to
be realized, the profession has come close and success is likely a matter of time. Medicare
reimbursement likely represents the counseling profession's top priority.

Though the strengths of the counseling profession have just been noted, the profession still
faces a number of challenges. The last four years have witnessed Medicare reimbursement for
counselors passing in both houses of the US Congress (Senate and House of Representatives),
but thus far no bill has cleared both houses of congress to be sent to the President to sign into
law. Other challenges remain. Though licensure has been achieved in all states and territories,
some licensure laws are very weak and allow professionals outside the counseling profession to

call themselves "counselors" (Cashwell, 2010, March). In some states, someone with no credentials may advertise themselves as a "counselor" so long as they do not refer to themselves as a "licensed" counselor (Remley & Herlihy, 2007). Some states have passed "title" laws which prohibit unlicensed providers from using the term "counselor"; but many states have yet to enact such legislation.

Finally, while ACA is the recognized flagship organization, many counselors have remained unaffiliated with ACA. The US Bureau of Labor estimated there are currently 655,000 counselors in the United States (2010–2011). Many of these counselors are almost certainly members of the 19 ACA professional affiliate divisions devoted to school counseling, mental health counseling, rehabilitation counseling, etc. But the fact that most counselors do not have membership in ACA, though they may hold membership in one of its divisions, is a concern for the profession.

Future directions

Only recently has the counseling profession begun to reach out to non-European cultures. As the United States becomes more culturally diverse, the counseling profession must work to remain culturally relevant in research and practice. As the world becomes more globally connected, it is likely counseling will be a part of that process. Counselors will likely seek employment overseas as job creation in certain geographic regions (e.g., Asian countries) offers growth potential. The international counseling movement remains small, though likely to increase substantially in the future, given growing international trade and increased mobility of workers.

Conclusion

Counseling psychology and professional counseling have undergone many changes through their respective evolutionary journeys. Both have gained a strong foothold in the mental health profession through accredited training, licensure, ability to bill insurance, multicultural competencies of practitioners, advocacy work, and research on evidence-based practice and clinical outcomes. As fast growing mental health professions, the future looks very bright. Still, challenges remain.

Note

1 For a comprehensive review of this topic, see Lichtenberg, Goodyear, and Genther (2008).

References

American Psychiatric Association. (2000). *Diagnostic and Statistical Manual-IV-text Revision (DSM-IV-TR).* Washington, DC: APA.

American Psychological Association. (2002). Ethical principles of psychologists and code of conduct. *American Psychologist, 57*, 1060–1073.

American Psychological Association. (2003). Guidelines on multicultural education, training, research, practice, and organizational change for psychologists. *American Psychologist, 58*, 377–402.

American Psychological Association. (2005). *American Psychological Association policy statement on evidence-based practice in psychology.* Retrieved August 15, 2008 from www.2.apa.org/practice/ebpstatement.pdf.

American Psychological Association, Commission on Accreditation. (2007). *Guidelines and Principles for Accreditation of Programs in Professional Psychology.* Washington, DC: APACA.

American Psychological Association, Commission on Accreditation. (2012). *Self-study Instructions: Doctoral Graduate Programs.* Washington, DC: Office of Program Consultation and Accreditation, APA.

Bronfenbrenner, U. (1995). Developmental ecology through space and time: A future perspective. In P. Moen, G. H. Elder, Jr., & K. Luscher (eds), *Examining Lives in Context: Perspectives on the Ecology of Human Development* (pp. 619–647). Washington, DC: APA.

Bureau of Labor Statistics (2010–2011). *Occupational Outlook Handbook.* Washington, DC: Bureau of Labor Statistics.

Cashwell, C. S. (2010). In CACREP perspective. *Counseling Today, 52*(11), 58–59.

Corey, G. R. (2009). *Theories and Practice of Counseling and Psychotherapy* (8th edn). Belmont, CA: Thomason.

Corsini, R. J. (2008). Introduction. In R. J. Corsini & D. Wedding (eds), *Current Psychotherapies* (8th edn) (pp. 1–13). Belmont, CA: Thomson Brooks/Cole.

Council for the Accreditation for Counseling and Related Educational Professions (2001). *CACREP Accreditation Standards.* Alexandria, VA: CACREP.

Council for the Accreditation of Counseling and Related Educational Programs (CACREP) (2009). *2009 Standards.* Retrieved from www.cacrep.org/doc/2009%20Standards%20with%20cover.pdf.

Daniel, J. H., Roysircar, G., Abeles, N., & Boyd, C. (2004). Individual and cultural diversity competence: Focus on the therapist. *Journal of Clinical Psychology, 25*(4), 255–267.

Fox, R. (1995). The rape of psychotherapy. *Professional Psychology: Research and Practice, 26,* 147–155.

Garrett, M. I. (2006). When eagle speaks: Counseling Native Americans. In C. Lee's (eds), *Multicultural Issues in Counseling: New Approaches to Diversity* (3rd ed) (pp. 25–53). Alexandria, VA: ACA.

Gladding, S. T. (2009). *Counseling: A comprehensive profession* (5th edn). Upper Saddle Hill, NJ: Merrill/Prentice-Hall.

Glasser, W. (2003). *How Psychiatry can be Hazardous to your Health.* Alexandria, VA: ACA.

Griner, D., & Smith, T. (2006). Culturally adapted mental health interventions: A meta-analytic review. *Psychotherapy: Theory, Research, Practice, Training, 43,* 531–548.

Harper, F., & McFadden, J. (eds) (2003). *Culture and Counseling: New Approaches.* Boston, MA: Allyn & Bacon.

Harold, M. (1985). Council's history examined after 50 years. *Guidepost, 27*(1), 4.

Hodges, S. (2009, March). Counseling in the twenty-first century: Challenges and opportunities. *Counseling Today, 51*(9), 44–47.

Hollis, J. W., & Dodson, T. A. (2001). *Counselor Preparation 1991–2001: Programs Faculty, Trends.* Greensboro, NC: National Board of Certified Counselors.

Hovarth, A. O., & Greenberg, L.S. (1994). *The Working Alliance: Theory, Research and Practice.* New York: John Wiley.

Hubble, M. A., Duncan, B. L., & Miller, S. D. (1999). *The Heart and Soul of Change: What Works in Therapy.* Washington, DC: APA.

Hochman, M., Hochman, S., Bor, D., & McCormick, D. (2008). *News Median Coverage of Medication Research.* Retrieved February 4, 2011 from http://jama.ama-assn.org/content/300/13/1544.full.

Imel, Z. E., & Wampold, B. E. (2008). The importance of treatment and the science of common factors in psychotherapy. In S. Brown and R. Lent (eds), *Handbook of Counseling Psychology* (4th edn) (pp. 249–266). New York: Wiley.

Ladany, N., & Inman, A. G. (2008). Counselor training and supervision. In S. Brown and R. Lent (eds). *Handbook of Counseling Psychology* (4th edn) (pp. 338–354). New York: Wiley.

Lee, C. (ed.) (2006), *Multicultural Issues in Counseling: New Approaches to Diversity* (3rd edn). Alexandria, VA: ACA.

Lichtenberg, J. W., Goodyear, R. K., & Genther, D. Y. (2008). The changing landscape of professional practice in counseling psychology. In S. D. Brown and R. W. Lent (eds), *Handbook of Counseling Psychology* (4th edn) (pp. 21–37). New York: Wiley.

Locke, D. C. (1990). A not so provincial view of multicultural counseling. *Counselor Education and Supervision, 30,* 18–25.

Lopez, S. J., & Edwards, L. M. (2008). The interface of counseling psychology and positive psychology: Assessing and promoting strengths. In S. D. Brown & R. W. Lent (eds), *Handbook of Counseling Psychology* (4th edn) (pp. 86–99). New York: Wiley.

McCormick, R., & Ishiyama, F. I. (2000). Counselling first nation's people in Canada. Special issue of *Canadian Journal of Counselling, 34*(1), 276–288

Myers, J. E., & Sweeney, T. J. (2005). *Counseling for Wellness: Theory, Research, and Practice.* Alexandria, VA: American Counseling Association.

National Board for Certified Counselors. (2011). *Understanding NBCC's National Certifications.* Retrieved February 4, 2011 from www.nbcc.org/Ourcertifications.

Norcross, J. C., Karpiak, C. P., & Lister, K. M. (2005). What's an integrationist? A study of self-identified integrative and (occasionally) eclectic psychologists. *Journal of Clinical Psychology, 61,* 1587–1594.

Psychotherapy Networker. (2007). *The Top Ten Most Influential Therapists of the Past Quarter-century.* Retrieved February 4, 2011 from http://psychotherapynetworker.org/magazine/populartopics/219-the-top-10.

Remley, T., & Herlihy, B. (2007). *Ethical, Legal, and Professional Issues in Counseling,* (3rd edn). Upper Saddle River, NJ: Pearson/Merrill-Prentice Hall.

Remley, T. P., Jr. (1995). A proposed alternative to the licensing of specialties in counseling. *Journal of Counseling & Development, 74,* 126–129.

Rollins, J (2010). 20/20 delegates reach consensus on definition on counseling. *Counseling Today* http://ct.counseling.org/?s=Jonathan%20Rollins

Roysircar, G. (2009). Evidence-based practice and its implications for culturally sensitive treatment. *Journal of Multicultural Counseling and Development, 37*(2), 66–82.

Roysircar, G. (2011). Foreword: Positive psychology, Eastern religions, and multicultural psychology. In E. Chang & C. Downey (eds), *Handbook of Race and Development in Mental Health* (pp. vii–xii). New York: Springer.

Roysircar, G. (2012a). Multicultural assessment: Individual and contextual dynamic sizing. In F. T. L. Leong and J. Trimble (eds), *Handbook of Multicultural Psychology.* Washington, DC: APA.

Roysircar, G. (2012b). Disaster counseling: A Haitian family case post January 12, 2010 earthquake. In S. Poyrazil & C. Thompson (eds), *International Case Studies in Mental Health* (pp. 155–180). Thousand Oaks, CA: Sage.

Roysircar, G. (2012c). American Indians and culturally sensitive therapy. Guest editor's introduction to special issue on American Indians and Native Alaskans. *Journals of Multicultural and Counseling, 40*(4), 66–69.

Roysircar, G., Dobbins, J. E., & Malloy, K. (2009). Diversity competence in training and clinical practice. In M. Kenkel & R. Peterson (eds). *Competency-based Education for Professional Psychology* (pp. 179–197). Washington, DC: APA.

Seligman, L. (1999). Twenty years of diagnosis and the DSM. *Journal of Mental Health Counseling, 21,* 229–239.

Seligman, M. E. P. (1998). Presidential statement. *APA Monitor,* May, 11–12.

Smith, T. B., Constantine, M. G., Dunn, T. W., Dinehart, J. M., & Montoya, J. A. (2006). Multicultural education in the mental health professions: A meta-analytic review. *Journal of Counseling Psychology, 53,* 132–145.

Sprinthall, N. A. (1981). A new model for research in service of guidance and counseling. *Personnel and Guidance Journal, 59,* 487–496.

Sue, D. W., & Sue, D. (2003). *Counseling the Culturally Different: Theory and Practice* (4th edn). New York: Wiley.

Sue, D. W., Arredondo, P., & McDavis, R. J. (1992). Multicultural counseling competencies and standards: A call to the profession. *Journal of Multicultural Counseling and Development, 20,* 64–88.

Sue, S. (1998). In search of cultural competence in psychotherapy and counseling. *American Psychologist, 53* (4), 440–448.

The Chronicle of Higher Education (2010, Sept. 24). *Diversity in academe,* Section B, p. B45. Washington, DC: Author.

Turner, E. H., Matthews, A. M., Linardatos, E., Tell, R. A., & Rosenthal, R. (2008). Selective publication of antidepressant trials and its influence on apparent policy. *New England Journal of Medicine, 358,* 252–260.

US Census Bureau (2010). State and country quick facts. www.census.gov/qfd/states/00000.html/. Author. Retrieved June 16, 2010.

Weinrach, S. G., & Thomas, K. R. (1993). The national board for certified counselors: The good, the bad and the ugly, *Journal of Counseling & Development, 71,* 105–109.

Zunker, V. G. (2006). *Career Counseling* (7th edn). Pacific Grove, CA: Brooks/Cole.

PART III

Counseling and psychotherapy in Asia

14

COUNSELING AND PSYCHOTHERAPY IN AUSTRALIA

Championing the egalitarian society?

Jac Brown

Introduction

Counseling and psychotherapy in Australia has evolved to meet the needs of a largely migrant population in a society where egalitarianism is enshrined in the minds of many. The convict settlement in the 1700s, inspired by Captain James Cook's exploration, left its mark in forming a society where authority is spurned and the myth that all are equal, despite many disparities created by money, power, and race. Australia is a country of approximately 22.7 million people (Australian Bureau of Statistics, 2011). While childbirth has decreased as in many Western countries, the growth in population continues mainly through immigration. In the earlier part of the last century, immigration consisted mainly of European migrants during the period of the "White Australia" policy (Australian Government Department of Immigration and Citizenship, 2009). This policy was reversed in 1966, when immigrants were assessed according to qualifications rather than skin pigmentation. The final vestiges of this policy were achieved in 1973. It was shortly after this time that there were many more migrants from Asian, African, and South American countries, fuelled by a number of factors including wars, genocide, and torture in the home countries of these refugees.

The changes in migrants also had implications for the growth of counseling and psychotherapy in Australia (Parliament of Australia, 2006). Immigrants from northern European countries were much more familiar with counseling than were those from southern European countries, leading to skepticism of counseling services from these new immigrants initially. However, many migrants to Australia came from countries where they were tortured or traumatized by wars, genocide, and restrictions of personal freedoms from repressive regimes, paving the way for counseling and psychotherapy for these victims of trauma. Difficulties with settling in Australia, including coping with unemployment, dealing with a new language, and facing racism in Australia resulted in a greater emphasis on these services. These factors paved the way for counseling to become more acceptable, and as a consequence of the broader cultural base, more models of counseling and psychotherapy began to focus on inter-cultural factors, making counseling relevant for a broader spectrum of Australians.

With the growth of increasing professionalization of the helping professions, including social work, psychology, counseling and psychotherapy, has come quality control through training specifications, ethical regulations, and professional development requirements (Brown & Corne, 2004). Non-pathologizing attitudes towards clients in these professions inspired by counseling were fostered by highlighting developmental issues rather than more pathological medical views of clients. This created an emphasis on psycho-education rather than remediation (Williams, 1978). Thus, focus on an egalitarian client-therapist relationship is fundamental to the work of counseling and psychotherapy in Australia and has had a major influence on the forms of counseling and psychotherapy that have evolved.

Brief history of counseling and psychotherapy

As counseling and psychotherapy are terms that have no legal definition or restrictions in Australia, it is not surprising that there are a number of different qualifications, ranging from high school to doctorate degrees, with the majority having bachelor's degrees (Pelling & Whetham, 2006). Counselors appear to be involved in a variety of specializations, including couple and family counseling, which began in the 1950s through the marriage guidance movement following the strain on relationships after the World War II (Simmons, 2006); career counseling which became established during the latter part of the 20th century and was formalized through a national association in 1989 (McMahon, 2006); and guidance and school counselors, who formed a national association in 1991 (Robinson, 2006).

Perhaps one of the most famous counselors in Australia is Michael White, who had a major impact on therapy in Australia and the world, and, in particular, family therapy. He was the founding editor of the *Australian Journal of Family Therapy* (which later became known as the *Australian and New Zealand Journal of Family Therapy*), which began in 1979. As editor, he created a context for dialogue between family therapists emphasizing the politics of experience particularly as it related to gender roles and the focus on effects of broader social issues that became influential during the 1980s (Denborough, 2009). These discussions stimulated an enormous amount of creative energy which is reflected in Michael White's extensive publications documenting his ideas, including externalizing the problem (White, 1988/89), re-authoring conversations (White & Epson, 1989), journey metaphors (White, 2002a), deconstructing failure conversations (White, 2002b), definitional ceremonies (White, 2003), scaffolding conversations (White, 2007), and narrative responses to trauma (White, 2004). He founded the Dulwich Centre, which has continued his work since his death in 2008 (Dulwich Centre, 2011).

The second half of the 20th century witnessed the establishment of numerous organizations that played a key role in the professionalization and specialization of counseling and psychotherapy in Australia. In 1974 The Australian Association for Cognitive and Behaviour Therapy (AACBT) (Australian Association for Cognitive and Behaviour Therapy, 2011) was formed. It currently offers training and continuing professional development that focuses on identifying unhelpful thoughts and behaviors and providing assistance in learning new thoughts and behaviors that promote healthy change.

The Australian and New Zealand Society of Jungian Analysts (ANZSJA) was established in 1977 (ANZSJA, 2011). The approach focuses on the individual interpretation of dreams, taking into consideration the often unconscious links between individuals and society in what Jung called the collective unconscious. Their training program, which includes individual psychotherapy for participants, involves training seminars which are rotated between Sydney, Melbourne, Canberra, The Gold Coast, and Auckland, New Zealand.

The Australia and New Zealand Association of Psychotherapy (ANZAP) was formed in 1987 (ANZAP, 2011). It originated out of the Psychotherapy Unit at the University of Sydney which was run at Westmead Hospital, focusing on Russell Mears' ideas, in conjunction with Robert Hobson, from the United Kingdom and was integrated through the ideas of Kohut's Self Psychology. This model became known as the Conversational Model (Mears, 2005). This model focuses on psychotherapy that integrates the self in relationship with unconscious traumatic memory. He continues to work in this area with a group of dedicated therapists, including a range of professions with training through ANZAP and the University of Sydney. In the same year, the Australian Association of Somatic Psychotherapists (AASP) (AASP, 2011) was established and is inspired by the work of biodynamic psychology and the neo-Reichians. They conduct training and therapy which is a holistic and experiential approach involving empathy, challenge, and understanding. Though united in somatic psychotherapy, their members are involved in a range of therapeutic interests including psychoanalytic studies, object relations, attachment theory, self psychology and intersubjectivity theory, neurobiology, infant observation, meditation, and various movement and bodywork disciplines, providing a model that encourages the integrative psychotherapy movement.

Counselor education programs, accreditation, licensure, and certification

For counseling psychologists, few university counseling psychology programs continue to operate in Australia. There has been considerable debate regarding the importance of counseling psychology to the discipline of psychology generally. Increasingly, this debate seems to be more focused on the general strategies and specific techniques that are central to counseling and psychotherapy, rather than the specialization as defined by the College of Counselling Psychologists. Pryor and Bright (2007) noted the relatively small percentage of College membership who are students in counseling psychology compared to other Australian Psychological Society (APS) Colleges. Brown and Corne (2004) cited the decreases in membership in recent years in the College of Counselling Psychologists, as well as the decrease in the number of university programs which still run professional master's degrees in counseling psychology throughout Australia. Five years ago there were six universities offering master's degrees in counseling psychology and today there are only three: Edith Cowan University in Perth, and Monash and Swinburn Universities in Melbourne. In a recent annual report for the APS, they reported almost three times as many members in the College of Clinical Psychologists as in the College of Counselling Psychologists (The Australian Psychological Society, 2011). While this trend has also been noted in American universities, the extent of the impact has been much greater in Australia due to the smaller number of universities involved. While this may have ramifications for professionals calling themselves counseling psychologists, it does not mean that counseling is disappearing, merely that is has become a more important foundational skill in most of the helping professions.

Recognizing the need for some form of regulation and a unified voice, counselors and psychotherapists are increasingly becoming members of organizations such as the Australian Counselling Association (Armstrong, 2006) and the Psychotherapy and Counselling Federation of Australia (Psychotherapy and Counselling Federation of Australia, 2011). Both of these organizations have developed ethical and training standards, addressed issues of continuing professional development, and continue to lobby government for forms of regulation or formal registration to guide consumers in obtaining high-quality counseling and psychotherapy. The

Australian Counselling Association has provision for membership through recognition by the Vocational Education Training or the Higher Education sectors. These state government bodies accredit qualifications that are recognized throughout Australia. Counselors are registered and placed on the register of this national association by having a Diploma in Counseling or a Bachelor of Counseling degree. Other health professional qualifications rarely meet the requirements of these counseling courses (Australian Counselling Association, 2011).

The Psychotherapy and Counselling Federation of Australia (2011) (PACFA) is the other national organization that maintains a national clinical register of counselors and psychotherapists. While it accredits member organizations with appropriate training standards, codes of ethics, and professional development requirements, it also maintains a clinical register of professionals who meet the requirement of a 3-year undergraduate training or a 2-year postgraduate specialist training in psychotherapy or counseling requiring a minimum of 750 client contact hours and 75 hours of postgraduate supervision over a period of 2 years (PACFA, 2011). Thus, there are significant attempts to obtain standardized training and recognition of qualified practitioners of counseling and psychotherapy even though the terms are not legally restricted to those possessing particular qualifications.

Counseling and psychotherapy is also central to the practice of psychology, and counseling psychologists are regulated through the process of becoming registered psychologists first, and subsequently becoming members of the Australian Psychological Society's (APS) College of Counselling Psychologists. This requires that counseling psychologists have master's degrees in counseling psychology as well as 1 year of supervised experience. These programs emphasize a range of models which focus extensively on the client-therapist relationship.

Currently, there are no formal recognized certification or licensure processes for counselors nor for psychotherapists, unless the particular counselor or psychotherapist is also a psychologist. The license which allows practice as a counseling psychologist is acquired through the registration process of becoming a psychologist and subsequently qualifying for the specialist title of counseling psychologist which is awarded by the Psychology Board of Australia (Psychology Board of Australia, 2011).

Current counseling and psychotherapy theories, processes, and trends

Counseling and psychotherapy in Australia as in other parts of the world, reacted to the psychodynamic models that were initiated by Freud which focused on unconscious processes and past family relationships, within the context of very long-term intensive therapy. Australia's reaction to the psychodynamic paradigm was experienced through two major influential paradigm shifts also noted around the world: The first paradigm shift was to humanistic psychology, represented by the work of Carl Rogers (1957; 1961). He focused on the key elements of accepting personal responsibility, focusing on the present, deciding how to manage personal problems, and emphasizing personal growth. The second paradigm shift was to cognitive psychology, which was evident in the cognitive behavior models of Albert Ellis (1962) and Aaron Beck (Beck, Rush, Shaw, & Emery, 1979). Both of these cognitive models defined thoughts as behavior, and were thus given scientific respectability which by and large, the humanistic models lacked. The models examined conscious thoughts and beliefs that were said to influence behavior and emotion, and provided new, more logical ways of thinking about problem situations of clients. Beck's model became more dominant, which continues to the present time, as it has been shown to be effective and is a short-term therapy for many, but certainly not all clients. While Roger's influence has also continued, there have been subsequent developments that have moved beyond this humanistic influence in these two major paradigm shifts.

The modernist view of reality which was supported by early advocates of humanistic psychology was challenged by the influences of social constructionism and postmodernism (Gergen, 1985). Parry (1991) defined postmodernism as " … what it means to live in a world where there is no longer any consensus concerning a fixed reference point" (p. 38). Postmodernism provided links between the multiple perceptions delineated by social constructionism, as it accounted for dominant views that were more widely accepted, and established these perspectives through language which seemed to be more influenced by culture than by mind. These ideas provided the backdrop for the solution-focused therapy of de Shazer (1982, 1985). De Shazer's work was influential because of its client-centered approach as well as its emphasis on very brief therapy which was popular with Australian state and federal governments who were attempting to limit costs. It emphasized finding out what clients were doing that was working and then attempting to increase the use of those solutions. Postmodern ideas were also fundamental to the developments of the narrative therapy of Michael White.

The other major model during this time was inspired by the work of the Milan associates (Selvini Palazzoli, Boscolo, Cecchin, & Prata, 1980). They developed a method of conducting therapy sessions, usually with entire families that focused on forming systemic hypotheses from which they developed a method of circular questioning within the context of a session where the therapist was seen to be relatively neutral (Selvini et al., 1980). The model of questioning has survived and has become influential in many forms of therapy, including cognitive-behavioral therapy (CBT), as these questions may provide challenges to client's unhelpful cognitions (James, Morse, & Howarth, 2010).

The second major influence of humanism on Australian therapy was through the work of Kohut (1984) and self psychology. His method of empathic enquiry is very similar to the work of Rogers (Kahn & Rachman, 2000) and was also influential in the subsequent developments of the conversational model of Russell Mears (2000; 2005). Despite these major influences towards client-centered therapies, there is a strong push, sparked by government bodies related to mental health, psychologists, and medical practitioners towards CBT. This influence is due to the amount of research that has been conducted on CBT and the nationwide push towards evidence-based practice. For instance, all 6-year clinical psychology training programs at universities include CBT training as an essential part of their training programs, ensuring a major influence by psychologists on counseling and psychotherapy generally. Often the evidence for other models of therapy is disregarded, in favor of the highly politicized emphasis on CBT by the APS and Medicare, the government system that provides rebates for psychologists for their services with clients. While the importance of the client-therapist relationship is acknowledged by CBT experts (e.g. Beck et al., 1979), there is little emphasis on training in this aspect of the therapy. Consequently, the divide between CBT and humanistic approaches is very real, creating considerable professional controversy.

Indigenous and traditional healing methods

As accreditation has been the focus for counseling and psychotherapy over the past 15 years, which has required enormous efforts, and possibly due to the belief that Australia was an egalitarian society, there has been little time devoted towards reflecting upon and forming links with indigenous and traditional healing. This also included any migrants bringing their traditional methods to Australia. However, some initiatives have begun, firstly in New Zealand, which spread quickly to Australia. There were also some subsequent initiatives in Australia. These initiatives have been linked to higher education in a number of universities.

The Family Centre (2011) in Wellington, New Zealand, developed a model for therapy with indigenous people which focused on the culture, gender, social, spiritual, economic, and psychological backdrops that seemed to provide the context for problems. This endeavor, which begun in 1979, was led by Charles Waldegrave and Taimalie Kiwi Tamasese. The program focused on issues of marginalization of indigenous people (Waldegrave, Tamasese, Tuhaka, & Campbell, 2003). Initially they employed two community development workers from the Maori and Pacific Island communities to facilitate justice and equality and to provide a context for mutual learning. This process recognized the wealth of information that traditional methods of healing, long before European settlement, could bring to the collective wisdom which often included simple solutions, and respectful non-intervention. These processes of course are fundamental to many counseling and psychotherapeutic approaches, but in the face of so many overwhelming problems, can often be forgotten in an attempt to solve these problems. The model became known as *Just Therapy*, and provided a more holistic approach for indigenous clients, as they became aware of the many limitations that impacted on these clients when they returned to their local communities, which included poverty, age and gender discrimination, racial harassment, and difficulties accessing services. This work has spread to countries beyond New Zealand, with a number of projects being conducted through the Family Centre Social Policy Research Unit at Massey University in Wellington (Massey University, 2009). This unit has now developed a 1-year postgraduate diploma in Discursive Therapies in conjunction with the Family Centre, which, with the completion of a thesis, can lead to a MPhil in Psychology.

The Bouverie Centre (2011) through its Indigenous Project Team in Melbourne has also been involved in conducting therapy and training designed for Aboriginal clients and workers. The Family Therapy Training and Consultation for Aboriginal Child and Family Workers in Community began in 2007, and focused on family therapy training, research, and consultation and policy development for Aboriginal child and family workers working in Aboriginal and mainstream communities across Victoria. The work involves consultation with an advisory group that consists of indigenous and non-indigenous representatives of Aboriginal Community Co-operatives and other organizations working with Aboriginal families. This work is being supported by an indigenous researcher, Robyne Latham, in partnership with La Trobe University's Indigenous Employment Scheme to conduct action research into the project to maximize the lessons learned in working effectively with Aboriginal families. Thus, these recent and pioneering efforts have been useful in beginning a dialogue with indigenous people and may form an important link for future development in this area.

Helping professionals within the immigrant population in Australia tend to move in a mainstream direction in regards to healing by enrolling in university programs in counseling and psychotherapy, rather than relying upon their own traditional methods used in their former countries. Thus working with immigrants by incorporating their traditional methods brought from their home countries has not emerged. This is probably not particularly surprising, given the limited efforts in embracing the Aboriginal traditional methods of healing in Australia.

Research and supervision

Research in Australia is largely supported by the Australian government through a system of grants that are awarded to academic and practice organizations who pair up with universities in order to work collaboratively on research projects (Australian Research Council, 2011). These grants are highly competitive and require a strong evidence-based background in order to receive funding. The major model that has a large, respectable research base is CBT. Thus, the major research coming out of Australia on therapy is related to CBT.

There is a general skepticism in psychological domains relating to qualitative research (Brown & Corne, 2004). This feeling makes it difficult to get research published that is not quantitative, and most of this research is published in overseas journals that specialize in CBT research. However, there are a couple of Australian journals that should be mentioned in relation to predominantly CBT research: *Clinical Psychology, Australian Psychologist* and *The Australian Journal of Psychology. The Australian Psychologist* will occasionally publish articles that are critical of CBT which embrace humanistic models of therapy. However this is rare. There is one other journal called *Psychotherapy in Australia* which publishes clinical papers on a range of therapeutic initiatives in Australia related to counseling and psychotherapy. The *Australian and New Zealand Journal of Family Therapy* publishes some quantitative and qualitative research, but focuses mainly on clinical issues. Finally, the *Dulwich Centre Review* is a journal that publishes work related mainly to narrative therapy which is also of a clinical nature. Thus, most evaluative research in Australia relates to CBT and is published locally, but predominantly is published in American and British journals.

Supervision is becoming more important in Australia, as professional bodies and government legislation and regulation exert a major influence. This has been coordinated by the Australian Health Practitioner Regulation Agency (2011) for many health practitioners, including psychologists. For psychologists, this involves 30 hours per year of professional development, of which 10 of those hours need to be supervision. This is the most prescriptive model in the requirements for professional development. Members of PACFA are required to complete 15 hours of professional development, but the components of this are not specified (PACFA, 2011). Thus, while ongoing supervision is desirable, specific requirements outside of a general guideline for professional development of some nature, are largely left up to the individual counselor or psychotherapist.

Strengths, weaknesses, opportunities, and challenges

Australia has moved a long way from its volunteer counseling beginnings in the 1950s. Its responsiveness to the worldwide trend towards professionalization and accreditation has been a necessary and important strength. For a country with a relatively small population, some important leaders in counseling and psychotherapy have emerged. Accreditation has resulted in many links with universities, which has been good for the universities as well as for the organizations that have been conducting the training, resulting in an excellent mix of theory and practice. Yet in some ways, the lack of accreditation meant that there was an air of creativity and exploration that allowed models related to the Australian culture to emerge. Accreditation has also meant that the public has been protected from poor standards of practice (Williams, 1978). Thus, while the professions of counseling and psychotherapy are quite young, progress towards professionalization has taken place relatively quickly. Australians have a very positive attitude to productivity and change, resulting in a very responsive environment for counseling and psychotherapy to thrive.

In many ways, the changes that have occurred have been in response to demands of the situation in a reactive rather than proactive manner. This is perhaps a weakness in the field that ought to be addressed. For example, when training standards were raised, this was related to government initiatives to set industry wide training standards rather than the training organizations themselves (Australian Qualifications Framework, 2011). Furthermore, these standards were also related to government initiatives to link counseling and psychotherapy to the national health system.

Further, Australians have been relatively slow in making connections with the indigenous population in relation to counseling and psychotherapy. This may be because of some of the negative attitudes that were developed towards Aboriginal and Torres Strait Islanders when Western development began, as well as the difficulties in integrating migrants who have come from many countries. Thus, the process has been much slower in this area than it might have been. However, the weaknesses are relatively small. The Australian ethos of egalitarianism and working hard towards goals that will benefit all Australians has had benefits to counterbalance some of these weaknesses that have been noted.

The distance of Australia from other major countries that have embraced counseling and psychotherapy has encouraged resourcefulness in Australians and provided opportunities to develop models and techniques for working with clients. This has allowed for a fresh approach in thinking creatively about human problems and how to address them. The government initiative in standardizing industry training across all sectors was a great opportunity for the counseling and psychotherapy industry to develop important training and accreditation standards (Psychotherapists and Counsellors Federation of Australia, 2011). Furthermore, the healthcare initiative of linking Medicare with counseling and psychotherapy services through social workers, occupational therapists, and psychologists has provided an opportunity for counseling and psychotherapy organizations to further professionalize to enhance the prospect of obtaining similar medical benefits for their members (Australian Government Department of Health and Ageing, 2010). Thus, the opportunities that have emerged have created carefully constructed and important initiatives for counselors and psychotherapists.

While there has been enormous change in counseling and psychotherapy, there are still further improvements required. It is with great frustration that counselors and psychotherapists (who are not social workers, psychologists or occupational therapists) wait for government acceptance of their training standards, ethical principles, professional development, and accreditation standards to develop to the level where the possibility of healthcare rebates could be offered through the medical healthcare system (Psychotherapists and Counsellors Federation of Australia, 2011). The body most closely associated with this process is PACFA, and this body represents a very broad and diverse range of counseling and psychotherapy strategies. While this may be seen as a strength, it is also a potential weakness as it raises concerns about what exactly has been accredited. At a time when evidence-based practice is gaining acceptance as shown through an emphasis on CBT, the question may also be asked as to how could such a broad range of therapeutic strategies be effective (Brown & Corne, 2004). Many of the modalities have not been evaluated for effectiveness, providing some skepticism. These issues need to be addressed in order for further growth to occur. The major difficulty in addressing this lack of research is the link between past research and new funding. While these models have not been adequately researched in the past, this makes it difficult to attract research funding in the present. Furthermore, many private practitioners who practice these models are not inclined to evaluate them as evaluation is an expensive exercise. These challenges appear to be difficult to deal with under current practices.

Future directions

The traditions of humanistic psychology and subsequent developments in social constructionism and postmodernism have been very influential in creating models that have been embraced by Australian therapists, which include solution focused therapy, post-Milan therapies, and narrative therapy. These models have such a strong base in Australia that they will continue into the future. However, in the future, there will probably be a new emphasis on this diversity. While these models have been established through emphasizing the differences, there will be increasing influences that highlight the commonalities in a way of working co-operatively rather than the current often divisive professional conflict. These models are often connected through the types of questions used in the therapy. There is also the common elements of the client-therapist relationship that are emphasized through the humanistic influence of non-directive therapy. These important influences will become more influential in the future, responding to current research that emphasizes the therapeutic benefit of the therapeutic alliance. In addition, the professional rivalry provided by the CBT establishment has only increased the resolve of those other practitioners who have been influenced by the humanistic movement (Brown & Corne, 2004). Thus, the future should lead to a greater emphasis on humanism, which may extend to CBT practitioners as they begin to place more emphasis on the client-therapist relationship and how all forms of therapy may be enhanced by a further move towards client-centered models of treatment.

Consequently, the influence of counseling models that emphasize the client-therapist relationship has also been felt in CBT, as the literature on the common elements continues to indicate that this relationship is responsible for a large proportion of the effectiveness of therapy (Wampold, 2000). Thus, it seems that the future for therapy in Australia may be a time of integrating models that have been perceived as very diverse, predominantly through emphasis on the common elements of therapy. Along with this emphasis is the important tradition of non-pathological conceptualizations. It seems that this tradition will move forward as therapists embrace more models that attempt to de-pathologize the client.

Conclusion

Counseling and psychotherapy has a great tradition of taking major models that have been influential particularly in the United States and the United Kingdom, and bringing them to Australia. In the process of this, changes are made, and new models develop that embrace the great Australian tradition of an egalitarian society. However, with the lack of a concerted effort to embrace traditional methods of healing, one could question how well egalitarianism has permeated Australian society. It is perhaps through further emphasizing the importance of the client-therapist relationship, the humanity and uniqueness of all clients and the environmental context of the client in explaining problems, as evident in all major models practiced in Australia and the two which originated in Australia of White's narrative therapy and Mears' conversational model, that such a society can be achieved.

References

Armstrong, P. (2006). The Australian Counseling Association: Meeting the needs of Australian counselors. *International Journal of Psychology*, *41*, 156–162.

Australia and New Zealand Association of Psychotherapy (ANZAP). (2011). *Training in the Conversational Model*. Retrieved from www.anzapweb.com/html/training/training-in-the-conversational-model.html.

Australian and New Zealand Society of Jungian Analysts (ANZSJA). (2011). *Homepage*. Retrieved from www.anzsja.org.au/index.php?page=home.

Australian Association for Cognitive and Behaviour Therapy. (2011). *Welcome*. Retrieved from www.aacbtqld.org.au/AACBT_QLD/Welcome.html.

Australian Association of Somatic Psychotherapists (AASP). (2011). *The Australian Association for Somatic Psychotherapists*. Retrieved from www.pacfa.org.au/memberassoc/list/asset_id/35/cid/4/parent/0/t/memberassoc/title/Australian%20Association%20of%20Somatic%20PsychotherapistsF.

Australian Counselling Association. (2011). *Homepage*. Retrieved from www.theaca.net.au/

Australian Bureau of Statistics. (2011). *Population clock*. Retrieved from www.abs.gov.au/ausstats/abs@.nsf/0/1647509ef7e25faaca2568a900154b63?OpenDocument.

Australian Government Department of Health and Ageing. (2010). *Department of Health and Ageing annual report 2009–10*. Retrieved from www.health.gov.au/internet/annrpt/publishing.nsf/Content/annual-report-0910-toc.

Australian Government Department of Immigration and Citizenship. (2009). *Abolition of the White Australia Policy*. Retrieved from www.immi.gov.au/media/fact-sheets/08abolition.htm.

Australian Health Practitioner Regulation Agency (2011). *Psychology board of Australia*. Retrieved from www.psychologyboard.gov.au.

Australian Qualifications Framework (2011). *The Australian Qualifications Framework*. Retrieved from www.aqf.edu.au/AbouttheAQF/TheAQF/tabid/108/Default.aspx.

Australian Research Council. (2011). *Annual Reports*. Retrieved from www.arc.gov.au/about_arc/annual_report.htm.

Beck, A. T., Rush, A. J., Shaw, B. F., & Emery, G. (1979). *Cognitive Therapy of Depression*. New York: Guilford Press.

Brown, J. E., & Corne, L. (2004). Counselling psychology in Australia. *Counseling Psychology Quarterly, 17* (3), 287–299.

Denborough, D. (2009). Some reflections on the work of Michael White: An Australian perspective. *Australian and New Zealand Journal of Family Therapy, 30,* 92–108.

De Shazer, S. (1982). *Patterns of Brief Family Therapy*. New York: The Guilford Press.

De Shazer, S. (1985). *Keys to Solution in Brief Therapy*. New York: Norton.

Dulwich Centre (2011). *About Dulwich Centre*. Retrieved from www.dulwichcentre.com.au.

Ellis, A. (1961). *Reason and Emotion in Psychotherapy*. New York: Lyle Stuart.

Gergen, K. (1985). The social constructionist movement in modern psychology. *The American Psychologist, 40,* 266–275.

James, I. A., Morse, R., & Howarth, A. (2010). The science and art of asking questions in cognitive therapy. *Behavioural and Cognitive Psychotherapy, 38,* 83–93.

Kahn, E., & Rachman, A. W. (2000). Carl Rogers and Heinz Kohut. A historical perspective. *Psychoanalytic Psychology, 17,* 294–312.

Kohut, H. (1984). *How does Analysis Cure?* Chicago, IL: The University of Chicago Press.

Massey University. (2009). *School of Psychology, Massey University: In Partnership with the Family Centre, Lower Hutt, Wellington, and the Taos Institute*. Retrieved from www.therapy.massey.ac.nz/

McMahon, M. (2006). Career counseling in Australia. *International Journal of Psychology, 41*(3), 174–179.

Mears, R. (2000). *Intimacy and Alienation: Memory, Trauma, and Personal Being*. New York: Brunner Routledge.

Mears, R. (2005). *The Metaphor of Play: Origins and Breakdown of Personal Being*. New York: Routledge.

Palazzoli Selvini, M., Boscolo, L., Cecchin, G., & Prata, G. (1978). *Paradox and Counterparadox: A New Model in the Therapy of the Family in Schizophrenic Transaction*. New York: Jason Aronson.

Parliament of Australia. (2006). *Australia's Settlement Services for Refugees and Migrants*. Retrieved from www.aph.gov.au/library/intguide/sp/settlement.htm.

Parry, A. (1991). A universe of stories. *Family Process, 30,* 37–54.

Pelling, N., & Whetham, P. (2006). The professional preparation of Australian counselors. *International Journal of Psychology, 41*(3), 189–193.

Pryor, G. L., & Bright, J. E. H. (2007). The current state and future direction of counseling psychology in Australia. *Applied Psychology. An International Review, 56*(1), 7–19.

Psychology Board of Australia. (2011). *General Registration*. Retrieved from www.psychologyboard.gov.au/Registration/General.aspx.

Psychotherapy and Counselling Federation of Australia (PACFA). (2011). *History of PACFA*. Retrieved from www.pacfa.org.au/aboutus/cid/9/parent/0/t/aboutus/l/layout.

Rogers, C. R. (1957). The necessary and sufficient conditions of therapeutic personality change. *Journal of Clinical and Consulting Psychology, 22,* 95–103.

Rogers, C. R. (1961). *On Becoming a Person: A Therapist's View of Psychotherapy*. New York: Houghton Mifflin Company.

Robinson, P. (2006). The Australian Guidance and Counseling Association: Meeting the needs of our members and Australian students. *International Journal of Psychology, 41,* 170–173.

Selvini Palazzoli, M., Boscolo, L., Cecchin, G., & Prata, G. (1980). Hypothesizing, circularity, and neutrality—Three guidelines for the conductor of the session. *Family Process, 19*(1), 3–12.

Simmons, P. (2006). Relationship and family counseling in Australia: A review of our history and current status. *International Journal of Psychology, 41*(3), 180–188.

The Australian Psychological Society. (2011). *About the APS.* Retrieved from www.psychology.org.au/ AboutUs/

The Bouverie Centre (2011). *Homepage.* Retrieved from www.bouverie.org.au.

The Family Centre. (2011). *Introduction.* Retrieved from www.familycentre.org.nz/Areas_of_Work/ Social_Policy_Research/index.html.

Waldegrave, C., Tamasese, K., Tuhaka, F., & Campbell, W. (2003). *Just Therapy—A Journey: A Collection of Papers from the Just Therapy Team, New Zealand.* Adelaide: Dulwich Centre Publications.

Wampold, B. E. (2000). Outcomes of individual counseling and psychotherapy: Empirical evidence addressing two fundamental questions. In S. D. Brown & R. W. Lent (eds), *Handbook of Counseling Psychology* (pp. 711–739). New York: J. Wiley.

White, M. (1988/89). The externalizing of the problem and the re-authoring of lives and relationships. *Dulwich Centre Newsletter.* Summer, Special Edition.

White, M. (2002a). Journey metaphors. *International Journal of Narrative Therapy and Community Work, 4*, 12–18.

White, M. (2002b). Addressing personal failure. *International Journal of Narrative Therapy and Community Work, 3*, 33–76.

White, M. (2003). Narrative practice and community assignments. *International Journal of Narrative Therapy and Community Work, 4*, 24–38.

White, M. (2004). Working with people who are suffering the consequences of multiple trauma: A narrative perspective. *International Journal of Narrative Therapy and Community Work, 5*, 45–76.

White, M. (2007). *Maps of narrative practice.* New York: W. W. Norton.

White, M. & Epson, D. (1989). *Narrative Means to Therapeutic Ends.* New York: W. W. Norton.

Williams, C. (1978). The dilemma of counseling psychology. *Australian Psychologist, 13*(1), 33–40.

15

COUNSELING AND PSYCHOTHERAPY IN CHINA

Building capacity to serve 1.3 billion

Doris F. Chang, Yuping Cao, Qijia Shi,
Wang Chun, and Mingyi Qian

Introduction

Although some of the earliest recorded theories regarding the cultivation of psychological wellbeing originated in China, counseling and psychotherapy as practiced today bear few traces of those cultural roots. Instead, counseling and psychotherapy in China today looks increasingly similar to professional practice in other industrialized societies, reflecting the sweeping social and economic changes that have transformed the country in recent years. On the one hand, this is a sign of remarkable progress. The state's growing recognition of the need and benefits of psychological services has led to increased investments in training and quality assurance efforts, expansion of mental health services in institutions such as schools and prisons, and funding support for research and foreign exchanges. On the other hand, there are also lamentable signs of traditions cast aside in the rush to modernity. Clinical relationships are increasingly replacing informal sources of social support as community structures weaken. Furthermore, as more and more foreign experts enter the country to disseminate knowledge developed elsewhere, the therapeutic potential of indigenous healing traditions and practices remains untapped.

An ancient civilization, dating from *c.* 2700 BCE, China has a population of more than 1.3 billion, making up one-fifth of the world's population (National Bureau of Statistics of China, 2011). The People's Republic of China (PRC) was founded in 1949 following an extended period of civil war that ended with the defeat of the Nationalist Guomindang armies. The PRC is a socialist republic, governed by the Communist Party of China, which has jurisdiction over 22 provinces, five autonomous regions (Xinjiang, Inner Mongolia, Tibet, Ningxia, and Guangxi), four municipalities (Beijing, Tianjin, Shanghai, and Chongqing), and two Special Administrative Regions (Hong Kong and Macau). Although 92% of the population is Han Chinese, 56 other ethnic groups including the Zhuang, Manchu, and Uighers make up a significant minority. Rapid economic growth since 1978 has led to substantial improvements in the overall standard of living, life expectancy, and literacy rates. However, wide economic and infrastructural disparities exist between the rural areas and the more prosperous coastal cities.

Brief history of counseling and psychotherapy

The first references to counseling and psychotherapeutic approaches in China can be traced back over 2,000 years to classical medical and philosophical writings. Theories of counseling and psychotherapy were initially described in the traditional Chinese medical text, *Huangdi's Internal Classics*, published around the 3rd century BCE. The text described how emotions and mental states may be improved by seeking consultation from a physician, diverting one's attention, and applying acupuncture. The authors also described what may be viewed as the first systematic psychotherapeutic approach based on Yin–Yang/five elements theory (Lin, 1980). The fundamental principles of the approach are as follows: "rage impairs the liver, sorrow prevails over anger; elation impairs the heart, fear prevails over elation; anxiety impairs the spleen, anger prevails over anxiety; grief impairs the lungs, joy prevails over melancholy; terror impairs the kidneys, anxiety prevails over fear" (Kang, 1999). According to these principles, mental diseases can be treated by activating particular emotions that can counteract dysfunctional mental states. In addition, the traditional Chinese medical techniques of *qigong* and *Moving Jing Changing Qi Therapy* (移精变气法) are very similar to modern relaxation approaches such as meditation and diaphragmatic breathing (Zhang & Zheng, 2011).

Beginning with Kuan-tzu's influential text, *Inner Enterprise* (内业), philosophers and scholars of ancient China including Confucius, Lao-tzu, Chuang-tzu, and Xun-tzu, emphasized the importance of mental cultivation, character development, and a flexible approach towards social and personal life. A number of ideas relevant to the enterprise of psychotherapy may be found in philosophical descriptions of practices such as "fasting of the mind" and "sitting and forgetting" (Chuang-tzu). The classic Taoist texts of Lao-tzu and Chuang-tzu have been especially influential in contemporary thinking about mental health.

Modern forms of counseling and psychotherapy date from the early 20th century, although the field's development has been periodically disrupted by war and domestic instability. One key event was Bertrand Russell's landmark 1920 lecture, "The analysis of mind," in which he introduced Sigmund Freud's theories to the Chinese intelligentsia. The Chinese Association for Mental Health was established in Nanjing in 1936. However, the association efforts were halted as a result of the War of Resistance against Japan (1937–1945).

After the establishment of the People's Republic of China in 1949, counseling and psychotherapy developed in two directions. First, psychotherapy practice was strongly influenced by neuropsychiatry models and behavioral approaches emerging from the former Soviet Union. Second, a few Chinese psychologists attempted to develop novel interventions such as comprehensive practice therapy by Li-Xintian and Li-Chongpei. However, these promising developments were interrupted during the tumult of the Cultural Revolution (1966–1976).

In the 1980s, following the end of the Cultural Revolution, mental hospitals and general hospitals resumed efforts to provide psychotherapeutic services to the severely mentally ill. As a result of political and economic reforms initiated in the late 1970s through the 1980s, the field of Chinese psychiatry began to thrive, aided by its re-engagement with Western scientific communities. These events ushered in a fertile period in the late 1980s and early 1990s that produced a number of innovations in Chinese psychotherapy. These include Li Xintian's comprehensive practice therapy (Li, 2003), Zhong Youbin's psychodynamically oriented Cognitive Insight Therapy (Zhong, 1999), Lu Longguang's dredging psychotherapy (Lu, 1996), and Zhang Yalin and Yang Desen's Chinese Taoist Cognitive Psychotherapy (Zhang & Yang, 1998). There was also renewed interest in traditional Chinese healing approaches such as Emotional Restriction Therapy and *qigong* (Yang, 2000; Zhang & Zheng, 2011).

In the 1990s, the fields of counseling and psychotherapy experienced rapid growth, spurred by the proliferation of advanced training programs organized by native and foreign experts.

Training programs in psychoanalysis, behavior therapy, cognitive therapy, cognitive-behavioral therapy, person-centered therapy, and family therapy served as important supplements to the nominal training provided by most medical schools at the time. In particular, the training program initiated by the German–Chinese Academy for Psychotherapy in 1997 fostered many of China's leading experts in counseling and psychotherapy today.

Since 2000, the level of professionalism and standardization within the field has continued to increase. Important events include the creation of a Psychologist Certification by the Ministry of Labor in 2002, the development of a Psychologist Qualifying Examination by the Ministry of Health in 2002, the registration of clinical and counseling psychologists and other mental health professionals by several professional organizations, including the Chinese Psychological Society beginning in 2007, and the publication of the Ethics Code of Conduct in Clinical and Counseling Psychology by the Chinese Psychological Society in 2007 (Chinese Psychological Society, 2007a, 2007b). In 2008, the Fifth World Congress for Psychotherapy was successfully held in Beijing, a sign of its current international stature in the global field of counseling and psychotherapy.

Counselor education programs, accreditation, licensure, and certification

Academic programs in clinical or counseling psychology were not established until the end of the Cultural Revolution in 1976 (Qian, 2002). A national survey conducted in the 1990s found that only 10 institutions reported having a graduate training program in clinical psychology or a related field such as medical psychology (Gong & Li, 1997). From 1980 to 1995, 87 graduates received their master's degrees, and 10 earned doctoral degrees from these 10 institutions.

It was not until the end of the 1990s that clinical and counseling psychology began to emerge as distinct subspecialties within the field of applied psychology in China. Today, psychology programs have been established in many universities. Combined with free-standing institutes of psychology, there are more than 240 programs dedicated to psychological training and education (Y. J. Su, personal communication, June 2009). The majority of undergraduate and graduate programs in psychology include courses related to clinical and counseling psychology.

Training programs in counseling psychology are predominantly master's level programs, although some universities do offer bachelor's degrees in counseling psychology. Programs in clinical or medical psychology also tend to be at the master's level, with a greater emphasis on both clinical science and practice. However, only a few training programs have a standardized curriculum and educational requirements. In many university psychology programs, there are no clear requirements with regard to practicum hours or supervision. In medical universities on the other hand, students are provided ample clinical practice opportunities, but only minimal coursework on topics such as psychological testing and assessment.

By the 1980s, few training programs in counseling and psychotherapy existed outside of university settings. However, by the late 1990s, several formal training programs in psychotherapy had been established, the most distinguished of which remains the Chinese-German Advanced Continuous Training Program for Psychotherapy, created by the German-Chinese Academy for Psychotherapy. The first cohort of participants (1997–1999) completed a 3-year curriculum of professional training courses held in the spring and fall in Kunming, Beijing, Shanghai, Wuhan, and Chengdu. The training encompassed three specialty areas: psychoanalytic psychotherapy, family therapy, and behavioral therapy. Over the last 10 years, the program has had a tremendous impact on the field of psychotherapy in China, elevating the standard of practice across the country. Similar international training programs have since emerged, including the Norway-Chinese Psychodynamic Training Program, German-Chinese Advanced Continuous

Training Program for EMDR, and the German–Chinese Continuous Training for Hypnosis (Guo, 2009; Xiao, 1998).

To elevate the quality of professional training and the delivery of psychological services, accreditation and certification of psychological counselors and psychotherapists began only about 10 years ago, with three regulatory bodies setting out separate standards and procedures. Beginning in 2002, the Ministry of Labor and Social Security released a set of accreditation standards for psychological counselors, which were revised 3 years later. From the first examination in 2003 to the end of 2010, nearly 200,000 people have passed the examination. However, the minimum training and education requirements for accreditation were considered by many to be too low (Wang, 2005), raising concerns about releasing unqualified counselors into the field.

A second credential is administered by the Chinese Health Ministry and the Chinese Ministry of Personnel. In 2002, the Chinese Health Ministry convened a group of experts to develop a qualifying examination for psychotherapists. The first examination was held in October 2002 and targeted medical professionals experienced in psychotherapy. There are three credential levels–primary, middle, and senior. To date, there over 2,000 people nationwide who have passed this exam, with none attaining the senior-level distinction.

The third credential is administered by the Chinese Psychological Society's Registered System for Professional Organizations and Individual Practitioners in Clinical and Counseling Psychology (RSPI) (Chinese Psychological Society, 2007a). Of the three credentials, only the RSPI is overseen by a non-governmental agency and the requirements are also the most stringent. Clinical psychologists and counselors who wish to be registered in the system must meet a set of competency standards pertaining to education and supervised clinical training experiences, which were modeled on standards outlined by the American Psychological Association and the American Counseling Association. Applicants must also submit a case report and letters of recommendation from two registered clinicians, counselors, or supervisors. Applicants must then pass an ethics exam. Once registered, individuals must complete at least 20 continuing education hours every 3 years and have no reported ethical violations (Qian, 2009). These procedures were implemented in 2007 and as of this writing, there were 175 registered clinical and counseling psychologists and 127 registered supervisors. An additional 108 members just passed the 2011 examination and will become formally registered in the system in 2012. As the field continues to develop, the Registered System will undoubtedly play an important role in elevating the standards of psychological training and practice, and assisting individuals searching for qualified professionals in their communities.

Current counseling and psychotherapy theories, processes, and trends

Contemporary forms of counseling and psychotherapy have been generally recognized as cultural imports from the West. As such, public and professional acceptance of psychotherapy in China has waxed and waned over the years, reflecting the changing sociopolitical context in which local experiences of distress are professionally labeled and transformed into curable entities. In the 1950s, Freud's theories were well-known among the intellectual elites. However, they were condemned for their emphasis on sexual drives, which were considered taboo at the time. During the Cultural Revolution, psychology was criticized as unscientific and mental health problems were criminalized and "treated" by a process of political re-education (Chang, Tong, Shi, & Zeng, 2005).

In the 1980s, the reform and opening policies initiated by Deng Xiaoping precipitated the development of the national economy and opened lines of communication with the West. Western counseling and psychotherapy models were reintroduced into China and reinvigorated the mental health field, sparking widespread interest in talk therapies and their healing potential

(Chang et al., 2005). Over the past 20 years, two national surveys of practitioners of counselors and psychotherapists have been carried out (Gong & Li, 1997; Qian et al., 2008) and highlight changes in practice trends over time.

The first large-scale survey was carried out in 30 provinces and cities by Gong Yaoxian (Gong & Li, 1997). Results indicated that the most frequently employed treatment was behavioral therapy, which was applied in 29% of the total cases described by participants. Other approaches included cognitive therapy (20%), supportive therapy (18.1%), psychoanalytic psychotherapy (11.3%), Morita therapy (7%), biofeedback (4.6%), hypnosis (3.9%), client-centered therapy (3.4%), and Zhang Youbin's cognitive insight therapy (2.7%).

The latest survey was conducted by Qian Mingyi (Qian et al., 2008) in six major field sites, involving 1543 subjects from 29 provinces, municipalities and autonomous regions. Cognitive therapy emerged as the most common treatment modality, followed by behavioral therapy, humanistic therapies, integrative therapies, psychoanalytic psychotherapy, and family therapy.

A comparison of the 1995 and 2008 surveys reveals a number of significant changes in clinical practice over time. First, cognitive therapy overtook behavioral therapy as the most common treatment approach in 2008. This change brings China in line with other countries in which cognitive approaches have become the dominant practice approach. Second, two popular indigenous treatments in 1995—Morita therapy and cognitive insight therapy, developed in Japan and China, respectively—disappeared from the list by 2008.

According to Wu Heming, the senior psychotherapist and deputy director of the Applied Psychology Institute at the Chinese University of Geosciences, patients were largely unwilling to pay for talk therapy in the 1980s and 1990s as it was not recognized as an effective cure for psychological problems. Morita therapy, on the other hand, exhibited many of the hallmarks of standard medical treatments—including a hospital stay and bed rest—and was therefore readily accepted by the general public (Shi, 2009). Since then, as individuals have acquired more discretionary income and are more aware of the curative effects of psychotherapy, more and more people are willing to pay for the "talking cure." By 2008, the most common treatment approaches were those that were developed in the West, reflecting the tremendous influence of foreign experts in shaping contemporary clinical practice in China.

In particular, integrative approaches have become a dominant paradigm in recent years. A strategy for collecting and integrating treatment techniques across schools of therapy, psychotherapy integration is viewed by many Chinese clinicians as a practical way to efficiently disseminate promising interventions to the public. From 2003–2008, German analyst Wolfgang Senf and Chinese psychiatrist Shi Qijia carried out a number of national training programs in psychotherapy integration (Senf & Shi, 2008) and a growing number of professionals describe their orientation as integrative (Tong, 2009).

The trend of psychotherapy integration in China has also been boosted by a series of events related in part to market forces. In early 2000, a new federal training program for psychotherapists was launched; of note, this program was developed under the auspices of the Chinese Ministry of Labor, rather than the Ministry of Health or the Ministry of Education. Entrance standards were minimal (a high school education) and the training period was only 3 months. As a result, large numbers of counselors were produced, leading many to seek additional training opportunities to improve their competitiveness in the job market. Many gravitated to the training programs led by the "senior experts" from America, France, Italy, Germany, and Norway. Exposure to different psychotherapy approaches within a compressed period of time led to confusion and the blurring of theoretical boundaries in practice, inadvertently laying the groundwork for a widespread movement in psychotherapy integration (Chen & Xia, 2009; Li, Jia, & An, 2006). While some Chinese students of psychotherapy choose to cultivate a deep knowledge base in a single theoretical perspective, this practice style is rare in China compared to other countries (Li et al., 2006).

Besides these changes in the dominant counseling approaches, the modes of service delivery have also evolved, reflecting both the increasing professionalization and popularization of counseling and psychotherapy in China. For example, a large number of specialty mental health clinics and state-supported hospitals for psychotherapy have been founded in recent years, including the Wuhan Hospital for Psychotherapy, the Chinese–German Hospital for Psychotherapy, and the Shanghai Mental Health Center. The quality of care within these centers is quite high, with many showcasing state-of-the art residential treatment programs and research centers engaged in treatment development and outcome research (Miao & Tong, 2004; Qiu & Shen, 1998). In addition, internet-based psychotherapy and counseling (or "e-therapy") have emerged as convenient if controversial alternatives to the traditional face-to-face treatment modality. A study conducted in December 2007 reported that there were already 156 websites providing psychotherapy and counseling services in mainland China (Cao, 2008). Meanwhile, the Chinese government has also increased its support for research and development of psychotherapeutic interventions, as evidenced by the prestigious National Key Technology Research and Development Program, organized by the Ministry of Science and Technology and the Ministry of Health.

Indigenous and traditional healing methods

Because nearly all of the psychotherapeutic treatments that are utilized in China are Western in origin, doubts have been raised about their applicability to the Chinese cultural context (Cheng, 1993; Young, 1996). In particular, the therapeutic value attached to emotional catharsis stands in contrast to the traditional Chinese avoidance of excessive emotion (Lin, 1980). For more tra-ditional Chinese patients, indigenous healing approaches such as *taiji quan, qi gong,* and acu-puncture are often preferred, with growing evidence of their effectiveness for the treatment of mood and anxiety symptoms in particular (Luo, Jia, & Zhao, 1998; Wang et al., 2010, Yang, 2000). However, because traditional Chinese medicine does not make a distinction between psychological and physiological functions (Lin, 1980), there are no specific herbs or recipes that are routinely prescribed for specific mental conditions, making it difficult to assess their efficacy.

In addition to these traditional healing approaches, indigenous forms of psychodynamic therapy (Zhong, 1988) and cognitive therapy (Zhang & Yang, 1998) have also been developed to improve their cultural accessibility with regard to content and structure. Across its long history, Chinese culture has been shaped by numerous philosophical influences, with Confucianism and Taoism leaving the deepest imprint on the modern Chinese psyche. Whereas Confucian values of social relationships and self-cultivation (McNaughton, 1974; Yip, 1999) have contributed to China's social, economic, and psychological development, Taoism's emphasis on the cultivation of personal harmony in relation to cosmological and natural spheres provides a sense of stability and comfort during times of crisis (Lin, 1980; Zhang & Yang, 1998).

After observing the ways in which Taoist-based coping was organically invoked in psychother-apy sessions with Chinese patients, Yang Desen and Zhang Yalin developed Chinese Taoist cognitive psychotherapy (CTCP) as a culturally grounded approach to cognitive therapy (Zhang & Yang, 1998). CTCP conceptualizes patients' maladaptive beliefs and behaviors as resulting from an intersec-tion of situational, cultural, and personality factors. Patients are instructed in how changing one's value orientation and interpretations of life events can alter one's emotional and behavioral reactions

Eight Taoist principles are presented as alternative approaches to managing stress and con-flict.[1] Similar to standard CBT, patients practice applying the principles through written assignments completed each week and regular review of core treatment components. CTCP has been found to be effective for the treatment of diverse patients including those with depression (Yang, Zhao, & Mai, 2005), anxiety (Zhang et al., 2002) and psychosomatic disorders (Zhu, Young, Xiao, & Liu, 2005). Preliminary trials demonstrate superior effects of CTCP over time compared to medications alone (Xiao, Young, & Zhang, 1998; Zhang et al., 2002).

Research and supervision

In China, most counseling and psychotherapy research is quantitative and outcome oriented in nature. Randomized controlled trials, single-subject designs and other effectiveness studies are common. However in recent years, researchers have turned to psychotherapy process research as a means to identify how psychotherapy works and under what conditions psychotherapy is effective (Elliott, Slatick, & Urman, 2001). Using a combination of qualitative and quantitative approaches, process research seeks to understand the unfolding process of therapy, including individuals' subjective experience of treatment as well as the mechanisms of change (Zhang, Xu, & Zhang, 2008).

Cognitive task analysis (CTA) is a qualitative approach that is being used by some researchers in China to explore cognitive processes occurring during psychotherapy sessions (Clark & Estes, 1996; Zhang & Yang, 2009a). CTA focuses on the cognitive elements involved in the process of performing a task effectively. Such elements include mapping the sequence of thoughts when the operator completes the task and acquires the knowledge needed in order to increase task competence; alternatively, the analysis may also identify cognitive deficits that may impede task performance.

In a comprehensive review of the literature Zhang & Yang (2009b) found that CTA is being used to analyze videotaped sessions of different psychotherapies in order to identify mechanisms of change, the critical treatment components, and strategies for improving treatment effectiveness. Although CTA has been used previously in North American contexts, this work is just beginning in China (Zhang & Yang, 2009a,b). We anticipate that mixed-method approaches combining quantitative and qualitative methods will become increasingly common in psychotherapy process and outcome research in China.

With respect to supervision, despite growth in the counseling and psychotherapy disciplines over the past two decades (Chang et al., 2005), professional guidelines and requirements for clinical supervision have yet to be instituted in China. Few therapists receive formal supervision although some institutes have recently acknowledged its importance and begun to offer supervision to its trainees. Li (2004) identified several reasons why supervision remains uncommon in the field. For example, because the practice of psychotherapy and counseling is a relatively new phenomenon in China, training tends to focus more on theory and clinical technique, and less on supervisory skills. The neglect of supervision as an important professional competency area is also reflected in the dearth of research and scholarship on the topic. As a result, many supervisors in China lack adequate training and guidelines for how to best foster the professional development of trainees.

Drawing upon supervision guidelines developed in other countries, Fan, Huang, and Feng (2002) recommended strategies for developing a formal practice of supervision in China. These strategies include encouraging the Chinese Association of Mental Health and the Chinese Psychological Society to establish supervisory criteria and evaluation systems, developing a system for vetting and registering qualified supervisors, and including training courses in clinical supervision in clinical and counseling training programs. In situations where access to supervision is limited, self-evaluation, self-learning, and peer supervision may serve as reasonable alternatives while the shortage is being addressed.

Strengths, weaknesses, opportunities, and challenges

As our review demonstrates, counseling and psychotherapy in China is evolving rapidly in response to the shifting social, cultural, and economic landscape. Below, we analyze some of the strengths, weaknesses, opportunities, and challenges involved in providing counseling and psychotherapy to the 1.3 billion individuals living in China today.

One important asset is China's rich cultural heritage and history, which has inspired adaptations and innovations in clinical theory and practice. Studying these culture-specific elements in counseling and psychotherapy may contribute to greater understanding of the universal and culture-specific elements of effective clinical practice. However, it is also important to recognize that Chinese society is evolving, integrating, and reinterpreting cultural influences from a variety of sources. As a result, patients' expectations and preferences for counseling and therapy are also changing, as evidenced by the psychotherapy surveys conducted in 1995 and 2008 (Gong, & Li, 1997; Qian et al., 2008).

As mentioned previously, a significant weakness is the lack of a modern Chinese psychotherapeutic worldview. The dominant counseling and psychotherapy approaches in China continue to be those originating in the West. Yet China's unique cultural and philosophical traditions argue for a more contextually grounded approach to counseling and psychotherapy. A second weakness of the field relates to its rapid pace of development. To meet the growing demand for counseling and psychotherapy services, numerous mental health agencies and clinics have sprung up over the past 10 years. However, the quality of care across these facilities remains uneven.

In terms of opportunities, improvements in the standard of living and increases in social stress, accompanied by a greater willingness to seek professional help have spurred the growth of counseling and psychotherapy over the past 30 years. The opening up of communications with the West, both politically and technologically speaking, have also allowed international developments in counseling and psychotherapy to reach Chinese practitioners, whether they are in a rural village in Hunan or the bustling metropolis of Shanghai. Another catalyst for growth is the renewed interest in traditional culture being expressed by Chinese youth. Because the ideas and practices of traditional Chinese culture were criticized and aggressively suppressed during the Cultural Revolution, an entire generation of Chinese grew up with little exposure to their cultural traditions. As a result, many have begun exploring traditional Chinese medicine and philosophy as sources of inspiration, wisdom, and guidance. Together, these societal trends suggest rich opportunities for the continued development of a model of practice that is tailored to the needs of the Chinese cultural context.

Seizing the aforementioned opportunities, however, requires the resolution of major challenges in the field. For instance, an estimated 50,000 individuals are practicing psychological counseling and psychotherapy in China today, a significant shortage compared to the estimated 860,000 professionals needed to meet the mental health needs of China's population of 1.3 billion (Qian, Chen, Zhang, & Zhang, 2010). Given the urgent need for qualified counselors and clinicians, a standardized training, licensure and certification process is sorely needed. At present, different organizations including the Ministry of Labor, the Ministry of Health, and the Chinese Psychological Society have separately attempted to develop a standard training curriculum and qualifying exam system. Integrating these different approaches to build a single, centralized system of training, licensure, and certification will be a vital task of the next 10–20 years.

Future directions

As this article describes, the fields of counseling and psychotherapy in China have made significant advances within a short period of time. Looking ahead to the future, we expect that professional standards and guidelines for clinical training, education, and practice will become more widely accepted and enforced through governmental and guild-based regulatory bodies. We also encourage continued efforts in research and scholarship aimed at clarifying the universality versus cultural-specificity of treatment processes and outcomes in China. In addition, future studies should consider the impact of Westernization and economic growth on constructions of the psychological and interpersonal self, and implications of changing patient and provider self-construals for the therapeutic relationship and treatment expectations. For example, practitioners should consider the relevance of key cultural assumptions underlying different treatment modalities, and tailor their approaches to the value orientations of their patients. Likewise, growing empirical support for indigenous psychotherapies such as CTCP suggests the potential for knowledge transfer from East to West and the dissemination of local innovations in clinical theory and technique to researchers and clinicians abroad.

Conclusion

Despite numerous setbacks over the past 100 years, the quality of counseling and psychotherapy services has improved significantly over the past 25 years as a result of increased public demand and governmental support (Chang et al., 2005). However, there remain a number of challenges to building a modern system of therapeutic practice that is contextually grounded and standardized with regard to training, education, supervision, and quality of service delivery. Because culture shapes individuals' thoughts, values, and behaviors, forms of counseling and psychotherapy that reflect China's rich cultural heritage and history and present-day influence in the global and political economy are needed to best suit the needs of China's diverse patient population.

Note

1 The CHED issued a curriculum guide stipulating that students in MP programs (Master of Psychology, a practitioner's degree) must take a six-unit field practicum in lieu of the thesis. The MA or MS in Psychology is defined as a teaching/research degree where a thesis is required, while the practicum course is up to the discretion of the school. In the Philippines, most large universities do require their students in MA (including MA Counseling) to undertake field practicum, usually a three-unit course.

References

Cao,Y. F. (2008). Establishment of an interactive information platform for internet-based psychological counseling in universities in China. *Journal of Changsha Railway University (Social Science), 9*(3), 253–298.
Chang, D. F., Tong, H., Shi, Q., & Zeng, Q. (2005). Letting a hundred flowers bloom: Counseling and psychotherapy in the People's Republic of China. *Journal of Mental Health Counseling, 27,* 104–116.
Chen, J. L., & Xia, Y. (2009). Problems in the training of psychological consultants from the perspective of its specialization: Reflections on Mainland China's eight years of training psychological consultants. *Psychological Science, 32*(4), 955–957.
Cheng, L.Y.C. (1993). Psychotherapy for the Chinese: Where are we going? In L.Y. C. Cheng, F. Cheung, & C. N. Chen (eds), *Psychotherapy for the Chinese* (pp. iv–viii). Hong Kong: The Chinese University of Hong Kong.
Chinese Psychological Society (2007a). Chinese Psychological Society registration criteria for professional organizations and individual practitioners in clinical and counseling psychology. *ACTA Psychological Sinica, 39,* 942–946.
Chinese Psychological Society (2007b). Code of Ethics for Clinical and Counseling Psychological Practice of Chinese Psychological Society. *ACTA Psychological Sinica, 39,* 947–950.
Clark, R. E., & Estes, F. (1996). Cognitive task analysis. *International Journal of Educational Research, 25,* 403–417.

Elliott, R., Slatick, E., & Urman, M. (2001). Qualitative change process research on psychotherapy: Alternative strategies. *Psychologische Beiträge, 43*, 69–111.

Fan, F. M., Huang, H. Y., & Feng, J. (2002). The meanings and roles of supervision on psychotherapy and counseling. *Chinese Mental Health Journal, 16*(9), 648–652.

Gong,Y. X., & Li, Q. Z.(1997). The survey and analysis on current training of clinical psychology as a profession in China. *Chinese Journal of Clinical Psychology, 5*(1), 1–7.

Guo, B.Y. (2009). A review of psychoanalysis in China's theoretical research and clinical applications during Reforming and Opening period – To commemorate the (1859–1939) 70th anniversary of Freud's death. *Chinese Psychotherapy in Dialogue (Psychoanalysis in China)* (pp. 1–6). Hang Zhou Publishing House.

Kang, J. (1999) Psychological thought in traditional Chinese medicine. In H. S. Ye (ed.), *The essence of psychological theories* (pp. 28–31). Fuzhou, China: Fujian Educational Press.

Li, B., Jia, X. M., & An, Q. (2006). Investigation about training in counseling and psychotherapy in today's China. *China Journal of Health Psychology, 14*(5), 514–516.

Li, L. Y. (2004). A discussion about clinical supervision. *Chinese Journal of Clinical Psychology, 12*(1), 96–99.

Li, X. (2003). Comprehensive practice therapy: A holistic psychotherapy. *Medicine and Philosophy, 24*, 56–57.

Lin, K.M. (1980). Traditional Chinese medical beliefs and their relevance for mental illness and psychiatry. In A. Kleinman, & T.-Y. Lin (eds), *Normal and Abnormal Behavior in Chinese Culture* (pp. 95–111). Dordrecht, Holland: D. Reidel Publishing Company.

Lu, L. (1996). *Dredging Psychotherapy*. Nanjing: Jiangsu Science and Technology Press.

Luo, H., Meng, F., Jia, Y., & Zhao, X. (1998). Clinical research on the therapeutic effect of the electro-acupuncture treatment in patients with depression. *Psychiatry and Clinical Neurosciences, 52 Suppl*, S338–S340.

McNaughton, W. (1974). *The Confucian Vision*. Ann Arbor: University of Michigan Press.

Miao, S. J., & Tong, J. (2004). Psychodynamic treatment in hospital settings. *Shanghai Archives of Psychiatry, 16*(5), 314–317.

National Bureau of Statistics of China (2011). *Press release on major figures of the 2010 National Population Census*, April 28. Retrieved October 14, 2011 from www.stats.gov.cn/english/newsandcomingevents/t20110428_402722237.htm.

Qian, M.Y. (2002). Psychotherapy in Asia: China. In A. Pritz (ed.), *Globalized Psychotherapy* (pp. 465–479). Vienna, Austria: Facultas Verlags-und Buchhandels AG.

Qian, M. Y., Chen, H., Wang, Y. P., Zhong, J., Yao, P., Xu, K. W., Yi, C. L., & Zhang, Z. F. (2008). An investigation of professional personnel and practice in psychotherapy and counseling in six major areas of China. *Psychological Science, 31*(5), 1233–1237.

Qian, M. Y. (2009). Chinese Psychological Society Registration System for Clinical and Counseling Psychology. In China Association for Science and Technology (CAST) (ed.), *2008–2009 Psychology Development Report* (pp. 91–100). Beijing: China Association for Science and Technology.

Qian, M.Y., Chen, R., Zhang, L, & Zhang Z. (2010). A prediction for requirement of counselors/psychotherapists in China. *Chinese Mental Health Journal, 24*(12), 942–947.

Qiu, Y. F., & Shen, D. Y. (1998). Morita therapy to treat 66 neurotic hospital patients. *Chinese Mental Health Journal, 12*(6), 361–362.

Senf, W., & Shi, Q. J. (2008). Psychotherapy in China. *Psychotherapy in Dialogue, 9*, 200–201.

Shi, Q. J. (2009). Psychoanalysis in China from last ten years. *Chinese Psychotherapy in Dialogue, 2*, 11–23.

Tong, H. Q. (2009). Answers to interviews of psychoanalysis in China from the last ten years, *Chinese Psychotherapy in Dialogue, 2*, 24–26.

Wang, X.J. (2005). Problems and coping strategies nowadays counselors' cultivate. *Chinese Mental Health Journal, 19*(10), 709–711.

Wang, C., Bannuru, R., Ramel, J., Kupelnick, B., Scott, T., & Schmid, C. H. (2010). Tai Chi on psychological well-being: Systematic review and meta-analysis. *BMC Complementary and Alternative Medicine, 10*(23), 1–16.

Xiao, S. Y., Young, D. S., & Zhang, H. G. (1998). Taoist Cognitive Psychotherapy for neurotic patients: A preliminary clinical trial. *Journal of Psychiatry and Clinical Neurosciences, 52 Suppl*, S238–S241.

Xiao, Z. P. (1998). Unusual training class: German-Chinese Continuous Training Program on Psychoanalysis in China. *Shanghai Archives of Psychiatry, 10*(1), 62–63.

Yang, D. (2000). Can *qi gong* treat neurosis and mental diseases? *Chinese Journal of Nervous and Mental Diseases, 26*(1), 52–53 (in Chinese).

Yang, J., Zhao, L., & Mai X. (2005). A comparative study of Taoist cognitive psychotherapy from China and *mianserin* in the treatment of depression in late life. *Chinese Journal of Nervous and Mental Disease, 31* (5), 333–335

Yip, K. S. (1999) Traditional Chinese Confucian, Taoistic and medical mental health concepts in pre-Chin period. *Asian Journal of Counseling, 6*(1), 35–55.

Young, D. (1996). Chinese people's mind and Chinese specific psychotherapy. In W. S. Tseng (ed.), *Chinese People's Mind and Therapy* (pp. 417–435). Taiwan: Gueiguan.

Zhang, H. & Zheng, W. (2011). A review of traditional psychotherapy methods. *Chinese Archives of Traditional Chinese Medicine, 29,* 160–162.

Zhang, J., & Yang, Y. C. (2009a). A self-analysis psychotherapy model and its qualitative research framework. *Medicine and Philosophy, 6,* 49–51.

Zhang, J., & Yang, Y. C. (2009b). Cognitive task analysis and application to the medical field. *Medicine and Philosophy, 3.*

Zhang, R. S., Xu, J., Zhang, W. (2008). Qualitative research on psychotherapy and counseling. *Psychological Science, 31,* 681–684.

Zhang, Y., Young, D., Lee, S., Li, L., Zhang, H., Xiao, Z., Hao, W., Feng, Y., Zhou, H., & Chang, D. F. (2002). Chinese Taoist cognitive psychotherapy in the treatment of generalized anxiety disorder in contemporary China. *Transcultural Psychiatry, 39,* 115–129.

Zhang, Y. L., & Yang, D. (1998). Chinese Taoist cognitive psychotherapy: Introduction of ABCDE technology. *Chinese Mental Health Journal, 12,* 188–190.

Zhong, Y. (1988). *Chinese Psychoanalysis.* China: People's Publications of Lian Nin.

Zhong, Y. (1999). *Cognitive Insight Therapy.* Guiyang: Guizhou Educational Publishing House.

Zhu, J. F., Young, D. S., Xiao, S. Y., Liu, S. X. (2005). The improvement of coronary heart disease patients' Type A behavior using Taoist cognitive therapy. *Chinese Mental Health Journal, 19,* 553–556.

16

COUNSELING AND PSYCHOTHERAPY IN INDIA

Professionalism amidst changing times

Tony Sam George and Priya Pothan

Introduction

India is a melting pot of diversity in castes, communities, geographical regions, languages, religions, and practices, within a geographical area of 32,87,263 kilometers, with 28 states and seven union territories. Although the notions of counseling and psychotherapy are Western, the process of mentoring and assisting individuals through their developmental issues was already present in ancient models of care in India, such as the Guru Shishya System,[1] the Joint Family Network,[2] and traditional healing. Counseling and psychotherapy do not exist as completely distinct disciplines in India. Although counseling grew out of a strong guidance format and led to a proliferation of trained and lay counselors and psychotherapy arose from a strong theoretical clinical psychology background, these differences are blurred in society. As Arulmani (2007) points out: "all that is termed as 'counseling' today was embedded within a complex support system of social relationships" (p. 70). Although these fields progressed, difficulties with accreditation exist. The Indian Association of Clinical Psychologists (IACP), along with other bodies such as the Counseling Association of India, offer discussions of matters related to psychotherapy counseling and clinical psychology, and provide the code of conduct in India (IACP, 1993).

Varma (1982) highlighted seven distinct features of the Indian population that strongly influence how counseling and psychotherapy are practiced and received by clients: mutual interdependence, lack of psychological sophistication involving introspective and verbal abilities, social distance between the doctor and the patient due to class hierarchies, religious belief in rebirth and fatalism and related accountability, guilt attributed to misdeeds in past life and social approval-related shame, and lower emphasis on confidentiality as society can be therapeutic allies. India is a collectivistic society wherein the self is relational (Roland, 2005), though recent socio-economic changes have resulted in a contradictory mix of traditional and modern elements in families (Murthy, 2003). Shah and Isaac (2005) note that relationship problems dominate themes in clinical interviews and in the process of individual, couple and family therapy sessions in India.

With the acute shortage of affordable professionals, rehabilitation services and residential facilities in India (WHO-AIMS Report, 2006), families have been more active in the past decade and assist as co-therapists (Murthy, 2011; Srinivasan, 2008). Religious leaders can also be effective change agents for the awareness and spread of mental health in the community. Besides yoga and meditation, visiting religious centers is commonly practiced for healing purposes in India (Raguram, Venkateswaran, Ramakrishna, & Weiss, 2002) as well as for Indians residing outside of India (Dein & Sembhi, 2001). Characters from religious texts and folklore are used in narrative work to enhance the therapy process. Taken together, the Indian model of psychotherapy is constantly defining its professionalism within its societal paradigms.

Brief history of counseling and psychotherapy

Counseling and psychotherapy in India has a long and varied past. In the early days of the discipline, counseling and psychotherapy were not differentiated and were akin to the guidance format provided by an expert. The earliest counselors in India were the elders in the community, be it within the family, local religious system, or in the local community. Counseling advice about marriage, parenting, and vocation were provided in a directive format but with considerations to the characteristics of the client. While psychotherapy has developed as a profession, counseling as a distinct discipline is still in its early stages.

Ancient Indian writings are resplendent with materials that point to sophisticated psychological concepts related to the mind (Mano) and knowledge (Vidya). Scholars have shown the startling similarities between these concepts and those put forward by Western psychology. As Neki (1975) points out: "If psychotherapy is defined as 'interpersonal method of mitigating suffering' then many psychotherapeutic systems have existed in India a long time". For instance, temple healing in India has catered to the psychological needs of individuals for years. Raguram et al. (2002) have documented how psychiatric conditions are remedied through temple healing in rural south India. Hence, even in ancient India, psychotherapy has existed in a diverse albeit similar format from its Western counterpart.

Modern Western psychotherapy was only introduced in India in the 1920s, with Girindrasekhar Bose as the first Indian psychoanalyst (Misra, 2011). Bose developed his theory of opposite wishes and treated his patients through an analytic method even before he became familiar with Freudian psychoanalysis. The Indian Psychoanalytical Society was founded in Calcutta in 1922 just 3 years after the British Psychoanalytical Society was formed (Psychoanalytic Therapy and Research Centre, 2011). Emilo Servido kindled psychoanalytic interest in Bombay, while Satyanand spread the Kleinian perspective in Delhi (Kumar, Alreja & Kenswar, 2010). Early psychotherapists such as Vasavada saw a parallel between psychoanalysis and an existential–yogic thought and merged the Eastern–Western divide on psychotherapy. However, Western psychotherapy was still limited in its popularity in India. As Hoch (1965) observed: "While most psychiatrists are carrying on some type of psychotherapy, at least of a supportive type, only a small number of orthodox analysts can be found in India, mostly in Calcutta and Bombay" (p. 3).

The first discontent of the practice of Western psychotherapy in India was expressed by Surya and Jayaram in 1964 (Rao, 1998). They emphasized the importance of local language and situational direct support among Indian patients, rather than their Western counterparts who require intrapsychic explanations (Surya & Jayaram, 1964). Indian therapists then delineated the role of Indian culture and philosophy with emphasis on spiritual independence and growth, in contrast to dependence on material, physical and emotional realms.

Counseling and psychotherapy have come a long way from their initial indigenous healing to their Western influences and are recognized as an important field in modern-day India.

Counseling psychology and clinical psychology, along with psychotherapy workshops and academic programs, have become common in the cities in India. Counselors and psychotherapists are constantly adapting interventions that will be cost-effective, utilitarian, and meet the needs of India's rural and urban population. As Varma (1982) rightly predicted, psychotherapy in India has gradually moved away from long-term psychotherapies to briefer contacts for specific crises and problems.

Counselor education programs, accreditation, licensure, and certification

The professional backgrounds of counselors and psychotherapists in India often vary. These normally include domains of psychiatry, clinical psychology, psychiatric social work, counseling psychology, and education. Psychiatrists typically spend 3 years of training to complete an MD degree in psychiatry after achieving a basic medical degree (MBBS). Postgraduate students of psychology often spend 2 years of clinical training leading to an MPhil degree in clinical psychology, which deems them fit to practice as mental health professionals. Similarly, social workers who have completed their master's degree in social work can gain an MPhil degree in psychiatric social work which provides them with competencies to function as counselors and psychotherapists.

In addition, India is witnessing a steady increase in the number of practitioner-based courses offered at the postgraduate level in counseling psychology or psychological counseling by university psychology departments. Arulmani (2007) cites the example of Bangalore University in India that focuses on developing a contextually relevant course at the postgraduate level to train effective counselors. Thomas (2011) surveyed university programs in counseling psychology and found that elements which contribute to personal and professional development varied across institutions based on the orientation and vision of individual colleges that offer these programs.

A number of private institutes also offer short-term counseling programs. These range from 6-month certificate courses in basic counseling skills to 1-year diploma courses in counseling. Many such courses are now offered by private social service trusts, nongovernmental agencies, university departments and educational institutes. Curriculum and foci depend on the particular needs of the organizations that have envisioned these courses.

There is no singular organization that accredits counselor education programs in India (Carson, Jain & Ramirez, 2009; Raney & Cinerbas, 2005). However, all university degrees are accredited by relevant governmental appointed accreditation systems such as the University Grants Commission or the Medical Council of India. The only legislation that provides licensing for professionals working in rehabilitation is the Rehabilitation Council Act of 1992, amended in the year 2000. Counselor education programs try to gain accreditation from international bodies for the courses they run. Recent efforts are being made by professional associations and university departments in India to develop professional standards in the training of counselors and psychotherapists.

Carson, Jain, and Ramirez (2009) point out that mental health training must consider important cultural aspects while delivering services to Indian clients. They contend that public views of mental health services are negative and this can be counterbalanced by paying attention to specific issues faced by clients in India. For instance, they discuss stigma, social embarrassment, and blame by the family and community as a specific issue to be tackled in mental health service delivery. Culturally held beliefs regarding the causation of mental health problems is another issue that comes in the way of seeking help. This conclusion is also explained by Saravanan et al. (2007) using findings of a qualitative study on clients seeking help for psychiatric conditions at Vellore, India. Carson, Jain, and Ramirez (2009) provide an exhaustive listing of issues and suggestions in both systemic public health delivery issues and cultural issues that impact counselling and psychotherapy. An example of a cultural issue they list is the older Indian clients' nonacceptance of counseling by younger professionals, especially in the area of marriage and family counseling. Another very specific example they cite pertains to how important it is to maintain community respect for clients, and any disruption in life due to counselling can be viewed by the clients as losing face in the community. These insights can be converted into material for training and education of counselors and psychotherapists in India.

Current counseling and psychotherapy theories, processes, and trends

Counseling and psychotherapy in India took on a formal structure in 1954 with the establishment of the All India Institute of Mental Health, which later became the National Institute of Mental Health and Neuro Sciences (NIMHANS, 2011). The establishment of departments of psychiatry, psychology, and social work and the interdisciplinary team approach to patient care as well as specialist units such as community psychiatry, family psychiatry, child and adolescent psychiatry, rehabilitation services, all saw the importance of extending psychosocial care to clients—most of which included counseling and psychotherapeutic services.

Psychotherapy within the behavioral and family therapy realms flourished in the early 1970s. Family therapy was introduced in India about the same time as its initiation in the West (Bhatti and Varghese, 1995). In 1971, Dr. Vidyasagar recognized the benefits of inclusion of treatment for families for patients who attended the services of the Amritsar Mental Hospital. Existential psychotherapy also found acceptance among Indian psychotherapy. Rao (1990) argued that existential philosophy is not alien to the Eastern culture and can be used effectively. India embraces the client-centered model in counseling practice and the client–counselor relationship has shifted from the authoritarian-driven guidance role to a more active collaborative process. While practice of psychotherapy in India is still more theoretically based and incorporates Western models of therapy in an eclectic fashion, psychological counseling has evolved to incorporate more indigenous elements. It is not uncommon for counselors to engage clients in meditative techniques and yoga in the practice of counseling. For instance, Clay (2002) cites examples of Indian psychologists who have blended meditation with psychotherapy in their clinical practice.

Owing to the scarcity of counselors and psychotherapists in India, they are often employed in a variety of settings. Mental hospital and general hospital settings continue to be places where these practitioners practice cognitive-behavioral therapy and supportive therapy with patients and their family members. Community psychiatry in India is now nearly four decades old (Murthy, 2011) and treatment for persons with severe mental illnesses has shifted from the hospital settings to the community setting. Private practice of counselors and psychotherapists has become an increasing phenomenon in urban India.

In terms of other trends, family courts are experiencing a rise in cases and the State Social Welfare Advisory Board has established family counseling centers throughout the country (Central Social Welfare Board, 2008). In recent times, families and couples have begun to seek professional help from family and marriage counselors especially in urban India. Further, counseling for man-made and natural disasters is also becoming a concern for Indian psychotherapists in the light of the terrorist attacks, earthquakes, droughts, and tsunamis faced by Indians in the last decade. Mental health professionals have recognized the need for preventive and promotive work in these settings (Maheshwari, Yadav & Singh, 2010), apart from early disaster management.

School counseling has grown in importance in recent years, when the Central Board of Secondary Education (CBSE) decided to have school counselors appointed in over 9,000 schools across the country in the recent years. They mandated at least 20 sessions of psychological counseling to every student in an academic session, with the involvement of parents and teachers (Central Board of Secondary Education Circular, 2008). This has led to other school boards creating posts for psychologists, counselors, and social workers to ensure the mental health of Indian children.

The rapid technological changes in the last decade in the country have led to the rise of several Multi-National Corporations and the introduction of employee assistance programs (Sengupta, 2010). These corporate counseling sessions cater to work and personal issues of clients to ensure better adjustment and higher work productivity. Along with spas and other rejuvenation centers, psychotherapists are also conducting wellness counseling and liaising with other health professionals such as nutritionists and physiotherapists. Hence, Indian mental health needs also have slowly shifted in the last few years from treatment and cure to prevention and psychological wellness (Mohan, Sehgal & Akansha, 2008). This has contributed to a higher societal awareness about the benefits of counseling and psychotherapy as well as an enhanced knowledge of common psychological concepts.

Indigenous and traditional healing methods

India's method of healing is ancient and has reinvented itself to meet modern-day needs The ancient Hindu text—the *Atharva Veda*—contains the earliest recorded account in the world of mental illnesses and their remedies and is the source of all Indian systems of medicine and psychotherapy (Veereshwar, 2002). According to the text, the human body consisted of three basic elements (*gunas*): wind (*vata*), bile (*pitta*) and phlegm (*kapha*). The three corresponding basic characteristics (*gunas*) of the mental structure were purity (*sattva*), eroticism (*rajas*) and evil (*tamas*). Balance in both sets of *gunas* ensures physical and psychological equilibrium and thereby health. Hence, treatment involved equilibrium through *Atharvanik Manas Chikitsa* (psychological control of the mind by the individual) and *Kaushik Chikitsa* (control of the physical body through factors external to self). The former includes treatments such as *Sankalpa* (auto-suggestion), *Sadesh* (suggestion), *Samvashikaran* (hypnosis), rituals, *Brahma Kavach* (psychological defensive belief), *Utarna* (transference), *Ashwasana* and *Upchar* (assurance, desensitization), *Daiviya Havan Chikitsa* (spiritual prayers), *Sweekarokti* (confession), *Tapa* (penance), and *Balidan* (sacrifice). The last one involves treatment through *angirasi* (endocrinal balance); *manushyaja* (medicines); and methods of *jal chikitsa* (hydrotherapy), *vaju chikitsa* (air therapy), *agni chikitsa* (heat therapy), and *sour chikitsa* (sun therapy).

These indigenous treatment practices are popular even today. As Naryanasamy and Naryanasamy (2006) point out, "Ayurvedic medicine is gaining popularity as part of the growing interest in New Age spirituality and in complementary and alternative medicine" (p. 1185). Another ancient text—the *Upanishads*—suggests that through the practice of meditation, one can have control over the inhibitory system, stability, and one-pointedness to achieve both worldly and other-worldly goals of salvation (moksha). This control facilitates all kinds of perceptions and problem-solving, leading to the realization of *Atman* (soul) (Ghorpade & Kumar, 1988). Meditation is another twin indigenous technique of self-realization wherein one learns to purify one's mind through focus and breathing exercises.

Patanjali's[3] eightfold path describes clearly the path to reach the peak state of consciousness (*samadhi*). Yogas can differ in its individual aspects such as yoga of action (*karma* yoga), belief and devotion (*bhakti* yoga). Yoga has resurfaced as an effective treatment method in the last decade and is advocated for several mental illnesses, even schizophrenia. Yoga has been associated with improved symptomology, socio-occupational functioning and facial emotion recognition (Behere et al., 2011). Yoga was also found to be an effective treatment for depression (Mehta & Sharma, 2010) and for the elderly population (Jaleel, 2010) in India. As Singh (2005) highlights, yogic approaches have also been successfully applied for a host of other illness such as "bronchial asthma, essential hypertension, mucous colitis, peptic ulcer, cervical spondylosis, chronic sinusitis, intractable pain, personality disorder, anxiety reaction, anxiety depression, gastritis and rheumatism" (p. 91).

Finally, another indigenous healing method worth mentioning is pranic healing. Pranic healing is based on the observation that the human body is surrounded by an energy field which reflects and influences health. The Pranic healers are trained to perceive, assess and modify the energy field and chakras[4] of the patient without any physical contact.

Research and supervision

A number of Indian journals are now dedicated to publishing research articles relevant to counseling and psychotherapy practice. Research on mental health epidemiology has been reported widely from India. However, Math, Chandrashekar, and Bhugra (2007) contend that epidemiological studies have failed to include some categories of mental health disorders and looked at limited explanatory variables.

Much research has also been done on testing the efficacy of various therapeutic models and practices across psychological problems and client groups. In comparison, process research in counseling and psychotherapy in India is scanty. Writing on the status of psychotherapy research in India today, Rao (2010) outlines the growth and documentation of psychotherapy research in India. Her review indicates that currently, there is research examining the benefits of psychological interventions in dealing with a variety of problems affecting children, adolescents, and adults, couples and families. Research has also examined the benefits of psychological interventions in comparison with pharmacological and biological therapies and usefulness of indigenous methods of psychotherapy, individual and group psychotherapy, and family and community approaches. Recent research by Parayil (2010) has examined the role of spirituality in counseling and psychotherapy. His research points out that Indian therapists and counselors actively use elements of Indian spirituality while working with client issues.

As for clinical supervision in India, Manickam (2010) comments that supervision is not adequately addressed in psychotherapy training programs in India. He states that the process of supervision is compounded due to differing linguistic backgrounds of clients, therapist, and their supervisors. Thomas (2011), however, points out that more systematic group and individual supervision mechanisms exist in recently established postgraduate courses in counseling psychology, which focus more on practice and supervision rather than purely theory. Supervised practicum and internship arrangements and self-development programs are seen as important by some master's level programs in India. Typically, master's courses in counseling psychology in these universities offer students within house individual and group supervision at least once a week. Supervision processes focus on client as well as supervisee issues using process recall questions and experiential methods within the supervision session. Presentation of audio- and video-tape verbatim is mandated in supervision. This trend contrasts with the didactic, client-focused supervision approaches practiced in training of mental health professionals in the past.

Thomas (2011) mentions that the above requirements now pose a greater challenge for the practice of counseling and psychotherapy as there are not enough professionally trained supervisors to meet the supervision needs of students graduating from these programs. Considering the dearth of supervisors, some centers have also initiated peer supervision groups and online peer supervision groups for mutual support and learning. Private sector companies that provide counseling services now insist on effective supervision practices within their agencies. It is also notable to see that a number of private trusts that run counseling courses insist on quality supervision as part of the course work.

Strengths, weaknesses, opportunities, and challenges

Counseling and psychotherapy in India is constantly evolving to meet the current-day needs of its people. The emphasis on specialized training at the university level, along with the increase in the number of universities offering these courses, indicates a growing trend towards professionalism. The Indian Association of Clinical Psychology was formed in 1968 and has been producing reports, newsletters, and conducting conferences to promote continuous education (IACP, 2011). The Counseling Association of India was established in 2005 and has organized conferences since its inception, with plans to start a multilingual research journal.

Stigma in India is related to the perception that an individual with a mental disorder would not recover (Bell et al., 2010). This is very different to the reason for stigma in other countries wherein stigma is attributed to the patient's level of dangerousness, unpredictability or difficulty in making conversations. While the importance of mental health professionals in India is growing, the social stigma is slowly reducing. The diversity inherent within the setting of an Indian counselor/psychotherapist is indicative of the development within the field. Counselors and psychotherapists in India are shifting from specialized roles of guidance and remediation to the community-based promotion of mental health (Patel, Flisher, Nikapota & Malhotra, 2008) and prevention of mental illnesses (Tiwari, Agarwal, Kumar, & Pandey, 2007). Indian counseling and psychotherapy is also increasingly borrowing its indigenous healing methods and the use of Ayurveda for treatment of mental disorders and promotion of mental health is being researched.

However, counseling and psychotherapy in India is still an advancing discipline that faces several obstacles. Patel, Kumar, Paul, Rao, and Reddy (2011) point out that India has one of the most fragmented and commercialized healthcare systems in the world, and due to the low public spending, the private out-of-pocket expenditure resort by most Indians is among the highest in the world. Hence, while the governmental expenditure on healthcare has gradually increased across the years, the effectiveness of these healthcare measures in India will arise only if guided by principles of equity, affordability and accountability. Counseling and psychotherapy need to become affordable services in India and increase their availability and accessibility.

In addition, special attention needs to be placed on reducing suicides among the youth and the poor in India. Youth suicide is found to constitute 30% of all recorded suicides (Shrivastava, 2003) and counseling and psychotherapy need to incorporate more preventive components to lower this rate. The increase in these services at a school and college level may hopefully pave the way to a decrease in the youth suicide rate in this country.

Ethics is an important challenge for counselors and psychotherapists in India. With the absence of a formal governing body, preservation of ethics within the psychotherapy hour is based on the personal accountability of the therapists/counselors. Isaac (2009) notes that clients in India may be less informed about their rights and these violations of ethical principles typically go unnoticed and unpunished. While clients are now becoming informed consumers, the implicit authority within the guru–chela paradigm of psychotherapist–client may also prevent clients from questioning the psychotherapist's therapy-based decisions.

Indian counseling and psychotherapy has tremendous scope for improvement. A balanced national mental health policy could pave the way for counselors and psychotherapists to use indigenous and Western methods in practice, as well as aid in uniformity and licensure. Appropriate attention to the treatment, prevention, and promotion of mental health can expand the field of counseling and psychotherapy and create diversity within the roles of these professionals. Community-based interventions with at-risk populations can also create more societal awareness and change the perception towards help-seeking. Kumar et al. (2009) note that while school mental health programs lead to positive student-oriented outcomes, these programs are scarce in India. Hence, despite socio-cultural changes, the advancement of the disciplines of counseling and psychotherapy is a must. Counselors and psychotherapists have the present-day challenge of maintaining professionalism amidst the changing times.

Future directions

In order for the field of counseling and psychotherapy in India to flourish, counselors and psychotherapists need to become unified to create formalized bodies to maintain professionalism. At present, counselors and psychotherapists collaborate within self-created communities and are also located in disparate locations across the country. In 1989, the dream of eliminating ill health by 2000 CE seemed difficult with the presence of only 1,500 psychiatrists and 600 clinical psychologists (Kishore, 1989). While these numbers have significantly increased, counselors and psychotherapists need to enhance community awareness, build help-seeking behaviors, and teach life skills in order for amelioration of the mental health needs in the country. For this objective, counselors and psychotherapists should not only collaborate with each other but also with the family members of the client, religious and community leaders. While the Westernized therapy model acknowledges the incorporation of family members into routine practice, the family members are already part of the caregiving process in India. Shankar (2002) reflects that in India, several barriers exist to the full optimization of the family potential in the recovery process, and interventions sensitive to the needs and concerns of caregivers are not considered as a priority. For effectiveness of psychotherapy in this context, this professional–familial collaboration is a necessity.

Conclusion

Indian counseling and psychotherapy is in a transition phase. It has progressed from the earlier Indian psychology days of traditional healers and community advisors to being influenced by the global developments. Although counseling and psychotherapy are still not clearly demarcated fields in India, there has been tremendous advancement in the formats, types, and methods used. Its history reflects attempts to enhance training, research and practice.

The reinvention of ancient healing practices has added a new dimension to the clinical practice. The use of these Indian traditional methods has been associated with positive outcomes such as promotion of mental health and treatment of psychosomatic illnesses (Singh, 1986). Mindfulness mediation and relaxation exercises are becoming common elements in routine practice both locally and internationally. Miovic (2008) notes the complementary nature of Indian traditional healing methods in Western psychotherapy. While he considers that Western psychotherapy can stabilize the emotional nature of the client and increase his/her capacity to engage in the larger aims of yoga, Indian psychology can expand the conceptual framework through provision of a consciousness perspective.

Despite the recent socio-economic changes, counseling and psychotherapy in India are two disciplines that are striving to maintain professionalism, create social awareness and contribute to the global development of therapy. In this process, counseling and psychotherapy have transformed to include a community format alongside modern wellness modes of counseling, work within families and with families as co-therapists, and to cater to the unique peculiarities in Indian society of culture and religion. In subsequent years, counseling and psychotherapy in

India will evolve to create a balanced model of mental healthcare on the global platform and the dream of helping the mentally ill in India will become a reality.

Notes

1 The Guru Shishya relationship refers to the ancient Indian tradition of mentoring students (shishyas) by a spiritual teacher (Guru) on matters of faith and life through a respectful, genuine relationship. The student in obedience to the teacher imbibes the values and teachings of the teacher.
2 The Indian joint family refers to the traditional Hindu joint family where parents, unmarried female children and married male children with their spouses and children live in one household sharing the work load of the house.
3 Patanjali was a sage in 400 BCE, who wrote the ancient text of Yoga Sutras, to analyze and explain the process of awakening and expanding the mind, intellect and the consciousness.
4 Chakras refer to whorls of energy that permeate from a point on the physical body and increases in a fan-shaped formation. Seven chakras exist along the spinal column and affect intelligence, vitality, emotional, and physical health.

References

Arulmani, G. (2007). Counseling psychology in India: At the confluence of two traditions. *Applied Psychology: An International Review, 56*, 69–82.

Behere, R.V., Arasappa, R., Jagannathan, A., Varambally, G., Venkatasubramanian, G., J. Thirthalli, & ... Gangadhar, B. N. (2011). Effect of yoga therapy on facial emotion recognition deficits, symptoms and functioning in patients with schizophrenia. *Acta Psychiatrica Scandinavica, 123*, 147–153.

Bhatti, R. S., & Varghese, M. (1995). Family therapy in India. *Indian Journal of Social Psychiatry, 11*, 30–34.

Bhatti, R. S., & Sobhana, H. (2000). A model for enhancing marital and family relationships. *Indian Journal of Social Psychiatry, 16*, 47–52

Bell, J.S., Aaltonen, S. E., Airaksinen, M. S., Volmer, D., Gharat, M. S., Muceniece, R., & ... Chen, T. F. (2010). Determinants of mental health stigma among pharmacy students in Australia, Belgium, Estonia, Finland, India and Latvia. *International Journal of Social Psychiatry, 56*(1), 3–14.

Carson, D. K., Jain, S., & Ramirez, S. (2009). Counseling and family therapy in India: Evolving professions in a rapidly developing nation. *International Journal for the Advancement of Counseling, 31*, 45–56.

Central Board of Secondary Education Circular. (2008). *All heads of institutions affiliated with CBSE: Counselling in Schools (Circular No 8)*. Retrieved from http://cbse.nic.in/welcome.htm

Central Social Welfare Board (2008). *Annual Report 2007–2008* (Ch. 9). Retrieved from http://wcd.nic.in/ar0708/English/Chapter-9.pdf

Clay, R. A. (2002). Psychology around the world: An indigenized psychology. Psychologists in India blend Indian traditions and Western Psychology. *Monitor on Psychology, 33*, 5. Retrieved from www.apa.org/monitor/may02/india.aspx.

Dein, S., & Sembhi, S. (2001). The use of traditional healing in South Asian psychiatric patients in the U.K.: Interactions between professional and folk psychiatries. *Transcultural Psychiatry, 38*, 243–257.

Ghorpade, M. B., & Kumar, V. B. (1988). *Introduction to Modern Psychotherapy*. Mumbai: Himalaya Publishing House.

Hoch, E.M. (1965). *Psychotherapy and Psychoanalysis in India*. Unpublished document.

IACP (Indian Association of Clinical Psychologists). (1993). Code of Conduct. Lucknow: IACP Secretariat.

IACP. (2011). *Home*. Retrieved from www.iacp.in.

Isaac, R. (2009). Ethics in the practice of clinical psychology. *Indian Journal of Medical Ethics, 6*, 69–74.

Jaleel, S. S. (2010). Effect of psychological intervention on anxiety and psychological well-being among elderly people residing in old age homes. *Indian Journal of Community Psychology, 6*, 290–301.

Kishore, R. (1989). Presidential address: Positive mental health for all by 2000 AD. *Indian Journal of Clinical Psychology, 16*, 1–4.

Kumar, D., Dubey, I., Bhattacharjee, D., Singh, N. K. Dotiwala, K. N., Siddiqui, S. V., & Goyal, N. (2009). Beginning steps in school mental health in India: A teacher workshop. *Advances in School Mental Health Promotion, 2*, 28–33.

Kumar, A., Alreja, S., & Kenswar, D.K. (2010). Current status of psychoanalysis. *RINPAS Seminars, 2*, 470–487.

Maheshwari, N., Yadav, R., & Singh, N. P. (2010). Group counseling: A silver lining in the psychological management of disaster trauma. *Journal of Pharmacy and Bioallied Sciences, 2*, 267–274.

Manickam, L. S. S (2010). Psychotherapy in India: Review article. *Indian Journal of Psychiatry, 52*, 366–370.

Math, S. B., Chandrashekar, C. R., & Bhugra, D. (2007). Psychiatric epidemiology in India. *Indian Journal of Medical Research, 126*, 183–192.

Mehta, P., & Sharma, M. (2010). Yoga as a complementary therapy for clinical depression. *Complementary Health Practice Review, 15*, 156–170.

Miovic, M. (2008). Therapeutic psychology and Indian yoga. In. K. R. Rao, A. C. Paranjpe, & A. K. Dalal (eds). *Handbook of Indian psychology* (pp. 449–470). New Delhi: Cambridge University Press.

Misra, G. (2011). Introduction. In G. Misra (ed.). *Psychology in India (Vol. 4): Theoretical and Methodological Developments* (pp. xv–xxii). New Delhi: Indian Council of Social Science Research.

Mohan, J., Sehgal, M., & Akansha, T. (2008). Psychological well being, spiritual well being and personality. *Journal of Psychosocial Research, 3*, 81–97.

Murthy, R. S. (2003). Emerging mental health programmes and changing families in India. In. R. S. Bhatti, M. Varghese & A. Raguram (eds). *Changing marital and family systems: Challenges to conventional models in mental health* (pp. 58–65). India: NIMHANS publication.

Murthy, R. S. (2011). Mental health initiatives in India (1947–2010). *The National Medical Journal of India, 24*, 98–107.

Naryanasamy, A., & Naryanasamy, M. (2006). Ayurvedic medicine: An introduction for nurses. *British Journal of Nursing, 15*, 1185–1190.

Neki, J. S. (1975). Psychotherapy in India: Past, present and future. *American Journal of Psychotherapy, 29*, 92–100

NIMHANS. (2011). *The genesis.* Retrieved from www.nimhans.kar.nic.in/aboutnimhans.htm

Parayil, T. J (2010). *Spiritual Ingredients in Counselling and Psychotherapy.* Unpublished M.Phil thesis. Christ University, Bangalore, India.

Patel, V., Flisher, A. J., Nikapota, A., & Malhotra, S. (2008). Promoting child and adolescent mental health in low and middle income countries. *Journal of Child Psychology & Psychiatry, 49*, 313–334.

Patel, V., Kumar, A. K. S., Paul, V. K., Rao, K. D., & Reddy, K. S. (2011). Universal health care in India: The time is right. *The Lancet, 377*, 448–449.

Psychoanalytic Therapy and Research Centre (2011). *History of the Centre.* Retrieved from www.psychoanalysis-mumbai.org/about-us.html

Raguram, R., Venkateswaran, J. R., Ramakrishna, J., & Weiss, M. G. (2002). Traditional community resources for mental health: A report of temple healing from India. *British Medical Journal, 325*, 38–40.

Raney, S. A. & Cinerbas, D. C. (2005). Counseling in Developing Countries: Turkey and India as examples. *Journal of Mental Health Counseling, 27*, 149–160.

Rao, K. N. (1990). Practical steps in existential psychotherapy and one year follow-up of a case. *Indian Journal of Psychiatry, 32*, 244–251.

Rao, K. N. (1998). *Psychotherapy Choices in the Indian Context.* Presidential Address to the Annual Conference of the Indian Psychiatric Society held at Devanagre, Karnataka, August 30th.

Rao, K. N. (2010).Psychological interventions: from theory to practice. In G. Misra (ed.), *Psychology in India (Vol. 3): Clinical and health psychology* (pp 317–360). India: Pearson.

Roland, A. (2005). Commentary on building multicultural counseling bridges. *Counseling Psychology Quarterly, 18*, 283–285.

Saravanan, B., Jacob, K.S., Johnson, S., Prince, M., Bhugra, D., & David, A. S. (2007). Assessing insight in schizophrenia: East meets West. *British Journal of Psychiatry, 190*, 243–247.

Shankar, R. (2002). Family-professional collaboration in India. In H. P. Lefley & D. L. Johnson (eds), *Family interventions in mental illness: International perspectives* (pp. 125–141). Westport, CT: Praeger Publishers/ Greenwood Publishing Group.

Sengupta, D. (2010). Dealing with emotional baggage: Cos take on role of counselors. Retrieved from http://articles.economictimes.indiatimes.com/2010-0621/news/27586812_1_counsellors-indian-companies-employees

Shah, A., & Isaac, R. (2005). Couple relationship and sexuality. *Indian Journal of Social Psychiatry, 21*, 32–40.

Shrivastava, A. (2003). Suicidal behaviour-A window to mental health: The Prerana initiative. In V. Patel & R. Thara (eds), *Meeting the Mental Health Needs of Developing Countries: NGO Innovations in India* (pp. 273–285). Thousand Oaks, CA: Sage.

Singh, R. H. (1986). Evaluation of some Indian traditional methods of promotion of mental health. *Activitas Nervosa Superior, 28*, 67–69.

Singh, A. N. (2005). Role of yoga therapies in psychosomatic disorders. In. C. Kubo & T. Kuboki (eds). *Psychosomatic Medicine: Proceedings of the 18th World Congress on Psychosomatic Medicine* (pp. 91–96). New York: Elsevier Science.

Srinivasan, N. (2008). *We are not Alone: Family Care for Persons with Mental Illness.* Bangalore: Action for Mental Illness.

Surya, N. C. & Jayaram, S. S. (1964). Some basic considerations in the practice of psychotherapy in the Indian setting. *Indian Journal of Psychiatry, 6,* 153–156.

Thomas, E. (2011) *Personal development components in post graduate counseling programs in Bangalore: An evaluation.* Unpublished M.Phil thesis. Christ University, Bangalore, India.

Tiwari, S.C., Agarwal, G. G., Kumar, A., & Pandey, N. M. (2007). Preventing illness: A community based behavioural intervention approach. *Psychological Studies, 52,* 77–84.

Varma, V. K. (1982). Present state of psychotherapy in India. *Indian Journal of Psychiatry, 24,* 209–226.

Veereshwar, P. (2002). *Indian System of Psychotherapy.* Delhi: Kalpaz Publications.

WHO-AIMS Report (2006). *A Report on Mental Health System in Uttarkhand, India.* Dehradun: WHO and Ministry of Health, Uttarkhand.

17

COUNSELING AND PSYCHOTHERAPY IN JAPAN

Integrating Japanese traditions and contemporary values

Shigeru Iwakabe and Carol Zerbe Enns

Introduction

Counseling and psychotherapy practices have evolved and become increasingly well developed in Japan since the middle of the 20th century (Nishizono, 2005). In the last 10 years, the field of counseling and psychotherapy has experienced dramatic development. The social climate has changed in response to economic recessions; and the psychological problems of school age children, adolescents, young adults, and senior citizens have led to societal demands for psychological services that address intrapersonal and interpersonal crises. The 2011 earthquake, tsunami, and nuclear energy concerns have also contributed to increased psychological and physical vulnerabilities. Although resilience following the 2011 earthquake is evident, fears about the future, grief about loss and death, survivor guilt, and anger about potential nuclear effects pose significant challenges.

The total population of Japan is 127 million people, with 22% of the population being over 65 years of age. The birth rate in 2008 was 1.37, which is one of the lowest among developed nations. Japan also has the highest life expectancy and the tenth highest living standard (Japan Ministry of Internal Affairs and Communications, 2008). However, a declining birth rate, the postponement of marriage as well as the aging population are often named as "threats" to the future of Japan, which has the world's third largest economy. As a highly developed nation, Japan is a leader in technology and industry, and educational attainment is high (99.8% literacy rate).

The official religion of Japan is Shinto, which is characterized by the worship of nature, ancestors, polytheism, and animism. Over 100 million Japanese people identify themselves as Shinto adherents, and 89 million as Buddhist adherents (Ministry of Education, Culture, Sports, Science and Technology, 2008). This dual religious background characterizes most Japanese people,[1] and along with Confucianism, contributes to its social values. In comparison to Buddhist and *Shinto* practice, the number of persons who practice Christianity remains relatively small, with 0.8% of the Japanese population identifying themselves as Protestant or Catholic. After the

1990s, a number of newer religious groups were formed, and some have been forcibly dissolved by the government because of their involvement in kidnapping, fraud, and mental torture.[2]

Japan is often represented as an intricate yet contradictory culture in which the elements of advanced technologies and cultural traditions coexist to create the moral rules and aesthetics that are difficult for outsiders to understand. This may be partly related to its history, which was characterized by openness to influences from the outside world followed by periods of isolation. The slogan of *Wa-kon Yo-sai,* which means "maintaining Japanese spirits and acquiring and integrating Western technology," has long mobilized Japanese people toward incessant efforts to advance its development while maintaining close emotional ties to traditional Japanese identity.

Brief history of counseling and psychotherapy

Psychoanalysis and other Western approaches of psychotherapy were introduced to Japan shortly after their inception. For example, Inoue's (1905) early psychotherapy book introduced parallels between Buddhism and psychotherapy (Kasai, 2009), child counseling clinics were established as early as 1910 (Fukuhara, 1989), and writings relevant to psychoanalysis appeared in the 1910s (Kitanaka, 2003). Jungian concepts were introduced in the 1920s and later elaborated and integrated with Buddhist concepts by Hayao Kawai (e.g., 1996), whose impact on the development of clinical psychology in Japan has been extensive. Indigenous counseling approaches also emerged during the first half of the 20th century, and person-centered psychotherapies were introduced during the 1950s (Muramoto & Hoffman, 2005). Over time, Japanese counseling and psychotherapy approaches have been enriched by the integration of Japanese and Western concepts.

For many years, psychotherapy was typically practiced by a relatively limited number of psychiatrists and academics who usually maintained small and informal practices in university settings. The tide started to shift in the 1980s when the economic growth and the ever growing consumerist culture contributed to changes in values and the traditional family unit, as well as the psychological problems of adolescents and their families. Major problems were identified as family violence (*katei nai boryoku*) of adolescent children toward their mothers and truancy in middle school, which received wide media coverage as one of the major educational problems (Honjo, 1983).

Counseling and psychotherapy in Japan expanded and developed rapidly since the 1990s in response to problems in education, such as the sharply growing rate of truancy and bullying in middle schools. In 1995, the Ministry of Education placed one school counselor who is a certified clinical psychologist in each public junior high school, where these problems were most severe. This initiative represented the first governmental enterprise in which clinical psychologists were involved. In the same year, the Kobe-Awaji earthquake hit Japan's second most populated area, causing nearly 6,434 deaths and 43,792 injuries, and destroying or badly damaging 249,180 buildings. Psychiatrists and clinical psychologists immediately responded to this disaster by establishing a psychological support center for victims. Their efforts contributed to the social recognition of the profession (Shimoyama, 2011). Knowledge about post-disaster health effects that were acquired from interventions developed following the Kobe earthquake is informing the efforts of mental health professionals following the most recent 2011 earthquake and tsunami. The psychology support center was established only four days after the incident to provide therapeutic services to the victims of tsunami and earthquake and training for psychologists and volunteer students.

The number of clinical psychologists is growing rapidly. The certification system for clinical psychologists started in 1988, growing from 1,595 initial members to 23,005 in 2011. A number of new graduate programs were established during the last decade, and approximately 1,500 new members have passed the certification test and joined the association of clinical psychologists (Foundation of the Japanese Certification Board for Clinical Psychologists, 2009).

The societal demand for the service of psychologists is increasing in a variety of areas. In the domain of family life, the problems related to child abuse in "ordinary families" due to *ikuji-fuan* (child-rearing anxiety) prompted the Ministry of Health, Labor, and Welfare to open nation-wide research and intervention programs to support young parents and their children (Misawa, 2004). As a result of changes in the social climate triggered by economic recessions, psychological problems related to work issues became a major concern. Many organizations started employee assistance programs in order to help workers cope with problems of depression and psychological dysfunction as well as to reduce the increasing rate of suicide due to work related issues such as burnout, power harassment, and office bullying (Ohta, Inadomi, & Tanaka, 2008). Work-related psychological dysfunctions are not isolated problems but rooted in the same social and economic structure that has gradually molded family life in Japan since the 1970s. Men typically work overtime, with little time left to get involved in parenting and child rearing activities. Many young mothers with *ikuji-fuan* are stay-at-home mothers in a nuclear family unit, left alone with a single child for most of their waking hours. Their anxiety is intensified by feelings of isolation, a sense of burden, and pressure to educate and discipline the child without their husband's involvement and in the "correct" way, and even feelings of resentment and loss for having their careers interrupted.

The current era is often referred to as "an era of mind (*kokoro no jidai*)." Most recently, it has been referred to as an era of depression (*utsu no jidai*) (Hiraki, Iwakabe, & Fukushima, 2011). The economic growth of the last 50 years that brought Japanese people wealth and a high standard of living has undeniably ended. Japan's citizens now face the difficult challenge of reflecting on and reappraising a value system that was heavily tilted toward the materialistic satisfaction, had long provided them with clear goals and meaning in life, and had structured their life style and social and gender roles (Saeki, 2003).

Counselor education programs, accreditation, licensure, and certification

The phrase "clinical psychology" has typically encompassed a variety of mental health and psychotherapy practices in Japan (Iwasaki, 2005; Shimoyama, 2001), and the use of this terminology (clinical psychology) throughout this chapter is consistent with this reality. When clinical and counseling practices are differentiated, clinical psychologists are more likely to provide psychological assessment and intervention, and counselors are more likely to work in multiple occupations that can range from advising consumers about products to providing assistance for crisis counseling hotlines (Seto, Becker, & Akutsu, 2006). Qualifications for counselors are also less standardized than for clinical psychologists.

A national licensing system for psychologists in Japan has not yet been established. Historically, Japanese clinical psychologists have been board certified by the Japan Society of Certified Clinical Psychologists since 1988. Following the establishment of an accreditation system (Foundation of the Japanese Certification Board for Clinical Psychologists) for master's degree programs in clinical psychology in 1996, many new graduate schools in clinical psychology were founded. By 2011, 160 accredited programs existed, including eight new professional schools of clinical psychology. These new schools have developed curricula that require an on-site practicum and replaced the master's thesis based on empirical research with an extensive case study.

To be certified as a clinical psychologist, one needs to complete a 2-year master's degree in an accredited clinical psychology program consisting of course work and practica. Courses cover topics such as theories of counseling and psychotherapy, psychological assessment, psychological interviewing, research methods, and specialized areas such as developmental psychopathology, play therapy, and group psychotherapy. Practicum experiences involve participating in a three-hour weekly case conference, providing counseling at a university training clinic, and completing an externship in an actual clinical setting.

Current counseling and psychotherapy theories, process, and trends

According to a survey conducted by the Japan Society for Certified Clinical Psychologists (2006), 73.7% of Japanese clinical psychologists identified themselves as having an eclectic orientation, 51.3% as humanistic, 42.3% as psychoanalytic/analytic, 39.7% as behavioral/cognitive-behavioral, and 16.5% as systems oriented. Another survey by Kanazawa and Iwakabe (2006), based on a relatively small random sample (N = 183), also revealed similar results. Seventy-eight percent of psychologists identified themselves as eclectic or integrative, endorsing major theoretical influences associated with psychodynamic and humanistic therapies. A strong Jungian influence was notable, with sandbox play therapy being endorsed widely for counseling children and adolescents (Kitanaka, 2003).

Mental health or counseling services are also provided by paraprofessionals. For example, Japan's 2001 domestic violence legislation mandated counseling services, and these services are often typically provided within Japan's public women's centers (Chan-Tieberghien, 2004). The training of counselors varies, with some domestic violence counselors holding academic degrees and others receiving training through more informal or nongovernment organizations (NGOs). Grassroots activism and volunteerism on the part of adult women have been an important tradition in Japan, and Japanese women have played an important role in developing mental health services for abused women (Hatashita, Hirao, Brykczynski, & Anderson, 2006).

Feminist therapy represents another form of counseling that first emerged as a grassroots movement during the 1980s. Japanese feminist counselors have emphasized consciousness raising and egalitarianism in relationships, and have offered a variety of counseling services that focus on self-esteem, body image, assertiveness, social support, and mother-daughter relationships (Enns, 2004; Matsuyuki, 1998). More recently, certified psychologists have also offered counseling that is consistent with feminist therapy goals, and academic psychologists have published a handbook on the psychology of gender (Aono, Akazawa, & Matsunami, 2008).

Another group of active paraprofessionals provide counseling for a suicide hot-line (*Inochi no Denwa*) that started in 1971. Over 7,000 volunteer counselors take calls 24 hours a day. Beyond the prevention of suicide, *Inochi no Denwa* provides supportive counseling for a variety of life issues, including survivors of the 2011 earthquake and tsunami. The number of calls has doubled in last seven years, exceeding 7 million. In 2008, 10% of calls were suicide related (Federation of Inochi no Denwa, 2008).

Indigenous and traditional healing methods

Japanese social life has often been characterized by collectivism and high-context communication. Although Japan has been experiencing rapid movement toward more individualistic values (Kasai, 2009), interdependence and interpersonal sensitivity remain important cultural ideals. The indigenous concept of *amae* represents an extension of collectivism and high-context communication, and can be defined as the ability to presume, depend on, and enjoy the benevolence and unconditional acceptance of another person. *Amae* involves mutual attachment and other-centeredness, security, and warmth between persons. It is communicated nonverbally, and considered relevant to relationships from cradle to grave (Doi, 1973; Iwakabe, 2008).[3]

Many indigenous Japanese psychotherapies can be referred to as non-talking cures in that many important therapeutic processes occur through silence, solitary introspection, or nonverbal interactions expressed through drawing and other artwork (Iwakabe, 2008). These nonverbal features are conspicuous in indigenous therapies such as *Morita* therapy and *Naikan* therapy, which have existed for over half a century. *Morita* Therapy incorporates a variety of concrete activities designed to unblock clients' psychological paralysis and facilitate productive action. Clients are asked to accept discomfort and anxiety rather than artificially attempting to change them, and to act constructively in spite of negative feelings. Clients learn to move from a self-focus, self-criticism, and avoidance behaviors to self-acceptance, direct action, and productive immersion in life tasks (Ishiyama, 2003).

Naikan involves participating in a series of systematic introspective exercises. Clients are taught to reflect on their attitudes and behaviors toward significant others, placing emphasis on three themes: (a) what they have received from others, (b) what they have offered in return, and (c) what difficulties or worries they have caused or placed on loved ones. They experience a type of cognitive reframing that redirects attention from inner symptoms or blaming others to appreciation and gratitude for what others have given them (Hedstrom, 1994; Ozawa-de Silva, 2006).

Hakoniwa[4] (box garden in English) is referred to as sandplay therapy in North America. This therapy allows individuals to express themselves nonverbally and construct a microcosm of their personal worlds by shaping sand and placing miniature figures in the sand (Enns & Kasai, 2003; Kasai, 2009). Prior to its introduction to Japan as a Jungian psychotherapy, Japanese persons often constructed *hakoniwa*, or miniature gardens, in small enclosures. This activity called participants to display the attitudes, self-discipline, and mindfulness associated with a variety of the Zen Buddhist arts such as tea ceremony, calligraphy, and flower arranging. Hayao Kawai (1996), who introduced *hakoniwa* as a therapy to Japan, viewed it as a method for integrating Buddhist, Japanese, and Jungian concepts.

A treatment structure that is often used for psychotherapy for children, adolescents, and their families is called mother–child parallel therapy (*boshi heiko mensetsu*) in which a mother and her child concurrently engage themselves in respective individual sessions from different therapists in the same clinical setting (Omata, 1999). Psychotherapy for the mother serves a psychoeducational purpose by providing her with information about parenting, child development, and the nature of her child's problems. More importantly, it gives the mother an opportunity to receive her own personal therapy for child rearing anxiety, and even marital problems that are suspected to lie beneath the problems manifested in the child. Mother-child parallel therapy is a creative attempt to maximize therapeutic effectiveness by involving the mother in the treatment of her child when fathers are not available or unwilling to participate. It also reinforces a commonly held social notion that parenting and child rearing responsibilities reside in the hands of mothers. Finally, in the case of *hikikomori* problems (described later), mothers often become clients and receive long-term consultation before children experiencing withdrawal agree to treatment.

Research and supervision

Most Japanese psychologists emphasize the importance of learning from unsystematic clinical case studies in which the therapist narrates the process of therapy. Consistent with this view, 60% of articles in the official journal of the Association of Japanese Clinical Psychology (AJCP) are clinical case studies, and the annual meeting has consistently featured a larger number of case presentations than research papers (Iwakabe, 2008; Kanazawa, 2007).

Clinical case studies are seen as symbolizing the inseparability of the knower and clinical knowledge, as well as research and practice (Hironaka, 2002; Kawai, 2002). Younger psychologists are strongly encouraged to write and present case studies as a sign of their professional development. In contrast, the case studies of senior psychologists are considered true clinical explorations. Unfortunately, there are no concrete methodological guidelines for conducting or writing up case studies. As a result, many case studies include only limited discussion of hypotheses and lack process and outcome measurements that can provide readers with client background information necessary to apply the understanding from such case studies. Major issues include the need for more methodological rigor (Shimoyama, 2011), concerns about accountability, and the increasing number of clinicians who are not involved in the examination of their own work.

The importance of supervision is strongly emphasized; however, the length and format of supervision vary from one graduate program to another. The Japanese Certification Board for Clinical Psychologists requires students to attend a three hour case conference each week for two years; however, there are no guidelines about supervision and its format. As the number of younger psychologists grows, more systematic measures will be needed to increase awareness about the importance of supervision in professional development.

Strengths, weaknesses, opportunities, and challenges

Strengths of counseling and psychotherapy practice in Japan include its well-developed history and efforts to integrate Western and Japanese concepts. For example, in 1932, Seisaku Kosawa studied psychoanalysis in Vienna and developed a theory of the Ajase Complex, an Asian alternative to the Oedipus Complex (Okonogi, 2009). Later, Japanese psychoanalyst Takeo Doi (1973; see also Okonogi, 2009) proposed the theory of *amae*, which focused on exploring features of Japanese interpersonal connectedness and has had a significant impact on psychotherapy practice. Indigenous psychotherapy approaches informed by Buddhist values have also existed since the early 20th century, and have gained popularity outside Japan (Hedstrom, 1994; Reynolds, 1995). These integrative efforts may show ways in which cultural factors are inter-woven into theories of psychotherapy that were developed in another culture (Iwakabe, 2008). Finally, concepts related to counseling and psychotherapy are becoming more familiar to the public, and acceptance of psychotherapy practice is growing.

Despite its well-developed history and growth, Sato (2007) described clinical psychology as "confused" (p. 133), "erratic" (p. 140), and as experiencing an adolescent phase of development. For example, a current hot debate centers on establishing a national licensing system for clinical psychologists, which has been a sensitive issue for Japanese clinical psychology throughout its history. Earlier attempts to develop a system of national licensure have failed, at least in part, because of divisions between two factions, one of which saw licensure as central to the future of clinical psychology, and another which viewed licensure as leading to bureaucratization and a potential drawback to the flexibility and social justice aims of clinical psychology (Shimoyama, 2011).

At present, multiple professional associations exist, and most are associated with major theoretical schools and orientations such as psychoanalysis, humanistic psychology, cognitive-behavioral therapy, and family therapies. Each group has over 1,000 members, and also sponsors a specialized certification system. The certificate for clinical psychologists, however, is often required for job applications. The presence of multiple systems of certification may limit unity and integration within counseling, clinical, and psychotherapy practice.

Although counseling and psychotherapy have gained visibility within Japan, members of the population remain hesitant to use the services of psychologists. Stigma about mental health remains, which limits help-seeking behavior. In addition, national health insurance does not cover psychotherapy services unless they are provided by psychiatrists, which further limits options for gaining access to psychotherapy services (Otake, 2008).

The present challenge for Japanese psychologists is to deal with psychological problems related to dramatic changes in the social and cultural climate. These changes include: (a) the availability of advanced information technology and an ever deepening consumerism that is changing the nature and mode of interpersonal relationships (Nishizono, 2005); (b) a clash between traditional and modern gender roles, gender role conflicts, increasing divorce rates, domestic violence, and other forms of sexual offense (Kingston, 2004; Kozu, 1999); and (c) the acute sense of economic insecurity due to a prolonged recession. For example, recent recessions and the increase of nonstandard employment have led to disillusionment among many young adults. A growing number of individuals are categorized as NEETs (Not in Education, Employment or Training) and Freeters (persons who work part-time and make frequent job changes) (Kasai, 2009). Among older adults, job loss has been associated with depression and suicide (Takano & Shima, 2006)

The Japanese *hikikomori* phenomenon has received substantial attention both within Japan and abroad (e.g., Jones, 2005; Zielenziger, 2006) and has been referred to as a silent epidemic. The Ministry of Health, Labor, and Welfare of Japan describes *hikikomori* as a pattern of social withdrawal that persists for at least 6 months, during which time persons with *hikikomori* do not participate in school, work, or other social activities. Individuals typically become home-bound, often maintaining only minimal contact even with family members (Kasai, 2009).[5]

Japan has one of the highest suicide rates in the world. For each of the past ten years, over 30,000 suicides have been recorded. A person living in Japan is three to five times more likely to die by suicide than in a car accident (Kawanishi, 2008; Kitanaka, 2009). Kawanishi (2008) indicates that approximately half of these suicides have been associated with financial difficulties. In Japan, suicide was traditionally thought of as conveying multiple meanings, including forms of apology, acts of resolve, or the acceptance of responsibility for the failings of an organization or group. More recently, however, suicide has been increasingly medicalized and associated with depression (Kitanaka, 2009). There is also growing concern about the potential rise of suicide following the 2011 earthquake and nuclear crisis (Parry, 2011).

One of the challenges of identifying and treating depression is that the term for depression (*utsubyo*) in Japan is indicative of a serious, biological psychiatric condition. In English, however, the word for depression is used to depict various levels of depression as well as more everyday variations of mood such as "feeling depressed" (Kirmayer, 2002). In addition, Japanese persons experiencing depression are likely to report physical symptoms (e.g., fatigue, sleep problems, body aches) and to seek treatment in psychosomatic clinics where anti-anxiety and other medications are often prescribed (Kanazawa, 2007; Kirmayer, 2002). It is important to note that feelings of sadness and melancholy are not necessarily seen as signs of distress in Japan; furthermore, those who are hardworking and show self-sacrificing devotion are considered model youths or model employees. In reality, they may be propelled by the anxiety and fear of not fulfilling the expectations of others or achieving the socially respectable norms, or may be overcome by the demands of others (Kitanaka, 2008). Someone who is overworked and fatigued may be regarded as a devoted and reliable person rather than someone who cannot control his or her life situation or engage in appropriate self-care.

Japanese culture may also support a "habit of hesitation" (Minami, 1971, p. 34) toward happiness. In Japan, experiencing positive and "happy" feelings is less likely to be linked to positive mental health and wellbeing than in Western countries (Oishi, 2002), and individually oriented states of personal "happiness" are less valued than socially oriented forms of wellbeing that are embedded in harmonious relationships (Lu & Gilmour, 2004). Although the recognition and treatment of depression and suicide is a major issue facing Japan, knowledge of how culture contributes to the presentation and experience of depression and other mood states is crucial to effective intervention.

Recent pharmaceutical marketing campaigns for SSRIs have introduced the phrase *kokoro no kaze*, which is translated as a cold of the heart, mind, or soul, as a way to demystify depression. Although scientific studies of SSRIs have raised doubts about the effectiveness of antidepressants for treating depression in Japan (Kirmayer, 2002; Watters, 2010), efforts to use new language (e.g., *kokoro no kaze*) to conceptualize depression may hold promise. Iwasaki (2005) suggested that terms such as *kokoro no care* sound "people friendly" (p. 137), and thus, can support an integrated mind-body-spirit approach to intervention, and may increase the willingness of persons in Japan to seek counseling.

Future directions

One of the major issues facing clinical and counseling psychologists concerns national licensing legislation. In 2006, legislation was introduced that would create a two-tiered national licensing system, which would give psychologists only limited opportunities to provide services relevant to medical domains. Some are opposed to this licensing system because it limits psychologists' roles in medical areas and may also undermine potential roles clinical psychologists may play in many other areas such as education, social welfare, and legal systems. In addition, the salaries of clinical psychologists vary substantially, and many do not have full-time positions that would allow them to "make a living" as psychologists. Many younger psychologists are quite concerned about financial security and appear to be waiting impatiently for the implementation of a licensure system.

A related issue is accountability. The majority of Japanese clinical psychologists provide open-ended long-term psychotherapy and seek limited outcome data. As the social demand for services and professionalization progresses, and as psychological service is incorporated within health services and educational services, psychologists will be required to demonstrate the effectiveness of their interventions in comparison to other treatments and interventions. Those with Jungian and psychodynamic orientations often feel that their work cannot be adequately assessed by the scientific methods accepted in the science community (Hironaka, 2002; Kawai, 2002). Nonetheless, an increasing social demand will focus on demonstrating mechanisms of change and the necessity for longer-term treatment.

Another important issue involves the need to develop more organized and systematic training programs in eclectic and integrative methods. As noted previously, over 70% of Japanese psychologists practice some form of eclectic and/or integrative therapies without adequate conceptual background and clinical training in integrating and synthesizing concepts and interventions from different therapies. Furthermore, although many psychologists working in school settings are expected to engage in consultation, psychoeducational approaches, and other community-based approaches, current training programs hold little space for these types of interventions. The two-year master's program may provide an essential basis for psychologists to launch their careers as psychologists, but continuing education and training are needed to support younger psychologists and their needs.

Finally, issues associated with the professional development of younger female psychologists need to be considered. Traditionally, many Japanese women were expected to leave their jobs once they married. Following the enforcement of the labor equity law, more women have continued to work after they have children; however, their participation in the labor force is still relatively low. For example, the proportion of working women with children under 6-years old is 35% for Japan, 78% for Sweden, and 61.5% for United States (Organization for Economic Co-operation and Development, 2001).

The contributions and employment of the many young female psychologists have not received sufficient attention from major committees of the Association of Japanese Clinical Psychologists and Educators. One particular issue is that many of these psychologists go through major life events such as marriage, pregnancy, and maternity leave. A qualitative study of clinical psychologists' experience of maternity revealed that they were often afraid of not being good mothers themselves, in spite of their clinical knowledge, and also not being able to find employment, though they all believed that their maternity experience helped them become better clinicians (Yamaguchi, 2007). To assist young female psychologists with tools to balance career and family roles, it will be necessary to include career and professional development issues in their training and continuing education programs. Mentoring systems as well as support systems are also important.

Conclusion

Clinical/counseling psychology and mental health counseling in Japan have grown rapidly during the last 10 years and the changes in Japanese society call for increased contributions to social problems at various levels in educational systems, organizational settings, families, and medical systems. The future health of counseling and psychotherapy practice will require attentiveness to Japan's 21st century challenges, the further creation of effective interventions, the continued development of training programs, and movement toward a national consensus about licensing. Our future and current goals are to demonstrate that we are, in fact, not only equipped to deal with these problems but also to effectively contribute to solutions.

Notes

1 Religious practice consists primarily of infrequent yet periodic visits to shrines and temples at the time of specific life events. A typical Japanese family visits *Shinto* shrines for celebration and purification rites, and manages funeral arrangements and anniversaries of ancestry within Buddhist temples.
2 One symbolic incident was a 1996 Sarin Gas terrorist attack in the Tokyo subway system by a group called *Aum Shinrikyo*.
3 The ability to "read" and enact social expectations and responsibilities is highly valued in Japanese culture. Nonverbal sensitivity is reflected in a variety of indigenous psychotherapies, and can also be seen in the "softer" form of eye contact used by many Japanese psychotherapists (Kanazawa, 2007).
4 Following the nonverbal phase of a *hakoniwa* session, the therapist often asks the client to describe the sandtray scene, and clients then describe new insights.
5 Estimates suggest that approximately 80% of those with *hikikomori* are male, and that up to 1 in 10 males between the ages of 14 and 20 may experience this pattern of social withdrawal, which may extend into adulthood (Zielenziger, 2006). Antecedents of *hikikomori* may include education pressures and school bullying, high personal sensitivity to criticism or shaming, family pressures, cultural expectations to "fit in," and the limited flexibility associated with adult roles (Borovoy, 2008; Furlong, 2008).

References

Aono, A., Akazawa, J., & Matsunami, T. (eds). (2008). *Jendashinrigaku no Handobukku* [Handbook of the psychology of gender]. Kyoto: Nakanishiya Syuppan.
Borovoy, A. (2008). Japan's hidden youths: Mainstreaming the emotionally distressed in Japan. *Culture, Medicine and Psychiatry, 32*, 552–576.
Chan-Tiberghien, J. (2004). *Gender and Human Rights Politics in Japan*. Stanford, CA: Stanford University Press.

Doi, T. (1973). *The Anatomy of Dependence*. New York: Kodansha International.

Enns, C. Z. (2004). *Feminist Theories and Feminist Psychotherapies* (2nd edn). New York: Haworth Press.

Enns, C. Z., & Kasai, M. (2003). Hakoniwa: Japanese sandplay therapy. *The Counseling Psychologist, 31*, 93–112.

Federation of Inochi No Denwa: FIND. (2008). *Toukei Jouhou* [The Annual Statistics]. Retrieved February 22, 2010, from www.find-j.jp/toukei/toukeidata/2008all.pdf.

Foundation of the Japanese Certification Board for Clinical Psychologists. (2009). Rinshoshinrishi Shikaku Nintei no Jisshi. Retrieved on February 22, 2010, from www.fjcbcp.or.jp/nintei_1.html.

Fukuhara, M. (1989). Counselling psychology in Japan. *Applied Psychology: An International Review, 38*, 409–422.

Furlong, A. (2008). The Japanese hikikomori phenomenon: Acute social withdrawal among young people. *The Sociological Review, 56*, 309–325.

Hatashita, H., Hirao, K., Brykczynski, K. A., & Anderson, E. T. (2006). Grassroots efforts of Japanese women to promote services for abused women. *Nursing and Health Sciences, 8*, 169–174.

Hedstrom, L. J. (1994). Morita and Naikan therapies: American applications. *Psychotherapy, 31*, 154–160.

Hiraki, N., Iwakabe, S., & Fukushima, T. (eds). (2011). *Shinseiki Utubyou-chiryou/Shienron: Togo Apurochi.* [Treatment, support, and prevention of depression in the new era: Integrative approaches]. Tokyo, Japan: Kongo Publishing.

Hironaka, M. (2002). Rinshoshinrigaku no Houhouron wo Meguru Mondai [Methodological problems in clinical psychology]. *Japanese Journal of Clinical Psychology, 2*, 51–55.

Honjo, S. (1983). The characteristics of school refusal accompanied by family violence. *Japanese Journal of Child and Adolescent Psychiatry, 24*, 27–43.

Inoue, E. (1905). *Psychotherapy*. Tokyo: Nankodo Shoten.

Ishiyama, F. I. (2003). A bending willow tree: A Japanese (Morita Therapy) model of human nature and client change. *Canadian Journal of Counselling, 37*, 216–231.

Iwakabe, S. (2008). Psychotherapy integration in Japan. *Journal of Psychotherapy Integration, 18*, 103–125.

Iwasaki, M. (2005). Mental health and counseling in Japan: A path toward societal transformation. *Journal of Mental Health Counseling, 27*, 129–141.

Japan Ministry of Internal Affairs and Communications. (2008). *The world statistics*. Retrieved on February 22, 2010, from www.stat.go.jp/data/sekai/pdf/2009al.pdf.

Japan Society for Certified Clinical Psychologists (2006). *Dai 4 kai "Rinsho-shinrishi no doukou narabini ishiki chousa" houkokusho* [The report on the fourth survey of The Japan Society for Certified Clinical Psychologists membership]. Tokyo: Author.

Jones, M. (2005). Shutting themselves in. *New York Times Magazine*, January 6, *15*, 5, 46–51.

Kanazawa, Y. (2007). Psychotherapy in Japan: The case of Ms. A. *Journal of Clinical Psychology: In Session, 63*, 755–763.

Kanazawa, Y., & Iwakabe, S. (2006, September). *Shinririnshoka no Shokugyouteki Hattatsu ni Kansuru Chosa (1): Seicho no Keiki* [Research on the professional development of clinical psychologists (1): Factors associated with professional growth]. Paper presented at the Annual Meeting of the Association of Japanese Clinical Psycholgy, Osaka, Japan.

Kasai, M. (2009). The role of Japanese culture in psychological health: Implications for counseling and clinical psychology. In L. H. Gerstein, P. P. Heppner, S. Ægisdóttir, S. A. Leung, & K. L. Norsworthy (eds), *International Handbook of Cross-cultural Counseling* (pp. 159–171). Thousand Oaks, CA: Sage.

Kawai, H. (1996). *Buddhism and the Art of Psychotherapy*. College Station: Texas A&M University Press.

Kawai, H. (2002). Rinshoshinrigaku no Kenkyuho [Research methodology in clinical psychology]. *Japanese Journal of Clinical Psychology, 2*, 3–9.

Kawanishi, Y. (2008). On karo-jisatsu (suicide by overwork). *International Journal of Mental Health, 37*, 61–74.

Kingston, J. (2004). *Japan's Quiet Transformation: Social Change and Civil Society in the 21st Century*. New York: Routledge/Curzon.

Kirmayer, L. J. (2002). Psychopharmacology in a globalizing world: The use of antidepressants in Japan. *Transcultural Psychiatry, 38*, 295–322.

Kitanaka, J. (2003). Jungians and the rise of psychotherapy in Japan: A brief historical note. *Transcultural Psychiatry, 40*, 239–247.

Kitanaka, J. (2009). Questioning the suicide of resolve: Medico-legal disputes regarding 'overwork suicide' in twentieth-century Japan. In J. Weaver & D. Wright (eds), *Histories of Suicide* (pp. 257–280). Toronto: University of Toronto Press.

Kozu, J. (1999). Domestic violence in Japan. *American Psychologist, 54*, 50–54.

Lu, L., & Gilmour, R. (2004). Culture and conceptions of happiness: Individual oriented and social oriented SWB. *Journal of Happiness Studies, 5*, 269–291.

Matsuyuki, M. (1998). Japanese feminist counseling as a political act. *Women and Therapy, 21*, 65–77.

Minami, H. (1971). *Psychology of the Japanese People*. Toronto, CA: University of Toronto Press.

Ministry of Education, Culture, Sports, Science and Technology. (2008). *Shukyo Tokei* [The annual statistics on religion]. Retrieved February 20, 2010, from www.mext.go.jp/b_menu/toukei/001/index39.htm.

Misawa, N. (2004). Kosodate shien no Tokushu ni Atatte [Preface to the special issue on parenting support]. *Japanese Journal of Clinical Psychology, 4*, 575–578.

Muramoto, S., & Hoffman, E. (2005). Humanistic psychology in Japan. *Journal of Humanistic Psychology, 45*, 465–482.

Nishizono, M. (2005). Culture, psychopathology, and psychotherapy: Changes observed in Japan. In W.-S. Tseng, S. C. Chang, & M. Nishizono (eds), *Asian Culture and Psychotherapy: Implications for East and West* (pp. 40–54). Honolulu, HI: University of Hawai'i Press.

Ohta, Y., Inadomi, H., & Tanaka, G. (2008). Shokuba no Mentaru Herusu no Genjyo to Mondaiten [Current status and problems of mental health in the workplace]. *Health Science Research, 21*, 1–10.

Oishi, S. (2002). Experiencing and remembering of well-being: A cross-cultural analysis. *Personality and Social Psychology Bulletin, 28*, 1398–1406.

Okonogi, K. (2009). Psychoanalysis in Japan. In S. Akhtar (ed.), *Freud and the Far East: Psychoanalytic Perspectives on the People and Culture of China, Japan, and Korea* (pp. 9–25). Lanham, JD: Jason Aronson.

Omata, K. (1999). Hahaoya to Kyoryokushitesasaeta Shishunki Joshi no Jirei [A case study of a female adolescent who was supported both by the therapist and her mother]. *Journal of Japanese Clinical Psychology, 16*, 538–549.

Organization for Economic Co-operation and Development. (2001). *Employment Outlook*. Paris, France: OECD Publishing.

Otake, T. (2008). Treating clinical depression a tall order. *Japan Times Online*, February 20.

Ozawa-de Silva, C. (2006). *Psychotherapy and Religion in Japan: The Japanese Introspection Practice of Naikan*. New York: Routledge.

Parry, R.L. (2011). Suicide cases rise after triple disaster. *Times* (United Kingdom), June 17, p. 50.

Reynolds, D. K. (1995). *A Handbook for Constructive Living*. New York: William Morrow.

Saeki, K. (2003). *Seichokeizai no Shuen: Shihonshugi no genkai to Yutakasa no saiteigi* [The end of economic growth: The limits of capitalism and the redefinition of wealth]. Tokyo, Japan: Diamond Publishing.

Sato, T. (2007). Rise and falls of clinical psychology in Japan: A perspective on the status of Japanese clinical psychology. *Ritsumeikan Journal of Human Sciences, 13*(2), 133–144.

Seto, A., Becker, K. W., & Akutsu, M. (2006). Counseling Japanese men on fathering. *Journal of Counseling and Development, 84*, 488–492.

Shimoyama, H. (2001). On the developmental task of clinical psychology in Japan. *Bulletin of the School of Education University of Tokyo, 41*, 273–281.

Shimoyama, H. (2011). Clinical psychology in Japan: Toward integration inside and recognition from outside. In H. Shimoyama (ed.), *An International Comparison of Clinical Psychology in Practice: West Meets East* (pp. 55–68). Tokyo, Japan: Kazama Publishing.

Takano, T., & Shima, S. (2006). Preventing suicide in those who are in the prime of life. *Japanese Journal of Psychotherapy, 32*, 568–576.

Watters, E. (2010). *Crazy Like Us: The Globalization of the American Psyche*. New York: Free Press.

Yamaguchi, K. (2007). *A Qualitative Study on the Experience of Professional and Family Roles in Female Clinical Psychologists: Examining Positive and Negative Spillovers*. Unpublished master thesis. Ochanomizu University, Tokyo, Japan.

Zielenziger, M. (2006). *Shutting out the Sun: How Japan Created its Own Lost Generation*. New York: Random House.

18

COUNSELING AND PSYCHOTHERAPY IN MALAYSIA

The joy and pain of (continuous) pioneering work

Wai Sheng Ng

Introduction

A developing country of 28.3 million in Southeast Asia, Malaysia is a multiracial, multilingual and multireligious society, consisting of Malays and other Aboriginal groups (e.g., Iban, Kadazan, Bajau, etc.) (67.4%), Chinese (24.6%), Indians (7.3%), and other ethnic minorities (0.7%) (Department of Statistics Malaysia, 2010). Each ethnic group retains their own cultural identity through their respective cultural language and customs; yet, they are also very much assimilated. Hence, Malaysian culture is known as "hybrid" in nature (Smith, 2003).

Among others, it is not uncommon to find Malaysians combining several languages and dialects, often interchangeably in a social conversation. Malay (the national language) and English are taught in all public and private schools. There are also vernacular schools that use ethnic languages (e.g., Mandarin or Tamil) as the medium of instruction. Ethnic dialects are commonly used in informal settings with family and friends. There are also about 18 aboriginal languages in Peninsular Malaysia and at least 54 indigenous languages/dialects in East Malaysia (Smith, 2003).

Islam is the official religion of the country and the mostly widely professed religion (61.3%), typically embraced by Malays and the indigenous groups. Other religions practiced include Buddhism (19.8%), Christianity (9.2%), Hinduism (6.3%), and Confucianism/Taoism/other folk religions (1.3%) (Department of Statistics Malaysia, 2010). Traditionally, Chinese and Indians practice Buddhism/Confucianism/Taoism, and Hinduism, respectively, although some also embrace Christianity/Catholicism or Islam. In addition, it is not uncommon that many local people maintain supernatural beliefs in their daily living, particularly relating to mental health issues.

Since its independence from British colonization in 1957, Malaysia has gone through rapid economical development, resulting in significant social changes. Through globalization, cultural values are also slowly changing, from a more traditional collectivistic worldview to more modern and postmodern individualistic worldviews, particularly among the younger generations. With increased pressure to achieve in society, coupled with greater disconnectedness in relationships, mental health concerns are also on the rise. According to the Ministry of Health, the annual cases of mental illness rose by 15.6% to 400,227 cases in 2010 (Xinhuanet, 2011).

While stigma towards counseling and psychotherapy is still very much prevalent in society (Sipon, 2007), there is certainly greater openness and demand for these services in the last two decades (See & Ng, 2010).

Quite a number of researchers have written on the topic of the development of counseling in Malaysia, from the earliest foreign researchers (e.g., Lloyd, 1987, as cited in See & Ng, 2010; Scorzelli, 1987), to local researchers such as Quek (2001); Ng and Stevens (2001); Pope, Musa, Singaravelu, Bringaze, and Russell (2002); and Salim and Mohd Jaladin (2005). In the last 5 years, three other reviews have been published, by Sipon (2007), Glamcevski (2008), and See and Ng (2010). On the development of psychotherapy in Malaysia, the following researchers have written on specific areas, including Varma and Azhar (1996) on cognitive therapy, Singh and Khan (1998) on behavioral therapy, and K. S. Ng (2003) on family therapy. Most recently, the author has also discussed the development of psychotherapists (Ng, 2007) and clinical psychologists (Ng, 2011). Therefore, in this chapter, the author will only provide a synopsis of the history, with added new developments in the field.

Brief history of counseling and psychotherapy

As early as 1938, guidance services were first introduced in the schools by the British Colonial Administrators (Salim & Mohd Jaladin, 2005). Initially, guidance work was practiced informally in schools by class teachers and hostel masters. Formal guidance and counseling services were first introduced in secondary schools in 1963 (Salim & Mohd Jaladin, 2005). Another 20 years passed before there were serious efforts to train local counselors in drug rehabilitation and school/university settings, to curb increasing drug abuse problems during the 1980s (Scorzelli, 1987). Most are not called "counselors" but are referred to as governmental "officers." They receive short-term (i.e., 8 weeks to 1 year) in-service training, and only practice counseling as a secondary responsibility (Scorzelli, 1987). Full-time school counselors were introduced in 1996, and by 2000, every secondary school had at least one full-time counselor (See & Ng, 2010).

The first professional milestone in the development of counseling in Malaysia was the establishment of the Malaysian Association of Counseling (Persatuan Kaunseling Malaysia [PERKAMA]) in 1982 (PERKAMA, 2004/2005). Subsequently, the Malaysian Psychological Association (Persatuan Psikologi Malaysia [PSIMA]) was established in 1988 (Abdul Rahman, 2005). In 1992, the counseling profession was further acknowledged by the Department of Public Services, with a created position called Head Officer of Psychology and Counseling (PERKAMA, 2004/2005).

In 1998, the Counselors Act (Act 580) was established, regulating for the first time the title of "counselor" and counseling practice in Malaysia (Lembaga Penyelidikan Undang-Undang, 1998). According to the Act, the Malaysian Counselors Advisory Council or Board of Counselors (Lembaga Kaunselor) is responsible in the implementation of the act. The Council also adopts the PERKAMA's Code of Ethics, which covers the counselor's qualifications, confidentiality, professional negligence, and informed consent, etc., similar to those of the American Counseling Association (ACA, 2006). To date, there are 2,090 registered counselors, as shown in the Council's online directory (Lembaga Kaunselor, n.d.). The Counselors Act, however, does not apply to other professionals such as 'psychotherapists' or 'psychologists'.

According to Azhar and Varma (2000), psychotherapy did not develop until the 1970s. It was mainly used for nonpsychotic (e.g., depressed, anxious, etc.) patients and first came to be practiced by local psychiatrists in major cities. Since these psychiatrists received their training overseas, the most common form of therapy in the 1970s to 1980s was psychoanalytic therapy. In line with that, some practice hypnosis and formed the National Association of Hypnosis in

Malaysia (Singh & Khan, 1998). Between 1980 and 1990, behavioral therapies and cognitive-behavioral approaches were introduced and practiced among those trained from abroad, such as Australia and United Kingdom (Singh & Khan, 1998; Varma & Azhar, 1996).

In the last few years, there have been more initiatives to benchmark the psychology profession to protect public safety and professional integrity. Among others, PSIMA appointed a taskforce to draft out a registration process and code of ethics for psychologists in Malaysia. The PSIMA's Code of Ethics draws upon Kitchener's (1984) ethical principles and adapts from the existing Code of Ethics from the American Psychological Association (APA, 2002) and the British Psychological Society (BPS, 2009).

In the meantime, the Malaysian Society for Clinical Psychology (MSCP) was registered in October 2010, with the objective to monitor and develop the clinical psychology profession in Malaysia. They too came up with an ethics code, with some overlap with the PSIMA Ethics Code, and adapting also from the existing Code of Ethics from APA (2002), BPS (2009) and Australian Psychological Society (APS, 2007). It is estimated there are about 90 clinical psychologists in Malaysia to date.

Furthermore, since 2009, the Ministry of Health has started drafting the Allied Health Professional Bill, in which clinical psychologist is the only psychology profession listed. The objectives of this Bill are to ensure the quality of services, monitor the treatment given and the safety of patients (My Sinchew, 2010). The Bill is expected to be tabled in parliament by the end of 2012.

Counselor education programs, accreditation, licensure, and certification

According to the online Malaysian Qualifications Register (2009), to date, there are 11 accredited counseling programs in Malaysia; seven in public universities and four in private. From the Register, all public universities offer a bachelor's degree in Counseling, three of the private colleges offer at the diploma level, and one at master's level. Nevertheless, the Register may not indicate programs that are undergoing accreditation. According to See and Ng (2010), four public and two private universities offer postgraduate degree in counseling, whereas a private college offers a twinning program with Taiwan universities at the bachelor level. Another source, however, reported four programs at the undergraduate level, six programs at master's level, and six programs at the doctoral level in the public universities alone (Salim & Mohd Jaladin, 2005). Overall, the current training programs still lack standardization across institutions (Salim & Mohd Jaladin, 2005). Neither PERKAMA nor Lembaga Kaunselor conduct program accreditation. The only accreditation requirements are by the Malaysian Qualifications Agency (MQA), under the Ministry of Higher Education.

In order to practice counseling in Malaysia, one needs to first register with the Lembaga Kaunselor and then apply for a practicing certificate. According to the Counselors Act, one is eligible to be registered if he/she is a citizen or permanent resident of Malaysia, not less than 21 years old, and possesses at least a diploma in counseling from an accredited institution. The practicing certificate is an additional requirement that authorizes a registered counselor to practice at a specified location, and is renewable every 2 years. The current standards allow both bachelor and master's level counselors to have the same licensing privilege (See & Ng, 2010).

There are currently no formal training institutes that teach psychotherapy per se, apart from the London College of Clinical Hypnosis Malaysia and Satir Institute of Malaysia, which offer diplomas in the particular therapeutic approach. There are also short courses or workshops organized by individuals, counseling/psychology programs, nonprofit organizations or private agencies.

The present systematic training of psychotherapists is shouldered by clinical psychology programs. To date, there are only three clinical psychology programs in the country, consisting of two public universities (Ng, Teoh & Haque, 2003) and a private university (W. S. Ng, 2008). Owing to the lack of program-specific benchmarking, each program has its own syllabus with varied standards on clinical training. Program accreditation is solely done by MQA, and not professional bodies.

To practice as a clinical psychologist, the minimal educational level is a master's degree in clinical psychology. There is currently no registration or licensure procedure required. With the impending enforcement of the Allied Health Professional Bill, all clinical psychologists will be required to register with a Council of Allied Health Professionals. The Bill will also delineate all the criteria for registration of individuals, codes of professional practice, as well as standard of the training program.

Despite much dispute, psychotherapy is listed as a chapter under the Malaysian Society for Complementary Medicine. Under the upcoming Traditional Complementary Medicine (TCM) Bill, psychotherapist is also listed as one of the professions. However, the definition of "psychotherapist" and the criteria of registration in the Bill remain ambiguous at the moment. This Bill is also meant to control the practice of indigenous and traditional healers in Malaysia (Ahmad & Teo, 2010).

Current counseling and psychotherapy theories, processes, and trends

According to the author's preliminary study of psychotherapists in Malaysia, the majority of participants reported their salient orientation as cognitive and behavioral approaches. Other orientations embraced by about a third of the practitioners include humanistic and client-centered approaches (Ng, 2006). Psychodynamic approaches are no longer widely practiced (or at least openly endorsed) apart from a small sect which has tried to revive the use of hypnotherapy. Creative therapies using art, sandtray, play, and drama, are also emerging in private practice.

From the author's preliminary findings, most counselors/therapists endorse a strong eclectic or integrative orientation in their practice (Ng, 2006). This seems to correspond with the pluralistic and "hybrid" nature of the Malaysian people. The majority of the counseling/therapy work (including working with couples and families) is individual based. Group therapy is rare, apart from some support/psychoeducation groups with specified area of interest. Only a handful of counselors and therapists are trained and practice family systems therapy (Ng, 2006).

Apart from that, religious psychology, specifically Islamic psychology and therapy, has grown significantly in Malaysia, as seen in the development of related institutes, seminars, and conferences (Haque & Masuan, 2002). Some local therapists reported positive results with their clients when they incorporated religious (i.e., Islamic) and sociocultural elements in cognitive therapy (Azhar & Varma, 1995a,b; Azhar, Varma & Dharap, 1994; Razali, Hasanah, Aminah & Subramaniam, 1998).

In addition, the potential of electronic counseling (or e-counseling) has been explored in Malaysia. Harun, Zainudin and Hamzah (2001) conducted a study among Malaysians to examine their willingness to participate in e-counseling. They found about half of the participants expressed willingness to participate in e-counseling, whereas others expressed reservation to the lack of physical presence of the counselor. The study also found that females and young people between the ages of 25 and 35 were more inclined to try e-counseling (Harun et al., 2001).

In terms of other trends, the author's preliminary study of clinical psychologists in 2004–2005 also showed that most of the participants were college/university faculty members (Ng, 2011).

As expected, many clinical psychologists in college/university settings were not practicing therapy as much because of heavy teaching load and other responsibilities (Ng et al., 2003). From the author's study, most therapy work was conducted in public outpatient settings and individual private practice (Ng, 2011); this is probably still true at present.

Indigenous and traditional healing methods

The help-seeking pathways of Malaysians reflect their cultural beliefs about mental health and illness (Razali & Najib, 2000; Rhi, Ha & Kim, 1995). Traditionally, Malaysians in general tend to attribute illness to humoral imbalance, whereby there is either a lack or overabundance of certain substance within the self, such as the inner wind (*angin*) and the spirit of life (*semangat*) (Laderman, 2001; Ng, 2003). Some also believe that illness is caused by "unclean" spirits, whom they have offended or sent by their enemies. Hence, traditional treatments range from attracting lost *semangat*, expelling accumulated *angin*, to casting out the "unclean" spirits.

Indigenous treatment approaches (e.g., Malay traditional healing, Chinese *sin-se*) are typically integrative in nature, seeking to restore the person physically, emotionally, socially, and spiritually. The specific practice of indigenous treatment approaches is closely associated with ethnic groups and religious beliefs (Edman & Koon, 2000; Haque, 2005). Even though these traditional healers are called different names and use different methods, their primary treatment goal is to restore patients to a harmonious state using a combination of herbal remedies, dietary adjustments, thermal treatments, and prayer rituals. Some also involve shamanism, which contains mixed elements of possession and exorcism.

The Malay traditional healer is called a *bomoh* or *pawang*. Although most *bomoh* primarily prescribe herbal medicine, some also perform Malay shamanism to bribe, threaten or exorcise spirits. According to Laderman (2001), Malay shamanic performance typically starts at dark and lasts well into the morning. Depending on the circumstances, they call on different spirits. The performance may combine music, song, dance, and poetry in colloquial language and humor. The patient's interaction with the healers and the spectators was thought to provide a cathartic effect and heighten one's feeling of self-worth (Laderman, 2001). Similar shamanic healing is performed by the Ibans in East Malaysia, who also emphasize communal presence as a significant contribution to healing efficacy (Harris, 2001).

Following folk religious beliefs, some Chinese seek mediums who might prescribe holy scripts or a talisman to be consumed or kept, in order to drive out uninvited spirits that cause emotional disturbance. Similarly, Indians have traditionally turned to their holy men for prayer rituals. Others may also use Chinese or Ayurvedic medicine to restore the balance of one's physical, mental, and spiritual functioning (Haque, 2005).

These traditional beliefs and practices are found among both rural and urban populations, regardless of socioeconomic status or education level (Azhar & Varma, 2000). While the younger generations endorsed less of the traditional beliefs about mental health, overall help-seeking behaviors remained pluralistic, combining the use of Western medicine, prayer, herbal medicine, and traditional healers (Edman & Koon, 2000). According to Rhi, Ha and Kim (1995), more than 60% of psychiatric patients in Malaysia first sought magicoreligious therapy, followed by psychiatric care; most other help-seeking pathways involved or combined magicoreligious therapy.

With the introduction of Western psychiatry and psychological practices, indigenous treatment approaches are increasingly seen as "backward," and less scientific and thus less professional. Most counselors/therapists follow major models of psychotherapy developed in Western countries and many tend to be more apprehensive or skeptical in integrating indigenous healing methods in their practice. Nevertheless, some preliminary attempts to customize therapy approaches by integrating indigenous beliefs of the patients showed a favorable outcome (Razali, Hasanah, Khan & Subramaniam, 2000; Varma & Azhar, 1996).

Research and supervision

Indigenous research and publication on the local psychotherapy condition is relatively scarce and not widely disseminated. Currently, there is only a counseling journal (*PERKAMA Journal*) and a psychology journal (*PSIMA Journal*). Both journals accept English and Malay articles; although, most articles published are in Malay language. These journals also have limited circulation among certain public universities. The types of research published range from qualitative to quantitative methodology, including explorative descriptive studies, case studies, correlational and experimental designs.

Some psychological or mental health-related research is also published in the *Malaysian Journal of Psychiatry* (published by the Malaysian Psychiatric Association, MPA) and the *ASEAN Journal of Psychiatry* (also under the management of MPA). Besides that, health psychology issues may be published in medical schools' journals, such as *Medicine & Health* (published by the Faculty of Medicine, National University of Malaysia) and the *Journal of University of Malaya Medical Centre*. In addition, school counseling issues are published in educational journals, such as the *Journal of Educational Research* (published by the Ministry of Education Malaysia) and the *Malaysian Journal of Education* (published by the Faculty of Education, National University of Malaysia). In recent years, there has been a surge of interest in qualitative studies among those in educational and counseling fields. Some of these studies are published in the *Malaysian Journal of Qualitative Research* (by the Qualitative Research Association of Malaysia). Currently, only a few of these journals permit free access of full texts on the World Wide Web to the public.

Traditionally, public universities offer more opportunities for research funding and time off for research than private institutions. In recent years, the government has opened up more funding opportunities in the form of research grants to both public and private sectors (e.g., the Prototype Development Research Grant Scheme, Long-term Research Grant Scheme, etc.). This is part of the government's effort to elevate the quality of higher education in the international platform. Along with that, many of the local public universities have been "re-categorized" as research universities, in order to push for more indigenous research work among local academicians.

There are few systematic studies on the counselors and psychotherapists in Malaysia. First, Bond et al. (2001) reported that the function of "psychotherapist" covers a broad range of professionals in Malaysia. Subsequently, between 2004 and 2006, a study carried out by the author of this chapter represented the first systematic research of the personal and professional characteristics of psychotherapists in Malaysia (Ng, 2006; 2011).

With respect to supervision, all trainees in counseling and clinical psychology must receive a specified amount of supervision in counseling/psychotherapy as part of graduation requirements. Nevertheless, the actual amount and quality of supervision vary across training programs and are not well monitored, considering the absence of program accreditation or regulation on training and supervision by professional bodies (Ng et al., 2003; See & Ng, 2010). Furthermore, there is no stipulation that requires continuous supervision after graduation.

Considering the limited number of practitioners in counseling and psychotherapy locally, there is an even greater shortage of eligible supervisors and practicum sites (Ng, et al., 2003; Salim & Mohd Jaladin, 2005; See & Ng, 2010; Ng, 2011). Those who are senior enough to supervise oftentimes are also burdened with other administrative and teaching responsibilities, which greatly reduce their availability to supervise (Ng et al., 2003). Moreover, those in private practice are less keen to take on trainees, given the lack of incentive other than an honorarium.

According to the author's preliminary study of clinical psychologists in 2004–2005, about a third of the participants belong to the "graduate" level (Orlinsky & Rønnestad, 2005) with 3.5 to 7 years of therapy experience. Despite being relatively young in age and in years of practice, about 50% of the participants were involved in providing supervision (Ng, 2011). Recognizing the need for more eligible supervisors in the field, professional bodies are working on providing supervision training for existing counselors and psychotherapists (See & Ng, 2010).

Strengths, weaknesses, opportunities and challenges

The greatest strength of the current counseling/therapy field in Malaysia is the youthfulness of the practitioners. According to Ng (2006), more than half of the current psychotherapists in Malaysia are below the age of 45; in fact, a third of them are below age 35. Although their relative inexperience could pose a potential challenge for therapists in Malaysia, their relative youthfulness also brings together much energy and creativity to mobilize development in a rapidly growing field.

From a structural perspective, the current professional systems in Malaysia, particularly for both counselor and clinical psychologists, are reaching pubescence (See & Ng, 2010). In local institutions, there is specialized training in counseling/psychotherapy conducted by local Malaysians. There are also professional bodies (e.g., PERKAMA, PSIMA, MSCP, Lembaga Kaunselor) as well as legal regulations (e.g., Counselor Act, Allied Health Professional Bill, Traditional & Complementary Medicine Bill) that govern the professions of counseling and psychotherapy in Malaysia. In addition, each of the professional bodies has established clear ethical standards for the local practitioners. Altogether, the current infrastructure shows the coming together of policy-makers, educators, and supervisors, practitioners, and researchers to uphold public welfare and professional integrity.

In terms of weaknesses in the field, currently there is still much ambiguity and inconsistency in the licensing requirements to practice counseling and psychotherapy in Malaysia, particularly among school counselors (See & Ng, 2010). There is also no differentiation in licensing privilege between a bachelor or a master's level counselor.

In addition, for those who are not trained in a counseling or clinical psychology program (such as marriage and family therapy (MFT), art therapy, music therapy and play therapy etc.), there is currently no local professional body to endorse their qualifications. And by placing all forms of psychotherapy under a single professional title of "psychotherapist" in the upcoming TCM Bill, this inevitably creates tension between the diversity of psychotherapy practices and forced uniformity under the guise of TCM.

Presently, psychotherapy services are concentrated in major cities. Access to services is also constrained by the language factor, as those in the governmental agencies use primarily Malay or English language (See & Ng, 2010). Individuals of lower socio-economical status typically can only afford public hospitals or social–welfare agencies, which have exceedingly high client load and inadequate follow-up services. Accordingly, attrition rate is high and therapeutic effect cannot be adequately monitored.

Besides that, significant improvement is needed in the area of knowledge management and sharing of information relating to the local scenario of counseling and psychotherapy. These include the circulation of local journals, studies and statistics, as well as maintenance of official websites for public knowledge.

With greater emphasis on research in local universities and governmental support in research funding, there are more opportunities for research on local mental health issues and counseling/

psychotherapy practices. More specifically, Salim and Mohd Jaladin (2005) nominated experimental-based and outcome evaluation research in counselor education programs as a targeted area for future growth. More research is also needed in the area of school counseling to "further define and refine its purpose and directions, theory and practice, and training framework," rather than letting the policy-makers dictate how it should be done (See & Ng, 2010, p. 20).

Further, the development of new professional bodies and policies on clinical psychology and psychotherapy rejuvenates the field towards greater professionalism and visibility in the local community. This is good timing, as mental health awareness and interest for psychological input are on the rise (Glamcevski, 2008; See & Ng, 2010). Projecting ahead, there will likely be more systematic endeavors to strengthen the area of continuous professional development among existing practitioners, benchmarking the standards of training and so forth. Such vibrant atmosphere is certainly an attractive platform for cross-cultural knowledge exchange, as exemplified by the research initiative by an American Fulbright Scholar Dr. Colleen O'Neal to improve the mental health of refugee children in Malaysia (Embassy of the United States in Kuala Lumpur, n.d.).

Several challenges still remain. The predominance of Western biomedical views in the mental health field pose a threat to the development of indigenous counseling/psychotherapy. With greater emphasis on the individual's pathology or symptoms, individual-focused treatments like psychiatric medications and cognitive-behavioral approach often take precedence over other therapeutic modalities. Furthermore, the indigenous value of holistic (body–mind–spirit) healing is also lost in the process of such "modern" treatment.

Besides that, the heavy reliance and indiscriminate application of Western-based theories of counseling/therapy also present a major challenge to a multicultural nation like Malaysia. This is partly related to the lack of indigenous studies that document the Malaysian experience. An example of a unique phenomenon noted in the author's study was that despite both Chinese and Indians are numerically a minority in Malaysia, up to 60% of Chinese participants did not endorse a minority status, while 75% of their Indian counterparts endorsed a minority status (Ng, 2006). Further investigation is warranted to explode the heterogeneous social-cultural identities among Malaysians.

Finally, the bureaucracy in certain governmental agencies (e.g., public hospitals or schools) can become stumbling blocks to the advancement of counseling/psychotherapy training in the country. In fact, most hospital facilities, social agencies and even schools do not provide the infrastructure for counseling/psychotherapy work (e.g., no private space, lack of assessment tools, etc.). Many private practice settings, despite their infrastructure, are also not ideal as a practicum site, because private clients often decline to see trainees, or refuse recording for training purpose.

Future directions

The current professional bodies will need to clarify and tighten the licensure requirements for trained counselors, for example to only master's level holders (See & Ng, 2010). This would also involve reviewing the standards and requirements of counselor education. Currently, the master's program in counseling or psychology degree, which means there is no difference in the entry knowledge level between a bachelor or a master-level counseling program. Additionally, considering that school counseling has its own unique concerns, it may be more practical to set different licensing and training standards for school counselors (Sipon, 2007). In regards to psychotherapists, a nationwide meeting among the diverse stakeholders is probably necessary to have a meaningful deliberation on the licensure requirements for their diverse professional titles.

As part of quality control, a key direction is to set minimum standards for training programs, practicum facilities and supervision (See & Ng, 2010). This would include the curriculum of training programs, requirements of supervised training, criteria of training sites, eligibility of supervisors and so forth. There should also be clear policies on grievance and due process for all parties involved (i.e., the student, the program, the site, and the supervisor). In addition, it is proposed that the provision of supervision, ideally pro bono, be counted as one of the factors for consideration in the renewal of license, to encourage more eligible practitioners to offer supervision services.

In their counseling/psychotherapy training, trainees should have opportunities to explore and learn various counseling/psychotherapy models, so as to widen their knowledge and skill repertoire. Moreover, part of the learning process should include examining the assumptions and philosophy of the existing counseling/psychotheraphy theories, and compare with one's own cultural values as well as clients' multicultural contexts. Not only is this instilling multicultural competency in their training as counselors/therapists, in the long run, ideas may germinate in regards to indigenous personality and psychotherapy models (Mohamad & Harun, 2006). Additionally, multicultural considerations should be incorporated in the formation of curriculum (e.g., exercises that facilitate reflection on therapists' own cultural identities), as well as the selection of staff and students for the program (e.g., consideration for mutilingual ability, particularly in indigenous languages/dialects).

As the field develops, there will likely be more standardization of service provision, similar to the development of managed care in the developed countries. The challenge is to ensure equal access of counseling/therapy services for the poor and marginalized. More research needs to be done to determine the efficiency, practicality, and cost-effectiveness of electronic counseling in the Malaysian context. Last but not least, knowledge management is the key to all continuous developments. All the professional bodies and policy-makers need to consider how to systematically store, maintain and disseminate local news, statistics, policy papers, and research findings, so that these knowledge can be easily accessible and fully utilized by the local and international communities.

Conclusion

This chapter provides an overview of the development of counseling and psychotherapy in Malaysia, including some contemporary issues of concern and anticipated future direction. As a growing field in a developing country, counseling and psychotherapy has fared well slowly but certainly. With still much room for growth and development, it presents a fertile field for those up for the adventure and challenges of pioneering and revolutionary work.

References

Abdul Rahman, W. R. (2005). History of psychology in Malaysia. In Z. A. Ansari, N. M. Noor & A. Haque (eds), *Contemporary issues in Malaysian Psychology* (pp. 1–17). Malaysia: Thomson Learning.

Ahmad, R., & Teo, A. (2010). *Malaysia to control faith healers as more seek spirit aid*, October 14. Retrieved September 15, 2011, from www.reuters.com/article/2010/10/14/us-malaysia-faith-healers-idUS TRE6 9D1D320101014

American Counseling Association (ACA) (2006). *Ethics*. Retrieved December 26, 2005, from www. counseling.org/Resources/CodeOfEthics/TP/Home/CT2.aspx

American Psychological Association (APA) (2002). Ethical Principles of Psychologists and code of conduct. *American Psychologist, 57*, 1060–1073.

Australian Psychological Society (APS) (2007). *Code of Ethics*. Retrieved September 30, 2011 from www. psychology.org.au/Assets/Files/Code_Ethics_2007.pdf

Azhar, M. Z., & Varma, S. L. (1995a). Religious psychotherapy as management of bereavement. *Acta Psychiatrica Scandinavica, 91*, 233–235.

Azhar, M. Z., & Varma, S. L. (1995b). Religious psychotherapy in depressive patients. *Psychotherapy Psychosomatics, 63*(3–4), 165–173.

Azhar, M. Z., & Varma, S. L. (2000). Mental illness and its treatment in Malaysia. In I. Al-Issa (ed.), *Al-Junun: Mental illness in the Islamic World* (pp. 163–186). Madison, MI: International Universities Press, Inc.

Azhar, M. Z., Varma, S. L., & Dharap, A. S. (1994). Religious psychotherapy in anxiety disorder patients. *Acta Psychiatrica Scandinavica, 90*, 1–3.

Bond, T., Lee, C. C., Lowe, R., Malayapilla, A. E. M., Wheeler, S., Banks A., ... & Smiley, E. (2001). The nature of counseling: An investigation of counseling activity in selected countries. *International Journal for the Advancement of Counselling, 23*, 245–260.

British Psychological Society (BPS) (2009). *Code of Ethics and Conduct.* Retrieved September 30, 2011 from www.bps.org.uk/sites/default/files/documents/code_of_ethics_and_conduct.pdf

Department of Statistics Malaysia (2010). *Population and Housing Census 2010.* Retrieved September 30, 2011, from www.statistics.gov.my/portal/download_Population/files/census2010/Taburan_Penduduk_dan_Ciri-ciri_Asas_Demografi.pdf

Edman, J. L., & Koon, T. Y. (2000). Mental illness beliefs in Malaysia: Ethnic and intergenerational comparisons. *International Journal of Social Psychiatry, 46*(2), 101–109.

Embassy of the United States in Kuala Lumpur (n.d.). *Fullbright Scholar Aims to Improve Mental Health among Refugee Children in Malaysia.* Retrieved September 30, 2011 from http://malaysia.usembassy.gov/progra m_ oneal_refugee_jun2011.html

Glamcevski, M. (2008). The Malaysian counseling profession, history and brief discussion of the future. *Counselling Psychotherapy and Health, 4*(1), 1–18.

Haque, A. (2005). Mental health in Malaysia: An overview. In Z. A. Ansari, N. M. Noor & A. Haque (eds), *Contemporary Issues in Malaysian Psychology* (pp. 19–41). Malaysia: Thomson Learning.

Haque, A., & Masuan, K. A. (2002). Religious psychology in Malaysia. *The International Journal for the Psychology of Religion, 12*(4), 277–289.

Harris, A. (2001). Presence, efficacy, and politics in healing among the Iban of Sarawak. In L. Connor & G. Samuel (eds), *Healing Powers and Modernity: Traditional Medicine, Shamanism, and Science in Asian Societies* (pp. 130–151). Westport, CT: Bergin & Garvey.

Harun, L. M., Zainudin, Z. N., & Hamzah, R. (2001). *E-Counselling: The Willingness Participate.* Paper presented at the International Education Conference in Selangor, Malaysia. Retrieved March 26, 2003, from http://cybercounsel.uncg.edu/articals /willing.htm.

Kitchener, K. S. (1984). Intuition, critical evaluation and ethical principles: The foundation for ethical decisions in counseling psychology. *The Counseling Psychologist, 12* (3) 43–55.

Laderman, C. (2001). Tradition and change in Malay healing. In L. Connor & G. Samuel (eds), *Healing Powers and Modernity: Traditional Medicine, Shamanism, and Science in Asian Societies* (pp. 42–63). Westport, CT: Bergin & Garvey.

Lembaga Kaunselor (n.d.). *Direktori kaunselor berdaftar* (Directory of registered counselors). Retrieved March 7, 2011, from www.lkm.gov.my/bm/default.asp? page = 4

Lembaga Penyelidikan Undang-Undang (1998). *Akta Kaunselor 1998 (Akta 580)* (Counselor Act]). Kuala Lumpur: International Law Book Services.

Malaysian Qualifications Register (2009). Retrieved October 4, 2011, from www.mqa.gov.my/mqr/english/eperutusan.cfm

Mohamad, M., & Harun, L. M. (2006). Western-based counseling theories: Adopt or adapt. *Journal PERKAMA, 12*, 71–84.

My Sinchew. (2010, July 12). Allied health professional bill ready by 2011. Retrieved March 7, 2011, from www.mysinchew.com/node/41651

Ng, K. S. (2003). Family therapy in Malaysia: An update. In K. S. Ng (ed.), *Global Perspectives in Family Therapy* (pp. 31–38). New York: Taylor & Francis Books, Inc.

Ng, K. S., & Stevens, P. (2001). Creating a caring society: Counseling in Malaysia before 2020AD. *Asian Journal of Counseling, 8*, 87–101.

Ng, L. O., Teoh, H., & Haque, A. (2003). Clinical psychology in Malaysia: A brief overview. *ASEAN Journal of Psychiatry, 6*, 11–16

Ng, W. S. (2006, August). *Personal and Professional Characteristics of Psychotherapists in Malaysia.* Paper presented at the 19th World Psychotherapy Congress, Kuala Lumpur, Malaysia.

Ng, W. S. (2007). Psychotherapy in Malaysia: An overview. *Mental Health & Learning Disabilities: Research & Practice, 4*(2), 205–217.

Ng, W. S. (2008, December). *Development of a Master's Program in Clinical Psychology: The Case of HELP University College*. Paper presented at the 3rd International Conference on Postgraduate Education, Penang, Malaysia.

Ng, W. S. (2011). Development of clinical psychologists in Malaysia. In A.H. Quek (ed.), *Multiple Perspectives of Psychology: Issues, Challenges and Future Directions* (Ch. 3). Kuala Lumpur, Malaysia: HELP University.

Orlinsky, D. E., & Rønnestad, M. H. (2005). *How Psychotherapists Develop: A Study of Therapeutic Work and Professional Growth*. Washington, DC: American Psychological Association.

PERKAMA (2004/2005). Pengenalan ringkas: Persatuan Kaunseling Malaysia (PERKAMA) [A brief introduction: Malaysian Association of Counseling]. *Jurnal PERKAMA, 11*.

Pope, M., Musa, M., Singaravelu, H., Bringaze, T. & Russell, M. (2002). From colonialism to ultra-nationalism: History and development of career counseling in Malaysia. *The Career Development Quarterly, 50*, 264–276.

Quek, A. H. (2001). *Career guidance and counseling in Malaysia: Development and trends*. Paper presented at the 9th Asia Regional Association for Career Development Conference, March, Singapore. Retrieved September 15, 2011 from www.spc.org.sg/9thARACD/CAREER%20GUIDANCE%20AND%20COUNSELLING%20IN%20MALAYSIA.doc

Razali, S. M. & Najib, M. A. M. (2000). Help-seeking pathways among Malay psychiatric patients. *International Journal of Social Psychiatry, 46*(4), 281–289.

Razali, S. M., Hasanah, C. I., Aminah, K., & Subramaniam, M. (1998). Religious-sociocultural psychotherapy in patients with anxiety and depression. *Australian and New Zealand Journal of Psychiatry, 32*, 867–872.

Razali, S. M., Hasanah, C. I., Khan, U. A., & Subramaniam, M. (2000). Psychosocial interventions for schizophrenia. *Journal of Mental Health, 9*(3), 283–289.

Rhi, B., Ha, K., & Kim, Y. (1995). The health care seeking behavior of schizophrenic patients in 6 East Asian areas. *International Journal of Social Psychiatry, 41*, 190–209.

Salim, S., & Mohd Jaladin, R. A. (2005). Development of counseling services in Malaysia. In Z. A. Ansari, N. M. Noor & A. Haque (eds), *Contemporary issues in Malaysian Psychology* (pp. 237–264). Malaysia: Thomson Learning.

Scorzelli, J. F. (1987). Counseling in Malaysia: An emerging profession. *Journal of Counseling and Development, 65*, 238–240.

See, C. M., & Ng, K. M. (2010). Counseling in Malaysia: History, current status and future trends. *Journal of Counseling & Development, 88*, 18–22.

Singh, R., & Khan, R. (1998). Behavior therapy in Malaysia. In P. O. Tian (ed.), *Behavior Therapy and Cognitive Behavior Therapy in Asia* (pp. 113–119). Australia: Edumedia.

Sipon, S. (2007). The status and future challenges of school guidance and counseling services in Malaysia. *Jurnal PERKAMA, 13*, 45–57.

Smith, K. J. (2003). Minority language education in Malaysia: Four ethnic communities' experiences. *International Journal of Bilingual Education and Bilingualism, 6*(1), 52–65.

Varma, S. L. & Azhar, M. Z. (1996). In the Field: Cognitive therapy in Malaysia. *Journal of Cognitive Psychotherapy: An International Quarterly, 10*(4), 305–307.

Xinhuanet. (2011, January 18). *Malaysia to Tackle rise in Mental Health*. Retrieved April 14, 2011 from www.news.xinhuanet.com/english2010/health/2011–01/18/c_13696388.htm.

19

COUNSELING AND PSYCHOTHERAPY IN PAKISTAN

Colonial legacies and Islamic influences

Humair Yusuf, Shabnum Sarfraz, and Linah Askari

Introduction

The population of Pakistan is estimated to be 187 million, with 70% of Pakistanis living in rural areas. While there are six distinct ethnic groups in Pakistan, 97% of the population consists of Muslims with small minorities of Christians and Hindus. Pakistani society is strongly patriarchal, collectivist, and family-oriented and the majority of the population lives in joint family residences (Federal Bureau of Statistics, 2011).

There has been considerable economic development since independence from Britain in 1947, but it has not been matched by improvements in social indicators such as health and literacy. Recently, Pakistan has suffered from political and economic instability, fragmentation across ethnic and sectarian divides, increasing religiosity, and a shift from the tolerant, Sufi-inspired version of Islam traditionally practiced in Pakistan to puritanical interpretations that tend to be hostile to Western culture and values (Armstrong, 2001). Meanwhile, conflict in neighboring Afghanistan has taken a huge toll on Pakistan, with terrorism resulting in over 5,000 civilian deaths over the last 3 years (Institute for Conflict Management, 2011).

The rural population relies primarily on traditional methods based on religious, tribal, and agrarian values for their mental wellbeing. In contrast, higher levels of education, access to media and exposure to Western culture through emigration have resulted in greater awareness of mental illness in the major cities. This awareness, along with the incorporation of Islamic values and practices into psychotherapy, has helped make it more acceptable and culturally relevant to Pakistani clients, and resulted in growing numbers of individuals seeking Western counseling and psychotherapy. In Pakistan the terms "counseling" and "psychotherapy" are used interchangeably to refer to clinical practice focused on mental illness, interpersonal relationships, and other aspects of applied human development. However, the lack of government resources and the low priority assigned to mental health means that the demand for counseling and psychotherapy is primarily fulfilled by private practitioners and paid for by clients and their families.

This chapter describes how counseling and psychotherapy in Pakistan evolved from colonial systems of treatment for mental illness to meet the emotional, cultural, and spiritual needs of contemporary Pakistani clients. It also discusses the challenges faced by clinicians in providing effective mental health services and explores ways of overcoming them.

Brief history of counseling and psychotherapy

Many of the pre-Islamic and Islamic healing techniques prevalent in the Indian sub-continent before British colonization in the 1700s are comparable to contemporary practices in counseling and psychotherapy (Hassan, 1990). During British rule, however, Western knowledge, education, and healthcare were emphasized while local knowledge and healing traditions were discouraged and devalued, resulting in parallel systems of treatment, especially for mental illness: a Western one for an Anglicized elite and an indigenous one for the general population (Zaman, 1991).

Beginning in Bombay in 1745, the British built a network of lunatic asylums (renamed "mental hospitals" in 1922) for the treatment of mental illness throughout India (Somasundaram, 1987). Described by Mubbashar (2000, p. 189) as "curative in their thrust and institutional in their approach," these hospitals, which were set up until the 1940s, reinforced the parallel systems of treatment and shaped attitudes towards mental illness after independence in 1947, resulting in an emphasis on psychiatry along with the confinement and segregation of individuals through hospitalization. Meanwhile, as early as 1929, Berkeley Hill, one of the first psychoanalysts in the sub-continent, began to draw attention to the shortcomings of such approaches and advocated focusing on prevention, rehabilitation, and mental hygiene (Nizamie & Goyal, 2010).

Colonization left a similarly problematic legacy in the teaching of psychology in Pakistan. Although the Government College in Lahore in collaboration with the Foreman Christian College established a psychology department headed by G. C. Chutterji in 1932, psychology was considered part of the philosophy curriculum with courses taught by the philosophy faculty (Ansari, 1967). Beginning with the University of Karachi in 1954, independent psychology departments were established in universities throughout Pakistan. However, Ansari (1967) reports that despite their independence these departments retained a philosophical orientation in contrast to the biological and sociological orientation of contemporary Western psychology.

In 1958, M. H. Shah and Afzal Habib formed associations for mental hygiene along the lines of the Indian Association for Mental Hygiene established by Berkley Hill in 1929 (Ahmed, 2008). Their efforts, however, had limited success and the origins of counseling and psychotherapy in Pakistan can be traced to the 1960s, when Western trained psychologists such as Hafeez Zaidi, Muhammad Ajmal, Shahabuddin Moghni, and Farukh Ahmad returned to teach in the newly independent psychology departments at local universities. Their return coincided with a surge of rural to urban migration and the associated decline of the extended family and the unavailability of elders, forcing individuals to turn to external sources to manage their distress. At the same time, guidance and counseling programs for women receiving higher education and entering the workplace provided an introduction to the notion of counseling for personal matters (Ibrahim & Almas, 1983).

Despite these shifts in social conditions and attitudes towards seeking help, the initial counselors and psychotherapists in Pakistan faced a number of challenges in being accepted as legitimate mental health professionals. In addition to the stigma associated with mental illness and traditional values of relying on family elders to solve problems rather than seeking help from outsiders, they had to contend with psychiatrists' domination of treatment (Zaman, 1991) and the perception of psychology as an academic discipline with a negligible role in managing distress (Ansari, 1967). Moreover, while the guidance and counseling programs described by

Ibrahim and Almas (1983) helped make psychotherapy more acceptable to Pakistani clients, they were directed at women and therefore reinforced the notion that while women could seek help from professionals, men had to manage their distress on their own (Tepper, 1999). As a result, the first generation of counselors and psychotherapists in Pakistan were largely marginalized and their role was limited to testing and assessment. Many of them turned to private practices, in which their clients tended to be limited to an urban, Anglicized, middle and upper class population (Zaman, 1997).

The establishment of the Pakistan Psychological Association in 1968 and the National Institute of Psychology in 1976 increased awareness of counseling and psychotherapy, while the Institute of Clinical Psychology headed by Farrukh Ahmad embarked on an ambitious agenda of research. It published extensively on therapeutic practice, developmental psychology and other areas (e.g., Ahmad, 1988; 1993), thereby providing the field with a measure of credibility that it had previously lacked. Clinicians, meanwhile, replaced psychoanalytic and gestalt approaches with behavioral and systemic ones that were more compatible to Pakistani culture and client expectations (Zaman, 1997). For example, in 1973, Rashid Choudhry established a halfway house that employed behavioral approaches towards rehabilitation and in 1975 Khalida Tareen began to provide specialized systemic treatment for children and families (Ahmed, 2008).

During the 1980s, when the military dictator Zia-ul-Haq was pursuing an aggressive agenda of Islamization, psychologists such as Muhammad Ajmal (1986) and Azhar Ali Rizvi (1994) supported the development of a uniquely Muslim psychology based on Islamic practices (Haque, 2000). The only significant result of such efforts, however, was an adaptation of rational emotive behavioral therapy (REBT) by Rahman (1991) for Pakistani clients through the identification of irrational beliefs regarding religion, deference to authority, relationships, and self-esteem.

A parallel development has been the use of counseling and psychotherapy in rehabilitation for drug addiction. The surge in heroin abuse during the 1980s overwhelmed government resources and led to the proliferation of private facilities for detoxification that relied exclusively on opiate reduction and symptomatic treatment (Gossop, 1989) without any follow-up or rehabilitation programs. Increasing awareness regarding the nature of addiction has led to the incorporation of behavioral therapies by clinicians such as Sadaquat Ali that focus on social skills, problem solving, discipline, and self-control, although detoxification rather than rehabilitation remains the priority in most facilities (R. M. Zaman, personal communication, September 24, 2010).

The last two decades have seen clinicians such as Haroon Ahmed attempt to provide holistic, culturally relevant, community-oriented, preventive, and educational mental health services through facilities such as the Institute of Behavioral Sciences (Ahmed, 2008). A corresponding development is the growing number of institutions offering master's and doctoral degrees in counseling and psychotherapy, along with an increase in the number of clinicians, although only a small minority are actively engaged in clinical practice (Karim, Saeed, Rana, Mubbashar, & Jenkins, 2004). Meanwhile, clients have become more familiar and comfortable with counseling and psychotherapy and clinicians more confident, resulting in an eclectic use of humanistic approaches such as narrative and client-centered therapy (Suhail, 2004) along with a somewhat flexible incorporation of Islamic beliefs and practices into cognitive and behavioral therapies (Murray, 2002). These integrative practices were in contrast to the rigorous and structured attempts of the 1980s and early 1990s.

Counselor education programs, accreditation, licensure, and certification

There are currently 28 departments of psychology in Pakistan, with 16 offering postgraduate programs and three offering doctoral degrees. In addition, there are a number of institutes, some affiliated with European or North American organizations, offering diplomas in humanistic counseling, rehabilitation, and occupational therapy (Ahmad, 2010; Rahman, 2009).

Until 2001, the only legislation regarding mental health in Pakistan was the Lunacy Act of 1912, which focused on the definition of insanity and issues of segregation, confinement, and inheritance. According to Karim et al. (2004), it was due to UN Resolution 46/119—Principles for the Protection of Persons with Mental Illness and the Improvement of Mental Health Care—and the ensuing Mental Health Act of 2001 that the rights of consumers of mental health services in Pakistan were formally recognized, guidelines regarding their treatment were established, and issues such as consent and complaints of misconduct or incompetence were addressed. Organizations such as the Pakistan Psychological Association and Pakistan Association for Clinical Psychologists are now using this act as a basis for further legislation to regulate the practice of psychology, psychotherapy, and counseling, and to establish criteria for accreditation and licensing. However, since counseling and psychotherapy are a low priority for the government, there is no legal framework to regulate practice and no formal credentials are required for the practice. Further, there are no specified requirements regarding training, supervision, and professional ethics, and there is no regulatory body empowered to address complaints of incompetence or misconduct (Zaman, 1997). Not only does the absence of such a body result in poor coordination amongst providers of mental health services and uneven accessibility to treatment, it places clients at risk of unethical and incompetent practice.

Current counseling and psychotherapy theories, processes, and trends

Estimates by Karim et al. (2004) suggest that there are less than a thousand trained counselors and psychotherapists in Pakistan, while Ansari (2001) adds that the majority are engaged in teaching, human resource management, and psychological assessment with only a small minority (7%) providing mental health services in clinical settings. Similar findings are reported by Murray (2002), who states that there are only 60 counselors and psychotherapists with master's degrees or post-master's diplomas practicing professionally in Pakistan. This limited number of clinicians means that specialization is uncommon and many psychotherapists provide treatment for mental illness, addictions, interpersonal and relational conflicts, developmental or behavioral problems, and issues related to sexuality, abuse, and trauma to children, adolescents, adults, couples, and families despite lacking adequate training (Z. Murad, personal communication, May 28, 2010).

Given that mental health is a low priority for the government and receives negligible funding, there is no concept of employing mental health practitioners in public sector hospitals, health centers, schools, or social welfare programs, and most counselors and psychotherapists in Pakistan are engaged in private practice (Akram & Khan, 2007; Suhail, 2004). Moreover, research by Khan and Reza (1998) indicates that in Pakistan primarily individuals suffering from severe mental illness who have attempted suicide, overdosed, or been hospitalized for substance abuse are likely to seek professional help. As a result, psychotherapy has an exclusively remedial focus with no attention paid to educational, developmental, or preventive issues.

Since most counselors and psychotherapists in Pakistan receive their training in either North America or Europe or in local universities following Western curricula, they tend to employ Western modalities (Rahman, 2009). In the context of Pakistan's conservative, religious, and family-oriented society, however, Zaman (1997) describes how psychoanalysis and Gestalt therapy are incompatible with the expectations of clients who often want concrete solutions rather than insight or opportunities to share emotions. Consequently, cognitive and behavioral approaches are the most widely used, and treatment is likely to be eclectic with elements of narrative, client-centered, process-experiential, and family systems therapy incorporated to meet client needs (Suhail, 2004). Although there have been no studies regarding the use of different approaches, there is considerable anecdotal evidence (for example, Ansari, 2001; Rahman, 2009; Zaman, 1991) to support this claim. It is unfortunate, however, that due to the stigma associated with mental illness, clients often demand immediate results and tend to become frustrated by the apparent lack of progress, resulting in missed appointments and premature termination (Khan, Islam & Kundi, 1996).

Given the significance of Islam in Pakistani society, religion has repeatedly been used to make counseling and psychotherapy culturally relevant and acceptable and to improve compliance with treatment. Ajmal (1986) and Ahmed (1993) used Jungian methods and Rahman (1991) developed a faith-based adaptation of REBT to address the religious inclinations of Pakistani clients. In the same vein, Murray (2002) reports that contemporary counseling and psychotherapy in Pakistan is increasingly likely to incorporate Islamic practices in response to the heightened religiosity of the client population. These approaches are typically based on Western principles such as behavior modification and cognitive restructuring, but utilize Islamic narratives and metaphors. For example, therapists may address anxiety by encouraging meditation through prayer and reading the Quran, or feelings of guilt, worthlessness and hopelessness by drawing attention to verses of the Quran that emphasize God's mercy and compassion. Proponents of such approaches, for example Awan (2003) and Rizvi (1994), argue that they help reduce the stigma of counseling and psychotherapy and make it culturally relevant and acceptable for Pakistani clients.

Ultimately, the main differences between counseling and psychotherapy in Pakistan and the West are due to social and cultural factors. Zaman (1997) describes Pakistani society as hierarchal and family oriented in which most problems, including emotional and interpersonal ones, are resolved through the advice and intervention of authority figures such as family elders. In this context, Pakistanis tend to relate to counselors and psychotherapists in the same way; that is, as authority figures or even "surrogate family elders" (Zaman, 1997, p. 75) who are expected to provide concrete solutions to their problems. Thus, in addition to being accepting, nonjudgmental and supportive, therapists are also required to play an active and directive role in helping clients, which is likely to involve engaging with family members and negotiating family relationships and hierarchies.

As a result of these dynamics between clients and therapists in Pakistan, the kind of therapeutic alliances expected in Western contexts are difficult or even impossible. By relating to therapists as authority figures or family elders, interaction tends to remain formal and deferential, with clients unlikely to express their true feelings towards therapists or bring up alliance ruptures. Zaman (1997) adds that such relationships often entail greater engagement in clients' lives than in Western contexts, as well as more self-disclosure from the therapist, making the establishment and maintenance of boundaries more challenging.

Indigenous and traditional healing methods

Owing to the stigma associated with mental illness and the shortage of counselors, psychotherapists, and psychiatrists in Pakistan, the majority of the population, especially in rural areas, relies on indigenous methods for the treatment of mental illness. These methods, which are primarily Islamic in nature, are compatible with agrarian and tribal values of not seeking help from outsiders since, according to Murray (2002), Islam instructs Muslims to keep their distress to themselves and rely on God. While this interpretation is commonly accepted in Pakistan, it is inconsistent with the historical contributions of Muslim scientists to psychology since the 9th century and has been challenged by scholars who argue that Islamic traditions require individuals to seek social, behavioral, medicinal, and spiritual cures instead of adopting a fatalistic attitude and passively accepting their suffering (Dein, Alexander, & Napier, 2008).

Mental illness in Pakistan is often attributed to a defective relationship with God or punishment for not fulfilling religious obligations (Rizvi, 1994). In addition, behaviors such as social withdrawal, aggression, or infidelity may be ascribed to possession by evil spirits or jinn (Gadit & Khalid, 2002). In such conceptualizations, healing is a process of moving closer to God and seeking His blessings. Individuals often attempt to improve their relationship to God through prayer and seeking recourse from the Quran. Majid (2001) describes how prayer helps individuals clear their minds, gain perspective on their problems and develop hope. In addition, since the Quran refers to itself as "guidance from your Lord and a healing for the diseases in your hearts" (10:57) individuals often read, recite or listen to audio recordings of the Quran (Bhui, King, Dein & O'Connor, 2008).

Individuals in distress often turn to healers who trace their lineage to Sufi saints (Dein et. al., 2008). Pirani, Papadopoulos, Foster and Leavey (2008) describe their treatment as being based on "ritualistic communication with the spiritual world ... based on dialogue with the spirits" (Pirani et al., 2008, p. 382). Interventions include prayer, recitation of the Quran, appeals to saints, singing and dancing, purification by drinking water that has been poured over the Quran and protection through the use of amulets containing Quranic verses. If the illness is attributed to possession, then healers may perform exorcisms that involve ritual cleansing, reading Quranic verses to agitate the jinn and persuade them to leave, or even a dialogue to convert the jinn to Islam.

Along with seeking help from particular healers, individuals also visit shrines associated with Sufi saints who are believed to have the power to mediate between God and ordinary individuals. At these shrines individuals live and worship together in a therapeutic community in which they share problems and express emotions without any adverse consequences and provide each other with acceptance, support and empathy (Pirani et al., 2008).

Research and supervision

Research on counseling and psychotherapy in Pakistan is primarily conducted at universities and funded by the provincial governments with additional financial support provided by the federal government (Osama, Najam, Kassim-Lakha, Gilani, & King, 2009). While there are no journals dedicated to counseling and psychotherapy, most studies are published by the main psychology journals, the *Pakistan Journal of Psychology*, the *Pakistan Journal of Psychological Research*, and the *Journal of Behavioral Sciences*. In addition to limited funding and opportunities for publication, Suhail (2004) adds that poor library resources and a lack of access to online databases such as PsychINFO hinder both the quality and the scale of research on counseling and psychotherapy in Pakistan.

While the initial philosophical orientation of psychology departments in Pakistani universities resulted in primarily theoretical research, studies by Ansari (1967, 1982, 2001) have revealed a shift towards empirical research employing quantitative methodology and statistical analysis. During the 1960s and 1970s, psychological research in Pakistan focused on social issues such as the impact of economic development on agrarian and tribal society and the migration of rural populations to urban centers (e.g., Zaidi, 1970). Beginning in the 1980s, the Islamization of academic institutions encouraged research on contributions to counseling and psychotherapy by Muslim scholars (e.g., Ajmal, 1986) as well as Islamic conceptualizations of mental illness (e.g., Rizvi, 1994). Along with Zaidi's (1979) initial critique on the ethnocentric nature of Western psychology being practiced in Pakistan and subsequent research on cross-cultural issues (e.g.,

Muhammad, 2002), these studies provided both legitimacy and a basis for the incorporation of Islamic practices into counseling and psychotherapy (e.g., Awan, 2003).

Pakistani researchers have published studies in most areas of counseling and psychotherapy, including therapeutic techniques and processes (e.g., Ahmad & Maniar, 1995), addiction (e.g., Khan & Reza, 1998), family and marital therapy (e.g., Munaf & Hassan, 2005), forensic psychology, (Suhail & Javed, 2004) the adaptation of Western tests and assessments (Dawood, 2008) as well as the development of indigenous measures (Rahman & Sitwat, 1997). In response to the recent spate of suicide bombings and terrorist attacks through the country, researchers are beginning to conduct studies on attitudes towards terrorism (e.g., Yousufzai, 2007) as well as its psychological consequences (e.g., Khan, 2008).

A comprehensive survey of research published in Pakistani journals by Haque (2000) revealed a focus on clinical practice (27%), followed by social issues (25%), assessment, and testing (17%), and industrial and organizational psychology (15%), with forensic, cross-cultural, developmental, and educational issues accounting for the remaining articles (14%). A more recent overview on articles published in Pakistani journals by Suhail (2004) indicated a shift towards social issues (38%) while Rahman (2009) reports a marked increase in research on developmental and educational psychology.

Clinical supervision in Pakistan remains neglected and often ignored altogether, despite an increase in the number of institutions offering advanced degrees in psychology and psychotherapy (Zaman, 1997). There is, however, a growing appreciation of the need for supervision, especially among the younger generation of counselors and psychotherapists, many of whom have, on their own initiative, established supervisory relationships with experienced clinicians from private practices and local universities (R. M. Zaman, personal communication, September 24, 2010). Supervision in Pakistan tends to be through informal groups holding fortnightly or monthly meetings focused on peer reviews, case conferences, referrals, and teaching sessions. Occasionally these informal meetings evolve into structured one-on-one supervision (Z. Murad, personal communication, May 28, 2010). While generally open, these groups are typically based on personal or professional networks, and thus liable to exclude counselors and psychotherapists seeking supervision who do not have access to these networks. To address this state of affairs, bodies such as the Pakistan Psychological Association are working towards establishing a formal framework for supervision.

Strengths, weaknesses, opportunities, and challenges

A small but dedicated group of clinicians and researchers forms the backbone of counseling and psychotherapy in Pakistan and is behind most efforts towards its development (Haque, 2000). According to Karim et al. (2004), this group played an important role in forcing the government to implement legislation to protect individuals with mental illness and improve the quality of care. Moreover, by establishing professional bodies such as the Pakistan Psychological Association and Pakistan Association for Clinical Psychologists, they have been able to coordinate their activities, especially towards establishing criteria for accreditation, licensing and the regulation of psychology, psychotherapy and counseling (Haque, 2000; Zaman, 1997).

By adopting an eclectic approach to treatment (Suhail, 2004) and remaining open to new ideas such as the incorporation of Islamic values and beliefs into clinical practice (Murray, 2002), these professionals have enabled counseling and psychotherapy to move beyond serving an anglicized, urban elite towards meeting the needs of a wider range of Pakistani clients. Many of them are also faculty members of psychology departments at local universities, where they have resisted government apathy towards research and maintained academic standards

(Rahman, 2009). As a result, Osama et al. (2009) argue that Pakistan is no longer exclusively dependent on North American and European institutions for the development of theories and processes in psychotherapy and the training of future generations of clinicians.

However, Zaman (1991) identified the lack of qualified practitioners along with minimal specialization—resulting in services for children, adolescents, and geriatrics being especially neglected—as fundamental weaknesses in the practice of counseling and psychotherapy in Pakistan. Studies by Suhail (2004) and Rahman (2009) suggest that despite overall improvement these weaknesses remain with an alarmingly low ratio of one mental health professional per 165,000 people.

Zaman (1991) also described how the treatment of mental illness in Pakistan is dominated by psychiatrists who focus on the treatment of psychopathology. Karim et al. (2004) report that although there are a few exceptions, this is still the case. In addition, financial constraints along with the lack of medical insurance mean that psychotherapy remains unaffordable for most Pakistanis (Zaman, 1991; 1997). Moreover, due to the absence of a legally recognized body to regulate counseling and psychotherapy, clients with financial resources are constantly at risk of being subjected to unethical, incompetent, or harmful treatment.

In terms of opportunities in the field, Pakistan is witnessing an ongoing reduction in the stigma associated with mental illness amongst the urban middle classes due to higher levels of education, workplace initiatives, exposure to mental illness through the media, and relatives who emigrated to the West. At the same time, the reduced influence and availability of extended family networks, from whom Pakistanis have traditionally sought help for emotional and interpersonal problems, has resulted in increasing numbers of Pakistanis seeking counseling and psychotherapy.

To meet the growing demands for mental health services, a number of institutions have begun offering master's level and post-master's diplomas in counseling and psychotherapy (Rahman, 2009) and charitable organizations have begun to subsidize or provide free mental health services to clients unable to afford treatment (Ahmad, 2010). Moreover, the incorporation of Islam into psychotherapy as described by Murray (2002) has made it culturally acceptable and relevant to clients from a wider range of social and economic backgrounds seeking counseling and psychotherapy.

In light of these developments, counselors and psychotherapists in Pakistan have a number of opportunities to expand the scale and scope of the field. These include improving awareness and extending services to rural areas where there is still considerable stigma attached to mental illness; further refining therapeutic theories and processes to meet the emotional, social, cultural, and spiritual needs of Pakistani clients; regulating practice to ensure ethical and competent treatment; collaborating with psychiatrists; and providing specialized treatment to neglected clients such as children, adolescents, and geriatrics. Urban populations, in particular, are also likely to be receptive to initiatives to push the boundaries of counseling and psychotherapy beyond the current remedial purposes of treating psychopathology towards preventive goals based on education, development, and wellbeing.

Notwithstanding the shift in awareness and attitudes, there is still considerable stigma attached to mental illness and help seeking, and as a result, individuals are routinely denied treatment in both urban and rural areas. While the incorporation of religion into counseling and psychotherapy aims to improve its relevance and appeal among Pakistani clients and reduce this stigma, increasing religiosity and the prevalence of puritanical and unforgiving interpretations of Islam threaten to replace the accepting and nonjudgmental basis of therapy with religious obligations, guilt, and fatalism. Moreover, given that counseling and psychotherapy are relatively new concepts for most Pakistani clients, misconceptions and unrealistic expectations often present additional challenges to clinicians.

Access, affordability, and quality of treatment remain problematic, especially in the absence of a regulatory body, and the recent trend of qualified practitioners emigrating abroad is likely to exacerbate the situation (Husain, 2001). For most Pakistanis, therefore, the only options for the treatment of mental illness are traditional religious healers or government hospitals where psychiatric care is often provided by general physicians. In this context it is not surprising that the unsupervised use of benzodiazepines and other psychotropic medication, which are cheap and easily available without prescriptions, is escalating and resulting in a corresponding increase in cases of dependence and overdose (Khan & Reza, 1998). Meanwhile, reports of traditional healers providing medical diagnoses and treating clients with medication (Karim et al., 2004) are a particularly disturbing development.

Future directions

The growing acceptability of counseling and psychotherapy, accompanied by the surge in institutions providing advanced degrees, is likely to translate into increased utilization of mental health services. In order to ensure competent and ethical treatment, it is imperative that Pakistani counselors and psychotherapists utilize their professional networks to establish a regulatory framework with clearly defined guidelines for training, supervision, and professional ethics. At the same, clients' needs can be more effectively met through increased specialization by clinicians, along with research into theories and processes that improve the acceptability, relevance, and efficacy of psychotherapy for Pakistani clients. Since a radical shift in government priorities is unlikely, clinicians, working in collaboration with professional and philanthropic organizations, will have to assume the responsibility of improving the availability and affordability of counseling and psychotherapy services.

Conclusion

Pakistan has made significant progress in counseling and psychotherapy since independence from British rule in 1947. Psychology departments have shed their philosophical orientation and established graduate programs with curricula similar to North American and European programs. Meanwhile, researchers have published empirical studies in most areas of counseling and psychotherapy and, in particular, been successful in adapting Western approaches to make them culturally acceptable and sensitive to the emotional, social, and spiritual needs of Pakistani clients. The increasing legitimacy and utilization of counseling and psychotherapy in Pakistan has enabled it to make inroads into the curative and institutional legacy of psychiatric treatment of mental illness left by the British.

While there is still a long way to go before the mental health needs of Pakistan's population are adequately met, the presence of capable and dedicated clinicians, university departments that are producing future generations of professionals, and philanthropic organizations working towards improving the availability and affordability of mental health services provide reasons for optimism. In particular, appropriate policies combined with resources channeled towards clinicians in community settings, qualified university faculty, specialized graduate study, and original research would ensure continuing progress in the field of counseling and psychotherapy in Pakistan.

References

Ahmad, F. Z. (1988). *Dependency in Psychotherapy*. Karachi: Institute of Clinical Psychology.
Ahmad, F. Z. (1993). *Child Rearing Practices and Mental Health in Pakistan*. Karachi: Institute of Clinical Psychology.

Ahmad, F. Z., & Maniar, S. (1995). Role of the therapist in the outcome of therapy. *Pakistan Journal of Psychology, 26*(2), 47–67.

Ahmad, M. (2010). *Karavan-e-Hayat Mission Statement.* Karachi: Karavan-e-Hayat.

Ahmed, D. S. (1993). *Islam and the West: A psychological analysis,* Unpublished manuscript, Lahore: National College of Arts.

Ahmed, H.S. (2008). *Development of mental health care in Pakistan: Past, present and future.* Retrieved May 22, 2011, from www.emro.who.int/mnh/whd/techpres-pakistan1.pdf.

Ajmal, M. (1986). *Muslim contributions to psychotherapy.* Islamabad: National Institute of Psychology.

Akram, M., & Khan, F. J. (2007). Health care services and government spending in Pakistan. *Pakistan Institute of Development Economics Working Papers, 32,* 22–40.

Ansari, Z. A. (1967). *Teaching and Research in Pakistan.* Islamabad: National Institute of Psychology.

Ansari, Z. A. (1982). *Psychological Research in Pakistan.* Islamabad: National Institute of Psychology.

Ansari, Z. A. (2001). Development of psychology in Pakistan. In S. H. Hashmi (ed.), *The state of social sciences in Pakistan* (pp. 97–108). Islamabad: Allama Iqbal Open University.

Armstrong, K. (2001). *The Battle for God: Fundamentalism in Judaism, Christianity and Islam.* London: Routledge.

Awan, M. A. (2003). Treatment of mental illnesses through Zikr Allah. *Al Murshid—The Spiritual Teacher, 24,* 4–6.

Bhui, K., King, M., Dein, S., & O'Connor, W. (2008). Ethnicity and religious coping with mental distress. *Journal of Mental Health, 17*(2), 141–151.

Dawood, S. (2008). *Development of an Indigenous Scale for Emotional Intelligence.* Unpublished dissertation. University of the Punjab, Pakistan.

Dein, S., Alexander, M., & Napier, D. (2008). Jinn, psychiatry and contested notions of misfortune among east London Bangladeshis. *Transcultural Psychiatry, 45*(1), 31–55.

Federal Bureau of Statistics. (2011). *Statistical Yearbook, 2011.* Islamabad: Government of Pakistan.

Gadit, A., & Khalid, N. (2002). *State of Mental Health in Pakistan: Service, Education and Research.* Karachi: Madinat-al-Hikmah

Gossop, M. (1989). The detoxification of heroin addicts in Pakistan. *Drug Alcohol Dependence, 24,* 143–150.

Haque, A. (2000). Development of Psychology in Pakistan. In A. E. Kazdin (ed.), *Encyclopedia of Psychology Vol. 6* (pp. 27–32). Oxford: Oxford University Press.

Hassan, I. N. (1990). An overview of Muslim spiritual therapy and other practices in dealing with mental health problems in Pakistan. In M. H. Mubbashar, & A. R. Saeed (eds) *Mental Health in Developing Countries* (pp. 67–89). Karachi: City Press.

Husain, I. (2001). Voting with their feet. In M. Shamsie (ed.), *Leaving Home: Towards a New Millennium: A Collection of English Prose by Pakistani Writers* (pp. 303–306). Karachi: Oxford University Press.

Ibrahim, F.A., & Almas, I. (1983). Guidance and counseling in Pakistan. *International Journal for the Advancement of Counseling, 6,* 93–98.

Institute for Conflict Management. (2011). *South Asia Assessment 2011.* Retrieved May 20, 2011, from www.satp.org/satporgtp/southasia/index.html.

Karim, S., Saeed, K., Rana, M. H., Mubbashar, M. H., & Jenkins R. (2004). Pakistan mental health country profile. *International Review of Psychiatry, 16,* 83–92.

Khan, M. M. (2008). *Living on the Edge.* Karachi: Dawn–Herald Publications.

Khan, M. M., Islam, S., & Kundi, A. K. (1996) Parasuicide in Pakistan: Experience at a university hospital. *Acta Psychiatric Scandinavia, 93,* 264–267.

Khan, M. M., & Reza, H. (1998). Benzodiazepine self-poisoning in Pakistan: Implication for prevention and harm reduction. *Journal of the Pakistan Medical Association, 48*(10), 292–295.

Majid, A. (2001). Healing power of faith and prayer: Religious and scientific perspectives. *Journal of Hazara Society of Science-Religion Dialogue, 8*(2), 33–39.

Mubbashar, M. H. (2000). Mental Illness in Pakistan. In I. Al-Issa (ed.), *Al-Junun: Mental Illness in the Islamic World* (pp. 187–203). Madison, MI and Westport, CT: International Universities Press.

Muhammad, G. (2002). Death by choice: Western and Islamic approaches. *Pakistan Journal of Psychology, 33* (1), 26–34.

Munaf, S., & Hasan, S. (2005). Parental divorce and the psychological well-being of children, *Journal of Psychology, 36*(2), 71–84.

Murray, B. (2002). Psychology takes a tenuous hold in Pakistan. *Monitor on Psychology, 33*(1), 33–34.

Nizamie H. S., & Goyal N. (2010). History of psychiatry in India. *Indian Journal of Psychiatry, 52,* 7–12.

Osama, A., Najam, A., Kassim-Lakha, S., Gilani, S. Z, & King, C. (2009). Pakistan's reform experiment, *Nature, 461*, 38–39.

Pirani, F., Papadopoulos, R., Foster, J., & Leavey, G. (2008). "I will accept whatever is meant for us. I wait for that—day and night": The search for healing at a Muslim shrine in Pakistan. *Mental Health, Religion & Culture, 11*(4), 375–386.

Rahman, N. (1991, October). *Rational emotive therapy and its application in Pakistan.* Presentation at the 8th Conference of the Pakistan Psychological Association, Islamabad.

Rahman, N. K. (2009). Psychology in Pakistan. In I. B. Weiner & W. E. Craighead (eds), *Corsini Encyclopedia of Psychology* (4th edn). Hoboken, NJ: John Wiley & Sons, Inc.

Rahman, N. K., & Sitwat, A. (1997). *Factor analysis of symptom checklist.* Presentation at the 11th International Psychiatric Conference, December, Karachi.

Rizvi. A. A. (1994). *Muslim traditions in psychotherapy and modern trends.* Lahore: Institute of Islamic Culture.

Somasundaram, O. (1987). The Indian Lunacy Act, 1912: The historic background. *Indian Journal of Psychiatry, 29*, 3–14.

Suhail, K. (2004). Psychology in Pakistan. *The Psychologist, 7*(11), 632–634.

Suhail, K., & Javed, F. (2004). Psychosocial causes of murder in Pakistan. *Pakistan Journal of Psychological Research, 19*, 121–32.

Tepper, M. S. (1999). Letting go of restrictive notions of manhood: Male sexuality, disability and chronic illness. *Sexuality and Disability, 17*, 37–52.

Yousufzai, A.W. (2007). *Attitudes and Perceptions of People towards Suicide Bombing: A Questionnaire Survey in Tribal Areas of Pakistan.* Presentation at the International Conference on Impact of Global Violence on Mental Health, May, University of the Punjab, Lahore.

Zaidi, S. M. H. (1970). *The Village Culture in Transition: A Study of East Pakistan Rural Society.* Honolulu, HI: East West Center Press.

Zaidi. S. M. H. (1979). Applied cross-cultural psychology: Submissions of a cross-cultural psychologist from the third world. In L. H. Eckenberger, W. Lonner, & Y. H. Poortinga (eds), *Cross-cultural Contributions to Psychology* (pp. 216–243). Amsterdam: Swets & Zeitlinger.

Zaman, R. M. (1991). Clinical psychology in Pakistan. *Psychology and Developing Societies, 3*, 221–233.

Zaman, R.M. (1997). The adaptation of Western psychotherapeutic methods to Muslim societies: The case of Pakistan. *World Psychology, 3*, 65–87.

20

COUNSELING AND PSYCHOTHERAPY IN THE PHILIPPINES

A discipline in transition

Maria Isabel E. Melgar

Introduction

The Republic of the Philippines comprises 7,107 islands of which 3,144 are named (National Statistics Office [NSO], 1997–2011). With Manila as its capital, the archipelago can be divided into three large island groups: Luzon, Visayas, and Mindanao. According to the latest census conducted in 2007, the Philippines has a population of 88.57 million (NSO, 1997–2011). In addition to its official languages, Filipino and English, there are eight major dialects. Approximately 81% of Filipinos are Roman Catholics and other religious groups include Protestants and Muslims.

The Philippines was occupied by Spain for almost 400 years from the 16th century to the end of the 19th century, and by the United States for the first half of the 20th century. In 1946, the largely agricultural country became formally independent with the local land-owning elite taking power. Philippine economic growth since then has at best been described as modest, with poverty incidence declining only slowly (Asian Development Bank, 2007). The new administration (2010–2016) of President Benigno Aquino III is seeking to restore the confidence and hope of Filipinos in their government by instituting massive reforms and by calling for a social transformation (Avendano, 2011).

The wide gap between the rich and the poor remains real with a handful of Chinese businessmen being the billionaires in Philippine society (Nam, 2011). Owing to the scarcity of jobs available in the country, vast numbers leave and work abroad. The foreign exchange remittances of overseas contract workers have in fact helped to keep the country's economy afloat. It is estimated that there are 8.2 million overseas workers (Mercene, 2009), contributing approximately 10% to the gross national product (NSO, 2010). Fueled by income coming from overseas workers, there is a recent boom in condominiums, shopping complexes, fast food chains, and restaurants. The Philippine's SM Mall of Asia is the third largest shopping mall in the world next to Jin Yuan Mall and the South China Mall (Eastern Connecticut State University, n.d.).

The rapid urbanization of key cities, deceleration of the agricultural economy, and a growing trend for fresh graduates from college to be working in urban cities where call centers and other outsourcing business companies (BPOs) are located (Eruma, 2011), as a result, lead to crowding particularly in Metro Manila. Nearly half of the Philippine population lives in urban areas (Collymore, 2011). In spite of the pressing economic and social problems, Filipinos are generally happy and optimistic people. The Philippines ranks 14th in the world and 2nd in Asia in the happiness index (New Economics Foundation, 2009). As a people, Filipinos' style of coping in times of adversity is perhaps strongly influenced by their Christian beliefs and faith in God.

The political, socio-economic and cultural background briefly described provides the context in which the development of counseling and psychotherapy in the Philippines occurs. Presently, it is a discipline that is gradually transitioning to a professional field. Counseling and psychotherapy are terms that are interchangeably used in this chapter, as both have been referred to in the Philippines as fields involving the application of psychological principles for understanding human behavior and helping clients in attaining personal growth and functioning.

Brief history of counseling and psychotherapy

Psychology in the Philippines was recognized as a discipline some 100 years ago. The earliest forms of psychology practice in the Philippines were in the areas of testing, counseling, and clinical psychology (Licuanan, 1989). They were established by individuals who obtained doctoral degrees in psychology or education from US universities.

The first half of the 20th century witnessed numerous milestones in the field of counseling and psychotherapy. The first psychological clinic was set up by Sinforoso Padilla in 1932 at the University of the Philippines (UP) (Licuanan, 1989). Testing, counseling and therapy were the main services offered. Padilla would later become the first president of the Psychological Association of the Philippines (PAP) in 1963. In 1933, Jesus Perfinan put up a psychological clinic at the Far Eastern University and in 1947, Jaime Zaguirre, psychiatrist and part-time instructor of clinical psychology, organized the first neuropsychological services unit at the V. Luna General Hospital (Pereira, n.d.). In 1948, the Institute of Human Relations was established by Estafania Aldaba-Lim, a clinical psychologist who supervised a staff of a guidance counselor, a psychiatric social worker, and psychiatrist consultants (Licuanan, 1989). Initially the institute confined its services to the Philippine Women's University but later extended its clinical services to other schools and to the community at large.

The second half of the 20th century was highlighted by the development of psychology as an academic department in colleges and universities while counseling psychology as a branch of specialization. This was the era when Master of Arts (MA) in counseling or clinical psychology was offered in a number of large universities in Manila. For instance, in 1960, renowned clinical psychologist Jaime Bulatao founded the psychology department at the Ateneo de Manila University (AdeMU) as well as the Central Guidance Bureau (now the Ateneo Center for Psychological and Educational Assessment [ACESS]) in the same university (ACESS, 2011). The Bureau primarily provided training opportunities for AdeMU practicum students and psychological services for the university population as well as clients not affiliated with AdeMU.

The last 50 years also marked the establishment of professional organizations such as the PAP, the Philippine Guidance and Counseling Association (PGCA), the National Association for Filipino Psychology (NAFP), and the Philippine Association for Counselor Education, Research and Supervision (PACERS).

The peak moment in the history of counseling in the Philippines occurred when the Philippine Guidance and Counseling Act and the Philippine Psychology Act were passed in 2004 and 2010, respectively (House of Representatives, 2004; Psychological Association of the Philippines, 2011). Both were laws of licensure aimed at professionalizing the practice of counseling in the Philippines. The advocates of the Guidance and Counseling Act were hopeful that the practice of counseling in various settings, especially the school setting, would be upgraded and the status of counselors improved (Villar, 2000).

Counselor education programs, accreditation, licensure, and certification

The first department of psychology was established at UP in 1926. Since then, the field of psychology has grown tremendously to some 171 colleges and universities offering a total of 249 psychology programs (Montiel & Teh, 2004). A third of these schools are located in Metro Manila while the rest are spread across the main islands. While some 21% of these listed schools do offer MA or Master of Science (MS) programs in clinical or counseling psychology, only a few of them (less than 4%) offer a PhD in Clinical Psychology. The latest Directory of Higher Education Institutions (Commission on Higher Education, 2006–2007) lists a total of 39 colleges and universities offering graduate programs in counseling. Most of the faculty members in psychology departments were academically trained in local universities, as scholarships for studying abroad depleted through time. The medium of instruction for these programs is English and practically all academic outputs are in English.

Prior to the establishment of the government Commission on Higher Education (CHED) in 1994, de Jesus (as cited in Montiel & Teh, 2004) wrote that PAP took an active role in assessing graduate programs and in convening various heads of the psychology departments to draw up standards for psychology programs, including counseling programs at various levels. However, since the PAP did not have a legal mandate to institute accreditation of academic programs, this initiative had limited impact (Montiel & Teh, 2004).

When the CHED was formed, a technical committee reviewed the curricula for both undergraduate and graduate programs in psychology. The CHED drew up policies and standards for graduate programs including the counseling programs (CHED, n.d.). Currently, MA degree programs require a total of 30 units where 15 units are allotted to major courses, nine units to core courses and six units to the practicum or thesis. For the Doctor of Philosophy (PhD) program, CHED requires a minimum of 45 units for those with an MA or MS degree in psychology or 66 units for those without an MA or an MS (CHED, 2010). With these units, a master's degree in counseling takes approximately 3 years while a doctoral degree takes anywhere from 3 to 5 years.

Academic institutions are given the flexibility to implement their own graduate curriculum based on CHED Policies and Standards for Graduate Programs (2010). As such, they may or may not impose MA practicum and PhD internship requirements for psychology graduate students (A. Bernardo, personal communication, November 1, 2011).[1] Two leading universities in the Philippines require 200 hours of field practicum at the MA psychology program while internship at the PhD level varies from 500 to 1,200 hours (C. Tarroja, personal communication, October 13, 2011). These practicum or internship hours are usually served in a government mental hospital, psychological centers, clinics, university guidance and counseling departments, government agencies, NGOs, pre-school, and professional societies. A few large private universities have put up their own counseling centers as a laboratory for their students (J. Reyes, personal communication, March 17, 2011; del Rosario & San Diego, 2009).

In addition to formal training within academic institutions, educational courses are offered to the public by the PAP, PGCA, and PACER; universities; private centers; testing agencies; and other organizations that counseling students and practitioners could attend for skills upgrading in counseling, psychological testing and research.

In terms of licensure, there are two laws that govern the licensure of counselors. A more recent one is the Philippine Psychology Act (Republic Act 10029), which was passed in 2010 to regulate psychologists who provide higher level psychological services to the public. A psychologist must possess at least a master's degree to qualify for licensure. According to this law, psychologists are those who provide psychological counseling, psychological assessment, psychosocial support, coaching, psychological debriefing, and other related interventions with individuals, groups and families (PAP, 2011). The licensure examinations for psychologists would cover advanced theories of personality, abnormal psychology, assessment, psychological counseling, and psychotherapy. The implementing rules and regulations of this law have yet to be drafted by the Professional Board for Psychology.

While there was no licensure law for counseling psychologists before 2010, the PAP in 2009 launched a certification program to promote a standard of practice of psychology in the country. Under this program, clinical or counseling psychologists may apply for certification as long as they have obtained a master's or doctoral degree and have practiced in a clinical setting for at least 3 years among PhD holders and at least 5 years among MA holders. This certification program remains to be active (PAP, 2009).

The other law which provides licensure among counselors is the Guidance and Counseling Act (RA 9258). This law refers to counseling as synonymous to and interchangeable with guidance and counseling. Furthermore, it also stipulated that counseling includes functions such as "counseling, psychological testing (as to personality, career interest, study orientation, mental ability and aptitude) research, placement, group processes, teaching and practicing of guidance and counseling subjects" (House of Representatives, 2004, p. 2). The practice covers the teaching of guidance and counseling subjects, particularly those covered in the licensure examinations and necessary in other human development services (House of Representatives, 2004). From this clause, psychologists who do counseling and psychological testing, among others, should comply with the licensure regulation if they wish to continue a legitimate practice. This expectedly drew protest and negative reactions from counseling psychologists who were employed in schools before the law was passed, as they derive their main income from this practice.

Current counseling and psychotherapy theories, processes, and trends

The Philippines was colonized by the Americans for 50 years. The Americans' strong influence on Filipino culture and lifestyle is attributed to the fact that the Philippine educational system was partially patterned after the US system (Dueck, Cutiongco, & Ramos, 2006).

In a survey of practicing Filipino psychotherapists (Teh, 2003), results showed that the majority of the respondents used a variety of Western techniques or simply labeling their approach as eclectic. The study found that popular techniques such as Rogerian, cognitive-behavioral, hypnotherapy, and spiritual approaches are being used by most practitioners who work with adult patients. A combination of humanistic, behavior modification and play therapy is employed by child counselors. Roger's client-centered approach is also popularly used as a guiding framework among guidance counselors.

In a qualitative study conducted by the author of this chapter (Melgar, 2009), it was found that not only diverse approaches were practiced among established therapists who are knowledgeable about Western techniques, but they also locally adapted these foreign techniques to the culture and context of their clients. For instance, counselors and therapists reported to be either followers of the Jungian, Gestalt, Rogerian, Eriksonian, or cognitive-behavioral models also claimed to adapt these modalities to meet the needs of their Filipino clients.

The trend to indigenize psychology was strong and well articulated only during the early seventies when Virgilio Enriquez arrived from his postgraduate studies from the US and taught at UP (Taboclaon, 2010). Enriquez was opposed to the wholesale importation of Western models developed in an industrialized country. He produced several works that focused on the Filipino psychology and identity, localization of methods of data collection and inquiry, Filipino personality theory, and Filipino social psychological constructs. While few psychologists in the Philippines are committed to indigenization, many clinical psychologists make efforts to integrate their clients' strong kinship ties and religious values into therapy (Stevens & Wedding, 2004) and adopt Enriquez's theoretical framework (Tanalega, 2004).

According to Bulatao (2002), the process of achieving a contextually sensitive psychology cannot be accomplished in isolation from foreign models. Western models are still welcomed but must match the context and culture in which they will be used. Bulatao expressed this idea and opined that this critical thinking process should start in the academia. He urged the PAP to set up norms where MA graduate students revalidate all American behavioral findings in a Philippine setting. PhD graduates, on the other hand, should be able to challenge American theory, create Philippine concepts, set up Philippine hypotheses and theories and challenge the validity of foreign tests.

Indigenous and traditional healing methods

The origins of Filipino traditional healing method date back to the pre-Hispanic period. The role of a female Babaylan (referred to as shaman in some cultures) in indigenous communities was documented as critical in healing the sick and the beleaguered. The Babaylans are known as ritualists, chanters, diviners, and they have the gift of traveling to the spirit world (Center for Babaylan Studies, 2010). In modern times, medical anthropology wrote about indigenous modes of healing which coexist with mainstream modern medicine in urban and rural centers in most provinces (Islam, 2005). Similar to the practice of Babaylans, traditional medicine and healing remain closely tied to the world of spirits. Traditional healers are generally believed to be empowered by gods or spirits.

The modalities of traditional healing may vary according to the community that practices it and to the geographical site in which it is located. The common principle shared by these modalities is a balance and harmony in the universe and in human relationships (Tan, n.d.). These traditional healing modes are recognized by the public but their use has slowly declined as the new generation of health workers emerge. However, there is still an accommodation of uniquely Philippine and Asian techniques that promote a body–mind–spirit therapy among contemporary counselors with Western influence. Some practitioners mix chi-gong, yoga (Melgar, 2011), religious, or psycho-spiritual interventions (Teh, 2003) and other Asian techniques with the usual Western counseling approaches. For instance, in the hospital where the author of this chapter consults as a psychologist, cancer patients are taught chi-gong and yoga alongside group therapy sessions to help them deal with psychological and physical stress. Spiritual counseling is also an essential part of these cancer support groups (Melgar & Dumlaon, 2010). In the academia, Bulatao offered a new course on Asian Psychotherapy for PhD students in clinical psychology as a way of introducing students to the Asian framework of integrating body, mind, spirit in the practice of therapy (J. Bulatao, personal communication, August 11, 2009).

Research and supervision

It is observed that while the number of psychologists with advanced degrees has grown tremendously in the Philippines, the amount of research and writing in the field has not advanced proportionately (Licuanan, 1989). However, the picture has slightly improved in recent years. The PAP conventions, for instance, have since changed its format from a mere meeting and sharing of professional experience to a vibrant presentation and discussion of research and practices.

Montiel and Teh (2004) attributed this low priority given to research to a lack of research skills and inadequate support resources to carry out research projects. However, Bernardo (2002) observed that there are many research efforts which do not see print. These studies are mostly commissioned research funded by the Philippine government or international agencies such as the UNICEF, Ford Foundation, and other foreign research institutions. Further, the emergence of new graduate programs in counseling over the years has yielded more student theses and dissertations, though very few have been published.

The two most established journals in the Philippines which publish articles on counseling and therapy are the *Philippine Journal of Psychology* and the *Philippine Journal of Counseling Psychology*. Some of the topics that have seen print were the application and evaluation of counseling with special groups such as children, adolescents, marginalized groups, and the family. Quite a number of studies involve validation studies of foreign psychological instruments or a validation of local assessment tools.

With respect to research supervision, the standard practice in university graduate programs in counseling is to assign a thesis adviser to a student towards the end of the academic program. A panel of reviewers is formed to provide advice to the thesis student either during the proposal or final thesis defense stage. There are a number of graduate courses in counseling that require students to conduct research, and supervision is mainly carried out by a faculty member. In practica or internships, an on-site system of close supervision and competent mentoring in the Philippines has yet to be developed, despite an abundance of sites for field or applied work. Some universities have tried to fill this gap by closely working with the sites through orientation and supervision skills training or maintaining a continuous line of communication with the on-site supervisors.

Strengths, weaknesses, opportunities, and challenges

Several strengths in the field of counseling and psychotherapy in the Philippines can be discerned. First, recent efforts to professionalize the practice of counseling have helped elevate the reputation of counseling as a professional field. As the public are more assured of the standards and quality of services provided by certified or licensed psychologists specializing in counseling, a growing demand for counseling and psychotherapy is evident.

Second, the media in the Philippines has been helpful in creating greater public awareness about the role of psychologists, as it frequently refers to them in its informative programs and TV talk shows. More and more publications feature interviews with notable psychologists whose opinions are often solicited on various relevant modern-day issues that the community and families confront, such as trauma, suicide, addiction, parenting, etc. The public visibility of a few counselors has strengthened the rapport of this specialty with many prospective clients who are hesitating to seek help because of the stigma attached to counseling.

There are two areas of weaknesses in the field that can be highlighted: one on the practice of counseling in schools and the other on the lack of productivity in terms of research in counseling. For quite some time, the practice of school counseling has been slow in progress or might have even deteriorated (Villar, 2000). The role of the guidance counselor has been misconstrued and even downgraded (Abrenica, 1999). Counselors in schools, for example, are given other assignments that deviate from their counseling role and promotion is slower. They are either assigned administrative duties or other tasks unrelated to counseling. Villar (2000) further lamented the unrealistic counselor–client ratio of 1:800–1,000 in schools serving the poorer sector of the community. Further, counselor training and education needs substantial updating to catch up with the evolving social problems brought about by the break-up of families, economic poverty and technological developments.

The research output in this specialty is also quite poor. There are a number of factors which account for this (Abrenica, 1999; Bernardo, 2002). Foremost of these is the lack of research resources such as the lack of available funds and technical support. Workload is also cited as a problem. Counselors in schools, for example, are expected to do more testing and counseling than research. Practitioners are keener in applying their therapy skills than their research skills. Another factor is the lack of research competence among professional counselors. However, Bernardo (2002) believes that there are misperceptions and myths that make research seem more difficult than it actually is.

The opportunities open to a professional psychologist in the Philippines, on the other hand, are vast considering we are now living in a globalized world. Students and practitioners have easier access to learning materials, scholarly journals, training modules, and other tools developed here and abroad. The chances of being approached for professional help have increased with the advent of websites, emails, and social networking. The clientele of counseling or clinical psychology is no longer confined to the guidance department of schools or to a local psychological center. As well, the practice of guidance and counseling in previous years has been predominantly school based, but the types of client problems have become more divergent extending beyond academic concerns of students. The public's growing need for more counselors is an opportunity for academically trained counselors to explore careers outside of the guidance and counseling centers in schools, such as those offered in NGOs, clinics, hospitals, and government institutions, and explore other applications of their expertise (Montiel and Teh, 2004).

There is also a growing opportunity for flexible merging with other disciplines such as health, social science, and social work. Psychologists who practice counseling find themselves collaborating with other professionals in government agencies, church-based organizations, local and international NGOs, psychological centers in tertiary institutions, health clinics, and recently in cyberspace. The field of psychological counseling has been flourishing and the demand for this service, coupled with psychological assessments, is increasing.

In emergencies, Filipino counselors are mobilized in numbers to debrief survivors of strong typhoons, great floods, earthquakes, and volcanic eruptions. The frontier of practice has therefore expanded to respond to emerging issues of national importance. Filipino psychologists have been called to assist survivors of political detention, torture, war-rape, and other forms of militarized brutality (Montiel & Teh, 2004).

Finally, opportunities to upgrade the quality and competence of many students and local practitioners in the Philippines lie ahead, as a network and interphase with Asian counterparts have been initiated by local universities and professional associations. For instance, countries in Asia such as Hong Kong and Singapore have been aggressive in mounting training workshops on varying counseling technologies. Travel has made the exchange of resources and information far easier and much less costly.

Nonetheless, there are challenges that professionals and leaders in the educational and professional fields must deal with while the institutional and legal accomplishments are in a fragile stage. In the Philippines, the discipline of counseling continues to grow and the number of professionals claiming credentials as practicing psychologists has significantly increased over the past decades (PAP, 2009a). As the practice of counseling continues to be open to people who come from other disciplines and lack the academic or professional training, this raises the question as to whether they are competent enough to handle sensitive or complex counseling issues. Another major challenge is the availability of resources in order for the profession to advance as a science through more research initiatives. The lack of research funds and organizational support as well as the availability of time to conduct research are among the barriers that need to be dealt with.

An additional challenge is for accredited counselors to take the initiative to update and upgrade what they know and continuously evaluate which counseling tools can be appropriately applied to the Filipino client, families, and communities. Most of the assessment instruments and counseling resources available in the market are imported from the US and Europe. In order for English standardized tests to be useful they must use Philippine norms that consider the distinctive characteristics of Philippine culture and normative behavior. Moreover, the translation or adaptation of English tests and counseling tools require time and resources. The challenge that counseling scholars and practitioners face is therefore to develop indigenous instruments and tools sensitive to the needs and culture of local clients.

Future directions

As previously mentioned, publications on experimental breakthroughs or trials of new models in Philippine therapy are limited. Local evaluation studies of foreign theoretical and practical models are lagging behind. To address this gap, there should be more collaborative partnerships between the academics and the professionals in the field, here and abroad. The academic researchers can provide the expertise in research methodology while the practitioners could share field experiences with their colleagues. Research hubs in academic settings could invite practitioners to assist in the conceptualization of field research. To further elevate the quality and standard of research, another scenario is to strengthen linkages with fellow practitioners in Asia so as to spur cross-fertilization of ideas and practices. Educators and practitioners of counseling should also strive to level up its communication with other disciplines such as medicine and social work for collaborative research and professional training. The academia must initiate and support more scholarly exchange among graduate students and faculty of different but related disciplines to expand knowledge on how the practice of counseling can be applied in other fields. This could be initiated by creating a system of connection and interfaces in the specialty. Shared access to information, resources, tutorials, library materials, and other professional concerns can be strengthened through joint or subsidized investments in these resources.

The role of educators in encouraging their students to do research should not be underestimated. There is a need to motivate and sustain educators to relentlessly lead students to experimentation and research in counseling and psychotherapy. The opportunities available at the universities should reinvigorate the call for more research and conversations on the exciting field of helping and healing other people.

Finally, educators should see to it that balancing students' learning experiences is maintained. Research and experimentation, while dominated by Western ideas, should not always mean a constant exposure to sophisticated new models posited by Western authors and scientists. Equally important is an awareness of contemporary local studies about the psyche of Filipino people. The concerns of the Y generation of young Filipinos, families split by migration, resiliency of Filipinos who survive all kinds of tragedies in life, spirituality of chronically ill patients, and personality disorders in the context of Philippine society are among the national concerns that counselors can respond to. They call for the need of a scientific psychology and robust practice that is Filipino.

Conclusion

The status of counseling and psychotherapy practice in the Philippines is gradually progressing to a state where the specialty of counseling is nationally recognized and professionalized. The developments are clearly reflected in the accreditation and governance of the counseling profession through licensure and certification of practitioners as well as the revision of the Code of Ethics for psychologists. These are significant developments which highlight the maturation of the field and the striving for quality in counseling services. On the academic front, the government has also made important contributions in standardizing the curriculum and providing opportunities for discussion and feedback on developing a relevant and culturally sensitive counseling curriculum at the MA and PhD levels.

However, the recent efforts at professionalizing the specialty have seen struggles and successes. The predominant influence of the Western world on local practice is seen both as an opportunity and as a barrier. The challenge in developing a truly Filipino approach towards counseling and healing Filipino clients continues to linger.

The window to the future of counseling and psychotherapy rests on the strengths and successes achieved by the community of committed professionals. Certainly, these historical moments should be celebrated; however, the momentum should be sustained. In order for these legacies to cascade down to the new generations of counselors, the dream should be embraced and lived out by all who identify themselves as current and future counselors and therapists.

Note

1 The CHED issued a curriculum guide stipulating that students in MP programs (Master of Psychology, a practitioner's degree) must take a six-unit field practicum in lieu of the thesis. The MA or MS in Psychology is defined as a teaching/research degree where thesis is required, while practicum course is up to the discretion of the school. In the Philippines, most large universities do require their students in MA (including MA Counseling) to undertake field practicum, usually a three-unit course.

References

Abrenica, A. (1999). *Counselor empowerment through research.* Workshop presented at the 22nd Annual PGCA Conference Workshop, Asian Social Institute in Manila, Philippines.

Avendano, C. O. (2011). *President Aquino: Filipinos caring again*, July 1. Retrieved from http://newsinfo.inquirer.net/20153/president-aquino-filipinos-caring-again

Asian Development Bank (2007). *Philippines: Critical development constraints* (*Publication No. 120907*). Mandaluyong City, Metro Manila: Author.

Ateneo Center for Psychological and Education Assessment (ACESS) (2011). *History.* Retrieved October 15, 2011 from www.pap.org.ph/?ctr=page&action=ra10029.

Bernardo, A.B.I. (2002). Psychology research in the Philippines: Observations and prospects. *Philippine Journal of Psychology*, *35*(1&2), 79–92.

Bulatao, J. C. (2002). Oh, that terrible task of teachers to teach psychology. *Philippine Journal of Psychology*, *35*(1&2), 32–37.

Center for Babaylan Studies (2010). *What is babaylan?* Retrieved September 29, 2011, from www.babaylan.net.

Collymore, Y. (2011). *Rapid population growth, crowded cities present challenge in the Philippines.* Retrieved October 29, 2011 from www.prb.org/Articles/2003/RapidPopulationGrowthCrowdedCitiesPresent ChallengesinthePhilippines.aspx.

Commission on Higher Education (2006–2007). *Directory of higher education institutions in the Philippines.* Quezon City, Philippines: Author.

Commission on Higher Education (n.d.). *What's new index.* Retrieved December 26, 2009 from www.ched.gov.ph/whatsnew/index.html.

Commission on Higher Education (2010). *CHED memoranda and issuances: CHED Memorandum Order No. 29.* Retrieved October 13, 2011 from http://202.57.63.198/chedwww/index.php/eng/Information/CHED-Memorandum-Orders.

del Rosario, H., & San Diego, C. (2009). *University of Santo Tomas Graduate School Psychotrauma Clinic.* Unpublished manuscript, University of Santo Tomas, Quezon City.

Dueck, A., Cutiongco, R., & Ramos, Z. (2006). *Patterns of indigenizing psychology in Puerto Rico and the Philippines*. Paper presented at the First World Congress of Cross-cultural Psychiatry, September, Beijing, China.

Eastern Connecticut State University (n.d.). *World's Largest Shopping Centers*. Retrieved October 29, 2011 from www.easternct.edu/~pocock/MallsWorld.htm.

Eruma, R. (2011, March). *State of the Philippine Contact Center Industry*. Lecture conducted at the College of Public Health, University of the Philippines, Manila.

House of Representatives (2004). *Downloads Center*. Retrieved October 13, 2011 from www.congress.gov. ph/download/index.php?d=ra.

Islam, N. (2005) Pluralism, parallel medical practices and the question of tension: the Philippines experience. *Anthropology Matters*, 7(2), 1–9.

Licuanan, P. B. (1989). *Psychology in the Philippines: History and Current Trends*. Manila: Psychological Association of the Philippines.

Melgar, I. E. (2011, July 6). *Philippine Experience in Creative Arts Therapy*. Presented at the Asian Creative Arts Therapy Summit, University of Haifa, Haifa, Israel.

Melgar, I. E. (2009). *Counseling Practice in the Philippines*. Unpublished manuscript, Ateneo de Manila University, Quezon City.

Melgar, I. E. & Dumlaon, J. (2010). *Cancer Support Groups in the Philippines*. Unpublished manuscript, St. Luke's Cancer Institute, Quezon City.

Mercene, F. M. (2009). The overseas contract workers. *The Manila Bulletin*. Retrieved from www.mb. com.ph/articles/208981/the-overseas-contract-workers.

Montiel, C. J., & Teh, L. (2004). Psychology in the Philippines. In M. J. Stevens & D. Wedding (eds), *Handbook of International Psychology* (pp. 467–500). New York: Brunner-Routledge.

Nam, S. (2011). *The Philippines' 40 richest*. Retrieved October 29, 2011 from www.forbes.com/lists/2011/ 86/philippines-billionaires-11_land.html.

National Statistics Office (NSO) (1997–2011). *NSO Philippines in Figures 2010*. Retrieved October 13, 2011, from www.census.gov.ph/

New Economics Foundation (2009). *The Happy Planet Index 2.0*. Retrieved November 1, 2011 from www.happyplanetindex.org/learn/download-report.html.

Pereira, M. E. (n.d). *History of Psychology: A Timeline of Psychological Ideas*. Retrieved October 13, 2011 from www.oocities.org/~emanoel/en_linha2.htm.

Professional Regulations Commission (2005). *Implementing Rules and Regulations for the Guidance and Counseling Act of 2004*. Quezon City: Professional Regulations Commission.

Psychological Association of the Philippines (PAP). (2009). *Certification of Psychology Specialists: Primer*. Retrieved September 1, 2011, from www.pap.org.ph.

Psychological Association of the Philippines. (2011) *2011 PAP Primer on RA 100029*. Retrieved October 9, 2011, from www.pap.org.ph/?ctr=page&action=ra10029.

Stevens, M. J., & Wedding, D. (2004). International psychology: A synthesis. In M. J. Stevens & D. Wedding (eds), *International Handbook of Psychology* (pp. 481–500). New York: Brunner-Routledge.

Taboclaon, MA. (2010). *Sikolohiyang Pilipino – The history of Philippine Psychology*. Retrieved October 13, 2011 from www.stumbleupon.com/su/2DjFxC/www.suite101.com/content/sikolohiyang-pilipino–the-history-of-philippine-psychology-a316940.

Tan, J. (n.d.). *The merging of Filipino traditional healing*. Retrieved September 29, 2011, from http://philwell. org/the_merging_of_filipino_traditional_healing.html.

Tanalega, N. (2004). *Counseling Filipinos … briefly*. Quezon City: Ugat Foundation.

Teh, L. A. (2003). A survey on the practice and status of Psychotherapy in the Philippines. *Philippine Journal of Psychology*, 3(1), 112–133.

Villar. (2000). Counselor professionalization: An imperative. *Philippine Journal of Counseling Psychology*, 3(1), 10–16.

21

COUNSELING AND PSYCHOTHERAPY IN SOUTH KOREA

Disciplines flourishing in a dynamic and challenging era

Eunsun Joo

Introduction

Korea has a long history of more than 5,000 years and throughout this time the country has developed a unique culture. Owing to its geographical situation of being surrounded by powerful nations, Korea has been invaded many times throughout its history. Through the painful experiences of frequent attack and occupation, Koreans learned to protect themselves socially by forming a group-oriented lifestyle as one of its unique cultural traits (Choi, 1976). In addition, traditionally as an agricultural society, tightly-knit groups were important since farming required highly collaborative work. In history, links with China have been strong. Much of the Korean heritage originated in China, from Confucianism, Buddhism, Taoism, to court culture. Though many traditions were imported from China, they have become so Koreanized that most Koreans no longer see them as foreign. Fuelling this adaptation and Koreanization of the imported tradition has been the continuing search for harmony. For example, in the case of Buddhism, the main doctrine is to seek a life lived in harmony with ultimate reality and with our own true inner nature. In terms of Confucianism, the basic philosophy aims to live life in harmony with our fellow human beings. Furthermore, in the case of Taoism, a life lived in harmony with natural course of things is emphasized (Howard, Pares & English, 1996; Kim, 1996). For several centuries, all these religious beliefs and doctrines were harmoniously incorporated in the everyday life of Koreans. The morals of Confucianism, the ascetic practices of Taoism, the concept of karma, the three states of existence from Buddhism, and the spiritual world of shamanism govern and influence the psychology of Korean people (Choi, 1996).

One of the biggest challenges in Korean history was the Korean War of 1950s. Owing to this tragedy, Korea was divided into North and South Korea. After the Korean War, the country was devastated, so in the 1960s economic development was the most critical challenge that

247

Korean people and society had to face. Social consciousness at that time focused on the urgent desire to modernize and develop the country. With the rapid economic development of the 1970s and exponential growth of the 1980s, the basic needs were being met, thus allowing the Korean people to begin to focus their attention on democracy and the rediscovery of traditional Korean culture and heritage. During the process of modernization and emulation of Western culture, Koreans began experiencing weakened cultural identity, and, to some extent, disintegration. With the stability of the Korean economy and political situation, the Koreans began to realize the importance of rediscovering their own identity and heritage. Currently, it can be interpreted that Koreans are in the self-reflecting stage. At the same time, Koreans are struggling with high rates of divorce, suicide, and emerging problems related to youth and children. Society in general is in need of psychotherapy and due to these demands the mental health field has been growing rapidly. Though psychotherapy is referred to as services provided for more severely disturbed people, often times, counseling and psychotherapy are used interchangeably in South Korea.

Brief history and counseling and psychotherapy

The concept of Western counseling and psychotherapy was first introduced to Korea in the 1930s (Rhi, 1972, 1985) by foreigners, but it was not until after the Korean War of 1950–1953 that clinicians actually began to practice psychotherapy. Historically, psychiatrists have been the most dominant group of helping professionals. During the 1950s and 1960s, most psychiatrists were psychoanalytically oriented having studied mainly in Germany, Japan, and the United States. However, it was not until the mid-1960s that all psychiatrists fully completed training in a psychoanalytic school.

Today, psychotherapy has become one of the booming professional fields in South Korea. Currently it consists of five main types of helping professionals: psychiatrists; psychologists (clinical and counseling psychology); counselors; social workers; a new and rising practitioner group including developmental psychologists, health psychologists, children and family therapists, play therapists, music and art therapists; and pastoral counselors.[1] They each follow a different historical trajectory which will be briefly presented below.

The first and oldest professional group in the field of psychotherapy is psychiatrists. As such they have had the most political power and professional jurisdiction (Abbott, 1988). Indeed, until 1996, psychiatrists were the only mental health professionals who were legally allowed to practice psychotherapy in Korea (Kang, 2002). The majority of the psychiatrists are members of the Korean Neuro-psychiatric Association, an active and powerful association established in 1968.

The second major professional group is psychotherapists in the field of clinical psychology. In 1974, the Korean Psychological Association (KPA) established a division of clinical and counseling psychology; however, this division became separated into two different divisions, a division of clinical psychology and a division of counseling and psychotherapy in the year of 1986.

The third professional group is counseling psychologists, who are also referred to as counselors in South Korea. Most of their backgrounds are either in psychology or educational psychology. In 2000, many professionals in the counseling field, who mostly have a non-psychology background, established the Korean Counseling Association (KCA) in an attempt to distinguish themselves from other professionals in the counseling field. They are perhaps the most sought after mental health professionals, as there appear to be fewer stigmas involved in seeing a non-medical counselor or therapist than going to a hospital for treatment by a psychiatrist. Recently, the increasing number of problems related to children and adolescents are becoming huge societal issues and parents are more likely to consult non-medical therapists, such as counselors, concerning the problems encountered by children and adolescents (Bae & Orlinsky, 1997; Joo & Han, 2000).

As in the case of the United States, the number of social workers is increasing in Korea. Initially, they were mostly involved in making and developing social policies; however, they soon developed a clinical domain. In 1985, the Korean Academy of Social Welfare (KASW) was established in response to the increasing number of social workers.

More recently, in the early 1990s, professionals with backgrounds in fields such as developmental psychology, child and family studies, art and music, health psychology and religion, started to enter the field of psychotherapy. In 1997, the Korean Art Therapy Association (KATA) was established, followed by the Korean Association for Play Therapy in 1998 and the Korean Music Therapy Association in 1999.

According to the Korean National Statistics Office (KNSO), in 1995, 50% of the population in South Korea report being religious, of which 40%, of them are Christian, which is the second largest religious group in Korea after Buddhism (46%). The Christian population is one of the fastest growing population in South Korea. Accordingly, pastoral counseling is fast gaining popularity and many religious institutions and centers have offered training programs and workshops to train counselors in this field.

Summarizing the history and professional aspect of counseling and psychotherapy in South Korea, the development of psychotherapy can be explained by different stages of the emergence of a new professional group of psychotherapists in South Korea. The first stage was established in the 1960s, which can be called the "Beginning Stage," when only psychiatrists who had medical backgrounds were allowed to practice therapy. The psychiatrists who studied abroad and returned essentially led the field. Then in the 1970s, psychotherapy transitioned into the "Emerging Stage." This is when non-medical professionals, who were mostly clinical psychologists, entered the psychotherapeutic field. However, their roles were mainly performing psychological diagnosis and assessment in the hospital setting and working for the psychiatrists. Economically, South Korea developed rapidly in the 1980s, thus increasing the public demand for mental health practitioners. This third stage can be called the "Developing Stage," a period when not only medical professionals, but also non-medical professionals, such as clinical, counseling psychologists and counselors, began to treat clients. This period also marked the formation of numerous professional organizations and provided the foundation for the further development of psychotherapy in South Korea. In the 1990s, professionals with various different backgrounds, such as developmental psychology, child and family studies, art, religion, etc., began to work as psychotherapists. This stage can be named as the "Booming Stage." In a relatively short period of time, many different professional groups have emerged in South Korea, with each seeking to establish its position in the field of modern psychotherapy.

Counselor education programs, accreditation, licensure, and certification

Currently, there are approximately 120 universities and graduate schools that offer counseling-related programs. In order to apply for the counseling licensures or certificates, one has to receive at least a master's degree in graduate schools. In general, it takes 2–3 years to finish a master's program in Korea and one has to take required courses such as Research Methodology, Counseling Theories, Psychological Testing, etc., and one can choose electives such as Group Counseling, Family and Couples Counseling, Psychopathology. Submission of a thesis is required. For a PhD, in general it takes 3–5 years to complete coursework as well as a dissertation. Courses in PhD programs are diverse and more specific such as a psychodynamic approach, cognitive-behavioral approach, person-centered theory and practice, to name a few. Owing to the increasing number of people interested in learning counseling in South Korea, professional graduate schools as well as cyber/on-line universities are alternative options to learn counseling.

Currently, there are no accreditation processes in South Korea that are similar to those in the United States or Canada. Associations issuing certifications regarding counseling and psychotherapy in South Korea acknowledge degrees earned from universities recognized by the Ministry of Education. This phenomenon remains a significant problem since the quality of educational services across many different educational settings varies significantly.

The licensure and certification process for psychiatrists is that one must complete 2 years of pre-medical school and 4 years of medical school. Then one can apply for the government board examination and become a general doctor. After that, 1 year of internship, 4 years of resident in a psychiatric unit, and successful completion of a specialized board examination are required to become a psychiatrist. It is a rigorous training of approximately 11 years and psychiatrists are the only professional group who can prescribe medication.

Prior to government licensing, the Korean Association of Clinical Psychology (KACP) issued professional certification to clinical psychologists to be qualified to practice psychotherapy. The certifications are called "Professional Clinical Psychologists (*Yim-sang Sim-li Chun-mun-ga*)" and "Clinical Psychologists (*Yim-sang Sim-li-sa*)." Owing to the constant request from non-medical mental health professionals, in 1996, the mental health welfare law was reformed and the government began issuing licensures of clinical psychologists called "Mental Health Clinical Psychologist (*jung-sin bo-kun yim-sang sim-li-sa*)." There are two types of mental health clinical psychologists, level I (1 *keup*) and level II (2 *keup*). However, in the field, the association-issued certificate and the government-issued licensure are treated similarly. This phenomenon creates confusion for many trainees.

The Korean Association of Counseling and Psychotherapy (KCA), a division of the Korean Psychological Association (KPA), provides certification for "Professional Counseling Psychologists" (*Sang-dam Sim-li Chun-mun-ga*) and "Counseling Psychologists" (*Sang-dam Sim-li-sa*). The KCA's certificate system consists of three categories: supervisor level professional counselor, professional counselor 1 *keup*, and professional counselor 2 *keup*. There are two types of government issued licensure for counselors: "Youth Counselor" by the Ministry of Gender Equality and Family and "School Counselor" by the Ministry of Education and Science.

As for social workers, the Korean government started to issue the "Mental Health Social Workers (*jung-sin bo-kun sa-hyo-bok-ji-sa*)" license to practice psychotherapy. There are two types of mental health social workers: level I (1 *keup*) and level II (2 *keup*).

In the field of developmental psychology and child and family studies, the Division of Developmental Psychology of the KPA issues certifications called "Professional Developmental Psychologist (*bal-dal sim-li chu-mun-ga*)" and "Developmental Psychologists (*bal-dal sim-li-sa*)." In terms of treating children, the Korean Association of Child Studies (KACS) started issuing certificates called "Professional Child Counselor," "Child Counselor 1 keup" and "Child Counselor 2 keup." Also, the Division of Health Psychology of the KAP issues certifications called "Professional Health Psychologist (*kun-kang sim-li chun-mun-ga*)" and "Health Psychologist (*kun-kang sim-li-sa*)." At the same time, in order to meet the demands of many different clientele groups, various therapy methods such as play, art and music therapy are rapidly gaining in popularity. In terms of art therapy, the certificate system consists of three categories: "Professional Art Therapist Supervisor," "Professional Art Therapist," and "Art Therapist."

Finally, with respect to pastoral counseling, the Korean Association for Pastor Counselor (KAPC) currently issues certificates called "Pastor Counseling Supervisor," "Christian Counseling Supervisor," "Pastor Counseling Specialist," "Christian Counseling Specialist," "Pastor Counselor 1 keup," "Pastor Counselor 2 keup," "Christian Counselor 1 keup," and "Christian Counselor 2 keup."

Current counseling and psychotherapy theories, processes, and trends

In terms of training and education, professionals have adopted systems practiced in the West, namely those from the United States and Germany. Most of the textbooks are imported from the United States and translated from English to Korean. Naturally, psychotherapeutic orientations are similar to those of the West: psychoanalytic/psychodynamic, humanistic, cognitive, behavioral, and systemic orientations. However, it is interesting to note that a recent study (Bae, Joo, & Orlinsky, 2003) on the practice characteristics of psychotherapists in Korea suggests that, compared to Western psychotherapists, there is a higher percentage of Korean therapists who practice based on humanistic orientation and non-salient theoretical orientations. This may be due to the generally humanistic Confucian cultural traditions (*In-bon-ju-euh Sa-sang*) in Korean society (Joo, 1996). It seems to be natural consequence given that the Korean culture values harmony in human relationships. Furthermore, in terms of work setting, a majority of Korean professionals reported practicing in public therapeutic settings and working at more than one setting, whereas the majority of Western therapists reported working in private settings, which provide more autonomy in therapeutic practice (Joo, Bae & Orlinsky, 2003; Orlinsky & Ronnestead, 2005).

Though Korea is rapidly becoming Westernized, the issue of applying a Western concept of psychotherapy in a non-Western society is a challenging task for many mental health professionals. Currently, in Korea, as a counter-reaction to rapid Westernization, there are some social movements toward re-examining traditional Korean heritage and values. Many Koreans are experiencing the drawbacks of rapid Westernization and are trying to seek wisdom from their historical roots. This trend is also true in the field of psychotherapy in Korea. Recently some Korean psychotherapists have been attempting to combine Western psychotherapeutic techniques with traditional values from Oriental medicine, Taoism, Zen Buddhism, and Korean Shamanism in order to better attune to the concept of psychotherapy at a time of renewed interest in Korean culture (Kang, 1995; Rhee, 1995; Rhi, 1991).

Indigenous and traditional healing methods

There are two traditional methods to which Koreans resort for solving physical and/or psychological problems: shamanistic healing and oriental medicine.

The basic function of Korean shamanism is to resolve human conflict and anxiety (Kim, 1972b). In traditional Korean society, shamanistic healing played a similar role to that of psychotherapy. Korean shamanism has been largely devoid of any form of religious theory, scripture, organizational, or ethical code. Its focus has been only on the idea of *bok* (meaning "blessing' or "bliss" in English) (Chung, 1985). The idea of *bok* is an important element in Korean mentality. It is fundamentally a belief that bliss, or happiness, is something that is granted by the supernatural forces, rather than something that men achieve through their effort. The opposite of *bok* is *wha*, which means "catastrophe." By *bok*, Koreans usually refer to longevity, material prosperity, health, many sons, and by *wha*, early death, sickness, poverty, and discontinuation of the family line. The fundamental function of the shaman is to placate the supernatural forces in order to avert the *wha* and bring forth the *bok* for his or her clients (Lee, 1983).

In shamanism, the cause of illness is most often attributed to spirit intrusion (i.e., a possession phenomenon). The supernatural beings which are most frequently believed to possess people are ancestral spirits who are angry with their surviving family members. The next most frequently made diagnosis is violation of taboo; for example, the shaman often says that gods have become infuriated because a dead ancestor is buried in the wrong place, or because moving, marriage, journey, or house repair has occurred on the wrong date. After giving the client a diagnosis in terms of the cause of his/her illness, a shaman instructs the clients to perform one of several healing ceremonies, depending upon the severity of illness, the nature of the cause, and the financial status of the client. Ceremonies vary from basic rites such as *son-bi-bim,* which entails giving simple offerings and prayer to the 12 gods to drive away evil spirits from the patients, to *kut,* a grand healing ceremony of chanting, drumming and dancing (Kendall, 1985; Kim, 1972a).

Along with shamanistic healing, Oriental medicine (*han-bang*) has formed an important element in traditional Korean culture through the centuries, and its impact to this day is still very strong. The theoretical framework of Oriental medicine stems from philosophical traditions of ancient China. It is based on the naturalistic view of the unity of man and nature and the mutual correspondence of macrocosm and microcosm, of natural phenomena and physiological phenomena (Colgrave, 1980). It is also based on the theory of *yin-yang* and the five elements. According to the theory, the universe and all objects and phenomena in it are the products of two counterbalancing and counter-playing principles. The two principles of *yin* and *yang,* and the five elements are thought to be in continuous interaction with one another, keeping the endless cycle of becoming and perishing in motion (Colgrave, 1980; Kim & Kim, 1973). The equilibrium state attained through their interaction, or the state of integration of these principles and elements, is thought to be the state of wellbeing in human life, in nature, or in history (Colgrave, 1980). This holistic view of Oriental medicine allows no single part of the human body to be considered separately from its relationship to the whole organism (Rhi, 1976), which also holds to the unity between psyche and soma (Colgrave, 1980).

Consequently, what Western medicine terms "emotional problems" are viewed in Oriental medicine as originating from the malfunctioning of certain organs. For example, depression is attributed to a dysfunction of the liver and the kidney; anxiety to that of heart; and mental confusion to that of the heart and spleen (Kim & Kim, 1973). Oriental medicine aims to strengthen certain weak physical organs (Kim & Kim, 1973; Rhi, 1977). Moreover, the malfunctioning of certain organs is believed to be caused by the organ's corresponding emotion, thoughts, or spirit. For example, one's kidney becomes weak because one is fearful, and one's liver becomes weak because one is depressed.

Rhi (1991) maintains that in Oriental medicine sustaining good emotional health is most important because physical health depends upon emotional health. The fact that Oriental medicine does not make a sharp distinction between psyche and soma has influenced Koreans' perception of illness, and this is especially clear when Koreans express psychological distress in terms of physical symptoms (Kim & Kim, 1973). Though slowly changing, for many Koreans an herbal doctor's diagnosis that a neurotic illness is caused by a bad heart or malfunctioning liver is much more understandable and acceptable than a modern psychiatrist's diagnosis. Furthermore, since traditionally mental illness has been regarded as a stigma in Korea, whereas physical illness tends to evoke sympathy, Koreans patients and their families prefer a physical diagnosis over a psychiatric one. Oriental medicine does not distinguish the psyche and soma from one another, it usually also treats mental patients with herbal medicine. Only in rare cases is some sort of psychotherapy used, and in such cases mainly a short-term, directive, problem-centered strategic type of psychotherapy is typically used. *Tong-Ui-Po-Kam,* the encyclopedia of Oriental medicine practiced in Korea, carries some examples of psychotherapy, all of them characterized by their short-term, problem-centered strategic approach. (Rhi, 1976).

In summary, the two main traditional healing methods in Korea provide some common points. First, the role of healer (a shaman or Oriental medicine doctor) is quite authoritative and directive. It is acceptable in Korean society for healers to demand that the patient or patient's family or even neighbors engage in certain behaviors, such as preparing for the ceremonial ritual and even participating in the process. Second, both methods are short-term, crisis-centered, and strategic. Koreans seek shamans or Oriental medical doctors when they have a specific problem or wish, and a healer is not interested in solving all the problems of a certain client but only in solving a specific problem that is urgent. As soon as the pressing problem is resolved, the therapeutic relationship ends until another urgent problem arises. In this respect, traditional healing in Korea contrasts greatly with the many psychotherapeutic approaches in Western societies.

Research and supervision

Korean counselors and psychotherapists have been actively engaged in conducting research on a variety of topics (Seo et al., 2007). Counselors in Korea need to publish a journal article in major journals if they wish to receive certification from the KCPA and/or KCA. Among several journals, *Korean Journal of Counseling and Psychotherapy* (KJCP), *Korean Journal of Counseling* (KJC), *Korean Journal of Youth Counseling* (KJYC) are the most recognized journals. Examining the studies published in journals, research topics vary, but most studies collected data from college students (approximately 40%), non-clinical adult populations (approximately 27%) and only 10% of studies used samples with actual clients (Seo, Kim, & Kim, 2007). Diversification of research practices and samples are recommended as part of the agenda.

Since there are no legislative restrictions on counseling practices, no standardized supervision model for counselors exist in South Korea. Owing to the lack of agreed-upon supervision models, several Korean researchers report that the content and quality of supervision varies from program to program (Choi & Kim, 2006; Lee, Oh, & Suh, 2007). A study on the counselor education and training program in South Korea suggests that there is a need for strengthening the internship program and supervision (Choi & Kim, 2006). For example in the United States, the Council for Accreditation of Counseling and Related Education Programs (CACREP) created a set of training and supervision standards and evaluates the content and quality of counseling programs seeking certification. A similar model may provide a useful guideline in South Korea for the development of securing counselor and psychotherapists' competence across various fields.

In terms of supervision, students in the Graduate School of Education have to take the Case Supervision course I & II, and in each course at least 10 cases need to be supervised in order to receive a "School Counselor" licensure issued by the Ministry of Education and Science. Another example is that in order to apply for a "Professional Counseling Psychologist" certificate issued by KCA, which is the most recognized certification in the field of counseling and psychotherapy, one has to have 40 individual counseling sessions, at least 30 hours of two group counseling cases, and 10 psychological testing cases supervised.

Strengths, weaknesses, opportunities, and challenges

The strengths of counseling and psychotherapy practice in South Korea include enthusiasm and a vast population of professionals in the field. Though there were conflicts among professional groups in the early stage of development of counseling and psychotherapy, slowly many are recognizing the collaborative work among different professionals. Instead of different professional groups competing with each other, a strong referring or network system is taking place. For example, in order to treat patients with eating disorders, currently, some physicians in the oriental medical institutions (*han-eu-won*) are working with clinical and counseling psychologists as a team. Secondly, government is recognizing the role of counselors and psychotherapists, and an increasing number of school counselors are placed in school settings. Also, government-related institutions such as Youth Counseling Centers, Seoul Elderly Welfare Counseling Centers, etc., are providing more counseling programs for public who are in need of services. Thirdly, mass media are providing opportunities for professionals to educate and promote psychotherapy to clients, potential clients, or the general public. Unlike clients in Western countries, the concept of modern psychotherapy is still new to many Koreans. Often, clients expect the therapist to provide direct answers to their problems. Their passive attitude in therapy often delays or results in a high drop-out rate from therapy. Television and radio programs regarding counseling and psychotherapy are providing valuable information about the field to the public and this leads to changes in perception of social stigma attached to receiving counseling services.

Many issues concerning the weakness of the counseling field in South Korea remain to be addressed. One issue is the confusion related to the licensure or certificate system. There are only three types of certificates (medical, clinical psychology, and social work) issued by the Korean government. However, except in psychiatry, professionals who have government-issued licenses to practice are not respected well socially or financially compared to other professionals with certificates issued by associations. This creates great confusion and financial burden for students or psychotherapists-in-training. Currently, without direction or guidance, they do not know which license to obtain for their career and end up pursuing many different certificates, resulting in wasteful effort and unwarranted expenses.

Also, psychotherapy research concerning patients or clients is lacking. However, studies from various fields such as clinical psychology, health psychology, education, and children's studies concerning the effects of a cognitive-behavioral approach on the psychological state of children and adolescents are increasing (Choi & Kim, 2005; Ha, Oh, Song, & Kang, 2004; Kang & Son, 1998; Lee & Choi, 2005; Yang, 2005). Hopefully, these studies will stimulate further research on psychotherapy process–outcome. Psychotherapy is a collaborative work between a therapist and a client; therefore, it is imperative to study expectations, needs, and experiences of clients in order to provide better services.

There are many opportunities in the field of counseling and psychotherapy in the context of a Korean society based on traditional cultural values that are undergoing Westernization and modernization. As mentioned earlier, the characteristics of traditional healing in Korea can be described as "directive" or "authoritative," "short-term" or "problem (crisis)-centered," and "psychosomatic." It is possible that Koreans have been accustomed to these characteristics of mental healing for more than 5,000 years. However, just within 50 years, Koreans have also been introduced to new modes of psychotherapy which have emphasized the egalitarian relationship between the therapist and the client. Also, clients' participation and involvement in therapy are strongly encouraged (Joo, 1998; Joo, 2009). In this regard, it can be argued that there is a certain gap between the psychotherapists and the general public. The gap is that psychotherapists are too Westernized and the general public is still in the process of becoming more Westernized with respect to the therapeutic relationship. For example, since Korean clients tend to expect a more directive and short-term approach in therapy, is the cognitive-behavioral approach more effective in the Korean setting than a long-term approach such as psychoanalysis (Joo & Orlinsky, 1994)? How can a Western trained psychotherapist in Korea explain or persuade clients about the effectiveness of a collaborative or egalitarian therapeutic relationship over the authoritative or directive approach (Joo, 1998; Joo, 2009)? Since Korea is known for its strong group-oriented culture, is group counseling or therapy more effective than individual therapy? Also, the family's value as a unit is prioritized rather than individual family member's needs in Korea. Does this mean that family therapy is a more desirable mode of therapy in Korea? How important a role do cultural differences vis-à-vis the West play in the therapeutic act? Also, South Korea is becoming an extremely multicultural society and in this context, how can we train counselors and psychotherapists to be multiculturally competent (Joo & Lee, 2010)? These questions are to be explored further for professionals to provide better services to the Korean public.

The mental health field in Korea has grown rapidly, but this development has been more focused on the quantity, rather than quality. Therefore, mental health professionals in the 21st century in South Korea are faced with new challenges related to quality control issues. Firstly, there are major issues with regard to the professional qualifications, ethical issues, and licensure system. Secondly, the education and training of psychotherapists needs to be re-examined. A recent study on the experience and characteristics of professional counselors in Korea suggests that counselors report a great need for specialty training (Joo, Bae & Orlinsky, 2003). Slowly, researchers are becoming aware of the importance of counselor education. Some researchers, such as Son, Yoo and Sim (2003) and Kim (2005) suggest "reflective practice" for the education and professional development of counselors.

Future directions

There are several suggestions for further development of psychotherapy in South Korea. Firstly, a "multidisciplinary" or "team approach" needs to be incorporated more often. Instead of different professional groups competing with each other, a strong referring or network system is needed. Secondly, government-related organizations or associations can play the role of regulators in the psychotherapy field. The organizations consisting of different professionals in the mental health field can issue all licenses in the mental health field and provide guidance or direction in the field. Thirdly, more education or promotion of psychotherapy to clients, potential clients, or the general public is needed. In light of clients' expectation of the therapist to provide direct answers to their problems, it may be helpful for clients to know ahead that their participation in therapy is crucial for effective treatment. Finally, as society becomes more complex and advanced in technology, developing new methods or techniques, such as cyber counseling and psychotherapy, should be explored. According to Kim & Joo (2001), adolescents in Korea often prefer cyber counseling to face-to-face counseling, and such media need to be developed further.

Conclusion

The last half of the 20th century has brought about a rapid and dramatic transformation in Korean society. As one of the Four Tigers of East Asia, South Korea has achieved an incredible record of growth and integrated into the high-tech modern world economy. Three decades ago, Koreans' GDP per capita was comparable with levels in the poorer countries of Africa and Asia. Today its GDP per capita is around $10,000, which is equal to the lesser economies of the European Union. This transformation is reflected in the life styles, values, and psychological attitudes of the Korean people (Chung, 1985).

In conclusion, the modern field of psychotherapy in Korea has developed tremendously within the last 50 years. Korea has given birth to many different professionals in the mental health domain: psychiatrists, clinical and counseling psychologists, counselors, social workers, developmental and health psychologists, play therapists, art and music therapists, and pastoral counselors. Based on the dramatic quantitative development of the mental health field in Korea, the 21st century is deemed a good time for psychotherapists to reflect and re-examine the development of psychotherapy in the context of the past and present. This may provide direction and guidance for the future counselors and psychotherapists in Korea as well as psychotherapists in other countries where they experience similar challenges.

Note

1 For the general public, professionals in the health psychology field are providing therapy for issues related to psychosomatic matters. As Koreans are more likely to report psychological problems as somatic problems, health psychologists are claiming that their role will be recognized soon. Currently, their roles in the field of psychotherapy are not clear.

References

Abbott, A. (1988). *The Systems of Professions*. Chicago, IL: The University of Chicago Press.
Bae, S. H., & Orlinsky, D. E. (1997, December). *Child and Adolescent Therapists in Korea*. Paper presented at the conference of the North American Society for Psychotherapy Research, Tuscon, AZ.
Bae, S. H, Joo, E., & Orlinsky, D. E. (2003). Psychotherapists in South Korea: Professional and practice characteristics. *Psychotherapy: Theory, Research, Practice, Training, 40*(4), 302–316.
Choi, H., & Kim, Y. (2006). A study on the graduate curriculum for the counselor education and training programs in Korea. *The Korean Journal of Counseling and Psychotherapy, 18*(4), 713–729 (in Korean).
Choi, J. (1976). *Social Characteristics of Koreans*. Seoul: Sam-Hwa.
Choi, J. (1996). Indigenous religion. In J. Kim (ed.). *Korean Culture and Heritage: Thoughts and Religion* (Vol. 2) (pp. 228–233). Seoul: Korea Foundation.
Choi, Y., & Kim, E. (2005). Social phobia with concern for offending others: reliability and validity of a Korean version of the TKS. *Korean Journal of Clinical Psychology, 24*(2), 397–411 (in Korean).
Chung, C. (1985). *The changes of Koreans value system before and after 1970's*. Seoul: Sung Kyun Kwan University Press (in Korean).
Colgrave, S. (1980). *Yin and Yang*. Berne and Munich: O.V. Barth Verlag.
Ha, E., Oh, K., Song, D., & Kang, J. (2004). The effects of cognitive-behavioral group therapy for depression and anxiety disorders in adolescents: A preliminary study. *Korean Journal of Clinical Psychology, 23*(2), 263–279 (in Korean).
Howard, K., Pares, S., & English, T. (1996). *Korea: People, Country and Culture*. London: The School of Oriental and African Studies.
Joo, E. (1996). *The Psychotherapeutic Relationship in Korea: Cross-national and Internal Cultural Comparisons*. Unpublished doctoral dissertation, University of Chicago, Department of Psychology, Mental Health Program, Chicago.
Joo, E. (1998). The psychotherapeutic relationship in Korea compared to Western countries. *Korean Journal of Clinical Psychology, 17*(1), 39–56.
Joo, E. (2009). Counselors in South Korea: A qualitative study of senior professionals. *Journal of Counseling and Development, 87*(4). 466–475.
Joo, E. Bae, S. H., & Orlinsky, D. E. (2003). The professional and practice characteristics of Korean psychotherapists: Based on the "International Study of Development of Psychotherapists (ISDP)." *The Korean Journal of Counseling and Psychotherapy, 15*(3), 423–439 (in Korean).
Joo, E., & Han, B. (2000). An investigation of the characteristics of "Classroom Alienated" middle school students in Korea. *Asia Pacific Education Review, 1*(1), 123–128.
Joo, E., & Lee, H. (2010). Qualitative research on the experiences of multicultural counselors working with internationally married female migrants. *Korean Journal of Psychology: General, 29*(4), 817–846 (in Korean).
Joo, E., & Orlisnky, D.E. (1994). The psychotherapeutic relationship in different cultures. In *Psychotherapy East and West: Proceedings of the 16th International Congress of Psychotherapy* (Revised edn) (pp. 82–90). Seoul, Korea: Korean Academy of Psychotherapists.
Kang, M. (2002). *Psychotherapists' Academic Background, Licensure and Practices*. Master's thesis, Duksung Women's University, Seoul, Korea (in Korean).
Kang, H., & Son, C.N. (1998). The effects of cognitive behavioral therapy and relaxation training on reduction of premenstrual syndrome. *Korean Journal of Health Psychology, 3*(1), 141–155 (in Korean).
Kang, S. H. (1995). Training and development of psychotherapy in Korea. In *Psychotherapy East and West: Proceedings of the 16th International Congress of Psychotherapy* (Revised edn) (pp. 337–340). Seoul, Korea: Korean Academy of Psychotherapists.

Kendall, L. (1985). *Shamans, Housewives, and Other Restless Spirits: Woman in Korean Ritual Life*. Honolulu: University of Hawaii Press.

Kim, E., & Joo, E. (2001). Clients' expectations of counseling: A sample of Korean adolescents. *The Korean Journal of Counseling and Psychotherapy, 13*(1), 51–77. (in Korean)

Kim, K. I. (1972a). Folk psychiatry in Korea: Part II. Shaman's healing ceremonies. *Korean Journal of Cultural Anthropology, 5*, 79–106.

Kim, K. I. (1972b). Psychoanalytic considerations of Korean shamanism. *Neuropsychiatry, 11*(2), 121–129. (in Korean)

Kim, K. J., & Kim, M. J. (1973). Socio-cultural problems in the treatment of psychiatric inpatients. *Neuropsychiatry, 12*(4), 245–254. (in Korean)

Kim, J. (1996). *Korean Culture and Heritage: Thoughts and Religion* (Vol. II). Seoul: Korea Foundation.

Kim, J. S. (2005). The significance and application of reflective practice in counselor education. *The Korean Journal of Counseling and Psychotherapy, 17*(4), 813–831. (in Korean)

Lee, J., & Choi, W. (2005). Effects of career group counseling based on the cognitive-behavioral therapy on career development by college students. *Career Education Research, 18*(2), 124–139.

Lee, K. T. (1983). Characteristics of the traditional "Bok" thought and their meanings today. In *The Essence and Realization of the Welfare Society: Collected Essays* (pp. 85–103). Seoul: The Academy of Korean Studies. (in Korean)

Lee, S. M., Oh, I. S., & Suh, S. (2007). Comparison study of Korean and American School counseling for developing a Korean school counseling model. *The Korean Journal of Counseling and Psychotherapy, 19*, 539–567. (in Korean)

Orlinsky, D. E., & Ronnestad, M.H. (eds) (2005). *The Psychotherapists' Perspective: Therapeutic Work, Professional Development and Personal Life*. Washington, DC: American Psychological Association.

Rhee, D. (1995). The Tao and Western psychotherapy. In *Psychotherapy East and West: Proceedings of the 16th International Congress and Psychotherapy* (Revised edn) (pp. 146–156). Seoul, Korea: Korean Academy of Psychotherapists.

Rhi, B. Y. (1972). The analysis in Korea. *Journal of Psychiatry, 11*(4), 209–216 (in Korean).

Rhi, B. Y. (1976). On the treatment of mental disorder in the book of Korean medicine: "Tong-Ui PO-Kam" with a special reference to the five examples of psychological treatment. *Neuropsychiatry, 15*(1), 20–27 (in Korean).

Rhi, B. Y. (1977). Psychosomatic relationship manifested in the book of Korean medicine: "Tong-Ui PO-Kam." *Neuropsychiatry, 16*(1), 23–29 (in Korean).

Rhi, B. Y. (1985). The psychotherapy: past and future. *The Seoul Journal of Psychiatry, 10*(2), 122–128 (in Korean).

Rhi, D. S. (1991). *Taoism and psychotherapy: Special volume for the celebration of D. S. Rhi's 70th birthday*. Tae-gu: Korean Religious and Cultural Research Center.

Seo, Y. S., Kim, D. M., & Kim, D. I. (2007). Current status and prospects of Korean counseling psychology: Research, clinical training, and job placement. *Applied Psychology: An International Review, 56*(1), 107–118.

Son, E., Yoo, S., & Sim, H. (2003). Counselors' self-reflection and professional development. *Korean Journal of Counseling, 4*(3), 367–380 (in Korean).

Yang, S. (2005). The effects of the play activities cognitive behavioral therapy on the perception about parental divorce. *Play Therapy Research, 9*(2), 79–93.

257

Part IV

Counseling and psychotherapy in Europe

22

COUNSELING AND PSYCHOTHERAPY IN BELGIUM

Towards accessible and evidence-based mental healthcare

Nady Van Broeck, Nele Stinckens, and Germain Lietaer

Introduction

Belgium has a total population of about 10 million people, 50% of which are women. The national languages are Dutch (approximately 6 million), French (approximately 4 million), and German (80,000) (National Statistics Office, 2011). The total number of clinical psychologists, psychotherapists, and counselors is unknown because registration is not obligatory. Because of the popularity of the program, every year approximately 700 students obtain their master's degree in psychology with an emphasis on clinical psychology from one of the seven universities[1] that organize the 5 years' university master's training. Estimations of the number of practicing clinical psychologists, psychotherapists, and counselors are not possible because of the variety of basic training among professionals and the lack of a clear definition of their professional activities.

In Belgium, clinical psychology refers to the application of theories, methods, and techniques of psychology in the prevention and treatment of health problems that manifest themselves by means of psychological and/or physical symptoms. Psychotherapy is a specific type of psychological intervention in which different psychological problems, conflicts, and disorders are diagnosed and treated by applying a systematic and coherent whole of methods based on a scientifically validated theory on human functioning and dysfunctioning. As for counseling, it is generally seen as an accessible, pragmatic, and goal-oriented form of social and psychological help aimed at clarifying and solving different problems that arise in various life situations by mobilizing the resources of the person, offering advice and support, and by developing new skills and competencies.

Different professionals with their respective training and competencies are active in the domain of mental healthcare. In primary care the medical general practitioner has an important function, next to several primary mental healthcare services such as centers for mental healthcare (GGZ), centers for community services, and private practices. Within institutions in the secondary (ambulatory) and tertiary (residential) level of healthcare, the responsibility is often carried by the psychiatrist. On these different levels of mental healthcare, multidisciplinary teams of psychiatrists, clinical psychologists, psychiatric nurses, social workers, and counselors work together to offer the best care for an individual and his or her family.

This chapter will discuss the practice of clinical psychology, psychotherapy, and counseling in Belgium, beginning with a brief overview of the field's history. Current training standards and programs will then be presented, along with some information on the key roles these professionals play in healthcare. Finally, current trends, traditional healing practices, issues associated with research, and supervision are described, as well as the field's strengths, weaknesses, opportunities, challenges, and future prospects.

Brief history of clinical psychology, psychotherapy and counseling

Clinical psychology, psychotherapy, and counseling have been present in the healthcare system in Belgium since the scientific developments of these disciplines in the 19th century. Counseling and psychotherapy developed out of the residential psychiatric care by progressive psychiatrists such as Dr. Joseph Guislain. In the beginning of the 20th century, open services in psychiatric hospitals were created, and the first ambulatory centers for 'mental hygiene' saw the light. In 1948, the care for the mentally ill was transferred from the authority of the Ministry of Justice to the Ministry of Health. Between 1945 and 1975, mental healthcare became a more important issue, as evident by the creation of psychiatric services in general hospitals. In the 1980s and 1990s the government decided to change the policy from investment in residential care in psychiatric hospital beds towards more resources for ambulatory mental health services for a larger amount of clients with various psychological problems (Cools, 2005).

This reconversion of hospital beds or tertiary care towards ambulatory mental health or secondary care enhanced the importance of mental healthcare workers such as clinical psychologists, psychotherapists, and counselors (Cools, 2005). The creation of several professional organizations of psychotherapists and counselors fostered the growth of this professional field. Various professional associations emerged and played an important role in developing training standards and enhancing the quality of the delivered work.

In the beginning of the 1990s, initiatives were taken to create a legal framework for the regulation of the practice of these non–medical mental healthcare practitioners. In 1993 a law was passed to protect the title of "psychologist." The Belgian Federation of Psychologists, an umbrella organization that represents the majority of psychological associations in Belgium, facilitated the passing of this law. This protected title of psychologist is delivered on the basis of training criteria and issued by the Ministry of the Independent Professions. The authorization to carry the title of psychologist is not associated with a regulation of the practice, control of quality, or respect of deontological rules. Subsequent law proposals in the last decade to extend the legal framework to the practice of psychologists, psychotherapists, and counselors have remained without success (Foissy, From, & Szafran, 2002; Van Broeck & Lietaer, 2008).

Counselor education programs, accreditation, licensure, and certification

Different Belgian universities offer a master's training in clinical psychology or health psychology. This formal university training recognized and financed by the government takes 5 years to complete, with internship included. Most clinical psychologists take postgraduate training in specialized areas such as clinical neuropsychology, psychodiagnostics, or psychotherapy.

Lacking a formal legal framework, there are no uniform university training requirements recognized by the Ministry of Education for the training of psychotherapists. Nevertheless, the Superior Council for Health proposed minimal training standards (Superior Council for Health, 2005). In this report, psychotherapy training is accessible to healthcare professionals having a master's degree training in a specified series of subject matters.[2] The specialization training consists of a total of 1,200 hours, 500 hours of which are spent in theoretical and technical training and the remaining in supervised clinical practice and a personal psychotherapy experience or learning therapy. These criteria are close to the training standards of the European Federation of Psychologists Associations (EFPA, 2011). The minimal training requirements to have access to this specialized training in psychotherapy are a master's degree in psychology or educational sciences or in medicine. When these minimal standards are not met, the applicant has to follow a complementary master's program in which the necessary basic knowledge and skills can be acquired.

At the moment, different training paths can be followed to become a psychotherapist, which leads to a great diversity of professionals with various levels of knowledge and skills. Five of the universities mentioned earlier offer postgraduate training courses in psychotherapy (Julie Renson Foundation, 2011). These postgraduate programs consist of a minimum 3 years of part-time training and some of them are organized in close collaboration with training institutes or professional associations outside the university. These postgraduate training programs offered by the universities meet the EFPA's criteria (EFPA, 2011) to apply for certification as a psychologist specialized in psychotherapy.

In addition, a range of private training institutes and professional associations of psychotherapists organizes training for psychotherapists. The content, length, and quality of these programs are very diverse. The access to these programs is often less stringent and applicants with various basic diplomas in the domain of human sciences on a professional bachelor level (like social workers, educators, and psychiatric nurses) can enroll (Julie Renson Foundation, 2011)

In Belgium, counselor education programs are mainly organized by private training institutes. Some universities and graduate schools provide postgraduate programs in counseling and continuing education in counseling skills, but there is no uniform academic training for counseling yet. The access to these counseling programs is quite open. There are only a few prerequisites in terms of prior knowledge or education. Applicants with a professional bachelor's degree in the broad domain of human sciences can enlist. The counselor education programs vary in length and educational scope. There are long-term (3–4 year) training programs that intend to develop broad relational and task-oriented counseling skills. There are also more specific training programs that focus on particular counseling settings (e.g. secondary school, palliative services, family work), client problems (e.g. stress symptoms, burn-out, grief and mourning, addiction), and types of counseling work (psychoeducation, crisis intervention, group dynamics). These programs mostly cover a short-term training period of 3–6 months (Julie Renson Foundation, 2011).

In 2004, the Flemish Association for Client-Centered and Experiential Psychotherapy and Counseling (VVCEPC) decided to include counselors as their members and explicitly mentioned this group in the naming of the association. Quality control is maintained over the practice of their counseling members through certification processes involving minimal educational and supervised practice standards. Counselor-members need to complete a postgraduate program that entails at least 3 years of part-time training. The program consists of a minimum 160 hours of theoretical and technical training, at least 120 hours of counseling supervision, and 120 hours for personal counseling experience or learning therapy. Practice standards include regular counseling sessions with a minimum of 5 hours a week. Since there is no legislation yet in Belgium for obtaining certification as a counselor, graduation from a program is not a general requirement; it is only a prerequisite for obtaining a counselor membership in the VVCEPC (VVCEPC, 2011).

The Julie Renson Foundation for mental healthcare publishes an overview of training programs in different areas of counseling and psychotherapy in the Dutch-speaking part of Belgium every 2 years. More than 25 training institutes (institutes for higher education universities and private training institutes) offer a range of 50 training programs in various psychotherapy and counseling methods (Julie Renson Foundation, 2011). Unfortunately, this foundation has not yet published a similar overview of the training programs in Wallonia, the French-speaking region of Belgium.

Because the professional activities of clinical or health psychologists, psychotherapists, and counselors in the domain of healthcare are not legally regulated in Belgium, there is no system of licensing that authorizes the practice of these professionals, and no register of authorized professionals. Further, there is no official accreditation process of training programs or training institutes, or a regulatory body that handles professional matters, complaints, and malpractice. In the last 10 years, however, efforts have been made to create a legal framework for these so-called 'new health professions' of clinical psychologists, psychotherapists and counselors. Although progress has been made in defining the different professions and their training requirements, at the moment a law has not yet been voted.

Current counseling and psychotherapy theories, processes, and trends

Most professionals delivering clinical psychological, psychotherapeutic and counseling services rely on the main theoretical frameworks in the domain of human mental functioning. Four main paradigms can be distinguished, namely the psychodynamic view, the client-centered and experiential approach, the cognitive-behavioral approach, and the family and systems view. A growing number of professionals describe their approach as integrative and combine elements of different theoretical models (Lietaer, Van Broeck, Dekeyser, Stroobants, & Trijsburg, 2005a). The combination of a cognitive-behavioral and system approaches is popular in the northern part of Belgium. In the southern part, the integration of the psychodynamic and the systems approach is more frequently used (Lietaer, Van Broeck, Dekeyser, Stroobants, & Trijsburg, 2005a). A possible explanation for this finding is the stronger influence of the Anglo-Saxon culture on the northern, Flemish-speaking part of the country (Lietaer et al., 2005a), whereas Wallonia is more heavily influenced by France and other Latin countries.

An interesting trend is the expansion of the scope of the work of clinical psychologists, psychotherapists, and counselors in somatic healthcare. Clinical psychologists, psychotherapists, and counselors work with somatically ill patients who often present with psychological difficulties. Hospitals actively engage psychologists, psychotherapists, and counselors in different medical specialisms, such as oncology, cardiology, nephrology, pneumology, gynecology, pediatrics, genetic counseling, and reproductive medicine (Lietaer et al., 2005a).

Another trend can be observed where the reimbursement of mental healthcare services is concerned. According to the actual regulations, mental healthcare delivered by medical doctors (i.e., general practitioners, psychiatrists, or other medical specialists) is reimbursed by the obligatory health insurance that covers a large part of the expenses of healthcare for all citizens. When these services are delivered by professionals that are not medical doctors they are not reimbursed. However, to meet the needs of their clients, different public and private health insurance companies offer partial reimbursement of these services delivered by clinical psychologists and psychotherapists. Patients or clients need to investigate themselves to find out whether their insurance companies will reimburse them for services received for a specific health problem from a particular clinical psychologist, psychotherapist, or counselor.

The most important trend in mental healthcare is the growing demand for a better, more accessible community-based primary mental healthcare (Cools, 2008; Kazdin & Blase, 2011; Van Audenhove, 2005). At various levels initiatives are taken to develop, finance, organize, and evaluate a variety of community-based and low threshold primary mental care services, in locations close to the client/patient and if necessary in the living environment by means of community outreach (Cools, 2008). The realization of this objective to offer qualitatively good, affordable, accessible, effective, and efficient mental healthcare to large numbers of people in the community can benefit from the development of new forms of social media. Indeed, the number of mental health services delivered by means of the internet and the social media is rapidly growing (Riper et al., 2011; White, 2010).

Indigenous and traditional healing methods

After a period of lesser interest in spirituality and religion, recently Belgium has witnessed a growing interest in this type of counseling. A large portion of the population seeks spiritual development and a better quality of life by doing yoga, meditation, and various types of practices that connect the body and mind (Leijssen, 2009). Training for these can be offered in a classical way or in a more contemporary format, such as the internet (Leijssen, 2009).

In the immigrant population it is possible that the use of mainstream mental health services is combined with traditional healing methods. First- and second-generation immigrants of North African origin, mainly Morocco, sometimes combine traditional healing methods with Western scientifically based medicine. However, Belgian policy makers are often worried about possible abuse of these methods, especially if patients or clients abandon regular treatment. A governmental organization in Belgium, the 'Centre d'Information et d'Avis sur les Organisations Sectaires Nuisibles (Centre of Information and Opinion on Harmful Sectarian Organizations, CIAOSN), undertakes the task of examining unknown health practices. In cases where there is a suspicion of practices that harm the mental or physical health of the client or patient, they file a report that can form the basis of a formal complaint.

Research and supervision

In Belgium, two different stands towards research in clinical psychology, psychotherapy, and counseling can be distinguished. A growing number of clinical psychologists and psychotherapists adopt an "Anglo-Saxon" research tradition with emphasis on empirically validated treatments. In order to enhance the quality of their clinical work, they strive towards the development and the use of empirically based methods of diagnosis and interventions (Lietaer, Van Broeck, Dekeyser, Stroobants, & Trijsburg, 2005b). Different universities have research groups working in the domain of experimental psychopathology and psychotherapy research. Via translational research they make efforts to translate their findings from the laboratory to clinical practice. In healthcare institutions, the effectiveness of different interventions is examined in randomized clinical trials. At the universities, clinical psychologists are trained to be "scientist-practitioners." Students in clinical psychology have to carry out a practice-oriented research project resulting in a master's thesis. Most of the scientific research in the domain of clinical psychology, psychotherapy and counseling is funded by the Fund of Scientific Research, the research funds of each university, important foundations, such as the King Baudoin Foundation, and European research funds.

At the same time, a group of clinical psychologists, psychotherapists, and counselors do not follow the Anglo-Saxon model. In line with their theoretical frameworks, they emphasize the importance of personal experience and growth, personality and relationship capacities, clinical practice, and evidence-based practice (Lietaer et al., 2005b). The personal psychotherapy process is often seen as the most important element in the specialized training as a psychotherapist, combined with supervised practice. In selecting research topics, they have a preference for single or multiple case studies and qualitative methods which they consider as more appropriate for research in the domain of individual psychological suffering.

Finally, an interesting research trend worth mentioning is the growing emphasis on evaluation of the effectiveness and efficacy of psychological, psychotherapeutic, and counseling interventions, and on the study of underlying processes of psychopathology and change (Hermans, Eelen, & Orlemans, 2006). Interesting research initiatives generated by the Flemish Association for Mental Healthcare (VVGG, 2008) and of the Catholic University of Leuven (Stinckens, Elliott, & Leijssen, 2009) are examples of this evolution.

In terms of supervision, supervised practice constitutes an important part of training programs of clinical psychologists, psychotherapists, and counselors. A clinical internship of 36 weeks under the supervision of a clinical psychologist is required to obtain a master's degree. Recently, an additional year of supervised training is required to obtain a Europsy diploma (EFPA, 2011). To obtain a postgraduate degree in psychotherapy and the certificate of psychologists specialized in psychotherapy of the EFPA, an additional period of supervised clinical practice of 1,200 hours is part of the training requirements, in combination with theoretical technical training and personal development (EFPA, 2011). In the training programs for counselors, the hours of required supervised practice vary depending on the program (Julie Renson Foundation, 2011).

Strengths, weaknesses, opportunities, and challenges

In Belgium, the education and training context represents a real strength. The formal university training program for master's in clinical psychology and other human sciences represents a good base for the further training of professionals that can deliver psychological and psychotherapeutic services of good quality. Different training programs in psychology, social work, and nursing at the bachelor's level prepare for specialization in various types of counseling work. The different postgraduate training programs in psychotherapy offer the opportunity to acquire specialized knowledge and skills. The model of clinical psychologists and psychotherapists as scientist-practitioners, adopted by some training institutes, accentuates the importance of the integration of scientific developments in practice.

The lack of a legal regulation of the professions of clinical psychologist, psychotherapist, and counselor, on the other hand, can be considered as a serious weakness. Quality control and control of ethical conduct is complicated when professionals work without licensing and registration. It also leads to patient misunderstandings, as it may not be clear to them which services can be obtained from what professionals. Absence of a legal definition complicates integration of these professionals and their services in the healthcare system (Van Broeck & Lietaer, 2008).

Another weakness is situated in the organization of mental healthcare in Belgium. In the mental healthcare system there is a lack of balance between the needs on the different levels of healthcare, on the one hand, and the financial investments on the other. In the Belgian mental healthcare system, investment in primary and secondary mental healthcare for large groups of people who need professional help with emerging social and psychological problems and acute mental health questions is insufficient (Cools, 2009; Van Audenhove, 2005). This leads to long waiting lists and missed opportunities to intervene at an early stage. Large investments are made in tertiary care, mostly on a residential base for a smaller group of patients with more serious and chronic mental health problems. Efforts are made to inverse this financing pyramid, but a lot of changes are still to be made.

Weaknesses in the field nevertheless open up new opportunities for improvement. At the moment, the federal government and the healthcare system are ready for the development of a better, more accessible, efficient, and effective primary mental healthcare. The current Minister of Health made the reorganization and development of primary mental healthcare one of his priorities (Van Deurzen, 2011). Different initiatives are taken to develop screening instruments that can distinguish clients who have to be referred to second-line ambulatory or third-line residential treatment from those who can benefit from first-line, short-term, problem-focused psychological help (Rijnders & Heene, 2010). Interesting projects for the development of a healthcare plan that reaches larger groups of clients by means of community-based interventions (White, 2010; Bennett-Levy et al., 2010) and internet-based programs (Riper et al., 2011) are welcomed as good examples. New programs for specific populations like children and adolescents by means of new forms of social media (e.g., Facebook and Twitter) and the development of "serious gaming" (games helping the gamer to acquire knowledge, insight, and skills in matters of mental health) are emerging rapidly.

A challenge for the years to come is the creation of a legal framework for the practice and training in clinical psychology, psychotherapy, and counseling in Belgium. This framework should be explicit about the content of graduate and postgraduate training and impose ethical and deontological standards of practice. Once this is achieved, efforts have to be made to integrate the new professions in the healthcare system at different levels in order to enhance the quality and the availability of these services for the clients and patients that need them. It will be a real challenge to enhance the accessibility and the quality of mental healthcare for the patients and at the same time avoid the negative side effects of a complex and overregulated set of rules.

Future directions

In Belgium the development of a sound legal regulation of the new health professions that clearly defines competencies and training is an important task for the near future. Clients and patients will benefit from regulation in which professional titles inform in a transparent way on the competencies of the professional. Counseling and psychotherapy are not seen as separate professions but as professional activities in which colleagues from different basic professions can be trained. Clients, for instance, will have the choice to ask the help of a psychiatrist-psychotherapist, psychologist-psychotherapist or nurse-counselor. Mentioning the basic training before the specialization trainings offers the possibility to address the professional that is most suitable to deliver the services a client requires.

Reversal of the financing system with more investments in primary and secondary mental healthcare for large patient groups and clients with new problems and demands is recommended. Recognition of the role of clinical psychologists, psychotherapists, and counselors would permit full integrate of these professionals within the different levels of the healthcare system. Definition of these professions would also be the first step to arrange reimbursement of services delivered by these professionals. Easy access to these services for patients and clients at risk is important to prevent the development, aggravation, and chronification of mental health problems and can contribute to the rehabilitation of clients and patients after recovery.

The urge of financing agencies to cut the costs by offering more efficient and effective help in a shorter period of time stimulates the development of treatment guidelines and promotes scientific evaluation of the effectiveness and efficiency of these treatment packages. The possible negative effects on the quality of care of this evolution can be limited by keeping in mind that the foundation of mental healthcare is the helping relationship, even if it is virtual. Mental healthcare is a multidisciplinary enterprise, in which different professions use their specific diagnostic and therapeutic knowledge and skills. An appropriate legal framework, in accordance with the regulations in other countries will permit society to control the quality of the services and respect ethical codes. It will also facilitate a clear communication to the patient so that people can easily find and have access to the help they need.

Conclusion

In Belgium there is a rather well-developed system of education and training in clinical psychology, psychotherapy, and counseling. The main theoretical models for psychological diagnosis and treatment are represented in the field of clinical psychology, psychotherapy, and counseling. Evolutions towards the integration of different models are on their way. The model of the clinical psychologist, psychotherapist, and counselor as scientist-practitioners becomes more important with the growing interest in research. This research interest considers the results of the intervention as well as the underlying processes of change and the importance of the helping relationship. More efforts are needed to translate scientific findings to everyday practice.

On a community level, information about mental health and low threshold access to primary mental healthcare in the community for common mental health problems such as stress, depression, and anxiety, and for educational and relational problems have to be developed.

On the first line we witness a growing investment in psycho-education, prevention, early detection, outreaching, and generalistic, short-term care for mental health problems. Use of the new social media and the internet in a scientifically controlled and qualitatively sound way can facilitate the realization of this objective.

Where secondary and tertiary psychological and psychotherapeutic help is concerned, a translation of the scientific knowledge in the domain of psychology to the practice of clinical psychologists, psychotherapists, and counselors can enhance efficiency and efficacy of their work in terms of mental healthcare. Emphasis on the importance of different relational and cultural contexts of the person fosters an evolution towards more contextual approaches or combinations of individual and family and group interventions. Furthermore, the ways of offering help will be expanded from the community, group, and individual interventions to other types of help offered by means of the internet.

We sincerely hope that our efforts to further develop scientifically based and accessible counseling and psychotherapeutic services at the primary, secondary, and tertiary levels of healthcare will result in the best possible help for a large number of people confronted with psychological and relational problems at a certain moment in their lives.

Notes

1 Catholic University of Louvain (KUL and UCL), Ghent University (UGent), Brussels University (VUB and ULB), Liège University (ULg), Mons University.
2 Psychotherapy training is open to professionals having obtained a master's degree in a training program containing all of the following subjects: anthropology, developmental psychology, neurosciences, psychopathology and psychiatry, learning theory, psychodynamic psychology, general and clinical psychological assessment and psychodiagnostics, introduction in psychopharmacology, basic counseling skills, introduction in psychotherapeutic methods and professional ethics (Superior Council for Health 2005).

References

Bennett-Levy, J., Richards, D., Farrand, P., Christensen, H., Griffiths, K., Kavanagh, D. & Williams, C. (eds) (2010). *Oxford Guide to Low Intensity CBT Interventions*. New York: Oxford University Press Inc.

Cools, B. (2005). Internationale ontwikkelingen in de geestelijke gezondheidszorg [International developments in mental health care]. *Psyche, 17,* 20–23.

Cools, B. (2008). Geestelijke gezondheid bevorderen en psychische problemen voorkomen [Fostering mental health and preventing psychological problems]. *Tijdschrift Klinische Psychologie, 2,* 119–139.

Cools, B. (2009). Geestelijke gezondheidszorg tussen subsidie en commercie [Mental health care between subsidy and commerce]. *Alert, 5,* 19–28.

Cools, B. (2009). Commercialisering geestelijke gezondheid: bedreiging of kans [Commercializing mental health: Threat or opportunity]. *Sociaal, 1,* 7–11.

EFPA, European Federation of Psychologists Associations (2011). *Training Standards for Psychologists Specializing in Psychotherapy.* Retrieved October 10, 2011 from www.efpa.eu/professional-development/training-standards-for-psychologists-specializing-in-psychotherapy.

Foisy, M.-L., From, F., & Szafran, W. A. (2002). Psychotherapy in Europe: Belgium. In A. Pritz (ed.), *Globalized Psychology* (pp. 39–70). Vienna: Facultas Universitätsverlag.

Hermans, D., Eelen, P., & Orlemans, H. (2006). *Inleiding tot de Gedragstherapie* [Introduction to behaviour therapy]. Halen: Bohn, Stafleu, Van Loghum.

Julie Renson Foundation. (2011). *Gids therapeutische opleidingen 2009–2011. Overzicht van psychotherapeutische programma's in Vlaanderen* [Guide for therapeutic training programs. Survey of programs in Flanders]. Retrieved July 22, 2010 from www.kbs-frb.be

Kazdin, A. E., & Blase, S. L. (2011). Rebooting psychotherapy research and practice to reduce the burden of mental illness. *Perspectives on Psychological Science, 6,* 21–37.

Leijssen, M. (2009). *Tijd voor de ziel. Spiritualiteit en zingeving vanuit psychotherapie* [Time for the soul. Spirituality and meaning in life: A psychotherapeutic perspective]. Tielt: Lannoo.

Lietaer, G., Van Broeck, N., Dekeyser, M., Stroobants R., & Trijsburg W. (2005a). Het professionele profiel van de psychotherapeut in België. Deel 1. Sociodemografische kenmerken, opleiding en werkkader [Professional profile of the Belgian psychotherapist. Part I. Sociodemographic characteristics, training and work setting]. *Tijdschrift voor Klinische psychologie, 35*(1), 7–29.

Lietaer, G., Van Broeck, N., Dekeyser, M., Stroobants R., & Trijsburg W. (2005b). Het professionele profiel van de psychotherapeut in België. Deel 2. Werkstijl, visies en attitudes ten aanzien van inhoudelijke aspecten van het beroep [Professional profile of the Belgian psychotherapist. Part II. Working style, views and attitudes relating to content aspects of the profession]. *Tijdschrift voor Klinische Psychologie, 35*(1), 30–54.

National Statistics Office (2011). *Bevolking* [Population]. Retrieved August, 20, 2011 from http//statbel.fgov.be/nl/statistieken/cijfers:bevolking

Riper, H., Spek, V., Boon, B., Conijn, B., Kramer, J., Martin-Abello, K., & Smit, F. (2011). Effectiveness of E-self-help interventions for curbing adult problem drinking: A meta-analysis. *Journal of Medical Internet Research, 13,* 42–49.

Rijnders, P., & Heene, E. (2010). *Kortdurende psychologische interventies* [Short-term psychological interventions]. Boom: Meppel.

Superior Council of Health (2005). *Psychotherapies: Definitions, practice, accreditation criteria (Hgr N° 7855 –* Approved by the workgroup on 21/06/2005 and validated by the Council on 13/07/2005). Retrieved May 5, 2011 www.health.fgov.be/eportal/SearchResults/index.htm.

Stinckens, N., Elliott, R., & Leijssen, M. (2009). Bridging the gap between therapy research and practice in a person-centered/experiential therapy training program. The Leuven systematic case study research protocol. *Person-centered and Experiential Psychotherapies, 8*(2), 143–162.

Van Audenhove, C. (2005). Psychiatrische thuiszorg als evidence based practice [Psychiatric home care as evidence based practice]. *Tijdschrift voor Welzijnswerk, 26*(6), 5–12.

Van Broeck, N., & Lietaer, G. (2008). Psychology in Health care: A review of legal regulations in 17 European Countries. *The European Psychologist, 13*(1), 53–63.

Van Deurzen, J. (2011). *Mental Health Policy Plan of the Minister of Health, Welfare and the Family of the Flemish Community.* Retrieved October 10, 2011 from www.ministerjovandeurzen.be/nlapps/docs/default.asp?fid=53

Vlaamse Vereniging voor Geestelijke Gezondheid (VVGG) [Flemish Society of Mental Health] (2008). *Home.* Retrieved October 2, 2011 from www.vvgg.be

Vlaamse Vereniging voor Cliëntgericht-experiëntiële Psychotherapie en Counseling (VVCEPC) [Flemish Society of Client-centered/experiential Psychotherapy and Counseling] (2011). *Home.* Retrieved October 2, 2011 from www.vvcepc.be.

White, J. (2010). The STEPS model: A high volume, multi-level, multi-purpose approach to address common mental health problems. In J. Bennett-Levy, H. Christensen, P. Farrand, K. Griffiths, D. Kavanagh, B. Klein, M. Lau, J. Proudfoot, D. Richards, L. Ritterband, J. White, & C. Williams. (eds), *Oxford Guide to Low Intensity CBT Interventions* (pp. 331–337). Oxford: University Press.

23

COUNSELING AND PSYCHOTHERAPY IN DENMARK

Counseling the "happiest people on Earth"

Nanja H. Hansen and Andrea L. Dixon

Introduction

In the 21st century the impacts of professional counselors/psychologists reach far beyond the borders of any nation or continent, and the mental health profession takes on varying forms from one country to the next. Denmark is one example of a nation that has a long history in the mental health profession and has much to offer the international counseling network. Denmark is consistently voted one of the "Best Countries in the World" to live in and consistently ranked as the "happiest place on Earth" (Statistics Denmark, 2010; White, 2007), and since the early 1970s the country has had a population of more than 5 million inhabitants. In January 2010, immigrants and descendants constituted 9.8% of the total Danish population (543,000 persons). Usually about 54% of all immigrants and descendants originate from Europe and represent about 200 different countries, including Turkey, Germany, Iraq, Pakistan, Somalia, and Arab countries (Statistics Denmark, 2010). Overall, Denmark remains a very homogenous country. Over 90% of the population is Danish ethnically, culturally, and in terms of spoken language.

The counseling/psychology profession has rapidly expanded and become more acceptable and affordable for individuals to access. Today, the current counseling/psychology theories, processes, and trends illustrate the need for counseling/psychology services and interventions for individuals throughout the country. It should be noted that a counseling degree in the United States is equivalent to a psychology degree in Denmark, and that individuals holding a degree in psychology practice psychotherapy (Dixon & Hansen, 2010). Therefore counseling/psychotherapy is used interchangeably throughout the chapter.

In this chapter, we offer an overview of the Danish counseling/psychology profession. First, we offer a brief history of counseling/psychology in the country. We then offer information regarding Danish counselor/psychology education programs, accreditation, and licensure and certification processes, as well as the current counseling/psychology theories, process, and trends in Denmark. Danish indigenous and traditional healing methods and current research and supervision trends are overviewed. Finally, we present our impressions of the strengths, weaknesses, opportunities, and challenges for the Danish counseling/psychology profession and for the country's future directions in mental health.

Brief history of counseling and psychotherapy

The history of counseling/psychology in Denmark stems from the philosophy movement, specifically influenced by Danish philosopher, Harald Høffding (Funch, 2000; Køppe, 1983; Lundberg, 2001; Pind, 2009). However, it was after the focused work of Alfred Lehmann, who established the first psychophysical laboratory (the University Psychological Laboratory, UPL) in Copenhagen in 1886, that psychology became a distinct discipline (Funch, 2000; Pedersen, 1990; Pind, 2009). Lehmann established the experimental approach as the main investigative tool at the UPL, today the second oldest psychological laboratory in the world (Funch, 2000), and Lehmann became the first professor in experimental counseling/psychology at the University of Copenhagen in 1919 (Hjørlund, 2000). Edgar John Rubin became the most well-known Danish figure in the history of counseling/psychology after Lehmann's death (Lundberg, 2001). Rubin succeeded Lehmann as manager of UPL in 1922. Best known for his ambiguous pictures (e.g., the vase/opposed profiles) illustrating the figure-ground phenomenon, Rubin's methodology was that of the old philosophical school (Funch, 2000; Pedersen, 1990). Although Rubin's work conflicted with Lehmann's ideology, he became a leader in Danish counseling/psychology, assuming instruction of experimental pedagogy and chairing the psychology department in Copenhagen from 1921 to 1951 (Pind, 2009).

The Danish counseling/psychological movement rapidly progressed until the end of the 19th century, and in 1905 The Association for Psychological Research was established in Denmark (Hjørlund, 2000). In 1914, the Association for Experimental Pedagogy was established, which marked the beginning of Danish school psychology (Hjørlund, 2000).

Throughout the 1920s and 1930s, numerous counseling/psychology-focused publications were produced by Danish professionals, and psychology in schools flourished. As a consequence of the World Wars, there was marked need for school psychologists and in the social services, prisons and military systems, and in business (Huey & Britton, 2002; Poulsen, 2007).

In 1947 the Danish Psychological Association (Dansk Psykolog Forening; DPF) was established (Hjørlund, 2000; Poulsen, 2007). By 1957, the need for licensure expectations and laws was raised by the joint council of Nordic countries, and in 1958 council members made recommendations; however, it took 37 years before psychological licensure guidelines/requirements took effect (Jensen, 2000). In the late 1940s, the first counseling/psychological treatment centers were established in Denmark, and in 1950 the first child psychology center opened at the University of Copenhagen (Almstrup, 2000; Hjørlund, 2000).

It was in the late 1960s that a student-led protest at the University of Copenhagen had great influence on the counseling/psychology profession in Denmark (Hjørlund, 2000; Karpatschof, 2000). The protest was a reaction to the Vietnam War, capitalism, and nuclear weapons, as well as the drastic increases in the number of students at the university. With no increases in the number of university professors, the student increases led to poor educational conditions (Hjørlund, 2000). After the highly publicized protest, international psychological ideas such as existentialism and Marxism were introduced into Danish counseling/psychology (Dixon & Hansen, 2010).

The 1980s was a period of great change in counseling/psychology. First, the number of international refugees relocating to Denmark throughout the 1990s (mainly from East Europe and Africa) created needs for additional applied counseling/psychological interventions (Alberdi, 2010; Hjørlund, 2000). In addition, in 1985 The Center for Brain Damage was founded at the College of Humanistic Studies at the University of Copenhagen by the neurological-psychologist Anne-Lise Christensen, which represented the focus on cognitive approaches in Danish counseling/psychology (Hjørlund, 2000). Finally, throughout the 1980s, the Nordic countries developed their own set of counseling/psychological ethical codes (Lunt, 1999), apart from the European Federation of Psychologists' Associations Charter of Professional Ethics for Psychologists (EFPA, 2011).

The increasing need for Danish counselors/psychologists continued in the 1990s for the purposes of working with emergency medical teams for crisis intervention situations. In the late 1990s, the number of counseling/psychology students had greatly increased and so had the membership of the DPA (Hjørlund, 2000). Overall, major expansion and development has continued throughout the 20th and 21st centuries, including the Danish government's work to make counseling/psychology services more affordable for individuals throughout the nation, and increases in research, training opportunities, and licensure opportunities.

Counselor education programs, accreditation, licensure, and certification

Currently, there are four main counselor/psychology education programs in Denmark, which are located at Copenhagen University, Århus University, Ålborg University, and Odense/South Danish University. All four universities offer a bachelor's and master's program in counseling/psychology. The structure of the counseling/psychology program is the same: a bachelor's degree in counseling/psychology takes 3 years to accomplish. Near the end of the third year each student must write a bachelor's thesis in order to fulfill the graduation requirements. A master's degree in counseling/psychology takes 2 years to complete. During the first year all coursework is completed. During the second year, each student completes 16 weeks of internship, which is followed by the mandatory writing of a thesis on a topic chosen by the student. While the bachelor's degree requirements and the structure of programs are the same at all four universities, the structure of the master's programs in psychology/counseling at the four universities shows some variation.

In Denmark, two additional degrees, the specialist and supervisor degree, can be earned throughout the counselor's/psychologist's career. Once licensed, Danish counselors/psychologists may continue education and earn a degree as a specialist in a multitude of areas, which are grouped into three main areas: (1) child psychology, (2) adult psychology, and (3) work and organizational psychology (Poulsen, 2007; Dansk Psykolog Forening [Danish Psychological Association] n.d.a).

Regarding the accreditation process of the training institutions in Denmark, the council of accreditation, ACE Denmark, was founded in 2007. Syddansk University's counseling/psychology program was the first to be accredited in 2009. Copenhagen, Århus, and Ålborg Universities are not accredited as of now. Though it has not been scheduled yet, the plan is for all three universities to have their counseling/psychology programs accredited by 2014 (I. Andersen & S. Poulsen, personal communication, October 8, 2010). Overall, ACE Denmark ensures the quality, and helps to make visible the quality and relevance of higher education in Denmark. As a foundation for its accreditations of the Danish training programs, the council makes a careful evaluation based on accreditation reports. The council must contribute to the visible quality of Danish university degrees, to their equivalence to international and European university degrees, and ensure that they meet the requirements of the highest international standards. Therefore, ACE Denmark actively seeks to draw in international experience and knowledge on accreditation in its work.

The accreditation process begins with meetings which are held by ACE and representatives from the different educational programs seeking accreditation. At the same time an accreditation panel is put together consisting of professional experts and students. The evaluation process begins once the documented report from the educational program is submitted. The documented report includes five criteria which must be documented by the educational program seeking accreditation. These five criteria are (1) a need for the degree (i.e., relevance and quality), (2) the degree is based on research and connected to a highly qualified and active research community, (3) the degree's professional profile and level including internal quality insurance, (4) the degree's structure and organization, and (5) continuous internal quality insurance of the degree (ACE Denmark, n.d.a).

Licensure in Denmark is not a requirement in order to work and use the title of counselor/ psychologist. Though licensure is elected by the individual counselor/psychologist, the majority do work towards licensure (Poulsen, 2007). Today, licensure can only be granted by the Danish Supervisory Board of Psychological Practice and the decisions of the board cannot be appealed to another authority (Psykolognævnet [Danish Board of Psychological Practice], n.d.a).

In order to achieve licensure, the counselor/psychologist has to have earned a master's of counseling/psychology, to have completed a minimum of 2 years of employment postgraduation, and to have received 160 hours of supervision from a previously licensed counselor/psychologist. Forty of those hours must come from an external supervisor and 40 hours must come from group supervision. In addition, a minimum of 500 contact hours are required in the area of assessment, and 500 contact hours are required in the area of intervention. Another minimum of 200 contact hours of group therapy is required (Psykolognævnet [Danish Board of Psychological Practice], n.d.b).

Certification, as it is known in the United States, does not currently exist in the same manner in Denmark. In Denmark the term "certified as a specialist in psychotherapy, child psychology" or "certified as a supervisor" is used (I. Andersen & S. Poulsen, personal communication, October 8, 2010). The counselor/psychologist receives a certificate showing/proving that he or she has fulfilled all the licensure, specialist, or supervisory requirements (I. Andersen & St. Poulsen, personal communication, October 8, 2010).

Current counseling and psychotherapy theories, processes, and trends

The field of counseling/psychology in Denmark is greatly influenced by the international counseling/ psychology community. The main theories currently used in Denmark are the psychodynamic (including both psychoanalytic and existential/humanistic theories), cognitive-behavioral, and systemic/narrative theories. In addition, developmental psychopathology and transcultural theories are emerging (B. Møhl, personal communication, October 6, 2010). With its roots in psychodynamic theory, Bateman and Fonagy's metallization based therapy (Jørgensen, Kjølbye, & Møhl, 2010) is gaining popularity in Denmark. Moreover, based in the more cognitive/ behavioral theories are dialectical behavioral therapy and acceptance and commitment therapy (Jørgensen et al., 2010), which has also been implemented within the public healthcare sector.

The systemic and narrative theories are more widely used by counselors/psychologists who are employed within private treatment facilities or corporate businesses, although systemic and narrative theories are also used by the Knowledge Center for Trans Cultural Psychology in the public healthcare sector (B. Møhl, personal communication, October 6, 2010). While a multitude of counseling/psychological theories are used by counselors/psychologists within the various private and public settings, the main theories used are those mentioned above.

There are a multitude of counseling/psychology and psychotherapy processes that currently exist in Denmark. Within the last 20 years a shift in the way Danish counselors/psychologists view and work within their theoretical framework has taken place. Twenty years ago, the majority of Danish counselors/psychologists were working from a psychodynamic framework. As cognitive-behavioral theories emerged, a sharp division between the two theoretical frameworks emerged. For years this polarization played a central role within the field of counseling/psychology in Denmark. Slowly, the two theoretical frameworks, (psychodynamic and cognitive-behavioral) began opening up to each other's framework and methods, and today a more integrative approach is used in working with clients especially within the public health-care sector (I. Andersen & S. Poulsen, personal communication, October 8, 2010). This process is seen in the implementation of theories and methods such as dialectical behavioral therapy, acceptance and commitment therapy, metallization-based therapy, and mindfulness based approaches which are currently being used within the counseling/psychological field.

Moreover, changes within school psychology have taken place. Previously, both school counselors/psychologists and clinical counselors/psychologists worked within the school system (Mortensen, 2000). School counselors/psychologists dealt with (and still do) testing and placement of children who had academic difficulties; whereas, clinical psychologists dealt with issues relating to their emotional health, whether it related to issues with other classmates or problems within the home (Mortensen, 2000). After the psychology law of 1994, when licensure for counselors/psychologists was introduced, it was decided to terminate the division of school and clinical psychologists at Pædagoisk Psykologisk Rådgivning (PPR) (Pedagogical Psychological Counseling Services). At this time both groups (school and clinical counselors/psychologists) had to go through the same educational standards in order to meet the qualifications for obtaining licensure (I. Andersen, personal communication, October 8, 2010). Previously, clinical counselors/psychologists had to have a 2-year supplementary education in clinical psychology (which in scope was equivalent to the licensure requirements), while school psychologists had to have a teacher's certificate. From the middle of the 1990s both clinical and school counselors/psychologists were defined as counselors/psychologists (I. Andersen, personal communication, October 8, 2010).

In addition, the process of implementing European counselor/psychologist certification requirements is in progress. The Danish Psychological Association has participated in developing a collective counselor/psychologist certificate since 1999. The aim of the project has been to develop a shared set of minimum standards for a counseling/psychology degree for the European countries so that the educational levels are heightened for the degree, and so that the mutual recognition of counselors/psychologists is simplified and the mobility of counselors/psychologists within European countries is made easier (Dansk Psykolog Forening [Danish Psychological Association], (n.d.c.). In 2009, the EFPA approved both the European counselor/psychologist certificate and the specialist degree in psychotherapy. The Danish Psychological Association is currently making arrangements to implement the two European certificates in Denmark. As of January 2012 the Danish Psychological Association has been able to begin awarding the EuroPsy certificate to Danish licensed counselors/psychologist.

Numerous trends currently exist in the counseling/psychology field in Denmark. In terms of professional trends, there are over 5,597 licensed counselors/psychologists practicing or training in Denmark at this time (Psykolognævnet [Danish Board of Psychological Practice], n.d.c), based on the most current statistics. Though there has been a shift in the number of counselors/psychologists going from working in the public sector to working in the private sector, 72% of all Danish counselors/psychologists still work within the public sector (Københavns Universitet [Copenhagen University], n.d.). Approximately 50% of Danish counselors/psychologists work within the healthcare and welfare institutions: hospitals, and inpatient and outpatient treatment facilities. The second largest area of public employment for counselors/psychologists is within higher education institutions, and the third largest is within public administration. Another trend which is seen today within the public healthcare sector is the implementation of developmental psychopathology as a way of understanding and studying psychiatric disorders. Instead of polarized models of etiology, developmental psychopathology attempts to integrate biological, psychological, and social reasons for the etiology of mental illnesses (B. Møhl, personal communication, October 6, 2010; Harder & Simonsen, 2010). Finally, a trend which is seen within the area of school counseling is that the Pædagoisk Psykologisk Rådgiving (PPR; Pedagogical Psychological Counseling Services) have shifted their focus from the individual to the context of the individual. This means that counselors/psychologists working at PPR focus their attention not only on the individual student as a separate entity but also on the milieu surrounding the student (classmates, parents, living environment, etc.). Again, an integrative approach to working with clients is used (I. Andersen, personal communication, October 8, 2010).

Indigenous and traditional healing methods

Indigenous and traditional healing methods as they are practiced in other countries have not been visible in Denmark in the past. Although Denmark has experienced a growing immigrant population, their indigenous and traditional healing methods are not currently practiced by Danish counselors/psychologists. However, *sjælesorg* (pastoral care) has a long history in Denmark, and continues to play a vital role in caring for the spiritual and mental health of Danish citizens. Pastoral care or *sjælesorg* as it is called in Denmark comes from the German word *Seelsorge*, which means care for the soul.

The religious ritual of confession may be seen as the early form of pastoral care (E. Due, personal communication, September 13, 2010). Before the reformation in 1536, the Catholic Church ruled in Denmark. Confession was mandatory if an individual wanted to obtain absolution. After the reformation, and with the influence of Martin Luther, confession became voluntary (E. Due, personal communication, September 13, 2010). In 1685 guidelines were established to help priests offer pastoral care to individuals who were possessed, prisoners, individuals being executed, and sick people. Furthermore, sick people sought evangelical comfort through conversations with the priest (E. Due, personal communication, September 13, 2010). During the 1800s, the number of individuals going to confession was cut in half (Due, 2003), and individual confession was substituted for communal confession. During the 1960s, communal confession disappeared and was replaced by communion. Communion was now considered the ritual for which the individual sought absolution (Due, 2003). This continues to be the practice today.

Today, most Danish pastors engage in what is called "ad hoc" pastoral care (E. Due, personal communication, September 13, 2010). This means that they offer pastoral care when their parishioners are in need. The majority of a pastors' pastoral care work is now done in connection with baptisms and weddings. They spend more time today than in the past with the couple before the ceremony talking about issues or questions that may arise due to the ritual. The pastors who do the majority of the pastoral care work in Denmark today are those working in the prison system or working at hospitals or hospices (E. Due, personal communication, September 13, 2010).

Currently in Denmark, the fields of theology and psychology exist side by side. While Danish pastors borrow tools of communication from the field of psychology, and have adopted supervision and practicum in the educational learning of how to care for the souls of their parishioners, pastoral care continues to be a theological discipline maintained by the pastors of the Danish churches.

Research and supervision

Currently, research is conducted at the four main universities in Denmark. Each university has many different research areas of interest. At the Department of Psychology at Copenhagen

University there are 15 different research areas. Within these different centers and research units multiple research projects are conducted each year with a variety of individuals from across Denmark. As an example, several studies of psychotherapy process and outcome are being undertaken at the Department of Psychology at Copenhagen University, e.g., a randomized controlled trial of cognitive-behavioral therapy (CBT) for bulimia nervosa and another randomized controlled trial of parent involvement in CBT for children with anxiety (S. Poulsen, personal communication, October 8, 2010).

Specific research areas at Århus University include social and personality psychology, cognition and learning psychology, developmental psychology, organizational psychology, clinical psychology, and pedagogical/educational psychology (Århus Universitet [Aarhus University], n.d.a). Furthermore, there is a research and educational anxiety clinic connected to the institute of psychology at Århus University which offers free treatment for individuals suffering from anxiety-related disorders primarily social phobias and panic attacks.

Research areas at Ålborg University can be divided into three different areas: experimental psychology, qualitative methods, and clinical psychology and music therapy. The cognitive psychological unit (CPU) located under the research area of experimental psychology aims to investigate "theoretical, empirical and applied aspects of human development, cognition and neurology" (Ålborg University [Aalborg University], n.d.). The center for supervision at Ålborg University collaborates with the center for supervision at Copenhagen University. Here, the aim is to conduct research which may strengthen or enhance the supervision for counselors/psychologists.

At Syddansk University, the center for psychological trauma engages in research on the psychological crisis that individuals experience when they have witnessed a life-threatening experience. The research projects focus on rape, incest, widowed elders, and catastrophes. The center currently has 83 ongoing projects (Syddansk Universitet [South Danish University], n.d.a). In addition, Syddansk University also has a research unit for work-related and organizational stress. They focus on intervention strategies, person-centered and organizational, that are applied in the treatment of work-related stress (Syddansk Universitet [South Danish University], n.d.b).

Supervision, is acquired through an internship course and through the various training clinics during training at universities. Furthermore, during the required internship course, the student must receive a minimum of 16 hours of supervision from the counselor/psychologist responsible for the intern (Århus Universitet [Aarhus University], n.d.b).

The counselor/psychologist usually receives supervision from his/her place of employment, and in most cases both individual and group supervision is offered. Guidelines for supervision have been established by Psykolognævnet (the Danish Supervisory Board of Psychological Practice). The main aim of supervision is for the counselor/psychologist to develop his/her skills in accomplishing relevant assessments and interventions. If professional development does not advance satisfactorily, the supervisor must make the supervisee aware of this. In order to provide supervision the counselor/psychologist has to be licensed by the Danish Supervisory Board of Psychological Practice and have worked as a counselor/psychologist for at least 3 years after obtaining a master's degree in psychology (Psykolognævnet [Danish Board of Psychological Practice], n.d.c).

If the counselor/psychologist has obtained a specialist degree the individual may add a 2-year supervisory degree (Lindhart, 2010). The requirements needed for the supervisory degree include working full-time as a counselor/psychologist for a minimum of 2 years after having obtained the specialist degree. The counselor/psychologist must have provided at least 120 hours of supervision to a minimum of two different counselors/psychologists, received 20 hours of supervision on the supervision provided or some other form of guidance, and participated in

30 hours of theory on the theory and method of the supervision process (Dansk Psykolog Forening [Danish Psychological Association], n.d.a.)

Strengths, weaknesses, opportunities, and challenges

There are a variety of strengths within the field of counseling/psychology in Denmark today. It has become popular and mainstream to seek help from a counselor/psychologist when needed, the field has political headwind, counselors/psychologists are used in a variety of work settings now as opposed to earlier, and a multitude of studies show that psychotherapy is helpful to individuals suffering from mental illnesses. Evidence-based treatment methods have become popular and integrated (Vendsbo, 2010).

A new degree for counselors/psychologists working within the area of psychiatry will surely prove to be an asset for counselors/psychologists (I. Andersen & S. Poulsen, personal communication, October 8, 2010). For the past 10 years the Danish Psychological Association has worked towards establishing this degree which will be financed by the government and not by the individual counselor/psychologist as has previously been the case. It is the first specialty degree in which the counselor/psychologist does not have to finance the education him/herself as is currently the case for many counselors/psychologists who obtain the specialist and supervisory degrees. The aim is to increase counselors'/psychologists' qualifications, and competences, increase salary, and provide counselors/psychologists with employment opportunities which entail an increase in responsibility and leadership. The start of the degree was launched in 2010 and is a great victory for the field of counseling/psychology in Denmark (B. Møhl, personal communication, October 6, 2010).

A weakness for counselors/psychologists, especially those working within the public health-care sector, is the increased attention on quality control (Simonsen & Møhl, 2010). Historically and culturally, Danes have not believed in the importance of quality control, because the consensus was that the quality of treatment was good and that people performed their jobs responsibly and up to standards. To a certain extent this has held true, but due to increasing international influence and international requirements and standards, new procedures for quality control have been and are currently being implemented. For example, Danish hospitals have been and are going through accreditations procedures, ensuring that joint procedures for patient safety and employee procedures are up to date. This change in the organizational structure and culture holds strengths, weaknesses, challenges, and opportunities for both personnel and patients. The aim is of course to provide a better service to the citizens of Denmark; however, counselors/psychologists who have been in the field for many years experience a shift in focus. They find themselves spending more time on administrative tasks and less time with the clients. This is a concern and a challenge for counselors/psychologists in Denmark (B. Møhl, personal communication, October 6, 2010; I. Andersen & S. Poulsen, personal communication, October 8, 2010).

Although it is a strength that current treatment methods are able to show evidence of their effectiveness, it may be considered a weakness that treatment methods, which have not undergone studies showing evidence of usefulness, are being discarded as ineffective. Owing to the current trend and popularity of evidence-based treatments, much practical expertise, which is not yet evidence-based, may in some areas of counseling/psychology be lost. A challenge therefore will be to maintain a multitheoretical universe in which both evidence-based and non-evidence-based treatment methods may exist and be used by counselors/psychologists (K. Pedersen, personal communication, October 8, 2010).

One opportunity for the field of counseling/psychology in Denmark has been to get treatment of some mental health illnesses out of the public health sector and into the private sector, so that counselors/psychologists in all areas may provide treatment for individuals with mental illnesses previously only treated within inpatient and outpatient psychiatric wards. Today, individuals who suffer from a psychological or physical illness can obtain treatment from a counselor/psychologist working in the private sector and have two-thirds of the payment covered by *sygesikringen* (the Danish healthcare provider) (Lindhart, 2010). Currently, individuals aged 18–37 years who are diagnosed with depression can also get their counseling/psychological treatment in the private sector covered by *sygesikringen*. The reason for the cut-off line of 37 years is purely an economical one. The field of counseling/psychology in Denmark continues to work towards providing treatment of mental illness in settings other than psychiatric units and at a cost which is affordable to the individual (I. Andersen & S. Poulsen, personal communication, October 8, 2010).

One challenge for Danish counselors/psychologists is to implement standards for the maintenance of their licensure, specialist, and supervisory certifications. Today, once the counselors/psychologists have met the requirements and obtained licensure and/or the specialist and supervisory degree, there are no requirements for maintaining the credentials (I. Andersen & S. Poulsen, personal communication, October 8, 2010).

Future directions

The field of counseling/psychology in Denmark is faced with many new opportunities and challenges and the future of the field appears promising and exciting. An area of growth for counselors/psychologists is the somatic area. Patients diagnosed with various forms of cancer and patients suffering from heart problems may benefit greatly from receiving treatment from counselors/psychologists. Currently there is a lack of counselors/psychologists connected to the somatic units at hospitals, and studies show that counselors/psychologists may help decrease recidivism and increase quality of life for these patients (I. Andersen & S. Poulsen, personal communication, October 8, 2010).

In addition, the Danish Psychological Association must continue to work towards improving continuing education and qualification requirements for counselors/psychologists in Denmark. Standards and requirements for maintaining licensure, specialist, and supervisory credentialing, must be implemented to ensure the highest quality of treatment for the citizens of Denmark.

Moreover, Denmark is currently faced with challenges from its growing immigrant population. Private counseling/psychological services working with minorities and immigrants exist in Denmark, and have previously maintained the majority of the treatment services (Alberdi, 2010). However, it is likely that we will observe a growing interest in non-traditional therapies and indigenous healing approaches as the immigrant population increases. While private organizations still work with ethnic minorities, trans-cultural psychiatry is now gaining increased importance and influence within the public healthcare sector, and the field of counseling/psychology may need counselors/psychologists who are educated to work with people of different nationalities, cultures, and ethnic backgrounds. Training opportunities may include introducing multicultural classes at the master's level for counselor/psychology students to improve their diversity and multicultural competencies and skills.

Conclusion

As the counseling profession continues to internationalize, counselors will want to remain informed about our profession's manifestations throughout the world. Counseling/psychology in Denmark has undergone many changes and there are still many forces at work to continue to improve the standards of the field of counseling/psychology within Denmark. We view this chapter as a first step in understanding the historical and current psychological trends in our profession's configuration in Denmark. We hope that our overview and the sharing of opinions from Danish psychologists aid international counselors' knowledge and comprehension of Denmark's approaches to professional counseling/psychology.

References

ACE Denmark (n.d.). Retrieved July 31, 2010 from http://acedenmark.dk/index.php?id=158

Alberdi, A. (2010). Transkultural Psykiatri [Transcultural psychiatry]. In E. Simonsen & B. Møhl (eds), *Grundbog i Psykiatri* (pp. 777–797). Copenhagen: Hans Reitzels Forlag.

Almstrup, O. (2000). U.B.K. Universitets børnepsykologiske klinik – glimt af en udvikling over 50 år [The University's psychological clinic for children – a glimpse of a development over 50 years]. *Psyche & Logos, 21*, 210–223.

Ålborg University (Aalborg University) (n.d.). Retrieved August 21, 2010 from www.cpu.aau.dk/

Århus Universitet (Aarhus University) (n.d.a). Retrieved August 21, 2010 from www.psy.au.dk/forskning/forskningsomraader

Århus Universitet (Aarhus University) (n.d.b). Retrieved August 21, 2010 from www.psy.au.dk/under visning/praktik/#c3047

Dansk Psykolog Forening (Danish Psychological Association). (n.d.a). *Association website*. Retrieved July 31, 2010 from www.dp.dk/Uddannelse/Specialist%20og%20supervisor.aspx

Dansk Psykolog Forening (Danish Psychological Association). (n.d.b). *Association website*. Retrieved July 31, 2010 from www.dp.dk/da/Om%20Foreningen/Foreningen%20i%20tal.aspx#Arbejdsomraader

Dansk Psykolog Forening (Danish Psychological Association). (n.d.c). *Association website*. Retrieved October 15, 2010 from www.dp.dk/da/Uddannelse/Internationalt.aspx

Dixon, A. L., & Hansen, N. H. (2010). Fortid, nutid, fremtid [past, present, future]: Professional counseling in Denmark. *Journal of Counseling & Development, 88*, 38–42.

Due, E. (2003). Før alt er forbi [Before everything is over]. *Tidsskrift for Sjelesorg, 3*, 213–223.

European Federation of Psychologists' Association (EFPA) (2011). (n.d). Association website. Retrieved September 20, 2011 from www.efpa.eu/ethics/ethical-codes

Funch, B. S. (2000). Psykologiens grundlæggelse i Danmark [The foundation of psychology in Denmark]. *Psyche & Logos, 21*, 116–134.

Grevbo, T. J. S. (2006). *Sjelesorgens Vei* [Pastoral care's road]. Oslo, Luther Forlag, AS.

Harder, S., & Simonsen, E.(2010). Udvik lingspsykopatologi. In Simonsen, E. & Møhl, B. (ed.), *Grundbog I Psykiatri* (pp. 101–115). Copenhagen, Hans Reitzels Forlag.

Hjørlund, B. (2000). Træk af dansk psykologis historie [An outline of the history of Danish psychology]. *Psyche & Logos, 21*, 11–31.

Huey, D. A., & Britton, P. G. (2002). A portrait of clinical psychology. *Journal of Interprofessional Care, 16*, 69–78.

Jensen, R. (2000). Knudepunkter I dansk psykologis udvikling i årene 1940–2000 [Conjunctures in the development of Danish psychology in the years 1940–2000]. *Psyke & Logos, 21*, 174–186.

Jørgensen, C. R., Kjølbye, M., & Møhl, B. (2010). Psykoterapi. In E. Simonsen and B. Møhl (eds), *Grundbog i Psykiatri* (pp. 595–621). Copenhagen: Hans Reitzels Forlag.

Københavns Universitet (Copenhagen University). (n.d.). Retrieved August 14, 2010 from http://studier.ku.dk/kandidatuddannelser/psykologi/

Karpatschof, B. (2000). Fra fænomenologidebat til studenteroprør – en revurdering af Københavnerfænomenologien 30 år efter [From a phenomenological debate to a student revolt – a reassessment of the Copenhagen phenomenon 30 years after]. *Psyche & Logos, 21*, 152–173.

Køppe, S. (1983). *Psykologiens udvikling og formidling i Danmark i perioden 1850–1980* [The devlopment and mediation of psychology in Denmark between 1850–1980]. Copenhagen. GEC Gads Forlag

Lindhart, A. (2010). Psykiatriens Organisering. In E. Simonsen & B. Møhl (eds), *Grundbog i Psykiatri* (pp. 876–887). Copenhagen: Hans Reitzels Forlag.

Lundberg, I. (2001). Zeitgeist, Ortgeist, and personalities in the development of Scandinavian psychology. *International Journal of Counseling/Psychology, 36*, 356–362.

Lunt, I. (1999). The professionalization of psychology in Europe. *European Psychologist, 4*, 240–247.

Mortensen, K.V. (2000). Lidt om udviklingen af klinisk børnepsykologi i Danmark [A little on the development of clinical child psychology in Denmark]. *Psyke & Logos, 21,* 224–242.

Pedersen, J.M. (1990). Psykologiens Historie [The history of Psychology]. *Temaer af Videnskabsteori og Psykologiens Historie, Psykologisk Laboratorium 1990,* 1–64.

Pind, J. L. (2009). A tale of two psychologies: The Høffding-Lehmann controversy and the establishment of experimental psychology at the University of Copenhagen. *Journal of the History of the Behavioral Sciences, 45,* 34–55.

Poulsen, A. (2007). School psychology in Denmark. In S. R. Jimerson, T. D. Oakland & P. T. Frarell (eds), *The handbook of international school psychology* (pp. 71–80). Thousand Oaks, CA, London, New Delhi: Sage Publications Inc.

Psykolognævnet (Danish Board of Psychological Practice). (n.d.a). Retrieved September 18, 2010 from www.pn.sm.dk/B2.Om.Nevn.Eng/0.TekstSiden.htm

Psykolognævnet (Danish Board of Psychological Practice). (n.d.b). Retrieved September 18, 2010 from www.pn.sm.dk/C.Ny-Design/0e.22Mapper.Sdrne/21.Love.Regler/0.LoveRegler.Frame.htm

Psykolognævnet (Danish Board of Psychological Practice). (n.d.c). Retrieved September 18, 2010 from www.pn.sm.dk/C.Ny-Design/0e.22Mapper.Sdrne/32.retn.l.010103/0.retn.l.010103.Frame.htm

Simonsen, E., & Møhl, B. (2010). Evidensbaseret Klinisk Praksis. In E. Simonsen & B. Møhl (eds), *Grundbog i Psykiatri* (pp. 555–566). Copenhagen: Hans Reitzels Forlag.

Statistics Denmark. (2010). *Denmark in figures 2010.* Retrieved September 25, 2010 from www.dst.dk/HomeUK/Statistics/ofs/Publications/dod.aspx

Syddansk Universitet (South Danish University) (n.d.a). Retrieved September 16, 2010 from www.sdu.dk/Om_SDU/Institutter_centre/Institut_psykologi/Forskning/Forskningsenheder/Videnscenter_for_Psykotraumatologi.aspx,

Syddansk Universitet (South Danish University) (n.d.b). Retrieved September 16, 2010, from www.sdu.dk/Om_SDU/Institutter_centre/Institut_psykologi/Forskning/Forskningsenheder/Forskningsenhed_for_Arbejdsrelateret_og_Organisatorisk_Stress

Vendsbo, P. (2010). Distriktspsykiatri [District Psychiatry]. In E. Simonsen & B. Møhl (eds), *Grundbog i Psykiatri* (pp. 687–700). Copenhagen: Hans Reitzels Forlag.

White, A.G. (2007). Global projection of subjective well-being: A challenge to positive psychology? *Psychtalk, 56,* 17–20. Retrieved February 15, 2007, from www.le.ac.uk/pc/aw57/world/sample.html

24

COUNSELING AND PSYCHOTHERAPY IN FRANCE

An evolving heterogeneous field

Valérie Cohen-Scali, Jacques Pouyaud,
Nicole Baudouin, and Emmanuelle Vignoli

Introduction

In 2010, France's population reached 63.1 million, making it the second most populated country in the European Union (EU) after Germany (The French National Institute for Statistics and Economic Studies, as cited in Pia & Beaumel, 2011). Furthermore, France has one of the lowest immigration rates in Europe (five times less than Spain for example) (The European Center for the Development of Vocational Training [CEDEFOP], 2008).

There are three specific demographic characteristics in France with direct repercussions on counseling activities. The first concerns discrimination against young people from immigrant families from southern Europe, the Maghreb and sub-Saharan Africa (Silberman & Fournier, 2006). The second concerns the specific difficulties and needs of people in the second stage or at the end of their career. The third characteristic concerns the general deterioration of working conditions in French companies. France is facing a high increase in the rate of suicides for professional reasons, ranking third in the world after Japan and Finland in 2005 (du Roy, 2009).

In France today, the term "counseling" is seen more as a useful metaphorical expression than a faithful representation of reality. In reality, it covers a broad range of practices in terms of methods, the professionals involved, and reference models. The professional field of counseling resembles overlapping networks of very different, unconnected people. This heterogeneity is reflected in the wide variety of terms used in France to describe the practices of helping others. However, these practices can be divided into three broad categories based on the problems dealt with and the people concerned. The first category covers activities related to issues of educational guidance and is directed towards adolescents and young adults. So, students of any educational level can take advantage of *guidance counseling,* which refers in part to the action of "holding council," and can be described as "taking action after deliberation" (Lhotellier, 2001). The second category of practice concerns adults going through a period of professional transition, looking for work or training. *Coaching* is a term that has been used for several years. In the fields of occupational integration, the term "to accompany" (or "support") is used to define a relationship based on assistance of a psychological nature over a period of several weeks. The type of assistance offered in these two categories is usually defined in French by the untranslated English word "counseling." In France, counseling is often used to describe *assistance* aimed at "normal" people, "taking into account their personal development during a challenging situation, drawing on existing strengths and integrating the dynamic between the person and his/her surrounding environment" (Paul, 2002, p. 45).

The third category covers psychotherapeutic practices offered to people suffering from identified psychological disorders. These practices are seen as distinct from those in the first two categories and are more homogeneous, better structured and longer established. As observed by Tourette-Turgis (1996), "For the French, counseling is far removed from the idea of therapy" (p. 25).

This chapter analyzes current counseling practices offered to these three client groups: young people at school, professional adults, and adults with psychological difficulties. It covers the main developments in practices aimed at these client groups, and the limitations and contradictions of a professional sector currently going through a period of unprecedented growth in France.

Brief history of counseling and psychotherapy

Traditionally, a distinction is made in France between psychoanalysis, psychotherapy, and counseling. Psychotherapy practices in the 20th century were inspired by the work of Janet, Bernheim, and Charcot, based on hypnosis and suggestion (Couchard, Huguet, & Matalon, 1995). But it was psychoanalysis which then gradually permeated the various therapeutic areas. Following Freud's meetings with Charcot (October 1885 to May 1886) and Bernheim (summer of 1889), psychoanalysis was born in Vienna and officially came to France a few years later. Under the leadership of Marie Bonaparte, Freud's patient, the Parisian Psychoanalysis Society (SPP) was created in 1926. Since then, psychoanalysis has spread widely in France because of the roles played by many psychoanalysts, such as R. Laforgue, D. Lagache, and F. Dolto for child psychoanalysis, and J. Lacan, who in 1954 was expelled from the International Psychoanalytic Association (IPA) and founded his own school.

The history of psychoanalysis in France was marked by many conflicts and divisions, which today translates into a multiplicity of associations or schools, each claiming a traditional Freudian psychoanalysis. For instance, the contributions of J. Lacan and the Anglo-Saxon currents developed by M. Klein and D. W. Winnicott became very important (Roudinesco, 1986). At the same time as psychoanalysis was growing in France, it entered the various fields of thought (psychology, philosophy, pedagogy) and influenced the practices of social work and care (psychiatry, counseling).

Currently, psychoanalysis still has a strong audience among intellectuals but is being increasingly challenged by cognitive-behavioral approaches and by Carl Roger's person-centered approach. These different approaches have strongly influenced current practices of counseling since the 1960s. While psychoanalysis settled in France, counseling activities for school and career guidance were gradually introduced. These were based on various schools of thought in psychology at the time, particularly analytic psychology and scientific psychology (Couchard et al., 1995). Counseling, like psychotherapy, involves suggestion. However, unlike psychotherapy, counseling in school and career guidance has always used standardized tests, particularly intelligence tests and skills assessment. These tools were inspired by Taylorism and the notion of matching the worker to the job ("the right man at the right place") (Kanigel, 1997). The counselor's aim was to help students choose a career path matching their skills and interests (Guichard & Huteau, 2001).

Assessment lay at the heart of career counseling practices in the 1950s. Piéron's work on intelligence, based on the notion of "intellectual types" rather than IQ (Guichard & Huteau,

2001), also contributed to the importance given to differential psychology in French research on career counseling from the 1960s through the 1980s. In the 1990s, a new conception of career counseling emerged following the introduction of vocational guidance education, aimed at adapting counseling practices to the new and more uncertain socio-economic environment. Practices arising from this development aimed to help young people build on their strengths in order to develop the most efficient strategies for adapting to their environment (Pelletier & Dumora, 1984). A large number of tools and methods inspired by this trend have been developed and used.

In addition, a new counseling field was developed in the 1960s, aimed particularly at couples and families. This field of activity was developed in France by Jean Lemaire, a psychiatrist and psychoanalyst, as part of the French association of marriage guidance centers (Tourette-Turgis, 1996). It is based on psychoanalysis, group psychology, and systems analysis, and stresses the importance of relationships, in line with the theses Rogers developed in the United States. Within this perspective, counseling is similar to a psychotherapeutic procedure. Despite these occasional overlaps, these two activities generally remain clearly distinct.

In the last 20 years, living conditions have led to increasing social needs for counseling. Most counselors in France today work in the fields of education, social integration, health, social work, and in companies. In education, the number of career counselors doubled between 1970 and 1980 as the school system became increasingly complex. Since 1981, those working with young people in schools have been called "school and career-counseling psychologists" (known as the "Conseillers d'orientation psychologues" [COP] in France) and are employed by the State.

Counselor training programs, accreditation, licensure, and certification

Overall, there are 50,000 professionals currently working in France as psychotherapists or counselors with young people and adults (Guichard & Huteau, 2001).

Most of them have at least a bachelor's or a master's degree, generally in human and social sciences and notably in psychology. They then specialize in the different counseling domains (e.g., vocational guidance, therapeutic counseling, integration counseling) through professional experience or additional training courses.

There are three university master's programs in the fields of school and professional counseling with adults: Paris Inetop-Cnam, Paris X Nanterre University, and Aix Marseille I University. There is also a professional state diploma course for school and career-counseling psychologists. This 2-year course is open to people with a degree in psychology, and the diploma confers the right to the title of psychologist and vocational counseling specialist. Faced with the growing demand for support in departments and companies, a number of degree-level diplomas focusing on short interventions are being set up (for example, there are six vocational degree specialties for occupational integration).

Psychotherapists also come from a wide range of backgrounds. They include psychologists, doctors, nurses, and social workers. Most of them follow specific psychotherapy training courses, varying from one institute to another depending on their theoretical approaches (e.g., transactional analysis, gestalt therapy, behavioral therapies). In general, participants of these training courses have a 4-year post-baccalauréat[1] level. The course organization varies but often includes practical work experience and supervision.

In contrast to the titles of "psychologist" and "psychotherapist," there is no legal protection for the use of the term "counselor" as an occupation in France. Two laws established by the French government regulate the titles of psychologist and psychotherapist. Since 1985, in order to earn the title of a psychologist, one must complete a master's degree in psychology with an internship of 500 hours (with supervised practice). The second law established in 2011 concerns the use of psychotherapist. Only those who complete a master's degree in the medical field or a master's degree in clinical psychology and psychoanalysis can be referred to as a psychotherapist. Furthermore, psychotherapists, psychiatrists, and psychologists must register with an accreditation list (ADELI List), which delivers a professional number. With these laws, abusive use of the title is legally pursued, but many other titles can be used for those who essentially do the same work as a psychotherapist or psychologist (e.g., psycho-practitioner, gestalt-therapist, psychoanalyst), which are then not controlled.

As all psychological practices are not yet well legally protected, many professional associations try to encourage ethical and quality control. In 1996, the Association des Educateurs Universitaires en Psychologie (University Psychology Teachers' Association, AEPU), the Société Française de Psychologie (French Psychological Society, SFP), and the Association Nationale des Organisations de Psychologues (National Association of Psychologist's Organizations, ANOP) wrote a code of ethics signed by 20 other associations. In 2011 this code is being rewritten. However, despite the fact that this code is accepted by a large community of professionals, these associations have no legal power to control quality, and the only legal code for practicing counseling, psychology or psychotherapy remains the French penal and civil code.

Current counseling and psychotherapy theories, processes, and trends

Three main aspects of counseling are presented. First, theories, processes, and trends related to counseling with adults and children with psychological difficulties are explored. Then, we evoke the same issues concerning career counseling in school and career counseling for adults.

In France, counseling practices with adults and children with psychological difficulties are traditionally rooted in psychoanalysis theory. It is based on the hypothesis that everyday behavior is influenced by unconscious mental processes. While it is still widely practiced, it is much less popular today than it was in the 1970s. Currently, modern psychotherapy methods in France are not only inspired by psychoanalysis, but they are also heavily influenced by cognitive-behavior therapies and systems analysis. Practitioners implement techniques such as association of ideas and suggestion, notably when using hypnosis and conditioning. Counseling with children with psychological difficulties, often inspired by psychoanalysis, uses mediators such as drawing and playing to overcome potential difficulties linked to language development, and occasionally involves the parents. The systems analysis approach was introduced in the 1970s (Watzlawick, 1978) in the field of counseling and broadly used in France with an aim of individual changes. Together, psychoanalysis, systems analyses, and cognitivism gave birth to a wide variety of therapeutic methods—between 300 and 400 forms of psychotherapy were identified (Moro & Lachal, 1996). Within these frameworks, the length of individual or group treatment varies widely. Short therapy courses, which are increasingly common in France, need to be distinguished from courses of psychoanalytic treatment, which are much longer in length.

Career counseling with adolescents and young adults in school is based on multiple approaches related to vocational development, mainly in the English-speaking literature (e.g. Holland, Gottfredson, and Super), and which have been translated and researched in France. French researchers in career counseling in schools are currently developing constructionist models with the aim of identifying ways that young people establish their identity in relation to work (Baubion-Broye & Hajjar, 1998; Guichard, 2005.).

Career counseling in school is carried out in group workshops about different jobs and is based, for example, on workers' biographies. Interviews are commonly used, sometimes associated with standardized tests, either as interest inventories or tests of intellectual potential. The primary objective is to help the client draw up a career project. Different forms of interview can be used, based on the client-centered principle. These interviews are further associated with decision-making techniques deriving more from cognitive and behavioral approaches (Brown & Lent, 1996; Hackett, 1995). The interview technique used by French school and career-counseling psychologists is a good example. It consists of an initial needs analysis phase. The second phase looks in more detail at the client's situation, resources, and limitations, his/her beliefs and values, and the impact of all these factors on solving the career problem. Finally, the third phase involves setting up an action plan based on realistic and achievable solutions (Tremblay & Lecomte, 1985). Another form of interview inspired by constructivism is currently being tested (Guichard, 2008).

Career counseling practices with adults are rooted in theoretical approaches aimed at explaining how the person can change his/her perception of work, jobs, and professions. Serge Moscovici's (1961) theory of social representations appears as a key reference for French career counselors with adults. Social representations are cognitive constructions (integrated sets of opinions, beliefs, attitudes, and knowledge) of reality which are socially constructed, shared by members of a group, and play a major role in communicating ideas and actions. Another theoretical approach is Kiesler's psychological commitment theory (Kiesler, 1971), which appears as a useful framework for supporting unemployed persons (Castra, 2003). Finally, counseling practices with unemployed adults are also largely inspired by work on self-esteem and self-efficacy, which aims at highlighting an individual's strengths and resources. Bandura's self-efficacy theory thus provides the basis of a large number of counseling activities.

Inspired by these main theoretical frameworks, two recent career counseling practices with adults have been developed for adults going through a period of professional transition: Competencies Elicitation Career Counseling (CECC) and Validation of Experiential Learning. All adults who have or have had a professional activity have a right to these two tools. The CECC was introduced in 1991 and can take place at the request of the worker or his/her employer. It involves the assessment of the worker's professional skills, motivations, aptitudes, and interests with a view to developing a professional or training project. (Aubret & Blanchard, 2005) The Validation of Experiential Learning, introduced in 2002, provides the possibility for anyone with a professional activity to obtain a diploma through recognition of their professional and/or personal experience. The validation process involves describing and proving the professional skills and knowledge acquired during an activity carried out for a minimum of 5 years.

Indigenous and traditional healing methods

Immigration in France massively increased from 1945 to 1975 (during what is generally called "the 30 glorious") with a stronger cultural diversification from the 1960s. The first wave of migrant workers came mainly from Mediterranean countries (especially Spain and Portugal), and the Maghreb, followed by Francophone African immigrants a decade later. However, topics surrounding cultural diversity have always provoked many debates in France. Cultural specificities have often been erased in the name of the republican ideology. As underlined by Munoz (1999), "the idea of the intercultural does not fit with French concept of nation and education ... French nation was built by reducing the regional languages and cultures, establishing a common language and culture in the service of a united nation" (p. 21). Institutions such as schools appeared as the main instruments of this unification. However, counselors, psychologists, and also social workers and healthcare workers, have experienced and identified daily unique and specific needs for these immigrant populations. The role of school counselors as mediators to facilitate the reception and integration of young immigrants was fundamental. They also took part in the detection of possible psychological disorders related to migration. Then it became obvious that specific knowledge about diverse cultures was necessary. According to Deen (2002), the counselor has to show "cultural empathy," a notion he refers to as the process of identifying values and expectations which can determine the client's behavior, and the significance that the client gives to the relationship with a professional who is external to his or her family and cultural group.

In terms of therapeutic interventions, psychological problems of immigrant populations have been primarily taken into account within the framework of ethnopsychiatry designed by Tobie Nathan. Before the 1990s, no psychiatric institution was capable of addressing these problems. This in turn prompted the establishment of the Georges Devereux[2] Center, which was founded in 1993 at the University of Paris 8. This center was the first where practices for clinical ethnopsychiatric interventions specialized in treating diseases related to migration could be developed. At the Avicenne Hospital, in the Paris region, consultations for children and teenagers suffering from pathologies connected to the immigration experience were also proposed in a psychiatric department managed by Moro (2002). According to Nathan (2001), migration can be such a psychological shock that it may produce pathologies several years later. In practice, ethnopsychiatric sessions are collective. They gather the patient and his or her family with a group of professionals (e.g., doctors, psychiatrist, psychologist), one of whom must speak the patient's native language. A partnership relationship is then established between caregivers and the family. Clients are encouraged to discuss the interpretations of their caregivers. They are also encouraged to make their own interpretations of their situation. The patients are thus considered as experts of their own culture and the role of caregivers is mainly to provide them additional insights.

Research and supervision

There are very few research teams currently working explicitly on counseling psychology. The research team of the National Institute of Vocational Training and Guidance (INETOP) is one of the most longstanding and most active in the field, with some of the research endeavors being funded by the state. It has conducted a number of studies which form the basis of much work on counseling today. These studies include: the processes of self-construction in school transition situations (Guichard, 2005; Pouyaud, 2008), situations combining work and training (Cohen-Scali, 2010), tools and evaluation methods (Bernaud, Gaudron & Lemoine, 2006), the functioning of social interactions (Olry-Louis, 2009), the assessment of individual situations (Chartier & Loarer, 2008; Guichard, 2005), and counseling adolescents (Baudouin, 2007; Vignoli, 2009). Specific counseling methods are being developed in the framework of these different studies.

Supervision is systematically carried out for psychoanalytic practice (which is not the case for all counseling practices) in France and is compulsory for all newly qualified professionals. Supervision involves a psychotherapist describing any specific difficulties encountered during the course of his/her work, in either a group or one-to-one situation, to an experienced psychoanalyst or psychotherapist. Advice may be given, and the therapist is also helped to analyze the counter-transfer processes at work in his/her practice.

In the field of career counseling, a recent practice has emerged called "practice analysis." This developed first in the field of health and social services following the work of Balint (1961), who initiated this approach with doctors in the 1950s. Counseling activities involve inter-individual relationships, and the counselor needs to be able to take a detached view, to question his/her methods and consider his/her role as a professional. Training courses for school and career-counseling psychologists include sessions for supervision, analyses of various professional practices, and learning about self-supervision in order to facilitate reflective practices.

During the first phase of practice-analysis workshops, counselors are invited to describe professional situations in which they have encountered difficulties. The objective is for each one to make sense of these situations and develop new and more efficient strategies. These groups take on different forms according to the presupposed underlying theories. Analysis is based on the situation presented by each counselor, from which a general point of view can be drawn. Sharing experiences in a group enables a deeper analysis of the situation and obliges each person to take a more objective and broader view. Each participant must think of strategies corresponding to the professional situation of the person presenting the problem (Blanchard-Laville & Nadot, 2004). After describing the situation, followed by questions and developing hypotheses, the practitioner is in a position to relate his/her professional way of working to personal scenarios (Blanchard-Laville & Fablet, 2002; Blanchard-Laville, 2004). Analysis is then centered on the practitioner, whereas in the first phase of workshop described above the work is essentially centered on the situation.

Strengths, weaknesses, opportunities and challenges

Highlighting individual responsibility for life-path choices has increased the need for all types of counseling. There are growing demands concerning all aspects of life (career, health, money, the family, the law, etc.). This now has political support, at both the national and the European level, with a new law recognizing the right to professional training, guidance, and information about training and jobs throughout life. Public services for employment, social security, and school and vocational guidance are being reorganized in a single service with the aim of covering the needs of individuals as a whole in a more structured way. This acknowledgement of counseling practices by French public policy authorities, by itself, is a strength (Guichard & Huteau, 2005).

The main weaknesses of the field lie in the fact that the growing demands for professional training, guidance, and information led to a sharp rise in the multiplicity of practitioners and their heterogeneity in terms of training, theoretical basis, and activity. This multiplicity makes counseling an ill-defined field in which individual professionals do not see themselves as belonging to the same professional family. Heterogeneity can also be seen in the scientific research into counseling within the different disciplines of human sciences. Counseling is considered as an applied branch of work psychology, social or clinical psychology, but rarely as a sector of multidisciplinary research; empirical multidisciplinary research and papers in the domain of counseling are in effect very rare. The major risk is thus that the single term "counseling" will be used to describe the wide variety of services on offer, with little scientific basis, and whose priority is economic efficiency (management of economic needs in terms of employment, organizational efficiency, etc.), and failing to put the client at the center (Cohen-Scali, 2009).

To overcome this problem, a quality assurance approach needs to be set up to differentiate between practices and thus protect clients and ensure they receive quality service. Practitioners will consequently need to organize themselves in professional associations in order to maintain an ethical counseling practice. This social context is also a historical opportunity that is given to practitioners, professional associations, scholars, politicians, employers, and syndicates to define and promote together scientific frameworks and guidelines for practitioners that ensure the quality of counseling services (Tourette-Turgis, 1996).

A major challenge for the years to come is to select the most relevant and state of the art practices on one hand, and to foster creativity among practitioners on the other. This involves developing scientific networks for counseling, with the aim of constituting a body of knowledge, research, and practices liable to lead to the formalization of counseling professions. It will entail scientists structuring a coherent field in which to continue developing research in a rapidly growing sector. However, the lack of interest shown by scientists in this subject has resulted in distancing the human and social sciences as sources of innovation and organization for the counseling professions.

Future directions

Owing to the heterogeneity and continuing increase in counseling activities in France (Bernaud, Cohen-Scali & Guichard, 2007), a real clarification of terminology and underlying theories is required, as well as a legal structure for actions in the field of counseling. An evaluative, qualitative, and ethical approach to these practices also appears essential.

To achieve this, more research in this field is needed that would help structure a body of knowledge within the scope of international scientific activities. Greater involvement of researchers in existing international bodies would enable international counseling issues to be compared with those developing in France. This would also foster cross-disciplinary and intercultural research, reviews, and meta-analyses. Setting up national bodies bringing together practitioners and researchers on the subject (similar to Division 17 of the APA) would also enable a clearer definition of the concept and its field of application. It should be recalled that in France a clear difference is made between counseling, available to all-comers, and psychotherapy, associated with the idea of treatment.

Alongside the development of research activities, developing initial and continuing training in counseling appears to be essential in constituting a more homogeneous professional group. The ever-increasing challenge of offering a service which can be measured and whose quality and efficacy are guaranteed can only be met though a major investment in terms of training specialist professionals. As such, supervision, which is commonplace in France in the therapeutic field, should be further defined, strengthened, and regulated by professional bodies in order to raise and maintain standards of care, particularly in light of the very high demand for practice analysis amongst these professionals who are frequently confronted with complex personal and social problems for which they are ill-prepared and insufficiently armed in terms of training (Cohen-Scali, Guichard, & Gaudron, 2009).

Finally, there is an urgent need for a legal and administrative definition making a clear distinction between the titles of psychologist, counselor, and psychotherapist according to their fields of application and places of practice. This definition would allow quality standards for counseling services to be laid down. These standards should concern first the professionals (in terms of competences, qualifications, professional experience, supervision, etc.), but also the structures and organizations providing these services (in terms of procedures, tools, status, initial interview procedures, funding, etc.).

Conclusion

In France, the professional field of counseling appears paradoxical. Indeed, the demands for counseling have increased rapidly according to the current needs of individuals and societies, but at the same time, this field is very imprecise as it is built around practices and practitioners that are widely different. The emergence of this social demand also contributes to the creation of institutionalized practices of counseling, especially in the field of career counseling.

However, two distinctions seem to be relevant to describe this professional field: the first one distinguishes counseling for youth and for adults, and the second one distinguishes support practices (non-pathological), and treatment practices (medical practices). Counseling in France (historically mainly based on the work of differential psychology, and that of Rogers) therefore differs significantly from the psychotherapeutic perspective, which is strongly influenced by psychoanalytic approaches.

The major challenge for France at the present time is to be able to structure this field around clearly identified practices based on psychology, practices that can be defined socially and ethically and associated with certified training programs. The process of overcoming such a challenge would undoubtedly strengthen both the counseling field and therapeutic practices, and thus ensure that a "quality approach" would be implemented.

Notes

1 Baccalauréat is a general certificate of education that can be obtained after 12 years of school.
2 Ethnopsychiatry was founded by George Devereux. After a visit to the United States, he developed research on Vietnamese people "the Sedang Moi", then on Indian tribes of North America. He occupied the first chair of ethnopsychiatry in France in 1963.

References

Aubret, J., & Blanchard, S. (2005). *Pratique du bilan personnalisé* [Personalised career development analyses practices]. Paris: Dunod.

Balint, M. (1961). *Le médecin, son malade et la maladie.* [The doctor, his/her patient and the illness]. Paris: PBP-Blanchard.

Baubion-Broye, A., & Hajjar, V. (1998). *Evènements de vie, transition et construction de la personne.* [Life events, transition and self-construction]. Sainte-Agne: Eres.

Baudouin, N. (2007). *Le sens de l'orientation: une approche clinique de l'orientation.* [The meaning of vocational guidance: a clinical approach of vocational guidance]. Paris: L'Harmattan.

Bernaud, J. L., Cohen-Scali, V., & Guichard, J. (2007). Counseling psychology in France: A paradoxical situation. *Applied Psychology: An International Review, 1,* 131–151.

Bernaud, J. L., Gaudron, J. P., & Lemoine, C. (2006). Effects of career counseling on French adults: An experimental study. *Career Development Quartely, 54,* 241–256.

Blanchard-Laville, C. (2004). L'analyse clinique des pratiques professionnelles: un espace de transitionnalité. [The clinical analysis of professional practices: A space of transition]. *Education Permanente, 161,* 17–31.

Blanchard-Laville, C., & Fablet, D. (2002). *Sources théoriques et techniques de l'analyse des pratiques professionnelles.* [Theoretical sources and analyses of professional practice methods]. Paris: L'Harmattan.

Blanchard-Laville, C., & Nadot, S. (2004). Analyse de pratiques et professionnalisation entre affect et représentations. [Analysis of professional practices and professionalization]. *Connexions, 82,* 119–143.

Brown, S. D., & Lent, R. W. (1996). A social cognitive framework for career choice counseling. *Career Development Quaterly, 44,* 354–366.

Castra, D. (2003). *L'insertion professionnelle des publics précaires* [Professional integration of unqualified people]. Paris: Presses Universitaires de France.

CEDEFOP (2008). *Vocational Education and Training in France.* Luxembourg: Office for Official Publications of the European Communities.

Chartier, P., & Loarer, E. (2008). *Evaluer l'intelligence logique.* [The assessment of logical intelligence]. Paris: Dunod.

Cohen-Scali, V. (2009). *Les évolutions récentes des professions et activités de conseil* [The occupations and counseling activities' new evolutions]. Proceedings of the 2007 symposium organized by the AFPA/INOIP, France.

Cohen-Scali, V. (2010). *Travailler et étudier.* [Working and studying]. Paris: Presses Universitaires de France.

Cohen-Scali, V., Guichard, J., & Gaudron, J. P. (2009). Career counseling in France: A growing practice among diverse professional groups. In L. H. Gerstein, P. P. Heppner, S. Aegisdottir, S.-M. A. Leung, & K. L. Norsworthy (eds), *International Handbook of Cross-cultural Counseling* (pp. 329–226). Thousand Oaks, CA: Sage Publications.

Couchard, F., Huguet, M., & Matalon, B. (1995). *La psychologie et ses méthodes.* [Psychology and its methods]. Paris: Le livre de poche.

Deen, N. (2002). Les jeunes nouveaux immigrés dans les sociétés européennes: implications pour l'éducation et le conseil [The young new immigrants in the European societies: Implications for education and counseling], *L'Orientation Scolaire et Professionnelle, 2*, 163–178.

Du Roy, I. (2009). *Orange Stressé.* [Orange under pressure]. Paris: Broché.

Guichard, J. (2005). Life-long self-construction. *International Journal for Educational and Vocational Guidance, 5*, 111–124.

Guichard, J. (2008). Proposition d'un schéma d'entretien constructiviste de conseil en orientation pour les adolescents et jeunes adultes. [Outline of a life designing counseling interview for adolescents and young adults]. *L'orientation scolaire et professionnelle, 3*, 413–440.

Guichard, J., & Huteau, M. (2001). *Psychologie de l'orientation.* [Career counseling psychology]. Paris: Dunod.

Guichard, J., & Huteau, M. (2005). *L'orientation scolaire et professionnelle.* [School and career counseling]. Paris: Dunod.

Hackett, G. (1995). Self-efficacy in career choice and development. In A. Bandura (ed.), *Self-efficacy in Changing Societies* (pp. 232–258). Cambridge: Cambridge University Press.

Kanigel, R. (1997). *The One Best Way, Frederick Winslow Taylor and the enigma of efficiency.* London: Brown & Co.

Kiesler, C. A. (1971). *The Psychology of Commitment: Experiments Linking Behavior to Belief.* New York: Academic Press Inc.

Lhotellier, A. (2001). *Tenir conseil. Délibérer pour agir.* [Holding a meeting. Deliberating for action]. Paris: Selin Arslan.

Moro, M. R. (2002). *Enfants d'ici venus d'ailleurs. Naître et grandir en Franc* [Children coming from abroad. To be born and grow up in France]. Paris: La Découverte.

Moro, M. R., & Lachal, C. (1996). *Introduction aux psychothérapies.* [Introduction to psychotherapies]. Paris: Nathan.

Moscovici, S. (1961). *La psychanalyse.* [The Psychoanalysis] Paris: Presses Universitaires de France.

Munoz, M. C. (1999). Les pratiques interculturelles en éducation. [Intercultural practices in education] In J. Demorgon & E. M. Lipiansky (eds), *Guide de l'interculturel en formation* (pp. 20–28). Paris: Retz.

Nathan, T. (2001). *La folie des autres* [The madness of others]. Paris: Dunod.

Olry-Louis, I. (2009). Effects of different forms of tutor action in a conditional reasoning task: An experimental approach to the tutorial dialogue. *European Journal of Psychology of Education, 2*, 169–180.

Paul, M. (2002). L'accompagnement: Une nébuleuse. [Counseling: A nebula]. *Education Permanente, 153*, 43–56.

Pelletier, D., & Dumora, B. (1984). Fondements et postulats pour une conception éducative de l'orientation [Foundations and postulates for an educational conception of the guidance]. In D. Pelletier & R. Bujold (eds), *Pour une approche éducative en orientation.* Chicoutimi, Québec: Gaëtan Morin.

Pia, A., & Beaumel, C. (2011). Bilan démographique 2010 [Demographic assessment 2010]. *Insee Première, 1332*.

Pouyaud, J. (2008). *Transition, construction de soi et développement vocationnel. L'exemple des collégiens s'orientant en lycée professionnel* [Transition, self-construction and vocational development. The case of junior high-school students in their transition to vocational high schools]. Thèse de doctorat nouveau régime [Doctoral Thesis]. Paris: Conservatoire National des Arts et Métiers.

Roudinesco, E. (1986). *Histoire de la psychanalyse en France. La bataille de cent ans, 1et 2* [The history of psychoanalysis in France. A battle of one hundred years, 1 and 2]. Paris: Seuil.

Silberman, R., & Fournier, I. (2006). Jeunes issus de l'immigration. Une pénalité à l'embauche qui perdure. [Young people from immigration. A penalty lasting during the recruitment]. *Bref, 226*, 1–4.

Tremblay, L., & Lecomte, C. (1985). *L'entretien d'évaluation en counseling d'emploi.* [Career counseling assessment interview]. Montréal: Institut de recherches psychologiques, INC.

Tourette-Turgis, C. (1996). *Le counseling* [Counseling]. Paris: Presses Universitaires de France.

Vignoli, E. (2009). Inter-relationships among attachment to mother and father, self-esteem and career indecision. *Journal of Vocational Behavior, 75*, 91–99.

Watzlawick, P. (1978). *The language of change: Elements of therapeutic communication.* New York: Basic Books.

25

COUNSELING AND PSYCHOTHERAPY IN GERMANY

Common past, different present

Petra Warschburger

Introduction

The act of counseling can be found throughout history in every society as task and privilege of the senior generation, but today these traditional "counseling offers" mostly no longer exist. Germany has seen social as well as dramatic political changes over the past decades with the fall of the wall in 1989—especially for people from the former German Democratic Republic. Germany comprises 16 different federal states. With a population of 82 million inhabitants and a surface area of 357,114 km^2, it is densely populated. Due to high life expectancy and low birth rate, 20.3% of the population is older than 65 years. About 15 million of the inhabitants have a migrant background, primarily from southeastern Europe (Federal Office of Statistics, 2010). There is a relatively high unemployment rate of 7–8%, which differs significantly between regions and educational backgrounds. In terms of religion, Germany is substantially Christian, though more and more secularized, and a growing prevalence of other religions can be noticed (with Islam being the next most important religion) (Bertelsmann Foundation, 2008).

On top of that, industrial nations such as Germany find themselves in a constant process of transformation: life and work contexts change and technological developments (e.g., in the sector of work or healthcare) offer opportunities, but also cause new moral dilemmas and ethical problems. These processes of diversification and specialization put high demands on the operational and decisional competence of the individual. Accordingly, an increasing spread and establishment of professional and non-professional counseling offers can be noted. Psychosocial counseling is an interdisciplinary field, where many professions such as psychologists, social workers, pastors, or special education teachers are concerned with questions of mental and social wellbeing.[1] There is free admission to counseling services, which are often maintained by the church.

In 1999, the so-called "Psychotherapy Act" established the term "psychotherapist" as a registered professional title. It also detailed explicit rules of usage and reimbursement and allowed psychotherapists to bill the health insurance companies directly.[2]

In the counseling domain, such an arrangement is still missing. Besides this major difference between psychotherapy and counseling, a huge overlap can be observed in practice, e.g., in the context of youth welfare. Hence, the differences and similarities of counseling and psychotherapy in Germany will be discussed in this chapter.

Brief history of counseling and psychotherapy

Counseling and psychotherapy share a long common history. Psychotherapy in Germany has been strongly influenced by two traditions: psychoanalytic and depth psychology, and since the 1960s the learning theory approaches. Later, a third strong influence appeared: Rogers' non-directive, client-centered approach. Traditionally, mainly psychologists and physicians practiced psychotherapy, mostly in psychiatric clinics and health provision institutions, but also in private practices. The treatment of mental disorders is at the forefront. A distinction between the terms "counseling" and "psychotherapy" could not be found until the mid-20th century. In Germany, steps towards independent development of counseling and particularly institutionalization of counseling services were first noticed primarily in the educational sector. Here, one can see the traditionally very strong association between counseling and social volunteer work as well as its deep embeddedness in the social science professions. Educational counseling services date back to the 18th century, when, in the then Prussian state, criteria for a compensatory education by the state were formulated. The first educational counseling service was founded for delinquent youths in 1903 by Cimbal, a crime psychiatrist. Over the next years, due to an initiative of dedicated physicians as well as of a volunteer association and clubs (the so-called "welfare movement"), more and more counseling services were established. Their focus was on diagnostics, and intervention played a minor role (Abel, 1998).

With the establishment of educational counseling services, the different focuses of counseling and psychotherapy became clear, with counseling no longer concentrating mainly on mental disorders and individuals, but also taking "normal variations" and systemic influences into account. School was more and more seen as a relevant socializing agent, and in 1922 the first school psychologist, Hans Lämmermann, took up employment. Even though behavioral observation and testing procedures to diagnose performance ability and personality were his main area of responsibility, he also offered counseling—not only for individuals but also for the whole organization (Möley, 2007). During National Socialism many educational counseling services were forced to discontinue their work or to offer diagnoses fitting to the core values of the national socialists (Abel, 1998; Möley, 2007). After World War II, counseling services were greatly expanded and more and more fields of application (such as sexuality, career and studies, health) and more and more target groups (such as migrants, children and youths, women, etc.) were served with specific counseling offers by public as well as independently funded institutions. At the same time, different contacting methods (e.g., telephone or online counseling) were established. Since the 1990s the number of institutionalized counseling services and above all the demand for counseling have grown significantly (Federal Conference for Educational Counseling, 2010).

Along with this development, the distinction between counseling and psychotherapy has been discussed in Germany, especially vigorously within the field of psychology, the profession which contributes to both fields. Dietrich (1983, 1987) was one of the first to handle the topic from the psychologist's perspective and who formed the term "counseling psychology." After the coming into force of the Psychotherapy Act in 1999 (German Federal Ministry of Justice), which defined the practice of psychotherapy as " ... every action using scientifically accepted psychotherapeutic methods to diagnose, heal or ease disorders with clinical significance [...] To the practice of psychotherapy do not belong psychological actions with the purpose of reprocessing or overcoming of social conflicts or other purposes" and explicitly excluded counseling, more efforts were made to create a "counseling law" and legal protection for the term "counseling". These efforts led to the foundation of the "German Association for Counseling," which to date includes 31 different professional associations and occupational unions (German Association for Counseling, n.d.). Its goals are, among others, to continue the sharpening of the profile of the manifold counseling professions and to establish a comprehensive quality management (German Association for Counseling, n.d.).

Counselor education programs, accreditation, licensure, and certification

In many professions, counseling is defined as an essential part of the job. So-called "counseling modules" can therefore be found in many study courses (e.g., teacher-training, education, special needs education, psychology, or medicine). The contents and methodical standards are developed by the respective academic institutions. There are no mandatory contents of teaching or a defined, generally accepted training course to become a psychosocial counselor. During the Bologna Process,[3] master's studies were designed, which explicitly use the term "counseling" and permit access to all professions. They are more common at universities of applied sciences than at universities (where most of the psychologists get their academic degree). Postgraduate training programs for (psychosocial) counselors are more widespread, and are partly affiliated to professional associations or to universities of applied sciences and universities. Thereby, many theoretical directions are represented, although in the psychosocial field, client-centered, and systemic family therapies are the most prominent directions. The German Association for Counseling strives towards standardized and legally binding standards for advanced training and published, for the first time in 2010, an agenda of detailed admission conditions, and the content and extent of theoretical and practical modules (German Association for Counseling, n.d.). Prerequisites are for example a university or university of applied sciences degree in an appropriate study course (e.g., social pedagogy/social work, education, psychology, medicine, theology, economics, law); also 570 hours of extra-occupational advanced training is proposed. The transfer of psychological, philosophical, religious, political, legal, and (inter-) cultural knowledge is emphasized to fulfill the diversity of the application areas. However, these regulations are voluntary guidelines, as there is to date no legally protected title of "(psychological) counselor."

Regarding accreditation processes in Germany, only three major forms of psychotherapy are listed as accredited psychotherapeutic techniques: analytic psychotherapy, depth psychology-based psychotherapy, and behavioral therapy. Other methods of psychotherapeutic treatment are not reimbursed by health insurance, and patients have to self-finance their treatment. Further training for psychological counselors is often offered at universities of applied sciences as a master's degree or as an additional qualification by the respective professional societies. A general rule of implementation does not exist at the moment.

In terms of licensure, the Psychotherapy Act established the term *psychotherapist* as a registered professional title available only to physicians, psychologists (master or diploma), and social workers (who are only admitted in psychotherapy programs for children and adolescents and not for adults) who successfully complete additional postgraduate psychotherapy training (segmented in programs for medical, psychological, and child and youth psychotherapists). The training takes place at state-approved institutes for psychotherapy training (currently more than 240 (Federal Chamber of Psychotherapists, 2010)). Psychotherapeutic training takes 3 years of full-time or 5 years of part-time study, and psychologists require 600 hours of theory training, 1,800 hours of psychiatric and psychosomatic internship, 600 hours of treatment under supervision, and 120 hours in self-consciousness raising groups, and ends with an oral and written exam, the approbation. Afterwards the newly licensed psychotherapist can apply for the right to become a provider under the local insurance scheme, which allows him to bill insurance companies directly. Admission depends on the regional supply situation.[4] It is also possible to offer psychotherapy and counseling as a non-medical practitioner according to legislation from the 1930s (i.e., the 1939 non-medical Practitioner Act, updated in 2001). Regional public health departments certify and grant the accreditation, because federal regulations do not exist. The accreditation permits acting as a psychotherapist or counselor (1999 Psychotherapy Act)—but without the possibility to bill the health insurance companies.

Finally, as for certification processes in Germany, psychotherapy training can be accomplished at one of the state-approved training institutes. Additional certification of the training institutes ensuring the quality of the training is not provided, but could be implemented according to the DIN EN ISO 9001 quality management system.

Current counseling and psychotherapy theories, process, and trends

Besides the guideline psychotherapies, we find a wide variety of client-centered and systemic and resource-orientated approaches, especially in the context of counseling. Many psychotherapists and counselors claim to have an eclectic orientation (Orlinsky & Rønnestad, 2005). Especially in psychotherapy-based counseling, traditional psychotherapeutic concepts are strongly used. The development of new theories related to counseling lags behind development within psychotherapy, whereas one can also observe a "rapprochement" of clinical counseling and psychotherapy by increasingly stressing systemic influences and the importance of resources (Krischke, 2009; Mattejat & Pauschardt, 2009). Nevertheless, counseling-specific theoretical approaches can very well be found in work and organizational or educational psychology (Bamberg, 2009; Schwarzer & Buchwald, 2009). In general, the reception of new theoretical concepts is strongly influenced by the Anglo-American area. To bridge the gap between different major psychotherapy approaches, integrative models are heavily discussed. Grawe, Donati and Bernauer (1994) carried out multiple meta-analyses on the efficacy of psychotherapy. On this basis, they postulated four general change mechanisms:

1. augmentation of coping competences (i.e. active support by the therapist/counselor)
2. clarification of meaning (i.e., reflection of experiences and behavior with regard to goals and values)
3. problem activation (i.e., problem-centered work in real settings)
4. activation of resources.

Within the discussion about a comprehensive theoretical foundation of counseling, Holm-Hadulla, Hofmann, and Sperth (2009) have presented an integrative model of counseling, which explicitly includes different aspects permitting the reflection of a problem from complementary perspectives. The so-called ABCDE model is based on a broad range of options for intervention, the modification of **B**ehavior (**B**) and the **C**hange of dysfunctional cognitions (**C**), the reflection of life/**D**ynamics (**D**) right up to the discussion of **E**xistential topics (**E**), all of which are to be combined with resource-orientated and solution-driven aspects. These techniques are embedded in a sustainable counselor–client **A**lliance (**A**) as described in the client-centered approach.

Also in the context of health counseling and health psychology—an increasingly important sector in Germany—integrative approaches like the transtheoretical model (TTM) of Prochaska and Norcross (2003), focusing on the process-like character of change and the question of matching a person's willingness for change and the particular intervention strategy, are increasingly applied. The self-management approach from Kanfer, Reinecker, and Schmelzer

(2006) is widely applied, especially in counseling and training of chronically ill people (also Domsch & Lohaus, 2009). This approach has also been transferred to other settings like educational counseling and is furthermore discussed as a general conceptual frame for counseling and therapy (Schmelzer, 2000). Despite the high prevalence of health problems and the increasing awareness of the need for effective prevention approaches, this area is clearly underrepresented both in practice and in research. Though there are evaluated prevention programs, their implementation and reception in broader contexts like schools lags behind. A lasting trend in Germany is the increasing publication of therapy manuals, guidebook literature (Krampen & Schui, 2006), and group programs.

Media-supported counseling has become more important over the past years. This topic comprises different styles of the so-called "distance counseling" (Haley, 2005), which, in contrast to classic face-to-face interaction in counseling, refrains from a temporal and/or local co-presence of client and counselor. Examples are telephone counseling, e-mail counseling, chat rooms and internet platforms, and simulated counseling or interactive modules. Although, distance treatment is categorically prohibited for psychotherapists and can only be conducted in well-grounded exceptional cases (Almer, 2008), media-supported counseling is used more and more often. Its advantages lie mostly in the local and temporal boundlessness and in the improved accessibility for underprovided groups of persons, e.g., youths, elderly people, or physically handicapped people. The ethical and legal questions linked to such services are controversially discussed (see Warschburger, 2009). The fields of applications reach from different prevention offers to treatment offers for physical (e.g. oncology) or mental disorders (e.g. eating disorders), with the field of aftercare and relapse prevention showing promising results (Bauer & Kordy, 2008).

Indigenous and traditional healing methods

Alternative and complementary therapies seem to be widespread for various somatic complaints. In a representative survey, 60% of the respondents indicated that they had practiced at least one classical natural (e.g., exercise therapy, herbal medicine, hydrotherapy, or medical massage) or alternative healing method (e.g., homeopathic therapy) within the last year. Furthermore, 6.4% contacted a non-medical practitioner (Härtel & Volger, 2004). Unfortunately, traditional healing methods were not listed in that study. According to Walach (2006), spiritual healing and healing through prayer are being used quite a lot, especially in rural areas. In general, traditional and folk healing methods seem to be more relevant and more prevalent in persons with a migrant background (Assion, Zarouchas, Multamäki, Zolotova, & Schröder, 2007). Assion (2004) reported that belief in djinns, the evil eye, or black magic is highly prevalent in Turkish migrants, and 70% had contacted a healer because of psychological problems. The practices applied most commonly were wearing an amulet ("musca"), reading the Koran, or drinking "hallowed water." Overall, around 70% of the patients had a positive or neutral attitude towards traditional healers. The charges for these approaches are usually not reimbursed by statutory health insurance.

Research and supervision

Unfortunately, there is a huge gap between practice and research in psychotherapy and counseling. On the one hand, current research results and theoretical developments are rarely adopted in practice (or even smiled at), on the other hand, researchers hardly notice developments that have arisen in the field. Therefore, only 6% of the publications in the field of counseling psychology originate from a non-academic setting (Kahn, 2005). Many different "root disciplines" play a part in the domain of counseling because of its interdisciplinary and multiprofessional character. For psychotherapy research in academic settings (e.g. university ambulances), behavioral approaches predominate and more empirical efficacy studies are published. With a range of special funding resources (e.g., the tendering of a psychotherapy network or of clinical studies by the Federal Ministry of Education and Research [BMBF] and the German Research Foundation [DFG]), psychotherapy research with high methodical standards (controlled RCT studies) has been considerably encouraged over the past years. No comparable funding initiatives explicitly support counseling research. Nevertheless, counseling has proved to be a dynamic field of research within psychology. Krampen and Schui (2006) assessed the proportion of counseling-related literature from 1967 until 2003. While the proportion of counseling-related publications in the international literature remains more or less constantly at 1.5%, it is 3–4% higher in the German-speaking literature. The papers mostly deal with psychotherapeutic counseling (international: career counseling) and partnership and pastoral counseling. New domains like genetic or intercultural counseling are attracting increasing interest. It is striking, however, that there is a lack of evaluation studies in the domain of counseling compared with well-established psychotherapy outcome research. Institutionalized counseling in Germany traditionally understands quality assurance as an integral part of its work. The framing conditions for institutional counseling (such as few contacts; strict data protection observances; insufficient cooperation networks with research institutions; lack of financial support) make, even forestall, large-scale controlled outcome studies difficult. Nevertheless, there are a number of effectiveness studies concerning educational counseling, particularly in the area of patient education (Warschburger, 2009). In general, empirical research and theoretical considerations are at an early stage in Germany (Auckenthaler, 1999; Strauß, Wheeler, & Nodop, 2010). As part of quality assurance, 10 years after the inception of the German law regulating the education of psychological psychotherapists and child and adolescent psychotherapists a nationwide survey concerning psychotherapy training in Germany was performed to assess the current situation in education and supervision (Glaesmer et al., 2009; Kohl et al., 2009; Sonntag et al., 2009; Nodop, Thiel, & Strauß, 2010).

Supervision is not only mandatory in psychotherapy training, it is also implemented in the guidelines for the training of psychosocial counselors. Freyberger (2010) criticizes that there are neither clearly defined prerequisites nor a consensus for the practical application of supervision nor required qualifications for supervisors and claims an increase in professionalism of supervision. The German Association for Supervision (DGSv, 2010) has worked out a systematic, comprehensive curriculum for the training of supervisors which is suitable for psychotherapy as well as for counseling. While clear guidelines for supervision during training exist, they are largely lacking after training is finished, although the importance of ongoing supervision is pronounced in professional associations and institutions (like psychosomatic clinics or educational counseling services). Representative data about the range of practicing psychotherapists accessing supervision are not available but seem to be high (Willutzki, 1995).

Strengths, weaknesses, opportunities and challenges

A major strength in the field of counseling and psychotherapy in Germany can be found in its well-established, multifaceted psychosocial supply network which for many years has guaranteed access to psychological treatment regardless of financial background. One pillar of this system is the Psychotherapy Act from 1999. Psychological psychotherapists and pediatric psychotherapists are two healthcare professions for outpatient treatment of mentally ill people equivalent to a medical specialist. This alleviates access to ambulant psychotherapy for many patients, because of the shortfall of financial constraints and social barriers like the "loop way via a referring physician". The act also established clear standards for professional qualification in line with training regulated by the state and guarantees of psychotherapeutic treatment when indicated. Since the Psychotherapy Act restricts this intervention only to curing a person with a mental disorder and therefore excludes subclinical problems or preventive efforts, the counseling services (often institutionalized and free of charge) constitute the second pillar in psychosocial basic care. In the Child and Youth Services Act (1990) there exists, for instance, a clear arrangement about the services exceeding counseling that parents and children can call upon without charge. Alongside these "free" services, there are also manifold charged services (e.g., non-medical practitioners providing psychotherapy as well as counseling).

In terms of weaknesses, the need of psychosocial assistance in different contexts of life like education or career, partnership and family, as well as health has risen dramatically while the means for psychosocial initiatives and establishments have been considerably reduced or even cancelled since the 1990s. In particular, counseling services are often financed by municipal or free providers (like churches and charity organizations), and certain services (e.g., special consultation hours for employed persons, prevention classes, etc.) depend on their funding resources. The means for the supply of school psychology counseling on site in some federal states have been reduced dramatically, and specialized staff are not available anymore. According to the Organisation for Economic Co-operation and Development (OECD) guidelines, there should be one school psychologist for 2,500 pupils. In Lower Saxony, a school psychologist is responsible for 10 times as many pupils (Jötten, 2007; The Association of German Professional Psychologists, 2010). Provision for children and youths, is an area where an enormous need for development exists (Sann & Landua, 2009).

In the field of psychotherapy, a considerable lack of provision can be noticed as well. The number of psychotherapeutic practices covered by health insurance is controlled by the state, and only in exceptional cases are health insurance companies willing to reimburse the costs of non-approved psychotherapists. Only about 10% receive appropriate therapy. This number is even lower for certain diagnoses and in rural regions (Wittchen & Jacobi, 2001).

Major opportunities in the field result from the demand for psychosocial counseling, which has massively grown over the past decades. One could almost call it a "counseling boom" and the prevalence of health-related problems is rising in our aging society. One can also notice a growing specialization and diversification of counseling concepts. Counseling is, in contrast to psychotherapy, not restricted to one specific vocational qualification, but plays an important role in many professions. The interdisciplinary character of counseling offers the chance to take a more comprehensive point of view on the etiology and chronicity of psychosocial problems. Specialists from different professions should conjointly develop new concepts and approaches. Such interdisciplinary collaboration can already be observed in several areas like media-supported or health-related counseling.

Nevertheless, many challenges still lie ahead. With the reimbursement by health insurance companies, an income-independent care of mentally ill persons should be guaranteed. However, ambulant psychotherapy is most often used by well-educated persons, women, and middle-aged persons, while younger and older people are hardly reached (Albani, Blaser, Geyer, & Schmutzel, 2010). Another challenge is the development of culturally sensitive counseling concepts for immigrants, since about 17% of the children and youths in Germany grow up in families with migration background. These children have poorer physical and mental health, while medical prevention services are rarely made use of (Robert-Koch-Institut, 2008). Cumulative social risks like poverty or low educational levels, well-known risk factors for health and quality of life, can often be found in these families as well (Lampert & Kurth, 2007). In particular, research is urgently needed to better understand the psychosocial and health situation of immigrants as well as their use of health-related services. Based on these data, psychosocial provision can then be adapted to specific requirements and needs (Lindert, Priebe, Penka, Napo, Schouler-Ocak, & Heinz, 2008).

Future directions

In Germany, institutionalized psychosocial counseling is an important pillar in psychosocial care. Counseling is characterized primarily by its interdisciplinary nature and low-threshold access. However, compared to psychotherapy, which is an integral part of the German statutory health insurance system with clear guidelines for reimbursement and qualification, professionalization is only at the very early stages. In order to establish itself as an additional, necessary pillar in psychosocial care besides psychotherapy, a distinguished theoretical background and professionalization within the field is needed. The various professions dealing with questions of counseling enrich the discussion on the one hand while on the other hand they present great demands when it comes to profiling (e.g. different theoretical backgrounds, different approaches). If the interdisciplinary character of counseling was taken seriously, the different professions could complement one another with their knowledge about the background of problems, as well as about the precise design of counseling work. Counseling approaches realized in medical settings seem to be a good example of how to reach that goal.

Conclusion

Within the Psychotherapy Act there exists a clear legal distinction between counseling and psychotherapy in Germany, but differentiation in terminology and theory is still lacking. Within clinical psychology, an obvious focusing on psychotherapy in research and practice has arisen over the past years, while educational, work and organizational, health or medical psychology have put the emphasis on counseling (and on training/education) as a form of intervention. Psychological professions still dominate the "classic" counseling institutions (like educational counseling, professional counseling, marriage and family counseling) and add classic clinical as well as therapeutic concepts (mainly from the field of client-centered and systemic orientation). Since the 1970s, new initiatives had been generated, first of all in the context of social work and special education, which has greatly enlarged the spectrum of counseling offers and concepts (e.g., youth counseling, migrant counseling, unemployment). However, in Germany one always has the impression that these "two waves of the counseling movement" did not interweave, but in contrast invested a lot of energy in a mutual delimitation. In light of the need to establish mandatory quality standards on a "booming market of counseling" and a registered title of psychosocial counselor so as to protect help seekers from ineffective and at times harmful interventions, counselors in Germany can profit from experiences in the field of psychotherapy.

Notes

1 There are about 12,500 psychosocial counseling institutions in Germany (Warschburger, n.d.) with about 5,180 psychotherapists working there (Federal Health Reporting, n.d.), among them about 2,400 in educational counseling (Federal Conference for Educational Counseling, 2010).

2 The majority of the German population are members of a public health insurance program which assures free access to medical as well as psychological treatment.

3 The Bologna Process is named after the Bologna declaration which was signed 1999 by ministers in charge of higher education. The general aim is to create a European Higher Education Areas (EHEAs) based on international cooperation and academic staff. Parts of these reforms are the establishment of

comparable degrees in higher education (e.g., bachelor, master, doctorate), the assurance of quality standards and the recognition of foreign degrees.

4 There are about 33,000 licensed psychological psychotherapists and child and youth psychotherapists. Beyond that, about 3,500 panel doctors work exclusively as psychotherapists (Federal Health Reporting, n.d.).

References

Abel, A. H. (1998). Geschichte der Erziehungsberatung: Bedingungen, Zwecke, Kontinuitäten [History of educational counseling. Conditions, goals, continuity]. In W. Körner & G. Hörmann (eds), *Handbuch der Erziehungsberatung* (Vol 1) (pp. 19–51). Göttingen: Hogrefe.

Albani, C., Blaser, G., Geyer, M., & Schmutzel, G. (2010). Ambulante Psychotherapie in Deutschland aus Sicht der Patienten. Teil 1: Versorgungssituation [Ambulant psychotherapy in Germany from the patients' view. Part 1: supply situation]. *Psychotherapeut, 6*, 503–514.

Almer, S. (2008). Das Fernbehandlungsverbot als rechtliche Grenze im Einsatz neuer Medien in der psychosozialen Versorgung. [The prohibition of distance treatment as legal borderline for the application of new media in the psychosocial care] In S. Bauer & H. Kordy (eds), *E-Mental Health. Neue Medien in der psychosozialen Versorgung* (pp. 13–17). Berlin: Springer.

Assion, H. J. (2004). *Traditionelle Heilmethoden türkischer Migranten* [Traditional healing methods of turkish migrants]. Berlin: VWB.

Assion, H. J., Zarouchas, I., Multamäki, S., Zalotova, J., & Schröder, S. G. (2007). Patients' use of alternative methods parallel to psychiatric therapy: Does the migrational background matter? *Acta Psychiatrica Scandinavica, 116*, 220–225.

Auckenthaler, A. (1999). Supervision von Psychotherapie. Behauptungen–Fakten–Trends [Supervision of psychotherapy: Claims, facts, trends]. *Psychotherapeut, 44*, 139–152.

Bamberg, E. (2009). Beratung in der Arbeits-und Organisationspsychologie [Counseling in work and organizational psychology]. In P. Warschburger (ed.), *Beratungspsychologie* (pp. 207–235). Berlin: Springer.

Bauer, S. & Kordy, H. (eds). (2008). *E-Mental Health. Neue Medien in der psychosozialen Versorgung* [E-mental health. New media in the psychosocial care]. Berlin: Springer.

Bertelsmann Foundation. [Bertelsmann Stiftung] (2008). *Bertelsmann Religionsmonitor Deutschland 2008. Charts* [Bertelsmann religion monitor survey Germany 2008. Charts]. Retrieved from www.bertelsmann-stiftung.de/cps/rde/xchg/SID-98B98026-0887BA33/bst/hs.xsl/85217_85220.htm

Dietrich, G. (1983). *Allgemeine Beratungspsychologie* [General counseling psychology]. Göttingen: Hogrefe.

——(1987). *Spezielle Beratungspsychologie* [Particular counseling psychology]. Göttingen: Hogrefe.

Domsch, H. & Lohaus, A. (2009). Gesundheitsberatung [Health counseling]. In P. Warschburger (ed.), *Beratungspsychologie* (pp. 155–173). Berlin: Springer.

Federal Chamber of Psychotherapists. [Bundespsychotherapeutenkammer] (2010). *Anerkannte Ausbildungsinstitute* [Accredited training institutions]. Retrieved from www.bptk.de/service/ausbildung/index.html

Federal Conference for Educational Counseling. [Bundeskonferenz für Erziehungsberatung] (2010.). *Inanspruchnahmequote* [Quota of demand]. Retrieved from www.bke.de/content/html/statistik/inan spruchnahme.show.html?id=233

Federal Health Reporting. [Gesundheitsberichterstattung des Bundes] (n.d.). *Beschäftigte Psychologische Psychotherapeutinnen und-therapeuten und Kinder-und Jugendlichenpsychotherapeutinnen und–therapeuten* [Employed psychological psychotherapists and pediatric psychotherapists]. Retrieved from www.gbe-bund.de/oowa921-install/servlet/oowa/aw92/dboowasys921.xwdevkit/xwd_init?gbe.isgbetol/xs_start_neu/& p_aid=3&p_aid=44434160&nummer=697&p_sprache=D&p_indsp=-&p_aid=27007749

Federal Office of Statistics. [Statistisches Bundesamt] (2010). *Statistisches Jahrbuch* [Statistical yearbook]. Retrieved from www.destatis.de/jetspeed/portal/cms/Sites/destatis/SharedContent/Oeffentlich/B3/Publikation/Jahrbuch/StatistischesJahrbuch,property=file.pdf

Freyberger, H. (2010). Professionalisierung der Supervision. Qualitätsmerkmale und Ausbildungserfordernisse von Supervisoren [Professionalization of supervision. Qualification features and training requirements of supervisors]. *Psychotherapeut, 6*, 465–470.

GEK. (2007). *GEK-Report ambulant-ärztliche Versorgung 2007* [GEK-report ambulant-medical supply]. Retrieved from http://media.gek.de/downloads/magazine/GEK-Report-Ambulant-aerztliche-Versor-gung-2007.pdf

German Association for Counseling. [Deutsche Gesellschaft für Beratung] (n.d.). *Essentials einer Weiterbildung/ Beratung/ Counseling* [Essentials of Advanced training/Counseling]. Retrieved from www.dachverband-beratung.de/dokumente/weiterbildungsstandards.pdf

German Association for Counseling. [Deutsche Gesellschaft für Beratung]. (n.d.). *Mitgliedsorganisationen* [Member organizations]. Retrieved from www.dachverband-beratung.de/mitgliedsorganisationen.php

German Association for Counseling. [Deutsche Gesellschaft für Beratung]. (2005). *Satzung* [Statutes]. Retrieved from www.dachverband-beratung.de/dokumente/Satzung.pdf

German Association for Supervision. [Deutsche Gesellschaft für Supervision] (2010). *Standards*. Retrieved from www.dgsv.de/pdf/Standards.pdf

German Federal Ministry for Family Affairs, Senior Citizens, Women and Youth [Bundesministerium für Familie, Senioren, Frauen und Jugend] (1991). *Kinder-und Jugendhilfe–Sozialgesetzbuch–Achtes Buch (KJHG)* [Children and youth welfare service–social statute book–8th book]. Retrieved from www.bmfsfj.de/BMFSFJ/gesetze,did=3278.html

German Federal Ministry of Justice [Bundesministerium der Justiz]. (1939/2001). *Gesetz über die Berufe des Psychologischen Psychotherapeuten und des Kinder- und Jugendlichen psychotherapeuten Heilpraktikergesetz* [Non-Medical Practitioner Act Psychotherapy Act].

German Federal Ministry of Justice [Bundesministerium der Justiz]. (1999). *Gesetz über die Berufe des Psychologischen Psychotherapeuten und des Kinder-und Jugendlichenpsychotherapeuten* [Psychotherapy Act].

Glaesmer, H., Sonntag, A., Barnow, S., Brähler, E., Fegert, J., Fliegel, S., … Strauß, B. (2009). Psychotherapeutenausbildung aus Sicht der Absolventen. Ergebnisse der Absolventenbefragung im Rahmen des Forschungsgutachtens [Psychotherapist training from the perspective of the graduates: Results of a survey of graduates in Germany]. *Psychotherapeut, 54*, 437–444.

Grawe, K., Donati, R., & Bernauer, F. (1994). *Psychotherapie im Wandel. Von der Konfession zur Profession* [Changes of psychotherapy. From confession to profession]. Göttingen: Hogrefe.

Haley, D. (2005). Technology and counselling. In D. Capuzzi & D. R. Gross (eds), *Introduction to the Counselling Profession* (pp. 121–152). New York: Pearson.

Härtel, U., & Volger, E. (2004). Inanspruchnahme und Akzeptanz klassischer Naturheilverfahren und alternativer Heilmethoden in Deutschland–Ergebnisse einer repräsentativen Bevölkerungsstudie [Use and acceptance of classical natural and alternative medicine in Germany–Findings of a representative population-based survey]. *Forschende Komplimentärmedizin und klassische Naturheilkunde, 11*, 327–334.

Holm-Hadulla, R., Hofmann, F.-H., & Sperth, M. (2009). Integrative Beratung. ABCDE-Modell zur psychologischen und psychotherapeutischen Beratung [Integrative counseling. An ABCDE model for psychological and psychotherapeutic counseling]. *Psychotherapeut, 54*, 326–333.

Jötten, B. (2007). Leitlinien und Idealskizze der Schulpsychologie [Guidelines and ideal sketch of school psychology]. In T. Fleischer, N. Grewe, B. Jötten, K. Seifried & B. Sieland (eds), *Handbuch Schulpsychologie* [Handbook of school psychology] (pp. 421–426). Stuttgart: Kohlhammer.

Kahn, J. H. (2005). Institutional research productivity, use of theory-thriven research, and statistical application in counseling psychology: Examining the research base. *The Counseling Psychology, 33*, 340–348.

Kamtsiuris, P., Bergmann, E., Rattay, P., & Schlaud, M. (2007). Inanspruchnahme medizinischer Leistungen. Ergebnisse des Kinder-und Jugendgesundheitssurveys (KiGGS) [Use of medical services. Results of the German Health Interview and examination Survey for children and adolescents (KiGGS)]. *Bundesgesundheitsbl–Gesundheitsforsch–Gesundheitsschutz, 50*, 836–850.

Kanfer, F. H., Reinecker, H., & Schmelzer, D. (2006). *Selbstmanagement-Therapie. Ein Lehrbuch für die klinische Praxis* [Self-management therapy. An instruction book for the clinical practice]. Berlin: Springer.

Kohl, S., Barnow, S., Brähler, E., Fegert, J., Fliegel, S., Freyberger, H., … Strauß, B. (2009). Die Psychotherapieausbildung aus Sicht der Lehrkräfte. Ergebnisse der Befragung von Dozenten, Supervisoren und Selbsterfahrungsleitern im Rahmen des Forschungsgutachtens [Psychotherapy training from the perspective of the trainers: Results of a survey made among lecturers, supervisors and leaders of self-awareness groups within the framework of the research report]. *Psychotherapeut, 54*, 445–456.

Krampen, G., & Schui, G. (2006). Beratung im Spiegel wissenschaftlicher Information und Dokumentation [Counseling in the mirror of scientific information and documentation]. In C. Steinebach (ed.), *Handbuch Psychologische Beratung* (pp. 134–146). Stuttgart: Klett Cotta.

Krischke, N. (2009). Beratung bei Psychischen Krisen [Counseling in mental crises]. In P. Warschburger (ed.), *Beratungspsychologie* [Counseling psychology] (pp. 235–255). Berlin: Springer.

Lampert, T., & Kurth, B. M. (2007). Sozialer Status und Gesundheit von Kindern und Jugendlichen. Ergebnisse des Kinder-und Jugendgesundheitssurveys (KiGGS) [Socioeconomic status and health in children and adolescents–Results of the German Health Interview and Examination Survey for children and adolescents (KiGGS)]. *Deutsches Ärzteblatt, 43*, 2944–2949.

Lindert, J., Priebe, S., Penka, S., Napo, F., Schouler-Ocak, M., & Heinz, A. (2008). Versorgung psychisch kranker Patienten mit Migrationshintergrund [Mental Health Care for Migrants]. *Psychother Psych Med, 58*, 123–129.

Mattejat, F., & Pauschardt, J. (2009). Beratung in der Klinischen Psychologie [Counseling in Clinical Psychology]. In P. Warschburger (ed.), *Beratungspsychologie* (pp. 173–207). Berlin: Springer.

Möley, S. (2007). Geschichte der Schulpsychologie in Deutschland [History of school psychology in Germany]. In T. Fleischer, N. Grewe, B. Jötten, K. Seifried, & B. Sieland (eds), *Handbuch Schulpsychologie* (pp. 17–26). Stuttgart: Kohlhammer.

Nodop, S., Thiel, K., & Strauß, B. (2010). Supervision in der psychotherapeutischen Ausbildung in Deutschland. Quantitative und qualitative Ergebnisse des Forschungsgutachtens [Supervision in the psychotherapeutic training in Germany. Quantitative and qualitative results of the research survey]. *Psychotherapeut, 55*, 485–495.

Orlinsky, D. E., & Rønnestad, M. H. (2005). *How psychotherapists develop: A study of therapeutic work and professional growth.* Washington, DC: American Psychological Association.

Prochaska, J. O., & Norcross, J. C. (2003). *Systems of psychotherapy: A transtheoretical analysis* (5th edn). Pacific Grove, CA: Brooks/Cole Publishing Company.

Robert Koch-Institut (eds). (2008) *Kinder-und Jugendgesundheitssurvey (KiGGS) 2003–2006: Kinder und Jugendliche mit Migrationshintergrund in Deutschland. Beiträge zur Gesundheitsberichterstattung des Bundes* German [*Health Interview and examination Survey for children and adolescents (KiGGS) 2003—2006: Children and adolescent with migration background*] Retrieved from www.kiggs.de/experten/downloads/dokumente/KiGGS_migration%5B1%5D.pdf

Rogers, C. S. (1951). *Client-centered therapy: Its current practice, implications and theory.* Boston: Houghton Mifflin.

Sann, A., & Landua, D. (2009). Systeme Früher Hilfen: Gemeinsam geht's besser! Ergebnisse der ersten bundesweiten Bestandsaufnahme bei Jugend-und Gesundheitsämtern [A systemic approach to early childhood prevention. Outcomes of a first nationwide survey of Youth Welfare and Health Care System in Germany]. *Bundesgesundheitsbl–Gesundheitsforsch–Gesundheitsschutz, 53*, 1018–1028.

Schmelzer, D. (2000). Hilfe zur Selbsthilfe. Der Selbstmanagement-Ansatz als Rahmenkonzept für Beratung und Therapie [Helping others to help themselves. The self-management approach as a conceptual framework for counseling and therapy]. *Beratung Aktuell, 4*, 1–20.

Schwarzer, C., & Buchwald, P. (2009). Beratung in der Pädagogischen Psychologie [Counseling in educational psychology]. In P. Warschburger (ed.), *Beratungspsychologie* (pp. 131–155). Berlin: Springer.

Sonntag, A., Glaesmer, H., Barnow, S., Brähler, E., Fegert, J., Fliegel, S., … Strauß, B. (2009). Die Psychotherapeutenausbildung aus Sicht der Teilnehmer. Ergebnisse einer Ausbildungsteilnehmerbefragung im Rahmen des Forschungsgutachtens [Psychotherapists' education from the perspective of trainees. Results of a survey in Germany]. *Psychotherapeut, 54*, 427–436.

Strauß, B., Wheeler, S., & Nodop, S. (2010). Klinische Supervision. Überblick über den Stand der Forschung [Clinical supervision. Review of the state of research]. *Psychotherapeut, 6*, 455–464.

The Association of German Professional Psychologists, Section School Psychology. [Berufsverband Deutscher Psychologinnen und Psychologen, Sektion Schulpsychologie]. (2010). *Versorgungszahlen Schulpsychologie* [Supply data for school psychology.]. Retrieved from www.bdp-schulpsychologie.de/backstage2/sps/documentpool/2010/2010_versorgungszahlen_schulpsychologie.pdf

Walach, H. (2006). Verfahren der Komplementärmedizin. Beispiel: Heilung durch Gebet und geistiges Heilen. [Procedures of complementary medicine. Spiritual healing and healing through prayer]. *Bundesgesundheitsblatt–Gesundheitsforschung–Gesundheitsschutz, 49*, 788–795.

Warschburger, P. (2009). *Beratungspsychologie* [Counseling Psychology]. Göttingen: Hogrefe.

Willutzki, U. (1995). Novizinnen und erfahrene Therapeutinnen: Brauchen alle dieselbe Supervisionsform? [Novices and experienced therapists: Do all need the same kind of supervision?]. *Verhaltensther Psychosoz Prax, 27*, 419–435.

Wittchen, H.-U., & Jacobi, F. (2001). Die Versorgungssituation psychischer Störungen in Deutschland. Eine klinisch-epidemiologische Abschätzung anhand des Bundes-Gesundheitssurveys 1998 [Met and unmet needs for intervention. Clinical-epidemiological estimations for mental disorders in the German Health Interview and Examination Survey]. *Bundesgesundheitsbl–Gesundheitsforsch–Gesundheitsschutz, 44*, 993–1000.

26

COUNSELING AND PSYCHOTHERAPY IN ITALY

Historical, cultural, and indigenous perspectives

Marco Gemignani and Massimo Giliberto

Introduction

Whereas the professional fields of clinical psychology and psychotherapy are strongly regulated, in Italy there are no specific laws or statutes that define the field of counseling and set minimum standards of training and practice. In this unregulated scenario, anyone can be a "counselor." Yet, at the same time, many schools of psychotherapy offer courses in counseling as part of the training curricula. In general, counseling is conceived as a practice that is limited in time and that focuses on human development, vocational orientation, problem solving, conflict resolution within small groups, and usually concrete goals.[1] Psychotherapy, instead, concerns psychological sufferance and pathology, and is usually conceived as being long term. Despite various attempts to separate the two professional figures of the counselor and the psychotherapist, in practice there is significant overlapping between the two of them. In effect, the Italian Order of Psychologists took a critical stance toward the field of counseling, maintaining that this practice corresponds to psychological consultancy and, since it is unregulated, it can easily lead to professional malpractice. Some psychology lobbies have even argued for the illegality of counseling because counselors perform activities that they are not authorized to do and that are within the professional domain of psychologists. This conflict is still ongoing.

Italy has a population of approximately 60 million. The Italian language is one of the few cultural dimensions that are common across the peninsula, even if it is important to acknowledge the political and cultural attention that has recently been dedicated to the numerous linguistic minorities that are mostly present in the border regions: Slovenian in the Friuli Venezia-Giulia region, German and Ladino in Trentino-Alto Adige, and French in Val D'Aosta. Although the Slovenian, German, and French can benefit from their formal recognition as co-official languages (Law n. 482, 15 December 1999), in Italy people speak many different dialects, some of which do not resemble the Italian language (e.g., Sardinian, Catalan, Friulan, etc.). Another input to Italy's linguistic and cultural multiplicity is immigration, which in 2010 accounted for 7.5% of the population (ISTAT, 2011).

The cultural contexts and sociological dimensions relevant for Italy's mental health profession are worth noting. First, migration has been a sociological presence and experience for Italians since the unification of the peninsula in 1861, and it is estimated that in the 100 years from 1876 to 1976, 25 million Italians left the country to escape from famine, poverty, and political persecutions in search of better life opportunities (Favero & Tassello, 1978). Often, emigration was a traumatic event in families, generating in those who stayed feelings of anger and the impression that their family life was never going to be the same as before the departure of the emigrant. Second, although gender equality is constitutionally granted in Italy, the difference between the presence of men and women in positions of political, economical, and social power is still striking (Gamba & Goldstein, 2009). The female presence in politics and in general positions of power is still among the lowest of Western countries. In the field of counseling and clinical psychology, although more women than men obtain university degrees in psychology, more men actually end up working as professionals in private practice or as university professors or researchers. Without any doubt, women in Italy face bigger challenges than men in their access to positions of responsibility and power. Lower levels of self-esteem and a high incidence of depressive symptoms are relatively common among Italian women, especially during adolescence (Pantusa, Berardi, Paparo, & Scornaienchi, 2006). Finally, being non-heterosexual in Italy is not easy, as Italy is still far from the political progress made by many of its European partners. The Roman Catholic Church plays an important cultural role in this context. Social discrimination and stigmatization are common daily experiences for non-heterosexual individuals, and internalized homophobia for Italian LGBTs has been linked to high levels of depression and suicide (Ciliberto & Ferrari, 2009). Homophobia runs high in the general Italian population, once again with significant differences among geographical areas and rural versus urban settings.

Besides the cultural, economic, and demographic challenges linked to the fast-changing social scenario of contemporary Italy, a historical view on the development of counseling and psychotherapy in the country may contribute to the understanding and appreciation of its complex and rich background.

Brief history of counseling and psychotherapy

The word "counseling" does not find a precise correspondent in the Italian language (Vitelli, Galiani, Amodeo, Adamo, & Valerio, 1998). In any case, although the history of counseling in Italy goes back to the 1920s, with activities in the area of social work, the words "counselor" and "counseling" were first used in the 1990s when a school of psychotherapy started to offer courses on counseling. Nowadays, despite the unregulated situation (or maybe exactly for this reason) and legal conflicts with the psychology and psychotherapy lobbies, there is great availability of counseling courses and counselors.

Psychotherapy in Italy started with Edoardo Weiss (1889–1970), who was a student of Freud and moved from Vienna to Trieste, where he became the first Italian psychoanalyst. In 1932, he co-founded the *Rivista Italiana di Psicoanalisi* (Italian Psychoanalysis Review) with Cesare Musatti (1897–1989), who is still today the most influential and famous of the Italian psychoanalysts. Despite the intellectual enthusiasm surrounding the development of psychology, the cultural climate of the period was unfavorable toward the field. As both the powerful Catholic church and the fascist regime deemed psychoanalysis a threat to their authority, they actively repressed its spread in Italy (Colombo, 2003). In 1923, the Gentile Reform of the education system decreed the abolition of psychology as a teaching subject in Italian schools and universities. Psychology was substituted for philosophy and pedagogy of idealistic orientation, thus forcing Weiss to migrate to the United States in 1934. A few years later, Cesare Musatti lost his university teaching position, which he regained only after World War II following the political shift to democracy and the publication of his influential *Trattato di Psicoanalisi* (Treatise on Psychoanalysis) in 1949. Despite these political controversies, psychoanalysis succeeded to set the bases for Italian psychology and mental health counseling: hereafter it would be the point of comparison for all other forms of psychotherapy.

After the end of World War II in 1945, the US experimental psychology and practices of mental health became a leading influence within Italian psychology. The post-war context was a time of deep societal changes in Italy. Especially in the 1950s and 1960s, the public demand for clinical psychology and psychotherapy became increasingly popular (Cancrini, 1982). Nonetheless, psychology achieved official scientific status only in in 1971, with the simultaneous launch of the first two psychology degrees at the universities of Padua and Rome. These openings into the rather conservative and elitist academic world became the main avenues through which new clinical theories and practices could enter the Italian university and scientific scene. Since then, and in just two decades, the theoretical diversity in mental health therapy has flourished.

The recognition of psychology as a scientific discipline came at the cost of reducing the scientific method to cognitive dimensions and measurable variables of human experience. Powerful lobbies within the universities deemed the human sciences and the interpretive aspects of mental health as being too unscientific. Yet, at the same time, interpretative practices of knowledge and the attention to social contexts and "subjectivity" were crucial aspects of public mental health services. Narrow definitions of science by the universities and the focus on "the lived experience" and the politics of knowledge (e.g., the strong anti-psychiatric movement of the 1960s in Italy) (Benvenuto, 1997) contributed to create an artificial separation between scientific and applied psychologies.

Inspired by phenomenology, the anti-psychiatric movement quickly developed in Italy thanks to the pioneering work of Franco Basaglia (1924–1980).[2] The anti-psychiatric lobby in Italy was able to become a vast and popular opinion movement, which, in 1978, led the Italian Parliament to establish Law 180 (May 13, 1978). Popularly called "Legge Basaglia" (Basaglia Law), the new regulation transferred the care of psychiatric patients from institutional settings of isolation, pathologization, and iatrogenesis to community practice, which included outpatient care, rehabilitation centers, patient cooperatives, and long-term residential facilities—e.g., apartment units (Piccinelli, Politi, & Barale, 2002).

Despite the relative lack of support from the Italian university system, psychotherapy has developed vigorously in Italy for the last 30 years, mostly in light of its popular (as opposed to academic) recognition as a healing or therapeutic practice. Initially the field suffered from not having a formal set of rules and standards that regulated both the training and the practice of psychologists and psychotherapists. With the development and implementation of such regulations in 1989, a number of professional schools opened. Nowadays, approximately 200 schools for professional psychology are present in the territory, with more than 300 active branches. While the majority of these schools are private, some are affiliated to public universities.

Different from what happened in other European countries, the laws that regulate the training and practice of professional psychology do not require or even recommend specific theoretical frameworks. This has ensured a rich and lively theoretical pluralism. The progressive decline of psychoanalysis has favored the development of therapeutic approaches that, for the most part, tend to adopt phenomenological, systemic, and constructivist philosophies.

Counselor education programs, accreditation, licensure, and certification

An array of training schools is present in Italy. The main distinction concerns whether they are affiliated to a public university or a private, for-profit institution. No private university in Italy offers training in professional psychotherapy. As of June 2009, the Ministry of Education, University and Research (MIUR) recognized 197 schools, but, since institutes may also have branches, the total number of training centers was 333. This long list of private schools is continuously evolving.

It is difficult and probably misleading to categorize the theoretical orientation of single schools simply by their names. Some of them may be too generic or non-denominational as to be able to understand their training practice. For instance, names such as "School for Comparative Psychotherapy" or "Cognitive Psychology Training Center" do not say much about their actual training or framework. It is usually more useful and informative to read the mission statements and didactic programs, which may be available on the schools' websites.

The level of theoretical sophistication varies extensively from school to school. Similar to US or Canadian PsyD programs, private psychotherapy schools in Italy tend to give a secondary role to research. This contributes to the misleading impression that systematic research or knowledge creation is the responsibility of universities or hospitals. To an extent, the low involvement in research is both cause and consequence of the relative international isolation of most Italian private schools. Just a few of these schools actively seek and establish connections with other countries through international networks or the exchange of didactic experiences and visiting professorships.

Public university schools are powerful players in the training of mental health professionals. Different from private training institutes, they are required to offer theoretically diverse training, although CBT seems to be quite dominant (Sanavio, 1999). Instead, private schools are usually devoted to a specific theoretical framework.

University schools are often the battlefield of competing academic politics, which further confuse the actual outcomes and the interpretation of benchmarks in the formation of professional psychologists. For instance, university specialization programs that can award a degree to practice psychotherapy are hosted within psychology departments with denominations as different as Clinical Psychology, Neuropsychology, Psychology of Life Cycle, Health Psychology, or Psychological Evaluation and Counseling. The number of specialization programs at public universities tends to vary from year to year.

The professional figure of the counselor is yet to be well defined in the Italian system of mental health. For instance, it is not clear how the work of a mental health counselor differs from that of a psychologist, educational psychologist, or social worker (Remley, Bacchini & Krieg, 2010).[3] There are no university academic programs dedicated to the training counselors, although this may soon change. There are, instead, many private courses. Remley et al. (2010, p. 31) cite a definition by the National Council of Economy and Labor, according to which, different from the psychotherapist, "the counselor is a professional who, after a 3-year training program of a specific school of theoretical orientation, can help to solve some existential difficulty that does not need a deep reorganization of personality" (CNEL, 2005, p. 93).

In relation to the accreditation of schools for the formation and training of professional psychologists, it is important to draw a clear separation between the legal recognition of a training institution by the MIUR and the school certifications issued within specific professional associations, like the Italian Society of Cognitive Behavioral Therapy. The latter have no legal value and, currently, there is no national professional association (like the American Psychological Association in the United States) that sets the minimum standards for the trainings and practice of psychotherapy.

In terms of licensure, four main professional figures can be licensed to perform clinical work in mental health or psychotherapy in Italy: the psychologist, the psychotherapist, the medical psychotherapist, and the psychiatrist. A fifth profession, the mental health counselor, is still under-regulated.

College graduates in psychology who want to start a professional practice need first to complete a year-long internship in clinical or counseling psychology, in which students typically shadow licensed psychologists and do not engage in direct clinical work with patients or clients. Upon completing this internship, students are eligible to take a state exam for psychologists that allows for the professional practice of clinical, counseling, or community psychology. This exam roughly corresponds to the licensure exam in North America.

Graduates in psychology or medicine can enroll in a training school in psychotherapy. Programs usually run at weekends and last for at least 4 years. They consist of a minimum of 2,000 hours of courses, tests, workshops, and direct face-to-face therapy (at least 100 hours). Students need to enroll on individual psychotherapy courses. At the end of their training, students take a final examination within the school and the state licensure exam that allows them to practice as psychotherapists. If they are registered physicians with the Medicine Association, medical psychotherapists can prescribe medications and perform pharmacological therapies. In general, the Italian criteria and norms for private schools of specialization are considered quite restrictive in comparison to the standards of the European Certificate of Psychotherapy (van Deurzen, 2001). For a detailed history of psychotherapy regulations in Italy, the interested reader may refer to Borsci (2005).

Similarly to the Anglo-Saxon world, the psychiatrist is a medical school graduate who undertakes a 4-year specialized training and an internship in psychiatry. Under the Italian regulatory system for the practice of psychology, the medical specialization in psychiatry is equivalent to psychotherapy training. Therefore, psychiatrists are allowed to take the licensure exam to become a psychotherapist. This is a contentious practice that indicates the power of the Medical Association, and that may be questionable from a professional standpoint since psychotherapy is an area of study and practice that is marginal and frequently absent in psychiatry trainings.

Regarding the professional figure of counselor, its legal status as a professional title is not recognized by the Italian State. We will further discuss this later on in this chapter.

Finally, with regard to certification processes, many national associations for counseling and psychotherapy are present in Italy autonomously from legal regulations, licensures, and laws. These associations generally promote exchange of knowledge between members, promote research, and provide certifications regarding standards for education and supervision practice. For instance, most Italian private schools of psychotherapy are members of the National Coordination of the Private Schools of Psychotherapy (CNSP), which establishes minimum standards, criteria for excellence in education, and ethical guidelines. In the absence of formal criteria for licensure or certification, the CNSP standards are particularly important for counselors and the associations to which they may belong, which find further recognition from the Federation of the Counseling Italian Association (FAIC).

Current counseling and psychotherapy theories, processes, and trends

As in most Western countries, in Italy as well the solitary supremacy of psychoanalysis has faded, taking out of its shadow a number of different clinical schools and orientations. A common consequence of the lack of a strong reference is the blurring of definitions and boundaries that could previously be taken for granted. Thus, despite numerous attempts to create consensus on the names and meanings of therapy traditions, the process of identifying and labeling a school of thought inevitably creates disagreements and arguments that are epistemological and historical as well as political (Legrenzi, 1980; Marhaba & Armezzani, 1988). The endorsement of certain schools by already established circles of power influences the reputation, acceptance, and degree of success of the specific school.

In brief, the Italian panorama on counseling includes the major theoretical approaches usually described in European and US literature. We compared a collection of essays about the 25 best-known schools of Italian psychotherapy (Marhaba & Armezzani, 1988) with Adami Rook, Ciofi, & Giannini's (1998) review of current Italian psychotherapy traditions and schools of thought. Although this study was conducted 13 years ago and cannot be considered exhaustive of the Italian psychotherapeutic context, it still reflects the vast majority of theoretical orientations in Italy. The following is a list of approaches that the two texts have in common: Adlerian individual psychology; bioenergetics; behaviorist, and cognitive-behaviorist therapy; brief cognitive therapy; cognitive therapy; constructivist therapy; Freudian, Lacanian, and Kleinian psychoanalysis; family system therapy; Gestalt psychotherapy; humanistic psychology; hypnosis; Jungian analytic psychology; object relations; psychodrama; psychosynthesis; rational emotive therapy (RET); and transactional analysis. In addition, Young (2008) reports body psychotherapy to be a fast-growing approach in Italy.

Contributions by local psychologists are also worth noting. Based on their originality and the attention they received in the international literature, we deem the following to be among the most innovative and long-lasting contributions of Italian psychologists: psychosynthesis developed from the works of Assagioli (1965; Ginger, 2003); family system therapy originated from the contributions of Selvini-Palazzoli, Boscolo, and Cecchin (Bertrando, 2003; Boscolo, Cecchin, Hoffman, & Penn, 2004; Palazzoli, Cecchin, Prata, & Boscolo, 1978), and Andolfi (1979); the cognitive approaches of Guidano and Liotti (Guidano, 1991; Guidano & Liotti, 1983); and the brief strategic therapy model of Nardone and Watzlawick (1990/1993; 1997/2004).

Indigenous and traditional healing methods

There are two ways to consider indigenous and traditional healing methods: the first rooted in tradition that is not attached to a scientific conception of psychotherapy and counseling; the second related to the idea of an indigenous psychology free from any intellectual colonialism.

Before modern psychology and medicine, traditional interpretations and healing methods were mostly connected to the power dynamics of the Church (i.e., the more or less direct sale of indulgence) or to what could be considered as superstition (e.g., possession by spirits, "malocchio" or bad luck given by someone to someone else). This last type of traditional method is as varied as the fabrics of cultural and regional identities in Italy. Still, for most psychological issues and dynamics (e.g., in the case of family counseling), the priest used to be the main referent and the "cure" entailed confession, dialogue with God, and typically some sort of personal sacrifice or deed.

It is interesting to think about the possibility for an indigenous and non-colonized psychology in Italy. While the historical location of an indigenous psychology is not marked by the presence of visible foreigners, like in post-colonial contexts, it would be challenging to deny the cultural influence and arguably dominance of some Western country over the development of Italian psychology and psychotherapy. Before World War II (WWII), the cultural influence of German-speaking scholars was instrumental in Italy to the development of psychology as a discipline that was separated from philosophy and theology. After WWII, the cultural and economic influence of the Anglo-Saxon world shaped the field and led to the creation of a scientific psychology that, at least in the universities, furthered the separation from philosophy and non-objective approaches to therapy.

In order to explore the possibility for an indigenous psychology in Italy, it would be interesting to analyze the cultural ramifications implicit in the strong political and economic influence of the US government on post-war Italian politics, for instance through the Marshall Plan and the endorsement of center-right-wing parties of Christian inspiration to contrast the surge of the Italian communist party. In addition, the USA played a key role in the collective fantasies of wealth and power, which was often popularized and romanticized in the Italian mass media. The Italians' "esterophilia" was maintained especially through assumptions of US scientific and technological superiority, which inevitably had an impact on Italian psychology as well. At times, Italian psychologists reacted to this cultural imperialism, as in the case of behaviorism, which was deemed by some to be "the expression of North American scientific and economic colonialism; and to be the ideological superstructure that reduced man and human relations exclusively to the realm of money" (Sanavio, 1999, p. 71). However, reactions of this sort are not exempt from ideological influences and they tend to represent multifaceted theoretical movements (like behaviorism) as a single corpus.

Research and supervision

Research on psychotherapy has significantly increased in Italy since the mid-1990s, despite being still significantly underfunded. Governmental funding is meager and almost exclusively granted to universities, although it is mostly private schools and institutions that train professional counselors and psychotherapists. Some of the most exciting developments in the field of psychotherapy research concern the creation of international, scientific networks that seek an international voice, collaboration, and support like the Italian section of the Society for Psychotherapy Research (SPR), and the establishing of specialized, bilingual journals, like *Ricerca in Psicoterapia/Research in Psychotherapy: Psychopathology, Process and Outcome*. The funding and coordination of the European Research Program is often instrumental to establishing these networks.

According to a recent editorial of *Research in Psychotherapy* (SPR, 2011), "SPR-Italy has always striven to establish a culture capable of responding [...] to all those who, from the perspective of hermeneutic hypersubjectivism or of pragmatic hyperobjectivism, consider psychotherapy of little interest to science" (p. 1). Current research tends to focus on socioeconomic circumstances and interpersonal styles as variables of therapeutic effectiveness. It is remarkable that, even when endorsing apparently reductionist approaches that assess therapy according to outcomes and discrete variables, many Italian researchers do not refrain from engaging in sophisticated theoretical and critical reflections, for instance on the political and cultural grounds of the mental health field (Salvatore, 2011). As we will discuss later, we deem this a major asset of Italian psychotherapy.

In addition to the above-named *Research in Psychotherapy*, other major peer-reviewed journals on clinical psychology in Italy are the *Rivista di Psicologia Clinica* (published in Italian and English), *Giornale di Psicologia, Psichiatria e Psicoterapia, Psicoterapia Psicoanalitica, Terapia Familiare, Giornale Italiano di Psicopatologia, Interazioni, Psicoterapia Cognitiva e Comportamentale, Rivista di Psichiatria, Ecologia della Mente, Psicoterapia e Scienze Umane,* and *Rivista di Psicoanalisi.*

According to the Italian normative on psychotherapy, all of the private training schools need to include "supervision of learners' practice" (art. 8, Ministerial Decree, December 11, 1998, n. 509). Although students are required to complete at least 100 hours of practical training in public mental health institutions or accredited private services, the Decree does not specify the minimum number of supervision hours and the format of supervision, which depend on the theoretical model adopted by the specific institute. This leaves quite a lot of discretion to single training schools. Public training schools, instead, are required to include in their curricula at least 60 educational credits of "supervised practice leading to the professional practice of psychotherapy" (art. 6, Ministerial Decree, July 24, 2006). As one educational credit corresponds to 25 working hours, this corresponds to 1,500 hours of supervised practice, which would be a huge difference from the standards of private schools. The ambiguity here is linked to the fact that, for university training, not all of the supervised hours need to be of clinical practice. The normative does not make a distinction between clinical supervision and other activities, like research or writing, which can be subject to supervision. Furthermore, the law for public or private training simply says that the supervisor needs to be "qualified," without specifying standards of legality, power, responsibility, and experience for the supervisor.

Strengths, weaknesses, opportunities, and challenges

In this section, we will reflect on some sociological and cultural phenomena that may be relevant to understand the development and performance of counseling psychotherapy in Italy.

In our opinion, one major strength in the field of counseling and psychotherapy in Italy is the philosophical and epistemological depth of Italian reflection on therapy. Italian scientists, professors, and even practitioners tend to pay great attention to theoretical sophistication. Most Italian clinicians are aware that practices such as interpretation, truth, assessment, intervention, culture, clinical setting, or wellbeing can be understood, explored, and deepened only through the careful interweaving of clinical and epistemological research and practice (Ceruti & Lo Verso, 1998). Interestingly, in the editorial of the first issue of the journal *Counseling*, the authors underscore that effective and competent counseling requires an epistemology of complexity (Di Fabio & Fulcheri, 2008). Such dedication to philosophical elaborations ensures theoretical coherence, originality, and creativity, as well as an overall consciousness of what therapists do and what happens in counseling. Counseling and psychotherapy are never neutral activities. As Basaglia (1968) and Foucault (1980) warned, the act of addressing mental health issues carries deep epistemological, social, and cultural implications for what the world is and how life can and, more or less implicitly, should be lived.

Finally, from our point of view, some of the main points of strength of the Italian psychotherapy panorama are found in the wide plurality of orientations practiced in the country, the link between philosophical awareness and professional practice, the precedence of ecological approaches to psychology over laboratory studies due to the socio-cultural aspects of Italian psychology, a growing emphasis on community psychology (Francescato, Arcidiacono, Albanesi, & Mannarini, 2007; Santinello, Martini, & Perkins, 2010), and the openness to multi-disciplinary interventions. Bertrando (2003, p. 101) suggests that one of the reasons why Italian therapists have been able to nurture complexity is because, "unlike what took place in the United States from the end of the 1970s, … [Italian] therapists have not given up the serious psychiatric pathologies, such as schizophrenia, mood or personality disorders." The plurality of theoretical orientations and the epistemological awareness that characterizes the clinical formation and practice of many Italian psychotherapists are assets to understand and work with the complexity of the fast-changing Italian society. In addition, the attention to the theoretical and philosophical bases of psychotherapy tends to challenge professional feudalism, to develop critical awareness on the limits and possibilities of psychotherapy, and to comfortably seek the collaboration with other professional figures (e.g., social workers, physicians, psychiatrists, educators, judges) who are involved in the clients' psychological wellbeing. If these assets of Italian therapists are valued, then psychologists and psychotherapists are well positioned to encourage dialogue among old and recent cultures and identities in Italy.

In our considerations of the "weaknesses" of Italian psychotherapy, it is important to bear in mind that Italian researchers are almost obliged to use the English language in order for their work to be recognized internationally. This requirement creates a gap between the English-fluent younger generation and the older academics, who often read but do not write in English. As Benvenuto (1997) writes, "Italian analysts lack an international audience because they write in a tongue which is spoken only in Italy." Most scholars publish in Italian and their works are very seldom translated into English. So, while the Italian academic context is strongly influenced by the English-speaking world, the reverse does not occur.

Some obstacles to the growth of clinical professions may be also found in the reticence of professional legislation and the slowness of the European Union, the European Association for Psychotherapy, and the European Association for Counseling to reach an agreement on minimum standards of and requirements for professional mobility. International mobility within Europe is still an unresolved issue. In addition, the almost frozen situation of the Italian university system, which is a victim of disastrous power games among its own administrators and professors, does not allow for innovative contributions from external researchers and scholars (Fava, 1997). Italian universities rarely attract foreign scholars or graduate students in the humanities and social studies. The brain-drain phenomenon deprives the university of some of its best scientists (ADI, 2001) and research in clinical psychology, psychotherapy, and counseling is limited and heavily dependent on contributions from the English-language world.

Finally, some weaknesses in the field can be attributed to the Roman Catholic church's deep influence on Italian society (Sanavio, 1999), particularly concerning the social and cultural acceptance of homosexuality. Gay couples are far from being legally recognized and therefore cannot enjoy the legal protection, institutional care, and social acceptance that they increasingly benefit from in other European countries. The Vatican actively lobbies some important political parties in the Italian parliament to oppose same-sex unions, which are seen as "a deplorable distortion of what should be a communion of love and life between a man and a woman in a reciprocal gift open to life" (John Paul II, 1999, chap. 23). Hence, while the church serves as a main player in the fields of humanitarian assistance, solidarity, charity, mental healthcare and prevention, the complex, conservative, and politicized side of the Catholic world would surely benefit from a more open and public dialogue between the conservative and the socially active forms of Catholicism.

In our opinion, one of the most exciting opportunities for an original development in Italian psychotherapy may come from capitalizing on the thorough theoretical and epistemological formation that most professional schools offer. We specifically see the recent social changes in Italy linked to immigration as an opportunity to translate into clinical practice such openness to theoretical complexity. In other words, psychology and mental health could become sites of dialogue and mutual learning that could significantly promote the transition toward a truly multicultural society.

Historical and cultural differences within Italy pose certain challenges to the development of counseling and psychotherapy throughout the country. Despite the presence of an Italian constitution and common regulatory system, Italy is a culturally diverse country, with wide differences of languages, traditions, practices, and values (Maiden & Parry, 1997) which reflect centuries of invasions and transitions. The concept of an Italian culture embodied in the Italian population cannot and should not be taken for granted. The expression "Italian culture" is controversial and may be more significant to an external observer than to an Italian living in Italy.[4]

While psychotherapy is usually a well-known resource to address mental health concerns in the north and in the center of Italy, in the south of Italy it is a much less common and a more stigmatizing practice, which cohabits with other practices and "practitioners" like wizards or healers—heritage of a past, although never completely vanished, paganism. It is not by chance that the majority of psychotherapy schools are concentrated in the north and the center of the country, although this gap in percentage terms is slowly decreasing.

Despite the historical obstacles to their development, such as little investment in scientific research, academic nepotism, Catholic conservatism and the language barrier, mental health professions in Italy are growing fast.

Future directions

We hope Italian psychotherapy will be able to capitalize on its strengths, which we see as mostly related to its theoretical and cultural diversity and its openness to undertake philosophical and political debates, which are rarely a focus of North American mainstream psychology. In addition, the shift to community-based clinical care for severely distressed patients and the shift to ecological contexts are two of the most remarkable Italian contributions to the international debate on chronic mental illness.

Italian therapists, scholars, and researchers would surely benefit from entering a constructive dialogue with the international community. A fundamental step in this direction is to increase publications in English-speaking journals, a process that may challenge the unidirectional rapport between the Anglo-Saxon and the Italian worlds of psychotherapy.

Conclusion

Understanding the complexity of psychotherapy and counseling in such a diverse and historically intricate country as Italy is not an easy task. The promotion of mutual dialogue with the Anglo-Saxon world of professional psychology, other healing traditions, and the recent cultural minorities in Italy represent fields of practice and concern from which Italian psychologists and counselors will most benefit in the future. As in other areas of the world with longer histories of immigration, racial, or ethnic tensions and intergenerational conflicts are likely to become delicate topics of social and psychological concern in Italy.

The field of counseling and psychotherapy in Italy holds great potential for being a community-grounded and scientifically sophisticated practice, from which the Italian society at large could benefit to shape its future growth as a multicultural and non-oppressive culture.

Notes

1 On its website, the Federation of Italian Psychotherapy Associations (FAIP, 2006) defines counseling as "a helping relationship that, starting from the analysis of the client's problems, aims at creating a new vision for such issues and at implementing an action plan to meet the client's goals, like decision making, relationships, awareness, feelings, emotion management, and conflict resolution."

2 Basaglia's (1968) movement, *Psichiatria Democratica* (Democratic Psychiatry), deeply shifted the professional's as well as the public's opinion toward an interpretation of psychological concerns as meaningful and contextualized within the patients' personal, social, and cultural reality or realities (Vitelli *et al.*, 1998).

3 The school system is one of the most important professional outcomes for counselors. As Remley *et al.* (2010, p. 31) write, "Schools in Italy need counselors and a counseling approach to help students make career decisions, to prevent violence and adolescent gangs, and to teach students how to mediate in order to solve interpersonal problems and conflicts."

4 A few years after the unification, Massimo d'Azeglio, a leading politician, asserted the famous motto: "Now that we made Italy, we need to make the Italians." This sentence summarized the complexity of the cultural and social dimensions of the unification.

References

Adami Rook, P., Ciofi, R., & Giannini, M. (1998). Nota per una storia della psicoterapia italiana [A remark for a history of Italian psychotherapy]. In D. K. Freedheim (ed.), *Storia della psicoterapia: Un secolo di cambiamenti* (pp. 1023–1122). Rome: Edizioni Scientifiche Ma.Gi.

ADI (Association of Italian PhD Holders and Students). (2001). *Cervelli in fuga: Storie di menti italiane fuggite all'estero* [Fleeing brains: Stories of Italian minds who flew abroad]. Rome: Avverbi.

Andolfi, M. (1979). *Family Therapy: An Interactional Approach.* New York: Plenum Press. (Original work published 1977)

Assagioli, R. (1965). *Psychosynthesis.* New York: Viking Press.

Basaglia, F. (ed.). (1968). *L'istituzione negata* [The denied institution]. Turin: Einaudi.

Benvenuto, S. (1997). Italy and psychoanalysis. *Journal of European Psychoanalysis, 5,* s/n. Retrieved from www.psychomedia.it/jep/number5/benvenuto.htm

Bertrando, P. (2003). The effects of family therapy. In K. S. Ng (ed.), *Global Perspectives in Family Therapy: Development, Practice, and Trends* (pp. 83–104). New York: Routledge.

Borsci, G. (2005). Psychotherapy regulation in Italy: History of law no. 56/1989 and current status of accredited psychotherapy schools. *Psicoterapia e Scienze Umane, 39,* 193–222.

Boscolo, L., Cecchin, G., Hoffman, L., & Penn, P. (2004). *La clinica sistemica: Dialoghi a quattro sull'evoluzione del modello di Milano* [System clinical practise: A four-people dialogue on the evolution of the Milan model]. Turin: Bollati Boringhieri.

Cancrini, L. (1982). *Guida alla psicoterapia* [Guide to psychotherapy]. Rome: Editori Riuniti.

Ceruti, M., & Lo Verso, G. (eds). (1998). *Epistemologia e psicoterapia: Complessità e frontiere contemporanee* [Epistemology and psychotherapy: Complexity and contemporary frontiers]. Milan: Raffaello Cortina Editore.

Ciliberto, J., & Ferrari, F. (2009). Interiorized homophobia, identity dynamics and gender typization: Hypothesizing a third gender role in Italian LGB individuals. *Journal of Homosexuality. 56,* 610–622.

CNEL (National Council of Economy and Labor) (2005). *Rapporto di monitoraggio sulle professioni non regolamentate* [Monitoring report on non-regulated professions]. Rome: Author.

Colombo, D. (2003). Psychoanalysis and the Catholic Church in Italy: The role of Father Agostino Gemelli, 1925–1953. *Journal of the History of the Behavioral Sciences, 39,* 333–348.

Di Fabio, A., & Fulcheri, M. (2008). Editorial. *Counseling, 1,* 1.

FAIP (Federation of Italian Psychotherapy Associations) (2006). *Definition of counseling.* Retrieved September 2009 from www.faipnet.it/

Fava, G. (1997). Psychotherapy research: Why is it neglected in Italy? *Epidemiologia e psichiatria sociale, 6,* 81–3.

Favero, L., & Tassello, G. (1978). Cent'anni di emigrazione italiana. In G. Rosoli (ed.), *Un secolo di emigrazione italiana: 1876–1976* (pp. 9–63). Rome: Centro Studi Emigrazione.

Foucault, M. (1980). *Power/Knowledge.* New York: Pantheon.

Francescato, D., Arcidiacono, C., Albanesi, C., & Mannarini, T. (2007). Community psychology in Italy: past developments and future perspectives. In S. Reich, M. Riemer, I. Prilleltensky, & M. Montero (eds), *International Community Psychology History and Theories* (pp. 263–281). New York: Springer.

Gamba, M., & Goldstein, A. (2009). The gender dimension of business elites: Italian women directors since 1934. *Journal of Modern Italian Studies, 14,* 199–225.

Ginger, S. (2003). The evolution of psychotherapy in Western Europe. *International Journal of Psychotherapy, 8,* 129–138.

Guidano, V. F. (1991). *The Self in Process.* New York: Guilford.

Guidano, V. F., & Liotti, G. (1983). *Cognitive processes and emotional disorders.* New York: Guilford.

ISTAT (National Institute of Statistics) (2011). Annual Report: The state of the Nation in 2010. Retrieved June 26, 2011 from http://en.istat.it/dati/catalogo/20110711_00/

John Paul II (1999, June 4). *Discourse to the participants in the XIV General Assembly of the Pontifical Council for the Family.* Retrieved January 20, 2004 from www.vatican.va/roman_curia/pontifical_councils/family/documents/rc_pc_family_doc_20001109_de-facto-unions_en.html

Law 180 (1978). *Forced and Voluntary Health Assessments and Treatments,* May 13. Official Collection of Legislative Acts of the Italian Republic.

Legrenzi, P. (ed.). (1980). *Storia della psicologia* [History of psychology]. Bologna: Il Mulino.

Maiden, M., & Parry, M. (eds). (1997). *The dialects of Italy.* London: Routledge.

Marhaba, S., & Armezzani, M. (1988). *Quale psicoterapia? Gli indirizzi psicoterapici in Italia: Confronto e analisi* [Which psychotherapy? Psychotherapeutic orientations in Italy: Comparison and analysis]. Padua: Liviana Editrice.

Nardone, G., & Watzlawick, P. (1993). *The Art of Change*. San Francisco, CA: Jossey-Bass. (Original work published 1990).

Nardone, G., & Watzlawick, P. (2004). *Brief Strategic Therapy*. Lanham, MD: Aronson. (Original work published 1997).

Palazzoli, M. S., Cecchin, G., Prata, G., & Boscolo, L. (1978). *Paradox and Counterparadox: A New Model in the Family in Schizophrenic Transaction*. New York: Aronson.

Pantusa, M.F., Berardi, M., Paparo, S., & Scornaienchi, C. (2006). Differenze di genere e sintomatologia depressiva in adolescenza: relazioni tra autostima, sintomi depressivi e ideazione suicidaria [Gender differences and depressive symptomatology in adolescence: Links among self-esteem, depressive symptoms, and suicidal ideations]. *Giornale Italiano di Psicopatologia, 12*, 407–414.

Piccinelli, M., Politi, P., & Barale, F. (2002). Focus on psychiatry in Italy. *British Journal of Psychiatry, 181*, 538–44.

Remley, T. P., Bacchini, E., & Krieg, P. (2010). Counseling in Italy. *Journal of Counseling & Development, 88*, 28–32.

Salvatore, S. (2011). Psychotherapy Research Needs Theory. Outline for an Epistemology of the Clinical Exchange. *Integrative Psychological and Behavioral Science, 45*, 366–388.

Sanavio, E. (1999). Behavioral and cognitive therapy in Italy. *The Behavior Therapist, 4*, 69–76.

Santinello, M., Martini, E. R., and Perkins, D.D. (2010). Community psychology in Italy: Introduction and prospects. *Journal of Prevention & Intervention in the Community, 38*, 1–7.

SPR (Society for Psychotherapy Research) (April, 2011). *Research in psychotherapy: Psychopathology, process and outcome*. Retrieved June 26, 2011, from www.psychotherapyresearch.org/associations/6344/files/EDITORIALE1_11EN.pdf

van Deurzen, E. (2001). Psychotherapy training in Europe: Similarities and differences. *The European Journal of Psychotherapy, Counselling & Health, 4*, 357–371.

Vitelli, R., Galiani, R., Amodeo, A. L., Adamo, S. M. G., & Valerio, A. (1998). Psychotherapy and counseling in Italy: A situation still in the phase of definition. *The European Journal of Psychotherapy, Counseling, & Health, 1*, 459–474.

Young, C. (2008). Body-psychotherapy in Europe: EABP & the EAP. *International Journal of Psychotherapy, 12*, 67–74.

27

PSYCHOTHERAPY AND CLINICAL PSYCHOLOGY IN THE NETHERLANDS

Settlement of five distinctive psy-professions

Giel J. M. Hutschemaekers and Fiona E. van Dijk

Introduction

The Netherlands is a West European country surrounded by the North Sea, Belgium, and Germany. The total Dutch population in 2011 is over 16.6 million people (50% women) (Statistics Netherlands, 2011). Approximately 24% of the population is below the age group of 20 years, whereas 15% is above the age group of 65 (Statistics Netherlands, 2011). The national language is Dutch. Almost 12% of the population has a non-Western origin.

Since 1986, the use of the term "psychotherapy" in clinical practice has been reserved for those interventions offered by psychotherapists, whereas "counseling" has become a generic term for psychological interventions offered by other healthcare professionals, such as social workers and psychologists. Nowadays counseling is mainly associated with the profession of social work, which in the Netherlands is a non-academic profession without legal recognition in the Dutch law BIG.[1] As such, this chapter will mainly focus on the development of psychotherapy, clinical psychology and the formal recognition of distinctive psy-professions by law.

The Netherlands has its own particular tradition concerning psychotherapy, clinical psychology, and counseling. In the literature it is called "the Dutch case." Originally the epithet Dutch case was used for the very early legalization in 1986 of a distinctive profession of psychotherapy. Nowadays it is mainly used for the broader formal building of disciplines in the domain of (mental) healthcare (Hutschemaekers & Staak, 2006). In other words, the Dutch case refers to the large number of disciplines that practice counseling and psychotherapy (the psy-disciplines).

The Dutch case could also be used in a third way, namely as label for the extraordinary expanse of the mental healthcare system (Hutschemaekers, 2000). In addition to the largely integrated mental health centers which include community mental healthcare centers as well as psychiatric hospitals and the psychiatric wards of general hospitals, a large number of private practices have been set up. The Netherlands has a large population of mental health

315

professionals. This, of course, is related to the high demand for mental health services; the Dutch seem to be rather high consumers of mental healthcare in general and psychotherapy in particular.

In this chapter we will present different aspects of the Dutch case. First, we will briefly recapitulate the history and development of psychotherapy, counseling, and clinical psychology in the Netherlands. Next we will focus on educational programs, present theories and practice, traditional approaches to healing, research traditions, and supervision issues, as well as the strengths, weaknesses, opportunities, and challenges of the field. Finally, we depict some desirable and further directions.

Brief history of counseling and psychotherapy

Psychotherapy was introduced to the Netherlands at the end of the 19th century by general practitioners such as Frederik van Eeden and Albert Willem van Renterghem, who used "those forms of medical treatment in which the disease is treated by psychological means through the use of psychic functions" (Hutschemaekers & Oosterhuis, 2004). Their private practice involved psychotherapeutic interventions in which the French traditions of moral treatment (Pinel) and dynamic psychiatry (e.g., Liébeault, Charcot, and Breuer) were combined (Oosterhuis & Gijs-wijt-Hoffstra, 2008).

During the first decades of the 20th century, psychiatrists took over the claim of practicing psychotherapy (Reijzer, 1993) and restricted it to psychoanalytic treatment. Their patients consisted of a small group of elite and upper-class individuals presenting with neurotic complaints. A reaction to this restriction occurred in the 1930s, when a group of psychiatrists tried to adopt a broader psychotherapeutic framework so that psychotherapy could also be offered to the larger public. The establishment of the Dutch Society of Psychotherapy (NVP) in 1930 was part of this movement, as was the foundation of the first Institute for Medical Psychotherapy (IMP) in 1940 (Hutschemaekers & Oosterhuis, 2004). The IMP was an outpatient clinic for "patients of limited means" who were suffering from disorders due to war conditions. The target group consisted of unstable people who, under "normal" conditions, would have kept their balance. For psychotherapists, the establishment of the IMP meant having their own institutional workplace.

After World War II, a process of differentiation started between psychotherapists and psychiatrists. The Dutch Society of Psychiatry and Neurology expressed the view that psychotherapy had no independent place and role within the field of psychiatric work, but a group of psychiatrists who advertised themselves primarily as psychotherapists did not accept this notion and successfully obtained recognition for their work from the Minister of Social Affairs (Reijzer, 1993). Moreover, they began collaborating with psychologists, who had made their appearance in Dutch mental healthcare in the late 1940s. In the early 1960s psychologists became permanent guests at the meetings of the society and after 1966 they became formal members. From then on, the practice of psychotherapy was no longer restricted to psychiatrists (Jongerius, 1987).

Meanwhile, a differentiation was also taking place within the professional group of psychologists. In 1961, 5 years before the NVP admitted psychologists to its register, a commission of the Netherlands Institute for Practicing Psychologists (NIP) introduced a formal distinction between psychological help (counseling) and psychotherapy (Hutschemaekers & Oosterhuis, 2004). Whereas counseling was part of the university program, psychotherapy had to be learned in a distinctive professional schooling program. This distinction was, however, never accepted among psychologists; accepting this viewpoint would imply the end of the unity of psychology.

The consequence was that counseling became one of the basic ingredients of psychotherapy, and that those psychologists who wanted to become counselors or psychotherapists left the NIP and joined the NVP from 1966 onwards (Hutschemaekers & Oosterhuis, 2004). Since 1966 three different disciplines have allowed entry to the profession of psychotherapy: the study of medicine, the study of psychology, and psychiatric specialization.

In the early 1970s entrance to the profession widened further through opening membership of the NVP to academics from outside the medical and psychological disciplines. For instance, in 1973, social workers with advanced studies were also allowed into the NVP. Further, between 1970 and 1986, psychiatrists, doctors, psychologists, pedagogics, philosophers, and even social workers could become psychotherapists. The psychotherapist became the professional par excellence who used systematic psychological interventions and counseling in mental healthcare. Counseling was considered as a special form of psychotherapy; those professionals who wanted to learn and use counseling had to become psychotherapists.

The broadening of the NVP membership to non-psychiatrists created all kinds of problems, such as the absence of a homogeneous training system. The NVP made a virtue of this need. It realized homogeneity by constructing its own nomenclature and creating a distinction between itself as the general psychotherapeutic society, and the other societies related to therapeutic schools as specialized societies (Hutschemaekers & Staak, 2006). Subsequently, it created a sophisticated system of grades in training, with general training in psychotherapy and specialized training in a therapeutic school. The combination of training elements led to registration as a psychotherapist by the NVP. In 1986 the NVP psychotherapist was formally recognized by a temporary law (Hutschemaekers & Staak, in press).

The permanent law, the Individual Healthcare Professionals Act (law BIG), was set up in 1993 as a quality control law to improve healthcare in general, as its goal was to acknowledge different disciplines and to specify the required competencies for each. The law guarantees these competencies by the use of professional titles such as "psychiatrist," "psychotherapist," "clinical psychologist," or "healthcare psychologist" (hereon referred to as HC-psychologist) (Drunen & Staak, 2011); only those who are formally registered as members of these specific professional groups (and have proven to have the needed competencies) are allowed to use these titles. The law formally recognizes three basic professions in the field of psychotherapy and counseling: medical doctors, HC-psychologists and psychotherapists. Within these three professions the law recognizes several specialisms: the psychiatrist as a mental health specialist within medicine and the clinical psychologist and the clinical neuropsychologist (formally recognized in 2008) as specialists of HC-psychology. Psychotherapists do not have their own specialism at the present time. At least five formally recognized disciplines practice counseling and psychotherapy. Here in this overview we will call them the "psy-disciplines."

Counselor education programs, accreditation, licensure, and certification

In the Netherlands, academic and professional schooling are formally separated; universities are responsible for education programs leading to bachelor and master's degrees as well as the postgraduate PhD (research), whereas the professional unions together with healthcare institutions and sometimes with educational organizations are responsible for professional schooling. Academic schooling falls under the responsibility of the Ministry of Education, whereas the Ministry of Health is responsible for (the quality of) professional schooling.

A master's degree in medicine, clinical psychology, pedagogics, and health sciences obtained at a university provides possible access to one of the mental health professions and the professional schooling program of doctors, HC-psychologists, and psychotherapists. Students in medical sciences may first become a general doctor, whereas students in clinical psychology, health sciences, and orthopedagogics could opt for the professional schooling program leading to registration as HC-psychologist or psychotherapist (CIBG, n.d.).

Below we provide a brief description of these professional schooling programs that lead to the titles of HC-psychologist, psychotherapist, clinical psychologist, clinical neuropsychologist, and psychiatrist. Government and regulatory bodies require these education programs to follow a specific curriculum. All these programs are obliged to follow accreditation procedures, and are audited, mostly every 4 years, by appropriate bodies.

The program for HC-psychologists takes 2 years and training includes a basic education in psychological assessment and treatment methods and takes place in approved mental healthcare institutes under the supervision of an experienced team of colleagues. One can either choose a program that focuses on adults and the elderly or a program that focuses on children and youth (SPON, n.d.). The program is currently being modernized using a competency-based framework (following the footsteps of the modernization process of the psychiatry program using CANmeds).

The program for psychotherapists takes 4 years and is open to general doctors as well as master's students in clinical psychology, health sciences, and orthopedagogics. HC-psychologists have access to a shorter training program to become psychotherapists, which takes 3 years. The training comprises education in the main psychotherapeutic frames of reference: cognitive-behavioral, client-centered, psychoanalytic, and family therapy. The program focuses on the treatment of complex problems in patients of various ages and backgrounds. Like the training for HC-psychologist it also takes place in approved mental healthcare organizations under the supervision of qualified colleagues. In addition to educational training, the future psychotherapist has to undergo personal learning therapy (CIBG, n.d.).

The programs of the specialisms of clinical psychologist and clinical neuropsychologist are open to HC-psychologists. Both programs take 4 years, comprise the complete psychotherapy program, require therapy learning, and also take place in approved organizations under the supervision of qualified tutors. Similarly, as in the HC-psychologist program, one can either choose to focus on adults and elderly or children and youth.

The program for psychiatrists is also currently being modernized and implemented. The new program takes 4.5 years of internships and follows the Canadian model, CANmeds, which has defined seven domains of competencies. It focuses not only on medical knowledge but also on communication and social skills, with examinations focusing on the seven core competencies. The program also allows trainees to focus on a specific population (children, adults, or the elderly) and select an area of specialty, such as addictions or forensic psychiatry. Post-master's degree doctors who specialize in psychiatry are also trained as psychotherapists, but this does not lead to BIG psychotherapist registration because the program does not follow the accreditation rules for psychotherapy schooling (CIBG, n.d.).

As mentioned in the previous section of this chapter, psychotherapeutic societies related to the different therapeutic schools, such as the Society for Client-Centered Psychotherapy and the Society for Cognitive and Behavioral Therapy, have their own training programs. Their programs lead to more specialized training in this specific therapeutic tradition and full membership of the society of choice.

Current counseling and psychotherapy theories, processes, and trends

Among the different psychotherapeutic traditions the cognitive-behavioral approach (CBT) is at the front. The CBT approach is dominant within academic centers, especially within academic outpatient clinics (Hutschemaekers & Neijmeijer, 1998). The CBT approach is also in the lead within integrated mental health centers which have organized their care based on evidence-based programs and systems of disease management. In the Dutch literature this form of psychotherapy is called *complaint-oriented psychotherapy* (i.e., protocolized CBT) (Hutschemaekers & Staak, 2006). The popularity of complaint-oriented psychotherapy is probably related to the rise of the evidence-based paradigm. It fits into the medical psychiatric paradigm, in which disorders are seen as diseases, and the research model that focuses on measurable symptoms by means of randomized clinical trials (RCT).

Within primary care a pragmatic model of psychotherapy has become dominant: a small number of sessions treating mainly clients with less severe problems. This kind of psychotherapy is called here *problem-oriented psychotherapy*. It focuses on the explanatory contexts in which the complaints have come about and consists of helping the patient to create a different interpretation of the onset of the complaints in reaction to changing circumstances such as events, stress, life-stages, etc. Much attention is paid to competencies and solutions, and therapeutic techniques are used to gain a sense of mastery by exerting more control over the provoking circumstances or the application of other strategies or styles. The general attitude of the therapist is twofold: helping patients to discover that under the burden of provoking circumstances it is quite normal to experience problems, and helping patients to discover that they have more competences at their disposal than they originally thought (Hutschemaekers, Brunenberg, & Spek, 1993).

The *person-oriented approach* is still dominant in private practices. It is called person oriented because therapy focuses on structural aspects of behavior, or habits that have existed for years. This form of psychotherapy uses the traditional psychodynamic, client-centered, and systemic frames of reference. Therapy here is usually more intense (more frequent, longer duration) and has more fundamental goals. Patients in private practice are, in comparison to patients in primary care or in mental health institutions, better educated and probably better integrated in society. Within the integrated mental health institutions the person-oriented approach is mainly used for the treatment of patients with a personality disorder. Examples are dialectical behavioral therapy (Linehan, 1993), schema-focused therapy (Young, 1999), mentalization-based treatment (Bateman & Fonagy, 2004), and short-term psychodynamic treatment (McCullough & Kuhn, 2003).

Although recent figures are not available, the general impression is that complaint-oriented therapy is mainly carried out by research-oriented HC-psychologists and clinical psychologists, whereas pragmatic problem-oriented therapy is executed by general practitioners, community-oriented psychiatric nurses, and HC-psychologists who work as "primary care psychologists." The traditional person-oriented therapy belongs mainly to the domain of psychotherapists working in specialized private practices. New forms of person-oriented psychotherapy are less often coupled with a specific discipline (Hutschemaekers & Staak, 2006).

Indigenous and traditional healing methods

In the Netherlands mainstream psychotherapeutic and counseling interventions could be considered as "traditional healing methods" par excellence. They not only have a history of more than a hundred years, but have also become part of the Dutch mental healthcare system and have deeply influenced our social representation of health and disease (Gijswijt-Hofstra, Oosterhuis, Vijselaar, & Freeman, 2005).

Other non-somatic methods are rarely used in formal mental healthcare in the Netherlands. Exceptions to this norm are specific treatments originating from the former colonial countries such as Indonesia and Surinam. Examples here are Winti or Vodoo healing techniques, in which rituals are used to chase away evil spirits that provoke psychic suffering. Within the official mental healthcare system, immigrants and patients of non-Western origin, however, are treated with more culturally sensitive techniques (Meekeren, Limburg-Okken, & May, 2002).

Outside the formally recognized mental healthcare, different forms of alternative care systems do exist. This alternative care, however, is not remunerated by social security assurances and is hidden from the view of policy makers, researchers, and official agencies such as the Healthcare Inspectorate (Reenen, Vandermeersch, & Hutschemaekers, 1997). Figures are scarce, but it is generally assumed that the number of patients who make use of it is almost as high as the number of patients in the official mental health setting. Techniques used originate from the New Age movement (healing, rebirthing, reiki) and descend from older traditions such as haptonomy, voice dialogues, bio-energetics, or even coming from classical psychotherapeutic traditions such as Gestalt therapy, psycho-synthesis, or Jungian therapy (Alternative Medicine Overview, 2011).

Research and supervision

Dutch research in clinical psychology follows the Anglo-Saxon research tradition. Four lines can be distinguished: an experimental approach focusing on psychopathological behavior; an RCT approach focusing on efficacy of psychotherapeutic interventions; a diagnostic-testing approach, which also focuses on indication variables for treatment; and finally a health services approach, which is mainly oriented on effectiveness of psychotherapy and the place of psychotherapy within the mental healthcare system.

In the *experimental* approach, the focus is on the neurocognitive aspects of psychopathology, combining research in human perception and cognition with the development of advanced methods in neuroscience. Several research groups have a specific interest in cognitive and emotional processes, mainly in anxiety disorders. One example is the study of characteristic biases of cognitive processes such as attention interpretation and memory in several anxiety disorders (Trumpf, Margraf, Vriends, Meyer, & Becker, 2010). A second focus is on the clinical neuroscience of psychopathology that is associated with the brain's reward system, with a special focus on addiction, anhedonia, and eating disorders (Wiers, Eberl, Rinck, Becker, & Lindenmeyer, 2011). The third focus is on developmental disorders (Groen et al., 2010).

We also have a research tradition focusing on the *efficacy* of psychotherapeutic interventions (Emmelkamp, 2004). There is a particular interest in the outcome of CBT. Several RCTs are being conducted, again with some emphasis on anxiety disorders, as well as on mood, somatoform disorders, and addiction (Schuck, Keijsers, & Rinck, 2011). There is also special research interest on the psychological understanding and treatment of personality disorders. Based on the RCT approach, we now have several protocols that are evidence based (Keijsers, Minnen, & Hoogduin, 1999). Most of them are cognitive-behavioral interventions, but also a protocol of interpersonal psychotherapy and a protocol of psychodynamic therapy carry the predicate "empirically validated psychotherapy." These are very desirable titles since decision makers and financiers use them to assess different psychotherapy approaches.

The *diagnostic testing* approach is currently not as popular as the other research traditions, but there is still an ongoing interest in it, mainly on the instruments for the measurement of personality (disorders). A well-known international instrument that receives a considerable amount of interest in the Netherlands is the Minnesota Multiphasic Personality Inventory (MMPI). Most recent research activities concern the convergent validity of the MMPI-2RF scales, but it is also frequently used in research contributing to the description of patients with, for example, addiction or forensic problems (Derksen, 2004). Also the Temperament and Character Inventory (TCI) is often used in research, particularly to describe and to help disentangle overlapping psychiatric diagnoses (i.e., addiction, ADHD, ASD, and the borderline personality disorder).

The *health services approach* focuses on testing healthcare systems, with topics like the implementation of evidence-based interventions, studies on the quality of healthcare, cost-effectiveness evaluations, clinical decision making, program evaluation, and population surveys (Bijl & Ravelli, 2000; Grol & Grimshaw, 2003; Grol & Wensink, 2000). Within the field of psychotherapy, health services research focuses on indications and contraindications for different psychotherapeutic treatments. Other topics in health services research are manpower planning and the positioning of the clinical psychologist and the psychotherapist within the Dutch Mental Health system (Hutschemaekers, Camp, & Hattum, 2001).

Although nowadays most Dutch scientific articles are published in international peer-reviewed journals, there are still some Dutch journals available for publishing scientific papers. Some of these journals are associated with professional societies, such as the *Journal for Psychiatry* (Tijdschrift voor Psychiatrie), the *Journal for Psychotherapy* (Tijdschrift voor Psychotherapie), and the *Psychologist* (De Psycholoog). Other journals are specific to the mental health sector, examples are the *Monthly for Mental Health* (Maandblad Geestelijke Volksgezondheid) and *Psy* (magazine of the Federation for Mental Healthcare). Also the specific psychotherapeutic associations have their own journals. Examples are the *Journal of Directive Psychotherapy*, *Journal for Behavioral Therapy*, and the *Journal for Person Oriented Experiential Psychotherapy*.

Research on clinical psychology, psychotherapy, and psychiatry is mainly funded by ZonMw (i.e., The Netherlands Organization for Health Research and Development). ZonMw funds health research and stimulates use of the knowledge developed to help improve health and healthcare in the Netherlands. ZonMw's main commissioning organizations are the Ministry of Health, Welfare and Sport and the Netherlands Organization for Scientific Research. More fundamental research is also granted by the Dutch Organization for Scientific Research (NWO). It funds thousands of top researchers at universities and institutes, and steers the course of Dutch science by means of subsidies and research programs.

As for supervision, it forms one of the cornerstones of the BIG law. It is an obligatory part of the schooling program of HC-psychologists, psychotherapists, clinical psychologists, and psychiatrists. Supervision can be more general, focusing on the development of a professional attitude and a personal learning capacity, or focused on psychodiagnostics or on specific treatment traditions such as CBT or psychoanalysis. Before the BIG law, supervision was mostly given outside the work setting in order to create optimum confidentiality for the trainee. Following its introduction in 1986, the training programs for psychotherapists, HC-psychologists, and clinical psychologists began to resemble the medical model (Baljon, 2008). Training in clinical practice is central and, for financial reasons, a supervisor is often someone connected to the department where the training takes place, thus leaving the trainee with little choice regarding the supervision. This model of supervision is characterized as educational counseling whereas the more traditional view of supervision (i.e., focusing on the personal professional development of the trainee) threatens to disappear (Pols, 2006). A demand is that supervision is clearly distinguished from educational counseling: supervision needs to fulfill a certain amount of hours and needs to be registered. For example, the program for healthcare psychologists dictates 90 hours of supervision.

Strengths, weaknesses, opportunities, and challenges

The Dutch case, a separate and formally recognized profession of psychotherapy, has been, for a long time, unique in the world. From the perspective of professionalization the settlement of a distinctive profession was a huge success. It not only created a new discipline, but committed psychotherapists to organize their discipline, to make explicit their domains and competencies and to establish their schooling programs. From this perspective it is perfectly understandable that the profession witnessed enormous growth, and psychotherapy has become one of most important treatment options in mental healthcare in the Netherlands. It is also probable that the success of psychotherapy (an interdisciplinary profession of doctors and of psychologists) opened the doors of the BIG law to other non-strictly medical professions such as clinical and HC-psychologists. Formal settlement of these five psy-disciplines reduced rivalries and disputes between professions, provided transparency in a number of professionals and what they do, and offered excellent opportunities for improvement of healthcare quality and professional schooling.

At the same time, however, one could argue that psychotherapy as a profession became a victim of its own success. Consequently, due to its interdisciplinary nature, neither medicine nor psychology fully adopted psychotherapy within their academic schooling and research programs. The result was a growing distance from the academic world, where psychotherapy does not have its own department or is not recognized as a distinct academic study. (Hutschemaekers & Staak, 2006). With the rise of empirical supported therapies (EST) (Chambless & Ollendick, 2001) and their translation into evidence-based guidelines (Hutschemaekers & Kalmthout, 2006), the gap between the psychotherapists and the academic world became even more aggravated. It led to the paradoxical situation where psychotherapists became more or less outsiders of the academic and scientific scene.

The complex and opaque ordering of the psy-professions, of course, could also be seen as a challenge to overcome. If these disciplines are able to develop a new and more rational division of the professional field, it would probably also lead to a clearer distinction between psychiatric and psychological help as well as psychotherapy and counseling. These major changes will, of course, have their consequences on the whole system of professional schooling and the inter-dependencies between different schooling programs. The new concept of learning guided by "competencies" could help to overcome the consequences of this major rebuilding of the professional schooling system.

Besides these interdisciplinary challenges, we expect some major concerns to result from the economic crisis. At this very moment psychotherapy is completely remunerated by health insurance companies. The Dutch Ministry of Health has already indicated that this situation will change. The consequence is that patients will have to pay for a large part of therapy themselves. For healthcare institutions as well as private practices, this will probably lead to a decline in patients. Moreover, we expect a further decrease in the number of therapy sessions.

Future directions

Although affairs of professionalization almost never develop in a rational way, we expect a transformation in the field of the psy-professions (Hutschemaekers & Staak, 2006). Hopefully the result will be a more transparent division of tasks and a clearer distinction between the basic disciplines and their specializations.

What other directions could be foreseen? Here too, we should be cautious. The future may develop in ways not assumed, based on contemporary trends. But if current topics continue for the next few years, we think the switch in focus from non-specific therapeutic factors towards specific interventions will continue. This trend implies the further rise of empirically supported therapies (Chambless & Ollendick, 2001) and implementation of evidence-based guidelines. The same trend will also continue in scientific research. Naturalistic studies will diminish and be replaced by RCTs. Similar trends will change schooling programs and clinical practice. Nowadays, students in psychotherapy learn as much about specific techniques as about non-specific therapeutic factors. We expect that specific techniques will become more central. In clinical practice the traditional person-oriented psychotherapies will disappear in officially recognized mental healthcare institutions and will be replaced by shorter forms of psychotherapy. In these therapies less attention is paid to the therapeutic relationship and the psychotherapeutic process. For instance, we see this development in the field of internet therapy: less personal interactions and more specific interventions. Finally, this shift is also reflected by the way Dutch mental health institutions have organized their primary work processes. The traditional organization was related to discipline and type of care (i.e., the department of ambulatory psychotherapy), whereas new organizational forms are often based on programs related to syndromes (i.e., department of anxiety disorders, etc.). (Hutschemaekers, Tiemens, & Winter, 2007)

Nevertheless, this shift towards further systematic use of evidence-based psychotherapeutic interventions will not necessarily lead to the disappearance of traditional person-oriented psychotherapies. On the contrary, we expect an increase of these psychotherapies outside the official mental healthcare institutions. In an alternative circuit all kinds of therapies will grow; some of them are based on psychodynamic theories or on the Rogerian tradition, others are based on more new-age insights and techniques. This alternative circuit will have its own finance system, but insurance companies will only remunerate a small part of it. We foresee that the size of this alternative health system will directly depend on the outspokenness of the formal system: the more outspoken the formal system, the greater the alternatives too.

Thirdly, we expect a further development in the treatment of patients with complex personality (disorders) and other comorbid disorders. These patients, who do not fit within regular treatment programs for chronic psychiatric patients, often function on a very "low level" and are regularly perceived as extremely "difficult" (Koekkoek, Meijel, & Hutschemaekers, 2006). They need treatment from an interdisciplinary team of a psychiatrist, psychotherapist or clinical psychologist, nurse, and social worker. The psychotherapeutic part of this treatment demands that therapists are able to manage the distance between the patient and the team. They also need elaborate training in setting and handling the therapeutic relationship with these patients. Hence, we expect that the professional schooling of these therapists will become part of regular educational programs of psychotherapists and that the treatment of these patients will become one of the new specializations within psychotherapy.

Conclusion

The development of counseling and psychotherapy in the Netherlands has been strongly influenced by the settlement of five distinctive psy-disciplines. The Netherlands was the first country with a distinctive profession of psychotherapists (Hutschemaekers & Staak, 2006). This formal settlement in 1986 gave psychologists their entry to the formally recognized mental healthcare professions. Later it also gave them the possibility to establish their own profession as HC-psychologists and clinical psychologists. Related to this formal settlement was the recognition of psychotherapeutic treatment by health insurance companies, which opened the door to this form of treatment for new patients. This resulted in a huge increase of patients receiving psychotherapeutic treatment.

At the same time, we have to admit that the settlement of five distinctive psy-professions created various very specific and difficult formal problems, such as defining the domains and competencies of these disciplines and setting their mutual borders. Professionalization topics are still under discussion and regularly lead to irritations, violent outburst, or defensive reactions from the professionals involved. One can compare this to an open wound which becomes more painful each time it is touched. This could be illustrated by the yearly negotiations on manpower planning and the settlement of the number of trainees for each discipline which inevitably leads to painful outcomes for each discipline.

One of the core problems to be solved in this professionalization tumult is the unclear distinction between the clinical psychologist and the psychotherapist. Other topics, such as defining the specialisms of the psy-professions and a better role distinction between the medical and the psychological disciplines, are directly related to this main problem. It is hard to predict how these professionalization topics will develop in the years to come and what will be the outcome of this process, but we can be sure that it will have important consequences for other developments in the field of psychotherapy. Ten years ago we predicted a merger between the professions of clinical psychology and psychotherapy. We have to admit, however, that to date no sign of such a merger has become visible.

Note

1 The Dutch law BIG (disciplines in individual healthcare) recognizes basic disciplines such as doctor, nurse, healthcare psychologist, and psychotherapist, as well as specialisms of these basic disciplines, such as the psychiatrist, the clinical psychologist, and the clinical neuropsychologist.

References

Alternative Medicine Overview. (2011). *Home.* Retrieved October 30, 2011 from www.alternatieve geneeswijzen-overzicht.nl/

Baljon, M. (2008). De tijden veranderen. De plaats van supervisie ten opzichte van de praktijkplaats [Times change. The place of supervision in clinical training]. *Tijdschrift Clientgerichte Psychotherapie, 46,* 265–266.

Bateman, A., & Fonagy, P. (2004). *Psychotherapy for Borderline Personality Disorder: Mentalization-based Treatment.* New York: Oxford University Press.

Bijl, R. V., & Ravelli, A. (2000). Psychiatric morbidity, service use and need for care in the general population: Results of the Netherlands Mental Health Survey and Incidence Study. *American Journal of Public Health, 90*(4), 602–607.

Chambless, D. L., & Ollendick, T. (2001). Empirically supported psychological interventions. Controversies and evidence. *Annual Review of Psychology, 52,* 685–716.

CIBG. (n.d.). *Specialization.* Retrieved from www.bigregister.nl/en/registration/inthebigregister/specialization/

Derksen, J. J. L. (2004). *Psychologische diagnostiek. Enkele structurele en descriptieve aspecten.* Nijmegen: PEN Publisher.

Drunen, P. v., & Staak, C. v. d. (2011). Van psycholoog in de gezondheidzorg naar gezondheidszorgpsycholoog [From psychologist in health care to health care psychologist]. In M. Verbraak, S. Visser, P. Muris & K. Hoogduin (eds), *Handboek voor gz-psychologen* (pp. 19–28). Amsterdam: Boom.

Emmelkamp, P. (2004). Behavior therapy with Adults. In M. J. Lambert (ed.), *Bergin and Garfield's handbook of Psychotherapy and Behavior Change* (pp. 393–446). New York: John Wiley & Sons.

Gijswijt-Hofstra, M., Oosterhuis, H., Vijselaar, J., & Freeman, H. (eds). (2005). *Psychiatric Cultures Compared. Psychiatry and Mental Health Care in the Twentieth Century.* Amsterdam: Amsterdam University Press.

Groen, W. B., Tesink, C., Petersson, K. M., Berkum, J., van der Gaag, R. J., Hagoort, P., & Buitelaar, J. K. (2010). Semantic, factual, and social language comprehension in adolescents with autism: An FMRI study. *Cerebral Cortex, 20*(8), 1937–1945.

Grol, R., & Grimshaw, J. (2003). From best evidence to best practice: effective implementation of change in patients' care. *Lancet, 362*(9391), 1225–1230.

Grol, R., & Wensink, M. (2000). *Implementatie* [Implementation]. Maarsen: Elsevier Gezondheidszorg.

Hutschemaekers, G. (2000). Wordt Nederland steeds zieker? Kengetallen en achtergrondanalyses [Are the Netherlands getting sicker? Figures and background analyses]. *Maandblad Geestelijke Gezondheidszorg, 55,* 314–335.

Hutschemaekers, G., Brunenberg, W., & Spek, H. (1993). *Beroep: psychotherapeut. Een verkennend onderzoek naar persoon, werk en werkplek van de psychotherapeut in Nederland* [Profession: Psychotherapist. A study on person, work, and workplace of the psychotherapist in the Netherlands]. (Vol. 93–14). Utrecht: NcGv.

Hutschemaekers, G., Camp, K. v. d., & Hattum, M. v. (2001). *Psychotherapie in getallen*. Utrecht: Trimbos-instituut.

Hutschemaekers, G., & Kalmthout, M. v. (2006). The new integral multidisciplinary guidelines in the Netherlands. The perspective of person-centered psychotherapy. *Person-centered & Experiential Psychotherapies, 5*(2), 101–113.

Hutschemaekers, G., & Oosterhuis, H. (2004). Psychotherapy in the Netherlands after the Second World War. *Medical History, 48*, 429–448.

Hutschemaekers, G., & Staak, C. v. (2006). The Dutch case. The rise and decline of an independent profession of psychotherapists in the Netherlands. *International Journal of Psychotherapy, 10*(1), 41–52.

Hutschemaekers, G., & Staak, C. v. d. (in press). Le Phénomène Hollandais. l'Histoire de la psychothérapie aux Pays Bas [The Dutch Case. The history of psychotherapy in the Netherlands]. In C. Fussinger & V. Barras (eds), *Psychothérapie en Europe*. Geneve: Bibliothèque d'histoire de la médecine.

Hutschemaekers, G., Tiemens, B., & Winter, M. d. (2007). Effects and side-effects of integrating care: The case of mental health care in the Netherlands. *International Journal of Integrated Care, 7*, e31.

Hutschemaekers, G. J. M., & Neijmeijer, L. (1998). *Beroepen in Beweging. Professionalisering en grenzen van een multidisciplinaire GGZ* [Moving professions. Professionalization and boundaries of a multidiscplinary mental health care]. Houten: Bohn Stafleu Van Loghum.

Jongerius, P. (1987). Le Phénomène hollandais, een geschiedenis van het psychotherapeutisch veld [The Dutch Case, a history of the field of psychotherapy]. In J. Vijselaar (ed.), *Ambulant in zicht. Verslag van het symposium op 17 januari 1986 te Zeist*. (pp. 120–136). Utrecht: NcGv.

Keijsers, G. P. J., Minnen, v. A., & Hoogduin, C. A. L. (1999). Protocollaire behandeling in onderzoek en praktijk: Recente ontwikkelingen [Protocol treatment in research and practice: Recent developments]. In G. P. J. Keijsers, v. A. Minnen & C. A. L. Hoogduin (eds), *Protocollaire behandleing in de ambulante geestelijke gezondheidszorg 2* (pp. 1–16). Houten: Bohn Stafleu Van Loghum; Cure & Care Development.

Koekkoek, B., Meijel, B. v., & Hutschemaekers, G. (2006). Difficult patients in mental health care: A review. *Psychiatric Services, 57*, 795–802.

Linehan, M. M. (1993). *Cognitive Behavioral Treatment of Borderline Personality Disorder*. New York: Guilford.

McCullough, L., & Kuhn, N. (2003). *Treating Affect Phobia. A Manual for Short-term Dynamic Psychotherapy*. New York: Guilford Press.

Meekeren, E. v., Limburg-Okken, A., & May, R. (eds). (2002). *Culturen binnen psychiatrie muren. Geestelijke gezondheidszorg in een multiculturele samenleving* [Cultures within psychiatry. Mental health care in a multicultural society]. Amsterdam: Boom.

Oosterhuis, H., & Gijswijt-Hoffstra, M. (2008). *Verward van geest en ander ongerief. Psychiaterie en geestelijke gezondheidszorg in Nederland 1870–2005* [Mentally confused and other nuisances. Psychiatry and mental health care in the Netherlands 1870–2005]. Houten: Bohn Stafleu van Loghum ism Nederlands Tijdschrft voor Geneeskunde.

Pols, J. (2006). *De psychiater als coach* [The psychiatrist as a coach]. Utrecht: De Tijdstroom.

Reenen, H. H. J. v., Vandermeersch, P., & Hutschemaekers, G. (1997). Alternatieve GGZ en Nwe Age. Verslag van een enquête onder alternatieve hulpverleners [Alternative mental health care and New Age. Report of an inquiry among alternative therapists]. *MGV, 52*(12), 1207–1218.

Reijzer, H. (1993). *Naar een nieuw beroep. Psychotherapeut in Nederland* [To a new profession. Psychotherapist in the Netherlands]. Houten: Bohn Stafleu Van Loghum.

Schuck, K., Keijsers, G. P. J., & Rinck, M. (2011). The effects of brief cognitive-behaviour therapy for pathological skin picking: A randomized comparison to wait-list control. *Behaviour Research and Therapy, 49*(1), 11–18.

Statistics Netherlands (2011). *Statistisch Jaarboek 2011* [Yearbook Dutch Statistics]. Den Haag: CBS.

SPON. (n.d.). *Homepage*. Retrieved October 30, 2011 from www.spon-opleidingen.nl/

Trumpf, J., Margraf, J., Vriends, N., Meyer, A. H., & Becker, E. S. (2010). Predicting anxiety: The role of experiential avoidance and anxiety sensitivity. *Journal of Anxiety Disorders, 24*(1), 109–114.

Wiers, R. W., Eberl, C., Rinck, M., Becker, E. S., & Lindemeyer, J. (2011). Retraining automatic action tendencies changes alcoholic patients' approach bias for alcohol and improves treatment outcome. *Psychological Science, 22*(4), 490–498.

Young, Y. E. (1999). *Cognitive Therapy for Personality Disorders: A Schema-focused Approach*. Sarasota: Professional Resource Press.

28

PSYCHOTHERAPY IN SPAIN

Rapid growth and the vicissitudes of clinical psychology

María Paz García-Vera, Jesús Sanz, and José M. Prieto

Introduction

Spain is the only country where a madman is the main character in the national literary canon: *Don Quixote*. For centuries, Spanish children in primary and high school have read simplified versions of this novel and they become accustomed to the idea of the insane as being worthy and genuine persons. In 1409, two centuries before Don Quixote, Joan Gilabert Jofré built a hospital in Valencia to provide care, including medical care, to people with mental disorders: the Hospital of the Innocents (Bassoe, 1945). Others were set up in Saragossa, Seville, Valladolid, and Toledo during 1425–1480. Philippe Pinel, the famed French reformer, visited the hospital in Saragossa and reportedly incorporated some of his observations into his revolutionary care program for the insane in France, referred to today as "moral treatment" (Bassoe, 1945).

In accordance with this Spanish millennial tradition of normalizing mental disorders and their treatment, Spain currently has a national health system supported by public funding, and based on the universality and gratuitousness of health services, which include individual, group, or family psychotherapies among the mental healthcare benefits.

This national health system covers virtually the entire Spanish population, which in January 2011 was 47.1 million inhabitants, including 5.7 million foreign nationals (12.2% of the total population) (National Statistics Institute [INE], 2011). The Romanies (Gypsies) are the one ethnic minority of long standing in Spain, with a population estimated at 650,000 (Open Society Foundations, 2010). There are ethnic minorities as a result of immigration, mainly foreign citizens from Romania (864,278), Morocco (769,920), and Ecuador (359,076) (INE, 2011). Spanish (or Castilian) is spoken all over the country and thus is the only language with official status nationwide, but four regional languages (Catalan, Valencian, Galician, and Basque) have co-official status in the six regions where they are spoken. Spain has no official religion, but about 72% of Spaniards self-identify as Catholics, whereas 2.4% self-identify with other faiths, and about 24% with no religion, among which 7.4% are atheists (Center for Sociological Research, 2011).

This chapter will review the current state of psychotherapy in Spain, mainly within the context of clinical psychology. Currently, the practice of psychotherapy in Spain is mainly related to the practice of clinical psychology and, to a smaller degree, to the practice of psychiatry. Thus, most of the professionals who are members of the Spanish scientific-professional associations that are specific to the sphere of psychotherapy are psychologists (around 70%) and, to a much lesser extent, psychiatrists (around 15%) (Spanish Federation of Psychotherapists Associations, 2010).

We will exclusively focus on psychotherapy since in Spain the field of counseling is not well developed: the profession of counselor does not exist, nor does any official education program in counseling, and counseling psychology is not considered a recognized professional profile by the Official Associations of Psychologists (in Spanish, *Colegios Oficiales de Psicólogos* or COP). In general, in Spain, psychological counseling is considered either a psychotherapeutic approach based on humanist theoretical orientations, especially on Carl Rogers' classic works, or a kind of psychological intervention focused on facilitating optimal personal development and used by clinical psychologists and educational-school, work-organizational, or sport psychologists.

Brief history of psychotherapy

The history of psychotherapy in Spain goes back to the beginning of the 20th century, when the process of institutionalization of psychiatry and psychology in Spain began and psychoanalysis was introduced into the country. The first work published by Freud about hysteria, written with Breuer in 1893, was translated to Spanish and published in a Spanish medical journal 1 month after it was originally published in German (Sánchez-Barranco Ruiz, Sánchez-Barranco Vallejo, & Sánchez-Barranco Vallejo, 2007). Subsequently, many other of Freud's works were translated and published in Spain, and soon psychoanalysis gained notoriety and caused controversy. However, it is not until the 1920s that we can find institutionalized psychiatry and applied psychology, which at that time were closely related to each other and were led by two physicians, Emilio Mira y López and Gonzalo Rodríguez Lafora, who contributed decisively not only to the development of the two disciplines, but also to the diffusion of psychoanalysis (Carpintero, 2004).

However, the first genuine Spanish psychoanalyst was Ángel Garma, who was trained in psychoanalysis in Berlin and joined the Psychoanalytical Association of Berlin in 1931. Although upon his return from Berlin, Garma said he had encountered a strong opposition to psychoanalysis among the physicians of Madrid, he nevertheless began to diffuse it through articles and conferences (Sánchez-Barranco Ruiz et al., 2007).

Unfortunately, the Spanish Civil War interrupted the progress of institutional psychiatry and psychology, because an important number of its figures were forced to go into exile after the war (e.g., Garma, Rodríguez Lafora, Mira y López). These intellectual losses, along with the international isolation that characterized the first years of the Francoist dictatorship, had dire consequences on the development of both disciplines and on psychotherapy.

Despite all this, the practice, training, and diffusion of psychoanalysis in Spain recommenced as of the 1950s and with greater force in the 1960s. However, this increasing diffusion did not reach the universities as intensely because, in the universities, a general attitude of clear rejection was adopted both in the sphere of psychiatry and in the sphere of psychology, based mainly on the dispute about the scientific status of psychoanalysis (Carpintero, 2004; Sánchez-Barranco Ruiz et al., 2007).

At the same time, scientific and academic psychology became progressively more consolidated in Spain. In 1948, the Department of Experimental Psychology was created within the Higher Counsel of Scientific Research (the most important public research organization in Spain), and 5 years later, university psychology studies in Spain began with the School of

Psychology and Psychotechnics created by the University of Madrid (currently the Complutense). This led to the appearance of the first individuals with a university degree in psychology who practiced clinical psychology, one of the three specialties that students could choose (Carpintero, 2004).

This laid the bases for a speedy expansion of university studies of psychology in the 1970–1980s. The first psychology faculty in Spain was created in 1980 in the Complutense University of Madrid. Other universities soon followed suit due to great demand by students (Carpintero, 2004).

As of the 1970s, cognitive-behavioral oriented psychotherapy began to be diffused in Spain, and, in a few years, underwent rapid expansion, so that already by 1986, most clinical psychologists chose behavioral models over psychoanalytic ones (48.8% vs. 37.6%) (Ávila, 1989). The 1970s and 1980s were also decisive in establishing Spanish Psychology at the professional level, with the creation in 1980 of the Official Association of Psychologists (COP) (Carpintero, 2004).

In the last 20 years, there have been some events that have led to the consolidation of clinical psychology and psychotherapy in Spain: the incorporation of clinical psychology in the Spanish National Health System; the inclusion of clinical psychology and psychotherapy in the services offered by private health insurance companies; the development and proliferation of professional training programs specializing in clinical psychology and psychotherapy for postgraduates, and the important increase in Spanish scientific research in the areas of clinical psychology and psychotherapy (Carpintero, 2004; García-Vera, Sanz, & Prieto, 2012; Sanz, 2001).

Psychotherapist education programs, accreditation, licensure, and certification

The structure of the Spanish educational system has undergone notable changes in the past 6 years as a result of its adaptation to the European Higher Education Area (EHEA), a political commitment endorsed by 47 European states to improve university education. This is done by adopting a series of common instruments, for example, a comparable degree system with three levels (bachelor, master, and doctorate), and a common unit of measure for academic credits (European Credit Transfer and Accumulation System or ECTS) that represents the quantity of student workload required to meet the training goals (one ECTS credit corresponds to 25–30 hours of work) (EHEA, 2011).

The only Spanish first-level university degrees currently providing specific training in psychotherapy are the licentiate's degree in psychology and the bachelor's degree in psychology, the latter only since October of 2008, enforced by the law of the new university titles adapted the EHEA, and which replaces the licentiate's degree.

The current bachelor's degree in psychology requires, by law, 6,000 hours of student workload over 4 years (240 ECTS credits), of which a maximum of 2,400 hours are theoretical or practical face-to-face classes. However, this degree does not provide sufficient training for the professional practice of psychotherapy because it offers few psychotherapeutic subjects (a mean of about 325 hours of student workload, including 130 of theoretical or practical face-to-face classes) and little clinical practice (an approximate mean of 350 hours of student workload) (García-Vera et al., 2012).

To receive more specialized and practical training in psychotherapy, the most frequent alternatives to the postgraduate level in Spain are (1) specialized health training via the residency system in the National Health System (training programs for the Intern-Resident Psychologist—PIR—and Intern-Resident Physician—MIR—for the specialty of psychiatry); (2) professionally oriented master's degrees organized by universities; and (3) master's degrees taught by scientific-professional organizations and assistance centers (García-Vera et al., 2012).

The PIR and MIR training programs in clinical psychology and psychiatry are regulated by the Ministry of Health and Social Policy and the Ministry of Education, and to access them, students must have a licentiate's/bachelor's degree in psychology or medicine and surgery and have passed the selective test held at the national level. Both programs last 4 years and are based on the occupational integration of the resident in hospitals and health centers of the National Health System through an occupational training contract to provide healthcare and simultaneously receive training. The programs involve programmed and supervised professional practice, with an increasing level of autonomy and responsibility, which is developed in diverse healthcare centers and facilities through which the resident receives training. Among the competencies the resident should acquire is the practice of psychotherapy: a key element of the PIR training program and, to a lesser extent, of the MIR training program in psychiatry (Yllá, Hidalgo, & Guimón, 2003).

Spanish universities offer two types of professionally oriented master's degree to train post-graduates in clinical psychology, psychiatry, or psychotherapy: the unofficial master's degree, which is certified by the awarding university, and the official master's degree, which is developed within the framework of the EHEA and is certified by the Ministry of Education. Most of the unofficial master's degrees include over 600 hours of face-to-face training distributed in two academic courses, whereas the official professionally oriented master's degrees have a mean of 90 ECTS credits (García-Vera et al., 2012).

Finally, a great number of scientific/professional associations of clinical psychology, psychiatry, or psychotherapy and private and public centers for psychological or psychiatric assistance offer non-university master's degrees in psychotherapy. The characteristics of these master's degrees are very diverse, although most of them include at least 500 hours of theoretical or practical face-to-face classes, distributed between two academic courses (García-Vera et al., 2012).

There are currently in Spain two main certificates to obtain accreditation as a psychotherapist, that of the COP and that of the Spanish Federation of Psychotherapy Associations (in Spanish, *Federación Española de Asociaciones de Psicoterapia*, hereafter FEAP), but the two accreditations are not officially acknowledged and in Spain the profession of psychotherapist does not exist in law. There are important differences between the criteria of both accreditations, especially concerning the necessary prior training to access specialized training in psychotherapy. The FEAP shares the position of the European Association for Psychotherapy (EAP), which maintains that psychotherapy is a different and independent profession from that of psychologist or psychiatrist, and, therefore, it is not necessary to have a prior university formation in psychology or medicine to access specialized training in psychotherapy (FEAP, 2010).

In contrast, the COP shares the same position about these issues as the European Federation of Psychologists' Associations (EFPA), of which the COP is a member. The EFPA is the organization that groups the national professional associations of psychologists of 35 European countries. The EFPA maintains that psychotherapy and its professional practice have their roots and foundations in psychology and in psychiatry, and, therefore, a psychotherapist cannot be considered a different profession from that of psychologist or psychiatrist, and its specialized training should be accessed from the basic university formation in psychology or medicine. Since 2007, EFPA has established criteria and procedures for the accreditation of psychologists specializing in psychotherapy and the COP is the organization in charge of its assessment in Spain (EFPA Standing Committee on Psychotherapy, 2005).

Current psychotherapy theories, processes, and trends

There are currently about 51,000 registered psychologists in the COP. According to Santolaya Ochando, Berdullas Temes and Fernández Hermida (2001), clinical psychologists represent approximately 68.4% of registered psychologists and 96.3% of them carry out psychological treatments.

The great majority (80%) of Spanish clinical psychologists work in the private sector (Santolaya Ochando et al., 2001). Although in the last 25 years, the employment of clinical psychologists in the public sector has not ceased to grow, it is still far from the standards of other developed countries that, like Spain, have an important public health system. In 2003, the Spanish public network of mental healthcare had 4.3 clinical psychologists for every 100,000 inhabitants (Salvador, 2005), whereas the median for high-income countries was 14 psychologists for every 100,000 inhabitants in 2005 (World Health Organization, 2005).

Given those figures and the organization of the national health system in Spain[1], the common therapeutic trajectory of most people in Spain who have psychological disorders and seek professional help is initially to receive treatment by a primary care physician (almost exclusively pharmacological) and, later, if there is a lack of response, to be referred to a public mental health center, and, if they do not find a satisfactory solution to their problems in the public mental health system, mainly due to its long waiting lists or its lack of time for psychotherapy, they usually go to private psychiatry and clinical psychology centers and consulting offices. If the patients have no economic resources to pay for private psychological attention, they usually remain in treatment in primary care centers or mental health centers. As detailed later, an increasing number of patients in Spain have access to private insurance that covers psychotherapy. All these reasons account for such a high rate of clinical psychologists working in private settings.

The cognitive-behavioral approach is the major theoretical approach to psychotherapy in Spain both among registered psychologists who ascribe themselves to the area of clinical psychology (Santolaya Ochando et al., 2001), among university professors in that discipline (Sanz, 2001), and among psychiatrists (Yllá et al., 2003). In Santolaya Ochando et al.'s (2001) study, 62.3% of the registered clinical psychologists reported that their theoretical orientation was cognitive-behavioral, whereas the following five most important theoretical orientations were the psychoanalytic (17.3%), eclectic (9.7%), systemic (5.3%), and humanist (4.3%) approaches. Among the university professors of clinical psychology and psychotherapy, the most frequent theoretical approach is also the cognitive-behavioral one, shared by 68.7% of the professors, followed far behind by the psychoanalytic and eclectic approaches, shared, respectively, by 11% and 8.2% of the professors (Sanz, 2001).

Indigenous and traditional healing methods

Psychotherapy in Spain falls within the framework of the European and North American academic psychotherapeutic tradition, and its conventional therapies are widely used by Spanish people. Nevertheless, in some regions of Spain, and, particularly, in rural areas, there are still traditional and indigenous healing methods for the treatment of diverse psychological disorders, including some supposedly culture-dependent syndromes such as the "evil eye" (*mal de ojo* in Spanish). These methods are mainly based on the use of herbs and/or symbolic–ritual procedures derived from Catholic religious traditions, operate outside of the official systems of health attention, and their use varies widely. For example, the use of herbs such as valerian is very frequent for anxiety and sleeping disorders, usually as a complementary therapy to conventional ones, whereas the use of charms for the evil eye seems to have diminished, since lately very few cases of this syndrome have been reported in the Spanish scientific literature (Carretero Ares, Ruiz Blanco, Yagüe Encinas, & Pérez Martín, 2001; Erkoreka, 2005).

The evil eye is not unique to Spain; other Mediterranean, Hispanic and Muslim cultures have similar superstitions of a look supposed to be capable of inflicting harm or illness to the person at whom it is directed for reasons of envy or dislike. However, the symptoms may vary among cultures. In Spain, people who believe they have been victims of the evil eye usually present a group of symptoms that resembles a depressive disorder: a general feeling of discomfort, decreased appetite, fatigue, insomnia, sadness, diminished interest in activities, crying spells without external triggers, weight loss, etc. Among the traditional remedies for the evil eye are the following: carry images of saints or religious charms; visit sanctuaries and being blessed with holy water, and visit folk healers (*curanderas* in Spanish), who apply charms, make the sign of the cross over the victim, or say prayers (Erkoreka, 2005).

Research and supervision

Based on Sanz's (2001) literature review, it can be estimated that psychotherapy research in Spain in the past 30 years has grown significantly, has been mainly carried out in the universities, has been mostly focused on cognitive-behavioral therapies, and has followed three pathways: the efficacy of the psychotherapeutic procedures, the development of new psychotherapeutic alternatives, and the study of the psychotherapeutic process itself.

Research on the efficacy of psychotherapy is the most important insofar as the number of works. Many research programs have addressed the assessment of the results of concrete psychotherapeutic modalities in the treatment of specific disorders by means of experimental or quasi-experimental designs. Almost all of these studies focused on cognitive-behavioral therapies, and among the mental disorders examined, the anxiety disorders are noteworthy (Echeburúa, Salaberría, de Corral, Cenea, & Berasategui, 2006; Labrador, Fernández-Velasco, & Rincón, 2006).

A second pathway has focused on the development of new therapeutic alternatives. For example, Spanish research groups have elaborated on a new multicomponent treatment (emotive performances) for specific phobias in children from 3 to 8 years (Méndez Carrillo, Orgilés Amorós, & Espada Sánchez, 2004), new techniques of awake hypnosis as adjuncts to cognitive-behavioral treatments (Capafons & Mendoza, 2010), or cognitive-behavioral therapeutic protocols based on virtual reality for the treatment of anxiety disorders (Tortella-Feliu et al., 2011).

The third pathway of Spanish psychotherapy research is a response to recent attempts to analyze the therapeutic process itself; this research is the most scarce. For example, there are works examining the processes of client–therapist verbal interaction that take place during therapy (Froján-Parga, Calero-Elvira, & Montaño-Fidalgo, 2009).

Supervised clinical practice is a core component of all the above-mentioned postgraduate-level alternatives to receive professional training in psychotherapy, but it varies widely in the number of hours and the type of setting in which the internship/practicum takes place.

A strong point of PIR and MIR training is the high number of hours of supervised clinical practice in very diverse contexts, which allows psychotherapeutic learning with many patients of all ages and with all types of mental disorders. However, this learning is, to some extent, diminished because of excessive patient load and the limited time that can be dedicated to patients in public healthcare facilities; thus, in most of these facilities, the main therapeutic activity is psychological advice, whereas full psychotherapeutic treatments are rarely or never applied (Virués Ortega, Santolaya Ochando, García Cueto, & Buela-Casal, 2003).

In contrast, university and non–university master's degrees in clinical psychology or psychotherapy require completion of many fewer hours of practical training and, besides, not all the practical training hours are dedicated to supervised clinical care of patients (García-Vera et al., 2012).

Concerning the two main certificates to obtain accreditation as a psychotherapist in Spain, the criteria of the COP accreditation require at least 500 hours of supervised clinical practice and 150 hours of supervision, whereas the criteria of the FEAP accreditation require a minimum of 280 hours of supervised clinical practice (300 treatment sessions of 45 minutes), plus 75 hours of supervision (100 sessions of 45 minutes).

Strengths, weaknesses, opportunities, and challenges

The vicissitudes of clinical psychology in Spain in the past 15 years have marked the recent history of psychotherapy, and they will no doubt mark its future.

A major strength in the field has been the consolidation of clinical psychology over the years. The basic structure of the profession of psychologist within the sphere of clinical psychology has advanced notably, but is still incomplete. On the one hand, the generic practice of the profession is acknowledged with the sole requirements of having a licentiate's/bachelor's degree in psychology and being registered in the COP. On the other hand, in 1998, the official title of Psychologist Specializing in Clinical Psychology was established by law. This involves a higher level of theoretical-practical training in diagnosis, assessment, treatment, and rehabilitation of mental disorders. One can only access this title through the above-mentioned PIR training. Subsequently, a law was passed in 2003 to regulate health professions; included among the certified and regulated health professions was that of the psychologist with the title of "Psychologist Specializing in Clinical Psychology," but not the psychology graduate. Lastly, also in 2003, another law established that only health professionals could work in health centers and services, either public or private.

These legal regulations have led to the consolidation of clinical psychology in Spain and, therefore, of psychotherapy as one of the main tasks carried out by clinical psychologists. Moreover, the demand of a high level of training to practice clinical psychology is no doubt a guarantee of quality for society and ensures to a greater extent that the people will receive adequate psychotherapeutic care.

A basic weakness of psychotherapy in Spain is its limited role in the National Health System and the few psychologists in the system. Since 1995, the portfolio of services of the Spanish National Health System includes mental healthcare based on individual, group, or family psychotherapies, although it expressly excludes psychoanalysis (understood as classic psychoanalysis or cure type) and hypnosis, an exclusion which is maintained in the latest portfolio of 2006. However, the real role of psychotherapy in the public health system is limited for several reasons. First, the majority of Spanish psychiatrists follow a biomedical model; they mainly prescribe pharmacological therapies and lack formal training in psychotherapy (Yllá et al., 2003). Second, there are no psychologists in primary care and their presence in specialized care is still scarce. Third, the excessive patient load of the public health centers and the short time that can be dedicated to patients in them hinder the application of psychotherapy in favor of therapeutic alternatives—such as the pharmacological one—that take less time and demand less skill and professional involvement.

These weaknesses are also reflected in the role of psychotherapy within the development of evidence-based treatment guidelines for mental disorders (e.g., anxiety disorders, depression in adults, depression in children and adolescents) by the Spanish health authorities. Although these guidelines are certainly necessary and their elaboration has followed a methodologically rigorous procedure with the participation of diverse professionals, the result tends to prioritize pharmacological treatment over psychological treatment, even when evidence shows that some of the psychological therapies are more effective than the pharmacological ones (e.g., anxiety disorders, depression in childhood and adolescence) or at least as effective (e.g., depression in adults).

How to solve these weaknesses represents a challenge to psychotherapy in Spain, but several other challenges still lie ahead. Up to 2003, psychology graduates without a specialist title could open a consulting office or a clinical psychology center and could be registered without any trouble on the health center registry. After passing the 2003 laws aimed to regulate health professions and centers, those psychologists were put in a difficult situation regarding work and juridical insecurity, because these laws not only affected the centers of the public health system, but also private centers, where, as mentioned, 80% of the Spanish psychologists who practice their profession in the clinical sphere are estimated to be working.

Fortunately, a large number of these psychologists have undergone an extraordinary process to obtain the title of Psychologist Specializing in Clinical Psychology (more than 14,500 requests were presented) and, therefore, their work situation has been regulated insofar as they have achieved the title (more than 7,000). However, psychology students who graduated after 1998 are worse off because, for them, the only possibility to obtain the title and, therefore, to be considered health professionals, is through access to PIR training. Currently, there are more than 56,000 students enrolled in psychology faculties and 40–50% of them chose curricular itineraries of clinical psychology. However, from 1998 to 2010, only between 60 and 135 PIR training places have been offered yearly. This high student-to-place ratio could be interpreted in terms of a discrepancy between the high number of psychology students and the actual possibilities of work in Spain. In fact, this discrepancy is quite real, but it is also obvious that such a low number of PIR places cannot ensure either the generational replacement among clinical psychologists or the psychotherapeutic care of a population that already exceeds 47 million inhabitants.

Therefore, although in the short term the high number of psychologists who have passed the extraordinary process to obtain the title of Psychologist Specializing in Clinical Psychology ensures that the psychotherapeutic care of the Spanish population is taken care of, in the medium and long term because of the lack of places for PIR training, the only official pathway to practice in the clinical sphere as a health professional, such care is at serious risk.

To solve the problems caused by the 2003 laws aimed to regulate health professions and centers, opportunities have arisen for the Ministry of Health and Social Policy, the Ministry of Education, and the professional and academic representatives of Spanish psychology to collaborate and work on the implementation of an official university master's degree in health psychology within the framework of the EHEA. The formation of such a degree will hopefully extend the possibility of being considered a health professional and will ensure higher training in clinical and health psychology than does the licentiate's/bachelor's degree in psychology.

Future directions

In 2006, the National Health System set, as one of the specific goals of its policy of mental healthcare, "to increase the percentage of patients with mental disorders who receive psychotherapy, according to the best practices available" (Gómez-Beneyto, 2010, p. 65). Unfortunately, 2 years later, assessment of this policy suggests that this goal is far from being met, but, hopefully, it remains as a goal to be pursued by the National Health System (Gómez-Beneyto, 2010).

This goal also seems to have been among the recent priorities of the Spanish private health insurance companies. In 2009, more than 8 million Spaniards had private health insurance, a booming market based on the promise of correcting the deficiencies of the public health system (e.g., speed in care of patients, shorter waiting lists). Since approximately 10 years ago, many of these insurance companies offer psychotherapy. The standard policy usually covers a maximum of 15–20 annual sessions of psychotherapy, excluding classic psychoanalysis and hypnosis, and the client must pay a small fee (copayment) for each session.

Finally, we note the recent initiatives of the COP and of diverse scientific and professional societies of Spanish psychology to achieve the incorporation of psychotherapy and adequately trained psychologists in the primary care services of the National Health System. As primary care constitutes access to the health system, and given the high prevalence of common mental disorders (anxiety, depressive, and adaptive disorders) among people who come to primary care centers and the demonstrated efficacy of the psychological treatments for these disorders, we hope such initiatives will have a positive impact on the evolution of psychotherapy in Spain in the future.

Conclusion

The history of psychotherapy in Spain goes back to the first years of the 20th century, and in the past 20 years, we have witnessed an impressive consolidation of clinical psychology and psychotherapy at all levels: training, research, and professional practice. Currently, the practice of psychotherapy in our country is mainly related to the practice of clinical psychology, so the vicissitudes of clinical psychology are closely linked to the situation of psychotherapy. Since 2003, the practice of psychotherapy in Spain has been characterized by the legal requirements to be able to practice as a clinical psychologist. By law, only psychologists who have the official title of Psychologist Specializing in Clinical Psychology, to which one only has access through PIR training, are considered health professionals and, as such, can work in public or private health centers in the psychological treatment of mental disorders. However, this triumph for Spanish psychology has caused serious problems because of the scarce number of places provided for PIR training, which does not ensure, in the medium or long term, either the generational replacement among clinical psychologists or the psychotherapeutic care of the Spanish population.

Perhaps the most important challenge facing psychotherapy in Spain is to increase its participation at all levels of the National Health System. Since the system is financed by taxes and provides almost universal coverage, and since there are efficient psychological therapies for most mental disorders, there is a need to increase the percentage of people with psychological disorders who receive psychotherapy. To achieve this, there will need to be an increase in the number of psychologists in specialized care (mental health) and the inclusion of psychologists in primary care.

Note

1 The Spanish national health system is organized at two levels: primary and specialized care. Primary care provides basic services to treat the most frequent problems through an extensive network of health centers and consulting offices where people are attended by family doctors, pediatricians, and nursing personnel. At specialized care level, patients are referred by primary care physicians. This level has more complex diagnostic and therapeutic resources in hospitals and diverse specialized centers, among which are the mental health centers where people are mainly attended by psychiatrists, clinical psychologists, and nursing personnel.

References

Ávila, A. (1989). La psicología clínica en España: Perspectiva de una década [Clinical psychology in Spain: Perspective of a decade]. *Papeles del Psicólogo, 36/37*, 84–89.
Bassoe, P. (1945). Spain as the cradle of psychiatry. *American Journal of Psychiatry, 101*, 731–738.

Capafons, A., & Mendoza, M.E. (2010). "Waking" hypnosis in clinical practice. In S. J. Lynn, J. W. Rhue, & I. Kirsch (eds), *Handbook of clinical hypnosis* (2nd edn) (pp. 293–317). Washington, DC: American Psychological Association.

Carpintero, H. (2004). *Historia de la Psicología en España* [History of Psychology in Spain]. Madrid: Pirámide.

Carretero Ares, J. L., Ruiz Blanco, A., Yagüe Encinas, E., & Pérez Martín, R. N. (2001). Medicina alternativa frente a medicina científica en un área básica de salud. ¿Un fenómeno emergente? [Alternative medicine vs. scientific medicine in a basic health area. An emergent phenomenon?]. *Medicina Clínica, 117*, 439.

Center for Sociological Research. (2011). *Barómetro de Julio 2011. Estudio nº 2909* [Barometer of July 2011. Study No. 2909]. Retrieved September 5, 2011, from www.cis.es

Echeburúa, E., Salaberría, K., de Corral, P., Cenea, R., & Berasategui, T. (2006). Treatment of mixed anxiety-depression disorder: long-term outcome. *Behavioural and Cognitive Psychotherapy, 34*(1), 95–101.

EFPA Standing Committee on Psychotherapy (2005). *Report to the General Assembly 2005 in Granada.* Retrieved September 30, 2011, from www.efpa.eu

Erkoreka, A. (2005). Mal de ojo: una creencia supersticiosa remota, compleja y aún viva [The evil eye: a remote superstitious belief, which is complex and still present]. *Munibe Antropologia – Arkeologia, 57*, 391–400.

European Higher Education Area (EHEA) (2011). *The official Bologna Process website 2010–2012. Main documents.* Retrieved September 30, 2011, from www.ehea.info

Froján-Parga, M. X., Calero-Elvira, A., & Montaño-Fidalgo, M. (2009). Analysis of the therapist's verbal behavior during cognitive restructuring debates: A case study. *Psychotherapy Research, 19*(1), 30–41.

García-Vera, M. P., Sanz, J., & Prieto, J. M. (2012). Current situation of undergraduate and postgraduate education in psychotherapy for psychologists in Spain. In S. McCarthy, K. L. Dickson, J. Cranney, A. Trapp & V. Karandashev (eds), *Teaching Psychology around the World*, Vol. 3 (pp. 311–329). Newcastle: Cambridge Scholars Publishing.

Gómez-Beneyto, M. (2010). *Evaluation of the Mental Health Strategy of the Spanish National Health System.* Madrid: Ministry of Health and Social Policy.

Labrador, F. J., Fernández-Velasco, M. R., & Rincón, P. P. (2006). Eficacia de un programa de intervención individual y breve para el trastorno por estrés postraumático en mujeres víctimas de violencia doméstica [Efficacy of a brief individual treatment program for the posttraumatic stress disorder in women victims of domestic violence]. *International Journal of Clinical and Health Psychology, 6*(3), 527–547.

Méndez Carrillo, X., Orgilés Amorós, M., & Espada Sánchez, J. P. (2004). Escenificaciones emotivas para la fobia a la oscuridad: un ensayo controlado [Emotive performances for phobia of the dark: A controlled trial]. *International Journal of Clinical and Health Psychology, 4*, 505–520.

National Statistics Institute (INE) (2011). *Preview of the Municipal Register at 1 January 2011. Press release of 4th April 2011.* Retrieved September 10, 2011 from www.ine.es

Open Society Foundations. (2010). *No data – no progress. Country findings. Data collection in countries participating in the decade of Roma inclusion 2005–2015.* New York: Open Society Foundations.

Salvador, I. (2005). El observatorio de salud mental: análisis de los recursos de salud mental en España [Mental health observatory: analysis of mental health resources in Spain]. *Revista de la Asociación Española de Neuropsiquiatría, 93*, 1–85.

Sánchez-Barranco Ruiz, A., Sánchez-Barranco Vallejo, P., & Sánchez-Barranco Vallejo, I. (2007). *El psicoanálisis en España: su pasado y presente* [Psychoanalysis in Spain: Its past and present]. Retrieved September 10, 2011 from www.psicoterapiarelacional.com

Santolaya Ochando, F., Berdullas Temes, M., & Fernández Hermida, J. R. (2001). The decade 1989–1998 in Spanish Psychology: An analysis of development of professional psychology in Spain. *The Spanish Journal of Psychology, 4*, 237–252.

Sanz, J. (2001). The decade 1989–1998 in Spanish Psychology: An analysis of research in personality, assessment, and psychological treatment (clinical and health psychology). *The Spanish Journal of Psychology, 4*, 51–81.

Spanish Federation of Psychotherapists Associations (FEAP) (2010). *Acreditación de psicoterapeutas y programas de formación* [Psychotherapist accreditation and formation programs]. Retrieved January 8, 2011, from www.feap.es/userfiles/file/Criterios de acreditacion FEAP – EAP.pdf

Tortella-Feliu, M., Botella, C., Llabrés, J., Bretón-López, J. M., del Amo, A. R., Baños, R. M., & Gelabert, J. M. (2011). Virtual reality versus computer-aided exposure treatments for fear of flying. *Behavior Modification, 35*, 3–30.

Virués Ortega, J., Santolaya Ochando, F., García Cueto, E., & Buela-Casal, G. (2003). Estado actual de la formación PIR: actividad clínica y docente de residentes y tutores [Current situation of PIR formation: Clinical and educational activity of residents and supervisors]. *Papeles del Psicólogo, 85*, 37–47.

World Health Organization. (2005). *Mental Health Atlas: 2005*. Switzerland: World Health Organization.

Yllá, L., Hidalgo, M.S., & Guimón, J. (2003). Orientación teórica de los psiquiatras españoles en 2003 [Theoretical orientation of Spanish psychiatrists in 2003]. *Avances en Salud Mental Relacional/Advances in Relational Mental Health, 2*, 1–3.

29

COUNSELING AND PSYCHOTHERAPY IN RUSSIA

Reunion with the international science community

Alla B. Kholmogorova, Natalia N. Garanian, and Valery N. Krasnov

Introduction

At 17,075,400 square kilometers, Russia is the largest country in the world, covering more than one-eighth of the Earth's inhabited land area. Russia is also the eighth most populous nation with 143 million people (Federal State Statistics Service, 2011). Russians have survived through numerous trials, which have dramatically influenced the demographic and mental health indices among the population. Today, there is a stable tendency towards depopulation in Russia and an unprecedented growth of early mortality, provoking serious isolation.[1]

Nicolas Eberstadt, a well-known demographist from the American Enterprise Institute, posits that the low life expectancy rates among Russians cannot be explained by well-known factors (e.g., alcohol abuse, unhealthy mode of life, and heart disease) (Eberstadt, 2010). Experts say that the chief factors behind the poor figures are depressive attitudes towards the future and high levels of anxiety. One of the leading Russian sociologists, Yu Levada, notes: "Russians are enormously scared by tomorrow. Instability—this is the chief phobia of our society. One more overwhelming fear—people are afraid of arbitrariness from the state" (Levada, 2004, p. 10).

One of the leading causes for the unprecedented growth of early mortality in the Russian male population is alcohol abuse (Nemtsov, 2009). The consequences of social instability and high alcohol consumption are extremely high rates of suicide and a rapid growth of socially disadvantaged families, and an orphanhood epidemic. Today, Russia's suicide levels are among the world's highest and it is in top position for the number of social orphans (Life is a Citizen of Russia, 2010). The adverse demographic situation in Russia requires complex government measures, particularly the extension of the psychological service system.

Clinical psychology, counseling, and psychotherapy in Russia are rapidly growing fields of professional activity. Clinical psychologists are allowed to practice psychotherapy but only in cooperation with doctors who have a medical background. The right to practice psychotherapy by clinical psychologists is a matter of constant and heated debate with Russian psychiatrists (Kholmogorova, 2010). Psychological counseling has not been yet identified as a separate specialization, but master's programs in counseling psychology have been established. Currently, every psychologist has a right to practice as a counselor, where counseling is referred to as the field of social population service and is not liable to licensing, according to the National Standard of Russian Federation (2003). As for psychotherapy, only doctors of psychiatry have the right to receive an *official* license to practice psychotherapy, but legislation and everyday practice diverge significantly. In reality, psychologists appear to be the most active in psychotherapy-related fields and are officially recognized under the label "psychological counseling," as previously mentioned.

Psychotherapy is not a free service under the Russian public health system. Therefore, it remains inaccessible to the masses. Publicly funded bodies for medical-psychological aid, however, have been established through initiatives by the Public Education Department. These are separate from the public health system. The psychotherapeutic network in regional primary care settings tends to provide medication alone.

Owing to the years of isolation from Western science and the long existing limitations of psychosocial interventions in the former Soviet Union, there remain a number of challenges to building a modern system of therapeutic practice that is contextually grounded and standardized with regard to training, education, supervision, and quality of service delivery. In light of the current critical demographic situation in Russia, establishment of an effective psychological service is one of the most important measures in overcoming this crisis. Resources and impediments to establishing this service are further analyzed in this chapter.

Brief history of counseling and psychotherapy

At the beginning of the 20th century, psychology and psychotherapy grew intensively in Russia. Publications by Freud and other psychoanalysts were actively translated into the Russian language. The newly originated approaches were also vividly debated. A significant step in promoting clinical psychology and psychotherapy was the development of psychological assessment methods. Lev Vygotsky was once the Russian equivalent of Stanley Hall and Lightner Witmer rolled into one: he was the founder of Russian developmental and clinical psychology based on his original *cultural-historical concept of human development*. Original ideas of this outstanding thinker, who was named the 'Mozart in psychology" by the famous British philosopher, author, and educator Stephen Toulmin (1981), require further refinement and development. Vygotsky's cultural-historical concept of human development sheds light on many disputable questions, and it continues to catch the attention of modern-day researchers.

In the 1930s, Vygotsky and his followers—the founder of activity theory, A. Leontiev; the founder of neuropsychology, R. Luria; the founder of Moscow clinical psychology school, B. Zeygarnik; and other scientists—became the target of official critique and political persecution. They were accused of being oblivious to the major tenets of Marxist philosophy, which was extremely dangerous in Stalin's time not only for the continuation of their scientific careers, but also for their personal freedom and physical integrity. Around 1936 a special governmental decree was passed that virtually placed applied psychology and psychotherapy under prohibition (Pseudology, n.d.). The long period of stagnation in the development of psychology and psychotherapy lasted until Stalin's death in 1953.

Luria's major work, *Human Higher Cortical Functions,* was published in 1962, and in 1966 it was translated into English (Luria, 1966). It contributed considerable insight into brain plasticity, describing both its exceptional potential and its limits. Luria borrowed the revolutionary views of the problem of mutual relations between brain and mentality, the biological and the psychological, from his teacher, Lev Vygotsky.

Research and treatment approaches in Russian psychiatry in soviet times traditionally focused on biological factors. The importance of the psychosocial variable was undeniably under-estimated. Mainstream psychiatry of that period primarily dealt with linear biological models of causality; furthermore, political attitudes could not admit the presence and influence of unfavorable psychosocial conditions in a "happy" soviet society. Psychotherapeutic interventions had minimal value, since biological factors were seen as playing the main causal role in the origin and maintenance of mental disorders.

The most important source of psychotherapy development in the former Soviet Union was the Leningrad School. Its establishment is closely tied with the founder of reflex studies, V. M. Bekhterev (1991), whose ideas heavily influenced J. B. Watson, the founder of behaviorism (Watson was also influenced by I. Pavlov, a renowned Russian physiologist and psychologist who was known for his competition with Bekhterev regarding the study of conditioned reflexes). Bekhterev also founded the Psychoneurological Institute in 1907, which became an important center promoting the development of clinical psychology and psychotherapy in Russia. Starting from 1939, the Institute was led by his follower, V. N. Myasishev, whose original concept of psychopathology was the first version of biopsychosocial models in Russian science (Myasischev, 1960). He also developed a theory of personality, which was rather influential and became the background for the original form of group psychotherapy developed by his follower, B. D. Karvasarsky, the editor of the most popular Russian handbook on psychotherapy (Karvasarsky, 2000).

Much has changed in the field since the Perestroika era, a period in the 1980s when drastic political and economic changes were implemented by the Communist Party. Psychoanalysis has long been the only therapy to receive support at the governmental level. Boris Yeltsin passed a decree to restore and develop psychoanalysis in Russia in 1996; since then, several Institutes for Psychoanalysis have been established (Rancour-Laferrierre, 2007). The development of other approaches has strongly depended on foreign visits by Western specialists who are willing to train local psychologists and psychiatrists for free, otherwise they simply cannot afford it. Also in 1996 the first faculty of psychological counseling (Counseling Psychology and Psychotherapy faculty) within the Moscow State University of Psychology and Education was created on the initiative of F. E. Vasiljuk, who has been running the faculty since its inception.

More recently, in 2003, the Russian Ministry of Public Health passed a special decree that reinforced the further development of psychotherapeutic aid. According to this initiative, a wide network of counseling centers, inpatient psychotherapeutic wards in psychiatric and psychosomatic hospitals and psychotherapeutic offices in primary care settings were to be established. This network was to be financed from local budgets at the discretion of local authorities. Further, multi-professional teams made up of psychiatrists, clinical psychologists, and social workers were to deliver care in these newly founded psychotherapeutic services (Decree of the Russian Federation Ministry of Public Health, 2003). On October 7, 2009, the Government of Moscow approved the Public Psychological Aid Act number 47 of Moscow City in order to provide available and high-quality public psychological aid (Garant, 2011). In accordance with this Act, psychologists are authorized to provide solely psychological counseling and so-called non-medical psychotherapy.

Counselor education programs, accreditation, licensure, and certification

The clinical psychology major takes approximately 5.5 years to complete and students accumulate 330 credits. Within this major are five different specializations that have various levels of connection to psychotherapeutic or psychological counseling training. All specializations have a basic mandatory part. This part is worth 150 credits, from which 15 credits (540 hours of workload) pertain to psychotherapy and psychological counseling. The intensity of any additional training in psychotherapy and psychological counseling varies within different specializations and largely depends on the specific university. For example, the Clinical Psychology and Psychotherapy Department of the Psychological Counseling School at Moscow State University of Psychology and Education requires an additional 40 credits (1,440 hours). In other words, throughout the entire education process about 2,000 hours are allotted to disciplines connected to the training of clinical psychology and psychotherapy (psychoanalysis, cognitive-behavioral therapy, existential and humanistic therapy, family therapy, group therapy, etc.). A large portion of the hours is given to practical courses as well as supervision.

As for institutions offering premiere certification for qualified psychotherapists, the authors offer two examples to illustrate the training process. The first example is the Division of Psychotherapy (Medical Academy for Postgraduate Education, St Petersburg), which provides several educational programs for specialists with different professional backgrounds (psychotherapists, psychiatrists, medical doctors, social workers). One of them is designed for professional psychotherapists who are willing to develop their competence (144 hours). Another is a 504-hour-long program that awards a certificate of psychotherapist to psychiatrists. In this course psychiatrists acquire theoretical knowledge and practical skills in psychodynamic, cognitive-behavioral, and humanistic approaches along with intensive self-experience. Doctors of internal medicine can acquire knowledge and skills in psychotherapy for somatic disorders, participating in the 144-hour program in the special psychosomatic cardiological department. Psychotherapists, psychiatrists, psychologists, and social workers can enter the next two 144-hour programs: one on psychotherapy for addictive behavior, another on psychotherapy for depressive disorders and schizophrenia.

The second example is the private training organization Society of Practicing Psychologists "Gestalt approach." It provides an advanced educational program for psychologists, medical doctors, pedagogues, and social workers who have chosen gestalt psychotherapy as a theoretical and methodological basis for their practical activities. The program mentioned includes 700–800 hours of theory study, optional specialized discipline (120–180 hours), lectures on psychiatry for psychologists, lectures on personality and developmental psychology for medical doctors, 240 hours of personal psychotherapy, 150 hours of supervision, and 400 hours of practical training. Certification requirements include three case write-ups, including one with regular supervision, participation in at least one conference, recommendations from the program's tutor, and demonstration of skills at the open session with an invited independent supervisor. Certification from this society gives no official right for legal practice; it acts as a sign of acknowledgment from the professional community.

Presently, there are no available public psychotherapists' unions in Russia that issue accreditation.

Current counseling and psychotherapy theories, processes and trends

With solid support from the International Association of Psychoanalysis, psychoanalysis has won a firm place in Russia. However, other psychotherapeutic methods that are currently popular appear to be psychodrama (Leutz, 1994), gestalt therapy (Perls, 2005), and the humanistic approach (Rogers, 2001). Wide acceptance of these methods may be due to the increased number of visits by Western experts specializing in these areas. Interest in existential and humanistic approaches, for example, was highly stimulated by visits from Carl Rogers and Viktor Frankl (2000). Today, the influence of existential orientations in Russia is attributed to the enthusiastic activities of Alfried Längle. Family systems psychotherapy is also growing in influence. Hanna Wiener, former President of the International Family Therapy Association (IFTA), trained the first groups of Russian professionals in family therapy. Cognitive-behavioral psychotherapy has been receiving greater popularity among Russian professionals over the last decade. Publication of Aaron Beck's books in Russian and training conducted by trainees from the Beck Institute for Cognitive Therapy and Research were rather influential in promoting this trend (Beck, Emery, Shaw, & Rush, 2003; Kholmogorova & Garanyan, 2000).

One of the most important trends in modern psychological counseling and psychotherapy in Russia is the creation of original integrative models combining the developments of Russian and foreign concepts. For instance, *personal reconstructive psychotherapy* integrates the developments of V. Myasishchev's relationships theory and group psychodynamic psychotherapy (Karvasarsky, 2000); *therapy with creative self-expression* integrates the principles of phenomenological and constitutional psychiatric approaches to severe forms of psychopathology and art therapy techniques (Burno, 1989); *integrative psychotherapy for affective spectrum disorders* is based on the original multifactorial model of these disorders, including macrosocial, family, personal, and interpersonal levels, integrating the developments of A. Beck's cognitive psychotherapy, family systems psychotherapy, social psychoanalysis, psychodynamic psychotherapy, and Vygotsky's cultural-historical concept (Garanyan, 2010; Kholmogorov & Garanyan, 1998; Kholmogorova, 2001, 2011); *co-experiencing psychotherapy* integrates the developments in Leontiev's activity theory and humanistic psychotherapy (Vasilyuk, 2007); and *reflexive activity approach to psychological and pedagogical counseling* integrates the developments of Vygotsky's cultural-historical concept, Leontiev's activity theory, Galperin's theory of intellectual activity formation, and Rogers's client-centered psychotherapy (Zaretsky, 2007, 2008; , 2010).

The first and second models are clinically oriented and applied primarily in the healthcare system. The third model is also clinically oriented; however, in addition to the healthcare service, it is also applied in psychological counseling within the education system (students and school children). The fourth and fifth models are oriented to psychological aid in the system of education and social security but they are not clinically oriented.

Finally, it should also be noted that in regions where local authorities and administrations provide favorable conditions, mental health service and rehabilitation programs are being developed intensively. For example, several cities in Russia (e.g., Moscow, Saint Petersburg, Omsk, Orenburg) have opened clinics to provide complex psychosocial aid to patients diagnosed with schizophrenia and suffering from their first psychotic episode (Gurovitch Shmukler, 2010).

Indigenous and traditional healing methods

According to the Russian Academy of Medical Science, 95% of folk healers in Russia do not have an educational background in medicine. Their activities often cause barriers to proper help and serious harm to public health. Although the field continues to be dominated by Western models of practice, many Russians look for modalities that are alternative to scientifically grounded psychotherapy and seek help from magicians and healers such as fortune tellers, astrologists, and Tarot card readers. This may be attributed to the fact that knowledge about the effectiveness of psychology and psychotherapy remains insufficient not only in the general population, but also among doctors, including psychiatrists. Owing to the high levels of belief in such practices in Russian society, many psychology specialists have generated manipulative names for the services they provide in order to attract clients (e.g., "Psychoanalysts and Mantics," "Removing Hexes with Scientific Methods").

In Russia, there has not been a marked interest among experts to integrate scientific methods with traditional healing methods. It is important to note, however, that there is a growing interest among some experts to develop a so-called "Christian psychology and psychotherapy" (Orthodox Psychology, 2008). A new type of Christian counseling specific to Russia is the "Russian Orthodox Psychotherapy," which integrates humanistic ideas and methods with basic ideas of the Russian orthodox religion and practice of praying. Among specialists in this approach are both Christian orthodox priests (who sometimes have a psychological or psychiatric education) and religious psychologists and psychiatrists.

Research and supervision

Psychotherapy process research is an emerging area of study in Russia that combines quantitative and qualitative methods to identify how psychotherapy works and under what conditions it is most effective. Along with RCT methodology, naturalistic studies with higher external validities and balanced (mixed) research methodology have emerged in Russia within the last several years (Kholmogorova et al., 2010). Projects aimed at fundamental theoretical problems in mental health are supported by the Russian Fund of Fundamental Research. Practice-oriented studies in the field of psychological counseling and psychotherapy are funded by the Russian Humanitarian Research Fund. The most representative journals in Russia are *Counseling Psychology and Psychotherapy, Social and Clinical Psychiatry,* and *Therapy of Mental Disorders.* The first on-line journal *Medical Psychology in Russia* was created in 2009. Many well-known Russian clinical psychologists and psychotherapists collaborate with this edition.

Educational standards for clinical psychologists and psychotherapists include supervision. For instance, according to the latest version of the state standard (proposed on December 24, 2010 by decree 2057 of the Ministry of Education and Science of the Russian Federation), basic professional training of clinical psychologists includes 200 tests, among which 32 tests are designated for different kinds of supervision. Ten of the 32 tests are directly connected with psychotherapy and psychological counseling. Nevertheless, the implementation of the above standard may be facing some impediments, such as the lack of qualified supervisors and clinical bases (hospitals and outpatient clinics where students can get hands-on experience).

Strengths, weaknesses, opportunities and challenges

A major strength in the field of counseling and psychotherapy in a Russian context lies in its historically innovative approaches to psychology. The cultural-historical approach developed by Vygotsky appears to be a great resource for further promotion of therapeutic theory and practice in a time when the voices of supporters of the biologically based approach to human mentality are getting stronger, and researchers in the field of psychotherapy face a fashionable temptation to reduce their research to seeking correlations between the processes in the nervous system, psychiatric diagnoses, and changes in the psychotherapy process.

Vygotsky's theories therefore provide a powerful tool for innovative models of psychopathology. For instance, key methodological problems of modern psychiatry, clinical psychology, and psychotherapy could be analyzed from the position of cultural-historical psychology: (1) the naturalization of mentality in the form of biological reductionism, and (2) the search for the new conceptual device for the description of processes and mechanisms underlying mental health and mental pathology (see Kholmogorova, 2011; Kholmogorova & Zaretsky, 2010)

Several weaknesses in the field which are practical in nature are worth mentioning. First is the shortage of well-trained specialists in Russia. The other unfavorable factor is the inability of

Russian medical insurance companies to cover psychotherapeutic treatment for patients. Other practical conditions that weaken the field include the lack of a solid and coherent system of training, supervision, licensure, and certification.

It is also very important to note that the lack of quality training in clinical psychology and psychotherapy in the system of medical education for psychiatrists results in the situation where the said specialists undervalue the role of psychosocial factors (and as a result the role of psychotherapists and social workers is also underestimated) in treatment and rehabilitation of patients suffering from mental disorders.

Finally, the managers in the education and healthcare systems who are responsible for the organization and creation of the psychological services are also poorly informed about the importance of this work as well as about the specific features that this work entails. For example, the managerial system pays insufficient attention to professional training in the field of evidence-based approaches in psychotherapy and underestimates the role of family in the problems of children. Experience (of this chapter's authors) suggests that in the majority of the state counseling centers little time and attention are being given to families, and psychological work is conducted only with children.

Despite the weakening conditions in the field of counseling and psychotherapy in Russia, major opportunities in the field lie ahead. One of the important opportunities in the development of psychotherapy paradoxically stems from the fact that Russia has historically lagged behind in this field due to the lack of established schools with well-developed traditions. This decreases scholarly commitment to one approach and facilitates the integration of various methods (Kholmogorova, 2011). As previously discussed, several integrative models of psychotherapy have emerged over the years and it is expected that this trend will continue.

Further, the growing exchange between foreign and local experts and possibilities of training and participation in international conferences with the support of Russian and foreign funds allow Russian professionals to integrate themselves within the international science community. For example, the collaboration between the US Institute of Mental Health (Director D. Regier) and Moscow Research Institute of Psychiatry (Director V. Krasnov) in terms of the joint initiative by our countries (State Secretary N. Gore and Prime Minister V. Chernomyrdin) in establishing a joint program on Detection and Treatment of Depression in primary care promoted, to a significant extent, an expansion of psychotherapeutic consulting wards at district polyclinics, higher levels of knowledge among general practitioners in relation to depressive disorders, publication of the first patient education materials, and the development of multidisciplinary teams across Moscow, Tver, Yaroslavl, and other cities of Russia (Krasnov, 2000; 2010; Krasnov, Dovzhenko, Veltischev, Kholmogorova, Garanyan, 2000).

Another example is the collaboration between the Russian clinical psychologists from the Institute of Psychology of the Russian Academy of Science and specialists from Harvard University on the topic of traumatic stress and its consequences. It allowed for the adaptation of an entire array of diagnostic instruments as well as outlining the aims of psychological help (Tarabrina et al., 1995a,b).

The major challenge in Russia is the continuation of scientific studies in the sphere of psychotherapy and psychological counseling, as financing is very poor in this sphere. This is especially important because Russian experts are unsatisfactorily informed about the scientific works in the field of psychotherapy and are very indiscriminate in selection of their methods. The few studies carried out by these experts and published as articles in Western journals and monographs in establishing bilateral exchange will require certain support on the part of the publishing houses.

The orphanhood situation in Russia is an example of yet another challenge faced by professionals in counseling and psychotherapy. Basically, there is no system of psychological support for troubled families, despite the fact that the number of children whose parents have lost parental custody continues to grow (UNICEF, 2009). There is no rehabilitation system for children that have been put into orphanages after their parents have lost parental custody and there is no system of psychological support for foster parents (Chepurnyh, 1998; Dementyeva, 2004; Iovchuk, 2009). The diagnosis of mental retardation is often a formality and is given based on the quantitative characteristics of the Wexler test (Sukhotina & Krijanovskaya, 2003). This results in a high incidence of misdiagnoses of mental retardation in social orphans, who have had no opportunity to be correctly educated, as well as in children who have experienced trauma and violence in their biological families (Kholmogorova, Volikova, & Stepina, 2011; Korobeinikov, 2002).

As for other national problems such as alcoholism, there is currently no legal system in place that mandates treatment for those suffering from alcoholism and drug addiction and those who have committed crimes. This leads to problems in the organization of a statewide comprehensive rehabilitation system for drug addicts as well as the rehabilitation of families with parental alcoholism. Considering the alarmingly high percentage of alcohol abuse in the Russian population, this situation is not only a challenge but also deemed a national health crisis (Nemtsov, 2009).

Finally, an extremely significant challenge to solving the aforementioned problems is the insufficient financing of scientific and educational programs and a gradual decrease in attractiveness of professions that would provide psychological and rehabilitation services to the aforementioned vulnerable populations, such as consultants, psychologists, and psychotherapists, due to the low salary that these specialists are offered at the governmental level.

Future directions

The development of professional standards and evaluation criteria is a necessary step in the professionalization of counseling and psychotherapy in Russia. In addition, it is extremely important to provide further integration of Russia into the international community and increase participation of Russian experts in international conferences, congresses, and seminars arranged by international and national associations of psychiatrists, psychologists, and psychotherapists. Because the income of Russian experts is not sufficient to pay for their participation fees and expenses of travels and accommodation, it is important to continue the international support for such participation through engagement with experts from various regions of Russia. The growth in the GDP of Russia has resulted in a very uneven distribution of income among the various population strata. Specialists in the sphere of healthcare and education are placed in a relatively low-paid category, especially in relation to postgraduate specialists. For example, an allowance of approximately US$100 per month is paid to a postgraduate doctor employed as an intern (resident).

Finally, it is important to assign scholarships for training and education at clinics in Europe and the United States; carry out translations and publication of the most important manuals and journal articles on psychotherapy and psychological counseling in Russian; and assign additional funds through Western foundations for joint projects in the sphere of psychological, consulting, and psychotherapy.

Conclusion

At the present time, Russia is characterized by a very intense development of practical psychology and psychotherapy and fast growth in the number of educational institutions which train specialists in psychology; however, the level of their training at most of these educational institutions is very low. In addition, governmental medical facilities employ over 3,000 clinical psychologists who are authorized to provide psychotherapy only in a team headed by a psychiatrist. Russian citizens may be provided with free psychological aid as a special service connected with educational (not medical) institutions; however, the quality of professional training for such services is relatively low. Russian science is developing original models of psychological aid based on integration of Russian and foreign developments which require further approbation and verification of their efficiency. Most developments in the cultural and historical psychology of Vygotsky and his successors seem relevant to the present realm of scientific psychology and psychotherapy and are considered major strengths in the field. However, numerous challenges and social conditions continue to hinder its progress. It is perhaps through further integration of Russian professionals in the international science community as a major stepping stone that this nation can begin to overcome the historically caused backwardness in the field of psychotherapy and psychological counseling.

Note

1 Russia takes one of the bottom places on average life span (66 years), lower than even poorer countries.

References

Alekseev, N. G. (2002). Designing of conditions of development of reflective thinking. *Personality Development*, 2, 92–116 (in Russian).

Beck, A., Rush, A., Shaw, B., & Emery, G. (2003). *Cognitive Therapy of Depression* (A. Tatlybaeva, Trans.). Sankt-Peterburg: Piter (First edn 1979 in Russian).

Bektherev, V. M. (1991). *General Reflexology*. Moscow: Nauka (in Russian).

Bolton, D. (2007). The usefulness of Wakefield's definition for the diagnostic manuals. *World Psychiatry*, 6 (3), 164–165. (in Russian)

Bruene, M. (2005). "Theory of mind" in schizophrenia: A review of the literature. *Schizophrenia Bulletin*, *31*(1), 21–42.

Burno, M. E. (1989). *Therapy by Means of Creative Self-expression*. Moscow: Academic Project (in Russian).

Chepurnyh, E. E. (1998) Children with special needs: social and educational support. In N. V. Vostroknutov (ed.), *Social and Spiritual Health of the Child and Family: Protection, Help, Bringing Back to Life* (pp. 3–8). Moscow (in Russian).

Cole, M. (2007). Philogenetic and cultural history tangle in ontogenesis. *Cultural–historical Psychology*, 3, 3–16 (in Russian).

Dementyeva, N. F. (2004). *Problems with Observing Human Rights in Psychoneurological Boarding Schools*. Retrieved from www.mhg.ru/english/3959925

Eberstadt, N. (2010) *Russia's Peacetime Demographic Crisis: Dimensions, Causes, Implications*. Retrieved from www.nbr.org/publications/specialreport/pdf/preview/Russia_demography_preview.pdf

Federal State Statistics Service. (2011). *Preliminary Results of the 2010 all-Russian Population Census*. Retrieved from www.perepis-2010.ru/results_of_the_census/results-inform.php (in Russian).

Fonagy, P., Steele, H., Moran, G., Steele, M., & Higgitt, A. (1991). The capacity for understanding mental states: The reflective self in parent and child and its significance for security of attachment. *Infant Mental Health Journal*, 13, 200–217.

Frankl, V. (2000). *The Will to Meaning* (D. Gurieva, Trans.). Moscow: April-press, EKSMO-PRESS (1969) (in Russian).

Garant (2009). *Law of Moscow on October 7, 2009 N 43: On the Psychological Care to the Population in Moscow*. Retrieved from www.garant.ru/products/ipo/prime/doc/292902/

Garanyan, N. G. (2010). *Perfectionism and Hostility as Personality Factors of Depressive and Anxious Disorders*. Unpublished doctoral thesis. The Moscow State University, Moscow (in Russian).

Gold, I., & Kirmayer, L. J. (2007). Cultural psychiatry on Wakefield's procrustean bed. *World Psychiatry, 6*(3), 165–166 (in Russian).

Gurovitch, I. Y., & Shmukler, A. B. (eds). (2010). *The Frst Psychosis Episode (Problems and Psychiatric Care)*. Moscow: Medpractica (in Russian).

Iovchuk, N. M. (2009). Characteristics of psychological disorders of orphans in boarding schools and foster families. In N.M. Iovchuk (ed.), *Children's and Teenager's Psychological Health Questions* (pp. 6–13). Moscow: Print on Demand (in Russian).

Karvasarsky, B. D. (2000). *Psychotherapy*. Leningrad: Medicine (in Russian).

Kholmogorova, A. B. (1983). Method for investigation of reflexive thought regulation's disorders (on the subject of concept definition). *The Moscow State University Bulletin, 14*(3), 64–68 (in Russian).

Kholmogorova, A. B. (2001). Cognitive psychotherapy and Russian psychology of thinking. *Moscow Psychotherapy Journal, 4*, 165–181 (in Russian).

Kholmogorova, A. B. (2010). *The clinical psychology handbook (vol. 1): General psychopathology*. Moscow: Academia (in Russian).

Kholmogorova, A. B. (2011). *Integrative psychotherapy of affective spectrum disorders*. Moscow: Medpractice (in Russian).

Kholmogorova, A. B., & Garanyan, N.G. (1988). Multifactorial model of depressive, anxious and somatoform disorders as a basis for their integrative psychotherapy. *Social and Clinical Psychiatry, 1*, 94–102 (in Russian).

Kholmogorova, A. B., & Garanyan, N. G. (2000). Cognitive and behavioral psychotherapy. In A. M. Bokovikov, A. (ed.), *Main trends of modern psychotherapy: Manual* (pp. 224–267). Moscow: Cogito-Center (in Russian).

Kholmogorova, A. B., Volikova, S. V., & Stepina, N. A. (2011). Concerning the negative consequences of diagnosing mental retardation in orphans in boarding schools. *Questions of Psychology, 5*, 66–75 (in Russian).

Kholmogorova, A. B., Pugovkina, O. D., & Garanyan, N. G. (2010). Efficiency factors of integrative psychotherapy of affective spectrum disorders. *Consultative Psychology and Psychotherapy, 2*, 77–109 (in Russian).

Kholmogorova, A. B., Zaretsky, V. K. (2010). *Whether the Russian Psychology can be Useful for the Solving of Actual Problems of Modern Psychotherapy: Reflection after XX Congress of International Federation of Psychotherapy (IFP)*. Retrieved from www.medpsy.ru/mprj/archiv_global/2010_4_5/nomer/nomer09.php (in Russian).

Korobeinikov, I. A. (2002). *Breaches in Development and Social Adaptation*. Moscow: PER SE (in Russian).

Krasnov, V. N. (2000). Program: Finding and treatment of depression in a primary medical network. *Social and Clinical Psychiatry, 1*, 5–9 (in Russian).

Krasnov, V. N. (2010). *Affective Spectrum Disorders*. Moscow: Practical Medicine (in Russian).

Krasnov, V. N., Dovzhenko, T. V., Saltykov, A. G., Veltischev, D. Y., Kholmogorova, A. B., & Garanyan, N. G. (2000). *Organizational Model of Assistance for Persons Suffering from Depression under Conditions of Territorial Polyclinics: Methodological Recommendations: Issue 107*. Moscow: Moscow Scientific Research Institute of Psychiatry (in Russian).

Leutz, G. (1994). *Psychodrama: Theory and Praxis*. Moscow: Progress-University (in Russian).

Levada, Ju. (2004). Money, power and fear. *Arguments and Facts (Newspaper), 51*, 10 (in Russian).

Life is a Citizen of Russia. (2010). *The Problem of Child Abandonment in Russia*. Retrieved from www.gosgra.ru/articles/790/ (in Russian).

Luria, A.R. (1966). *Higher Cortical Functions in Man*. New York: Basic Books.

Myasischev, V. N. (1960). *Personality and Neurosis*. Leningrad: Medgis (in Russian).

Nemtsov, A. V. (2009). *Alcohol History of Russia: The Newest Period*. Moscow: Bookshop "LIBROKOM." (in Russian).

Nikolaeva, V. V. (1992). *The Person in the Conditions of Chronic Somatic Disease*. Unpublished doctoral thesis. The Moscow State University, Moscow (in Russian).

Orthodox Psychology. (2008). *Homepage*. Retrieved from http://dusha-orthodox.ru (in Russian).

Perls, F. (2005). *Gestalttherapie* (M.P. Papush. Trans.). Moscow: Institute of General Humanistic Studies. (First edn 1951 in Russian).

Pseudology. (n.d.). *Party Central Committee (B): Resolution*. Retrieved from www.pseudology.org/Documets/Pedologia.htm

Rancour-Laferrierre, D. (2007). Observations on psychoanalysis in contemporary Russia. *Clio's Psych, 13*, 201–204.

Roder, V., & Medalia, A. (eds). (2010). *Neurocognition and social cognition in schizophrenia patients: Basic concepts and treatment*. Switzerland: Karger Press.

Rogers, K. (2001). *On Becoming a Person* (M. M. Isenina. Trans.) Moscow: EKSMO-PRESS. (1961) (In Russian)

Sartorius, N. (2007). A new way of reducing the prevalence of mental disorders? *World Psychiatry, 6*(3), 162–163.

Sukhotina, N. K., & Krijanovskaya, I. L. (2003). Results of the psycho-psychiatric evaluation of the children in one of the psychoneurological boarding schools. In N.M. Iovchuk (ed.), *Children's and teenager's psychological health questions* (pp. 44–48). Moscow: Print on Demand (in Russian).

Tarabrina, N. V., Lazebnaya, E. O., Zelenova, M. E., Misko, E.A., Orr, S., Lasko, N.V., Pitman, R. (1995a). Physiological responses to loud tones in Russian combat veterans. *XI Annual Meeting of The International Society for Traumatic Stress Studies*, 62.

Tarabrina, N. V., Lazebnaya, E. O., Zelenova, M. E., Misko, E.A., Orr, S., Lasko, N.V., Pitman, R. (1995b). Psychophysiological and psychological assessment of posttraumatic stress disorder imagery in Chernobyl disaster worker: Book of abstracts. *Fourth European Conference on Traumatic Stress*, 144–145.

Toulmin, S. (1981). Mozart in psychology. *Voprosy Philosophii, 10*, 127–137 (in Russian).

Vasilyuk, F. E. (2007). Coexperiencing psychotherapy: Psychotechnical system construction. Psychological counselling and psychotherapy. *Humanitarian Researches in Psychotherapy, 1*, 159–203 (in Russian).

UNICEF. (2009). Children in Russia-2009: New study launched in Moscow. Retrieved from www. unicef.org/ceecis/media_13801.html

Wakefield, J. C. (2007). The concept of mental disorder: diagnostic implications of the harmful dysfunction analysis. *World Psychiatry, 6*(3), 149–156 (in Russian).

Zaretsky, V. K. (2007). Zone of proximal development: What Vygotsky had not time to write about. *Cultural-Historical Psychology, 3*, 96–104 (in Russian).

Zaretsky, V. K. (2008). Reflexive-activity approach in work with children with difficulties in training. In I. Y. Kulagina (ed.), *Educational Psychology* (pp. 81–98). Moskau: Sfera (in Russian).

Zaretsky, V. (2010). *Zone of proximal development as the basis for psychological help to children with learning problems*. Paper presentation at the FMPP Annual Congress of Psychiatry and Psychotherapy and the 20th IFP World Congress of Psychotherapy, KKl, Luzerne, Switzerland.

Zaretsky, V. K., & Kholmogorova, A. B. (1983). Regulation of creative task's solving. In J. A. Ponomarev (ed.), *Researches of Psychology of Creativity* (pp. 62–101). Moscow: Nauka (in Russian).

Zeygarnik, B. V., & Kholmogorova, A. B. (1985). Disorders of self-regulation in cognitive process among schizophrenic patients. *S. S. Korsakov Journal of Neuropathology and Psychiatry, 12*, 1813–1819 (in Russian).

Zeygarnik, B. V., Kholmogorova, A. B., & Mazur, E. S. (1989). Behavior self-regulation in norm and a pathology. *Psychological Journal, 2*, 122 –132 (in Russian).

30

COUNSELING AND PSYCHOTHERAPY IN THE UNITED KINGDOM

Future of talk therapy

Del Loewenthal

Introduction

As of mid-2010, the estimated resident population of the UK was 62.2 million, increased by 470,000 from the previous year (Office for National Statistics, 2011). Britain is still a predominantly White society, with at the turn of the millennium 92% of its population forming the White majority. This is changing, however, with a rapidly increasing diversity of ethnic groups and cultures. The fastest growing group was "Black African," more than doubling during the period 1991–2001. Bangladeshi, Pakistani, and Chinese groups also saw rapid growth (Lupton & Power, 2004).

Counseling and psychotherapy in the UK are, after a period of gradual development, in a state of flux due to government intervention. At the start of the 21st century the UK government has been exceptionally proactive in attempting to bring about change in the provision of what are termed the "psychological therapies" (counseling, psychotherapy, psychology, and art therapies). This has included an attempt to separate the regulatory from the professional functions of existing psychological therapy training organizations through the Health Professions Council (which will be renamed the Health and Care Professions Council [HCPC] following Royal Assent of the Health and Social Care Bill 2011), to which it was proposed that psychotherapy and counseling organizations would be forced to cede their regulatory function (previously, other professions such as art therapies and more recently the practitioner psychologists, have volunteered to do this) (British Psychological Society [BPS], 2000–2011a).

The use of ideas from population-based medicine to plan a national strategy for free access for all to certain psychological therapies through focusing on anxiety and depression has led to a rapid expansion in the number of psychological therapists under a government program entitled "Improving Access to Psychological Therapies" (IAPT). These psychological therapists, who are called "high and low intensity workers," are not required to have come from previous Health

Service or counseling/psychotherapy professions. They are trained for work in the National Health Service (NHS) according to prevailing notions of evidence-based practice which are determined by the National Institute for Health and Clinical Excellence (NICE). The standard of this new service is monitored within the Department of Health (DH) (IAPT, 2011a) itself and not by existing professional bodies, whose own futures are consequently less secure.

What follows is an exploration of counseling and psychotherapy in the United Kingdom in terms of a brief history of these practices in the UK; counselor education programs, accreditation, licensure, and certification; current counseling and psychotherapy theories, processes, and trends; indigenous and traditional healing methods; research and supervision; strengths, weaknesses, opportunities, and challenges; future directions and conclusion.

A brief history of counseling and psychotherapy

In this discussion of counseling and psychotherapy in the UK, examination of the more recent history is given primarily in terms of accreditation, attempts at regulation, and organizational change. This is, for some, perhaps understandable in a culture increasingly dominated by managerialism.

For the UK, Freud's arrival in London in 1938 and his presence there together with that of Anna Freud and Melanie Klein greatly assisted the development of a British tradition in psychoanalysis. This included Bion (1961; 1962), Bowlby (1997), Winnicott (1971; 2000) and, more controversially, R. D. Laing (1960). Since that time there have been further developments in psychoanalysis, alongside the development of UK traditions in humanistic (Heron, 1996; Mearns, 1999; Rowan, 1993; Thorne, 1991), existential (Deurzen, 1997, 1998; Loewenthal, 2011; Spinelli, 1997, 2005), and behavioral therapies (Clark, 1986; Salkovskis, 1996). It should be noted that the authors cited tend to straddle the modality categories used here for simplicity.

It is now nearly 40 years since the Foster Report of 1971 first raised the proposal that psychotherapy should become a regulated profession (Shepherd, 1979). In 1981 it was proposed again when a Private Member's Bill was brought in the House of Commons—this also failed to become passed into legislation. In 1982 the then British Association for Counselling (now the British Association for Counselling and Psychotherapy) organized a symposium at Rugby which formed a Professions Joint Working Party. This led to a second symposium and then to the founding of the United Kingdom Standing Conference for Psychotherapy (UKSCP) in 1989 (UKCP, 2011a).

A year before the UK National Register of Psychotherapists came into being in 1993 (the forerunner of the UKCP) there was a break-away movement from the UKSCP. This resulted in the formation of the British Confederation of Psychotherapists (BCP), which later renamed itself the British Psychoanalytic Council (BPC), with 12 organizations under its umbrella (BPC, n.d.a). The reason given for this breakaway was that a few organizations, led by the British Psycho-Analytical Society, felt that their seniority was not sufficiently recognized. Another version of the subsequent political machinations is described by Young (1999).

As previously mentioned, the HPC is one of a number of UK health professions regulators. It was created by the Health Professions Order in 2001 to protect the public by setting and maintaining standards for the professions it regulates (HPC, 2011). At the time of writing, it regulates 15 professions. In its White Paper *Trust, assurance and safety: The regulation of health professionals in the 21st century* (HPC, 2007) the UK government again proposed that the professions of counseling and psychotherapy should be regulated, and had identified the HPC as its regulator. The strong objections from the profession to the HPC becoming the statutory regulator, based in part on what some considered the inappropriateness of applying a medical framework to these practices, resulted in a judicial review which seriously challenged and demoted the HPC from this position.

This most recent attempt at regulation should be seen in the context of the government's increasing involvement in the field through its implementation of IAPT from 2007 onwards (IAPT, 2011a). This program is primarily concerned with the "modernization" of psychological therapies within the NHS and added further to the most recent debate about statutory regulation, particularly in relation to which psychotherapies should have been eligible. This is because IAPT has prioritized the provision of therapies under the NHS based on the recommendations from NICE about effective therapeutic interventions. This has resulted in a move away from the provision of medication alone for anxiety and depression and existing primary care counseling services to short-term, evidence-based therapies such as cognitive-behavioral therapy (CBT) (Waller, 2009).

Another government initiative has been the creation of Skills for Health (SFH), which is essentially a think-tank concerned with developing National Occupational Standards for the psychological therapies and delivering "a skilled and flexible UK workforce" in order to improve health and healthcare (Skills for Health, 2011). The SFH Strategy Reference Group was set up and chaired by Lord Alderdice, who in 1999 proposed a Private Members Bill for the self-regulation of the psychotherapies, which could have given more autonomy to the professional bodies than HPC would have done.

More recently, following the change of UK government in 2010, the 2011 Command Paper, *Enabling excellence: Autonomy and accountability for health workers, social workers and social care workers* (DOH, 2011) marked a change of policy away from statutory regulation and a move towards enhanced voluntary registers. As a result, counseling and psychotherapy organizations started talks with the Council for Healthcare Regulatory Excellence (CHRE, shortly to be renamed the Professional Standards Authority [PSA]) with a view to establishing the foundations of a "Quality Assured Voluntary Register".

Under this scheme each individual membership organization will be assessed against certain criteria defined by the PSA and, if approved, be "kitemarked" as an Assured Voluntary Register. At the time of writing the HPC are also proposing setting up their own voluntary register which practitioners can decide to join independently from their own modality-specific professional organization's register. Recommendations from the previous government to regulate certain professions by statute through the Health Professions Council seem no longer likely to be taken forward.

Counselor education programs, accreditation, licensure, and certification

This section will describe the main stakeholders involved and their role in the education of counselors, accreditation, and certification. In the UK the term "licensure" is not used, and instead the terms "approved," "accredited, "and "registered" can be found.

There are various psychological therapy training organizations in the UK, which include The Association of Child Psychotherapists (ACP), The British Association for Behavioural and Cognitive Psychotherapies (BABCP), The British Association for Counselling and Psychotherapy (BACP), The British Psychoanalytic Council (BPC), The British Psychological Society (BPS), The College of Psychoanalysts UK (CP UK), The Health Professions Council (HPC), Improving Access to Psychological Therapies (IAPT), Skills for Health (SFH), The United Kingdom Council for Psychotherapy (UKCP), and the Universities Psychotherapy and Counselling Association (UPCA).

With the development of professionalization of counseling and psychotherapy, the approach to training has become more structured and some courses are accredited. This means that they lead to automatic membership to the corresponding professional organization once the training is validated. Each such organization has distinct training requirements—for example, the training period is a minimum of 4 years at postgraduate level for BPC (BPC, n.d.b) and UKCP (UKCP, 2011a), and 3 years for BPS (BPS, 2000–2011b). For BACP it is 1 year full-time or 2 years part-time at either undergraduate or postgraduate level (BACP, 2010a). Counseling psychologists are trained at a doctoral level in universities whilst in the UK clinical psychologists are not usually regarded as psychotherapists or counselors (though more recently they are taking an important role primarily in the supervision of CBT based IAPT programs).

The UPCA currently accredits training in counseling and psychotherapy in nine universities, and the BPS and the BABCP between them list 39 IAPT accredited courses (IAPT, 2011b). In addition there are a significant number of private and charitable training institutes and professional agencies whose courses are externally accredited by universities. Each training course will follow a defined theoretical approach (the main ones being psychodynamic, integrative, person-centered and CBT) and in turn will open the possibility for the therapist to register and be accredited by the appropriate corresponding membership organization.

At the time of writing, there are no legal minimum qualifications necessary to practice as a counselor in the UK. Since 1988 BACP has its own accreditation scheme for individual counselors (BACP, 2010b). Here any substantial core counseling course which requires a supervised placement may be counted for accreditation purposes. Courses eligible to apply for BACP accreditation are those training courses likely to be of 1 year full-time duration or 2–3 years part-time with a notional minimum of 450 contact hours (BACP, 2010b). It is not necessary, however, to have undertaken a BACP accredited course in order to apply for individual accreditation with BACP, though ongoing clinical supervision and Continuing Professional Development (CPD) is a requirement for all.

UKCP (2010) defines its nine modality colleges as collections of members (individual and organizational), who share a philosophy of psychotherapy. The colleges each hold associated standards for education, training and practice and are responsible for accepting members, both individual and organizational, into full membership of UKCP which recently added the title of "psychotherapeutic counselor" together with the previously established one of "psychotherapist" (UKCP, 2010). They also have the responsibility of reaccrediting (individual) or reviewing (organizational) membership on a cyclical basis. Each college will specify its own requirements for personal therapy whilst training.

One distinguishing factor between the different professional bodies is the minimum number of times trainees are required to have personal therapy: for the BPC (BPC, n.d.a) one to three times a week, for the UKCP (UKCP, 2011b) zero to twice a week, and for the BACP (BACP, 2010a) and IAPT (IAPT, 2011a) none is required. Overall this represents a significant reduction in these requirements.

Current counseling and psychotherapy theories, processes, and trends

Historically the trends that were favored in the UK were psychodynamic and humanistic approaches. The UK continues to be influenced by developments in North America and perhaps to a lesser extent by those in continental Europe. Within psychoanalysis there is increasing interest in relational psychoanalysis (this interest being mirrored in psychotherapy in general) (Hargaden & Schwartz, 2007; Loewenthal, 2010; Mitchell & Aron, 1999) and mentalization-based treatment. Within humanism, the person-centered approach as well as integrative approaches have come more to the forefront (see for example Tudor & Worrall, 2006).

In the last 20 years following the rise of CBT, the trend within the UK is currently towards what are regarded as evidence-based practices (see Roth & Fonagy, 2005). With regard to CBT there has been a growing interest in broadening its definition including what has been termed third-wave approaches (Hayes, 2004). Critiques have highlighted, however, that the overall standard of what is taken as evidence determined by NICE favors CBT as it shares an underlying set of assumptions with the preferred research methodology of randomized control trials (RCTs) (Guy, Loewenthal, Thomas, & Stephenson, 2012). As a result, CBT has subsequently formed the basis of the nationwide High and Low Intensity training programs funded by the DOH. Consequently and as evidenced by the number of IAPT accredited courses mentioned above, universities are increasingly involved with providing CBT training, whereas previously they were involved in more psychoanalytic and humanistic modalities.

In response to the growth of evidence-based practices there are calls for a greater focus on the use of practice-based evidence—a research approach which raises the question of whether "psychotherapy and counseling can themselves be forms of research?" (Loewenthal & Winter, 2006, p. xviii). There are a number of papers which argue in favor of consideration of the service user's perspective regarding therapy they have received, including Barkham et al. (2001); Foskett (2001); Macran, Ross, Hardy, & Shapiro (1999); and Mellor-Clark & Barkham (2003). A key element of this form of research is the use of self-report questionnaires such as the Clinical Outcomes for Routine Evaluation (CORE) system, which according to Aveline (2006, pp. 19–20) is "one of the most promising" of several "reliable, relevant and sensitive psychometric systems for routine use" which have been developed to monitor psychotherapeutic outcomes at both an individual and service level.

Indigenous and traditional healing methods

The estimates suggest that across England and Wales, between 2001 and 2009, the population in non-"White British" groups grew by an average of 4.1% per year (Office for National Statistics, 2011). White Irish were the only non-White British group to decrease in size over this period, with Chinese being the fastest growing at an estimated 8.6 per cent per year (Office for National Statistics, 2011).

The UK is therefore developing an increasingly ethnically diverse population, in particular in specific urban areas, and each of these ethnic groups are bringing to the UK their own traditions and alternatives to healing. For instance, prevalent amongst some of the UK's Muslim communities are concepts such as "Jinn" (Khalifa & Hardie, 2005) whereby "according to Islamic belief, jinn are real creatures that form a world other than that of mankind, capable of causing physical and mental harm to human beings. An example of such harm is possession" (Khalifa & Hardie, 2005, p. 315). Such concepts have been shown to influence the uptake of psychological therapy services in the UK by these populations (Khalifa & Hardie, 2005; Loewenthal, Murkhopadhyay, Ganesh, & Thomas, 2011).

The UK has a tradition of Christian healing, as exemplified by the healing ministry within the Religious Society of Friends (otherwise known as Quakers) (Harrell, 1976). Spiritual healing available within the UK may thus be based on Christian or Pagan philosophies. Professional organizations for Spiritual Healers in the UK include those such as the Healing Trust, who have set national standards of training, accreditation for trainers, require a minimum 2 years' training period with national standards of final assessment and who publish a professional code of conduct and disciplinary procedures (the Healing Trust, 2011).

The UK also has a tradition of 'complementary therapies', including, for example, homeopathy for the treatment of psychological conditions, an approach which has received attention in terms of efficacy research (see, for example, Pilkington, Kirkwood, Rampes, Fisher, & Richardson, 2005).

More generally, for some there is a danger that what was previously regarded as part of the responsibility of the teacher, parent, or religious leader has now become part of a professional therapeutic framework (Ecclestone & Hayes, 2008), encouraging individualism at the expense of a sense of community (House & Loewenthal, 2009; Layard & Dunn, 2009). The danger here is that individualism is seen as being about autonomy and putting oneself first, in contrast to heteronomy and putting the other first (Levinas, 1969). Hence, individualism can be seen as lying at the heart of frameworks such as psychoanalysis and person-centered therapy, in which there are seen to be intra-psychic mechanisms (or psychogenic) causes for distress (Kihlstrom, 2002). This focus reduces or eliminates the significance of the role played by the community/society in which the person lives.

Research and supervision

As has already been indicated, the current research debate in the UK centers on the appropriateness of using RCTs for researching psychotherapy. The debate can be characterized as being between three main points of view: those who believe the use of RCTs is not only an appropriate research methodology for the field but the best one; those who believe RCTs sometimes can be appropriate but should not be privileged above other approaches; and those who believe RCTs to be completely inappropriate and who advocate a more practice-based approach to research (Guy et al., 2012).

Latterly a fourth position has also arisen—those who see there being no choice but to accept RCT methodology in an attempt to secure the future of relational counseling services within the UK NHS (Cooper, 2011). Whilst those such as Cooper fear for the future availability of free (at point of service) counseling and therefore advocate pragmatically compromising and "working with the system" (Cooper, 2011, p. 16), there are those who offer an alternative vision for such service delivery beyond the NHS. Rather than attempting to secure "a slice of the NHS pie in 'proving' (on others' terms) that relational, explorative therapies are as good as State approved ones, we might instead strive to offer a genuine choice, a counter-cultural alternative, with practices and research methodologies consistent with our core therapy values" (Rogers, Maidman, & House, 2011, p. 39).

Finding research funding in the UK is not easy. There are no specific bodies that offer funding for counseling or psychotherapy. In their advice to would-be researchers, the BACP suggests that depending on the area of research it may be worth approaching the Economic and Social Research Council (ESRC) "the UK's leading research funding and training agency addressing economic and social concerns" (Richards, 2010). Alternatively, some researchers have success in securing funds from European sources (see the Community Research and Development Information Service, CORDIS, 2011).

The major journals where research is published include the *British Journal of Guidance and Counselling*, the *British Journal of Psychotherapy*, *Counselling and Psychotherapy Research*, the *European Journal of Psychotherapy and Counselling*, *Psychodynamic Practice*, *Counselling Psychology Quarterly*, *Psychotherapy Research*, and *Psychology and Psychotherapy Theory Research and Practice*.

Supervision requirements vary greatly from one organization to the other but are widely acknowledged as being a core element of training and practice. At some point in training, students will be expected to work with clients and to present their clinical material both orally—often in weekly supervision groups—and in the written form of assignments (clinical supervision is carried out separately to academic supervision).

Regardless of the organization, receiving supervision is generally a requirement of ongoing registration as part of an individual member's CPD, even if some aspects of the underlying philosophy of supervision may differ between organizations from practice monitoring to relational and personal development. The BACP for example considers their supervision policy to be based on a "developmental" rather than a "deficiency" model of the person and is intended to be ongoing and part of a counselor or psychotherapist's commitment to CPD (Mearns, 2002). Specifically for BACP, supervision is not about the monitoring of an individual's practice, but, instead, they state their aim is to develop a relationship in which the supervisor is regarded as "a trusted colleague" who can help the counselor to reflect on all dimensions of their practice and, in doing so, to develop their counseling role.

As a general rule, supervision is not a mandatory requirement of Chartership (the name given to the qualification necessary for practice as a psychologist in the UK) but is strongly encouraged for those in clinical practice.

Strengths, weaknesses, opportunities and challenges

One strength of the IAPT program is that talking therapies are given an increasing primacy over medical intervention as well as being far more available to everyone. The Layard report (2006) cited statistics showing that the majority of people in treatment under a general practitioner would prefer therapy to medication and that therapy is as effective as medication in the short term, and that "in the longer-run, therapy has more lasting effects than drugs" (p. 10). Prior to the implementation of the IAPT program, it was estimated that waiting times for access to a mental health professional were, on average, 9 months. The National Mental Health Development Unit estimated in 2007 that, of the 6 million persons in the UK suffering from anxiety and depression disorders, only 25% of these were in treatment. In response, the IAPT program aims to cut this waiting time significantly.

It has been argued (Cooper 2009), however, that closer examination of the IAPT program reveals certain weaknesses concerning its theoretical basis, logistics, and research methodology, and casts doubt on its advantages over alternative approaches. Clark et al. (2009) states that empirical findings on IAPT are limited to descriptive data from the two demonstration sites in Doncaster and Newham, whose mission was "to test the effectiveness of providing significant increases in evidence-based psychological therapy services to people with the common mental health problems of depression and anxiety disorders" (IAPT, 2011c) and that no systematic statistical analysis is yet possible. They went on to suggest, however, that whilst uptake of the new service appears to be good, with well over 5,000 referrals in 1 year, 40% of patients were deemed unsuitable, declined therapy or dropped out after a single session. Cooper (2009) argues that a further weakness of IAPT is that it gives the impression that happiness is the only desirable mental state and that it is inextricably linked to economic prosperity.

In addition, it is argued that the IAPT demonstration project's core purpose was defined (while it was still in progress) as being "to collect evidence of delivery to substantiate the development of a business case for a national roll-out of the IAPT service model" (IAPT, 2007, p. 1). This is the language of business management, not of empirical investigation. The fact that at the time of the demonstration project resources had already been allocated for the next phase of the rollout of IAPT (called 'Pathfinders') strongly suggests that a political decision to go ahead was taken before any pilot results were available.

A further weakness is the inability of research (of which there is a growing interest) to provide evidence for therapies which are perhaps not measurable from a positivistic standpoint. The DOH website states that "in the last five years, a wealth of evidence has emerged about which practices are effective and which are not" (DOH, 2008). This "wealth of evidence" has been based on the "gold standard" of RCTs and other experimental, clinical outcomes data. With this in mind, whilst there is evidence to show that CBT can be effective for people with simple, uncomplicated, mild depression, there is less evidence for its effectiveness in helping people with more complicated or prolonged depression, including depression arising from early trauma—the sort of people who are more likely to be on long-term benefits (Ferguson, 2006).

One of the potential opportunities in the UK is a growing interest in common factors and in exploring where theoretical differences are there more for the psychological therapist than may be helpful for the client. In broad terms, this conceptualization (Beutler, Machado, & Neufeldt, 1994; Hubble, Duncan, & Miller, 1999; Bohart & Tallman, 1999) suggests that common factors involve other dimensions of the treatment setting, including the therapeutic alliance (which RCTs may be inefficient in researching) and expectancy variables.

In addition to the challenge to convince NICE to include non-RCT research in evaluating psychological therapies, sits a higher level challenge which concerns the extent to which the State should be involved in determining the population's mental health. There are those who think that the State should not be involved in determining the mental health of the population (Parker & Revelli, 2008). They are concerned that such State regulation would be a very serious infringement on individual liberties and could lead to a further dumbing down of standards. Some might see a further challenge is the extent to which personal therapy is helpful in the training of psychological therapists (Risq, 2011), as the government understandably wants to fund those approaches which, in avoiding personal therapy, will cost less.

Future directions

As reported in Mace, Rowland, Evans, Schroeder, & Halstead (2009) with the advent of government intervention in terms of service delivery, training standards, the use of evidence-based practice and professional regulation it might be hoped that a more unified and larger psychotherapeutic profession will emerge. This is in contrast to the tradition in the UK of distinct boundaries between professional associations with competing treatment models as well as allegiances to other professions.

There is, however, a significant group, as discussed (see for example, Parker & Revelli, 2008) who have been concerned that such State regulation would be a very serious infringement on individual liberties and could lead to a reduction in of standards. Some might see the attempt at regulation as already being coupled with a decline in standards, with for example increasingly more counselors calling themselves "psychotherapists" and psychotherapists calling themselves "psychoanalysts" whilst simultaneously there is a reduction in the number of times the trainee therapist is required to have personal therapy, if at all.

Furthermore, more research should focus on the idea of theory, not only from the perspective, as discussed, of common factors but also in terms of the cultural implications of, for example, the work of Wittgenstein, as to the importance of practice and language rather than theories (see, for example, Heaton, 2010; Loewenthal, 2011). Linked with this last point, and perhaps what is most important, is what developments our managerialist culture will take, for without it, we might have a very different idea of what constitutes the nature of evidence and how we might see we are caught up in a compulsive need for happiness rather than being able to think about our increasing alienation.

Conclusion

The conclusion to this chapter is presented as a series of questions: To what extent will therapeutic interventions continue to be carried out as individual interventions and to what extent will they increasingly be at the level of community/society? It would appear that in the 21st century in the UK, stress (previously named alienation) is creating an insatiable demand for individual counseling and psychotherapy. It is expected that the level of interest in counseling and psychotherapy at the level of the organization will at least be maintained through, for example, employee assistance programs. There is also a question as to whether counseling and psychotherapy will become increasingly indistinguishable and whether psychoanalysis will continue to maintain its more separate position. There is a further question that as our cultural practices change, how will what we regard as research, including our current narrow notions of evidence, change; and how will this affect what we regard as "good" psychotherapy and counseling? With regard to government intervention it is unclear whether the IAPT program will increasingly come to dominate psychotherapy and counseling and will be a form of state regulation through the back door, and, on the other hand, what will happen when the ring-fencing of current funding is removed. The final question concerns the extent to which the UK's growing multicultural society will contribute to the emergence of new approaches to counseling and psychotherapy.

Acknowledgement

My thanks to Anne Guy, Rhiannon Thomas, Betty Bertrand-Godfrey, Research Assistants at Roehampton University, for their help in researching this chapter.

References

Aveline, M. (2006). Issues in psychotherapeutic research. In D. Loewenthal & D. Winter (eds), *What is Psychotherapeutic Research?* (pp. 3–28). London: Karnac.

British Association for Counselling and Psychotherapy (BACP). (2010a). *Introduction.* Retrieved October 6, 2011 from www.bacp.co.uk/join_bacp/

BACP. (2010b). *Training.* Retrieved October 6, 2011 from www.bacp.co.uk/information/education/training.php

Barkham, M., Margison, F., Leach, C., Lucock, M. P., Mellor-Clark, J., Evans, C. ... & McGrath, G. (2001). Service profiling and outcomes benchmarking using the CORE-OM: Toward practice-based evidence in the psychological therapies, *Journal of Consulting and Clinical Psychology, 69,* 184–196.

Beutler, L. E., Machado, P. P. P., & Neufeldt, S.A. (1994). Therapist variables. In A. E. Bergin & S. L. Garfield (eds), *Handbook of Psychotherapy and Behavior Change* (4th edn) (pp. 229–269). New York: Wiley.

Bion, W. R. (1961). *Experiences in Groups.* London: Tavistock.

Bion, W. R. (1962). *Learning from Experience.* London: William Heinemann.

Bohart, A. C., & Tallman, K. (1999). *How Clients Make Therapy Work: The Process of Active Self-healing.* Washington, DC: American Psychological Association.

Bowlby, J. (1997). *Attachment and Loss* (2nd edn). London: Pimlico.

British Psychoanalytic Council (BPC). (n.d.a). *About the BPC.* Retrieved October 6, 2011 from www.psychoanalytic-council.org/main/index.php?page=10099

BPC. (n.d.b.). *Clinical Trainings.* Retrieved October 6, 2011 from www.psychoanalytic-council.org/main/index.php?page=10102

British Psychological Society (BPS). (2000–2011a). *Regulation of psychology.* Retrieved October 6, 2011 from www.bps.org.uk/what-we-do/bps/regulation-psychology/regulation-psychology.

BPS. (2000–2011b). *Undergraduate and post graduate psychology.* Retrieved October 6, 2011 from www.bps.org.uk/careers-education-training/undergraduate-and-postgraduate-psychology/undergraduate-and-postgraduate-

Clark, D. M. (1986). A cognitive approach to panic. *Behaviour Research and Therapy, 24,* 461–470.

Clark, D. M., Layard, R., Smithies, R., Richards, D., Suckling, R., & Wright, B. (2009). Improving access to psychological therapy: Initial evaluation of two UK demonstration sites. *Behaviour Research and Therapy, 47*(11), 910–920.

Cooper, B. (2009). *Strange bedfellows: Economics, happiness and mental disorder.* Retrieved from www. tumoronline.it/articoli.php?archivio=yes&vol_id=446&id=5282

Cooper, M. (2011). *Meeting the demand for evidence-based practice.* Retrieved from www.therapytoday.net/ article/show/2447/

Community Research and Development Information Service (CORDIS). (2011). Retrieved from http:// cordis.europa.eu/guidance/welcome_en.html

Department of Health (DoH). (2008). Mental Health, Retrieved September 2008 from http://webarchive. nationalarchives.gov.uk/20080910134953/dh.gov.uk/en/healthcare/nationalserviceframeworks/mental health/index.htm

Department of Health (DoH). (2011). *Enabling excellence: Autonomy and accountability for health workers, social workers and social care workers.* Retrieved September 2011 from www.dh.gov.uk/en/publicationsand statistics/Publications/PublicationsPolicyAndGuidance/DH_124359

Deurzen, E. (1997). *Everyday Mysteries: Existential Dimensions of Psychotherapy.* London: Routledge.

Deurzen, E. (1998). *Paradox and Passion in Psychotherapy.* Chichester: Wiley.

Ecclestone, K., & Hayes, D. (2008). *The Dangerous Rise of Therapeutic Education.* London: Routledge.

Ferguson, I. (2006). *Richard Layard: Inequality and the 'Science' of Happiness.* Retrieved from www.socialist worker.co.uk/art.php?id=10280

Foskett, J. (2001). What of the client's-eye view? A response to the millennium review. *British Journal of Guidance and Counselling, 29*(3), 345–350.

Guy, A., Loewenthal, D., Thomas, R., & Stephenson, S. (2012). Scrutinising NICE: The impact of the National Institute for Health and Clinical Excellence Guidelines on the provision of counselling and psychotherapy in primary care in the UK. *Psychoanalytic Psychotherapy, 18*(1), 25–50.

Hargaden, H., & Schwartz, J. (eds) (2007). Relational psychology in Europe. *European Journal of Psychotherapy and Counselling, 9*(1).

Harrell, E. (1976). *All things are possible: The healing and charismatic revivals in modern America.* Hoboken, NJ: John Wiley & Sons.

Hayes, S. (2004). Acceptance and commitment therapy, relational frame theory, and the third wave of behavioral and cognitive therapies. *Behavior Therapy, 35*(4), 639–665.

Heaton, J. (2010). *The Talking Cure: Wittgenstein's Therapeutic Method for Psychotherapy.* London: Palgrave Macmillan.

Heron, J. (1996). *Co-operative Inquiry: Research into the Human Condition.* London: Sage.

House, R., & Loewenthal, D. (2009). *Childhood, Wellbeing and a Therapeutic Ethos.* London: Karnac Books.

Health Professions Council (HPC). (2007). *Trust, Assurance and Safety: The Regulation of Health Professionals in the 21st Century.* London: Health Professions Council.

HPC. (2011). *The Health Professions Order.* Retrieved October 20, 2011 from www.hpc-uk.org/publications.

Hubble, M. A., Duncan, B. L., & Miller, S. (eds) (1999). *The Heart and Soul of Change: What Works in Therapy.* Washington, DC: APA Press.

Improving Access to Psychological Therapies Programme (IAPT) (2007). IAPT outline service specification. Retrieved September 29, 2011 from www.iapt.nhs.uk/silo/files/iapt-outline-service-specification.pdf

IAPT. (2011a). *IAPT Pathfinder Programme.* Retrieved September 8, 2011 from www.iapt.nhs.uk/about-iapt/iapt-pathfinder-programme/

IAPT. (2011b). *Accreditation.* Retrieved October 6, 2011 from www.iapt.nhs.uk/workforce/accreditation/? keywords=accreditation

IAPT. (2011c). *Demonstration sites.* Retrieved from www.iapt.nhs.uk/about/demonstration-sites

Khalifa, N., & Hardie, T. (2005). Possession and Jinn. *Royal Journal of the Society of Medicine, 98*, 351–353.

Kihlstrom, J. F. (2002). To honor Kraepelin … : From symptoms to pathology in the diagnosis of mental illness. In L. Beutler & M. Malik (eds), *Rethinking the DSM: A Psychological Perspective* (pp. 279–303). Washington, DC: American Psychological Association.

Laing, R. D. (1960). *The Divided Self.* London: Penguin Books.

Layard, R. (2006). The depression report: A new deal for depression and anxiety disorders'. Retrieved from http://cep.lse.ac.uk/textonly/research/mentalhealth/DEPRESSION_REPORT_LAYARD.pdf.

Layard, R., & Dunn, J. (2009). *A Good Childhood.* London: Penguin Books.

Levinas, E. (1969). *Totality and Infinity, An Essay on Exteriority.* Pittsburgh, PA: Duquense University Press.

Loewenthal, D., & Winter, D. (eds) (2006). *What is Psychotherapeutic Research.* London: Karnac Books.

Loewenthal, D. (2010). The magic of the relational? Introduction to the relational in psychotherapy and counselling– cutting edge or cliché. *European Journal of Psychotherapy and Counselling, 12*(3), 201–205.

Loewenthal, D. (2011). *Post-existentialism and the Psychological Therapies.* London: Karnac Books.

Loewenthal, D., Murkhopadhyay, S., Ganesh, K., & Thomas, R. (2012). Reducing the barriers to accessing psychological therapies for Bengali, Urdu, Tamil and Somali communities in the UK: Some Implications for training, policy and practice. *British Journal of Guidance and Counselling, 40*, 1, 43–66.

Lupton, R., & Power, A. (2004). *Minority Ethnic Groups in Britain*. Washington, DC: Center for Analysis of Social Exclusion.

Mace, C., Rowland, N., Evans, C., Schroeder, T., & Halstead, J. (2009). Psychotherapy professionals in the UK: Expansion and experiment. *European Journal of Psychotherapy and Counselling, 11*(2), 131–140.

Macran, S., Ross, H., Hardy, G. E., & Shapiro, D. (1999). The importance of considering clients' perspectives in psychotherapy research. *Journal of Mental Health, 8*(4), 325–337.

Mearns, D. (2002). *S1: How much Supervision Should you Have?* Leicestershire: BACP.

Mearns, D., & Thorne, B. (1999). *Personal-centred Counselling in Action* (2nd edn). London: Sage.

Mellor-Clark, J., & Barkham, M. (2003). Bridging evidence-based practice and practice-based evidence: Developing a rigorous and relevant knowledge for the psychological therapies, *Clinical Psychology and Psychotherapy, 10*(6), 319–327.

Mitchell, S. A., & Aron, L. (eds). (1999). *Relational psychoanalysis: The emergence of a tradition*. Mahwah, NJ: Analytic Press.

Office for National Statistics. (2011). *Mid 2010 Population Estimates*. Retrieved September 22, 2011 from www.ons.gov.uk/ons/publications/re-reference-tables.html?edition=tcm%3A77–231847

Parker, I., & Revelli, S. (2008). *Psychoanalytic Practice and State Regulation*. London: Karnac Books.

Pilkington, K., Kirkwood, G., Rampes, H., Fisher, P., & Richardson, J. (2005). Homeopathy for depression: a systematic review of the research evidence. *Homeopathy, 94*(3), 153–163.

Richards, K. (2010). *Information sheet R12: Finding Research Funding, BACP Website* Retrieved September, 22, 2011 from: www.bacp.co.uk/admin/structure/files/repos/384_r12_finding_research_funding.pdf

Risq, R. (2011). Personal therapy in psychotherapeutic training: Current research and future directions. *Journal of Contemporary Psychotherapy, 41*(3), 175–186.

Rogers, A., Maidman, J., & House, R. (2011). The bad faith of evidence based practice: beyond counsels of despair', *Therapy Today, 22*(6), 26–29.

Roth, A. D., & Fonagy, P. (2005). *What Works for Whom? A Critical Review of Psychotherapy Research*. New York: Guilford Press.

Rowan, J. (1993). *The Transpersonal: Spirituality in Psychotherapy and Counselling*. London: Routledge.

Salkovskis, P. M. (ed.). (1996). *Frontiers of Cognitive Therapy*. New York: Guildford Press.

Shepherd, M. (1979). Psychoanalysis, psychotherapy and health Services, *British Medical Journal, 2*(6204), 1557–1559.

Skills for Health. (2011). *Homepage*. Retrieved from www.skillsforhealth.org.uk/

Spinelli, E. (1997). *Tales of Un-knowing: Therapeutic Encounters from an Existential Perspective*. London: Duckworth.

Spinelli, E. (2005). *The Interpreted World: An Introduction to Phenomenological Psychology* (2nd edn). London: Sage.

The Healing Trust (2011). *About the Healing Trust*, Retrieved October 6th 2011 from www.thehealingtrust.org.uk/about/the-healing-trust.

Thorne, B. (1991). *Person-centred Counselling: Therapeutic and Spiritual Dimensions* (Counselling & Psychotherapy Series) (2nd edn). London: Wiley-Blackwell.

Tudor, K., & Worrall, M. (2006). *Person Centred Therapy: A Clinical Philosophy*. London: Routledge.

United Kingdom Council for Psychotherapy (UKCP). (2010). Constitutional change: What it means for you. *The Psychotherapist, 46*, 36–37.

UKCP. (2011a). *Homepage*. Retrieved October 6, 2011 from www.psychotherapy.org.uk/

UKCP. (2011b). *Supervision, Personal Therapy and Clinical Practice*. Retrieved October 13, 2011 from www.psychotherapy.org.uk/iqs/dbitemid.144/sfa.view/students_and_trainee_therapists_frequently_asked_questions.html

Waller, D. (2009). Psychotherapy in Europe: An emerging professional project. *European Journal of Psychotherapy and Counselling, 11*(2), 203–209.

Winnicott, D. W. (1971). *Playing and Reality*. London: Tavistock

Winnicott, D. W. (2000). *The Child, the Family and the Outside World* (2nd edn). London: Penguin Books

Young, R. M. (1999). *Psychoanalysis and Psychotherapy: The Grand Leading the Bland*. Retrieved February 8, 2011 from www.human nature.com/rmyoung/papers/pap101h.html

PART V

Counseling and psychotherapy in the Middle East

31

COUNSELING AND PSYCHOTHERAPY IN IRAN

Flourishing perspectives

Behrooz Birashk

Introduction

The Islamic Republic of Iran, located in the Middle East between the Caspian Sea and the Persian Gulf, has a population of more than 77 million (Central Intelligence Agency [CIA], 2011), and of the total population 70% live in towns and cities. The religion held by the majority of the Iranian population is shiite Muslim, 89%, and Sunni Muslim 9%. The remaining 2% of Iranians are from other religions, primarily Zoroastrian, Christian, and Jewish (CIA, 2011). The main ethno-linguistic minority groups are the Azeris, Kurds, Arabs, Baluchis, Turks, Armenians, Assyrians, Jews, and Georgians (CIA, 2011). Examples of major tribal groups include the Bakhtiaris, Khamseh, Lurs, and Qashqai.

Iran, with its very long heritage and important history, has benefited from traditional medical systems stemming from several thousand years ago. Origins of counseling and psychotherapy in Iran can be traced back to Zoroaster's[1] teaching in Avesta (Zoroaster's book), who emphasized good thinking in accordance with realities; good speaking, in which hopefulness and encouragement can be expressed and maintained; and good behavior that brings positive consequence to life (Ghobari, 2006). Early Muslim physicians like Tabari, Avicenna, Rhuzes, and Jorjani have devoted long sections of their books to a discussion of mental disorders under the general title of "the diseases of the head and the brain" (Birashk, 2004).

Modern psychiatry, psychology, psychotherapy, and counseling were introduced to Iran in the 20th century at the newly established medical schools and universities. Following the worldwide adoption of modern theories and approaches to counseling and psychotherapy by academic institutions, universities in Iran started developing similar curricula and introduced this discipline into their regular training programs. Recent developments in the training and practice of counseling and psychotherapy are responses to the increasing demand for such services across Iranian society.

Brief history of counseling and psychotherapy

Iran, a remnant of the Old Persian Empire, has a rich and long history of 7,000 years. Unfortunately there is not much written history before the emergence of Islam, except for some writings of Zoroaster the prophet, and his book the Avesta (Shamloo, 2000). The Zoroastrian literature refers to three types of physicians: herbal therapists, surgeons, and divine world healers, who may be thought of as the first psychiatrists in Iran (Javanbakht & Sanati, 2006). In ancient Iranian texts, there are references to mental illnesses and their treatment, both with and without drugs, particularly in the Avesta—the philosophy of mental health, namely Good Thinking, Good Speaking, and Good Behavior—and later by Iranian scholars, physicians, and philosophers, including Avicenna, Zakariya-e-Razi, Rhuzes, Nasir al-Din Tusi, and Seyed Esmael Jorjani, who shaped the foundation of present psychotherapy without drug treatments (Mehrabi et al., 2000). Also among their books are guidance and suggestions that help children and youths in choosing academic majors and appropriate careers, which resemble what is now career and academic counseling.

During the Islamic civilization 14 centuries ago, a movement in human sciences especially in the domain of counseling and psychotherapy took place (Ghobari, 2006). The Koran introduced indexes of healthy life styles, and differentiated them from unfulfilling pathways of life. In addition, it categorized people according to their personalities and ensuing behaviors in accordance with their personal characteristics (Ghobari, 2006).

About a thousand years ago, Avicenna,[2] (Ibn Sina, 980–1037), one of the Iranian philosophers, derived ideas concerning cognition, perception, and structure of the personality from the Koran and Prophet Mohammad's tradition. Such formulation is illustrated in his book *Science of Soul* and can be considered as antecedents to modern approaches to psychological paradigms (Ghobari, 2006).

Long before Sigmund Freud introduced the structures of the mind, namely Id, Ego, and Super ego, Iranian thinkers during the 8th century believed that human mind or personality consisted of three parts or Nafs,[3] quite comparable to Freud's concept of personality, only much more extensive (Javanbakht & Sanati, 2006).

Iranian scholars had remarkable ideas about the psyche and the relationship between mind and body. From an Islamic view and according to the Koran, mankind is created from dust and God breathed his spirit into man. Mulla Sadra (also known as Sadr Aldin Shirazi, 1572–1640), in his book *Asrar al Ayat* (Nasr, 1996) further illustrated the meanings of Koranic verses. In his other book *Al Hikmat al Mutaaliya*, he also provided an in-depth discussion of the field of psychology (Ghobari, 2006).

Iranian mystics also had interesting ideas regarding the psychic apparatus and growth. Apart from man's apparent behavior, they believed in man's inner world, which was called Baaten. This concept described the individual and collective unconscious (Javanbakht & Sanati, 2006). Only an inquiring individual who follows a master (pir = old wise man) that mirrors the seeker can gain insight to the mysteries of Baaten. In fact, this master is a kind of analyst, who, apart from being a mirror, should be believed by the seeker to be a masterful medium between himself and God.

Modern psychology in Iran began in 1933, when the late Ali Akbar Siassi established the first laboratory of psychology by the order of the then Minister of Culture in Dar al Moalemin (Birashk, 2004). Teheran University was established in 1934 and included traditional schools such as medicine, law, literature, and human sciences. Ali Akbar Siassi, president of the university at the time, was interested in psychology and introduced the first psychology courses there in 1938 (Birashk, 2004). The department of psychology eventually became independent of philosophy, and a degree in psychology (BA) was offered. Later on, as new universities were established in Isfahan, Shiraz, Tabriz, and Mashhad, they too introduced psychology programs and began offering degrees in psychology.

Clinical psychology became a recognized field of study in the 1960s. The first clinical psychology course was taught in 1965 in Tehran University (Birashk, 2004) and its first master's degrees in clinical psychology were awarded in the 1970s at the psychiatry department in Rouzbeh Hospital.

Following the Islamic Revolution in 1979, the MA program at Rouzbeh Hospital closed down after 5 years of training graduate students in clinical psychology (it was later reactivated and the hospital initiated its first PhD program in 2011). Instead, after the Revolution, Tehran Psychiatric Institute, a faculty branch of Iran University of Medical Sciences, began to offer an MA in clinical psychology in 1985 (Birashk, 2004). In the 1990s the Ministry of Health and Medical Education agreed to permit the MA degree in clinical psychology at the Welfare and Rehabilitation Sciences University in Tehran. Similar university programs in other cities soon followed suit.

The existing counseling movement dates back 54 years, despite the fact that traditional counseling and guidance have a long history in Iran. Since its establishment, this discipline has been through four main periods (Sanaie Zaker, 2008): (1) the traditional counseling and guidance period, (2) the pioneer period, (3) the interval period, and (4) the rebirth and progress period.

During the first period, or the *traditional counseling and guidance period*, the Koran was a major source to draw upon when seeking counseling and guidance. For instance, The Koran, the holy book of counseling and guidance, has spoken of the importance of counseling in some Surahs,[4] such as Al-Omran[5] and Shura.[6] As well as The Koran, Shiite Imams and Iranian philosophers, thinkers, and poets such as Avicenna, Ferdowsi, Birouni, and Saadi have also pointed out the importance of counseling and guidance, for example, on self-knowledge, human needs, and issues surrounding children and parenting (Nasr, 1996).

The *pioneer period* (between 1965 and the 1979 Revolution) was characterized by the arrival of non-traditional education from the West (though Dar al-Funun, Iran's first modern institution of higher learning based on Western models, was already established in 1851) and the trend to send Iranian students abroad for education. The pioneer and founder of the first movement was Dr. Mohammad Mashayekhi, who focused his activities on revising the educational system in Iran. He brought his idea of counseling to Iran from his experiences in France (Sanaie Zaker, 2008).

During the *interval period* (during the 10 years following the 1979 Revolution), an attempt was made for all majors of humanities to become Islamic (known as the Cultural Revolution [1980–1987]). While the Cultural Revolution achieved its goal of ridding the universities of Western influence, it led to the emigration of numerous academics and technocrats, which inevitably weakened Iran in the field of science and technology. For about 6 years there was a halt to counseling training at the universities, but as a result of continued efforts on the part of a group of counselors, counseling training programs were finally reinstalled in universities and were accepted by the Higher Council (Sanaie Zaker, 2008).

Finally, during the *rebirth and progress period* (following 1988 and the end of the Cultural Revolution) there was a dire need for revising and updating new university counseling programs and including counseling courses at the MA level in their curricula. Following these revisions, all the major universities in Tehran and other large cities have developed general counseling at the MA level, while some universities admit students in four specialized majors as follows: Educational Counseling, Occupational Counseling, Family Counseling, and Rehabilitation Counseling.

Since the rebirth and progress period, by accepting counseling as an approved field of study and acknowledging the role of counselors in Iranian society, nearly all universities in the country have followed suit and proceeded to accept counseling students in their universities. The past two decades have witnessed a striking increase in the number of counseling students enrolled at the BA, MA, and PhD levels and the augmentation of university departments by offering four specialized fields of counseling at the MA level. All universities have counseling centers for students and other non-student clients, and private counseling centers are active all over the country. Many governmental institutions have even established counseling departments.

Counselor education programs, accreditation, licensure, and certification

The master's degree is generally the basic qualification level required for practicing counseling and psychotherapy. Applicants to graduate school must pass another nationwide entrance exam administered annually by two ministries—the Ministry of Health and Medical Education and the Ministry of Higher Education. This process leads to the selection of a small number for the interview and final selection. Usually about half of the applicants pass the interview and start studying towards a 2-year-long master's degree in clinical psychology or counseling (Khodayarifard, 2007). Islamic Azad University, however, has its own entrance examination with a similar selection process.

The master's programs (MSc or MA) in Iran entail 2 years (or four semesters) of training and require the completion of 32 credit hours, among which four to six credits are dedicated to thesis work. In addition, students must pass a course titled "Muslim Scholar's Views on Psychology." This course reviews the theories of Islamic philosophers and scientists about the soul and psyche, and provides students an opportunity to discuss the relationships between psychological conditions and somatic disorders (Birashk, 2004).

The graduation requirements for a PhD program in Iran include 42–50 credit hours of course work as well as a 1-year internship (for clinical psychology). Students in clinical psychology and counseling have to pass a comprehensive examination before starting their internship (only for clinical psychology students), as well as 20 credit hours of dissertation.

According to the statistics in Iran (Ministry of Higher Education, 2008), there are 25,713 BA students in psychology and counseling, 1,500 MA or MS students in these disciplines, and 120 students are involved in the PhD program. Twenty-five universities offer bachelor degrees in counseling and psychology, including departments of clinical psychology. There are 13 departments in clinical psychology and 10 in counseling psychology at MA level. At present six universities offer doctorate degrees in clinical psychology and four universities offer doctorate degrees in counseling.

The Board of Clinical Psychology based at the Ministry of Health and Medical Education is responsible to evaluate and accredit clinical psychology programs at the medical universities. Clinical psychology and counseling programs in non-medical universities that are regulated under the Ministry of Higher Education, however, are accredited by the Ministry itself.

In terms of licensure, the Iranian Psychology and Counseling Organization (PCO) was founded in 2004 by a law passed in Parliament that required mandatory licensure for counseling/psychology practitioners. The aim has been to regulate the practice of psychologists and counselors and to ensure that the public could access authentic services. For instance, to be licensed, accredited, and certified for private practice, supervision during counseling training and additional postgraduation supervised practice are required. The organization also monitors the work of practitioners and protects their legal rights as well as those of their clients (Khodayarifard, 2007).

Since 1995, several associations have been established with the permission of the Ministry of Science, Research, and Technology and the Ministry of Health and Medical Education to extend the border of scientific knowledge as well as developments of new therapeutic procedures which are supported by the PCO. At present there are six organized non-governmental psychological bodies in Iran.

Current counseling and psychotherapy theories, process, and trends

In terms of professional trends, the number of psychologists, counselors, or psychotherapists in Iran is growing rapidly, but the exact number in different specialties is hard to estimate. They work in public and private psychiatric hospitals and in psychiatric wards in general hospitals, as well as in schools and counseling centers (Mehrabi et al., 2000). In addition, many psychologists, counselors, and psychotherapists are working in the private sector in either mental health clinics or with psychiatrists in private practice (Birashk, 2004).

At present the dominant psychotherapeutic theories in Iran are those borrowed from Western countries, mainly the United States and Europe (Ghobari, 2006; Shamloo, 2000). Psychology and counseling students are taught all theories in psychology, counseling, personality, psychopathology, and psychotherapy. However, most clinical and counseling psychologists use behavior therapy, psychoanalysis, humanistic approaches, rational-emotive-behavioral therapy, client-centered, psychodynamics approaches, transactional analysis, short–term psychotherapies, group therapy, family therapy (all the main approaches), marriage counseling, and recently "third wave" or new approaches like schema therapy, dialectic behavior therapy, meta-cognitive therapy, mindfulness-based cognitive therapy, acceptance-commitment therapy, or acceptance-based behavior therapy (Khodayarifard, 2007).

Cognitive behavioral therapy (CBT) in Iran was primarily initiated by psychologists interested in behavior therapy (Birashk, 2004). This interest was partly inspired by the gradual integration of cognitive processes as important dimensions of learning about emotionally loaded experiences in particular. As with other converts to CBT, their main source of inspiration was the work of Aaron T. Beck.

A major reason for the rapid growth of interest in CBT was its resonance with Iranian culture, which has long recognized the close link between thoughts and emotions. As a reflection of this cultural tradition it may be of interest to note that a line by Rummi, a well-known Iranian Sufi poet, has attained the status of a frequently quoted proverb: "O brother, you are but your thoughts, the rest of you are no more than bone and tissues."

Since late 1980s, CBT has been the main approach to psychotherapy at the Institute of Psychiatry, Rouzbeh Psychiatric Hospital, and many other major training centers, such as the Institute for Cognitive Science Studies (ICSS) (Birashk, 2004). A large number of students have devoted their MA and PhD theses to the application of CBT to different individuals with varied mental health/life problems. A good deal has also been learnt regarding the limitations and comparative advantages of CBT in Iranian culture (Birashk, 2005).

Following the Islamic Revolution in 1979, there was a widespread pessimistic attitude towards psychoanalysis and Freud's ideas on sexuality. During the first few years of the war with Iraq, there was no place for psychoanalysis in universities and academic settings. Therefore, psychoanalysis was removed from the academic system and was only practiced in private therapy offices (Javanbakht & Sanati, 2006). However, situations have changed since then and currently psychoanalysis is a part of psychotherapy training.

Finally, the Institute for Cognitive Science Studies (ICSS), established in Iran in 1977, is a non-governmental organization (NGO) dedicated to explore the nature of the human cognition and how it affects human behavior and social interactions. In pursuing this goal, ICSS promotes scientific collaboration and knowledge exchange among academics and researchers from a number of traditionally separate disciplines, including psychology, psychiatry, neuroscience, computer science, artificial intelligence, linguistics, and philosophy.

Indigenous and traditional healing methods

Zar is one of the common primitive techniques of mental healing associated with spirit possession beliefs in the southern region of Iran. The *Zar* spirit may communicate from the possessed, and the victim will be in a state of hysterical trance, which is followed by temporary amnesia (Sabaye Moghaddam, 2009).

Special ceremonies are held to pacify the *Zar* and alleviate the patient's symptoms. These ceremonies, called by a leader, bring together the patient and those previously afflicted by the *Zar* and involve incense, music, and movement.

Based on records and interviews regarding the *Zar* ceremony, roughly two phases in the ritual can be recognized: separation and incorporation. The separation phase begins with a person complaining to cult leaders (*Baba Zar* or *Mama Zar*) about feeling ill. The cult leaders then help the patient control his *Zars*. In treatment ceremonies by the group, everyone gathers in a circle with the patient in the center while a piece of cloth, with eggs, dates, confetti, and aromatic herbs, is spread on the floor. During the incorporation phase, after the patient's head is covered with a piece of white cloth to keep him/her from view of strangers, a tray holding aromatic herbs on charcoal is passed around and the patient and the participants are frequently enveloped in incense from the smoke from the mixture. The *Zar* leader takes charge with music (drums) and musicians and others present follow.

The leader usually knows the name of the *Zar* and the music (drums) that goes with them. *Baba* or *Mama Zar* also sings and the participants respond in turn. During the singing of the incantations, which are sung in different languages or dialects (Sabaye Moghaddam, 2009), every piece of music accompanies a specific spirit; and with each type of music, some members of the cult may start moving and shaking. The reaction is usually expressed as a swinging of the upper body, vertical movements of the head, and shaking of the shoulders. The leader speaks with the spirit through the patient and asks the *Zar* about the reasons behind the affliction as well as its demands for leaving the patient alone (Saedi, 1961).

Despite close to half a century of government opposition to these practices (Saedi, 1961), *Zar* beliefs and practices have not ceased to exist in the southern part of Iran and many other countries in the Middle East.

In recent years, after the establishment of a music therapy association in 1997, some therapists use music in their psychotherapy. But in some parts of Iran, there are still some traditional music therapies practiced by local musicians, who use their music for treatment of ill people. For example, *Gwat* is a kind of mental illness (similar to epilepsy) known to the Iranians which is observed more in women than in men. The melody used for its treatment is accompanied by dancing, and dancers claim to enter a world of ecstasy. The ceremonies are continued for 3–7 days and last between 1 and 4 hours.

In recent years some psychologists and psychotherapists have shown innovations in psychotherapy based on traditional concepts and techniques used in ancient times in Iran (Shamloo, 2000). For instance, *story therapy* is carried out by reading and analyzing a story relevant to the patient's problem, thus giving him some problem-solving insights (Rizvi, 1988; Pezechkian, 1974). *Poetry therapy* has been a long tradition in Iran's medical history and in recent years some specialists have made extensive use of poetry from classical poets, such as Rummi, Saadi, Hafez, and Khayyam in therapy (Farvardin, 1984, Noorbakhsh, 1965; Shamloo, 1998). Incorporating *selflessness* is an ancient therapy technique based on Gnosticism and its purpose is to relieve the patient's egotistic and narcissistic tendencies, while the incorporation of *forgiveness* allows the patient to forgive those who have hurt him in the past (Khodayarifard, et al., 2001). Finally, *meditation* and *silence therapy* (which is an offshoot of meditation using a special technique, different from those used in South East Asian countries) (Ghobari, 2006) are commonly practiced in Iran.

Research and supervision

Research is an important part of the counseling and psychotherapy training programs in Iran. During their study, students are required to conduct research projects related to their areas of interest and have at least one or two published articles in Farsi or English in scientific journals for their final defense of their education or degree. In addition, many symposiums and conferences are held yearly in Iran in the areas of psychology, psychiatry, psychotherapy, counseling, or related areas, and all presentations are expected to be research oriented. Finally, there are many Farsi and English scientific journals published by the universities, and all articles are research based and authored by psychologists, psychiatrists, psychotherapists, and counselors. Many articles are published in international journals or presented at international congresses. The topics of the research touch on new approaches to therapy or counseling as well as areas of need in Iranian society (Khodayarifard, 2007). In the last decade, however, Iranian researchers have turned to psychotherapy processes, outcomes, and effectiveness.

Many of the counseling and psychotherapy research projects and also MA and PhD theses are effectiveness studies or comparisons between therapeutic approaches (CBT is the approach most often compared). A review of the SID (Scientific Information Database) in Iran shows that we can classify these topics into different categories, such as personality disorders, sexual disorders, neurological disorders, schizophrenia, addiction, depression, health, family therapy, phobias, and learning disorders. These types of research are conducted using both qualitative and quantitative methods.

There are certain popular journals that most Iranian psychologists, counselors, and psychotherapist refer to and in which most Iranian research on therapy and counseling is published, such as *Iranian Psychiatry and Clinical Psychology, (Andisheh va Raftar)*, published by the Tehran Psychiatric Institute; *Quarterly Journal of Tazeha Ye Olum e Raftari*; *Journal of Behavioral Science*; *International Journal of Psychology* (in English); and *The Journal of Tazeha Va Pazhoheshhaye Moshavereh* (Ghobari & Bolhari, 2001).

With respect to supervision, MD residents and PhD intern students, and even most MA students in the last semester of their studies gain practical experience under direct supervision to improve their clinical and therapeutic skills at university-affiliated clinics and hospitals. To make direct supervision possible, these clinics for the most part are equipped with one-way mirrors or camera systems. Hence a team of students and supervisors may observe the therapy sessions (Khodayarifard, 2007). Supervisors are also able to communicate with trainees through walkie-talkies to direct the course of therapy if need be. Observed sessions are only allowed with the consent of the clients.

Many psychotherapists work in universities or other types of public clinics, but most have private practices as well. In the majority of clinics, a group works together as a team comprising at least one professional from the various fields of psychology, psychiatry, psychometric, and social work. However, there are some clinics in which a number of psychologists, psychiatrists, and counselors work independently. To work independently as a counselor or clinical psychologist, one must have at least 750 hours of supervised work after graduation. Supervised experience at the PhD level is 1,500 hours.

Strengths, weaknesses, opportunities, and challenges

General health indicators have been improving in Iran. These achievements have been possible because of the primary healthcare (PHC) system (Shadpour, 2000). Local staff run health networks, and this model has spread to most parts of the country and has brought about immense changes in the promotion and maintenance of community health. Many counselors, psychologists, and psychotherapists have played an important role in this improvement.

Further, the increasing number of Western trained psychologists and counselors returning to Iran, new graduates acquiring more experience and knowledge, annual research and publications, and training opportunities and workshops have strengthened the development of therapeutic services in Iran.

However, due to many factors and changes that have taken place in Iran over the past several decades, the progress in the field of psychology has stagnated and has not been able to reflect the rich philosophical and cultural conceptualization of human nature and its psychological condition. For these reasons, the field of psychology in Iran has not flourished beyond what one might have expected, given its strong potential.

In reviewing the status of the field, one can identify a number of weaknesses that may have contributed to the stagnation evident in the field. One major weakness is the abandonment of the concepts and philosophical viewpoints that have been advanced by influential Iranian thinkers over many centuries (Kimiaei, 2008). Although many of these concepts and viewpoints have been reiterated by Western philosophers and theorists and then brought back to Iran in the form of Western theories of human nature and psychology, Iranian psychologists have been content with adopting the Western views uncritically. This approach has led to pessimistic or negative distrustful views from a number of institutions which regard Western theories in various fields of social, psychological, political sciences, and economics adversarial to Iranian and Islamic cultures. Unfortunately, little effort has been put forth by renowned Iranian psychologists in developing psychological theories based on Iranian culture and Islamic views and concepts, albeit that Western psychology emphasizes the undisputed role of cultural factors in psychological processes. Tied to this is the weakness that there is an absence of a specific theory that could capture the essence of Iranian culture and depict the psychology of Iranian people.

Further, Khakpour (2008) has mentioned some of the shortcomings in Iranian educational programs: an insufficient number of required and necessary courses; inappropriate number of units disproportionate to the nature and objective of the field; inappropriate titles and contents based on the objectives of the course, and weakness in teaching lessons in practice and absence of adequate clinical supervision in training.

These shortcomings have led to realization that in order to advance the field, there is a need for the PCO and other psychological associations to work together with governmental institutions to conceive a coherent system of training. In recent years, major steps have been taken to improve psychology and counseling programs. For example, revisions of program contents have been initiated and opportunities for students to be trained in a variety of psychotherapeutic modalities have increased. In the new curricula there will also be more opportunities to incorporate cultural and Islamic points of view.

Further, there is a growing potential for the field of psychology to strengthen, in light of the ever-increasing interest among students to choose psychology and counseling as their major field of study. Also an increasing number of journals, books, educational opportunities, and workshops has led to the development of counseling and psychological services.

Although there is a rich history of psychology and treatment backgrounds in Iran and counseling and psychotherapy practices have advanced greatly in recent years, we still face numerous challenges along the way. For instance, the attitude of the general population towards mental illness and counseling and psychotherapy is still clouded by some misconceptions and stigmas, and one may expect that the status of psychology should have advanced further than it has. Fortunately, due to the active presence of counselors and psychologists in Iranian society and the media and the ongoing publications of articles and books, stigma surrounding mental illness has decreased significantly, especially among the educated population. The future of counseling and psychotherapy in Iran is therefore promising.

Future directions

As mentioned above, at present the status of counseling and psychotherapy is promising in Iran. However, there are several areas that require specific attention in order to improve the quality of training and services.

One major task for academics is to introduce an integrated method of counseling and psychotherapy to include cultural entities into the current and contemporary Western approaches. Other areas for future focus in training counselors and psychotherapists are to further develop marital therapy, family therapy, and health psychology, areas that would address some of the unique needs of Iranian society. Facilitating access to psychological services via extending national health insurance coverage to this field is another future plan for the bodies responsible for public health. This is of particular importance when consideration is given to the following facts in Iran: a relatively high prevalence of depression and anxiety among both sexes, especially women; drug addiction, especially among young adolescents; and the increase in HIV/AIDS in recent years due to drug use through injections or unprotected sexual activities.

Conclusion

In spite of the aforementioned shortcomings and challenges, psychotherapy and counseling in Iran have developed significantly over the years. The recent movement is to progress towards a new era in which national cultural entities are integrated into psychotherapeutic theories and practice. Part of this diligence includes the incorporation of specific cultural, religious, and spiritual concepts associated with psychological processes into current psychological theories. Accordingly, psychotherapy and counseling are in the process of developing a new identity that respects and integrates local cultural and philosophic roots into the prevailing Western scholars' products for the ultimate goal of optimizing acceptance and efficacy. This will eventually earn this nation a prominent standing within the international community of counselors and psychotherapists.

As a developing country, Iran faces a great deal of work with respect to developing a mental health field that responds to the needs of its growing population. In addition, keeping up with the ever-emerging approaches and techniques of the field and firmly adopting these innovative methods will also remain as part of the continuing evolution of this discipline in Iran.

Acknowledgment

My gratitude and appreciation to my dear friend and colleague Dr. Akbar Bayanzadeh for his wonderful and very valuable remarks and editorial suggestions and his efforts to accomplish this work.

Notes

1 A prophet in ancient Persia.
2 The first example of the word-association method was practiced by Avicenna. As an example: A prince was in severe fever and no doctor seemed able to help. Avicenna understood that the prince was in love, and diagnosed "love fever." The prince denied it and did not express the name of the girl. Avicenna while taking his patient's pulse, named neighboring counties, and one caused a rise in the pulse rate. He then began naming the streets, and one caused the pulse to rise again. Finally, he named the

girls on that street and the pulse rate revealed the name of the girl. He advised the parents to let the marriage happen and the prince was cured (Javanbakht & Sanati, 2006).

3 The first kind of Nafs was Nafs e Ammare, which drove man toward basic instincts (roughly similar to Id). The second component, Nafs e Lavame, contained conscience and would criticize man on his immoral and instinctual behavior (reminiscent of super ego). Third, Nafs e Motmaenne was a transcendental, or perfect, human ego.

4 Verses from the Koran. The Koran has 114 chapters (Surahs) and 6,236 verses (Ayahs).

5 A verse from the Koran : " ... and consult with them up on the conduct of affaires" (Verse 159).

6 A verse from the Koran: " ... and they do their work after the consultation with others" (Verse 38).

References

Birashk, B. (2004). Psychology in Iran. In M. Stevens & D. Wedding (eds), *Handbook of International Psychology* (pp. 405–418). Brunner: Rutledge.

——(2005). *Cognitive behavior therapy in Iran*. Paper presented at the 5th International Congress of Cognitive Behavior Therapy, Thessaloniki, Greece.

Central Intelligence Agency. (2011). *Iran*. Retrieved October 18, 2011 from https://www.cia.gov/library/publications/the-world-factbook/geos/ir.html

Farvardin, A. (1984). *Poetry Therapy*. Tehran: Dehkhoda Press.

Ghobari, B. (2006). Counseling in Iran. *Newsletter, Division of Counseling Psychology of the International Association of Applied Psychology, 2*(3), 13–17.

Ghobari, B., &, Bolhari, J. (2001). The current state of medical psychology in Islamic Republic of Iran. *Journal of Clinical Psychology in Medical Settings, 8*(9), 34–43.

Javanbakht, A., & Sanati, M. (2006). Psychiatry and psychoanalysis in Iran. *Journal of the American Academy of Psychoanalysis and Dynamic Psychiatry, 34*, 405–414.

Khakpour, R. (2008). Basic education in counseling. *Papers on Seventh Seminar of Iranian Counseling Association*, 27–49.

Khodayarifard, M. (2007). Psychotherapy in Iran: A case study of cognitive-behavioral family therapy for depression. *Journal of Clinical Psychology, 63*(8), 745–753.

Khodayarifard, M., Ghobari Bonab, B., & Faqihi, A. (2001). *Application of forgiveness in psychotherapy (with emphasis on Islamic view)*. Conference presentation at the 1st International Conference on Religion and Mental Health, April, Tehran, Iran.

Kimiaei, S. A. (2008). Challenges of counseling and counselors in Iran. *21st Century. Papers on Seventh Seminar of Iranian Counseling Association*, 157–163.

Mehrabi, F., Bayanzadeh, S. A. Atef-Vahid, M. K., Bolhari, J., Shahmohammadi, D., & Vaezi, S. A. (2000). Mental health in Iran. In I. Al. Issa (ed.), *Al Junun: Mental Illness in the Islamic World* (pp. 134–161). Madison, WI: International Universities Press.

Ministry of Higher Education. (2008). *Annual Reports from the Number of Psychology Students and Universities*. Tehran: Iran.

Nasr, S. H. (1996). Mulla Sadra: His teaching. In S. H. Nasr & D. Leaman (eds), *History of Islamic Philosophy* (pp. 634–652). London: Routledge.

Noorbakhsh, J. (1965). *The Role of Poetry in Psychotherapy*. Tehran: Tehran University Press.

Pezechkian, S. (1974). *Using Stories for Psychotherapeutic Aims*. New York: Springes-Verlog.

Rizvi, S. A. (1988). *Muslim Tradition in Psychotherapy and Modern Trends*. Lahore: Institute of Islamic Culture.

Sabaye Moghaddam, M. (2009). *Negahi be eteghadat va marasem-e Zar* [Considering the beliefs and rituals of the Zar]. Najva-ye Farhang.

Saedi, Gh. (1961). *Ahl-e hava* [The possesing spirit]. Tehran: Amir Kabir Publication.

Sanaie Zaker, B. (2008). Historical perspective of current counseling position in Iran. *Papers on Seventh Seminar of Iranian Counseling Association*, 165–188.

Shadpour, K. (2000). Primary health care networks in the Islamic Republic of Iran. *Eastern Mediterranean Health Journal, 6*(4), 622–625.

Shamloo, S. (1998). *Mental Health* (14th edn). Tehran: Roshd Publication.

——(2000). *Psychotherapy in Iran*. Presented at International Congress of Psychotherapy in East and West Tehran.

32

COUNSELING AND PSYCHOTHERAPY IN ISRAEL

Milestones, disputes, and challenges

Rebecca Jacoby

Introduction

Since Israel's establishment in 1948 its population has grown almost tenfold, today reaching a total population of about 7.7 million, with a clear majority (75.6%) of Jews who migrated to Israel from all over the world (Central Bureau of Statistics, 1997–2011). Although immigration from Europe began before World War II, the largest waves of immigration consisted of Holocaust survivors, followed by immigrants from North and South Africa, South America, and more recently from Ethiopia and the former Soviet Union. The Jewish population in Israel can be classified by varying levels of religiousness, including the orthodox-religious population, the traditional population, and the secular one, each differing in their world views, values, and customs. The non-Jewish population consists of 16.9% Moslems, 2% Christians, 1.7% Druze, and 3.8% others (Central Bureau of Statistics, 1997–2011). The result is a mosaic of people divided into numerous communities differing in ethnic background, religion, traditions, and values, and characterized by cultural, economic, and social disparities.

Psychological and counseling services in Israel are provided free of charge by educational services, public mental health centers, child development institutes, and psychiatric or general hospitals. These services are financed by governmental and municipal agencies. Psychological treatments not received through the above options are not included in the "health basket," but some are subsidized through complementary health insurance policies provided by Health Maintenance Organizations (HMOs) at hospital clinics and at clinics run by academic institutes. Clearly, however, these limited services are unable to address the growing needs of the entire population.

This chapter discusses the development of the field of psychotherapy in Israel while examining education and training programs, recent approaches, and areas of dispute. The field of counseling is not accredited in Israel, so there are currently no training programs for psychological counseling. However, counseling is provided in the education system (school counseling) and in the occupational field (career counseling).

Brief history of counseling[1] and psychotherapy

Two factors have most significantly influenced the development of psychotherapy in Israel—concurrent international developments in the field and the unique needs of the Israeli population, leading to the development and implementation of innovative approaches.

Prior to the declaration of the State, at a time when the country's Jewish population comprised only about 600,000 people, counseling and psychotherapy services were relatively limited. Attempts made by intellectuals of that period to spread psychoanalytical theory did not gain much public attention, mostly because at the time the Jewish population was struggling for survival and because the prevailing Zionist and socialist ideologies renounced personal aspirations for the common good (Ben-Ari & Amir, 1986; Levinson, 1997).

Following the migration of a group of psychoanalysts from Germany to Israel during the 1930s, psychoanalytic thought began to gradually permeate Israeli awareness. This was manifested in the establishment of the Israel Psychoanalytic Society in 1933/4, the Psychoanalytic Institute in 1934 (The Israel Psychoanalytic Society, 2009), and later in the application of psychoanalytic principles to education and medicine.

The Jewish population's rapid growth in the years following the establishment of Israel required immediate solutions for new immigrants' absorption, occupation, and education, leading to new approaches in counseling and psychotherapy as well as to the development of mental healthcare institutions and educational and welfare services.

The Israel Psychological Association was founded in 1957. During the same year the first Psychology Department was launched at the Hebrew University of Jerusalem. In 1958 a Psychology Department was opened at Bar-Ilan University and later also at Tel Aviv University (1966), Haifa (1966), Beer Sheba, and others.

The 1960s introduced a process of institutionalizing the country's psychological services in various fields including health, education, and welfare. During this period, the three main areas of specialization available in psychology were clinical, educational, and occupational (Levinson, 1997). In addition, the Israel Association of Analytical Psychology was founded by Erich Neumann in 1962. It was also during the 1960s that the family-system therapy approach began to attract professionals. Kaffman (1985), founder of the family therapy approach in Israel, established a national network of family care units, inviting leading international figures including Satir, Whittaker, Andolphi, and especially Minuchin, who trained an entire generation of family therapists (see Elizur, 1998). Eventually family therapy was included in academic curricula, followed by the establishment of the Israeli Association for Marital and Family Therapy and Family life Education (IAMFT) in 1977 (IAMFT, n.d.).

The first psychotherapy training program was opened in 1971 at the Tel Aviv University Medical School (Tel Aviv University, n.d.). The program, intended for certified clinical psychologists, psychiatrists, and clinical social workers, adopted an analytical-dynamic orientation. In later years, additional psychotherapy programs were opened in academic and non-academic institutions alike.

During the 1970s, mental health professionals who traveled abroad to complete their education (due to the very gradual inclusion of psychology PhD programs in Israel), became exposed to new approaches being developed, especially in the United States. The first was the behavioral approach, which was met with a certain level of opposition from the psychoanalytical establishment. It was closely followed by the cognitive approach, which at that time began to take a central position in the world. The Israeli Association for Behavioral Therapy was founded in 1972, later adding the cognitive element to its name, and becoming The Israeli Association for Behavioral-Cognitive Psychotherapies (ITA) (ITA, n.d.).[2]

During the 1980s, the Israeli therapeutic community continued to encounter new issues in therapy. The country had grown, its population matured and birth rates were on the rise. All of these changes brought forth emerging therapeutic issues related to child development, chronic diseases, road accidents, war and terror casualties. During this period, new specializations emerged, including rehabilitation psychology, medical psychology, and developmental psychology (Levinson, 1997). In 1987, "Amcha" was founded (Amcha, n.d.) providing emotional and social support to Holocaust Survivors and their families.

Since the 1990s, groups of psychotherapists have engaged in establishing joint projects of Israeli and Palestinian psychotherapists (for a review see Zelniker, Sarraj, & Hertz-Lazarowitz, 2007). Regrettably, these initiatives are routinely interrupted due to the security situation.

The end of the 20th century and the beginning of the 21st introduced new problems, some of which are characteristic of Western societies in general, while others are more specific to immigrant populations and their special needs. Thus, the therapeutic system was required to provide solutions to social issues such as absorption difficulties, violence, addictions, sexual abuse (Somer, 2005), and personal and family issues, including homosexuality, single-parent families, and issues of individuality in a developing society (see Strenger, 1998; 2004).

War, suicide bombers and missile attacks created additional unique difficulties which also required appropriate interventions. The special needs among these populations stimulated the development of unique therapeutic approaches as well as crisis intervention models (Lahad, 1997) and centers, such as the Community Stress Prevention Center located in the northern border town of Kiryat Shmona (CSPC, n.d.) and Natal—Israel's Trauma Center for Victims of Terror and War (Natal, n.d.). The model developed at Kiryat Shmona has since been widely implemented internationally.[3]

Education programs, accreditation, licensure, and certification

The pursuit of psychotherapy in Israel has not been officially legislated and therefore there is no clear definition of the field,[4] of the professionals authorized to engage in it, or of the required training. This situation has resulted in the fact that a large number of study and training programs have appeared in Israel, with much variability between them.[5]

The first professionals who practiced psychotherapy in Israel were psychiatrists, followed by clinical psychologists. Later on social workers and art therapists began taking advanced programs in psychotherapy. Over the years the field has gained professional prestige and attracted growing interest. Recently additional professionals also wish to work in the field, including family doctors, philosophers, criminologists, coaches, and others.

Currently, psychology is the primary profession offering a comprehensive academic training in psychotherapy. The basic courses required for practicing psychotherapy are included in the MA curricula of all applied disciplines. Each program provides courses dedicated to specific therapeutic approaches relevant for that specialty.

Despite the above, training provided during graduate studies and internship cannot cover the entire scope of knowledge, theoretical developments, and therapeutic techniques. Therefore, many professionals enroll in advanced training programs in psychotherapy. The range of psychotherapy training programs in Israel is not only classified according to the various schools they represent, but also according to their targeted populations, therapeutic framework, therapeutic tools, duration of therapy, and training framework.

Generally speaking, the three central approaches to psychotherapy in Israel include the psychoanalytic-dynamic approach, the cognitive-behavioral approach, and the family-systems approach.

In addition to the Psychoanalytic Institute and the Tel Aviv Institute of Contemporary Psychoanalysis, specific training programs are identified with central theoreticians from the

Psychoanalytic-Dynamic approach such as Jung, Melanie Klein, Winnicott, Kohut, and Lacan, while other programs represent specific schools of thought such as object relations, inter-subjectivity, or relational psychotherapy. Yet other training programs focus on specific pathologies such as primary mental states and incorporate a number of approaches or theoreticians.

A growing number of cognitive-behavioral training programs take place at academic institutes as continuing education programs, while others are held at medical institutions or at public or private institutes. The ITA organizes workshops in the field and hosts local and international experts.

While the majority of psychotherapy programs in Israel focus on individual therapy for adults, there are a number of programs which focus on children and youths, on dyadic relationships, and on group therapy (e.g., Group Psychoanalysis based on Bion).

In terms of accreditation, all psychology programs in universities require accreditation by the Council for Higher Education. This, however, does not apply to the various psychotherapy programs offered in Israel, as these are considered continuing education programs. Study programs in psychotherapy (whether within or outside universities) may choose whether to belong to a professional association such as The Israeli Association for Psychotherapy or The Israeli Association for Psychoanalytic Psychotherapy and to meet their criteria, or function independently.

With regard to licensure, two professional bodies deal with all legal, ethical, and professional issues which concern the vocation and practice of psychology in Israel—the Israel Psychological Association (IPA) and the Council of Psychologists (COP). The former is responsible for formulating and implementing the ethical code for Psychologists while the latter is responsible for implementing the Law of Psychologists (legislated in 1977) and serves as an advisory body to the Minister of Health on all matters related to psychology. The COP nominates members of professional committees responsible for internship programs, training institutions, exams, and qualification of supervisors (for detailed description see Jacoby, 2004).

A psychologist who has completed his MA studies and internship and passed the Ministry of Health examinations is granted a license to practice psychology, including psychotherapy. Psychiatrists and social workers as well as art therapists who wish to practice psychotherapy complete their studies in one of the psychotherapy training programs available throughout the country.

As mentioned above, a "Law of Psychotherapy" has not been legislated in Israel, and therefore, actually, anyone can practice psychotherapy. Paradoxically however, psychology is the only profession in which the practice of psychotherapy has been regulated.[6]

The term "certification" does not apply to the practice of psychotherapy in Israel. However, certain fields of therapy such as family therapy, sexual therapy, and hypnosis require special training. Hypnosis in Israel, for instance, may be practiced only by certified physicians or psychologists and is supervised by the Israeli Hypnosis Association.

Current counseling and psychotherapy theories, processes and trends

Two parallel directions can be identified in the field of psychology in Israel today. One takes place in academia and the second in the field. Not only are these two directions not necessarily compatible, but also the gaps between them are often quite significant, to the point that we can say they represent different world views. For instance, within the academic world there has been a growing demand to adhere to an evidence-based approach to psychotherapy. This demand has been supported by an international committee nominated by the Council for Higher Education to assess psychology curricula in Israel. Its report published in 2009 states that clinical programs should be required to train students to acquire proficiency in at least two evidence-based approaches, including empirically supported treatments (Council for Higher Education, 2008).

Recently, some have raised concerns that the wish for evidence-based treatment may deteriorate into a "tyranny," by which any therapeutic approach not immediately empirically supported becomes disqualified (e.g. Berman, 2010). An opposite "tyranny" is expressed by the professional committees, which are composed mostly of field people, thereby often making it difficult for psychologists who have trained abroad to obtain accreditation. This is mostly relevant for cognitive psychologists who do not meet the committee's training requirements, often considered anachronistic.

As mentioned earlier, the analytical-dynamic approaches to psychology in Israel represent a wide range of theoreticians as can be seen from the variety of study programs in psychotherapy, seminars, advanced studies, and publications. A wide corpus of analytical literature has and is being translated into Hebrew, and professional articles in the field are being published in major local journals and on the website *Hebrew Psychology*.

The cognitive-behavioral approach in Israel has also been following world developments. The currently prevalent therapeutic approach in this field is compatible with the third wave in psychotherapy, which emphasizes the broad constructs of values, spirituality, relationships, and mindfulness (see Yovel, 2009).

In addition to their common constructs which have been outlined by Beck and Ellis, training programs also present more updated therapeutic approaches such as Acceptance and Commitment Therapy, Dialectical Behavior Therapy, Mindfulness-Based Cognitive Therapy, Mindfulness-Based Stress Reduction, Schema Focused Therapy, and others (The New School, n.d.).

Additional developments have taken place in unique directions, well suited to Israeli reality. For instance, training programs have been dedicated to treating trauma and post-trauma patients, while focusing on a number of therapeutic tools including Eye Movement Desensitization and Reprocessing (Shapiro, 2001) and Prolonged Exposure Therapy (Foa, Hembree, & Olasov-Rothbaum, 2007), and on specific approaches such as Cognitive Grief Therapy (Malkinson, 2007). Recent developments in the cognitive sciences, which resulted in a deeper understanding of the damage caused by traumatic brain injury (TBI), have opened the possibility of cognitive rehabilitation for this population (see Hoofien et al., 2011).

Despite the fact that even today we can see remnants of the historical antagonism between the analytical-dynamic and the cognitive-behavioral approaches, parallel processes have been taking place, marking attempts for dialogue and integration between the two (see Berman, 2011). These processes have been initiated mainly by those psychotherapists able to contain the differences between the approaches while also seeing their common aspects, and who are not pressured by ideology, but rather see the benefit of their patients at the forefront of their work. Examples can be seen in discussions currently taking place at online forums such as Ofakim[7] and the Israeli Psychoanalytic Research Group.

The family-systems approach in Israel is represented by a number of therapeutic approaches; the most prominent ones being Strategic System Therapy, Narrative Therapy, and recently also Functional Dialectic System approach (Almagor, 2011). Other empirically supported family-based treatments being used in Israel include: Attachment Based Family Therapy, Multi-dimensional Family Therapy, Emotion Focused Couples Therapy, Imago Therapy and Internal Systems Family-work.

In addition to the approaches presented above, a number of other training programs in psychotherapy can be found in Israel, based on existential (Yalom, 1980) and spiritualistic approaches (Buddhism, Daoism). These, as well as some elements of the narrative approach (see Frank, 1995), are implemented in treatment of patients suffering from terminal diseases. Further, recent years have brought a growing awareness to the body's presence in psychotherapy, leading to the implementation of compatible therapeutic approaches (for instance, Somatic Experiencing or

Focusing). In parallel, researchers and practitioners of the more conservative approaches have begun to discuss the matter in seminars and publications (Jacoby, 2011).

Finally, in line with recent international trends, Positive Psychology has taken its place in Israeli therapeutic thought, although certain people tend to be "swept away" towards this new wave (see Held, 2004).

Indigenous and traditional healing methods

As mentioned above, although psychology as a profession has been regulated by law, the field of psychotherapy is still lacking legislation, thus creating fertile ground for various types of healers.

One of the reasons causing people to opt for these healing methods is due to cultural background. Israel is a multicultural country and in some cultures, seeking psychotherapy is considered taboo and sometimes may reduce the chances of marriage. Thus, for instance, religious people tend to consult with Rabbis, some of whom provide psychological education. Jewish immigrants from Ethiopia and Morocco and also Moslems tend to consult with traditional healers. Israeli Arabs may also consult with their Sheikh[8] with regard to personal, interpersonal, and family problems.

Therapeutic methods used by traditional healers can be classified into actions and objects. "Diagnostic" actions include "reading" coffee and opening tarot cards. "Therapeutic" actions include rubbing oils, administering potions, distributing amulets, and performing healing ceremonies, usually at sacred places bearing a mystical-religious meaning (Ben-Dror, 1993; Minuchin-Itzigsohn, Youngman, & Zara, 1997).

Another specialization in traditional medicine is exorcism (Bilu, 1993). Although exorcism ceremonies originate from traditional healing methods, their principles can be applied to the practice of psychotherapy (Al Krenawi & Graham, 1997; Somer, 1993).

In recent years, in light of influences from Eastern cultures, people returning to Israel from the Far East, often with no professional training in therapy, began offering various "therapies." Among them are a number of charlatans who take advantage of people's plight, for instance, by offering instant healing to people suffering from physical diseases or by using hypnotic suggestions without being trained or licensed to do so. The code of ethics does not apply to these "treatments" and some of them have been exposed by the press as being involved in financial exploitation, dependence, sexual abuse, and even rape.

An additional trend which has become increasingly common in Israel is that of Kabbalah[9] studies. These studies emphasize spiritual growth and are usually held in groups at the various Kabbalah centers established around the country (Kabbalah Center, n.d.). This trend coexists with similar global trends focusing on spiritual growth, often used for coping with emotional and physical distress. Over the years Israel has become a spiritual center with many Kabbalah students from abroad visiting the country, mostly on Jewish holidays and festivities.

Research and supervision

The vast majority of research studies in psychotherapy are conducted within academic institutions and university hospitals. Cooperation between Israeli researchers and their international counterparts is also prevalent.

The combination of external threats and internal tensions tax a high price from individuals in both the emotional and physical domains, thereby transforming Israel into a "stress laboratory" (Breznitz, 1983, p. 269). This condition has in turn influenced the work and research of Israeli mental health professionals. Extensive research has been dedicated to the evaluation of mental and emotional impairments sustained by holocaust survivors (e.g., Gampel & Mazor, 2004; Shmotkin, Blumstein, & Modan, 2003), veterans and prisoners of war (e.g. Lieblich, 1994; Solomon & Shalev, 1995), and victims of terrorist attacks (Witztum & Kotler, 2000), as well as their impact on second and third generations (Bar-On, 1995; Dasberg, 1987; Gampel, 2005; Lev-Wiesel & Amir, 2000). Other studies have focused on the influence of war-related stress on the quality of life among various populations such as young children (Sadeh, Hen-Gral & Tikotzki, 2008), Jews and Arab adolescents (Braun-Lewensohn & Sagy, 2010), immigrants (Slonim-Nevo, Sharaga, & Mirski, 1999), and other population groups including settlement evacuees (Nuttman-Shwartz, 2008; Sagy & Antonovsky, 1986).

The move towards evidence-based psychotherapy has led to research focusing on assessing and comparing the efficacy of therapeutic methods or interventions for targeted populations (e.g. Gilboa-Schechtman et al., 2010). Another research direction focuses on therapist–patient interaction (Ziv-Beiman, 2010). The high cost of psychological treatments and the willingness of public HMO's to participate only in a limited number of sessions have promoted studies on the efficacy of short-term therapy (Shefler, Dasberg, & Ben Shakhar, 1995; Tishby, Assa, & Shefler, 2006).

In fact, many recent studies have proven the efficacy of cognitive-behavioral therapy in treating various psychological disorders (Marom, Gilboa-Schechtman, Mor, & Meijers, 2011). As for research in psychoanalysis, although it still lacks a formalized conceptualization of its central processes, interactions, and outcomes, it has significantly evolved in Israel in recent years. One of the most interesting discussions held at the Israeli Psychoanalytic Research Group (IPRG) was triggered by Schedler's (2010) article and focused on whether finding empirical support for psychoanalytic therapy is possible. This and other discussions held in IPRG and Ofakim serve to enlighten group members, stimulate thought and act as fertile ground for development of new research directions.

Recent years have also seen a substantial rise in the number of qualitative studies in psychotherapy, allowing researchers to gain an intimate perspective on patients' experiences and to learn how they perceive and experience psychotherapeutic processes, what is meaningful to them and which variables do they perceive as curative (Shapira, 2008).

With regard to supervision, the practice of psychology is regulated by the Ministry of Health and requires a master's degree in psychology as well as an internship period supervised by professional committees nominated by the Council of Psychologists.

During their studies, psychology students participate in a 10-month weekly practicum, 2 days a week. Each student works with several patients, and his/her work is closely monitored and supervised by senior psychologists. Weekly personal and group supervision takes place in the field as well as at the university. For advanced study psychotherapy programs, personal and group supervision are also included as part of their basic requirements during studies.

During internship, which lasts for 4 years and takes place at a recognized institution for internship, interns receive constant supervision by at least two supervisors. The number of hours required for internship has been determined in the internship guidelines. Even after completing their exams and obtaining their license, psychologists continue to receive supervision, whether at their work places or privately. Only after 3 years of work as specialists are psychologists authorized to commence the process of qualifying for supervision, which takes 2 years to complete.

In general it can be said that psychology as well as advanced psychotherapy programs and work places (Ministry of Health institutions or at HMOs) in Israel maintain a high level of supervision and ensure that students and practitioners receive the required amount of supervision hours.

Strengths, weaknesses, opportunities, and challenges

The science of psychology, including the field of psychotherapy, is thriving in Israeli universities. The field's strengths can be attributed to the universities' internationally acclaimed researchers, who are recognized for their innovative and solid contributions.[10] International research ties also greatly contribute to reciprocal work, theoretical developments, and updated applications of developments in psychotherapy (e.g. Shahar et al., 2010).

Three main weak points can be noted: the lack of a clear definition of psychotherapy, the absence of legislation, and the lack of sufficient governmental resources to provide psychotherapy to all who need it but cannot afford private care. Owing to the high cost of private therapy, coupled with the fact that there is no legislative control over the profession, patients will often opt for lower-priced "therapeutic" alternatives, in many cases offered by non-professionals.

Israeli reality has dictated circumstances which have made way for opportunities to understand difficulties as well as coping capabilities of the individual, which in turn facilitated an implementation of the knowledge for therapeutic work. While Israel may have been perceived as a stress laboratory, its inhabitants can also be viewed as possessing unique coping resources manifested in hardiness, sense of coherence, optimism, and hope.

Owing to the profusion of cultures in Israel, therapists encounter a variety of populations, exposing them to an ongoing learning process on the complexity of the human spirit and challenging them towards developing therapeutic methods suitable for these populations.

The psychotherapeutic community today, however, continues to face academic, professional, cultural, and social challenges. The academic challenges focus on the development of evaluation and measurement methods of processes taking place in psychotherapy, including deciphering mediating variables which take part in this important process. An especially important challenge is in strengthening the understanding of reciprocal relations existing between psychological and physiological processes. In addition, further investment and study is required towards the development of unique therapeutic measures compatible with technological developments, such as the use of virtual reality (see Wallach & Bar-Zvi, 2007; Wallach, Safir, & Bar-Zvi,2009), internet-based therapy for immobile populations, etc. The professional challenges we face include defining the profession, developing legislation for the field of psychotherapy and setting professional standards according to accepted international ones.

Being a multicultural country committed to the absorption of immigration, Israel is required to conduct an ongoing process of reassessing the unique needs of different cultures and religions, including Ultra-Orthodox Jews (Bilu & Witztum, 1994; Witztum & Bilu, 1994), Bedouins (Al Krenawi, 1999), Arabs (Al Krenawi & Graham, 2000), immigrants from the former Soviet Union (Mirski, 2001, Slonim-Nevo et al., 1999) and from Ethiopia (Youngmann, Minuchin-Itzigsohn, & Barasch, 1999), foreign workers and their families, and others. Cultural challenges include matching therapeutic methods to unique populations and training therapists from all sectors (including Arabs, Bedouins, and Jews of Ethiopian descent), while social challenges are focused on increasing community services accessible for populations having a low socio-economic status and who are unable to pay for private therapy. Recently, as a response to the growing social protest movement in Israel (Warshavsky, 2011), an association has been formed by psychology interns (Psychology Interns Association, n.d.) aimed at improving public psychological services in Israel, striving to achieve high-quality, accessible, available, and affordable services for the entire population.

Future directions

In order to provide quality psychotherapy in Israel it is important to continue to develop the field and to find the right balance between the various prevalent approaches.

One of the main issues being discussed by psychotherapists and researchers in Israel today is the debate over evidence-based vs. tailored psychotherapy. The growing demand for evidence-based therapy is well based scientifically, economically, and consumer-wise. However, even among supporters of this approach, many have expressed their reservations as to the "technical" aspect of some therapies which make use of protocols, arguing that it overlooks the therapeutic process and relationship.

The question is whether each type of psychotherapy needs to meet the sometimes too strict requirements of the evidence-based approach, or that maybe in a world comprising such variability between individuals and cultures, there is enough room also for dialogue between different approaches, integration, or a tailored approach to psychotherapy.

Recently, Prof. Golan Shahar has been appointed as editor of the *Journal of Psychotherapy Integration*, published by the American Psychological Association and sponsored by the Society for the Exploration of Psychotherapy Integration (SEPI). Consequently, Shahar and others have been attempting to promote a dialogue and integration encompassing various therapeutic approaches. The fate of such attempts will be determined over the next few years.

Conclusion

The editors of this book have raised the idea of therapy without borders in the age of globalization. However, experience has taught us that often in order to succeed in therapy, it is necessary to gain specific familiarity with the patient's culture, beliefs, and symbols typical to that culture. The tendency today is to train representatives of different cultural groups, so that they would be able to treat familiar populations, in an attempt to prevent mistakes and injustices resulting from misinterpretations.

Some of the questions currently being discussed by the therapeutic community in Israel are relevant to the entire community of psychotherapists regardless of their physical location. We are hopeful that in the coming years, professionals will succeed in finding the balance between evidence-based and tailor-made psychotherapy, between model-based interventions and a narrative approach based on life stories, between long- and short-term therapies, and between the skill of therapy and its art.

Acknowledgment

The author wishes to thank her colleagues in Israel for their valuable input and support in preparing this chapter.

Notes

1 As explained above, in Israel the field of counseling is not accredited.
2 ITA is a member of the European Association for Behavior and Cognitive Psychotherapies.
3 Teams of trained psychotherapists traveling abroad to assist in coping with severe stress situations such as war, earthquakes, and terrorist attacks.
4 According to Corsini (2000, p. 10), there are over 400 international definitions of psychotherapy.
5 Academic programs in psychotherapy span 2–3 years, while other training programs take only a few months to complete. Some programs admit only clinical psychologists, psychiatrists, and social workers,

others are open to a wider range of professionals having at least an MA degree, and still others are open to more general populations including teachers, counselors, nurses, etc.

6 According to the 1977 Law of Psychologists, only clinical psychologists were permitted to engage in "psychotherapy." As a result, other psychological disciplines which gained recognition in Israel in the following years were permitted to practice "psychological treatment" only. The distinction between the two was never defined, but over the years the term psychotherapy became more prestigious. In recent years, initiatives to revise the law were met by strong opposition from a union of clinical psychologists, who claimed they have a monopoly over the practice of psychotherapy. In 2010 the law was revised by the Israeli Parliament (the Knesset), suggesting that licensed psychologists may practice psychotherapy (Knesset, 2011.)

7 Ofakim is a professional society joining psychologists from the academy and the field with the purpose of promoting a dialogue between science and applied psychology.

8 Sheikh means leader and/or governor. It is commonly used to designate an Islamic scholar who gained this title after completing the basic Islamic school where he became familiar with the laws of the Koran.

9 The Kabbalah is an ancient wisdom aiming to reveal how the universe and all aspects of life work.

10 Prof. Berman has recently won the 2011 Sigourney Award for his contribution to the field of psychoanalysis.

References

Al Krenawi, A. (1999). Explanation of mental health symptoms by the Bedouin-Arab of the Negev. *International Journal of Social Psychiatry*, *45*(1), 56–64.

Al Krenawi, A., & Graham, J. R. (1997). Spirit possession and exorcism: The integration of modern and traditional mental health care systems in the treatment of Bedouin patient. *Clinical Social Work Journal*, *25*, 211–222.

Al Krenawi, A., & Graham, J. R. (2000). Culturally sensitive social work practice with Arab clients in mental health settings. *Health and Social Work*, *25*(1), 9–22.

Almagor, M. (2011). *Functional Dialectic System Approach to Therapy with Individuals, Couples and Families*. Minneapolis, MN: University of Minnesota Press.

Amcha (n.d.). *Amcha's Mission*. Retrieved October 15, 2011 from www.amcha.org/indexEn.htm.

Bar-On, D. (1995). *Fear and Hope. Life Stories of Five Israeli Families of Holocaust Survivors Three Generations in a Family*. Cambridge MA: Harvard University Press.

Ben-Ari, R., & Amir, Y. (1986). Psychology in a developing society. The case of Israel. *Annual Review of Psychology*, *37*, 17–41.

Ben-Dror, M. (1993). *Craftsmen, Healers and Miracle Workers in the Galilee*. Jerusalem: Ariel Publishers (in Hebrew).

Berman, E. (2010). Psychotherapeutic fundamentalism. *Dialogue: Israel Journal of Psychotherapy*, *24*(3), 305–306 (in Hebrew).

Berman, E. (2011). The dialogue is essential: Some thoughts following Shahar's article. *Dialogue: Israel Journal of Psychotherapy*. *25*(3), 288–290 (in Hebrew).

Bilu, Y. (1993). *Without Bounds: The Life and Death of Rabbi Yaacov Wazana*. Jerusalem: The Magnes Press, the Hebrew University (in Hebrew).

Bilu, Y., & Witztum, E. (1994). Cultural sensitivity in psychotherapy: guidelines for working with ultra-orthodox patients. *Dialogue: Israel Journal of Psychotherapy*, *8*(2), 114–119 (in Hebrew).

Braun-Lewensohn, O., & Sagy, S. (2010). Coping resources as explanatory factors of stress reactions during missile attacks: Comparing Jews and Arab adolescents in Israel. *Community Mental Health Journal*, *47*(3), 300–310.

Breznitz, S. (1983). *Stress in Israel*. New York: Van Nostrand Reinhold Company Inc.

Central Bureau of Statistics (1997–2011). *National population census, 2008*. Retrieved October 14, 2011 from www.cbs.gov.il/census/census/pnimi_sub_page_e.html?id_topic=11&id_subtopic=1.

CSPC, Community Stress Prevention Centre (n.d). *Homepage*. Retrieved September 11, 2011 from www.icspc.org/?CategoryID=176.

Corsini, R. J. (2000). Introduction. In R. J. Corsini, & D. Wedding (eds), *Current Psychotherapies* (6th edn) (pp. 1–15). United States: Thomson.

Council for Higher Education (2008). *Evaluation reports of the committee for the evaluation of psychology and behavioral sciences study programs*. August 2009. Retrieved August 30, 2011 from www.che.org.il/template/default_e.aspx?PageId=423.

Dasberg, H. (1987). Psychological distress and Holocaust survivors and offspring in Israel, forty years later: A review. *Israel Journal of Psychiatry and Related Sciences, 24*, 243–256.

Elizur, Y. (1998). The development of family therapy in Israel: a review of major issues and future challenges within the wider socio-political context. *Bamishpacha, 40*, 109–133 (in Hebrew).

Foa, E. B., Hembree, E. A., & Olasov-Rothbaum, B. (2007). *Prolonged Exposure Therapy for PTSD: Emotional Processing of Traumatic Experiences: Therapist Guide.* New York: Oxford University Press.

Frank, A. W. (1995). *The Wounded Storyteller.* Chicago, IL: The University of Chicago Press.

Gampel, Y. (2005). *Ces parents qui vivent a traves moi* [The parents who live through me]. France: Fayard.

Gampel, Y., & Mazor, A. (2004). Intimacy and family links of adults who were children during the Shoah: Multifaceted mutations of the traumatic encapsulations. *Free Associations, 11*(4), 546–568.

Gilboa-Schechtman, E., Foa, E. B., Shafran, N., Aderka, I. M., Powers, M. B., Rachamim, L. & Apter, A. (2010). Prolonged exposure versus dynamic therapy for adolescent PTSD: A pilot randomized controlled trial. *Journal of the American Academy of Child and Adolescent Psychiatry, 49*(10), 1034–1042.

Held, B. S. (2004). The negative side of positive psychology. *Journal of Humanistic Psychology, 44*, 9–46.

Hoofien, D., Barak, O., Bar-Lev, N., Weissman, D., & Shushan, T. (2011). Selection biases and efficacies of three neuropsychological rehabilitation programs: Comprehensive interdisciplinary day-center, pre-vocational workshops and individually tailor-made Programs. *Journal of the International Neuropsychological Society, 17*, 245.

ITA, Israeli Association for Behavioral-Cognitive Psychotherapies (n.d). *Homepage.* Retrieved October 14, 2011 from www.itacbt.co.il.

Israeli Association for Marital and Family Therapy and Family life Education (n.d.). *Homepage.* Retrieved August 18, 2011 from www.mishpaha.org.il/.

Jacoby, R. (2004). Psychology in Israel. In D. Wedding & M. Stevens (eds), *Handbook of International Psychology* (pp. 419–435). New York: Brunner/Routledge.

Jacoby, R. (2011). Psychotherapy: Where has the body gone? Manuscript submitted for publication.

Kaffman, M. (1985). Twenty years of family therapy in Israel: A personal journey. *Family Processes, 24*(1), 113–127.

Knesset (2011). *Legislated laws.* Retrieved September 15, 2011 from www.knesset.gov.il/laws/heb/template.asp?type=1.

Lahad, M. (1997). BASIC Ph: The story of coping resources. In M. Lahad & A. Cohen (eds), *Community Stress Prevention* (pp. 117–145). Kiryat Shmona, Israel: Community Stress Prevention Center.

Lieblich, A. (1994). *Seasons of Captivity: The Inner World of POWs.* New York: New York University Press.

Lev-Wiesel, R., & Amir, M. (2000). Posttraumatic stress disorder symptoms, psychological distress, personal resources and quality of life in four groups of Holocaust child survivors. *Family Processes, 39*(4), 445–459.

Levinson S. (1997). Psychology in Israel. *Psychologia: Israel Journal of Psychology, 1*(1), 109–120 (in Hebrew).

Malkinson, R. (2007). *Cognitive Grief Therapy: Constructing a Rational Meaning to Life Following Loss.* New York: W. W. Norton.

Marom, S., Gilboa-Schechtman, E., Mor, N., & Meijers, J. (2011). *Cognitive Behavioral Therapy for Adults.* Tel-Aviv: Dyonon (in Hebrew).

Minuchin-Itzigsohn, S., Youngmann. R., & Zara, M. (1997). *Meetings with Traditional Healers from the Ethiopian Community in Israel.* Jerusalem: American Jewish Joint Distribution Committee – Israel (in Hebrew).

Mirski, J. (2001). Psychological independence among immigrant adolescents from the former Soviet Union. *Transcultural Psychiatry, 38*(3), 363–373.

Natal, Israel's Trauma Center for Victims of Terror and War (n.d). *Multidisciplinary Trauma Studies Center.* Retrieved October 14, 2011 from www.natal.org.il/English/?CategoryID=287.

Nuttman-Shwartz, O. (2008). From settlers to evacuees: Is forced relocation is a traumatic event? *Group, 31*, 265–280.

Psychology Interns Association (n.d). *News.* Retrieved October 14, 2011 from http:www.mitmachim.com/

Sadeh, A., Hen-Gal, S., & Tikotzki, L. (2008). Young children's reactions to war-related stress: A survey and assessment of an innovative intervention. *Pediatrics, 121*(1), 46–53.

Sagy, S., & Antonovsky, H. (1986). Adolescents' reactions to the evacuation of the Sinai settlements: A longitudinal study. *The Journal of Psychology, 120*(6), 543–556.

Schedler, J. K. (2010). The efficacy of psychodynamic psychotherapy. *American Psychologist, 65*, 98–109.

Shahar, G., Porecerelli, J., Camoo, R., Czarkowsky, K., Magriples, U., Epperson, C. N., & Mayes, L. (2010). Defensive projection, superimposed on simplistic object relations, erode patient-provider relationships in high risk pregnancy: An empirical investigation. *Journal of the American Psychoanalytic Association, 58*, 953–974.

Shapira, A. (2008). *Patients' experiences in psychodynamic therapy. A qualitative study.* Unpublished thesis. Tel Aviv Yaffo Academic College, Tel Aviv Yaffo.

Shapiro, F. (2001). *Eye Movement Desensitization and Reprocessing: Basic Principles, Protocols and Procedures* (2nd edn). London: Guilford Press.

Shefler, G., Dasberg, H., & Ben Shakhar, G. (1995). A randomized controlled outcome and follow-up study of Mann's time limited psychotherapy. *Journal of Consulting and Clinical Psychology, 63*(4), 585–593.

Shmotkin, D., Blumstein, Z., & Modan, B. (2003). Tracing long-term effects of early trauma: a broad – scope view of Holocaust survivors in late life. *Journal of Consulting and Clinical Psychology, 71*(2), 223–234.

Slonim-Nevo, V., Sharaga, Y., & Mirski, J. (1999). A culturally sensitive approach to therapy with immigrant families: The case of Jewish emigrants from the former Soviet Union. *Family Processes, 38*, 445–462.

Solomon, Z., & Shalev, A. Y. (1995). Helping victims of military trauma. In J. R. Freedy & S. E. Hobfoll (eds). *Traumatic stress: From theory to practice* (pp. 241–261). New York: Plenum Press.

Somer. E. (1993). Possession Syndrome in a hysterionic personality: Exorcism and Psychotherapy. *Dialogue: Israel Journal of Psychotherapy, 3*(1), 40–47 (in Hebrew).

Somer, E. (2005, February). *Psychotherapy in Israel in face of reality: Road accidents, violence, rape, terror and the expectation towards efficient treatment.* Conference presentation at the Psychotherapy 2005 Conference organized by the Israeli Association for Psychotherapy, Herzelia.

Strenger, C. (1998). *Individuality, the impossible project.* Madison, WI: International Universities Press. Paperback Edition. Reprint: New York: Other Press, 2002.

Strenger, C. (2004). *The Designed Self.* Hillsdale, NJ: The Analytic Press.

Tel Aviv University. (n.d.). *Sackler Faculty of Medicine, Program of Psychotherapy.* Retrieved October 14, 2011 from http://medicine.tau.ac.il/index.php/psychotherapy/psychotherapy.

The Israel Psychoanalytic Society. (2009). *Homepage.* Retrieved October 14, 2011 from www.psychoanalysis.org.il/default.aspx?lang=en-US.

The New School (n.d.). *Homepage.* Retrieved October 14, 2011 from www.TheNewSchool.co.il.

Tishby O., Assa, T., & Shefler, G. (2006). Patient progress during two time-limited psychotherapies as measured by Rutgers psychotherapy process scale. *Psychotherapy Research, 16*(1), 89–90.

Wallach, H. S., & Bar-Zvi, M. (2007). Virtual reality assisted treatment of flight phobia. *The Israel Journal of Psychiatry and Related Sciences, 44*(1), 29–32.

Wallach, H. S., Safir, M. P., & Bar-Zvi, M. (2009). Virtual reality cognitive behavior therapy for public speaking anxiety. A randomized clinical trial. *Behavior Modification, 20*(5), 1–28.

Warshavsky, E. (2011) *Israel Social Protest* [Video file], July 26. Retrieved October 14, 2011 from www.youtube.com/watch?v=EdiHr9NycgE.

Witztum, E., & Bilu, Y. (1994). Cultural sensitivity in psychotherapy: Guidelines for working with ultra-orthodox patients. *Dialogue: Israel Journal of Psychotherapy, 8*(3), 190–199 (in Hebrew).

Witztum, E., & Kotler, M. (2000). Historical and cultural construction of PTSD in Israel. In A. Shalev, R. Yehuda, & A. Mcfarlane (eds). *International Handbook of Human Response to Trauma* (pp. 103–114). Dordrecht, Netherlands: Kluwer Academic Publishers.

Yalom, I.D. (1980). *Existential Psychotherapy.* New York: Basic Books.

Youngmann, R., Minuchin-Itzigsohn, S., & Barasch, M. (1999). Manifestation of emotional distress among Ethiopian immigrants in Israel: Patient's and the clinician's perspective, *Transcultural Psychiatry, 36*, 45–63.

Yovel, I. (2009). Acceptance and Commitment Therapy and the new generation of cognitive behavioral treatments. *Israel Journal of Psychiatry, 46*(4), 304–309

Zelniker, T., El Sarraj, E., & Hertz-Lazarowitz, R. (2007). Palestinian-Israeli cooperation on mental health training: Gaza Community Mental Health Program and Tel-Aviv University 1993–2007. In J. Kuriansky (ed.), *Beyond Bullets and Bombs: Grassroots Peace Building between Israelis and Palestinians* (pp. 307–313). Westpoint, CT: Praeger Publishers.

Ziv-Beiman, S. (2010). *Therapist Self-disclosure: Its Effects on Treatment Outcome and Patient Perception of the Therapist.* Unpublished dissertation. Tel Aviv University, Tel Aviv.

33

COUNSELING AND PSYCHOTHERAPY IN LEBANON

Towards a Lebanese framework of psychology

Brigitte Khoury and Sarah Tabbarah

Introduction

Lebanon is a small country in western Asia, on the eastern shore of the Mediterranean. In 2009, the Lebanese population was estimated to be at around 4 million people (World Health Organization [WHO], 2009).There is no state religion in Lebanon; however, the republic recognizes 17 religious sects of Christianity, Islam, and Judaism (Lebanese Global Information Center [LGIC], 2005). The capital of the republic of Lebanon is Beirut, and the official language is formal Arabic. Lebanon's geographical location between the orient and the occident give it a cosmopolitan character and a rich multicultural heritage (Embassy of Lebanon, 2002). Owing to its location, the country has been considerably influenced by the West. Many Lebanese study in French or English schools and universities, and are versed in the three languages Arabic, French, and English.

Psychology's presence in academia has long been seen since it was one of the earliest majors taught at a number of universities in Lebanon. It is also present in the clinical setting, in hospitals, private clinics, and other treatment centers. Counselors are employed in most of the main universities in Lebanon. They are also found at the school level. In Lebanon, counselors deal mostly with student populations at schools and universities whereas the clinical psychologist's clientele is more diverse and not limited to these settings. Although both clinical psychology and counseling involve conducting psychotherapy, clinical psychologists work in settings where there is a higher level of severity and/or chronicity of mental illness, such as psychiatry units in general hospitals, community mental health centers, psychiatric hospitals, and governmental agencies. Despite the long presence of psychology in Lebanon, legislation and guidelines for practice are still missing, hence making it impossible to control all psychological practices in the field.

Lebanese society has been more aware that psychological practice is different from psychic readings, astrology, religious rituals, and others (Attieh, 2008). Psychology has developed as a path of its own, independent of medicine. Although medicine, specifically psychiatry, has been known to be the treatment of choice in treating mental disturbances, there is more awareness of the importance of psychological treatment either standing on its own, or complementing the medical treatment. Most models of treatment in Lebanon follow the biopsychosocial model of treatment; hence the presence of psychologists as part of the treatment team is becoming an essential component for any service provider. This recent movement gave more credibility to the field and specifically to psychotherapy.

The present chapter will provide a brief history of the field of clinical psychology and counseling in Lebanon in addition to a description of its current status and future prospects.

Brief history of counseling and psychotherapy

The history of psychology in Lebanon is closely related to the history of psychiatry and the establishment of the first asylum for the mentally ill in Lebanon, Syria, and the Middle East in the late 19th century by the Swiss Quaker Theophilus Waldmeir (Ichimura & Kemsley, 2002). Fifty years later, the Psychiatric Hospital of the Cross opened its doors, and is still present now, providing inpatient and residential care to individuals who need it. Around the same time, the first psychology program in Lebanon was founded at the American University of Beirut, closely followed by the other leading universities, such as St. Joseph University (established by the order of Jesuits) and the Lebanese University (Chamoun, 1984). In the early 1980s, the Institute for Development, Research, Advocacy, and Applied Care (IDRAAC) and its sister institution the Medical Institute of Neuropsychological Disorders (MIND) were established and contributed significantly to mental healthcare and research in Lebanon and the rest of the Arab region (Medical Institute of Neuropsychological Disorders [MIND], n.d.; Syndicate of Hospitals, 2011). Over the years, the presence of psychology has penetrated many areas such as schools, hospitals, institutions for the mentally ill, special treatment centers, and industry (Saigh, 1984; Khoury, 1992; Salloum, 1992).

Psychology in Lebanon came from two perspectives (Attieh, 2008). The first perspective states that mental disorders were the specialty of psychiatrists with the majority of them combining medication and psycho-education for treatment. However, most of the time, the treatment they provided was only through medication, although some did try to guide their patients. There were not enough guidance counselors and psychologists present early in the 20th century to draw the dividing line between psychiatry and psychology. Their presence was found only minimally in schools and with juvenile delinquents. The second direction that psychology in Lebanon took was that of guidance and counseling psychological issues in regular schools and social institutions for special needs. Family therapy, adult psychotherapy, and geriatric therapy came at a later time around the 1950s and 1960s.

The many civil wars and multiple crises that Lebanon has been through in the past 30 years made psychologists more involved with field interventions, both individual and group, providing consultations, contacting victims of war and violence and offering them services, helping at guidance and counseling centers, and addressing addictions and delinquency (Attieh, 2008). These interventions were either done in private clinics or in hospitals, or in specialized centers for mental health services. Psychologists worked also in orphanages, homes for the elderly, and centers for handicapped persons. It was clear that the war and the range of service needs which came out of it helped in promoting the field of clinical and counseling psychology and raised awareness to these needs with the general population.

Starting in the 1970s and 1980s, but mostly after the end of the civil war in 1992, a number of universities held multiple seminars and conferences to find out how psychological science can meet the people's demands by assessing their psychological needs and increasing the credibility of the field (Attieh, 2008). These seminars and conferences presented the issue of psychotherapy as an independent profession aside from psychiatry, focusing not only on mental disorders but also on academic problems, deviant behavior, aggression, and delinquency. One main goal of these meetings was to spread awareness about the behavioral and learning dimensions of psychological disorders and how they can be treated. Another aim was to allow the networking of professionals and to call for the establishment of specialized centers for assessment and treatment.

Throughout the years, many societies and associations were established in Lebanon to acknowledge, expand, and regulate the profession of clinical psychology and counseling (Attieh, 2008). One such society is the "Société des Practiciens en Psychothérapie et Consultants" (SPC), which was founded in 1960 at the Lebanese University. It aims to unify practice, despite the differences in modalities between practitioners and its own inclination towards psychoanalysis. The Lebanese Society for Psychological Studies is the second oldest society after the SPC. This society is interested in the clinical practice of psychology and aims to communicate with other Arabs to widely spread an Arab psychology. Moreover, it is connected with the Arab psychology database "Arabpsynet." The Lebanese Society for Psychoanalysis was first established in 1980 at the St. Joseph University by Dr. Mounir Chamoun (who also founded "Le cercle d'Études Psychanalytiques" [CEP] in 2000) (Louis D. French Institute of Intercultural Anthropology, 2004), but shut down during the Lebanese civil war which took place from 1975 to 1991. After the war ended, in 1995 it was revived and renamed as the Arab Center for Psychopathological and Psychoanalytical Research (ACPPR). The ACPPR is complemented with SPC. The Lebanese Psychological Association (LPA) was established in 2003 by university professors and clinicians (among them is the founding president, Dr. Brigitte Khoury, main author of this chapter) representing leading universities and community psychologists, to support and strengthen the academic face of psychology as a preliminary step towards regulating professional practice (Attieh, 2008). The LPA played a major role in raising the awareness of the public about mental health issues, working on setting up rules and regulations of practice with governmental bodies, and pulling together the majority of psychologists into a network of Lebanese professionals. More recently in 2011, Khoury also established the Arab Center for Research, Training and Policy Making at the American University of Beirut Medical Center, which ultimately aims to build capacity for mental healthcare and research in the region.

Currently, the presence of psychologists is found in a range of services and settings, where most of them follow the Western scientist-practitioner model. They are mostly found in private clinics, hospitals, academic institutions, schools, and university counseling centers, as well as centers for specialized care (i.e., cognitively challenged, physically challenged). A large number work in schools, as well as in non-governmental organizations. Some work on a consulting basis under the request of national or international institutions. Nowadays psychologists are also found in the military, industry, companies, businesses, research services, legal system, and other areas where their skills are needed (Attieh, 2008).

Counselor education programs, accreditation, licensure, and certification

Different universities for higher education offer degrees in graduate (MA) and postgraduate studies (Doctor of Philosophy, Psychological Practitioner Diploma) in addition to the undergraduate degree (BA, license) (Attieh, 2008; American University of Beirut [AUB], 2009; Beirut Arab University [BAU], 2009; Chamoun, 1992; Haigazian University [HU], 2009; Khoury & Tabbarah, 2012; Lebanese American University [LAU], 2009; Notre Dame University [NDU], 2008; University of Balamand [UOB], n.d.; Saint Esprit University of Kaslik [USEK], 2009; USJ, 2009).The type of training and its quality depend on the training site, the supervisor, and his/her experience.

Most of these universities follow a Western education system and teach clinical as well as educational psychology. For instance, St. Joseph University (USJ) and the Lebanese University (LU) follow a French curriculum whereas the American University of Beirut (AUB), the Lebanese American University, Hagazian Univeristy (HU), Notre Dame University (NDU), and University of Balamand (UOB) follow an American curriculum. Most universities teach psychology at undergraduate and graduate levels with a few offering postgraduate degrees (such as St. Joseph University, St. Esprit University of Kaslik, University of Balamand, Beirut Arab university, and the Lebanese university). None of the universities so far offers accredited clinical psychology programs. The University of Balamand is currently putting together a professional master degree in cognitive and behavior therapy (Institute for Development Research Advocacy & Applied Care [IDRAAC], n.d.). The Psychology Department, at the American University of Beirut is also in the process of establishing a graduate program in Clinical Psychology, with a master's degree as its terminal degree (T. El-Jamil, personal communication, September 16, 2011).

Licensing and accreditation have been some of the main problems for the field of psychology in Lebanon. Licensing requirements, qualifying exams, exams of practice, or revision of credentials are non-existent. There is no official mechanism that has been put in place to control for malpractice or professional misconduct (Saigh, 1984). Up until now, the work of clinical psychologists has not been recognized by the Ministry of Health (Salloum, 1992).

These matters are still unresolved due to the complexity of the matters, the variety of programs and degrees seeking equivalence. In addition, it has been quite difficult for a body of psychologists to agree on common licensing and practice guidelines regulations despite the many attempts to draw guidelines of practice and licensing regulations. In 2005–2006, a task force made up of psychiatrists and psychologists from the Lebanese Psychological Association joined forces to draft a document discussing guidelines for the practice of psychology. It had to be presented to the Order of Physicians (the licensing body for physicians and hence the representative of all health matters to the government), which would endorse it and present it to the Lebanese parliament. Its aim was to establish clear rules and regulations for the practice of psychology in Lebanon and to have a regulating body governing it. This project was delayed, primarily because of the fragile political and security situation in the country. Recently, it has been revived and it is only a matter of time before clear guidelines for practice are established (Khoury, 2010).

A psychology governing board is needed in order to ensure the quality of services provided to clients (Attieh, 2008). It also sets the minimum degree necessary for professional practice, irrespective of the university guidelines or the country's culture. The board sets rules of practice and establishes doctor–patient relationship rules based on human rights and integrity and the code of honor for the profession. Legislation is needed in Lebanon to protect the title of "psychologist," in order to prevent it from being assumed by ineligible persons. So far Lebanon has no regulating body for the profession of psychology. The Lebanese Psychological Association is working closely with the Ministry of Public Health and the health commission in parliament in order to establish a certification process and practice guidelines (L. Dirani, personal communication, September 20, 2011).

Current counseling and psychotherapy theories, processes and trends

As mentioned previously, most psychotherapists in Lebanon are either trained in the West or adhere to a Western model of treatment. Hence many schools of thought and orientation are found and practiced among clinicians, such as psychoanalysis, cognitive-behavioral, gestalt, and humanistic therapies. Many clinicians also are trained in different modalities of therapy such as individual, couples, family, and child and adolescent, which are applied following the clinician's theoretical background and training (Chamoun, 1992).

A large number of psychologists in Lebanon are trained under the French school of thought and travel to France for their graduate studies, hence making them mostly trained in psychoanalysis and practicing psychoanalytic psychotherapy. In the last 10 years, however, and after the civil war ended, the country witnessed an influx of therapists trained in North America and therefore following more the cognitive-behavioral theory and humanistic theories. A few of them even follow the Gestalt school of thought and use it in their practice (Attieh, 2008).

Although the education and training of many clinical psychologists and counselors is Western based, care is taken to adapt these learned theories and psychotherapeutic techniques to the Lebanese context. The importance of the social context in the lives of Arab patients is highly recognized by therapists in the region. A full assessment of contextual factors (e.g., individual-family interdependence/independence, traditional/liberal gender role orientation, cultural beliefs and values, sources of external pressures, sources of support, status of the client in the family, efficiency of social coping mechanisms, religiosity) that would affect the psychotherapeutic process is recommended when dealing with Arab patients. Given the centrality of the family in the lives of Arabs, preventing the patient from getting into harsh confrontations with family members is advised (Dwairy, 2006). An assessment of contextual factors such as intra-familial conflicts, intra-familial coalitions, and status of the client in the family usually guides the treatment and enables the therapist to help the patients negotiate with the family effectively using culturally appropriate methods (Dwairy, 2006). Sometimes, the therapist dealing with Arab patients involves family members in the treatment and treats them as allies instead of shutting them out and risking having them as obstacles to the therapeutic process (Khoury, 2012). Religion is another aspect of the lives of Arab patients that has been emphasized and that may need to be taken into account and incorporated in the treatment (Dwairy, 2006).

With the increasing availability of mental health professionals following different theoretical orientations and the heightened awareness of cultural issues pertinent to the therapeutic process, the future of psychotherapy and counseling in Lebanon seems promising. Moreover, an atmosphere of continuous learning is being promoted among Lebanese clinical psychologists who are making a noticeable effort to bring their community closer through the societies and holding conferences and workshops throughout the year. They are also reaching out to one another through the internet by establishing a Facebook group for the Lebanese Psychological Association and inviting all students, graduates, practitioners, and others who are part of the field, whether in Lebanon or abroad, to join the group and communicate and share information.

Indigenous and traditional healing methods

People in Lebanon find alternatives for treatment of their psychological disturbances other than psychotherapy and counseling. Some resort to herbal medications, a movement that has gained huge momentum and media coverage in recent years. One of the oldest traditions of healing has been Arab medicine, which relies mostly on herbs and natural products to treat any ailment. It also applies to some psychological problems. Another group has turned to religious answers and so-called "religious" practices to get them through their hardship. These practices exist for both Christians and Muslims and have more to do with folkloric traditions and popular beliefs than religion. These alternative cures may range from the acceptable to the incredible.

There has been a dramatic increase in "religious" healers and their clients in Lebanon (Al-Issa & Al-Subaie, 2004). The seer and the fortune teller combine diagnosis and treatment. An "imam" or "mullah" is a caretaker of a mosque who serves as the leader of group prayers or as a teacher. His treatment consists of reading Koranic verses over the patient or doing "maho," which refers to writing verses in saffron on a paper to be soaked in water for the patient to drink or wash certain body parts. This person deals with behavioral and emotional problems more than physical ones. He also may perform exorcisms.

Many universal factors are involved in the therapeutic process. These include the healer's shared worldview with his/her patient, labeling of the disease, the attribution of the cause of the disease, the expectations of the patient, and the importance of suggestion (Al-Issa & Al-Subaie, 2004). Muslims are mainly guided in medical matters by their holy book, the Koran, and the prophet-tradition, the "Hadith." Arabs were later influenced by the traditions of the countries they conquered as well as their supernatural beliefs, magical practices, and miraculous healings. These are entirely independent of Islam. Seeking help from sorcerers, diviners, astrologers, fortune-tellers, and the like is forbidden in Islam because it contradicts the Islamic belief in God's absolute knowledge and power of healing ("tawheed"). Most native healing is believed to be heretic innovations by Islam.

One explanation of physical and mental illness that has been present throughout the history of humanity is spirit possession. The evil eye is also present across a number of cultures, including the Middle East, and with Christians and Muslims alike (Al-Issa & Al-Subaie, 2004). It is attributed to symptoms involving the afflicted person's health, family life, and social functioning. Envy and jealousy are major emotions accompanying the evil eye (Al-Issa & Al-Subaie, 2004). It is also powered by the magical law of association by contrast, meaning that praising or admiring of something may cause the opposite to occur.

For Muslims, the best protection from the evil eye is to turn to God and recite a specific verse of the Koran (Al-Issa & Al-Subaie, 2004). For Christians, the use of topaz beads (also used by Muslims), little crosses and Christian icons of saints can be used for preventive as well as curative measures by having the person wear them on a chain, or attached to clothes by a safety pin (Al-Issa & Al-Subaie, 2004). Other practices include throwing dust after suspected perpetrators or cracking salt in fire. Another popular method in Lebanon to counteract the effects of the evil eye is to have the native healer pour a melted piece of lead into a bowl of water over the head of the afflicted person. The lead make as cracking sound when it touches the water and solidifies in the image of the perpetrator. The safest precaution is to prevent exposure altogether. Other precautionary measures include keeping things or children dirty so they do not invite admiration of others, and readily handing over the admired object to protect from the eye's evil consequences.

The jinn are supernatural creatures that are different from humans (Al-Issa & Al-Subaie, 2004). One type is the "afrit" and it has remarkable strength. When it possesses a person, the person becomes manic, strong, and brave. A second type is the "shaytan" (Satan). It influences thinking and behavior and is responsible for the possessed person having obsessive thoughts or deviant or sexual behavior (such as wet dreams). The practice of sorcery is forbidden in Islam and Christianity (Al-Issa & Al-Subaie, 2004). Sorcerers claim they control the jinn by offerings and actions that violate religious traditions. Treatment of disorders caused by jinn possession is either exorcising them or establishing a symbiotic or working relationship with them.

The World Health Organization (WHO) conducted a survey of 17 countries to assess the mental health services they used for anxiety, mood, and substance disorders (Wang et al., 2007). Results showed that over half the respondents (53%) resorted to general medical services for treatment, while only 18% of the Lebanese respondents declared using mental health specialists for treatment of problems related to emotions, nerves, mental health, or use of alcohol or drugs. Eleven percent of respondents sought services provided by religious or spiritual advisors, social workers, or counselors in any setting other than a specialized mental health setting.

Herbal remedies have been also used to cure mental illness. St. John's Wort is one of the most common herbs used in treating anxiety and depression (Kallassi & Tabbarah, 2006). It has been used throughout history. St. John's Wort has shown good results in treating mild to moderate depression. It also has also shown comparable results to other drugs and is effective in the short term. One institution in Lebanon that uses herbal remedies is Life Long. An interviewed herbalist practicing at this center uses valerian root and St. John's Wort to treat anxiety (Kallassi & Tabbarah, 2006). He treats depression using St. John's Wort and cayenne pepper. The herbalist claimed that using herbal remedies is very safe and suggested that patients observe effects almost immediately. Treatments usually last around 6 months and the ultimate aim is to stop using Western medicines altogether.

Research and supervision

The importance of research in psychology has recently increased with the establishment of research centers in psychology. Two main centers are IDRAAC, which is affiliated with the St. George Hospital, and the Center for Behavioral Research, hosted at AUB. They are both strong advocates of research and have produced many important projects in the field (Khoury & Tabbarah, 2012). A new center was also recently established at the American University of Beirut Medical Center (AUBMC), namely the Arab Center for Research, Training and Policy Making in Mental Health. This center is directed by Dr. Brigitte Khoury and ultimately aims to enhance mental healthcare and research in the region. This center received initial funding from the WHO and from the Faculty of Medicine at AUB for its establishment.

Research is often emphasized in academic settings and as a requirement for promotion of faculty members, making it an essential part of the academic life and curricula. Researchers at the university level conduct national or regional studies and may also participate in international projects. Most research adopts a quantitative approach relying primarily on the use of surveys. Experimental clinical research is mostly found in hospital settings or medical centers. The validation and standardization of psychological instruments has increasingly become a necessity and caught the interest of many mental health researchers.

Besides academic milieux and the research centers mentioned above, research in psychology is still lagging behind due to lack of funding and to the lack of a research culture in the Middle East in general and in Lebanon in particular. Researchers seek various funds at the national, regional, and international level. The National Council for Scientific Research is a funding body located in Lebanon that supports social sciences research. Most regional funding sources do not clearly specify mental health as one of their priorities but they could be useful for certain types of project that involve capacity building and development. Examples of regional funders are the Qatar Foundation and the King Faisal Foundation (King Faisal Foundation, 2011; Qatar Foundation, 2011).

Supervision is one of the main criteria in the training of practitioners in psychology in Lebanon. Although the requirements vary depending on the program, it is found at varying degrees in all programs. Supervisors are primarily senior psychologists in the field or faculty members from the academic programs students are enrolled in. Psychiatrists are present to a lesser extent in some programs. Owing to the lack of clear practice guidelines, supervision of psychology trainees is not homogeneous and varies by academic program and training site.

Strengths, weaknesses, opportunities, and challenges

One of the main strengths of the field of psychology in Lebanon is the variety of academic programs and curricula that exist and that provide a rich heterogeneity in the training of psychologists. The combination of American, French, and Arab schools of thought in psychology provides a variety in content and process and allows for a dialogue among different professionals to resolve mental health issues. As a result, effort is being made to raise awareness about the need for psychology in Lebanon. This is accomplished by the regular participation of psychologists in the media, community outreach, government lobbying, and by establishing associations and societies for psychology. This exposure and normalization of psychological issues encourages those in need to seek help. It also fights the stigma that equates seeking therapy with being crazy and makes people realize the depth and breadth of the field of psychology and all the services that it can offer. Another strength that is worth mentioning is the increasing interest of Lebanese psychologists to establish societies and associations aimed at enhancing communication and collaboration between the members of the field and regulating their activities.

A major weakness in Lebanon's clinical psychology field is that it suffers from the lack of having an "Arab psychology framework" where theories, diagnostic categories, and treatment options are based on the Arab culture, language, traditions, and value system (Khoury, 2010). A framework where family and religion, the two pillars of Arab and Lebanese society, are taken into account and given importance in clinical intervention, and psychological interpretations is needed. As highlighted earlier, the work of psychologists in Lebanon is based on their Western training, which is based on Western theories, and diagnostic and treatment modalities, which may sometimes lead to misinterpretation, misunderstanding, and mistreatment of individuals seeking psychological help. Such a framework is essential in moving psychology forward in the Middle East and Lebanon, whether on an educational, research, or clinical level.

With the increasing global focus on the need to reduce the mental health treatment gap worldwide especially in low- and middle-income countries (Kohn, Saxena, Levav, & Saraceno, 2004; Okasha & Karam, 1998; World Health Organization, 2011), building capacity for mental healthcare in the region has become increasingly urgent. Funding bodies across the world are called to invest in mental health research to enhance the delivery of mental health services in developing countries (Tomlinson, Rudan, Saxena, Swartz, Tsai, & Patel, 2009). This is a conducive environment for change, and Lebanese mental health specialists should seize that opportunity to strengthen their mental healthcare system. As an example, one of the main aims of the Arab Center for Research, Training, and Policy Making is to reduce the mental health gap by building capacity for mental healthcare and research.

An important challenge facing Lebanese mental health researchers is the lack of assessment and measurement tools which are standardized on a Lebanese population. Many Western tests are translated then used, creating problems in their use, obtaining results, and their interpretation. Lack of funding and lack of standardized tests has been one of the major obstacles which psychologists face. Though many clinicians are aware of this problem and use such instruments with caution, it is imperative to have the proper tools which reflect real results with Lebanese individuals.

Another challenge in the field is the confusion among psychologists about the nature of their expected roles and responsibilities (Attieh, 2008). That is why psychologists start to fulfill multiple roles beyond their specialties which often lead to their frustration and problems with their employers. For instance, child clinical psychologists in Lebanon are often confronted with the need to fulfill the role of a social worker in addition to that of a therapist when dealing with young patients and their families. This adds a lot of pressure to these psychologists who end up working overtime and being underpaid.

Future directions

The field of psychology is still at its beginning in Lebanon, but many institutional and personal initiatives look promising for its growth. The main factors playing a role in that direction are the well-trained professionals who are raising people's awareness and are the best ambassadors in the field and its guardians from charlatans and self-claimed healers. They are raising the standards of care and work with the people's best interest in mind. The need to collaborate and join forces among each other as well as with other complementary professions is an important step in the recognition of the field of psychology as an important one in the field of health services. Hopefully this joining of professionals will eventually result in an Arab framework, and Lebanese framework of psychology, which takes culture into consideration. The fact that psychologists are entering more work areas, not just the traditional ones, is an indication of the growth and recognition of the field.

Conclusion

The presence of clinical psychology and counseling in Lebanon is becoming more apparent as time passes. The increase in awareness of the services that psychology has to offer and the increase in recognition of the existence of the career have helped in destigmatizing the field. Granted, there is still much to accomplish in the realm of academics and the government. The move from psychology associations to a professional board with guidelines and regulations is a necessary step in helping professionals do their work properly and to help protect the public. One hopes that if the advancement of the field of psychology continues as such, more professional clinical and counseling psychology will soon arise.

References

American University of Beirut. (2009). Faculty of arts and sciences department of social and behavioral sciences psychology program. Retrieved December 3, 2009, from http://staff.aub.edu.lb/~websbs/Psychology/index.htm

Al-Issa, I. & Al-Subaie, A. (2004). Native healing in Arab Islamic societies. In U. P. Gielen, J. M. Fish & J. G. Draguns (eds), *Handbook of Culture, Therapy, and Healing* (pp. 343–365). Mahwah, NJ: Lawrence Erlbaum Associates.

Attieh, N. (2008). *Current developments of psychological practice in Lebanon: A plea toward certification and formal licensing.* Retrieved June 24, 2009, from www.arabpsynet.com/HomePage/Psy-books.htm [in Arabic].

Beirut Arab University. (2009). Faculty of arts department of psychology. Retrieved December 3, 2009, from www.bau.edu.lb/department.php?id=89&&faculty=5.

Chamoun, M. (1984). Start of psychology in Lebanon. *Liban la memoire culturelle jalons et tournants*, 49–61.

Chamoun, M. (1992). Quarante ans de psychologie au Liban [Forty years of psychology in Lebanon]. *Psyché, 1*(1), 9–21.

Dwairy, M. (2006). *Counseling and Psychotherapy with Arabs and Muslims.* New York: Teachers College Press.

Embassy of Lebanon. (2002). *Profile of Lebanon.* Retrieved August 15, 2011, from www.lebanonem bassyus.org/country_lebanon/history.html

Haigazian University. (2009). *Why choose HU.* Retrieved December 3, 2009, from www.haigazian.edu.lb/ProspectiveStudents/Pages/Overview.aspx

Ichimura, J. & Kemsley, R. (2002). Lebanon hospital for mental and nervous disorders. In *Mundus: Gateway to missionary collections in the United Kingdom.* Retrieved June 24, 2009, from www.mundus.ac.uk/cats/4/1065.htm.

Institute for Development, Research, Advocacy, & Applied Care. (n.d.). *Clinical training.* Retrieved August 15, 2011, from www.idrac.org.lb/sub.aspx?ID=179&mid=59&pid=31&secid=31

Kallassi, P. & Tabbarah, S. (2006). *Alternative healing practices in the treatment of anxiety and depression.* Unpublished paper, American University of Beirut, Beirut, Lebanon.

Khoury, B. (2010, March). *The future of psychology in the Arab region: The need for an Arab framework.* Paper presented at the 1st International Conference for Psychological Sciences and Applications: Why we do what we do. Al Ain University, United Arab Emirates.

Khoury, B. & Tabbarah, S. (2012). The history of psychology in Lebanon. In D. Baker (ed.), *Oxford Handbook of the History of Psychology*. Oxford University Press.

Khoury, B. (2012). Case study of a female with anxiety and depression: Psychotherapy within a Lebanese cultural framework. In S. Poyrazli & C. Thompson (eds), *International Case Studies in Mental Health* (pp. 85–100). Thousand Oaks, CA: Sage Publications.

Khoury, M. (1992). Le psychologue dans l'institution pour les enfants handicapés mentaux [The psychologist in the institution for mentally handicapped children], *Psyché, 1*(1), 23–24.

King Faisal Foundation (2011). Philanthropic grants. Retrieved September 21, 2011 from www.kff.com/EN01/KFF/KFFPhilanthropicGrants.html

Kohn, R., Saxena, S., Levav, I., & Saraceno, B. (2004). The treatment gap in mental health care. *Bulletin of the World Health Organization, 82*(11), 858–866.

Lebanese American University. (2009). *Academics*. Retrieved December 3, 2009, from www.lau.edu.lb/academics/programs/ba-psychology.php

Lebanese Global Information Center. (2005). *General information*. Retrieved March 26, 2010, from www.lgic.org/en/lebanon_info.php

Louis D. French Institute of Intercultural Anthropology Chair. (2004). *Programme de la conference internationnale "Le defi euro-mediterraneen: pour un partenariat des deux rives"* [The euro-Mediterranean challenge: for a partnerships on both sides]. Retrieved 19 August, 2011, from www.caic.usj.edu.lb/pdf/defiem.pdf

Medical Institute for Neuropsychological Disorders. (n.d). Staff. Retrieved August 15, 2011, from www.mindclinics.org/Staff.aspx?pageid=9026

Notre Dame University. (2008). Faculty of humanities, department of social and behavioral sciences. Retrieved December 3, 2009, from www.ndu.edu.lb/academics/fhum/dsbs/ba_psychology.htm.

Okasha, A. & Karam, E. (1998). Mental health services and research in the Arab world. *Acta Psychiatrica Scandinavica, 98*(5), 406–413.

Qatar Foundation. (2011). Qatar National Research Fund. Retrieved September 21, 2011 from www.qf.org.qa/science-research/science-research-institutions/qatar-national-research-fund

Saigh, P.A. (1984). School psychology in Lebanon. *Journal of School Psychology, 22*, 233–238.

Salloum, S.R. (1992). La psychologie au Liban: Formation des psychologues et domains d'application [Psychology in Lebanon: Training of psychologists and areas of applications]. *Psyché, 1*(1), 35–51.

Syndicate of Hospitals (2011). The Department of Psychiatry & Clinical Psychology at St Georges University Medical Center won the Hamdan bin Rashid Al Maktoum award, April. *Human & Health, 15*, 39–42. Retrieved August, 15, 2011, from www.syndicateofhospitals.org.lb/magazine/apr2011/english/8.pdf

Tomlinson, M., Rudan, I., Saxena, S., Swartz, L., Tsai, A. C., & Patel, V. (2009). Setting priorities for global mental health research. *Bulletin of the World Health Organization, 87*, 438–446.

University of Balamand (n.d.). Faculty of arts and sciences department of psychology. Retrieved December 3, 2009, from www.balamand.edu.lb/english/Arts.asp?id=1131&fid=117

Saint Esprit University of Kaslik. (2009). Faculty of Philosophy and Human Sciences. Retrieved December 3, 2009, from www.usek.edu.lb/usek08/Content/Faculties_Nod450/Philosophy_Nod592/Pge593/FR/index.asp

Saint Joseph University (2009). Psychology. Retrieved December 3, 2009, from www.usj.edu.lb/admission/cursusdoma.htm?dipl=103

Wang, P. S., Aguilar-Gaxiola, S., Alonso, M. J., Angermeyer, M.C., Borges, G., Bromet, E. J., & … Bruffaerts, R. (2007). Use of mental health services for anxiety, mood, and substance disorders in 17 countries in the WHO World Mental Health survey. *Lancet, 370*, 841–850.

World Health Organization (2009). Countries. Retrieved August 15, 2010, from www.who.int/countries/lbn/en/index.html

World Health Organization (2011). WHO Mental Health Gap Action Programme. Retrieved August 15, 2010 from www.who.int/mental_health/mhgap/en/index.html

34

COUNSELING AND PSYCHOTHERAPY IN PALESTINE

Between occupation and cultural colonialism

Rana Nashashibi, Anan Srour, and Roney Srour

Introduction

The Palestinian Occupied Territories are the areas to the West of the River Jordan which were occupied by Israel in 1967. As of 2010, the total population of the Occupied Territories (Palestinian Central Bureau of Statistics [PCBS], 2010) is 3.935 million with 54.4% of the population under the age of 20 years and 9% above 50 years of age. Approximately 60% of the population is living in 400 villages and 27 refugee camps[1] (PCBS, 2010). Arabic is the official and main language and Arabs constitute the main ethnic group. Religious groups include Muslims and Christians in addition to a very small Jewish minority (the Samaritans in the Nablus district).

The Palestinian territories are still under Israeli military control in spite of the fact that a Palestinian Authority (PA) is in place and is trying to manage the daily life of the people in those areas. The PA is very dependent on foreign aid. Consequently, the quality and availability of mental health services in Palestine are affected by the donor's policies.

Counseling, psychotherapy, and psycho-social programs are used alternatively in this chapter to describe the existing therapeutic, preventive, or developmental interventions of a psychological nature. The terminology used to describe the services alternates depending on what ideologies surrounding human nature are involved; however, alternations are mostly due to funding purposes. Psycho-social programs became a term used in Palestinian society to describe programs implemented by paraprofessionals and organizations whose mandate is not particularly in psychological interventions or mental health. Women's organizations, youth clubs, or human rights organizations added psycho-social programs to their work with no clear mandate or proper training in order to receive funding (Giacaman, 2004)

There are many definitions for counseling and psychotherapy, some of which capture the content, others the form, and others the degree of intrusiveness in the role of the counselor/therapist (Gilliland & James, 2002). An interesting definition is given by Adler who defines counseling as the younger sibling of psychotherapy with an inferiority complex, while psychotherapy is the older sibling with a superiority complex (Flanagan & Flanagan, 2004). It is the same in Palestine as it is in other places, where counseling refers to psychological interventions which take place outside clinical settings, such as in schools, protective shelters for women and children, courts prior to divorce, community centers, or detention centers. Psychotherapy, on the other hand, is connected to clinical settings and is geared to treat people with clear pathologies as described in the Diagnostic and Statistical Manual (DSM). In the Palestinian context, counseling is a more socially accepted term, because it implies normalcy. In other words, they are interventions provided to individuals or groups who are "imbalanced" temporarily due to external forces such as war but are otherwise "normal."

As we will explain later, the field of counseling and psychotherapy is a young one in the Occupied Palestinian Territories and has not been investigated yet. Most of the sources used in this chapter are based on interviews with key persons, planning and reporting documents (that have not been published), and the literature that has been written about this issue. A lot of our reporting and suggestions is based on our impressions and experiences in the Palestinian field. Nonetheless, the small community of counselors and psychotherapists in Palestine (about 4,000 people) has helped us identify tendencies and trends easily.

Brief history of counseling and psychotherapy

Counseling as a field of study and practice is relatively new worldwide and its introduction in Palestine can only be traced to the beginning of the 1980s (M. Awad, personal communication, August 22, 2010). The evolution of the field has never been documented before, but in reviewing relevant literature and interviewing primary sources four major milestones can be identified: (1) the establishment of the Palestinian Counseling Center (PCC), (2) the outbreak of the first Intifada,[2] (3) the coming of the Palestinian authority, and (4) the second Intifada.[3]

Probably the most important figure associated with counseling in Palestine is Dr. Mubarak Awad, an American-Palestinian clinical psychologist born in Jerusalem. Awad believed that counseling Palestinians in nonviolent ways to resist Israel's occupation of the West Bank and Gaza Strip is one of the ways that Palestinians can fight occupation. Additionally, he believed that "the rehabilitation of the young and who are in need with a healthy attitude is a political statement that we can take care of our people" (M. Awad, personal communication, August 22, 2010). He recalled that upon visiting his family in Jerusalem back in 1982 he put an advertisement in the paper to announce a training course in counseling. Three hundred people responded, of whom he chose 80 with backgrounds in nursing, social work, and education. At the time none of the national universities was offering an academic degree in psychology. The people who attended the course along with some social activists formed the founding group of the PCC, which was established by the great efforts of Awad in 1983. Awad was an advocate of the Rogerian client-centered approach with "counseling" as an intervention technique, and with its emphasis on health versus pathology. The acceptance of his approach stemmed from people's need to address daily concerns which affect their wellbeing.

The PCC was supported by the local community and funded first by Palestinian organizations and individuals, and later by a multitude of local and international donors. It offered services such as training and coaching of university graduates in a client-centered approach to therapy; training and placement of counselors in schools to work with children, teachers and parents; working with street kids and drug addicts to find rehabilitation programs or boarding facilities; rehabilitation and reintegration of released political prisoners from the Israeli jails; counseling young Palestinian couples who are in mixed marriages; and vocational counseling and awareness raising.

Establishing a counseling center and offering such services was a major breakthrough in the Palestinian community. For many years the field was completely dominated by the conception of dichotomy of health and pathology. Mental healthcare in Palestine was based on a biological model and psychiatrists played the primary role in service provision. In addition, the mental hospital located in the city of Bethlehem (with 200 beds and 60–70% occupancy) was governed by the Israeli military occupation's health administration (Gordon & Murad, 2002), and it was the only place for care of the psychologically disturbed. Awad best described the dire situation of the services offered to Palestinians by stating that, "It is difficult for a military occupation like Israel to deal with mental health and mental well-being. This is not on their agenda, or in their program of occupation; Israel saw counseling, social work, mental health, as advancing Palestinians' self esteem and therefore the more primitive and scarce the services offered to Palestinians the better it is" (M. Awad, personal communication, August 22, 2010). Nonetheless, in 1974 a mental health clinic was established in the city of Nablus to the north of the West Bank as a satellite clinic for the hospital in Bethlehem.

The second milestone in the history of counseling/psychotherapy in Palestine resulted from the outbreak of the first Intifada in 1987, which brought about a major shift in conception and significant changes in the development of the mental health services (Ashhab, 2005). The escalation of Israeli violence had affected every family in Palestinian society. There was at least a martyr, injured, or incarcerated member in every family, which led to the increase and diversity of services offered (Arafat, 2003). More people were suffering from depression, post-traumatic stress disorder (PTSD), anxiety and somatization disorders and therefore complaints of psychological ailment became the norm, not the abnormal. In consequence, stigmatization and labeling decreased so people began to feel more at ease to seek help. It was important to respond to people's needs for services and therefore a number of local and international non-governmental organizations, like the Gaza Community Mental Health Program in Gaza, and Medicines Sans Frontiers (MSF) in the northern areas of the West Bank, began to establish services to help victims of Israeli violence with an emphasis on women and children. In addition to specialized psychosocial organizations, organizations that treated the Intifada injured, like the YMCA and Bethlehem Arab Society for Rehabilitation, developed counseling programs as part of their services.

The third milestone coincided with the coming to power of a Palestinian authority, which was a result of the Oslo Accords signed between Israel and the Palestine Liberation Organization (PLO) in 1993. This meant that the Palestinians had to set up public services to run their own lives. Ministries were set up to provide services which were formerly the responsibility of Israel—the occupier (Gordon & Murad, 2002)—though they were not always provided.

The Ministry of Health assumed responsibility for healthcare of the Palestinian people and among its responsibilities was mental healthcare. Nevertheless, the ministry did not give mental health much importance and even now, in the year 2011, there is no mental health plan for Palestinians. Nonetheless, a service organizational plan was prepared in 2004 with the help of the WHO and the French and Italian governments where "Deinstitutionalization and Reintegration" of mental health patients was the main goal of the plan. The Ministry of Education, on the other hand, launched a school counseling program in 1996, employing 624 school counselors working in public schools in the West Bank and Gaza Strip. The school counselors provide individual and group counseling in addition to vocational counseling. Students suffering from psychological disorders and problems that need specialized interventions are referred to specialized care in the public or NGO sector.

Another ministry was established in 1998 (WAFA, 2010) for ex-detainees to look after the needs of ex-prisoners, including their psychosocial needs. This group constitutes about 40% of the adult male population of Palestine (WAFA, 2011).[4] An NGO with mental health professionals was established to care for torture victims. According to different sources, the number of

NGOs providing programs in psychosocial and mental health services doubled in the period between 1999 and 2004, from 16 to 35 (Giacaman, 2004).

The final milestone in the field resulted from the second Intifada in 2000, which led to an escalation of violence. The mental wellbeing of children and adults deteriorated and was expressed through severe and chronic reactive psychological syndromes, including PTSD, anxiety, and behavioral problems (Sarraj & Qouta, 2004). This resulted in the Palestinian professional community being flooded with funding for training in trauma work. The years between 2001 and 2005 witnessed an "abnormal growth" and mushrooming of services in healing the trauma.

Nonetheless, research into the specific manifestations of traumatic events on the people in the Occupied Territories was very limited and often unreliable. Therefore, programs designed to deal with trauma remained funding dependent and were not integrated properly in the mental health scene in Palestine. Many institutions which had been established especially or had modified their work to deal with the so-called traumatic reactions discontinued their work when the funding dried up. Presently the field is better organized. Organizations which survived the funding spree are able to provide professional services and have a qualified team.

Counselor education programs, accreditation, licensure, and certification

Several Palestinian universities teach psychology as the basis for counseling, yet often an undergraduate degree in psychology is offered under the Faculty of Education, thus giving it a specific nature that limits it to working with children. Careful examination of the educational courses and modules indicates a compliance with the international requirements for this type of science, with the exception of research and statistical methodologies, which are addressed superficially by Palestinian universities. This might be one of the causes for the lack of independent research work in Palestine in general.

In fact, many students in Palestine view psychology as the last resort; in other words, the choice for those who have no other options. The required average for admission to studying psychology is one of the lowest in Palestinian universities with adverse consequences on the motivation of students who embark on their studies from a relatively low starting point. The situation is further exacerbated by the shortage of educational staff for these types of courses in Palestine. This is mainly due to the unattractive conditions prevalent at Palestinian universities given the low salaries, scarcity of research centers or funds allocated to research, forcing educational staff to travel abroad or work in the private sector instead of investing their skills and capabilities in research.

The other academic specialization that relates to counseling is social work. Social work graduates find themselves in a relatively better position due to their field training rather than their academic qualifications. All social work courses offered in Palestine have integral field training aspects, allowing students to graduate with good knowledge of what to expect in the field. Unfortunately, the theoretical tools that students acquire to be capable of working in the field are basic and incomprehensive, particularly in terms of working in a complex field of specialization. To put things into perspective, one needs to be aware that students who obtain the first degree (BA) in psychology or social work are not expected to work in the field, since the first degree usually focuses on the theoretical rather than the practical aspects of the profession. However, in the Palestinian context, and given the absence of several required components, which will be addressed later, new graduates become workers in the field of mental health prematurely (Giacaman, 2004).

It is important to shed light on another more difficult problem, namely the absence of courses in clinical psychology at the Palestinian universities and the absence of other therapy-oriented courses. Most courses focus on pedagogical counseling and are usually incorporated under the Faculty of Education. These courses deal with children and students only, and do not address adults. The clinical aspect of mental health continues to be absent from counseling and therapy courses at Palestinian universities. Recently, and in light of pressures by the WHO, some universities have introduced courses in community mental health where the teaching focuses on dealing with psychological disorders with community resources. The introduction of these courses is the first example of interventions by external parties in an attempt to influence the field of mental health in Palestine. The WHO, as a medical organization, is trying to shift attention to the biological and environmental aspects of mental health rather than the intra-psychic aspects.

Under these conditions and in view of the scarce qualified staff resources, the field depends on graduates of universities from outside Palestine, namely American, European, and Israeli universities. These graduates have received a Western education in counseling and psychotherapy and attempt to apply it or customize it to correspond with the local culture, which often meets with little success. Here too, the lack of research on Palestinian counseling and psychotherapy poses a challenge to closing the gap.

In 2005, the union of psychologists and social workers developed and submitted a draft licensing law to the Palestinian Legislative Council (PLC) in session number 16 on August 23, 2005 (Palestinian Legislative Council, 2005). However, the PLC was paralyzed for political reasons and as such the law remained as pending review and endorsement for several years. In the absence of such a law, the profession remains under threat and unclear for those who practice it and for the beneficiaries of its services.

The contents of the law raised a lot of internal controversy between the union and its supporters on the one hand and the network of mental health institutions known as "Building Balance" (a network of 11 organizations that work on lobbying and advocacy for laws and procedures in the field of mental health in Palestine) on the other. The main controversy revolved around two main issues.

First, as a source of power the union tried to assume the responsibility of issuing the licenses. Building Balance wanted licensing to be the responsibility of the ministries, who should take care of the quality of the services provided to citizens. The second issue concerns the suitability of the law in the Palestinian context. The proposed law adopts Israeli standards for psychological professionals and is deemed not suitable in the Palestinian context according to the claims of the Building Balance network. For instance, Israeli law imposes high demands on students wanting to obtain the title of specialized psychological specialist since they have to obtain a master's degree in psychology first, then go through a long process of specialization (4 years at least). Trainees in counseling will not have the possibility to obtain this title due to the unavailability of the required educational courses. As for specialization, the criteria were drafted accurately and in detail within the proposed law and taken from Israeli law, but lack substance since the organizations that are positioned to accept the specialists are unavailable particularly in terms of schools. Hence, when these requirements were applied to the Palestinian context, it became obvious that the number of people who will obtain the title of psychological specialist will be very low.

Currently, the Ministry of Health has issued licenses in accordance with special procedures that were not derived from the law. Therefore, recognition of these licenses is limited and nonbinding. For the field of counseling in Palestine to move forward, a clear vision is needed, including a vision regarding the future counselor and therapist in Palestine. Until we reach such a stage, there is a need to follow procedures and enact transitional laws based on what exists today towards what is desired. The ideal solution currently might be to issue temporary licenses preconditioned by the completion of specific issues.

Current counseling and psychotherapy theories, processes and trends

A study conducted by Giacaman (2004) on psycho-social and mental healthcare in the West Bank and Gaza found that counselors and mental health workers use "an eclectic range of intervention approaches" (Giacaman, 2004, p. 15). The counselors and directors of organizations working in mental health reported that they provide both individual and group counseling. A higher percentage (54–65%) of counselors use cognitive, behavioral, and cognitive-behavioral approaches, with a smaller proportion also citing psychodynamic approaches (34%). Many counselors use Rogerian and other humanistic related approaches like Gestalt or transactional analysis (TA) but do not clearly identify themselves as humanistic counselors. "Eighty eight percent of counselors cited using crisis debriefing techniques and 12% reported using EMDR" (Giacaman, 2004, p. 15).

Clinicians apply therapeutic models which were developed and utilized in other settings without properly testing their efficacy and applicability to the Palestinian context. Such practice is quite unacceptable for many professionals. Dwairy (2006) argues that the Palestinian society is an Arab society where individual needs are compromised to the collective needs, and therefore Western interventions not customized to suit the culture are not useful. He proposes a culturally sensitive approach based on metaphoric and indirect interventions.

In Palestine, like many war-stricken areas, many interventions are geared towards working with traumatized people. With a background of conflicts and occupation, Palestine became a testing ground for many intervention techniques and for developers who wanted to test their models on the traumatized population. Among these models were debriefing, somatic experiencing, EMDR, class-based intervention, and expressive arts therapy. Miller (2002) argues that "much of our clinical knowledge of how to evaluate and treat victims of terrorist trauma and their surviving loved ones must be adapted from work with analogous cases of traumatic bereavement" (p. 285). Such a practice is not followed in Palestine. Many Palestinian mental health and community workers were trained by local and international experts to use debriefing in response to traumatic exposure, usually caused by people who were passive or active victims of Israeli violence. The technique, though widely used especially following the events of the second Intifada, was also criticized for not being used properly and often untimely. "The professionals and the general population were bewildered by the debriefing techniques" (Ashhab, 2005, p. 82).

Several Palestinian mental health workers were also trained in EMDR. Some Palestinian organizations like the YMCA and the Torture Rehabilitation Center conducted training with the help of international trainers from the United Kingdom, United States, and Turkey (Wright, 2006).

Expressive Arts Therapies is a new and emerging field within psychotherapeutic practice in Palestine. The trained therapist plays an important role in introducing the intervention with those experiencing secondary trauma, like ambulance drivers, aid workers, and journalists who were in the middle of violent events, especially in the Israeli incursions to West Bank towns and villages in 2002 (Abu Sway, Nashashibi, Salah, & Shweiki, 2005). Presently, expressive arts are used as a therapeutic intervention model with individuals and groups, and this has been used as a model for empowerment and building capacities of professionals and paraprofessionals.

Indigenous and traditional healing methods

Fertility and mental health are two of the most important problems where people eventually resort to traditional treatments and healing methods, since they are the subject of many misconceptions and are usually linked to evil spirits, devils, or Jinn (Al Krenawi & Graham, 1999). The prevalence of ignorance and traditional ways of thinking render the work of charlatans easy as they use ideas derived from religion in "treatment" or "healing." The official religious establishment in Palestine clearly fights these phenomena and usually offers scientifically based psychological counseling as an alternative. In order to fight against witchcraft covered by Islamic beliefs, several awareness-raising activities undertaken by organizations seek help from Muslim public figures to refute the claims of charlatans and their methods. However, these methods continue to be prevalent in rural areas in Palestine.

Over the last decade, new methods of healing originating from the Far East started to gain ground, such as Reiki and other forms of energy healing (Masarwah-Srour, 2011). These methods are now being practiced by religious individuals (sheikhs) who imprinted into these methods Islamic concepts and molded them to empower and strengthen individuals. These methods became widespread as part of new-age practices amidst many who fought against charlatans and who attempted to practice methods that were less complicated than psychological counseling.

However, a phenomenon that strongly indicates that Palestinian society is moving towards accepting psychological counseling is the opening of departments at religious courts for family counseling. This constitutes a modern approach that the religious authorities are undertaking in giving counseling a positive tone which alleviates the stigma associated with its recipients. Recently, many coalitions formed against charlatans propose counseling as an alternative. Among these efforts are awareness-raising efforts at schools and neighborhoods and the approach of lawyers and legal professionals, but exposure to the Western and Arab world through TV channels that present psychological counselors and specialists as experts for addressing for mental health problems, remains the most influential factor.

Research and supervision

Palestinian universities are more like colleges given their lack of research centers and where most of the work focuses on education due to the lack of qualified staff and scarce financial resources and laboratories. A quick search, conducted for the purposes of this article, in the PsyNet database, listed 1,282 items containing the word Palestine or Palestinian. Most of the topics address the conflict (377 items), the war (177 items), violence (157 items), Jews (143 items), terrorism (132 items), peace and conflict resolution (113 items), and only 92 items addressing cultural differences.

In mental health research, the Palestinian context is being addressed as a laboratory for armed and non-armed conflict. As such, research related to trauma and its symptoms become prevalent, as if these are the only problems that Palestinians suffer from. Further, as in the case of counseling services that are greatly influenced and dependent on foreign funding, so is the research work. Research on counseling topics in Palestine depends entirely on international funds and is prepared by foreign researchers who engage in partnerships with local researchers as the gateway to the field. It is important to note that the Palestinian universities' boycott of Israeli universities has limited this phenomenon by Israelis, yet it is still common for European and American universities.

In terms of supervision, professional supervision is considered an essential practice in the qualification process of counselors. However, this is still a voluntary choice that depends on personal motivation and the availability of material resources. Historically, professional supervision as we know it today started in the late 1980s upon the return of a number of counselors and psychologists who had graduated in the USA and Europe (based on our personal knowledge of the supervisors). The new practitioners felt the need to be supervised in their work and asked their organizations to provide them with professional supervisors. The organizations were reluctant to respond positively, mainly because they were not aware of the significance and added value of professional supervision, and also because they lacked the human and financial resources. But thanks to the persistence of the newly graduated psychologists and counselors, supervision became a tradition in some organizations. Because its value was understood, supervision through the years became common practice in Palestine among many organizations in spite of the fact that it is not obligatory under law.

Contrary to NGOs that provide professional supervision that focuses on the counselor, public institutions and the United Nations Relief and Works Agency (UNRWA), for example, provide administrative supervision instead. The latter focuses on work procedures and on the counselee (UNRWA, 2010). This supervision model is usually adopted by large governmental institutions and UNRWA in order to respond to the great need for supervision with the limited financial resources at hand. The low salaries offered to counselors in public institutions and in UNRWA make it difficult to attract highly qualified counselors, which makes the need for supervision all the more important.

Since the outbreak of the second Palestinian Intifada in 2000 and the resulting emergency situation in Palestine, programs in mental health and psychosocial interventions almost always include supervision and capacity building. This is mainly due to the increased awareness among counselors and therapists of the importance of professional supervision and also to the fact that capacity building has become a strategy adopted by most mental health donor agencies.

Strengths, weakness, opportunities, and challenges

A major strength in the field of counseling and psychotherapy in the Occupied Palestinian Territories concerns its response to the needs of the community. As described earlier in the chapter, life under oppressive occupation like that of the Israeli occupation has taken its toll on the Palestinian people and has affected their mental wellbeing. This fact motivated Palestinian mental health professionals to improve their skills and services and to rise to the challenge. The Palestinian mental health scene is constantly advancing and there is serious work being done on many levels of services, such as therapy, prevention, crisis intervention, and rehabilitation. Palestinian professionals organized crisis intervention teams to respond to the emergency situation in the aftermath of the Israeli attacks in 2002. In comparison to other war-stricken areas, such as the Balkans, Sudan, and Iraq, Palestinian professionals were at the forefront in their crisis response work. Some Palestinian professionals as individuals and organizations were also called to intervene and provide training in war-stricken areas such as Iraq and Sudan.

Weaknesses in the field relate to the dependency Palestine has on foreign aid, such as the WHO, and Italian Cooperation and French Cooperation through co-projects with the Ministry of Health. Although mental services have improved and community mental health centers have been set up in almost all the towns in the West Bank and Gaza Strip, international funding, especially European and American government funds, is seen as a means to deal with the consequences of occupation rather than uprooting it (Roy, 1999). Therefore it fluctuates according to the atrocities of the Israeli occupying authorities. When the number of casualties increases, the international community's response always comes through with increasing funds. Roy in an article titled "Strangled by Aid" claims that "Aid has depoliticized the root causes of Palestinian suffering." By focusing exclusively on the humanitarian aspects of the occupation, donors effectively deprive Palestinians of their voice and right to self-determination (Palestine Monitor, 2010).

The opportunities concealed in the need for counseling in the community and the numbers of people affected by the occupation are enormous and therefore there is willingness among

Palestinians to seek professional help. The statistics show a continuous increase in the numbers of people frequenting mental healthcare in the public, private and UNRWA services in both the West Bank and the Gaza Strip (UNRWA, 2010). The increase in numbers may also be attributed to the fact that the medical profession has traditionally been valued highly and people trust what is recommended by the doctors. Owing to the positive rapport between the medical and mental health fields and a recent movement to integrate mental health into primary healthcare, the number of people referred to counseling and psychotherapy by the medical professions is on the rise. Moreover, the high involvement of the community and especially the family in the care of people with disabilities in general and mental disabilities in particular has further facilitated the work of mental health professionals (Mannan & Turnbull, 2007).

Although there are some positive changes, there are still significant challenges facing the mental health field in Palestine. These include the need for the support of decision and policy makers and a strengthened commitment to a new approach to mental health services. These also include the absence of the required structure within the Ministry of Health for mental health, and some resistance on the part of certain professionals, especially psychiatrists, towards the new mental health strategies. The scarcity of financial and human resources is also a factor that severely impedes mental health development in the territory. Finally, a major challenge is the unavailability of a mental health plan in Palestine. The health ministry and its major donors insist on a service organizational plan which is updated every 3 years. The claim is that the situation in Palestine is too volatile and therefore long-term holistic planning is impractical. The problem which results is that there is no analysis of responses provided at the macro-level and the ensuing plans are restricted to the public sector, which leaves the private sector and NGOs completely outside the plan. With the absence of a national mental health plan there is no organization of services. There is excess in some services on one hand and lack of services on the other.

Future directions

It is imperative here to clarify that the future directions for counseling and psychotherapy in Palestine involve different stakeholders. The stakeholders include the beneficiaries, the governmental agencies, the civil society actors and the academic institutions. The future also involves developmental and organizational matters. On the developmental level it includes therapy, prevention, and capacity building, while the organizational level involves legislation and availability and best use of resources.

When it comes to the beneficiaries or clientele there is a movement to reach out and make services available to people living in distant villages far away from the city centers where most of the services are concentrated. This will not only lead to the availability of services to marginalized populations but it will also reduce the stigma attached to counseling and psychotherapy in that the services will become part of the facilities available in the community. The services combine group gatherings to raise the awareness on mental health issues and primary interventions like post-meeting individual consultations for those who seek them. This leads to secondary interventions held in therapy rooms.

Civil society actors, whether they are NGOs, private sector, or religious organizations, should focus on model building, lobbying, and ensuring that both clients and mental health professionals are protected. The most important role could be developing culturally sensitive models of interventions designed for specific target groups like chronically ill patients, children with developmental disorders, victims of torture or political violence, and families with marital problems. Such models should be transferred to the public sector after proving their efficacy through evidence-based research.

Finally, although Palestinian academic institutions are working on improving the professional capacities and qualifications of the people working in the field by providing more specialized and qualification programs, more resources need to be allocated to research centers and universities to produce research and epidemiological studies which can better guide the work of professionals and the service provision centers.

Conclusion

Counseling as a discipline is relatively young in Palestine, having begun about three decades ago. Development of the field has been dependent on two things: the needs of the population that mainly stem from political violence and its implications, and funding, which in most cases is driven by an international political agenda.

Palestinian counselors who were educated in Western countries were the first to bring the discourse on mental health to the Palestinian occupied territories, a topic that was avoided for fear of stigmatization. However, the political situation and the link between mental health and political victimization facilitated the entry and acceptance of counseling as a tool to maintain resistance against the occupation. Although there has been a significant improvement in the provision of counseling in terms of both quality and quantity, counseling in Palestine is still far from being satisfactory. The main challenge that faces counseling today is to develop a discipline capable of taking cultural differences into consideration. In order to do this, there is a need to improve academic programs and encourage independent research that will provide local knowledge rather than rely on Western or even Arab sources. This knowledge should be evidence based, examined over extended periods of time and conducted in a systematic manner. Taking into account all these challenges, the accumulated experience in this young field is sufficient to serve as a base for building a system that every Palestinian counselor can work with.

Notes

1 Palestinian refugees who were expelled out of their homes in what is now the State of Israel. In 1948 Israel destroyed and depopulated 400 Palestinian villages and their inhabitants became refugees living in refugee camps in different areas of the West Bank, Gaza Strip, Jordan, Lebanon, Syria, and other countries (Khalidi, 1992).
2 A Palestinian uprising against Israeli occupation from 1987 to 1993.
3 A Palestinian uprising against Israeli occupation from 2000 onwards.
4 750,000 Palestinians were incarcerated between 1967 and 2011 according to WAFA the Palestinian information agency.

References

Abu Sway, R., Nashashibi, R., Salah, R., & Shweiki, R. (2005). Expressive arts therapy: Healing the traumatized: The Palestinian experience. In D. Kalmonowitz & B. Loyd (eds), *The Palestinian Experience in Art Therapy and Political Violence: With Art, Without Illusion* (pp. 154–171). New York: Routledge.
Arafat, C. (2003). *A psychological assessment of Palestinian children*. Retrieved from http://domino.un.org/unispal.nsf/bc8b0c56b7bf621185256cbf005ac05f/6bb117b13425504685256ea90055c8ab/$FILE/assessment.pdf
Ashhab, B. (2005). An update on mental health services in the West Bank. *Israeli Journal of Psychiatry and Related Science, 42*(2), 81–83.
Al-Krenawi, A., & Graham, J. R. (1999). Gender and biomedical/traditional mental health utilization among the Bedouin-Arabs of the Negev. *Culture, Medicine and Psychiatry, 23*(2), 219–243.
Dwairy, M. (2006). *Counseling and Psychotherapy with Arabs and Muslims: A Culturally Sensitive Approach*. New York: Teachers College Press.

Flanagan, J., & Flanagan, R. (2004). *Counseling and Psychotherapy Theories in Context and Practice*. Hoboken, NJ: John Wiley and Sons.

Giacaman, R. (2004). *Psycho-social/mental Health Care in the Occupied Palestinian Territories: The Embryonic System*. Palestine: Birzeit University.

Gilliland, B., & James, R. (2002). *Theories and Strategies in Counseling and Psychotherapy* (5th edn). Boston, MA: Allyn & Bacon.

Gordon, H., & Murad, I. (2002). Psychiatry and the Palestinian population. *The Psychiatrist*, *26*, 28–30.

Khalidi, W. (1992). *All that Remains: The Palestinian Villages Occupied and Depopulated by Israel in 1948*. Washington, DC: Institute for Palestine Studies.

Mannan, H., & Turnbull, A. (2007). A review of community based rehabilitation evaluation: Quality of life as an outcome measure for future evaluation. *Asia Pacific Rehabilitation Journal*, *18*(1), 29–45.

Masarwah-Srour, A. (2011). *Reiki, Islam and Body*. Lecture presented at the "Talking about the Body, Talking from the Body Conference", June, at the Hebrew University, Jerusalem.

Miller, L. (2002). Psychological interventions for terroristic trauma: Symptoms, syndromes, and treatment strategies. *Journal of Psychotherapy: Theory, Research, Practice Training*, *39*(4), 283–296.

Palestinian Central Bureau of Statistics (PCBS) (2010). *The Status of the Total Population of the Palestinian Territory at Mid 2010*. Ramallah: PCBS

Palestinian Legislative Council. (2005). *Draft law no. 195/2005*. Palestine: Ramallah.

Palestine Monitor. (2010). *Strangled by Aid*. Retrieved from www.palestinemonitor.org/spip/spip.php?article1556

Sarraj, I., & Qouta, S. (2004). Prevalence of PTSD among Palestinian children in Gaza Strip. *Arabpsychnet Journal*, *2*, 8–13

Roy, S. (1999). De-development revisited: Palestinian economy and society since Oslo. *Journal of Palestine Studies*, *28*(3), 64–82.

United Nations Relief and Works Agency (UNRWA) (2010). *The annual report of the development of health*. Retrieved from http://www.unrwa.org/userfiles/2011052062220.pdf

WAFA. (2010). *Organizations which cater for Palestinian prisoners*. Retrieved from www.wafainfo.ps/atemplate.aspx?id = 3795

WAFA. (2011). *An international committee expresses concern over the situation of Palestinian prisoners*. Retrieved from www.wafa.ps/arabic/index.php?action=detail&id=115498

Wright, J. (2006). *EMDR part II training in Bethlehem*. Retrieved from www.globalministries.org

35

COUNSELING AND PSYCHOTHERAPY IN TURKEY

Western theories and culturally inclusive methods

Şenel Poyrazlı, Süleyman Doğan, and Mehmet Eskin

Introduction

Turkey is a republic that was founded in 1923, following the collapse of the Ottoman Empire. It is strategically situated to the east of Europe and north of the Middle East. Countries that surround Turkey by land are Greece, Bulgaria, Georgia, Armenia, Iran, Iraq, and Syria. The population is 72.5 million, with 50% being below the age of 29 (Central Intelligence Agency; CIA, 2011). The largest ethnic group in Turkey is the Turks (70–75%), followed by Kurds (18%). Other minority groups such as Armenians, Arabs, and Jews make up 7–12% of the population (CIA, 2011). The majority of the people are Muslims; however, Jews and Christians also live in Turkey. The official language is Turkish, while Kurdish, Arabic, Greek, Armenian, and Circassian are among other minority languages that are spoken by different groups (CIA, 2011)

Currently, counseling and psychotherapy in Turkey are practiced by psychiatrists, psychologists, and counselors. While there were practices to treat mental disorders in older Turkic States, the modern treatments of mental disorders started at the end of the 1800s by the efforts of psychiatrists during the late years of the Ottoman Empire. Later, the science of psychology was introduced to Turkey at the beginning of the 1900s (Dogan, 2000). The historical development of counseling in Turkey, on the other hand, is closely related to the history of educational practice and problems in schools and dates back to the 1950s (Dogan, 2000). It may be contended that although psychiatrists conduct psychotherapy, they mainly tend to use pharmacotherapy in treating mental disorders. Thus, counseling and psychotherapy are usually practiced by counselors and psychologists in Turkey. In this chapter, we provide a summary of the history of psychology and counseling in Turkey. While describing the development of counseling and psychotherapy, we will also assess the current state of the field, and discuss opportunities (e.g., inclusion of multiculturalism) and challenges (e.g., supervision and consultation) that the field faces.

Brief history of counseling and psychotherapy

According to Kağıtçıbaşı (1994), the year 1915 marks the beginning of psychology as a scientific discipline in Turkey. It is clear that initially European and then American influences have played significant roles in the establishment of psychology departments and in the conceptualization of research interests in Turkey (Acar & Şahin, 1990). Kağıtçıbaşı (1994) states that many Turkish psychologists are either trained in the United States or are exposed to the idea that American mainstream psychology is the model to be followed. Thus, the scientific reference group is American (or more generally Western) psychology, with its norms and values.

There are two important milestones in the development of psychology in Turkey. The first one is related to the importation of knowledge and skills through professionals who were educated abroad during the early 1960s. These professionals introduced the field to psychoanalytic psychotherapy and cognitive-behavioral therapy. The second milestone relates to the establishment of professional associations for psychology and psychotherapy. These organizations aimed to protect the rights of psychologists, generate and disseminate knowledge, and/or provide training (see, for example, Turkish Psychological Association, 2011). The year of 1976 marked the founding of the professional organization of psychologists, which was named the Turkish Psychological Association. Later, other organizations specific to treatment models were also established (e.g., Halime Odağ Psychoanalysis and Psychotherapy Foundation, the Turkish Association for Cognitive and Behavioral Psychotherapies, the Gestalt Therapy Association, the Transactional Analysis Association).

The Turkish counseling movement exists separately from psychology. Turkey has a 60-year history of counseling and derives largely from advances and developments in the system of counseling in the United States, such as Rogers' person-centered approach. The history of counseling in Turkey can be divided into six periods: taking the initial steps, the formative years, establishing counseling services in schools, establishing undergraduate programs in counseling, assigning counselors to schools, and attempts to restructure and accredit counseling undergraduate programs (Dogan, 2000).

During the first period (1950–1956), the visits of some American counselor educators and the efforts of pioneer counselor educators trained in the United States played a significant role in bringing counseling concepts into Turkish education in the 1950s (Baymur, 1980; Tan, 1986). This period witnessed several important developments in counseling. Two of the most important of these developments occurred when the Ministry of National Education set up a Test and Research Bureau in 1953 and then implemented the first Guidance and Research Center in 1955 (Dogan, 1996).

Following the initial steps were the formative years (1957–1969). This period included the adaptation and development of some group tests and rapid changes in school curricula (Oner, 1977). The importance of delivering counseling and guidance services, especially career counseling, to secondary school students was pointed out in national policy during the 1960s. Some Turkish universities began to set up either undergraduate or graduate counselor education during this time as well (Kuzgun, 1993; Ozguven, 1990).

Between 1970 and 1981, the formative years transitioned in a period that officially marked the beginning of professional counseling practice in schools. Both the Tenth National Education Council in 1981 and the Eleventh National Education Council in 1982 focused on the need for counselors in education settings and how school counselors should be trained. These councils also recommended "counselor" as a title for graduates and confirmed "guidance" as a specialty field in education (Dogan, 1990).

The following period witnessed the establishment of undergraduate programs in counseling and the formation of a professional association (1982–1995). During this period, the Turkish universities began admitting students to a 4-year bachelor of education program with a major in guidance and counseling after the Higher Education Law (no. 2547) came into effect in 1981. The professional organization of counselors was founded in 1989, called the Turkish Psychological Counseling and Guidance Association (Dogan, 2000).

Between 1996 and 2003, a rapid increase in the appointment of counselors took place. Some new steps were being taken to establish a new structure for elementary schools, including counseling, after the extension of national obligatory education from grades 1 through 5 to grades 1 through 8 in 1997 (Dogan, 2000). Additionally, the discussions about the idea of restructuring counseling undergraduate programs began among academics during this period.

Since 2004 Turkey has entered a new period in which attempts to restructure and accredit counseling undergraduate programs have been made. After the unsuccessful attempt to restructure an undergraduate counseling program by the Council of Higher Education (CHE) in 1996, the first remarkable work to restructure counseling undergraduate programs was one that started with the initiative of counseling and guidance departments at colleges. This work continued for 4 years and was completed with the creation of a "New Counseling and Guidance Undergraduate Program" in 2004 (Turkish Psychological Counseling and Guidance Association, 2004). This program was implemented by a few universities for a couple of years but was ultimately abolished. Then the CHE prepared a counseling undergraduate program and mandated that all colleges implement this program starting with the 2007–2008 academic year. However, some of the academicians of the field objected to this program since it did not largely represent inclusion of training components for important counselor competencies.

Counselor education programs, accreditation, licensure, and certification

Counselors in Turkey are predominantly trained at the undergraduate level. Most of the universities in Turkey are making remarkable efforts through the training of potential counselors at the undergraduate level with a view to meet the needs of school children. Therefore, potential counselors are trained primarily to function as school counselors.

Since the Turkish pioneer counselor educators were trained in the United States, the Turkish counselor education model was greatly influenced by the American counselor education model. However, the Turkish counselor education model has become a unique model over time in that it mirrors neither counselor education models in the United States nor those in Europe (Council for Accreditation of Counseling and Related Programs [CACREP], 2011; Dogan, 2008). Currently, the number of counseling programs is more than 50, demonstrating a sharp increase over three decades. Moreover, there are now 21 master's degrees and 14 doctoral programs in the area of counseling.

Today, Turkey is one of the rare countries in the world that has been carrying out counselor education at three levels (undergraduate, master's, and doctoral). Counselor education programs at each level are officially titled "Guidance and Counseling Programs" by the CHE. The curriculum of counselor education at each level largely includes courses which represent psychological, social, and educational foundations; statistics and research foundations; and the field of counseling. Despite the fact that this model of counselor education is offered at three levels, the education program at each level is generic. In other words, the programs follow a continuum and repeat each other and do not offer specialization in different counseling areas.

Current counseling undergraduate programs in Turkey aim to equip counselor trainees with generic counseling competencies, focusing on school counseling specifically. Although the counseling undergraduate programs train counselors who may work as practitioners, the curriculum weighs more heavily on delivery of knowledge than the development of applied skills.

In order to work as a counselor in public or private institutions in Turkey, it is sufficient to have an undergraduate degree. Despite this right, there seems to be a broad consensus that a 4-year program in counseling as a basic science does not prepare counselor trainees to become specialists in any area of counseling and that at least 1 year of graduate work beyond the undergraduate degree is necessary for specialization. However, a master's degree program in counseling functions as a step that has to be taken in order to continue to a doctoral program, rather than master's programs being independent programs that train counseling specialists who may work as practitioners. The doctoral programs basically train potential faculty members that are needed by universities. Essentially, doctoral education as the highest academic degree in the area of counseling is expected to train professional counselors with advanced skills in clinical practice, teaching, supervision, and research (West, Bubenzer, Brooks, & Hackney, 1995).

The accreditation of undergraduate programs in counseling, like all other undergraduate programs, is statutorily carried out by the CHE; there is no other body that professionally regulates counseling training in Turkey. The accreditation work done by the CHE only aims to create unity in course titles, credit/hours, and course definitions. It can be said that this accreditation process has not generally been accepted and internalized by most of the counselor educators. On the contrary, there is no consensus among counselor educators on which counselor competency domains and counseling competencies and courses should be included in a counseling undergraduate program.

Counseling graduate programs, while they are accredited by the CHE, are the responsibility of the university faculty senate of the respective universities in terms of approval and implementation of the specifics of the program. However, the CHE defines common guidelines for all graduate programs such as the quality and the quantity of the faculty, the length of the program, course descriptions, and credit/hours. It is impossible to carry out a graduate program without meeting the criteria of the CHE for graduate programs (CHE, 2011).

Accreditation of undergraduate and graduate counselor education programs is considered increasingly important for the development of counseling in Turkey (Korkut, 2006). However, it is essential that the profession is monitored, that practitioners demonstrate their competency and become licensed or certified, and that unethical practices are more closely regulated through professional boards (Bemak & Hanna, 1998). At the moment, counselors in Turkey do not require a license or certificate to practice other than a university degree in counseling. Essentially, licensing or certification in Turkey is not mandated for the other helping professionals, either.

Generally, clinical psychologists are expected to be one of the groups of professionals who practice psychotherapy in Turkey. However, the number of clinical psychology graduate programs and clinical psychologists is limited. Although the number may change in time, there are about 10 graduate programs that train clinical psychologists in Turkey. Consequently, clinical psychologists do not meet the demands of various sectors. In this sense, although individuals with a psychology undergraduate degree have very limited skills and either no or very little practicum experience to conduct psychotherapy, they take positions as clinical psychologists.

Since psychology undergraduates are employed as mental health professionals in various settings, we will also discuss psychology undergraduate education in detail. Psychology undergraduate programs are 4-year programs. Today, there are 19 undergraduate psychology programs in Turkey, being housed in psychology departments within the Faculty of Science and Letters at both state and private universities. A perusal of the curricula of these programs reflects a wide spectrum of psychology courses and theoretical perspectives, a concern with methodological sophistication, and a largely North American approach (Bolak-Boratav, 2004). The CHE centrally awards and recognizes academic degrees in only five specialties of psychology: developmental psychology, experimental psychology, applied (clinical, organizational, and school) psychology, social psychology, and psychometrics (Gülerce, 2006). The accreditation of the psychology undergraduate and graduate programs is similar to counselor education programs as mentioned earlier. Moreover, similar to counselors, licensing or certification is not mandated for psychologists.

Current counseling and psychotherapy theories, processes, and trends

The counseling field is primarily Rogerian in orientation, while an increase in the use of cognitive-behavioral therapies is being noticed. Psychotherapy practices, on the other hand, often utilize cognitive-behavioral approaches. However, a wide range of other theories (e.g., Albert Ellis' Rational Emotive Behavior Therapy, Bowenian Theory, Gestalt Theory) are also being used in both fields (Dogan, 2000; Kurter, Jencius, & Duba, 2004; Poyrazli, 2003).

Utilization of a wide variety of counseling and psychotherapy theories offers individuals in Turkey an opportunity to receive the type of help they may need. Historically, psychotherapy in Turkey started with psychoanalysis and psychoanalytic psychotherapy. Currently, the practice of and training for psychoanalysis and psychoanalytic psychotherapies are offered by psychiatry residency and psychology graduate programs and private practice (Erten & Aydın, 2009; Vahip, 2007); however, the influence of these theories in psychiatric training has diminished considerably (Yüksel, 2001). Transactional analysis has become more popular in recent years; the theory is taught in a few psychology departments and is used in some private practice settings (Akkoyun, 2001; Aydın, 2009). Gestalt therapy has also gained popularity within the past two decades and a journal devoted to gestalt therapy is published (Daş, 2009).

Within the past three decades, the practice of cognitive-behavioral psychotherapies has become widespread. Training in cognitive-behavioral psychotherapies is offered in the curricula of psychiatric residency training, psychology departments, counselor education programs, psychiatric nursing education, and social work programs. The increase in the number of books published on cognitive-behavioral therapies is an indication of this trend (e.g., Eskin, 2009; Köroğlu, 2005; Türkçapar, 2007).

Some changes in Turkish society have impacted the structure of the family and have given way to the teaching and use of family and couples theories (e.g., Bowenian). The divorce rate is increasing in the country (Uçan, 2007) and the dissolution of traditional family ties have made it a necessity for counselors and therapists to work with the family. Therefore, the demand for family and couples therapy services is an increasing trend. The need to work with family and couples is deeply felt in clinics and private practice. To address this need, many chapters on family and couples therapy have been added to counseling and psychotherapy books (e.g., Eskin, 2007; Kılınç, 2009).

Some other counseling and psychotherapy approaches are also practiced in clinics and private practice in Turkey. Psychodrama (Göka, 2009) is becoming more and more popular among practitioners both in private clinics and in educational institutions. The demand for sex therapies shows an increased need in the population, and education and training programs for sex therapy have been developed and are offered mostly on a private basis. Group counseling and psychotherapy are also utilized both in the public and in the private sectors.

While these Western theories are widely taught and used in Turkey, a word of caution is that they may not be applicable in a Turkish context in exactly the way they were developed. Carl Rogers' theory, for example, emphasizes and promotes individual goals, while not addressing the person's cultural obligations to his or her family and social group (Poyrazli, 2003). In addition, because of the authoritarian nature of the culture and communication styles, the non-directive approach in this therapy method may leave clients dissatisfied and disappointed with the counseling process. Similarly, other theories that are mentioned above need to be critically examined to see if and how they may apply to a Turkish cultural context.

Indigenous and traditional healing methods

Publications and clinical practices related to the use of indigenous and traditional healing methods in Turkey are extremely limited. A content analysis that was conducted by Ongel and Smith (1999) indicated that research published in a prominent psychology journal, *Turkish Journal of Psychology*, showed no tendency or evidence toward indigenization of psychology theories or practices. On the contrary, North American counseling and psychotherapy theories and treatment models were the focus of application oriented-articles. However, many practitioners in Turkey have pointed out the need for an indigenous knowledge base to help with the development of the field and for providing effective practices (Bolak-Boratav, 2004; Gergen, Gulerce, Lock, & Misra, 1996). Owing to its traditional culture, there are many indigenous or traditional practices in Turkey that could easily be included within the healing process. For instance, because of religious and spiritual beliefs, many individuals seek traditional ways of healing their mental illnesses. Visiting religious leaders to receive advice or praying in sacred places and tombs are some methods utilized to gain a greater mental health balance and deal with psychological problems (Raney & Cinarbas, 2005). When individuals pray in sacred places or visit a tomb, there are different rituals they practice. Lighting a candle, touching the tomb, or circling the sacred site are a few examples. People believe that when they engage in these rituals, they will gain emotional strength and their prayer (e.g., for an unwell relative to get better) will likely be answered.

As Bolak-Boratav (2004) acknowledges, different aspects of the culture are typically not integrated into the training of practitioners in Turkey. However, she points out one exception in the form of a new graduate level course at Ankara University which promotes understanding of individual differences and teaches aspects of indigenous cultures such as Sufism. Sufism is a mystical belief system; movement, meditation, and chanting are used to help the person connect with their inner self and with God. "The goal of Sufism is to enable people to live simple, harmonious, and happy lives" (Pedersen & Pope, 2010, p. 847). While the utilization of indigenous and traditional methods is in its infancy, it is clear that many cultural beliefs and practices could be incorporated into treatment models to increase their validity and applicability in Turkey.

Research and supervision

Funding for research in Turkey is supported by the government and also through the European Union. National research institutes receive research proposals and decide if they should be funded. Research projects are also funded by university type institutions through small internal grants.

Within the counseling and psychotherapy fields, generally descriptive and correlational research is employed; however, there is also a limited amount of experimental or process and outcome research studies. In addition, while written material on counseling and psychotherapy in Turkey is flourishing, research in both fields is in its beginning stage.

There is an abundance of research about several psychological variables related to college students as a general group in Turkey. This is primarily because college students are an easy-to-reach population. However, some other studies have examined clients' or patients' satisfaction levels regarding the treatment they received (e.g., Sayin et al., 2008; Şentürk, Arslan & Çevik, 2006).

Randomized controlled effectiveness studies are rare in counseling and psychological research in Turkey. Though rare, there are some research efforts related to the effectiveness of counseling and psychotherapy. These studies have compared the effect of counseling and psychotherapy while using "no-counseling/psychotherapy" as a control. In addition, there is very limited research comparing counseling and psychotherapy to drug treatment (see, Ataoglu, Ozkan, Tutkun, & Maras, 2000).

Cognitive-behavioral psychotherapies have, within the past three decades, gained a significant importance in clinical application and training in Turkey and made their way into experimental research. As one example in a randomized controlled clinical trial, Eskin, Ertekin and Demir (2008) have tested the efficacy of a structured problem solving therapy (PST) in reducing depression and suicide potential in adolescent and young adults.

In terms of psychotherapy supervision in Turkey, it is integrated into the clinical psychology graduate education programs which are very few. Those with bachelor's degrees in psychology mostly rely on supervision on a private basis. The Turkish Psychological Association and the Psychiatric Association of Turkey provide a forum for psychotherapy training and supervision. Most supervision, however, occurs in the professional associations or foundations such as Halime Odağ Psychoanalysis and Psychotherapy Foundation, the Turkish Association for Cognitive and Behavioral Psychotherapies, Psychodrama Institutes, the Gestalt Therapy Association and the Transactional Analysis Association. Psychotherapy supervision in Turkey is neither regulated nor structured.

Supervision in counseling is also similar to the situation of psychotherapy supervision in Turkey. Undergraduate and graduate students receive supervision for their practicum and internships in their departments from a faculty member. Very limited additional supervision is provided at these students' practice sites. In more recent years, however, many practitioners in the field have developed training models that include in vivo supervision.

Strengths, weaknesses, opportunities, and challenges

There are a number of strengths within the field of counseling and psychotherapy in Turkey. Both undergraduate and graduate counseling and psychology training programs have been increasing in number since 1982 (Center for Student Selection and Placement, 2011). The number of counselors and psychologists have also been increasing through the years. Interest and motivation in the profession are high among counselors and psychologists. Moreover, the need for counseling and psychotherapy among Turkish people has been rising in the recent years despite the general consensus that Turkish society is a collectivist society and Turkish people would not prefer professional help. Accordingly, the government has been highly encouraging universities to open more counseling programs.

A major weakness in the field involves the quality of training. Counseling and psychology undergraduates are hired for positions that require them to function as mental health specialists because the number of qualified counselors and clinical psychologists with advanced degrees is inadequate to meet the demands of the people in Turkey. In fact, there are no graduate programs in Turkey similar to the mental health counseling programs or counseling psychology programs in the United States (Raney & Cinarbas, 2005). Another fact is that practicum and internship experiences are not required in most of the counseling and psychology training programs.

Moreover, the dearth of Turkish literature has impacted the quality of the counselor education programs negatively. Most research is survey and exploratory based. In addition, there is limited clinical process and outcome research. There is still much dependence upon Western literature for research findings.

Consequently, a major opportunity and an area of growth related to counseling and psychotherapy in Turkey lies within research. Scholars should be encouraged to increase their research efforts within Turkey and disseminate their findings through journal articles and books so that the dependence upon the US literature lessens.

Another area of growth lies within the supervision of counselor trainees. Most supervised clinical training is provided in each educational institution while the student is working towards his or her degree. However, there could be some additional supervision at the internship or practice sites which could help the student develop to be a more efficient counselor or therapist.

Finally, counseling could make the necessary expansions through going out of the education sector and leaning toward society as a professional mental health service in Turkey. If counseling continues to grow and gain a broad base of acceptance in the country, it could be instituted and implemented in community and mental health centers where individual, group, and family counseling can be offered.

In terms of present-day challenges, the recent growth in the number of training programs seems to be problematic and raises the need for standardization and accreditation of counseling and psychology training programs in Turkey. A second challenge is that professional mental health positions such as counseling and psychotherapy do not require an education beyond a bachelor's degree in Turkey. On the other hand, there are no formally recognized requirements or certifications for mental health professionals (Dogan, 2000). Indeed, the debates on how to train mental health professionals and how to regulate their practices have been ongoing. Some attempts to pass a law, which has not covered counselors, to regulate practices of psychologists have been undertaken by the Turkish Psychological Association for many years. However, this proposed law has not been passed yet because of the objection from the psychiatrists.

It is contended that Turkish people still seem to be close to the collectivist end while at the same time striving for individualism (Mocan-Aydin, 2000). As a result, the public demand for counseling and psychotherapy is limited, even in urban areas. In addition, many people who interface with the mental health system are legally seen by psychiatrists, and generally treated with pharmacotherapy rather than counseling and psychotherapy in Turkey (Bolak-Boratav, 2004).

A final challenge is that counseling in Turkey has largely been identified with school counseling and most individuals who have an undergraduate degree in counseling are employed in schools. Counselors are therefore not yet officially accepted as mental health professionals in Turkey.

Future directions

Counseling and psychology in Turkey are yet to assume professional status. Counseling and psychology need more development work and organizational structures to establish their professional identities. They have to establish standards for certification; standards for licensing members or potential members. Consequently, there is a great need for a careful regulation of all mental health-related fields in Turkey. Essentially, there is an urgent need for professional codes that recognize counseling and psychology as independent professions, bring clarity to the professional titles, and mandate the regulation of the ethical practice of counseling and psychotherapy by a professional board.

There is a growing awareness of the benefits of counseling and psychotherapy in Turkey, but the rate at which people seek the assistance of counselors and therapists is still low. Integrating Turkish cultural values into an emerging philosophical concept of counseling and psychotherapy is vital for counselor and therapist education in Turkey. Raney and Cinarbas (2005) contend that more integration of culturally sensitive, indigenous counseling approaches with mental health approaches is needed to better serve the Turkish people. In addition, multiculturalism is expected to be an important component of counseling and psychology education in the future.

It is our hope that training, accreditation, and standards would be clearly laid out for counseling and psychology to gain a professional identity and obtain a legitimate role among human services professions. It is expected that issues related to specialization, practicum and internship experiences, licensure and certification will be resolved in the future. Despite legal issues and public confusion, we believe that counseling and psychotherapy have an optimistic future. We expect that the public and the legal recognition and appreciation of counseling and psychotherapy will continue to grow.

It is obvious that the Turkish culture, the academic structure, and the legal system of Turkey will shape the future of counseling and psychotherapy. Research, publication, and training programs in counseling and psychology have advanced and will continue to advance the counseling and psychotherapy movement in a way that is necessary in a modern, democratic, and humane society.

Conclusion

The need for counseling and psychotherapy in Turkey has been increasing. This is largely as a result of changes in society and the family structure, economic crisis, an increase in the overall daily stress experienced by Turkish individuals, and a knowledge increase among people about how counseling and psychotherapy could be helpful. However, the current forms of degree programs that instill limited practical skills, a limited amount of process and outcome research, a lack of consideration of Turkish culture when utilizing theories and methods, and limited supervisory experience lead to having this need not met fully. Revamping of degree programs, increasing the number of qualified mental health professionals, considerations of Turkish cultural practices to adapt theoretical practices, developing methods that include indigenous ways of healing, and development and implementation of licensure and certification laws and ethics are among steps that must be taken to advance counseling and psychotherapy in Turkey.

References

Acar, G., & Sahin, D. (1990). Psychology in Turkey. *Psychology and Developing Societies, 2,* 241–256.

Akkoyun, F. (2001). *Transaksiyonel analiz* [Transactional analysis]. Istanbul: Nobel Yayın Dağıtım.

Ataoglu, A., Ozkan, M., Tutkun, H., & Maras, A. (2000). Alprazolam and Cognitive Behavior Therapy in treatment of panic disorder. *Turkish Journal of Medical Sciences, 30,* 167–171.

Aydin, E. (2009). Transaksiyonel analiz therapisi [Transactional analysis psychotherapy, in Turkish]. In E. Köroğlu & H. Türkçapar (eds), *Psikoterapi Yöntemleri: Kuramlar ve Uygulama Yönergeleri* (pp. 215–228). Ankara: Hekimler Yayın Birliği.

Baymur, F. (1980). Türkiye'de rehberlik calismalarinin baslangici, gelisimi, ve bugunku sorunlari [The beginning, the development, and the current issues of guidance activities in Turkey]. In N. Karasar (ed.), *Egitimde Rehberlik Arastirmalari* (pp. 3–7). Ankara: Ankara Universitesi Egitim Arastirmalari Merkezi Yayini.

Bemak, F., & Hanna, F. J. (1998). The twenty-first century counsellor: An emerging role in changing times. *International Journal for the Advancement of Counselling, 20,* 209–218.

Bolak-Boratav, H. (2004). Psychology at the cross-roads: The view from Turkey. In M. J. Stevens & J. Wedding (eds), *Handbook of International Psychology* (pp. 311–330). New York: Taylor & Francis.

Center for Student Selection and Placement. (2011). Yükseköğretim programları ve kontenjanları kılavuzu [Higher education programs and quotas]. Retrieved October, 2 from www.osym.gov.tr/belge/1–2629/a-condensed-english-version.html.

Central Intelligence Agency (2011). *The World Fact Book.* Retrieved from https://www.cia.gov/library/publications/the-world-factbook/geos/tu.html

Council of Higher Education (CHE) (2011). Lisansüstü eğitim ve öğretim yönetmeliği [Regulation for graduate education and instruction]. Retrived October, 2 from www.yok.gov.tr/content/view/417/183/lang,tr/.

Daş, C. (2009). Gestalt Terapi [Gestalt Therapy]. In E. Köroğlu & H. Türkçapar (eds), *Psikoterapi Yöntemleri: Kuramlar ve Uygulama Yönergeleri* (pp. 171–214). Ankara, Turkey: Hekimler Yayın Birliği.

Dogan, S. (1990). Turkiye'de rehberlik kavrami ve uygulamalarinin gelisiminde milli egitim suralarinin rolu [The role of national education councils in development of guidance concept and practices in Turkey]. *Psikolojik Danisma ve Rehberlik Dergisi, 1*(1), 45–55.

Dogan, S. (1996). Türkiye'de psikolojik danisma ve rehberlik alaninda meslek kimliginin gelisimi ve bazi sorunlar [The development of professional identity in the counseling and guidance field in Turkey and related problems]. *Psikolojik Danisma ve Rehberlik Dergisi, 1*(7), 32–44.

Dogan, S. (2000). The historical development of counseling in Turkey. *International Journal for the Advancement of Counseling, 22,* 57–67.

Dogan, S. (2008, April). *Türkiye'de psikolojik danisman egitiminin rotası [The route of counselor education in Turkey].* Paper presented at the Psychological Counseling and Guidance Conference, Istanbul, Turkey.

Erten, Y., & Aydin, E. (2009). Psikanaliz ve psikanalitik psikoterapi [Psychoanalysis and psychoanalytic psychotherapy]. In E. Köroğlu & H. Türkçapar (eds), *Psikoterapi Yöntemleri: Kuramlar ve Uygulama Yönergeleri* (pp. 9–23). Ankara: Hekimler Yayın Birliği.

Eskin, M. (2009). *Sorun çözme terapisi* [Problem solving therapy]. Ankara, Turkey: Hekimler Yayın Birliği.

Eskin, M. (2007). Aile terapileri: Temel ilke, kavram ve seçilmiş modeller [Family therapies: Principles, concepts and selected models]. In E. Köroğlu & C. Güleç (eds), *Psikiyatri Temel Kitabı* (pp. 623–635). Ankara: Hekimler Yayın Birliği.

Eskin, M., Ertekin, K., & Demir, H. (2008). Efficacy of a problem-solving therapy for depression and suicide potential in adolescents and young adults. *Cognitive Therapy and Research, 32,* 227–245.

Gergen, J. J., Gulerce, A., Lock, A., & Misra, G. (1996). Psychological science in cultural context. *American Psychologist, 51,* 496–503.

Göka, E. (2009). Psikodrama [Psychodrama]. In E. Köroğlu & H. Türkçapar (eds), *Psikoterapi Yöntemleri: Kuramlar ve Uygulama Yönergeleri* (pp. 315–340). Ankara: Hekimler Yayın Birliği.

Gülerce, A. (2006). History of psychology in Turkey as a sign of diverse modernization and global psychologization. In A. C. Brock (ed.), *Internationalizing the History of Psychology* (pp. 75–93). New York: New York University Press.

Kağıtçıbaşı, C. (1994). Psychology in Turkey. *International Journal of Psychology, 29*(6), 729–738.

Kılınç, E. (2009). Aile terapileri [Family therapies]. In E. Köroğlu & H. Türkçapar (eds), *Psikoterapi Yöntemleri: Kuramlar ve Uygulama Yönergeleri* (pp. 229–271). Ankara: Hekimler Yayın Birliği.

Korkut, F. (2006). Counselor education, program accreditation and counselor credentialing in Turkey. *International Journal for the Advancement of Counseling, 29*(1), 11–20.

Köroğlu, E. (2005). *Düşünsel duygulanımcı davranış terapisi* [Rational emotive therapy]. Ankara: Hekimler Yayın Birliği.

Kurter, M. F., Jencius, M., & Duba, J. D. (2004). A Turkish perspective on family therapy: An interview with Hurol Fisiloglu. *The Family Journal: Counseling and Therapy for Couples and Families, 12,* 319–323.

Kuzgun, Y. (1993). Türk egitim sisteminde rehberlik ve psikolojik danisma [Guidance and counseling in Turkish education system]. *Egitim Dergisi, 6,* 3–8.

Mocan-Aydin, G. (2000). Western models of counseling and psychotherapy within Turkey: Crossing cultural boundaries. *The Counseling Psychologist, 28,* 281–298.

Oner, N. (1977). *Psychology in the schools in international perspective,* 2. (International School Psychology). Columbus, OH: U.S. Department of Health Education & Welfare National Institute of Education (ERIC Document Reproduction Service No. ED 147 257).

Ongel, U., & Smith, P. B. (1999). The search for indigenous psychologies: Data from Turkey and the former USSR. *Applied Psychology: An International Review, 48,* 465–479.

Ozguven, E. (1990). Ulkemizde psikolojik danisma ve rehberlik faaliyetlerinin dunu ve bugunu [The past and the present of psychological counseling and guidance activities in our country]. *Psikolojik Danisma ve Rehberlik Dergisi, 1*(1), 4–15.

Pedersen, P., & Pope, M. (2010). Inclusive cultural empathy for successful global leadership. *American Psychologist, 65,* 841–854.

Poyrazli, Ş. (2003). Validity of Rogerian Therapy in Turkish culture: A cross-cultural perspective. *Journal of Humanistic Counseling, Education, and Development, 42,* 107–115.

Raney, S., & Cinarbas, D. C. (2005). Counseling in developing countries: Turkey and India as examples. *Journal of Mental Health Counseling, 27,* 149–160.

Sayin, A., Karslioğlu, E. H., Sürgit, A., Şahin, S., Arslan, T., & Candansayar, S. (2008). Perceptions of psychiatric inpatients about therapeutic factors of group psychotherapy. *International Journal of Group Psychotherapy, 58,* 253–263.

Şentürk, V., Arslan, E., & Çevik, A. (2006). Evaluation of therapeutic factors with Q sort method in group therapy period in inpatients. *Türkiye Klinikleri. Journal of Medical Sciences, 26,* 232–239.

Tan, H. (1986). *Psikolojik danisma ve rehberlik* [Psychological counseling and guidance]. Istanbul: Milli Egitim Basimevi.

The Council for Accreditation of Counseling and Related Programs (CACREP) (2011). Standards. Retrieved from http://67.199.126.156/doc/2009%20Standards.pdf.

Turkish Psychological Association (2011). *TPD Tarihçe* [History of Turkish Psychological Association]. Downloaded from www.psikolog.org.tr/Tarihce

Turkish Psychological Counseling and Guidance Association (2004, April). *Psikolojik Danisma ve Rehberlik Anabilim Dallari Toplantisi, III* [The third meeting of counseling divisions]. Denizli: Pamukkale University, Turkey.

Türkçapar, H. (2007). *Bilişsel terapi* [Cognitive therapy]. Ankara, Turkey: Hekimler Yayın Birliği.

Uçan, Ö. (2007). Boşanma sürecinde Kriz Merkezine başvuran kadinlarin retrospektif olarak değerlendirilmesi [A retrospective assessment of women applying to a crisis center during the divorce process]. *Klinik Psikiyatri, 10,* 38–45.

Vahip, I. (2007). Psikanaliz, psikoanalitik yönelimli psikoterapi ve destekleyici psikoterapiler [Psychoanalysis, psychoanalytically oriented psychotherapy and supportive psychotherapies]. In E. Köroğlu & C. Güleç (eds), *Psikiyatri Temel Kitabı* (pp. 571–574). Ankara, Turkey: Hekimler Yayın Birliği.

West, J. D., Bubenzer, D. L., Brooks, D. K., & Hackney, H. (1995). The doctoral degree in counselor education and supervision. *Journal of Counseling and Development, 74,* 174–176.

Yüksel, N. (2001). Prof. Dr. Leyla Zileli ile psikanaliz, psikoterapi, içgörü geliştirme üzerine [An interview with professor Leyla Zileli on psychoanalysis, psychotherapy, insight]. *Klinik Psikiyatri, 4,* 219–224.

PART VI
Conclusion

36

COUNSELING AND PSYCHOTHERAPY AROUND THE WORLD

Current state and future prospects

Juris G. Draguns

Counseling and psychotherapy in its contemporary form originated in Europe and North America. As the foregoing 35 chapters demonstrate, these services have by now been extended to all regions of the world. This volume provides a realistic and up-to-date account of both the achievements of this worldwide endeavor and the obstacles encountered in its path. What remains to be done is to identify some of the current trends in the evolution of counseling and psychotherapy across nations and to sketch some of the discernible directions of its future developments.

Legal and professional contexts

Both counseling and psychotherapy constitute purportedly powerful activities that can affect clients' lives and their wellbeing for good or ill. Thus, they are not applied in a legal or social vacuum. Beginning with the earliest stirrings of the helping professions, institutionalizing, codifying, and legitimizing the activities of counselors and psychotherapists and monitoring their competence has been a major concern for the public authorities, practitioners, and recipients of services, proceeding from the beneficence principle, "let no harm be done." Yet the road to legal recognition of the professional activity has been long and tortuous, and conflicting interests and claims of the several professional and consumer groups involved have slowed down the process, sometimes to a prolonged standstill. Nonetheless over the past several decades, considerable progress has been achieved in a great many countries.

Understandably, those nations in which widespread application of psychotherapy and/or counseling services had a head start lead the way, and it is not surprising that such countries as the United States, Canada, The Netherlands, Denmark, Belgium, and Germany have the most elaborate, differentiated, and comprehensive provisions for licensing qualified professionals to provide services as well as specifying educational and experience requirements and setting ethical standards, Even in these countries, however, the process of credentialing professionals, protecting the public, and assuring the legitimacy of services is as yet not complete, as several of the chapters in this volume attest. On the other side of the ledger, even in countries in which psychotherapy and/or counseling services have been initiated recently, efforts toward securing a legally protected status to procedures and/or service providers have made a surprising degree of headway. Cases in point include the Philippines and South Korea which by now feature modern, streamlined credentialing systems, which have enabled psychologists to extend and solidify their services. Indeed, there are only few chapters whose authors unequivocally state that psychotherapy and counseling remain completely unrecognized and unregulated as far as the public authorities are concerned.

Against this background, the following trends are detectable. The earliest stage in the credentialing process has been to restrict the provision of psychotherapy services to physicians or doctors of medicine and to designate psychiatry as the medical specialty for providing treatment, including psychotherapy, to mentally ill patients. By now, however, most countries represented in this volume explicitly recognize properly trained, typically, though not exclusively, clinical psychologists as qualified independent psychotherapists, and the right to practice psychotherapy is also granted in a great many jurisdictions to members of other helping professions such as social workers, counselors, and nurse practitioners on the basis of their education, training, and practicum. German legislation is unusually explicit in both describing the three kinds of psychotherapy that are eligible for insurance reimbursement and drawing a sharp line between psychotherapy and psychological treatment, the former reserved to clinical psychologists and psychiatrists and the latter included within the scope of counseling psychologists and members of other professions. Somewhat similarly, French legislation contains a distinction between counseling and psychotherapy, with clear consequences for practice, even though, as pointed out in the chapter on Canada, the workplace activities of clinical and counseling psychologists are virtually indistinguishable. The Netherlands, however, have pioneered comprehensive legislation that has culminated in the recognition of the profession of psychotherapist, overlapping but not coextending with clinical psychology and psychiatry, and the specification of practicum and academic requirements for the independent practice of psychotherapy.

Internationally, counseling is less rigorously and consistently regulated than psychotherapy. A multitude of professions include counseling in the repertoire of their services, and defining the core of counseling and penetrating its fuzzy boundaries presents a formidable challenge. Moreover, counseling differs depending on the settings in which it is applied: school, work, family, and personal. Different levels of counseling activity are also envisaged on the basis of degrees and levels of education, doctoral, master's, baccalaureate, and diploma. For all of these reasons, no nation represented in this volume has succeeded in including all counseling activities under one comprehensive credentialing umbrella. The chapter on the United Kingdom provides an especially detailed and instructive guide through the maze of the professions and procedures subsumed under the designation of counseling.

Professions and procedures

Historically, psychiatry and psychoanalysis were among the first providers of psychotherapy in many countries, and they were recognized as such, both administratively and legally as well as by the public at large. Data in several chapters of the book, however, point to a strong trend across nations of psychologists exceeding psychiatrists in numbers and percentages of psychotherapists. It would seem that at long last a differentiation between the two professions is taking place, with the psychiatrists' expertise being focused on biological interventions, possibly with other, including psychological, ancillary procedures, and clinical psychologists concentrating on psychological therapies.

As far as theories and schools of thought are concerned, for a long time psychodynamic treatment approaches held sway in Europe and North America. In the last three decades, however, cognitive-behavioral therapy (CBT) has radiated from the United States and Canada to assume prominence in Western Europe, Australia, Israel, Japan, China, and beyond. An exception to this trend has been noted in Russia following the collapse of the Soviet Union. As reactance theorists would have predicted, schools of practice and thought that had been proscribed under the Soviet regime such as psychoanalysis and also humanistic and existential psychology, experienced rapid growth. Elsewhere, humanistic, phenomenological, and existential approaches have been developed in response to the public's quest for meaning. In the process, these procedures have assumed the status of the third force in psychotherapy.

Doan in the chapter on Australia has detected another trend that is compatible with a shift toward a postmodern and post-positivist orientation. Increasingly, the quest for objectivity in applied scientific endeavors, including counseling and psychotherapy, has given way to the interpretive, hermeneutic study of the various personal narratives which constitute the raw data of the counseling and psychotherapy experience. The objective of helping services within this framework has shifted toward enabling help-seeking clients to tell the stories of their lives and to give voice to those who so far, have not had a chance to be heard. This orientation is more compatible with the exploratory and open-ended humanistic schools of thought than with the directive and focused methods characteristic of CBT. Doan sees a differentiation emerging, with counseling more oriented toward promotion of self-expression and facilitation of personal choice and decision making and with psychotherapy increasingly focused on the change of dysfunctional behaviors and cognitions and reduction of distress and disability. This is a daring and novel hypothesis which deserves to be further explored and, eventually, systematically investigated across time and space.

Who are the therapists and counselors who provide these services across nations? The past few decades have seen a tremendous increase in educational programs and training facilities in Europe, North America, and Australia as well as several countries in Asia and Africa. A master's degree or an equivalent appears to be evolving as the general world standard for independent professional practice. The number of doctoral-level practitioners is also growing. These developments create problems for baccalaureate level persons who in several countries, such as Turkey, Brazil, and Argentina, are trained to assume counseling and psychotherapy responsibilities and to fill a niche in providing needed services. In the differentiated credentialing systems of several European countries, provision has been made for psychological assistants and other occupational designations which would secure official status for people with appropriate training and practical experience below the master's level. A special situation exists in South Africa, where the demise of the apartheid system sparked demand for mental health service providers that is provisionally being met by intensive training within 2-year programs. Clearly, social change demands innovation, and progress creates new dilemmas and problems that should be resolved in a realistic manner for the maximal benefit to those who are in need of help, with fairness to and recognition of all parties involved in the counseling transaction. In virtually all the countries on which pertinent data have been reported, there has been a marked shift in gender balance. Worldwide, the percentage of women who are active in counseling and psychotherapy is increasing, and the proportion of men is declining.

Feminization of psychology, as Marsella (2011) has called it, transcends geography, culture, ideology, and religion and holds everywhere around the globe, from Denmark to India and from Japan to Argentina. As noted in the chapter on Italy, men are still disproportionately represented in positions of prestige and leadership, especially in university hierarchies. In any case, none of the chapter authors have as yet identified the emergence of any problems with this trend. Potentially, there may be a mixture of positive and negative consequences to this shift, ranging from greater empathy and caring, purportedly more compatible with women's role in many cultures to the antagonistic attitude toward men and their problems, especially in connection with their loss of status or power, real or imagined (Gerstein, Heppner, Ægisdóttir, Leung, & Norsworthy, 2009). Somewhat paradoxically, feminist trends are prominently featured only in a few chapters, such as those on Japan and the United States.

Research and practice: toward a worldwide network of contributions

Only a few decades ago, there was a gulf separating the service providers and researchers in counseling and psychotherapy. What research findings were extant were rarely deemed relevant to the practical concerns of the practitioners. Moreover, most of the research results originated in the United States, Canada, and the United Kingdom, and were thought by many not to be directly applicable within service settings, especially those in non-Western cultures. At best, research findings trickled through from retrospective studies of psychotherapy and counseling to actual practice (Goldstein, 2009).

As this book demonstrates, the situation has radically changed in both respects. Ambitious and extensive research programs exist in France, Germany, The Netherlands and several other European countries. Research has made inroads in the rapidly expanding therapy and counseling enterprise in China, Korea, and Japan, and it thrives in Israel. No longer do information, knowledge, and expertise flow one way, and psychotherapists and counselors in the major English-speaking countries stand to benefit from advances and developments elsewhere in the world. Examples include Assagioli's psychosynthesis, a distinctive variant of systematic family therapy pioneered by Maria Selvini-Palazzoli and her associates, and a creative blend of psychodynamic tenets and cognitive-behavioral techniques developed by Vittorio Guidano and Giovanni Liotti, all of which originated in Italy. As constraints have been removed from conceptualization and practice, Russian psychologists have turned to the heritage of Lev Vygotsky in order to apply it to the development of new and original therapy procedures that mark a shift from an evolutionary biological approach to a cultural historical orientation. The pivotal concept for psychotherapy is reflexion, or a person's capacity to cognize his or her own self-attributions and to regulate cognition, emotion, and behavior. From Germany has come the specification by Klaus Grawe of the four fundamental change mechanisms in psychotherapy, namely strengthening of coping strategies, clarification of meaning, problem activation, and utilization of resources, as well as a comprehensive formulation of psychotherapy on a neuropsychological basis by the same author (Grawe, 2007). Holm-Hadulla, Hoffman, and Sperth have offered the ABCDE model of psychotherapy as consisting of behavior modification, change of dysfunctional cognitions, dynamic-unconscious conflicts, and existential conflicts, all of them addressed in the context of therapeutic alliance. In France, contributions have been made to the development of constructivist interviews for young adults and adolescents to reveal their design of life (Guichard & Huteau, 2001) and the concept of social representation by Moscovici has been integrated with psychotherapy and psychoanalysis. Psychologists in Spain have developed a multiplicity of novel and specialized techniques, mostly within the CBT framework. They are briefly introduced, but remain to be more thoroughly described, for potential application elsewhere.

García-Vera, Sanz, and Prieto start their chapter by offering a new and provocative idea: Has Don Quixote's madness in ideation and behavior had an impact on Spanish attitudes toward the mentally ill by increasing tolerance, understanding, and empathy and by reducing rejection and prejudice? This notion deserves to be taken seriously, even though it can be only indirectly tested and then from a variety of perspectives and by a combination of methods.

The three major countries of East Asia, China, Korea, and Japan offer by now a panoply of psychotherapeutic and counseling services, many of which originated in the Euroamerican West. Some of these procedures, however, have arisen out of indigenous sets of beliefs and helpful interventions. A case in point is the Chinese Taoist Cognitive Psychotherapy, a blend of traditional Taoist techniques and teachings with CBT designed to promote spontaneity, flexibility, and harmony with nature. In Japan, Morita therapy is well known and has been copiously described, also with a view toward its potential application in the West (Reynolds, 1980; Tanaka-Matsumi, 2004). Before the publication of this book, little was heard about Hakaniwa therapy, which apparently represents a combination of Zen procedures and Jungian concepts. Both Japanese and German therapists and counselors have made forays into distance therapy, powerfully stimulated by information technology, with the full understanding of the risks of venturing into this unchartered territory. Tentatively, they have concluded that there is more room for exploring these innovations within some forms of counseling than of incorporating them into psychotherapy.

At different points of the globe, counselors and psychotherapists have been called upon to respond to unanticipated conditions of acute or chronic stress brought about by nature or by humans in the form of war, terror, oppression, and persecution. In Israel, the experiences in a border community subject to intermittent shelling and attack have led to the development of the Kiryat Shmona model of community stress prevention that is applicable at other sites experiencing similar stressful conditions. On the other side of the Arab-Israeli conflict, the chapter on Palestine presents a unique glimpse of counselors, psychotherapists, other professionals, and even laypersons pooling their efforts in improvising, developing, and applying interventions under conditions of constant, yet unpredictable stress. Children, in particular, as potential or actual victims of violence are in dire need of both prevention and intervention.

Another unique situation pertains to South Africa where the psychological conceptions and practices of the apartheid era had to be dismantled and replaced by an emancipatory, egalitarian, and multicultural orientation that would begin to fulfill the needs of all segments of the South African population, specifically in helping to overcome the sequelae of oppression and shape change as well as adapt to it.

In the United States, Canada, and the United Kingdom, counselors and psychotherapists are responding to the challenge of developing and delivering services to all components of the multicultural population of these countries. In the process, they have made their interventions more meaningful and sensitive to their ethnoculturally heterogeneous clientele and have narrowed, if not altogether bridged, the cultural divide separating service recipients from service providers. In the process, a more collaborative relationship has emerged between the ethnic communities and human services. These efforts continue and are being constantly extended and diversified, especially in light of the increased global mobility not only in North America and Great Britain, but in many countries throughout the world (Gerstein, Heppner, Ægisdóttir, Leong, & Norsworthy, 2009). In addition to this volume, Pedersen, Draguns, Lonner, and Trimble (2008) and Sue and Sue (2008) provide compendia of useful information from applying multicultural interventions in the United States and Canada.

Toward evidence-based treatment: a universal standard of helping services?

The application of evidence-based treatment (EBT) is a relatively new development in mental health and human help services. It has assumed prominence in the United States, the United Kingdom, and several countries in Northern and Western Europe. Originated in medicine, it has been extended to the assessment of efficacy of psychological interventions, including psychotherapy and personal counseling. A working definition by the American Psychological Association Presidential Task Force on Evidence-Based Practice in Psychology (EBPP) (2006) posits that "EBPP is the integration of the best available research with clinical expertise in the context of patient characteristics, culture, and preferences" (p. 271). This statement incorporates a number of specifications that go beyond the automatic and identical manualized treatment and recognize the weight of the professional's experience, patient's expectations, and cultural context. In the multicultural setting of the United States, Griner and Smith (2006) demonstrated in a meta-analysis of mental health interventions that cultural accommodation in therapy techniques and delivery of services significantly improves the outcome of mental health services to four major ethnocultural groups: African Americans, Asian Americans, Hispanic Americans, and American Indians. CBT lends itself especially well to the EBT format as its procedures are specifically described and are relatively easily applied with a considerable degree of consistency (Tanaka-Matsumi, 2008).

As EBT is extended beyond the milieus where its validity was established, a number of problems are encountered. Such pivotal aspects of therapy and counseling as the therapeutic alliance, the spontaneity of a patient's or client's communication, a therapist's expression of empathy, and the complexities of mutual social perception defy being incorporated within the confines of EBT structure, even if the cultural characteristics of the therapy encounter are taken into account. More fundamentally, as Zeldow (2009) has pointed out, rigid adherence to EBT would inhibit a therapist's reflective response to unique individuals facing unanticipated challenges in an unforeseen and uncertain situation. Therapy just cannot be reduced to following rules, and although EBT is unquestionably an advance in increasing the potential efficacy of a therapist's interventions within and across cultures, it is, however, only one criterion among many. In venturing beyond one's own culture and in designing and implementing helping services in a new setting, improvisation is essential, and EBTs validated somewhere else may need to be revised and supplemented.

Extending psychotherapy to new cultures

There are many cultures in Africa, Asia, and elsewhere, where, in the words of the authors of the chapter on Francophone West Africa, "most people have neither heard nor seen a psychologist, a counselor, or a psychotherapist." In general, as the chapters on Malaysia, Turkey, and Pakistan illustrate, psychotherapy and counseling have spread slowly and gradually, proceeding from the modernized, Westernized, urban, educated, and often Anglophone (or Francophone) elite and expanding to broader strata of the population. Another pathway of imported psychological services involved the most seriously disturbed for whom the local ministrations had failed.

These unfortunate individuals were confined to the asylums where most of them received only minimal custodial care. It is not surprising that many members of traditional non-Western cultures do not take readily to psychotherapy that is predicated on verbal communication, introspection, self-disclosure, and a trusting relationship with a stranger. Moreover, the stigma associated with craziness has not disappeared even in the West and may be widespread or even ubiquitous in many other locales. Moreover, the format of a one-to-one encounter and being torn away from the members of one's family and thus being deprived of one's customary sources of support, constitutes additional obstacles to recognizing the positive, helpful aspects of these encounters.

Beyond these surface concerns, the resistance against psychotherapy and counseling has deeper roots. It concerns the implicit, yet fundamental concept of personhood (Kirmayer, 2007) and is embedded in a usually nonverbal set of unquestioned assumptions about the world and reality. Chapters on English-speaking countries of East Africa and the Caribbean and on the Francophone nations of West Africa lift the curtain on the traditional mentality of the local populations. A holistic worldview prevails where the distinctions between mind, body, and spirit are blurred or obliterated. Children's upbringing is entrusted to the entire community with the parents playing a key role, but not being their exclusive agents of socialization. Something akin to the Western notion of lifespan development is posited, with each of the stages of life having its distinctive tasks, all of them at the service of building up a person's resiliency and solidifying his or her identity, as a member of one's family and community. Externalization prevails over internalization. Under these circumstances, biographical, reconstructive, individually centered psychotherapy or counseling becomes irrelevant. Best results are achieved by time-limited brief interventions focused on specific beneficial outcomes. In the optimal case these results become a wedge for building a more enduring and trusting relationship that may form a foundation for further intervention.

Another obstacle to psychotherapy is fatalism. As the authors of the chapter on Pakistan report, keeping one's suffering to oneself and relying on God are principles by which a lot of Pakistanis abide. Although there is a coherent set of therapeutic beliefs and practices that are explicitly derived from the Koran and are integrated with modern psychotherapeutic principles (Al-Issa & Al-Subaie, 2004). It is not clear, however, to what extent they are practiced, and in what contexts. More widely diffused are various folk beliefs and remedies, such as practices to ward off the evil eye. On the basis of the chapter in this volume, Egypt has a wide range of psychotherapy and counseling services of which some, however, are regarded as incompatible with Islam. Rational emotional therapy and possibly CBT, apparently pose few if any problems in this respect.

Traditional and patriarchal cultures prefer directive and prescriptive approaches and have little patience or tolerance with the person-centered techniques that invite clients to express themselves or to seek an optimal solution on one's own. There may also be little understanding for process and discovery, as opposed to instantaneously given authoritative directions. It is interesting that, with the growth and expansion of the mental health services in the People's Republic of China, clientele preferences have shifted from explicitly assigned activities that are part and parcel of Morita therapy imported from Japan to the more self-expressive and open-ended techniques of humanistic and integrative therapy. However, in both of the surveys conducted 12 years apart, behavioral and cognitive therapies were ranked highest. Finally, it is not surprising to discover that there is a bias in favor of interventions of local provenance as opposed to imported procedures. Explicitly demonstrated in Kenya, it is probably characteristic in a great many other cultures. Consistent with this expectation, upon conducting a meta-analysis of the effects of the Chinese techniques of acupuncture and quijong, Lei, Askeroth, Lee, Burshteyn, and Einhorn (2004) commented that "if you happen to grow up in a certain culture in which some healing modalities come to you naturally as an indigenous method to alleviate illness, you are more likely to enjoy its efficacy, because of your belief in the modality itself could contribute to the placebo effect (in addition to the method's specific effect), regardless of whether it really manipulates your system in the way the healer expects it to do" (p. 243).

Indigenous healing methods and their unfulfilled promise

Although the focus of this volume is upon the modern treatment methods and counseling approaches all of which claim to be empirically based and to be traceable to the time span of less than the last two centuries, the predecessors of modern psychotherapists were traditional healers who ministered to the body, mind, and spirit simultaneously, integratively, holistically, and intuitively, with a lot of mystery and magic thrown in. Counseling was approximated in the transmission of practical wisdom and cultural and personal beliefs and norms of conduct by men and women whose status and age gave authority to their advice and pronouncements.

In this day and age healers survive in Africa, Asia, South America, and among the First nations of Canada and the United States. Their modi operandi have been extensively scrutinized by anthropologists, psychiatrists, and psychologists (e.g., Jilek & Draguns, 2008; Krippner, 2002; Moodley & West, 2005). Not only do the traditional healers perform an important social function, but they often do that in an effective and culturally sensible manner. Indeed, they have often succeeded where modern therapists have failed, by couching their interventions in a culturally sensible and familiar manner. There is no cultural gulf to be crossed, and there is no bafflement. Everything makes sense if the perspective within the culture is adopted. Traditional healing practices play an important role in countries as diverse as Brazil, Cuba, the English-speaking islands of the Caribbean, India, Nigeria, and the Francophone nations of West Africa. Little is known of the therapeutic effectiveness of these services, and often the distressed person's options are between the imported, but locally untested, EBTs and the familiar indigenous services with no scientific rationale and no systematic observations on their outcome. The goal of culturally sensitive planners of mental health services involves integration of traditional healing into comprehensive treatment programs. So far, it has been rarely attained. The pioneering contributions of A. Thomas Lambo in creating psychiatric villages are mentioned in the chapter on Nigeria, as is the description of the two systems of care by Henri Collomb in Senegal in the chapter on Francophone West Africa. The chapter on Argentina describes the healing procedures of Mapuche shaman incorporated into a mental health program designed for Mapuche Indians.

Several reasons account for this apparent paradox. For one, there is mutual distrust, often shading off into disdain or suspicion on the part of both modern and traditional purveyors of mental healing. Interest, fascination, and receptivity may mark the explorers and investigators of these services, but the attitudes of the working professionals who attempt to provide modern, scientifically based services where they have not existed before may be very different and pronouncedly negative. On the other side of the divide, there may be, often well founded, fears and concerns of exploitation, duplicity and worse. Moreover, not all traditional healers are benevolent or competent. The assumption that all of them are psychotherapists' counterparts in traditional trappings is as misleading as equating all native practitioners of psychological intervention with malevolent and incompetent witch doctors. In the meantime, the practices of traditional healers remain a resource to be tapped, but cautiously and judiciously. More broadly and less directly, Heppner, Ægisdóttir, Leung, Duan, Helms, Gerstein, and Pedersen (2009) see a great potential in incorporating the effective therapeutic components of traditional healers' interventions into modern counseling and psychotherapy programs designed for First Nation or American Indian populations as well as for components of potential clientele in various locations in Africa, Asia, Australia, and elsewhere.

Responding to problems in space and time

To a surprising degree the problems of persons seeking help from psychotherapists are remarkably alike. Anxiety, depression, alienation, loneliness, inability to get along with other people or to tolerate oneself recur throughout the world and are featured, although in somewhat different guises, throughout the world. On the national scale, the challenge of preventing suicide and providing help to survivors is prominently mentioned in the chapters on France and on Japan.

The authors refer to the era of depression in Japan, and the chapter on Russia describes a widespread depressive attitude toward the future, anxiety due to uncertainty, and fear of arbitrariness from the state. The current world economic crisis is perhaps too recent to be reflected in the chapters of this book, but looking at the social problems of time and place through the prism of the complaints brought to psychotherapy and counseling is a worthwhile undertaking. Moreover, it may be instructive to compare psychotherapy and counseling services in a country known for its high happiness indicators, such as Denmark, with a nation such as Russia where reported levels of stress are high and pessimism is widespread.

Summing up and looking ahead

Through the multiple processes of globalization, the world is fast becoming a global village (Marsella, 1998). This book attempts to make its readers aware of the developments and problems in all parts of the world and of their relevance to the day-to-day professional concerns here and now. Wherever practiced, counseling and psychotherapy are amalgams of the unique and the generic, the universal and the particular. Each of the chapters provides something new to its readers and, beyond the cultural trappings, there lurk a great many locally adaptable features. The challenge now is to go beyond a passive receptivity to information and to engage in an active and continuous process of exchange and mutual enrichment. Following the recommendations by Heppner et al. (2009), this objective can be accomplished by active and bilateral exchanges, continuous electronic contact, and active, long-term collaborations.

As Heppner et al. (2009) and Marsella (2011) emphasize, it is essential that these programs be construed as occurring between equal partners where both sides can teach and learn. Any appearance of a patronizing, quasi-colonial attitude are to be avoided.

Of necessity, the 35 chapters of this book throw in bold relief the identical or similar modes of intervention, especially in the developed Western countries of the world, with but an occasional dab of local color. It is good to know that not only CBTs but psychodynamic and humanistic therapies are so widely applicable. However, there is a cultural component to many counseling and psychotherapy interventions that only comes to the fore if an inside look is taken at these operations. This is virtually impossible to do in a global survey and it remains a task for the future. It is also necessary to begin identifying cultural characteristics that make a difference in designing and delivering counseling and psychotherapy services. Finally, globalization will continue to impact all aspects of life, not excluding human services.

Such terms as therapeutic alliance (Castonguay, 2011) and empathy (Draguns, 2007) have rarely been mentioned in this volume. Yet, they have been deemed crucial components of therapeutic influence in North America and elsewhere. Whether they play an essential role worldwide remains to be established on the basis of cross-cultural research that would systematically explore the intrapersonal experience of the client. And if empathy does matter, how important is it in different cultures and in what ways is it expressed, communicated, and experienced? Moreover, empathy's major role has been posited in psychotherapy and it is by no means obvious that it should automatically extend to the multiple modalities of counseling as well. The same unanswered questions apply to the newer concept of therapeutic alliance, and the psychotherapeutic relationship is subject to cultural shaping as are self-experience and self-disclosure. The counseling or psychotherapy relationship may be mainly vertical or authoritarian or pronouncedly horizontal or egalitarian. Pedersen, Crethar, and Carlson (2008) have made the concept of empathy central for personal counseling in the multicultural North American milieu. Inclusive cultural empathy that they have proposed may be potentially applicable in interventions across cultures and nations as well.

By way of additional cultural variables that are relevant for cross-cultural counseling, the dimension of individualism-collectivism has been repeatedly proposed (Norsworthy, Heppner, Ægisdóttir, Gerstein, & Pedersen, 2009; Draguns, 2008; Triandis, 2001). Is the culturally approved goal of psychotherapy and counseling the actualization of the individual's potentials and resources or is it the achievement of harmony, solidarity, and integration into one's family and community? How does an individualist fare in a culture in which the collective is paramount and a collectivist, in a setting where individualism is honored and promoted? And what kind of helping services are provided for persons who do not fit comfortably into their culture's designed slots?

Finally, globalization is often invoked as a prepotent, yet vague force which shapes the lives of the denizens of this planet and impacts them in a multitude of unpredictable and uncontrollable ways. Does it promote a sense of helplessness or is its net effect to empower individuals? And how do the various threads of globalization find their way into counseling and psychotherapy encounters? Certainly, the timely appearance of this book and the creation of a worldwide network of authors would not have been possible without globalized developments and trends such as comprehensive and instantaneous communication. However, rapid social and technological change has the potential for producing disruptive consequences. To what extent, if any, do they impinge upon individuals, families, communities, cultures, and the entire humankind in the form of depression, anxiety, and confusion to which counselors and psychotherapists are called upon to respond?

Against the background of these ongoing challenges, the present volume constitutes a progress report on the various efforts to help individuals to cope with distress and overcome dysfunction, ultimately on the basis of optimal helping resources grounded in worldwide experience.

References

Al-Issa, I. & Al-Subaie, A. (2004). Native healing in Arab–Islamic societies. In U. P. Gielen, J. M. Fish, & J. G. Draguns (eds), *Handbook of Culture, Therapy, and Healing* (pp. 343–367). Mahwah, NJ: Erlbaum.

American Psychological Association Task Force on Evidence-Based Practice (2006). Evidence-based practice in psychology. *American Psychologist, 61*, 271–285.

Castonguay, L. G. (2011). Psychotherapy, psychopathology, research, and practice: Pathways of connection and integration. *Psychotherapy Research*, 125–140.

Draguns, J. G. (2007). Empathy across national, cultural, and social barriers. *Baltic Journal of Psychology, 8*, 5–20.

Draguns, J. G. (2008). From speculation through description toward investigation: A prospective glimpse of research in psychotherapy. In U. P. Gielen, J. G. Draguns, & J. M. Fish (eds), *Principles of multicultural counseling and therapy* (pp. 393–418). New York: Routledge.

Gerstein, L. H., Heppner, P. P., Ægisdóttir, S., Leung, S. M. A., & Norsworthy, K. L. (2009). Cross-cultural counseling: History, challenges, and rationale. In L.H. Gerstein et al. (eds), *International handbook of cross-cultural counseling* (pp. 3–32). Thousand Oaks, CA: Sage.

Goldstein, R. (2009). "Blowin' in the wind": Holding on to values in the face of regulation in Britain. In L. H. Gerstein et al. (eds), *International Handbook of Cross-cultural Counseling* (pp. 281–290). Thousand Oaks, CA: Sage.

Grawe, K. (2007). *Neuropsychotherapy. How the Neurosciences Inform Effective Psychotherapy*. Mahwah, NJ: Erlbaum.

Griner, D., & Smith, T.B. (2007). Culturally adapted mental health intervention: A meta-analytic review. *Psychotherapy: Theory, Research, Practice, Training, 43*, 531–548.

Guichard, J., & Huteau, M. (2001). *Psychologie de l'orientation* [Psychology of career counseling]. Paris: Dunod.

Heppner, P. P., Ægisdóttir, S., Leung, S. M. A., Duan, C., Helms, J. E., Gerstein, L. H., & Pedersen, P. B. (2009). The intersection of multicultural and cross-national movements in the United States: A complementary role to promote culturally sensitive research, training, and practice. In L. H. Gerstein et al. (eds), *International Handbook of Cross-cultural Counseling* (pp. 33–52). Thousand Oaks, CA: Sage.

Jilek, W. G., & Draguns, J. G. (2008). Interventions by traditional healers: Their relevance within their cultures and beyond. In U. P. Gielen, J. G. Draguns, & J. M. Fish (eds), *Principles of Multicultural Counseling and Therapy* (pp. 353–372). New York: Routledge.

Kirmayer, L. J. (2007). Psychotherapy and the cultural concept of the person. *Transcultural Psychiatry, 49*, 232–257.

Krippner, R. (2002). Conflicting perspectives on shamans and shamanism: Points and counterpoints. *American Psychologist, 57*, 962–978.

Lei, T., Askeroth, C., Lee, C. T., Burshteyn, D., & Einhorn, A. (2004). Indigenous Chinese healing: A criteria-based meta-analysis of outcomes research. In U. P. Gielen, J. G. Draguns, & J. M. Fish (eds), *Handbook of Culture, Therapy, and Healing* (pp. 213–252). Mahwah, NJ: Erlbaum.

Marsella, A. J. (1998). Toward a global community psychology: Meeting the needs of a changing world. *American Psychologist, 53*, 1282–1291.

Marsella, A. J. (2011). Twelve critical issues for mental health professionals working with ethnoculturally diverse populations. *Psychology International*, October 2011. Retrieved from www.apa.org/international/pi/2011/10/critical-issues.aspx

Moodley, R., & West, D. (eds) (2005). *Integrating Traditional Healing Practice into Counseling and Psychotherapy*. Thousand Oaks, CA: Sage.

Norsworthy, K. L., Leung, S. M. A., Heppner, P. P., & L. Wang (2009). Crossing borders in collaboration. In L. H. Gerstein et al. (eds), *International Handbook of Cross-cultural Counseling* (pp. 125–140). Thousand Oaks, CA: Sage.

Pedersen, P. B., Crethar, H. C., & Carlson, J. (2008). *Inclusive Cultural Empathy*. Washington, DC: American Psychological Association.

Pedersen, P. B., Draguns, J. G., Lonner, W. J., & Trimble, J. E. (2007). *Counseling across Cultures* (6th edn). Thousand Oaks, CA: Sage.

Reynolds, D. K. (1980). *The Quiet Therapies. Japanese Pathways to Personal Growth*. Honolulu: University Press of Hawai'i.

Sue, D., & Sue, D. W. (2008). *Counseling the Culturally Diverse: Theory and Practice* (5th edn). New York: Wiley.

Tanaka-Matsumi, J. (2004). Japanese forms of psychotherapy: Naikan therapy and Morita therapy. In U. P. Gielen, J. M. Fish, & J. G. Draguns (eds) *Handbook of Culture, Therapy, and Healing* (pp. 277–292). Mahwah, NJ: Erlbaum.

Tanaka-Matsumi, J. (2008). Functional approaches to evidence-based practice in multicultural counseling and psychotherapy. In U. P. Gielen, J. G. Draguns, & J. M. Fish (eds), *Principles of Multicultural Counseling and Therapy* (pp. 169–198). New York: Routledge.

Triandis, H.C. (2001). Individualism and collectivism: Past, present, and future. In D. Matsumoto (ed.) *The Handbook of Culture and Psychology* (pp. 35–50). New York: Oxford University Press.

Zeldow, P. B. (2009). In defense of clinical judgment, credentialed clinicians, and reflective practice. *Psychotherapy: Theory, Research, Practice, Training, 46*, 1–10.

INDEX

Psychological Association of the Philippines (PAP)
238, 239, 240, 241, 242
Psychological Society of South Africa (PsySSA)
64, 68, 69
Psychopathologie Africaine 35–36, 46
psychosocial counseling: Francophone West Africa
30–31, 36; Germany 292, 294, 297, 298–99;
Israel 373; Russia 338, 339, 343; Sub-Saharan
Africa 76
Psychotherapy Act (Germany, 1999) 292, 293–94,
297, 299
Psychotherapy and Counselling Federation of
Australia (PACFA) 173, 174, 177, 178
PsySSA *see* Psychological Society of South Africa
PTSD 13, 57, 76, 395, 396

qigong 183, 187
Quebec 108, 114
Qur'ran/Koran 23, 230, 231, 296, 362, 363,
388, 423

Rachman, Stanley 63
rational emotive behavior therapy (REBT) 161,
228, 230, 408
Regla Lucumi 133–34
regulation *see* certification/licensing
relational cultural therapy (RCT) 121
religious healing 20, 23, 56, 121–22, 194, 219,
409; *see also* Ayurvedic medicine; Buddhism;
Catholicism; Christian healing; failth/spiritual
healers; Hinduism; Islam; pastoral counseling
religious obsession 56, 57
research: Argentina 90–91, 92; Australia 176–77;
Belgium 265–66, 268; Brazil 100, 101, 102–3;
Canada 110, 111–12; China 188; Cuba 133,
134; Denmark 273, 276–78; Egypt 24, 25;
English-speaking Caribbean 122–23, 124;
France 12, 287–88, 289; Francophone West
Africa 35–36; Germany 296–97; India 198–99;
Iran 367; Israel 376–77, 378; Italy 308, 309–10;
Japan 208–9; Lebanon 389; Malaysia 220,
221–22; Mexico 140, 141, 145–46, 147, 148;
Morocco 56–57, 58; Netherlands 320–21;
Nigeria 42, 45–46, 47, 48; Pakistan 228,
231–32, 234; Palestine 13, 396, 399–400, 401;
Philippines 241, 242, 243, 244; Russia 342;
South Africa 66–67, 68; South Korea 249, 253;
Spain 328, 331–32; Sub-Saharan Africa 77–78;
Turkey 405, 409–10; United Kingdom 352,
353–54, 354, 355; USA 157–58, 163–64
Rizvi, Azhar Ali 228, 230, 231
Rogers, Carl 65, 96, 141, 174, 284, 293, 340,
408; *see also* client-centred therapy;
person-centered/oriented theory
role definition 418; Argentina 87; Australia 179;
Belgium 261, 266, 267; Brazil 97, 101, 102;
Canada 106, 109–10, 113, 114; Egypt 22, 26,

27; France 284–85, 418; Germany 292, 293,
294; Israel 378; Lebanon 386, 390; Netherlands
12, 317, 322, 323–24; Russia 337–38; South
Korea 253, 254; Spain 327, 329, 332, 333, 334;
Turkey 411; USA 164
Roman Catholicism *see* Catholicism
Rubin, Edgar John 272
Russia 12, 130, 337–45, 420, 425
RVOE *see Official Recognition of Studies Validity*

St. John's Wort 388–89
SAJP *see South Africa Journal of Psychology*
sandtray/Hakoniwa therapy 10, 207, 208, 218, 421
Santería 133–34
SAPA *see* South African Psychological Association
Scheeffer, Ruth 96
schizophrenia 45, 66, 67, 197, 340, 341, 367
school/student counseling 12, 283, 284, 285, 286,
287, 288; Belgium 263; Canada 107, 109, 110,
112; China 182; Denmark 272, 275, 276;
France 282, 283, 284, 285, 286, 287, 288;
Francophone West Africa 33; Germany 293,
296, 297, 298; India 196–97, 199, 200; Israel
371; Japan 205, 211; Lebanon 383, 384, 385;
Malaysia 216, 220, 221, 222; Mexico 139, 142,
146; Nigeria 41–42, 43, 44, 46; Palestine 394,
395, 397; Philippines 238, 239, 240, 242–43;
Russia 341, 345; South Africa 64, 65–66, 67;
South Korea 250, 253–54; Sub-Saharan Africa
73, 76; Turkey 404, 405, 406, 407, 411; USA
154, 160, 163
self-actualization 5, 37, 38, 197
self-diagnosis 6
Senegal 8, 30, 31, 32, 33, 34, 35–36, 38, 424
sex therapy 21, 54, 63, 146, 158, 367, 374, 408
sexual orientation 2, 12, 130, 161, 162, 304, 311
Shahar, Prof. Golan 379
Shamanism 11, 77, 90, 219, 241, 247, 251–52, 253
Shinto 204
sjælesorg 276
Smuts, Jan Christiaan 62, 63
social historical perspectives 130, 132–33, 135
social media 5, 267, 268, 296, 387
social/cultural-historic approaches 130, 132–33,
135, 338, 341, 342, 345, 420
Sociedad Cubana de Psicología 132, 134
solution-focused therapy 109, 133, 175
somatic healthcare 54, 173, 264, 279, 296, 340
South Africa 9, 61–69, 72, 74, 75, 421
South Africa Journal of Psychology (SAJP) 66–67
South African Psychological Association (SAPA) 63
South Danish University 273, 277
South Korea 11, 247–56
Spain 12, 326–34, 420
Spanish Federation of Psychotherapy (FEAP)
329, 332
spirituality *see* religious healing